# SUPPLEMENT TO THE HANDBOOK OF MIDDLE AMERICAN INDIANS

## Volume 1  Archaeology

# SUPPLEMENT TO THE HANDBOOK OF MIDDLE AMERICAN INDIANS

 VICTORIA REIFLER BRICKER, General Editor

VOLUME ONE

# ARCHAEOLOGY

JEREMY A. SABLOFF, Volume Editor

With the Assistance of Patricia A. Andrews

UNIVERSITY OF TEXAS PRESS, AUSTIN

Copyright © 1981 by the University of Texas Press
All rights reserved
Printed in the United States of America

First Edition, 1981

Requests for permission to reproduce material
from this work should be sent to
    Permissions
    University of Texas Press
    Box 7819
    Austin, Texas 78712

Library of Congress Cataloging in Publication Data
Main entry under title:

Archaeology.

    (Supplement to the Handbook of Middle
American Indians; v. 1)
    Bibliography: p.
    Includes index.
    1. Indians of Mexico—Antiquities—
Addresses, essays, lectures.  2. Indians of
Central America—Antiquities—Addresses,
essays, lectures.  3. Mexico—Antiquities—
Addresses, essays, lectures.  4. Central
America—Antiquities—Addresses, essays,
lectures.  I. Sabloff, Jeremy A.  II. Andrews,
Patricia A.  III. Series.
F1219.A76      972'.01      81-4353
ISBN 0-292-77556-3

To the memory of
ROBERT WAUCHOPE
General Editor of the *Handbook of Middle American Indians*
Teacher, scholar, friend, gentleman

# CONTENTS

This volume is the first in a series sponsored by the University of Texas Press to update and supplement the *Handbook of Middle American Indians*. By 1976, when the last volume of the *Handbook* was published, some of the earlier volumes were already out of date, and it was also apparent that research on Middle American Indians had developed in directions that had not been anticipated in 1956, when the series was planned (see Marcus and Spores 1978 for a history of the *Handbook*). The Press responded to these problems by choosing a more flexible format for a series of supplementary volumes that would permit the continuous updating of information on a rotational basis by discipline.

Of all the disciplines covered by the *Handbook*, archaeology became outdated most quickly, and therefore the first volume of the *Supplement to the Handbook of Middle American Indians* is devoted to this subject. The volume editor, Jeremy A. Sabloff, chose to focus on the most important excavation projects that have been completed during the past twenty years. Other projects, still underway or recently completed, can be the subject of later archaeological volumes.

The second volume of the series, which will be devoted to language and literature, will supplement, rather than update, the *Handbook of Middle American Indians*. It will provide grammatical descriptions of languages not represented in the *Handbook*, and it will, for the first time, include Middle American Indian literature in its coverage. In recent years, Middle American linguists have become interested in discourse and style, and the decision to combine language and literature in a single volume recognizes that trend. Munro S. Edmonson is the editor of the second volume of the *Supplement*.

Another major development in the last twenty years is that "documentary ethnology" (Spores 1973:25) has come into its own, and we now have more information on Colonial Indian social organization and cultural institutions than was available to the planners of the *Handbook* in 1956. At the same time, ethnographers have begun to look for historical explanations of conditions in modern Indian communities. As the boundary between ethnohistory and ethnography disappears, what were formerly two disciplines become part of a single discipline, "ethnology." These developments will be represented in later volumes of the *Supplement*.

The physical anthropology volume of the *Handbook* will also be updated and supplemented from time to time. Since that volume was published (in 1970), research in osteology, genetics, nutrition, and growth and development has flourished, and demography and body composition have been added to the fields of inquiry pursued by physical anthropologists in Middle America. The results of their recent investigations will be summarized in a forthcoming volume of the *Supplement*.

The *Supplement* will not replace the *Handbook of Middle American Indians* as the standard reference work on the native peoples and cultures of Middle America. The four volumes of the *Handbook* entitled "Guide to Ethnohistorical Sources" will probably never be outdated, and most of the other volumes contain basic factual information that will not be repeated in the *Supplement*. The *Supplement* is conceptually linked to the *Handbook* and should be used in conjunction with it.

V. R. B.

## VOLUME EDITOR'S PREFACE

*The Handbook of Middle American Indians,* produced under the general editorship of the late Robert Wauchope, is one of the most valuable resources ever produced for anthropologists interested in this area. Unfortunately, with the rapid advance of knowledge in the past two decades, many of the articles are now considered out of date. This volume will rectify this situation by providing a useful follow-up to the original archaeology volumes.

In formulating the outline for this *Supplement,* I was faced with a number of possibilities. For example, I could have asked the original authors to update their chapters, or I could have tried a new encyclopedic approach. Instead, after much thought, I decided that professionals and students alike would find a discussion and an evaluation of the major archaeological achievements of the past two decades of greatest interest and utility. Accordingly, I chose a number of the most significant archaeological projects of the last twenty years and asked their directors to (1) discuss the most important findings of their projects and (2) personally evaluate how these findings have changed our conceptions

of Mesoamerican archaeology. The projects which they report on here range from those which concentrated on individual sites such as the great urban center of Teotihuacan to those which focused on regions such as the Valley of Oaxaca.

I also decided to crosscut these chapters with a series of three general chapters on some of the topics which hold great interest to today's Mesoamerican archaeologists. These topics are the rise of sedentary life, the rise of complex society (civilization), and the rise of urbanism. Rather than choose the archaeologists most often associated with these subjects, I asked three relatively younger archaeologists, whose achievements in the field are just being recognized, to write the chapters. I believe that these scholars have produced important, fresh new perspectives on these topics.

Finally, to open the volume, I asked the distinguished American archaeologist Gordon R. Willey to provide introductory comments on the thirteen chapters in the volume and place their contributions in the general context of the recent developmental trends in Mesoamerican archaeology.

Clearly, I have not attempted to provide coverage for all of Mesoamerica either geographically or chronologically. Given the size limitations for the *Supplement* which were agreed upon by the University of Texas Press, Victoria Reifler Bricker (the series editor), and the volume editors, I was faced with some very hard decisions about what to include in this volume. The final contents which appear here were shaped by the vicissitudes of space constraints, my own biases, the inability to participate in the volume of several authors who had been invited to prepare articles, and the fact that some very significant projects are still in the field phase, thus making assessment of their impact on Mesoamerican studies difficult.

In sum, I feel that while this volume will supplement the original *Handbook*, it also will offer new viewpoints and ideas, as the volume editor and eleven of the authors were not contributors to the original *Handbook* volumes. The *Supplement* provides its readers with a review of some of the principal archaeological accomplishments in the past two decades and a "state of the art" perspective on some of the most significant issues with which Mesoamerican archaeologists are concerned.

J. A. S.

# Part I. Introduction

# 1. Recent Researches and Perspectives in Mesoamerican Archaeology: An Introductory Commentary

*GORDON R. WILLEY*

WHAT HAVE BEEN the most significant new findings in Mesoamerican archaeology? And how have these changed our thinking about the Mesoamerican Precolumbian past? In attempting to answer these questions, the editor of this volume has assembled a series of summary reports on several major archaeological research programs which have been in progress in the past twenty years, or from about 1960 to 1980. The 1960 date is the approximate cut-off line of archaeological research and opinion as recorded in the original *Handbook of Middle American Indians*. Since that time, as the editor has indicated, archaeological research in the Mesoamerican area has proceeded at a great rate. In making his assignments for this *Supplement*, the editor has been forced to be very selective. He has chosen ten research undertakings that are well known among Mesoamerican archaeologists and that have produced substantive information generally regarded to be of great importance to the field. He has also added to this list by soliciting three other chapters. These last are on broad developmental themes which crosscut the data of the research summaries as well as synthesize other recent Mesoamerican archaeological data. In addition, they have theoretical implications of a general nature which transcend the Mesoamerican setting and lead on to wider comparative perspectives.

The purpose of the introductory commentary which follows is to provide an overview of all of these chapters. By offering short summary statements of each it is my hope to make it possible for the reader to see more readily their relationships one to another. In such a summary of summaries, brevity is obviously indicated, and I will be brief. This demands an even greater degree of selectivity than that which has already been exercised by the editor and the several authors. Over their selections I must place my own.

## SOME PRELIMINARY REMARKS

As a prelude to my introductory review, a few preliminary remarks seem in order. Two issues or themes come to mind. The first of these concerns the term and concept "Mesoamerica." In a sense it defines the arena or sphere of all of the papers, the principal exception being the earlier cultures with which some of the authors treat. The idea of "Meso-america" was first formally essayed by Paul Kirchhoff, in 1943, as a culture area defi-nition. Geographically, it referred to the southern two-thirds of Mexico, all of Belize, Guatemala, and Salvador, and western or southern portions of Honduras, Nicaragua, and Costa Rica. The substance of the defini-tion was culture content—traits, trait com-plexes, and their patternings. Kirchhoff drew upon both ethnohistoric and archaeological information for his definition, and consider-able Prehispanic time depth was taken for granted. Mesoamerica was, in effect, a cul-ture-area-with-time-depth, a vast interaction sphere. Since Kirchhoff's original "Meso-american" formulation, further attempts have been made to refine and give sharper defini-tion to the concept, especially with reference to its specific time depth and to the fluctua-tions of its geographical boundaries through time. One such discussion is offered in the original *Handbook* (Willey, Ekholm, and Millon 1964; see also Willey 1966: Ch. 3). I raise the matter here in this review of recent Mesoamerican archaeological developments to indicate that the most signal advance in a reconsideration of the Mesoamerican con-cept is that made by Jaime Litvak King (1975) in an article in which he examined the nature of the intercommunication network among the various subareal and regional cultures within the Mesoamerican sphere. In so do-ing, he has provided a dynamic, chrono-logical perspective on the growth and de-velopment of the Mesoamerican cultural tradition which helps explain its function-ings. Thus, what had been a rather static cul-ture area–classificatory device has been re-cast to give us greater understanding of what went on in the Mesoamerican past. In partic-ular, this *Supplement* will review some of the investigations into the roots of the Meso-american tradition or interaction sphere and its antecedents. These had been glimpsed in only a very preliminary way twenty years ago.

The second issue that needs a word or two in these preliminary remarks is that of Meso-american area-wide chronology schemes. Early area chronologies tended to blur the distinction between strictly defined chron-ological periods and developmental stage for-mulations (Armillas 1948; Wauchope 1950, 1954; Willey 1950, 1955, 1978a; Willey and Phillips 1955). Mesoamerican regional cul-tures were seen as passing through "For-mative," "Classic," and "Postclassic" periods and/or stages in a more or less synchronous manner. But as research progressed it be-came apparent that this was not the case. As a result, there was a trend toward defining major Mesoamerican archaeological periods by chronological criteria alone. This was done by retaining the old names but releas-ing them from any evolutionary or develop-mental meaning. An example would be the Willey, Ekholm, and Millon (1964) chronol-ogy in the original *Handbook*. More recently, however, some archaeologists have put for-ward a new chronological system which em-ploys a whole new terminology designed to eliminate any developmental implications in its period names (Price 1976). Without enter-ing here into the pros and cons of this termi-nological issue, these taxonomic differences should be called to the reader's attention, for some of the authors of the present volume have followed the old system, others the new. For a concordance or correlation between the two, the reader may consult the book *Chro-nologies in New World Archaeology* (Taylor and Meighan, eds. 1978), especially the arti-cles by Lowe (old system), Tolstoy (new sys-tem), and Willey (for a concordance).

Two other matters deserve very brief com-ment here. The first relates to radiocarbon dating citations. Most of the dates cited in the chapters in this volume, and all of those referred to in this commentary, are uncor-rected. Where corrected or calibrated dates have been used, they have been so specified by the author.

Finally, I should note that bibliographic references are kept to a minimum in this in-troductory commentary. The several authors have amply documented their presentations.

4

What few citations I shall make pertain to specific observations of my own.

## THE RESEARCH REPORTS
### Tehuacan

Richard S. MacNeish, quite properly, lists his long preceramic-to-ceramic sequence as the backbone of the Tehuacan contribution. His earlier work in Tamaulipas had prepared Mesoamerican archaeologists for the idea that the rise of agriculture was a long, slow process rather than a sudden "revolution"; the Tehuacan data drive the point home with even greater force. Following a Paleoindian Ajuereado phase, the heart of MacNeish's contribution begins with El Riego, an Archaic-type culture with both artifactual and ecological similarities to the North American Desert tradition. Significantly, however, El Riego, with its first steps toward plant cultivation, showed a trend toward the formation of what was to become the Mesoamerican cultural tradition. What seems to be a further emphasis in this direction is also seen in a relatively elaborate burial ceremonialism for El Riego, incorporating the feature of human sacrifice. The slow pace of the agricultural transformation continued in the succeeding Coxcatlan phase (5000–3400 B.C.), with related settlement evidence testifying to the importance of seasonality and residential shifting in subsistence adjustments. By the Abejas phase (3400–2300 B.C.) domesticated plant foods had risen in importance, and this was reflected in a greater degree of sedentarism with the establishment of seasonal macroband camps.

In tracing this out, MacNeish makes a number of important observations. One is that the Tehuacan Valley was not the only place where early experiments in domestication were taking place. In both Coxcatlan and Abejas, plants were appearing in the dry cave stratigraphies that were not in their natural habitat in the upland Tehuacan Valley but, apparently, had been under cultivation in different Mesoamerican environmental niches. MacNeish also comments that the

Tehuacan data indicate that economically successful agriculture may precede fully sedentary life, as in the Abejas phase, and, conversely, that it is possible that sedentary life preceded agriculture in other Mesoamerican regions, such as along the tropical littoral. Farther along we will see that Barbara L. Stark takes up this alternative in the settlement-subsistence history of ancient Mesoamerica.

The Purron phase (2300–1500 B.C.) marks the appearance of pottery in the Tehuacan sequence; and this, along with the Pox complex pottery of the Guerrero coast, is the earliest appearance of ceramics known for Mesoamerica. Regrettably, settlement and subsistence data for Purron are extremely limited, so we do not know for certain if the "threshold" of sedentary farming life can be said to have occurred in this phase, although it seems highly probable. The subsequent Ajalpan phase (1500–900 B.C.), with ceramics, pottery figurines, and sedentary villages, is fully representative of the Mesoamerican Early Formative, as this may be conceived of either as a stage of development or a culture period. Again, we will see that Stark, in her summary of the rise of farming and sedentary life, points to the time interval of the Purron culture—her Initial Period of ca. 2500 to 1400 B.C.—as a crucial transitional one in Mesoamerica and one, unfortunately, for which data are still relatively few.

The later phases of the Tehuacan sequence are somewhat less unique in the information they impart to the archaeologist than those of the preceramic time ranges. In Santa Maria (900–150 B.C.), MacNeish found evidence for irrigation, a discovery now seen as consistent with what we know of Middle and Late Formative cultures elsewhere in upland Southern and Central Mexico. MacNeish characterizes Santa Maria and Palo Blanco (150 B.C.–A.D. 700) cultures as chiefdoms. In general, the degree of sociopolitical development in the Tehuacan Valley in these times was somewhat less than that achieved in other contemporaneous parts of Mesoamerica. The region was becoming slightly marginal, and this marginality persisted through the Venta Salada phase (A.D. 700–1520) with the rise of what MacNeish characterizes as a "not very successful city-state." Presumably, the comparative standards he has in mind here would be the achievements of the Mixtecs, Toltecs, or Aztecs.

MacNeish treads rather warily in his theoretical formulations deriving from the Tehuacan work. He sees environmental setting and population pressure as factors in the rise of agriculture but as insufficient in themselves to explain it, noting that such things as subsistence scheduling, food storage facilities, and the diffusional interchange of plant products among regions must also have played important roles. Still, from his Tehuacan point of vantage, he has no hesitation in saying that agricultural intensification through irrigation does precede the rise of a chiefdom or nonegalitarian social order, although cautioning that population growth, irrigation, agriculture, and sociopolitical complexity all operate in a positive feedback syndrome in which it is difficult, if not impossible, to extract initial causality. For the origin of state-type societies he concedes that a certain population-agricultural productive base is necessary but not enough to be the triggering cause. He leaves it like this, adding only that such institutions as trade and warfare perhaps play important roles at this point. He devotes some space to methodological innovations in his research, emphasizing the importance of orchestrating interdisciplinary research in the archaeological endeavor. Much of what he has to say here will be taken for granted by a younger generation of archaeologists; but, as deployed on a large scale, such an approach marked a "first" in Mesoamerican studies.

## Preceramic and Formative Oaxaca

As of the mid-1960s, Oaxacan archaeology was known largely from the explorations carried out by Alfonso Caso and his associates at the great valley hilltop site of Monte Alban. From these it was clear that Oaxaca had been the seat of an impressive regional cultural development, one associated with the Zapotecs and the Mixtecs, in which architecture and the arts, hieroglyphic writing and calendrics, and statecraft had rivaled those of other important Mesoamerican centers of civilization such as the Maya area or the Valley of Mexico. The earliest Monte Alban occupation and construction dated to Middle Formative times, although the beginnings and origins of this Monte Alban I phase were undetermined. Vague stylistic Olmecoid resemblances were pointed to, but antecedents were generally unknown. The long-term Valley of Oaxaca program, initiated and run by Kent V. Flannery and his associates, has greatly expanded our knowledge. The culture sequence has now been extended backward in time through Early Formative cultures and through the preceding several millennia of preceramic occupation. Research has utilized extensive settlement pattern surveys, has coordinated these with an excavation program, and has leaned heavily upon ethnohistoric studies in interpreting the archaeological evidence. The Flannery, Marcus, and Kowalewski chapter reports on this.

The Oaxaca sequence begins with a Naquitz phase (8900–6700 B.C.) that discloses a hunting-collecting economy not greatly different from that of the Tehuacan El Riego phase. Plants utilized appear to have been mostly wild, although *Lagenaria* and *C. pepo* may show results of domestication. In subsequent preceramic phases additional food plants were added to the inventory. By what is known as the Blanca phase (3295–2800 B.C.), domesticated maize was probably widespread. Existence was semi-sedentary, much as at Tehuacan, and it is of interest that one site of the Jicaras phase was a macroband camp with a stone-bordered ceremonial or "dance" area (5000–4000 B.C.). There are various artifactual links with the Tehuacan sequence—as well as some differences. One notable similarity is the appearance of stone bowls in both sequences in the last centuries before the appearance of pottery. Concerning the processes that led to the rise of farming, Flannery and his colleagues state: ". . . the Oaxacan agricultural revolution can be simulated without resorting to population pressure, environmental change, or any of the major 'prime movers' sometimes relied on. All that is required is a set of relatively simple policies which result in a resilient, diversified strategy for coping with an unpredictable succession of wet, dry, and average years—a strategy which evaluates its own procurement efficiency on an annual basis and modifies itself bit by bit by selecting from a limited series of alternative moves." As is evident, this is not far different from the way MacNeish looks at the causal forces behind agriculture, although, in the present writing, Flannery and colleagues go to somewhat greater lengths to spell out the processes.

With regard to Oaxacan Formative developments, the same authors set as their goals identification of "the processes leading to the establishment of sedentary life; the rise of societies with hereditary ranking; and the eventual evolution of stratified, class-endogamous societies and the Zapotec state." The first glimpse of the beginnings of this developmental sequence is in the Espiridion complex, which dates somewhere in the 2000–1400 B.C. interval. It has ceramic ties to the Purron phase of Tehuacan, and there are evidences of wattle-and-daub houses; but, as with Tehuacan, the data for this crucial transition to sedentarism are few. The Tierras Largas phase (1400–1150 B.C.) is a more firmly documented and recognizable Mesoamerican configuration. Pottery includes tecomates, flat-based bowls, red-rimmed ware, and dentate-stamped decoration. Sedentary village settlement is indisputable, and at one site, the largest and principal community, there are corporate labor constructions. It is noted that this hint of nonegalitarian society definitely precedes any Olmec influence or Olmec iconography. Olmec-like designs are seen on the pottery of the succeeding San Jose phase (1150–850 B.C.) during which the principal site of the valley (San Jose Mogote)

greatly outstripped the other communities in size, had a number of public buildings, and was clearly the seat of a rising elite class. In 1968 Flannery had advanced the interesting hypothesis that such a locally-arising Oaxacan elite was in contact with and imitating the wealthier and more sophisticated Gulf Coast Olmec (1968b). This argument is not emphasized here, and, further along, it will be seen that David C. Grove, in his chapter, questions the nature of Olmec "influence" in the rise of Early and Middle Formative Mesoamerican cultures. The succeeding phases of the Middle Formative (850–450 B.C.) saw general population increases in the valley and widespread use of agricultural irrigation techniques. San Jose Mogote continued as an important center, but it may have been rivaled by two others, Huitzo and Tomaltepec; and the suggestion is made that these three may have combined forces to construct a new center or "capital" at Monte Alban. By Monte Alban II times (after 200 B.C.) a Zapotec state was in position with a four-tiered settlement hierarchy directed from the Monte Alban capital. Flannery and colleagues' definition of this condition is that of a strong centralized government, with an elite and professional ruling class that had divorced itself from its kinship bonds with supporting commoner populations. The final processes of this development, they believe, were in situ ones which took place in the Monte Alban I phase (450–200 B.C.). Foreign conquest or influence is not seen as vital in this development.

## Oaxaca: Monte Alban and After

Richard E. Blanton and Stephen A. Kowalewski's chapter takes off from the founding of Monte Alban and traces the growth and vicissitudes of that city in its valley context. The story is a complex one in which the authors attempt to consider and balance demographic, economic, political, and social variables. They describe settlement and population concentration in and around Monte Alban, with an increase from 5,000 to 16,000 persons in the city during the Monte Alban I phase. There were secondary and tertiary administrative centers in the valley during this time, but these were situated at some distance from the Monte Alban capital. In Blanton and Kowalewski's opinion, an increasing need for control of regional interaction within the valley was the principal causal force in the centralization they describe. The demographic profile for Monte Alban II (200 B.C.–A.D. 250) is, however, more difficult to interpret. While the full emergence of the power of the state is placed in this phase, Blanton and Kowalewski state that there was a population decrease, at least in the central part of the valley; and they state that this may be related to expansion of state powers, and revenue extraction, to regions outside of the valley. In Monte Alban IIIA (A.D. 250–450) and IIIB (A.D. 450–700) the city continued to grow, reaching a climax population in the latter period estimated at 24,000. This simple summary statement glosses over the details of site and valley history in these centuries, including fluctuations in agricultural exploitation of alluvium and piedmont lands; but, in general, events seem to confirm the increasing consolidation of state power and class development. There was a trend toward architectural seclusion of the main politico-religious precincts of Monte Alban and the growth, outside of these, of elite residential units. There are also some indications that the boundaries of the Monte Alban–controlled valley system were contracting, although it still maintained outlying subadministrative centers at places like Zaachila, Cerro de Atzompa, and San Pedro Ixtlahuaca. The authors also state their belief that the main functions of Monte Alban, during its lifetime and especially at its height, were administrative and interpret only 10–15 percent of the city's population as having been engaged in craft production.

Blanton and Kowalewski tackle the old and difficult problem of Monte Alban IV and V. Were these sequential phases or essentially contemporaneous cultures of different ethnic origins? They prefer the first explanation—

and in this I am inclined to agree. Lambityeco is the type site for Monte Alban IV (A.D. 700–1000). It was one of 10–12 communities of size in the Valley of Oaxaca after the breakup of the Monte Alban IIIB centralized state. A much-reduced Monte Alban itself may have been another. In attempting to understand why the great Monte Alban state of the Classic came apart, Blanton and Kowalewski note that phases I, IIIA, and IIIB were each characterized by population growth, an extension of piedmont agricultural lands, and increased governmental centralization. After each development, problems must have arisen. Population seems to have declined, at least for brief periods, piedmont agricultural expansion was discontinued, and governmental control and centralization may have waned (although this last seems in conflict with statements in the previous Flannery, Marcus, and Kowalewski chapter that focus attention on Monte Alban II as the point at which the centralized state emerged). Why, then, the earlier recoveries and the failure to recover at the close of IIIB? Blanton and Kowalewski offer the explanation that the fall of Teotihuacan, in Central Mexico, ca. A.D. 700, removed an external threat of pressure and competition and allowed for decentralization. While this is certainly a possibility, I think we should also keep in mind that the Late Classic throughout much of Mesoamerica was a time of drastic change in old social orders. Indeed, only the Maya Lowlands seem exempt from such a crisis of change; theirs was to come a century or two later. Attributing all of this to the collapse of Teotihuacan may be too simple, or, at least, may lead us to overlook or fail to search for more complex and interesting chains of processes.

Blanton and Kowalewski carry the story on into Monte Alban V (A.D. 1000–1500) and the complexities of Zapotec and Mixtec relations. This period saw a continuance of the political "balkanization" of Oaxaca. Blanton sees in this the processes which he outlined so well in an earlier article on Central Mexico, Teotihuacan, and the Postclassic aftermath of the end of the dominance of that city (Blanton 1972a). Economic links provided the integration now, rather than governmental decisions radiating out of one great extractive center. These processes, fueled by greater demands for specialized products, doomed the old, costly centers like Monte Alban and Teotihuacan. This "decline"(?)— or an arrangement more complex and flexible(?)—is, I believe, the key characterizing difference between the Mesoamerican Classic and Postclassic cultures. To my way of thinking, the Lowland Maya city-states never adjusted successfully to these processes. The Aztec state was attempting—not altogether successfully—to implant a new political integration on this system of relationships at the time of the Spanish Conquest.

## San Lorenzo Tenochtitlan

Michael D. Coe's earlier account of his excavations at San Lorenzo Tenochtitlan, published in the late 1960s (M. Coe 1968), gave archaeologists a post-*Handbook* knowledge of that site and its important sequence and also a much better understanding of Olmec influences throughout the Mesoamerican area. In his chapter in this volume he updates this, presumably just prior to the publication of his final report (Coe and Diehl 1980). The first occupation of the San Lorenzo "plateau," a natural hillock in the Gulf Coastal Lowlands of southern Veracruz, occurred in the Ojochi phase (ca. 1500–1350 B.C.). This was a relatively small settlement, presumably of riverine farmers, who had an Early Formative pottery complex which Coe characterizes as a less sophisticated version of the Ocos phase pottery from the Chiapas Pacific coast—thin-walled tecomates, flat-bottomed bowls, narrow-necked bottles, with gadrooned, fluted, and red-banded decoration. Figurines are a part of the artifact complex, and a limited amount of grey obsidian was recovered. In brief, there was nothing very Olmec about the assemblage. In the succeeding Bajio phase (1350–1250 B.C.) there must have been a much larger

population at the site; great amounts of earth fill were heaped up on the natural plateau, and the whole was arranged into what appears to have been a giant effigy of a bird, about 1,200 m in length. Temples or public constructions were a part of this site planning and building, and complex sociopolitical organization can be inferred. Ceramics and figurines from this phase are more elaborate than those of Ojochi. There are some continuities out of the earlier phase, but there are also many innovations, including black-white fired pottery, rocker-stamping, and hollow figurines. The latter are technically similar to later Olmec figurines, although no Olmec "baby-faced" figurine heads were recovered. Bajio is followed by the Chicharras phase (1250–1150 B.C.) occupation of the hill, with white and white-rimmed black wares and hollow and solid figurines. Some of the latter have heads that Coe describes as having "vaguely Olmec features." There are also some indications that the famous Olmec monumental sculptural style in stone began in this phase.

The San Lorenzo phase (1150–900 B.C.), divided into A and B subphases, saw the site at the peak of its population growth as well as the florescence of the Olmec art style. Most of the stone monuments were carved at this time, mound complexes were constructed on the "plateau," and a complex system of stone drains was put in. Ritual ceramics display carved jaguar-paw-and-wing, flame-brow, and fire-serpent symbols—all a part of the repertoire of Olmec iconography. Figurines are of the characteristic baby-face style; and there is a rich inventory of lapidary work in ilmenite, magnetite, and hematite, as well as the presence of prismatic obsidian blades. All of this last is indicative of contact with other and distant parts of Mesoamerica, such as Oaxaca and other upland regions; and in the San Lorenzo B subphase, foreign figurine styles show an increasing involvement with such outside regions.

The Nacaste phase (900–700 B.C.), and the Palangana (600–400 B.C.) and Remplas (of Late Formative date) represent later occupations. The first two show some Olmec or epi-Olmec traits in both pottery figurines and small stone carvings, but it is clear that these cultures are not a part of the early and strong Olmec stylistic horizon.

Coe discusses the chronology of monuments at the site. These were all destroyed and buried at the close of San Lorenzo B, and there is little doubt that they were carved in the San Lorenzo phase and, possibly, in the earlier Chicharras. They must have been carved at some location other than the site, perhaps in the Tuxtla Mountains a considerable distance away. As in his earlier writings, Coe attributes the economic and social basis of the San Lorenzo achievement to the extremely rich agricultural soils of the local river levees, and he briefly reviews models and theories for the spread of Gulf Coast Olmec influence to other regions of Mesoamerica. Within the Olmec heartland, problems also remain. Was La Venta the successor and conqueror of San Lorenzo? What was the relationship of these two sites to the unexplored Laguna de los Cerros, another Olmec center of great size and many monuments?

*The Basin of Mexico*

The prehistoric settlement survey of the Basin of Mexico conducted by William T. Sanders and his associates is one of the most ambitious long-term archaeological projects of the Americas. As an aside, I can remember when Sanders, as a graduate student, told me that he wanted to embark on such a venture, and I was inclined to put it down as an unrealistic dream prompted by the enthusiasm of youth. I said that it would take a long time. It did, but Sanders has brought it off with the appearance of the final publication (Sanders, Parsons, and Santley 1979), of which his chapter in this volume is a précis. Sanders' coverage is close to total. Of the approximately 7,000 sq km that make up the surface area of the Basin of Mexico, 1,000 sq km of surrounding mountain slopes were not surveyed; 1,000 sq km bordering lakes were only partially surveyed; 1,000 sq km under

alluvium could not be surveyed; and the approximate 500 sq km of modern Mexico City could not be effectively examined. However, the remaining 3,500 sq km were examined in detail, both from low-level aerial photographs and on the ground. Sanders discusses the many problems in procedures and methods, explains his excavation strategy in connection with surface explorations, and recounts his use of ethnohistoric sources in connection with the archaeological program. The need for population estimates at all times and places—a corollary of population pressure and sociocultural evolutionary hypotheses and questions—began with the reconstruction of population as of A.D. 1519 through use of early Spanish tax records. A figure of 800,000–1,200,000 was arrived at for the basin plus the Tula region to the north. The many problems of "back-projecting" to earlier times from this base-line estimate are outlined in Chapter 6 in some detail.

Sanders' chronological perspective is as far-ranging as his survey enterprise. He employs the "new" chronology:

| | |
|---|---|
| Lithic 1 | 30,000–12,000 B.C. |
| Lithic 2 | 12,000–5000 B.C. |
| Lithic 3 | 5000–2500 B.C. |
| Initial Ceramic period | 2500–1500 B.C. |
| Early Horizon | 1500–1150 B.C. |
| First Intermediate period | 1150 B.C.–A.D. 300 |
| Middle Horizon | A.D. 300–750 |
| Second Intermediate period | A.D. 750–1350 |
| Late Horizon | A.D. 1350–1519 |

But this is overlaid with a broad scheme of ecological adaptation which relates to ecological systems, population pressure, and sociopolitical adjustments:

Stage I    23,000–6000 B.C.
    Hunting (large game) and wild plant collecting

Stage II    6000–900 B.C.
    Hunting-collecting with agriculture as adjunct

Stage III   900–100 B.C.
   Rapid population growth and agricultural
   expansion and intensification

Stage IV   100 B.C.–A.D. 1350
   Population stabilization, continued agricultural intensification, fluctuating political centralization and fragmentation

Stage V   A.D. 1350–1519
   Climax of Precolumbian population
   growth and intensive land use as well as
   urban and sociopolitical evolution

For Stage I, Sanders is talking about such
finds as Tlapacoya and later Tepexpan and Ixtapan. Populations were very small. No food-
grinding implements have been recovered.
   Stage II begins with the Playa phase (6000–
4500 B.C.) at the Zohapilco site, with its plant
collecting and probable very early plant domestication, and continues through the
Zohapilco phase (3000–2000 B.C.) of the
same site, when food collecting was augmented by definite cultivation. Initial period
ceramics and sites in the Basin of Mexico
have not been clearly defined; but Early
Horizon occupations are better documented,
and these small sedentary settlements are
found mainly in the southern and western
portions of the valley and gradually spread
northward from there. The economic role of
farming, vis-à-vis wild plant–collecting, is
mainly to be speculated upon, but Sanders
emphasizes a mixed resource base.
   Stage III (900–100 B.C.), which falls entirely in the First Intermediate period following the Olmec-related Early Horizon, is
seen as a stage of very rapid population
growth. In its three subphases, valley-wide
population estimates are set by Sanders at
20,000, 80,000, and 140,000, respectively;
and there were also some interesting demographic shifts in settlement in that large nucleated villages grew to regional centers of
considerable size. In the second subphase
Cuicuilco, in the southern valley, was the
largest aggregation, with 10,000 people; by
the close of the third subphase Teotihuacan
had outstripped it with 40,000. Some interesting processes can be observed during
the period. Subsistence was now largely or
wholly agricultural, and populations first increased in the prime agricultural regions of
the basin, especially in the south and the
west. There was a population fissioning to
marginal areas, but then irrigation techniques—at first operated on a relatively
small scale—began to give demographic superiority to these marginal areas. Such is one
processual explanation of the rise of Teotihuacan, in its northeastern basin region, over
its southern rival Cuicuilco, although it also
seems fairly certain that the latter site suffered from volcanic activity toward the end of
the stage. But, whatever the reasons, by the
end of Stage III, Teotihuacan was the great
center of the Basin of México—and, indeed,
of Mesoamerica shortly thereafter.
   Stage IV (100 B.C.–A.D. 1350), including
the latter subphases of the First Intermediate period, the Middle Horizon, and the Second Intermediate period, saw the extraordinary centralization of population and power
at Teotihuacan. The population of the entire
Basin of Mexico is estimated at a Middle
Horizon peak of 230,000, with 150,000–
200,000 of these concentrated in the city of
Teotihuacan. Throughout the stage there was
a cyclical alternation of centralization and
fragmentation, with clear correlations of population maxima at times of centralization and
minima during periods of fragmentation.
Sanders sums this up as 700 years of centralization at Teotihuacan, 200 of political fragmentation or decentralization, another two
centuries or so of the Tula Toltec centralization, and this followed by the "Chichimec"
era fragmentation prior to the rise of the
Aztecs. While he speaks of population "minima," it should be noted that the estimate figures remain high during the Second Intermediate period, with a 120,000–180,000
range for the Basin of Mexico.
   Stage V (A.D. 1350–1519) is the Late Horizon or the Aztec horizon. This was the climax
of population size and intensity of land use,
as well as urban and political evolution.
Much of rural population was in dispersed

settlements which blended together. As of 1519, the basin had between 60 and 65 principalities. Each had a center or shared a center with another principality. Most of these centers had relatively small populations of 6,000 or under, although some, such as Texcoco, were in the 10,000–30,000 range. Tenochtitlan-Tlatelolco, the Aztec great capital, had an estimated 150,000–200,000 persons in its 12–15 sq km, a total size comparable to that of Teotihuacan at its height, although more densely settled in its smaller area; however, it should be noted that Tenochtitlan's essentially non-food-producing 150,000–200,000 residents contrast with Teotihuacan's population of about the same size in that 70 percent of the latter's residents are assumed to have been farmers. Tenochtitlan drew upon a much larger immediate area of 600 sq km, with 400,000 people. This population lived around the lakes of the basin, and Sanders estimates that 60 percent of them were engaged in agricultural production. It is Sanders' further contention and interpretation that the Late Horizon period and stage was characterized by much more commercial and craft specialization than in previous eras, with the attendant professional classes related to these functions. The Aztec social and political order is, of course, well known—the aristocracy, the middle classes, a peasantry with communal land rights, and an emerging landless urban poor, many of whom were of slave or semislave status. Tenochtitlan's power and apparatus of taxation were wider than those of either Teotihuacan or Tula, its effective political domain greater.

While Sanders is fully aware of, and refers to, such factors as trade and militarism, and the systemic and multicausal complexities in the rise of civilization, it is probably fair to say that his story looks more directly to subsistence ecology and to demographic pressures as being the principal causes—as Blanton and his Valley of Oaxaca colleagues charge. However, the reader has an obligation to follow out the intricacies of the arguments in each case. What is certain is that the data amassed and examined, both in the Basin of Mexico and in the Valley of Oaxaca, and the closeness and detail in which these have been studied, are infinitely greater than they were twenty, fifteen, or even ten years ago.

## Teotihuacan

If the Basin of Mexico settlement survey was one of the largest and most ambitious Mesoamerican archaeological projects of its kind, René Millon's companion study of the huge metropolis of Teotihuacan was another. The Millon study is, of course, linked to the wider Sanders settlement program in that any meaningful study of urban growth must be viewed in wider regional perspective. Millon and his associates also benefited from the Mexican government's program of large-scale excavations of the 1960s in and around the major buildings of "downtown" Teotihuacan.

A major focus of the Millon study was the residential apartment compounds which are found in great numbers within the Teotihuacan city. Prior to 1961 a few of these had been explored, but it was not known that they were such a common architectural-residence type. These were stone, mortar, wood, and plaster constructions of one story, averaging about 60 × 60 m. Each appears to have been planned and built in a single constructional operation. They are divided into rooms and apartments, usually with a central courtyard. They were clearly residential in function, although many of them incorporate shrines or temples. It is estimated that they accommodated 60–100 people each, presumably living in several nuclear households. The degrees to which the apartment compounds were kin unit settings, places of corporate economic activities, ritual foci, or perhaps served all of these functions remains largely speculative; however, biological-anthropological studies on human skeletons found buried within the compounds do support the kin hypothesis with indications of virilocal residence. As Millon suggests, also, the apartment compounds would have been effective units of administration, social con-

12

trol, and taxation, serving as means for the "Teotihuacanization" of the heterogeneous urban populations, allowing for a certain freedom of customs within the compound walls and, at the same time, some city-wide uniformity. Interestingly, the apartment compounds were not common in the early centuries of the city's history, becoming the fashion only after about A.D. 300. As the enormous Teotihuacan population buildup took place a few centuries before this, it cannot be reasoned easily that their invention and employment was in immediate response to population increase. It should be noted that the apartment compounds are not built to a uniform plan. They share certain formal characteristics, but they vary in size, internal organization, and elaborateness; thus, they would appear to have been built not by the state but by corporate groups exercising differential controls over wealth and resources.

On a residence organizational level above that of the individual apartment compound, Millon found evidences for *barrio*-type clusterings of compounds. These appear to be analogous to similar neighborhood divisions in later Aztec Tenochtitlan. Again, they may have had kin significance, and some were definitely craft *barrios* where obsidian workers, figurine makers, or potters were living together. Wealth and status differences were noted between *barrios*; in many cases there was a "most important" apartment compound within a *barrio*, and this principal compound had the largest temple of the *barrio*.

Because of its length, data and interpretive richness, and interrelated complexity, Millon's chapter does not lend itself to easy short summarization; but it is accurate to say that, after his initial settlement and architectural descriptions of Teotihuacan, he is mainly concerned with higher levels of inference and interpretation. Teotihuacan society was a stratified one of six or more levels. At the top, the aristocratic high leadership are believed to have lived in the Ciudadela palace complex; several thousand members of a priestly and administrative bureaucracy held the next step down on the social scale; below were three levels of apartment compound dwellers, ranked in accordance to the wealth and elaborateness of such residences; and at the bottom a lowest class can be discerned from small, humble, noncompound dwellings, scattered in among the compounds and on their peripheries. Millon estimates that almost three-fourths of the city's total population (estimated in the 150,000–200,000 range for the Middle Horizon [A.D. 300–750]) were engaged in agricultural pursuits outside of the perimeters of the city. From this it follows that many compound dwellers must have been farmers, although some, as noted, were *barrio*-settled craftsmen and almost certainly full-time craftsmen. The lowest social order could also have been agricultural workers, although some may have been servants to palace and compound dwellers. One is reminded of Tenochtitlan's "urban poor," a class emerging in the wake of state centralization and urbanization. Millon concurs with Paul Wheatley's concept of the city as an instrument for the organization of dependent territories and for the social transformation of its surrounding area through the influence of its urban institutions. In other words, the state is not strictly synonymous with the city itself, but the city is the locus of power of the state. In this broader, regional perspective his presentation obviously overlaps with that of Sanders. In state growth he emphasizes the importance of the "autonomous goals" of a leadership that is evolving toward a control of social relations, the economy, and politico-religious centralization.

That some of these "autonomous goals" were achieved early in the city's history can be seen in the regional reorganization and resettlement prior to A.D. 300, expressed most dramatically in the massing of population within Teotihuacan and the depletion or abandonment of outlying centers. Later, there was a planned resettlement of smaller regional centers, established for administrative, extractive, and trading purposes by the centralized power of the state. Exchange and marketing are discussed at length. Millon

13

feels that most day-to-day economic activities, centering in the great market of Teotihuacan, were not state supervised but that the state did control large-scale movements in raw materials, produce, and finished goods. This last was tied to Teotihuacan's expansion outside of the Basin of Mexico, into Morelos, Hidalgo, Tlaxcala, and the Puebla Valley. In the Middle Horizon Millon estimates a Teotihuacan political and economic domain comprising 25,000 sq km and embracing 300,000–350,000 people. He examines some very difficult questions: to what extent was Teotihuacan the seat of a political "empire," to what extent a vast economic system, a religious force, or all of these? Millon concludes that each case of the Teotihuacan "presence" must be examined in situ with as full a contextual analysis as possible—as, for instance, at Kaminaljuyu or Tikal.

That there are no easy answers to complex questions posed by archaeological data is emphasized again in Millon's consideration of "why Teotihuacan." What were the roots of its greatness, the causes behind this particular social phenomenon? Environment and ecology alone cannot explain it; force alone cannot explain it; an expanding economy with all of its requirements does not seem in itself sufficient cause; nor can we attribute the rise and greatness of the city to religious ideology alone. But, taken together, they do explain Teotihuacan, or, at least, they do offer an interactive and intersystemic model that demonstrates the workings of the processes in the city's growth. For those who are satisfied only by simple, single-causal explanations this may not be enough. Personally, I do not think we will ever arrive at these because I do not think that they exist. But, whatever position one may wish to take on this philosophical issue, Millon's treatment of the forces and factors behind the rise of Teotihuacan is fully consistent with and highly representative of the archaeological approach to such problems in Mesoamerica of 1980.

His description of the decline and fall of Teotihuacan is in the same vein. The imme-

diate destroyers of the city were probably rival polities, centers which had been under Teotihuacan's control or economic hegemony. A cited example is Xochicalco, and there are other possibilities. But, again, why? Was it because the territorial extent of the Teotihuacan domain had grown too great, too bureaucratically overloaded administratively and economically? The possibility of factional disputes within the city, perhaps supported from the outside, must also be considered. Certain facts are known. Militaristic symbolism is more prominently displayed in the city's art in the last or Metepec phase than previously, suggesting troubles and the resort to force rather than persuasion. It is also known that the "burning of Teotihuacan" was not a vast, city-wide looting, pillaging, and burning, but a ritual destruction of the main monuments and buildings—following an old Mesoamerican tradition. This destruction was, though, effective. There was probably continued and certainly later settlement at the site, but old great Teotihuacan was gone, never to rise again. Its impress on Central Mexican and Mesoamerican history was not forgotten, however. The Aztec emperors are said to have come here to commune with the spirits of these former glories, as self-appointed guardians of a great tradition.

## The Tlaxcala Region

When Cortez entered Central Mexico in 1519, one of the regions and native states that came most to his attention was that of the Tlaxcalans. Situated east of the Basin of Mexico, in effect, between the sea and the Aztec center at Tenochtitlan, Tlaxcala and its inhabitants were strategically situated to play a role in the Conquest. That they did is a matter well known in history. Long-time enemies of the more powerful and threatening Aztecs, they looked upon the Spanish, for a brief time at least, as allies and saviors. Aside from this place in ethnohistory, the Tlaxcalan region more or less disappeared from view, at least as far as archaeology was concerned, until the last few years. Angel García Cook

14

has remedied this in an important chapter which, more than any other in this volume, brings to most Mesoamericanists what are essentially new data; it provides a whole new regional sequence to place alongside those of the Valley of Mexico, Tehuacan, and elsewhere. This is based upon fieldwork of the 1970s and the integration of the results of this work with what little had been provided earlier by Eduardo Noguera and Sigvald Linné. My relatively brief treatment of García Cook's chapter should in no way be taken as a slight to this highly important contribution. Most of what he has to say is entirely new to me, so I am in the process of digesting it and attempting to fit it into what I know of the rest of Mesoamerica. The reader should do the same with a close study of what he has to say.

The García Cook sequence begins with a Tzompantepec phase (1600–1200 B.C.). The findings seem in line with this dating. The culture is one of small sedentary villages, presumably the first of the region on this Early Formative level. Tlatempa (1200–800 B.C.) follows, with larger villages, the first signs of religious structures, and the beginnings of complex society. There are slight Olmec influences, or at least Olmec stylistic tinges, to the assemblages, a circumstance, again, in keeping with the Early-to-Middle Formative dating. The remainder of the Middle Formative is the time of the Texoloc phase (800–400/300 B.C.). Tlalancaleca is the principal center. As for contemporaneous cultures in the Tehuacan Valley, there are evidences of agricultural intensification techniques—terraces and canals. The Late Formative Tezoquipan phase (400/300 B.C.– A.D. 100) shows effects of the rise of Teotihuacan, especially in what looks like a population loss toward the end of the phase; but it should be added that Tezoquipan culture contributed to the rise of both the Teotihuacan and Cholula cultures and domains. The succeeding Tenanyecac phase (A.D. 100– 650) was a contemporary of Teotihuacan's greatness, and its relationships with that power throw light on the political develop-

ment of the Central Mexican Highlands. It displays evidences of militarism, more notable than before, and explainable in terms of the Tlaxcala regional need to maintain some degree of independence against Teotihuacan and Cholula. Eventually, the Tenanyeca played a part in the fall of Teotihuacan, in García Cook's opinion. Tenanyeca was, thus, one of the Classic period rivals of the great Basin of Mexico metropolis, probably undergoing varying periods of subjugation, semi-subjugation, and near-independence in the struggles and processes of rival state formations. A Texcalac phase (A.D. 650–1100) saw a fully independent Tlaxcalan polity, well consolidated after A.D. 850. And the final Late Postclassic period Tlaxcala phase, and state, was, again, engaged in a power struggle for its independence, vis-à-vis the Aztecs, at the time of the Spanish Conquest.

It is only to be added that this chronological skeleton does not do justice to García Cook's narrative with its concerns for the processes of history and sociopolitical change.

### Tula

Tula and the Toltecs have long been recognized as an important force in Mesoamerican prehistory. Perhaps here we should qualify this by saying "prehistory becoming history," as the Central Mexican Postclassic period began to usher in a kind of semilegendary traditional history of which the Toltecs and their doings mark the first recognizable landmark. As of the date of the *Handbook of Middle American Indians*, our knowledge of Tula derived largely from the field researches of Jorge R. Acosta and the important 1941 ethnohistorical research paper of Wigberto Jiménez Moreno. The latter convinced the archaeological community that Tula was the Tollan of the historical sources. Previously, some scholars had linked Tollan to Teotihuacan; and George C. Vaillant (1941), in his synthesis, had attempted to resolve the ethnic identification issue by referring to Teotihuacan as the seat of the "Classical Toltecs," with Tula the base for the Postclassic or "New

15

Toltecs." Richard A. Diehl, in his introductory remarks, indicates agreement with the Tula-Tollan identification, although I think there is at least the possibility, considering the reverence and awe in which the name Toltec was held in the historical sources, that Teotihuacan may have been a still earlier Toltec capital, a more ancient Tollan.

In recent years both the Mexican government and the University of Missouri have conducted further field research at Tula, in Hidalgo, north of the Basin of Mexico, and Diehl offers a synthesis of their results in his summary paper. There are important chronology revisions to be reported. Robert H. Cobean (of the University of Missouri team) has produced a fine-grained ceramic chronology linked to radiocarbon dates. A Prado phase (A.D. 700–800) is the earliest at the site, and it shows both Coyotlatelco (early Post-Teotihuacan) ties and similarities to contemporaneous developments on the northwestern Mesoamerican frontier, this last suggesting population movements from these regions into Central Mexico. These same ceramic traditions—Coyotlatelco and northwestern frontier—also characterize the succeeding Corral phase (A.D. 800–900). By this time the site occupation was larger, and the Tula Chico ceremonial center was the focus of activity. A brief Terminal Corral phase (A.D. 900–950) follows. This is designated as a "critical" time, just before the rise of great Tula. The Tollan phase (A.D. 950–1150/1200) is the great phase. The end date for this phase is still open to question, and Diehl says that there is the possibility that it may be one hundred years earlier than the above dates. This was the phase of the building of the Tula Grande center, the main and well-known one at the site. Of particular note is that the dominant pottery of the Tollan phase is not Mazapan or Tula-Mazapan as was so long thought. Instead it is a continuation of the Coyotlatelco tradition. There are, however, many interesting trade wares at the site, occurring in quantity. These include Tohil Plumbate, polychromes from Lower Central America, Huasteca V types from the

Gulf Coast, and ceramics from the northwest. The only well-known trade ware absent from the Tollan phase assemblages (in some instances these look like traders' warehouses) is the Early Postclassic Fine Orange of southern Gulf Coast and Maya Lowland provenance.

Tollan phase Tula was an urban site covering 13 sq km and with an estimated population of 35,000. Its subsistence economy was agricultural, and there are evidences of terracing and some limited clues to Prehispanic irrigation. It was a great craft center, and there are indications of obsidian workers' *barrios* and probable pottery workshop areas. Tula, at this time, controlled the famous Pachuca green obsidian sources which had formerly been a part of the Teotihuacan system. Considering the widespread nature of Tula products, it seems likely that a *pochteca*, or government-controlled trading cadre, was a Toltec institution. The extent of Tula's state boundaries is estimated by Diehl to have been, minimally, as far to the north and east as the Pachuca obsidian deposits on the edge of the Sierra Madre Oriental and west to Michoacan; but political power, and certainly trading power, far outran these limits. Ties to central and northern Veracruz were very strong, and, of course, Tula Toltec influence in the monumental art of the distant Maya Lowland city of Chichen Itza is well known. As with Teotihuacan, the nature of this extended Tula presence, in its various manifestations, is still to be investigated.

Diehl emphasizes that Tula could not have been a causal force in the decline and fall of Teotihuacan, as Tula was not in existence at that time. It seems quite possible that some population elements of the Prado and Corral phases came into Tula from the Basin of Mexico after the fall of Teotihuacan; others were probably immigrants from the northwestern frontier country.

Diehl offers an interesting comparative discussion of Tula, Teotihuacan, and Aztec Tenochtitlan, the three great urban centers of Central Mexico. Of the three, Tula was by far the smallest, in both population and territorial size. Teotihuacan shows the greatest degree of planning of the three, Tula the least. The Tula residential unit shows some similarities to the Teotihuacan apartment compound in that many of the site's court-yard residences must have housed several nuclear families; however, single nuclear family residences are also common at Tula. Neighborhood or *barrio* units are also present in the Tula settlement layout.

Three later phases are represented at Tula. Fuego phase corresponds to what would be the Aztec II–III transition in the old chronology. The site at this time—following its fall—was only a modest-sized community. In the Palacio phase (Aztec III and IV) there was a much larger community here, presumably under the Aztec imperium, and this continued on into a Tesoro phase (Colonial period).

No new data are available on the causes and nature of the fall of Tollan phase Tula. It probably perished as the result of strife in an era of militarism. Such militarism is well exemplified in Tula Toltec art at that capital and elsewhere.

*Tikal*

Of generally comparable magnitude to the Teotihuacan study is the research carried out at Tikal, Department of Peten, Guatemala, in the 1956–1965 period by University of Pennsylvania archaeologists. This has been further supplemented by a continuance of the program, for the 1965–1970 period, by the Guatemalan government. Christopher Jones and his colleagues, William R. Coe (who directed the Pennsylvania work) and William A. Haviland, have given us a brief summary of the highlights of these investigations. These authors summarize the outstanding substantive achievements at Tikal under headings of "Epigraphy and Rulership" and "Demography and Subsistence." It should be added that, to date, there has been little published on this very important Tikal work in the way of final and formal monographs. These are being readied for an early

release, but preliminary statements and various other articles incorporating Tikal results have already had a tremendous impact on Maya studies.

While a full translation of Maya hieroglyphs is probably still some years away—and, according to some authorities, may never be attained—there can be little doubt that some significant advances have been made. These pertain, especially, to the identifications of rulers, dynasties, and their seats of power and to a fascinating network of intermarriages and dynastic connections ranging widely over the Maya Lowlands in the Classic period. The epigraphic and iconographic data from Tikal form a major node in this network. A Tikal king list has been documented with beginnings traceable back to the third century A.D. In this documentation hieroglyphic texts and monuments have been linked to specific tombs and burials. Of special interest has been the identification of an early ruler of Tikal as a probable foreigner or at least a personage associated with dress, symbols, and paraphernalia indicative of connections with distant and non-Mayan Teotihuacan. This takes on particular importance as archaeologists attempt to understand the processes of widespread trading and political connections. It also appeals to a humanistic interest as we begin to identify and sketch in individuals and personalities from what had been, heretofore, a fully "prehistoric" past.

The old Lowland Maya problem about the nature of the great Maya sites—were these true cities or vacant ceremonial centers?—has been clarified greatly by the Tikal investigations. There is now little doubt that Tikal was a metropolis, with urban dimensions and urban functions. This is seen in the settlement layout. Around the mammoth acropolises, pyramids, and palaces of its central zone, small residential mounds occur in great numbers. Between A.D. 480 and 830 this dense settlement extended over an area of about 120 sq km. That this had been conceived of as a vast settlement unit by the ancient Maya is verified by the presence of defense walls about 5 km to the north and south

17

of the city center. The eastern and western edges of this urban sprawl are defined by natural swamps or *bajos*. Within the 120 sq km the archaeologists have counted an average of 112 small structures per sq km. While there is some open territory between and among residential units, this is not believed to have been sufficient for maize cultivation but was, rather, utilized in an "infield" or "kitchen garden" manner for vegetables and orchard crops. How then was the Tikal urban population—estimated at 72,000 for the 120 sq km zone (personal communication from Haviland to Willey, 1980)—sustained in the production of major food staples? This question, posed by the Tikal investigations as well as elsewhere in the Maya Lowlands, has led to inquiries into the whole matter of Maya subsistence. Among other modes of food production intensification, it has now been well documented that the Maya farmers, in addition to swidden or milpa cultivation, practiced a raised field cultivation in low-lying riverine and swamp locations. For further information on this the reader is referred to an important recent publication, *Prehispanic Maya Agriculture* (Harrison and Turner 1978). With immediate reference to Tikal subsistence, Jones and his coauthors cite the *bajos* adjacent to that site as having been the settings for such raised field cultivation and a major source of agricultural production for Tikal's huge populations.

These two lines of research advance, epigraphic-dynastic and demographic-subsistence, while focusing attention on important new data and changes in interpretation, do not cover all of the significant findings in the Tikal work. New architectural and ceramic data from the site have expanded our knowledge in the substance of these specialities and have helped to integrate this with what was known from other Lowland Maya sites and regions.

## Dzibilchaltun

Another Lowland Maya site selected for a report here is the huge center of Dzibilchal-

tun in northern Yucatan. In the original *Handbook* the then recent excavations at that site provided the basis for E. Wyllys Andrews IV's summary statement on the Northern Lowlands. Since then, continued investigation and analysis of the Dzibilchaltun data have provided new information, supplementing and modifying what had been known. E. Wyllys Andrews V outlines this important northern culture sequence from Dzibilchaltun.

The Nabanche phase (800–300 B.C.) represents the Middle Formative beginnings. To date, the only earlier pottery found in northern Yucatan has been that from the Mani Cenote and from the Loltun cave. During the earlier half of the phase the settlement was a simple village location; formal public architecture began appearing in the latter half, along with population and settlement growth. The ceramics are described as pertaining to the Mamom sphere of the Southern Lowlands but with regional differences. In general, the northern ware slips tend to be harder and glossier than those of the south, and Andrews also observes that this northern Mamom tradition variant is characteristic of the Edzna and Rio Bec regions. The implications of this last would be that by the Middle Formative at least, if not before, there were the beginnings of a ceramic split between north and south, with the line falling somewhere along the northern boundary of the Guatemalan Peten. The origin of northern Yucatecan Formative ceramics is still uncertain. Southern (Peten) influences probably were involved, but it may be that, on an Early Formative level, ties were stronger to the southern Gulf Coastal Lowlands. The Dzibilchaltun Xculul 1 phase (300–50 B.C.) saw the kind of first big building that characterized the Late Formative period in many places in Mesoamerica. This building—and the implications that it carries of a development of a complex and more centralized society—should be looked upon not as derivative from elsewhere but as a response to local conditions of population growth and the need for control of agriculture and trade. This does not preclude contacts with other regions, and these can be seen in certain architectural similarities to northern Belize and in a participation in a Chicanel ceramic sphere; but, with relation to this last, Andrews cautions that there are numerous ceramic differences between Dzibilchaltun Xculul and Peten Chicanel. Trade from distant parts is signaled by the appearance of jade in Komchen contexts, but, as in all Dzibilchaltun Formative phases, there is very little obsidian. Andrews speculates that some of Dzibilchaltun's greatness could be attributed to the salt export trade from reasonably nearby coastal locations which were under its control. Toward the end of the Xculul phase (300 B.C.–A.D. 150) there was a decline in public architecture and population. The reasons are unknown. Overpopulation? A disintegration of coastal trading patterns and a loss of control of the salt trade? One can only add that this particular period in Maya Lowland history, in some places referred to as the Protoclassic period, saw similar declines in some places and regions although considerable vigor in others. Readjustments, realignments, and changes in seats of political and economic power seem to have been going on after the Late Formative "boom" in population growth and agricultural expansion in the area.

The Piim and Early Copo 1 phases fall in the A.D. 250–700 period. Dzibilchaltun was resettled and public architectural construction resumed after the Late Xculul collapse. Teotihuacan architectural elements (tablero-talud terraces) occurred at about A.D. 600. Were these the work of a small group of outsiders in some way connected with the salt trade? But by A.D. 700, or the Late Copo 1 phase, there was a resurgence at Dzibilchaltun, comparable in many ways to the resurgence or renaissance seen elsewhere in the Late Classic period. In less than a century Dzibilchaltun became one of the most populous centers in northern Yucatan. Edward B. Kurjack's settlement pattern studies in and around the site have produced data for urbanism on a scale comparable to that of Tikal. Residences of different sizes and elaborations

speak of differences in wealth. A number of temple-palace complexes, sometimes connected by causeways, suggest that governance of the metropolis may have been handled on a rotational basis among the more powerful lineages. There are relationships in architectural features to Usumacinta and Palenque, and a Teotihuacan theme in big architectural orientation (15.5° east of north) is observed. There seems little doubt that Dzibilchaltun now controlled a large portion of the salt trade, and the city imported jade, obsidian, and Belize chert in quantity. Between A.D. 830 and 1000, in the Copo 2 phase, Dzibilchaltun buildings displayed Puuc architectural styles. These had arisen almost 100 years earlier in the Puuc Hill sites. There would seem to have been even greater wealth and class differences in Copo 2 than earlier; however, in the closing century of the phase there are signs of population fall-off and constructional decline. The rise of Tiho, the location of modern Merida, some little distance to the south, may have drained people and power from Dzibilchaltun. From this point Dzibilchaltun ceased to be a place of great importance and would appear to have become a pawn in the struggles of the Postclassic. Andrews gives us some insight into the complexities of these. Among other things, it is now fairly clear that there was a Mexican presence in northern Yucatan before A.D. 1000. For another, the big sites of the Puuc Hills probably were not abandoned until some time after the first Toltec architectural and artistic features appeared at Chichen Itza. In the Dzibilchaltun Zipche phase (A.D. 1000–1200) there were some Mexican Chichen ceramic types, and in the latter part of that phase some modest public building. A very small population lived at the site in the Chechem phase (A.D. 1200–1540), and in this final Precolumbian period it seems to have served as a small ceremonial center. Andrews surmises that the salt trade of the Postclassic had passed into the hands of Mexican-controlled Maya and, later and more specifically, into the control of the sea-faring Putun of Cozumel and Mayapan.

## THE TOPICAL SYNTHESES
### *The Rise of Sedentary Life*

Barbara L. Stark's treatment of the rise of sedentary life, derived primarily from recent Mesoamerican data, necessarily treats with much of the same information reviewed by MacNeish, Flannery and colleagues, and Sanders—that is, the antecedents to settled agricultural communities, the transition to that condition, and the results of this important change. She prefaces her remarks by saying that hers will be a multicausal-model approach to the explanation of the processes involved, taking account of the factors of population growth, environmental conditions and ecology, cultivation and domestication of plants, food storage, distance costs (in transporting food), and sedentarization. A reading of her chapter will confirm that she has addressed all of these, individually and in concert, and that her theoretical outlook is not greatly at variance with that of MacNeish, Flannery, and Sanders.

Her Paleoindian periods are essentially background to the stage of transition. Paleoindian I (before 14,000 B.C.) subsumes about what Sanders did in his Lithic I period—the edge-retouched pointed flints below bifacial points in the Hueyatlaco complex of the Valsequillo stratigraphy, Tlapacoya, El Horno, El Mirador, and like finds. Stark expresses some doubt about it all by asking whether these Mesoamerican evidences for such a stage are truly valid and whether other comparable discoveries in the New World are valid. She leans toward a positive answer, as, I think, most American archaeologists would do. While this has generally been considered an "unspecialized hunting" stage, Stark puts two other interesting questions. How can we be sure that the hunters of Paleoindian I were not as good at "big game hunting" as those of Paleoindian II? And, if they were not, why did not their rather generalized subsistence scrounging of miscellaneous game, plants, and seeds lead on to agriculture at this earlier time? Obviously, we do not yet know enough to answer these questions. Paleoindian II (14,000–7000 B.C.) is the bifacially-flaked-point, big-game-hunting stage. The "big-game-hunting" characterization has been challenged. Big Pleistocene fauna was hunted and killed at this time, but how often? Some early culture complexes, such as those of Tehuacan and Oaxaca, date to the period but reveal mixed economies and no big game. All in all, the subsistence of Paleoindian II is still not well understood. How important, respectively, were big game, small game, and wild plant foods? The best conclusion for now seems to be that hunting was more important in the Paleoindian era than later.

The Archaic period (7000 B.C. to the first pottery at ca. 2500 B.C.) saw the two changes Stark is most concerned with: the development of sedentarism and the development of agriculture. Sedentarism is defined as more or less steady, continuous occupation of the same site and agriculture as plant cultivation and domestication, with concomitant changes in the plant genotype. While sedentarism and agriculture are each possible without the other, it must be recognized that there is a strong (and apparently intercausal) relationship between the two in the highlands of Mesoamerica. As is shown in MacNeish's account, there was definite cultivation in the Tehuacan Valley before 5000 B.C., and a significant increment of subsistence was dependent upon domestication in the Abejas phase (3400–2300 B.C.). Full sedentarism there may have been later, although the record, even in this most detailed Archaic period sequence of Mesoamerica, remains somewhat ambiguous on the exact timing between sedentary life and economic dependence on plant domestication. As we move more deeply into the problem of the relationships between the two, there are a number of puzzles, and Stark airs these very conscientiously. There seems little question that population growth and sedentarism are linked, as there is considerable ethnographic evidence for a shorter birth-spacing among humans under sedentary conditions. But to adjust to these population increases, what pressures led to the continuation of plant-cultivation experiments? Selection and cultivation is more work than wild plant gathering for what would appear to have been little or no increased gain in food materials at first. What was the role of storage? Were cultivated domesticates, such as maize, more easily stored than wild foods? This seems not altogether certain. Might not the successful storage of some wild foods, such as mesquite, have slowed down maize domestication? The factor of travel costs is also considered. Cultivation and domestication would have concentrated food resources so that less time and energy would have been devoted to more widespread foraging. There is also the matter of social interaction and its desirability and advantages in sedentary, single-locus living throughout the year. In examining the pros and cons of all of this, Stark has taken us about as far as present data and thinking permit. There are no final answers—and there may never be—but the multicausal complexities of the problem are revealed.

Stark also observes that there is more than one developmental course possible in the rise of sedentary life and farming, even within the area of Mesoamerica. Lacustrine, riverine, and coastal niches appear to provide settings different from those of the uplands. The Chantuto phase of the Chiapas coast, as an example, gives evidences of possible sedentarism, with house floors, postmolds, metates, and manos. Palo Hueco of the Veracruz coast, dated at ca. 3000 B.C., is another case in point, as is the Ostiones phase of the Guerrero coast, which is of comparable age. These were all preceramic cultures, and all would appear to have had an economic dependence heavily weighted on the side of shellfish, fish, and, very probably, plant foods. Was their apparent sedentarism fully preagricultural? All were, indeed, late enough to have begun to adapt to plant cultivation through contacts with inland groups. It may also be argued that the natural environmental potential in such littoral settings would have allowed for greater populations sustained by fishing and collecting,

and these populations would have been predisposed to adapt to farming to sustain their increasing numbers. While such an assumption may be, and has been, challenged, it is obvious that Mesoamerican archaeologists need to examine further the interrelationships and interplay between upland niches such as the Tehuacan Valley and those of the lowland tropical coasts. For one thing, plants in early stages of domestication often undergo genetic changes very rapidly when they are moved from one environmental niche to another. For another, it is now becoming increasingly apparent that Mesoamerican agriculture did not have a single regional base but was, instead, built up of contributions from many diverse regions.

As I have already noted, Stark and others in this volume point to the crucial period of from about 2500 to 1400 B.C. as the time in which the sedentary-agricultural "revolution," if we wish to call it that, was finally achieved, at least in the southern portions of the Mesoamerican area. Whatever the pace of the moves toward sedentarism, the rise of plant domestication, and the interaction between these two processes, the village farming tradition was a fact by the later date. Unfortunately, this particular millennium has something of the aspects of a "black box"; we see many of the elements feeding into it from earlier times; and we see the results; but we do not as yet have a clear picture of how and why they came about. Beyond the village farming threshold a number of things were permitted, if not immediately caused by, sedentarism. Stark lists some of these. The nuclear family settlement allows for production for prestige-related social activities. The village setting, once established, is the context for these activities and also a unit offering its members defensive advantages against competitors. Ritual and social mechanisms to settle disputes and increase solidarity of the community are devised. The feedback relationships between a reliance on farming and population increase are accelerated. The "filling in" of the landscape through growth and fissioning occurs. Exchange is facilitated:

21

there are more customers, better storage of produce, and easier communications. Differential access to resources, such as good lands, makes for social differentiation. As yet, we do not fully understand how ecological and other factors favor the development of social hierarchies, but progress toward such understanding is promised. Finally, as Stark concludes, there can be little doubt that sedentary farming life changed the nature of intra- and intercommunity relations in Mesoamerica in a most profound way. The social differentiation and complexity of societies that developed rapidly after 1400 B.C. attests to this.

## The Evolution of Complex Culture

David C. Grove continues the story from the point where Stark leaves off. To study the rise of complex societies over and above the sedentary farming, simple village-based community of the Early Formative "floor," he reviews the evidence from four of the best-known Mesoamerican regions: (1) the Olmec Gulf Coast, (2) the Valley of Oaxaca, (3) Central Mexico, and (4) the Pacific Coast and slopes of Chiapas and Guatemala. Three of these regions have already been examined in the updated research reports, so I will be brief in this summary. From an archaeological point of view, Grove selects such things as big public architecture, monumental and portable art objects, iconography on pottery, figurine development, and the presence of finely worked jades. Although he does not specifically list it in his criteria, it is also fair to say that he depends to some extent on differentiated settlement sizes and central-place organization. It is his intent to emphasize cultural continuity from an in situ point of view in his regional analyses, but the importance of diffusion or external contacts is not ruled out. As he puts it, in situ complexity attracts external interactions in cultural development.

For the Gulf Coast, the Ojochi-to-Bajio phase transition (ca. 1350 B.C.) was the first

step up from simple to complex society. This judgment is based upon the construction of the huge artificial plateau for residences at the San Lorenzo site. Insofar as we know, it was the biggest public works project of its time in Mesoamerica, and such a construction implies organization over and above that of an egalitarian society. Figurines in the Olmec style appeared at this time, foreshadowing the later monumental expressions of this style in the succeeding phases. In the San Lorenzo phase what appear to be rulers were portrayed on the stone monuments, and these were accompanied by finely made and ornamented small goods and evidences of trade in exotic goods. The Early-to-Middle Formative period changes in Olmec culture, as represented by La Venta and other finds, appear to be largely shifts in stylistic and artistic choices; or at least Grove makes no attempts to relate these to any particular line of sociopolitical evolutionary reasoning. Unfortunately, there are few wider regional settlement data for the Olmec Gulf Coast, so that it is impossible to say anything about the nature of a central-place hierarchy or the number of levels involved in such a hierarchy if one did exist. Perhaps there were only two such levels, one of the major sites or centers, such as San Lorenzo and La Venta, and the other of small peasant hamlets—but we do not know. Later on in his paper, Grove expresses the opinion, also held by Michael Coe, that highly productive river levee agriculture was the foundation for this ranked Olmec society; and he further links this with the appearance of hard kernel maize in the Gulf Coast region in the Ojochi phase, some 400 years earlier here than is known for any other part of Mesoamerica. The cited archaeological evidence for this is the presence of stone metates and manos in Ojochi.

In Oaxaca the first public constructions also date to the Early Formative (the Tierras Largas phase), although these are of a much more modest size than the Bajio plateau construction of the Gulf Coast. There was an increase in this kind of constructional activity in the San Jose phase (1150–850 B.C.), and this was associated with Olmec-style motifs on ceramics. This leads Grove to wonder about the significance of the "Olmec presence" here and elsewhere in Mesoamerica at this early time. Was it the result of trade contacts or even the imitation of prestigious foreign items? Or are archaeologists dealing with a very widely held and ancient ideological or mythic base for southern Mesoamerica—something that was once registered in perishable media and, in the course of social evolution, was carried on, quite independently in a number of places, to ceramics and stone? I am less convinced of this than I am of the trade-contact explanations. The complexity and specificity of the designs of Olmec art are such that contact seems to me to be the only way they could have been replicated from region to region. Furthermore, I would see the emergent chiefdom level, as represented by the Oaxacan Tierras Largas phase, as providing the more likely social milieu for the diffusions responsible. But to return to the Oaxacan sequence, the Guadalupe and Rosario phases, spanning much of the Middle Formative period, featured the development of secondary centers. That is, a central-place hierarchy was being built up, a very definite testimony for complex society. And it was at this point, near the end of the Middle Formative period, or at about 500 B.C., that Monte Alban was founded as the valley-wide capital and the head of a central-place network of at least three hierarchical levels, a further evolutionary step in social complexity toward the level of the state.

In treating with Central Mexico, Grove begins by noting the clarifications in the Formative sequence which have now placed the Olmec-influenced Tlatilco culture as a part of an Early Horizon Ixtapalapa phase (1250–900 B.C.). This is definitely earlier than the Zacatenco and El Arbolillo phases. Initial period or Early Formative ceramics of Central Mexico still remain somewhat nebulous for the earlier time ranges of ca. 2000 B.C., a point made in the review of Sanders's chapter, although the Nevada phase (1400–1250 B.C.) pottery is now better known. One assumes, on what evidence there is at hand, that these Initial period or Early Formative period cultures of the Valley of Mexico were on an egalitarian village level of social development. For the Early Horizon, the nature of the burials, ceramics, and figurines at Tlatilco and at other Ixtapalapa phase sites argues for a ranked society, although evidences for mound building or public construction are somewhat ambiguous. By the Middle Formative, however, such constructions and important central sites are well in evidence. Chalcatzingo, in Morelos, and the earlier building stages of Cuicuilco, in the Valley of Mexico, would be examples.

On the Chiapas-Guatemalan Pacific Coast there is a substantial and well-known Early Formative development—that of the Barra and Ocos phases—and the Ocos phase, which probably lasted until 1150 B.C., may be associated with public architecture. There are Olmec influences in this coastal region, and these may date to the Early Horizon Cuadros phase (1150–800 B.C.), although Grove suspects that they are a bit later than this in the Middle Formative. By the Middle Formative Conchas phase (800–600 B.C.) there were a number of pyramid and mound platform sites in the region.

Grove's review leaves us with the picture of the earliest big public constructions dating to Early Formative times in the Olmec Gulf Coast country, with public architecture not being much later than this in Oaxaca. Such constructions seem to have begun still later in Central Mexico and in Pacific Chiapas-Guatemala, where they are not securely documented until after 1000 B.C. or into the Middle Formative. By ca. 800–600 B.C. central-place sites, marked by intensive labor constructions, were a general feature of southern Mesoamerica; and from this evidence one assumes that complex society and culture were well under way. We are left to wonder about the role of Olmec culture in this. Its possible slight priority in the signs of complex social organization, the diffusion or spread of its symbols to other Mesoamerican regions in the ca. 1200–900 B.C. period, and the more or less contemporaneous appearance of public building in these regions at about that time do leave us with at least a tentative model of an Olmec dissemination of "high culture." While I think that the weight of the evidence does suggest strongly that the Olmec Gulf Coast was the hearth for this symbolism, I think that we must view with extreme caution the "culture-bearer" role of the Olmecs as the causative force in these rather widespread changes. As can be seen in several of the chapters in this volume, there were forces of in situ cultural and social evolution at work in various regions of Mesoamerica during the Early and Middle Formative periods.

As indicated, Grove reviews the relationships of agricultural productiveness to the rise of complex culture, and he makes clear that, while there is indeed a relationship, there are no easy one-to-one answers. He also comments upon the probabilities of South American diffusion into Mesoamerica having had a role in such things as the development of early pottery styles (e.g., Ecuador to Barra-Ocos, or Peru and Ecuador to various parts of West Mexico), the spread and exchange of food plants, architectural features, and ideological elements. The Mesoamerican archaeologist, in an attempt to be as comprehensive as possible, cannot ignore any of this; but, as with the geographically more limited phenomena of Olmec symbols, the archaeologist cannot depend upon the "borrowings" of things or ideas to explain all the processes in the rise of complex cultures.

## The Rise of Cities

Richard E. Blanton is concerned with a continuation of the evolution of social and cultural complexity which Grove has traced. This is best subsumed under the concept of the "rise of the city." What is manifest in the Mesoamerican archaeological record of the growth of institutions capable of organizing regions and peoples through integrated systems of government, commerce, or both? This regional perspective is the keynote of

Blanton's approach, and he leans heavily upon the geographer's models and studies of central-place functions. This means an examination of sites with reference to their arrangements in central-place hierarchies and with reference to their functions. For example, marketing centers and administrative centers are not always the same, and whether they are or are not tells us something about the society and its economy. It is an axiom that "higher-order" central places serve a wider territory and more people and have more functions than lesser-order centers; therefore, it is expectable that these "higher-order" centers will have larger populations. Such a circumstance leads to an urban aspect or dimension of a city, but Blanton emphasizes that sheer population numbers, in themselves, are not the criterion of city definition. His definition is essentially a functional one: a city is a higher-order central place in any system of central places. Such a definition not only avoids hard-to-agree-upon population-numbers criteria but also stands aside from ethnocentric criteria.

Mesoamerican field research has provided many new data for the study of the rise of the city, and Blanton addresses these data from his central-place theoretical standpoint. The best-known example of the early Mesoamerican city is, of course, Teotihuacan. From a regional point of view, with reference to the Basin of Mexico and even to a more widely defined Central Mexican region, Teotihuacan was a mammoth "primate" center. It was larger than any of the satellites in its system by a magnitude of ten times or more. It was vastly more wealthy than any of its subordinates. Such a Teotihuacan regional system— a "solar" type system—does not conform to the rank-size distributions of marketing places of Walter Christaller's predictions. Interestingly, these predictions are more closely matched by the Basin of Mexico and Central Mexican site distributions of the Late Postclassic (Aztec) period. Does this tell us something about the inherent weaknesses of the Teotihuacan system and the city's fall? Perhaps so. Teotihuacan's overwhelming primacy in its region meant that all of the rest of the region was economically disadvantaged through an absence of marketing choices and through physical distance from the center. How is this Teotihuacan "solar" system to be explained? Blanton feels that what he considers the "cultural ecological" point of view, as represented by Sanders and his associates, is insufficient to explain Teotihuacan's great growth and size at the expense of the rest of the region. He argues that "more powerful" explanations than those of agricultural production or resource access advantages are needed.

Blanton contrasts the Teotihuacan regional pattern with that of Monte Alban and the Valley of Oaxaca. The Monte Alban hegemony over the Valley of Oaxaca was not, in his view, comparable to that of Teotihuacan in its setting. The Monte Alban system was not a "solar" system. There were other large centers in the Valley of Oaxaca before the rise of Monte Alban, but these were not afterward foreclosed as were Teotihuacan's rivals. Instead, they continued to function as important, if second-level, central places, both administratively and commercially. To support this interpretation Blanton develops various lines of evidence which I will not go into in this quick summary, but the summation of his thesis is that the Monte Alban–Valley of Oaxaca system more closely approximates the predictions of the geographer's central-place theory than the Teotihuacan system.

Why the differences in the two courses of city development? Blanton is unwilling to accept the factor of population pressure as the main cause. This, he feels, is the cultural ecologist's error—despite the fact that Sanders and his colleagues do admit other factors in their causative equation. In the Blanton view, population growth—city growth—is as much a reflection of changes in societal structure as a cause of those changes. For the present, he leaves it there, with only the directive that the regional perspective in the study of central-place hierarchies will permit analyses that are more sophisticated, and more likely to give us insights and explana-

tions into the rise of the city, than the cultural ecological approach. As the reader will realize, this is one of the most complex and knotty problems that the archaeologist faces in the Mesoamerican data. It is clearly unresolved as yet. Blanton's insistence on the regional perspective and the importance of the study of central-place hierarchies is certainly justified. On the other hand, I do not think he has given Sanders and cohorts sufficient credit for their employment of a regional perspective, and it remains to be seen, in the Teotihuacan and Oaxacan settings, what further explanations may be elucidated from the central-place frame of reference.

## Some Concluding Comments

The new perspectives and developments in Mesoamerican archaeology of the past twenty years abound with substantive discoveries. Many of these are reviewed in the research reports of this *Supplement*. They concern such things as cultural-distributional data, sequences changes and additions from many regions, contextual "filling out" of cultures, and the space-time systematics of interregional relationships. Despite the wealth of these data offered here, it should be added that many regions and sites not mentioned have been similarly explored, including the vast territories of western Mexico lying to the north of Oaxaca and Central Mexico, Central and Northern Veracruz, and, in the far south and east, the Mesoamerican peripheries that blend with Lower Central American cultures in Salvador, Honduras, Nicaragua, and Costa Rica. In general, there has been less work here than in the better-known regions, but this is being rapidly remedied. There is little said in this volume about the interrelationships of Mesoamerican cultures with those to the north in North America or to the south in Lower Central America and South America—themes treated in the original *Handbook*—but there have also been data and interpretive advances along these lines.

From methodological and theoretical

standpoints, the research of the last two decades has emphasized a number of things. One of the first and most obvious that comes to mind is in the realm of interdisciplinary research, the coordinating of archaeological investigations with those of scholars from the natural and physical sciences. As some of the following chapters will detail, these coordinated researches have paid off enormously well in better and more accurate understandings of cultural settings and culture content.

A second, and more immediately archaeological, improvement has been in a greater concern with and control of context. The pottery debris, the flint or obsidian tools, the animal bones or organic refuse, the house floor, and the temple and its fine sculptures are being viewed together as cultural-societal wholes rather than as series of objects studied without reference to each other. The "telephone-booth-sized" test pit is being replaced with the exploration of the house floor living unit of a past time (Flannery 1976a), the basis for a beginning of behavioral understanding.

This theme of contextual control can be extended to include the great strides that have been made in settlement pattern study. The Central Mexican, Oaxacan, and Lowland Mayan examples to be described here are outstanding instances of both data gathering and interpretation. Settlement pattern relates directly and immediately to the regional perspective and the importance of and necessity for such a perspective in our attempts to even begin to understand the rise of such phenomena as the great Precolumbian cities and state formations.

Mesoamerican research is also becoming fully indoctrinated into the tenets of the "new archaeology" as its practitioners strive to get beyond the potsherd, house floor, or palace mound and to see these material residues as byproducts of ancient social and cultural systems, institutions, and behavior patterns. The archaeologist now asks questions as a preliminary to field investigations. The latter are geared to these questions through hypotheses that are formulated to be tested

by the materials found in the field. There is also a greater sophistication now in the framing of these questions and in the expectations as to answers. All of the chapters which follow will demonstrate this. The rise of sedentary life, farming, complex societies, or the city and the state are not thought of as simple events attributable to single, easily comprehended causes. The human story is recognized as vastly more complex. Systemic, multicausal explanations now dominate the field. Perhaps this is a vogue, and perhaps we will come back to a greater simplicity in attempting to understand the whys and hows of culture change; but, if so, it will be a new level of simplicity that has been attained only after an upward struggle through the maze of complexity that now seems to confront us.

Can we predict the future directions of Mesoamerican archaeology? Not really, or at least only within very general limits. It is a commonplace to say that explorations will be pushed into regions as yet unexplored or that we shall increase our chronological control of the data through the filling of regional and sequence gaps and the more extensive and refined deployment of dating aids. I think that within a very few years the long preceramic periods will be much better known, and we shall also have considerably more data on that shadowy time band that corresponds to the earlier part of the Early Formative period (now estimated at ca. 2500– 1500 B.C.). Even with these new data, it remains to be seen whether we shall truly understand this vital transition in human society and culture any better than we do now. And the same applies to the later transitional "thresholds" that are discussed in this volume. Archaeologists can only redouble their efforts in their application of scientific techniques and in the systematization of their own data to approach scientific standards and keep on trying. Whether these advances will lead to the explanation of cultural process is difficult to predict. There is, however, one encouraging aspect of Mesoamerican archaeology. This is its retention of its old, rich humanistic tradition. It is expressed in the way that the subject is embedded in a marvelous ethnographic and ethnohistoric context, and in some of the following chapters it can be seen how this tradition and these contexts have been further enriched and deepened by hieroglyphic and iconographic studies of the very recent years that help us tell the story of the past and, I think, better understand that story in direct, documented human behavioral terms. Is this a moving away from Mesoamerican archaeology's progress as a science? Some of our colleagues might think so, but I would see it as a reinforcement, a betterment as we move forward on a broad front.

# Part II. Some Significant Archaeological Researches of the 1960s and 1970s

# 2. Tehuacan's Accomplishments

*RICHARD S. MacNEISH*

HAVE BEEN ASKED to discuss in thirty typewritten pages the principal accomplishments of the Tehuacan Project and my opinion of how these achievements have altered archaeologists' basic conceptions of prehistoric Mesoamerican development. This is a tough task to undertake even in a book (MacNeish 1978), let alone in thirty pages, but I will give it a try. Obviously, there are two separate questions involved. The first, and the easier one, is what I consider to be the main contributions of the Tehuacan projects that started in 1961 (and still are continuing). This may be discussed in terms of (1) concrete new and significant findings that lead to (2) new hypotheses or theoretical considerations concerned with prehistoric Mesoamerican development (Byers 1967; MacNeish, Nelken-Turner, and Johnson 1967; MacNeish, Peterson, and Flannery 1970; Johnson 1972; MacNeish et al. 1975). The second question is how the above have altered other archaeologists' basic conceptions of prehistoric Middle American cultural change. At the outset, let me say that it often seems that some archaeologists working in Mesoamerica never

change their minds no matter what the new data (Lathrap 1977), or if they do, they never admit it (Lorenzo 1975). Further, there is a great deal of provincialism in respect to both time and space among Mesoamerican archaeologists, so that sometimes they may change their minds about one aspect, usually an aspect that concerns their narrow problems, and not change their minds about other conceptions. Altogether, it is difficult to judge just how much each and every one of the Mesoamerican archaeologists—rugged individualists par excellence—have altered their basic conceptions. Therefore, the best I feel I can hope to accomplish in this brief chapter is to give my judgments about how the Tehuacan accomplishments *should have* altered the basic conceptions of prehistoric Mesoamerican development of archaeologists who work in this area, not how they actually did.

Thus, I shall give my opinions about the Tehuacan Project in terms of three general categories. First, I shall consider the new (as of 1960) finds that the project brought to light. This I shall do in terms of my nine sequential archaeological phases running from before 10,000 B.C. to the time of the Spanish

Conquest. Second, I shall discuss how basic conceptions of prehistoric Mesoamerican development should be or seemingly have been altered by these "new" Tehuacan findings. This will be done in terms of five general theoretical problems: (1) the process of the peopling of the New World; (2) the original domestication of plants and the problem of the origin of agriculture; (3) the beginning of settled life and the concept of the Neolithic revolution; (4) the transition from village (tribal) life to town or urban (sometimes civilized) life (chiefdoms and/or priestdoms); (5) the origin of the state and/or national states—the shift from chiefdoms to primitive states. Third, I shall be concerned with how and why these findings that altered concepts occurred, and here, obviously, I must talk of the techniques, methods, kinds of analyses, and approach that the Tehuacan Project used or developed.

## SUBSTANTIVE ACCOMPLISHMENTS

The earliest phase, Ajuereado, which dates from before 10,000 B.C. to about 7000 B.C., or better, 7600 B.C., is not well represented, as only about 20 small sites or components and only a few thousand artifacts have been found in the Tehuacan Valley (MacNeish et al. 1975). Yet, never before these 1960 endeavors had so many Early Man sites been found in so small a region. Furthermore, before that, there were hints that in this time period, people lived in small groups as nomadic bands. The Tehuacan data supported such a hypothesis. Also, this culture, with its various types, clearly showed that a Mesoamerican, Early Man level culture, while having general relations with Early Man cultural traditions such as Clovis, Plainview, etc., to the north, was clearly a distinct, separate culture tradition. Tehuacan gave proof of Mesoamerica's independence from the north, even on the Early Man level.

The long estimated length of this poorly defined Ajuereado phase also had important implications about Early Man and other discoveries in this field that were to come later.

First, Ajuereado spanned the period of the extinction of megafauna, and our analysis hinted that while man may have had a hand in the extinction of the Pleistocene beasts, the loss of this biomass for whatever reason was also one of the causes of the cultural development from the Ajuereado phase to El Riego or, more generally, from the Early Man to the Archaic period. Second, the long period showed that Early Man had not only slowly developed better and better hunting techniques, but also a series of other subsistence options. In fact, as I have pointed out before, "these people in the so-called big-game hunting stage or mammoth-hunting period were far from being the great hunters they are supposed to have been. As one of my colleagues said, 'they probably found one mammoth in a lifetime and never got over talking about it,' like some archaeologists we know" (MacNeish 1964a:532). In fact, in Tehuacan, we had begun digging Early Man occupation sites, not kill sites, and for the early sixties this was a whole new approach which was to give a whole new outlook on the way of life of Early Man, an approach that is still being developed. The final implication concerned associations of the earliest materials of Ajuereado with extinct animals, in apparent Pleistocene contexts with obvious connections to Juan Armenta Camacho's (1978) and Cynthia Irwin-Williams' (1967a) new, very early finds from nearby Valsequillo Dam on the outskirts of Puebla. These facts, coupled with Alex D. Krieger's then new article about pre–projectile point cultures (1964) and my earlier Diablo materials from Tamaulipas (MacNeish 1958), hinted that the hypothesis of a 12,000-year limit for Early Man in America was probably incorrect (Martin 1973) and that a new flood of earlier finds would occur not only in Mesoamerica, but elsewhere in the New World. Thus, our Tehuacan finds were involved in the development of this new revolutionary concept and provided evidence that the best was yet to come in the field of archaeology— a statement that still holds true in spite of the conservative doubts of some of my col-

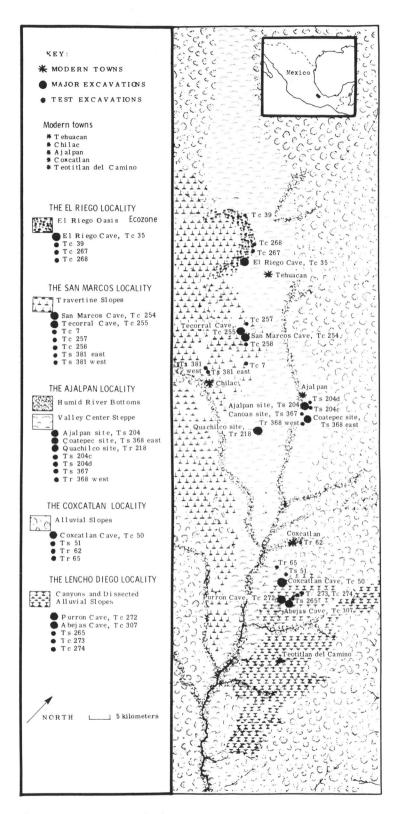

KEY:

✳ MODERN TOWNS

● MAJOR EXCAVATIONS

• TEST EXCAVATIONS

Modern towns

✳ Tehuacan
✳ Chilac
✳ Ajalpan
✳ Coxcatlan
✳ Teotitlan del Camino

THE EL RIEGO LOCALITY

El Riego Oasis Ecozone

● El Riego Cave, Tc 35
• Tc 39
• Tc 267
• Tc 268

THE SAN MARCOS LOCALITY

Travertine Slopes

● San Marcos Cave, Tc 254
● Tecorral Cave, Tc 255
• Tc 7
• Tc 257
• Tc 258
• Ts 381 east
• Ts 381 west

THE AJALPAN LOCALITY

Humid River Bottoms

Valley Center Steppe

● Ajalpan site, Ts 204
● Coatepec site, Ts 368 east
● Quachilco site, Tr 218
• Ts 204c
• Ts 204d
• Ts 367
• Tr 368 west

THE COXCATLAN LOCALITY

Alluvial Slopes

● Coxcatlan Cave, Tc 50
• Ts 51
• Tr 62
• Tr 65

THE LENCHO DIEGO LOCALITY

Canyons and Dissected Alluvial Slopes

● Purron Cave, Tc 272
● Abejas Cave, Tc 307
• Ts 265
• Tc 273
• Tc 274

NORTH  └─┘ 5 kilometers

FIGURE 2-1. Location of Tehuacan.

33

leagues. In any case, by the end of the Valse-quillo and Tehuacan endeavors, we could write considerably more about Early Man in Mesoamerica than the one paragraph of Willey and Phillips 1958 or the three short paragraphs of Armillas 1964.

As has been shown, even our flimsy evidence from our earliest phase had important new implications for prehistoric Mesoamerican developments, and, not surprisingly, so did our materials from our second, much better documented, El Riego phase, dating from roughly 7600 to 5000 B.C. in radiocarbon time, or perhaps 8000 to 5800 B.C. in sidereal time. Here, we had materials from over 41 components, of which 25 were excavated. Although some of the earlier ones did not have much preserved foodstuffs or feces, most had abundant cultural features, artifacts, chips, bones, and other ecofacts, concentrated in definite activity areas on each floor. There was obviously a mass of new data, but did it signify anything really new, conceptually? After considerable soul searching, I decided it did, for while many had thought of the culture of this general Archaic time period as being analogous to that of Julian H. Steward's seasonal basin-plateau bands, no one had ever attempted to test this hypothesis with archaeological data. In fact, what had usually been done was to consider site size, grinding stones, and food collecting artifacts for their subsistence implications and ecological aspects, decide these features were analogous to those of the Great Basin cultures, and then apply the rest of the patrilineal-bands cultural features in the reconstruction of an archaeological culture.

The more we analyzed our El Riego data, the more apparent it became that Steward's band type was simply a hypothesis to be tested or modified by archaeological data. Thus, we set out to get seasonal indicators for each of our activity areas to determine not only whether they were contemporaneous and whether they represented microbands or macrobands, but also to determine in what season certain ecozones were occupied and what activities were carried out. In other

words, we attempted to see if our archaeological cultures were like the ethnographic, seasonal calendar-round ones, and we tried to reconstruct their seasonally scheduled subsistence systems and their band way of life from the archaeological data, not by ethnographic analogy. It was found that, while our archaeological El Riego type of band had some general similarities to those of Steward (1938) and Sahlins and Service (1960), it also had some significant differences from the ethnographic examples.

First, and foremost, we found evidence that these Mesoamerican bands were experimenting with plants such as mixta squash, peppers, chile, avocado, and perhaps corn and slowly taking the first faltering steps toward their domestication or cultivation, unlike any bands recorded in the ethnographic record. Second, there was evidence that these bands, unlike most ethnographic bands, had a complex burial ceremonialism that implied strong shamanistic leadership, as well as mechanisms for population control via the ceremonial use of infanticide and (female) human sacrifice.

Thus, our El Riego findings gave us not only new data about a prehistoric developmental stage of Mesoamerica but also new information about ancient types of bands in Mesoamerica as well as hypotheses about plant domestication, cultivation, and band structure that could be tested by further archaeological work. Michael Coe's and Pedro Armillas' records of 1962 and Gordon R. Willey and Philip Phillips' of 1958 (M. Coe 1962; Armillas 1964; Willey and Phillips 1958), which were all written just as the Tehuacan Project began or slightly before, contained no information on these subjects. Thus, I believe our El Riego materials did introduce new data with theoretical implications that should have altered basic conceptions.

That the next phase, Coxcatlan, dating from 5000 to 3400 B.C. in radiocarbon time, did give new data is much more obvious, for here is where we obtained our basic information about the domestication of corn. Although opinions and interpretations about how corn was domesticated have changed since Paul C. Mangelsdorf's initial statement, the fact remains that even twenty years later we have obtained no new, better, or more complete archaeological data on the subject (Mangelsdorf, MacNeish, and Galinat 1967). Corn is still thought to have developed from wild corn, teosinte still seems to be a later development from corn in terms of the archaeological evidence we have, and the process of domestication still appears to have taken place somewhere in the Oaxaca-Puebla area in the general period from 7000 to 5000 B.C., whether one uses the more extensive Tehuacan information or the less reliable pollen data from Oaxaca (Schoenwetter in press) and the Valley of Mexico (Lauro González Quintero, personal communication).

Figures 2-2 and 2-3 and Table 2-1 chart H. Garrison Wilkes' (1967) and my thoughts on the domestication of corn (as well as the development of teosinte). As we suspected before the Tehuacan Project began, domestication took a long time, as did all pristine agricultural developments; such developments were not initially revolutionary, and their first effects were slight and slow. With the Tehuacan sequence, we had solid evidence that this was true, and the older concepts of rapid domestication became invalid. Further, the sudden occurrence in Coxcatlan levels of fully domesticated avocado, chile pepper (C. E. Smith 1967), black and white sapotes, bottle gourd, moschata squash (Cutler and Whitaker 1967), and common beans (Kaplan 1967)—all plants unrelated to any growing wild in Tehuacan—strongly suggested multiple origins of domestication in Mesoamerica and indicated that the old concept of a hearth, or single place, in Mesoamerica where all plants were domesticated was also invalid. Thus our Coxcatlan phase not only gave us significant new data on changing culture but also provided information concerning the process of incipient agriculture and horticulture.

The following Abejas phase (3400–2300 B.C.) gave more data to confirm these generalizations, and in addition it produced the first preceramic pit house of Mesoamerica. Furthermore, it showed that the increasing growing of cultivars and domesticates for storage was associated with longer and longer stays in band encampments, until it was possible to stay in one place all year and be sedentary. Before the Tehuacan Project we had no data to document the way in which this process occurred in Mesoamerica; now we have obtained some initial data, though we still need a great deal more.

The next phase, Purron, dating from 2300 to 1500 B.C. plus or minus a few hundred years, yielded the earliest pottery for Mesoamerica, as well as some evidence of increasing production of food by the use of hybrids. These were both firsts, and we have learned little more about them since then. These findings were more important for raising new questions than for altering basic conceptions, but they were certainly a major accomplishment, since they are so hard to duplicate.

With the Ajalpan phase, dating from 1500 to 900 B.C., we were on much firmer ground, for a great deal had been written on the Early Formative before the Tehuacan Project. Some of the earlier theories could be shown by our ceramic and radiocarbon studies to be erroneous. First, there was the whole problem of chronological alignment of the Early Formative cultural manifestations. Originally, the Valley of Mexico materials, early El Arbolillo, and sometimes early Zacatenco, were considered to belong to the Early Formative period, while early Tlatilco manifestations, or those with Olmec affinities, were thought to be Middle Formative (Piña Chan 1955b). We straightened out this chronology with our trade sherd study, and now Paul Tolstoy's initial digging (Tolstoy and Paradis 1970) and Christine Niederberger's later digging (Niederberger 1976) on Tolstoy's Tlapacoya site have provided us with some real Early Formative materials and have put El Arbolillo and Zacatenco where our Tehuacan data indicated they belonged, in Middle Formative times. Much the same could be said of the poorly documented

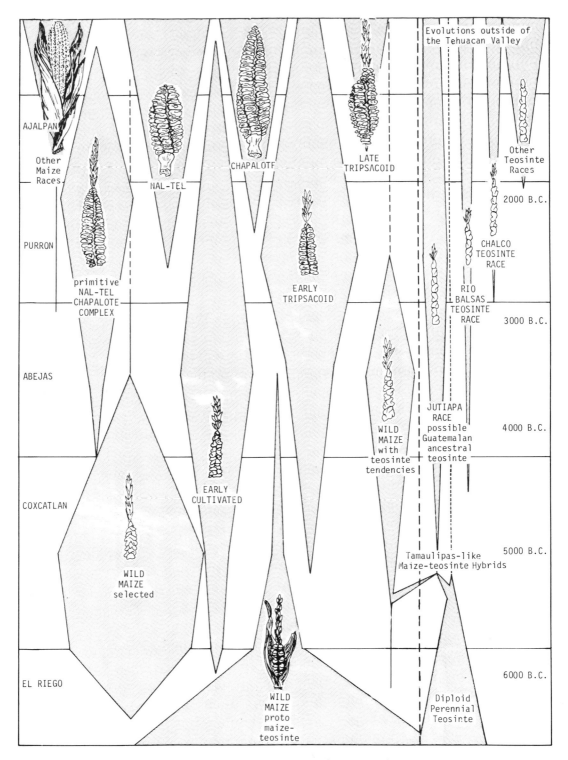

FIGURE 2-2. Schematic drawing of the evolution of corn and teosinte: alternate 1.

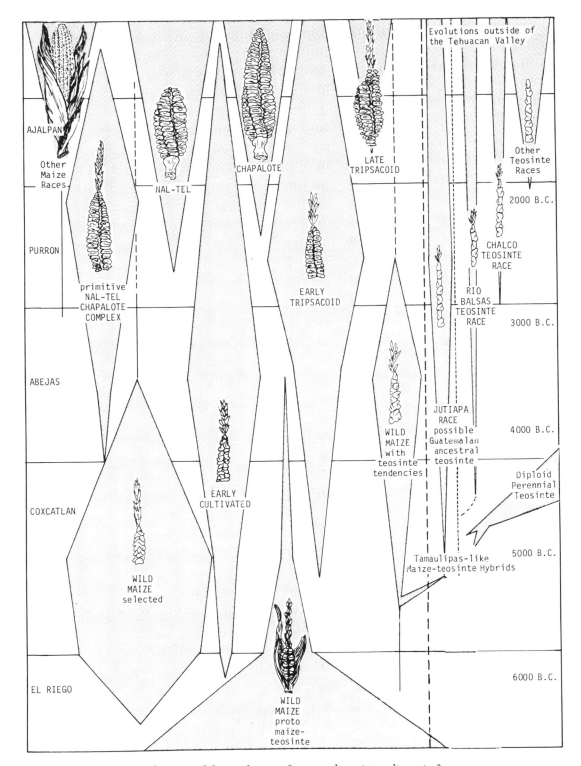

FIGURE 2-3. Schematic drawing of the evolution of corn and teosinte: alternate 2.

Text within the figure:

AJALPAN

Other
Maize
Races

PURRON

primitive
NAL-TEL
CHAPALOTE
COMPLEX

ABEJAS

COXCATLAN

WILD
MAIZE
selected

EL RIEGO

NAL-TEL

CHAPALOTE

LATE
TRIPSACOID

EARLY
TRIPSACOID

EARLY
CULTIVATED

WILD
MAIZE
with
teosinte
tendencies

WILD
MAIZE
proto
maize-
teosinte

Evolutions outside of
the Tehuacan Valley

Other
Teosinte
Races

2000 B.C.

CHALCO
TEOSINTE
RACE

RIO
BALSAS
TEOSINTE
RACE

3000 B.C.

JUTIAPA
RACE
possible
Guatemalan
ancestral
teosinte

4000 B.C.

Diploid
Perennial
Teosinte

5000 B.C.

Tamaulipas-like
Maize-teosinte Hybrids

6000 B.C.

TABLE 2-1. Early Corn Races from Tehuacan Levels Which Are the Basis for Figures 2-2 and 2-3

| Level | Wild Wild Maize-1 | Cultivated Wild Maize-2 | Early Cultivated or Domesticated | Evolved Wild Maize-3 | Early Tripsacoid Maize-Teosinte | Proto Nal-Tel Chapalote | Pure Nal-Tel Race | Pure Chapalote Race | Complex Late Tripsacoid |
|---|---|---|---|---|---|---|---|---|---|
| *(characteristics)* | proto maize-teosinte; 4 rows; deeper than wide cupules; 6 spikelets; soft glumes | selected, perhaps planted; 8 rows; wider than deep cupules; 6–9 spikelets; soft glumes | planted and selected; 8–10 rows; wider than deep cupules; 8–19 spikelets; soft glumes | evolving teosinte tendencies; 8 rows; deeper than wide cupules; 6–19 spikelets; indurated glumes | various crosses, backcrosses; 4–12 rows; deeper than wide cupules; 8–20 spikelets; indurated glumes | selected primitive hybrids; 8–12 rows; width, depth about equal; 10–25 spikelets; soft glumes | bred for orange pericarp; ave. 11 rows; much wider than deep cupules; 16–30 spikelets; soft glumes | bred for brown pericarp; ave. 12.3 rows; much wider than deep cupules; 25–50 spikelets; moderate glumes | various complex crosses; 12 rows; width, depth about equal; 20–40 spikelets; hard glumes |
| Tc254, Zone C¹ Late Ajalpan—1200 B.C. | | 37 | 43 | | 86 | 4 | 2 | 2 | 1? |
| Tc272, Zone J Late Ajalpan—1850 B.C. | | | 2 | | 6 | 2 | 1 | 1 | |
| Tc272, Zone K, K-K1 Purron—2500 B.C. | | | | | 3 | | | | |
| Tc50, Zone VIII Late Abejas—3500 B.C. | 1 | 1 | 7 | 3 | 3 | 1 | | | |
| Tc50, Zone IX | | 7 | 18 | | | | | | |
| Tc50, Zone X | | | 1 | | | | | | |
| Tc254, Zone D Early Abejas—4000 B.C. | | 58 | 38 | 1 | | | | | |
| Tc50, Zone XI | 1 | 19 | 3 | 1 | | | | | |
| Tc254, Zone E Late Coxcatlan—5000 B.C. | | 24 | | 1 | 1 | | | | |
| Tc50, Zone XII | | 5 | | | | | | | |
| Tc50, Zone XIII | 2 | 15 | | | | | | | |
| Tc254, Zone F Early Coxcatlan—5800 B.C. | 1 | | | | | | | | |

NOTE: Dates are for specific zones and do not necessarily correspond to general dates for phases given in text.

Highland Guatemala sequence, in which Arevalo, Majadas, and sometimes Las Charcas had often been placed in Early Formative times (Shook 1951). Even Monte Alban I had sometimes ended up in the Early Formative (Paddock 1966) and often in the Middle Formative (Caso, Bernal, and Acosta 1967), but our studies resulted in the placement of the former in the Middle Formative and the latter in the Late Formative.

Thus, our Ajalpan relationships helped align the complexes of Early Formative times in the highlands and also showed that they represented a general village Formative way of life. Also, our data helped confirm Covarrubias' not very well accepted idea that Olmec culture on the coast began in this time period. Only Squier (1964) really had evidence of this, and he had placed San Lorenzo in this period. His later testing at La Venta, as well as Michael Coe's magnificent excavation at San Lorenzo, confirmed these Tehuacan indications (MacNeish, Peterson, and Flannery 1970). However, what was more important was that these data underscored the newly formed concept that developments on the coast and in the highlands were quite different, with the highlands emphasizing secular development and the lowlands, sacred. In fact, Mesoamerican developments were multilineal rather than unilineal, or even unicausal.

Somewhat connected with this highland-lowland, secular-sacred problem was our study of the distribution of figurine types in various house areas of the Ajalpan and Coatepec Early and Middle Formative sites. Here, we were attempting to discern the evolution from sodalities connected with kin-aggregate groups to supernatural beings associated with some sort of cult. No one had tried this before our Tehuacan endeavors, but now there is increasing interest in understanding changing social organization and problems of information flow. We were grappling with the problem of what these clusters of artifacts in the archaeological activity areas meant, and how to interpret them. Although we never really came to any definite conclu-

sions ourselves, at least we contributed new hypotheses and well-documented data for others to theorize about.

These distinctive areal developments become even more noticeable in Middle Formative times, 900 to 450 B.C., during the heyday of great coastal ceremonial centers like La Venta that were contemporaneous with the not very striking highland villages of early Santa Maria in Tehuacan; San Jose, Guadalupe, and Rosario in Oaxaca (Drennan 1976a); and El Arbolillo and Zacatenco in the Valley of Mexico (Tolstoy and Paradis 1970).

Perhaps the most startling "new accomplishment" connected with the Santa Maria phase (900–150 B.C.) was the finding of Purron Dam, with the indications from foodstuffs from nearby Purron Cave that the peoples of the Santa Maria phase had a subsistence system based on irrigation agriculture. Karl A. Wittfogel, Pedro Armillas, Angel Palerm, Julian H. Steward, and William T. Sanders had long suspected this, but they had not been able to prove it. Moreover, Robert McC. Adams had written a monograph (1966) claiming that early irrigation did not exist in Mesoamerica and was not a significant factor in the rise of the state in Mesoamerica (or the Near East): good anti-Wittfogel stuff, or what my friends call "throwing the baby out with the canal water" (Wittfogel 1957:447). Purron Dam laid this ghost to rest (or should I say drowned it), and more recent investigations by Kent V. Flannery in Oaxaca (see Chapter 3 of this volume), by Angel García Cook in Tlaxcala (see Chapter 8 of this volume), by Melvin L. Fowler near the city of Puebla, and by Sanders and his colleagues in the Valley of Mexico have turned up many more early "hydraulic" features, as did the earlier Tehuacan investigations of Richard B. Woodbury and James A. Neely (1972). These findings should be altering archaeologists' basic conceptions, so that they include "water control" as a basic consideration or ingredient in any theory or hypothesis about early prehistoric Mesoamerican developments. Thus, our Santa Maria phase materials not only yielded new pottery and figurine types, new subsistence and settlement pattern information, etc., and helped solve chronological problems in the Formative, but also had important theoretical implications.

However, in terms of the Tehuacan Project's orientation toward the "rise of agriculture and concomitant development of village life," our materials from the Santa Maria phase, as well as the Palo Blanco phase, dating from 150 B.C. to A.D. 700, were of peripheral interest. Nevertheless, our Palo Blanco ceramic studies and dates did help in the overall chronological alignment of the various so-called Classic sites or periods and did correct a serious misconception about this stage. Before our endeavors in Tehuacan it was generally assumed that the Maya Lowland Classic (M. Coe 1966), dated calendrically from A.D. 100 or 300 to about A.D. 960, was contemporaneous with the so-called Classic of the highlands: Teotihuacan I–IV and Monte Alban I–IIIB (Willey and Phillips 1958; F. Peterson 1959). Our studies of Palo Blanco relationships pretty much convinced us that the early part of the Highland Classic, represented by Palo Blanco, Monte Alban II, Teotihuacan I and II, etc., was in fact in existence before the Maya Classic (which began about A.D. 300) and in fact was roughly contemporaneous with the Maya Protoclassic. Further, our late Palo Blanco phase had trade sherds of San Martin–stamped and Fresco-decorated wares from Teotihuacan II and III (Tlamimilolpa) (R. Millon 1966b) as did the Early Classic Esperanza phase of highland Guatemala (Kidder, Jenning, and Shook 1946) and Tzakol phase of the Peten, while the Maya Late Classic sherd type, San Juan Plumbate, did not occur in Tehuacan until the early Venta Salada phase of the Postclassic (A.D. 700–1520). These discoveries mean that the Maya Late Classic was in fact contemporaneous with the Highland (Tehuacan) Postclassic, the period when militarism was starting in the highlands. This has important implications for "the fall of the Maya Empire," and one has to acknowledge that the expanding Highland Postclassic militarism

may have been a factor in the Maya collapse.

This brings us to the significance of our Postclassic Venta Salada finds. As indicated above, our chronological work indicated that the Postclassic in highland Mexico was far longer, roughly A.D. 700–1520, than our previous estimates (A.D. 960–1520), with the obvious implication that the Postclassic developed much less suddenly than we had thought. Further, our rich Venta Salada materials shed light on the gradual rise of a not very successful city-state, trying to be an empire. We even turned up a sixteenth-century map of the *señorío* of Coxcatlan and found out that our survey had rediscovered most of the ruins of its tribute towns (Sisson 1973–1974). Our ceramic studies, our weaving analysis, flint knapping investigations, studies of salt ruins, and other excavations also gave us hints of the sort of full-time specialists and industries that were in Coxcatlan and Venta Salada. Somewhat to our surprise, we also uncovered evidence, in the form of carved glyphs on our pottery, that the peoples of the Tehuacan region were possibly responsible for the *Codex Borgia* and probably the whole Borgia school of codex writing (Chadwick and MacNeish 1967). Not only did these discoveries, plus the finding of Xantiles (anthropomorphized urns or incense burners) in certain rooms of most of the house compounds, give us new glimpses of Postclassic gods, cosmology, and theology, but such finds also had exciting possibilities for understanding the ancient inhabitants' social organization. We are still trying to understand the implications of these finds, but even now many of our basic conceptions of Postclassic Mesoamerican development have been altered.

## THEORETICAL ACHIEVEMENTS

However, our major achievements in terms of altering basic conceptions were in the theoretical field. These I should like to discuss in terms of the specific problems that were changed by what we did in Tehuacan. One of these, which I alluded to earlier, concerns how our finds helped change archaeologists' concepts of how much earlier man was in the New World than they had previously thought, how slow his migrations must have been, and how great Early Man development must have been over this more-than-50,000-year period. However, this was not the major accomplishment of the Tehuacan Project, and much of the basic data came from later finds made elsewhere. The major theoretical change that the Tehuacan Project brought about had to do with the problem of the domestication and cultivation of plants and the development of agriculture, not only in Mesoamerica, but perhaps in all the pristine centers of development in the world.

Pertinent to the understanding of this process was the finding that, with the extinction of animals in the Tehuacan Valley, there was a shift from a relatively unscheduled subsistence pattern by microbands with limited subsistence options, to the El Riego system with good evidence of a seasonal scheduling subsistence and settlement pattern system and increasing numbers of subsistence options, including storage. Our studies of the El Riego phase seem to show that in the dry seasons microbands lived mainly by hunting in the oasis and along the river banks of the valley Center Steppes, with only occasional brief forays into the eastern Alluvial Slopes or, more rarely, into the canyons of the western Travertine Slopes. In the spring, microbands moved into the Dissected Canyons, the western Travertine Slopes, and the eastern Alluvial Slopes for longer stays, collecting seeds. In the lusher years, some of the microbands in the Travertine Slopes and the eastern Alluvial Slopes may have coalesced into macrobands during this season. These same microenvironments (though not necessarily the same spots) continued to be exploited during the wetter summer months as the people continued to collect seeds and pick fruit. With the coming of fall and its diminution of food supplies, the microbands began moving back to their winter abodes. This behavior constitutes a regular pattern of economic seasonality. Since the pattern

seems so regular for so long a period, one can suspect that it was culturally determined, and that the temporal ordering of where groups moved in the various seasons was governed, consciously or unconsciously, by the selection of certain subsistence techniques (subsistence options) in order to exploit the various seasonally available resources (resource options) in the various microenvironments. Thus, the seasonality pattern was a scheduled one (MacNeish et al. 1975).

Studies of the food remains in these seasonally scheduled occupations also showed the evolution of the subsistence pattern. Near the end of the phase there was evidence of new uses of plants that seemed genetically different from their previously used wild relatives or ancestors: avocado, chile, amaranth, and mixta squash would be examples showing this shift at this time, although corn, ciruela, cosuhuico, chupandilla, etc., would not. These data seemed to show the gradual development of new subsistence options that I termed hydro-horticulture and *barranca*-horticulture subsistence systems, which others often lump under the term "incipient agriculture." This process seems to have evolved during the 2,000-year span of the El Riego phase and to have continued into the Coxcatlan phase. It was no sudden explosion but a very minor, slow, accumulative increment. El Riego people were still basically plant collectors.

Looking at other changing plant materials in their seasonal contexts, we attempted to reconstruct this process of domestication and cultivation as follows. Two new subsistence options occurred very late in El Riego: seed planting, which had grown imperceptibly out of seed collecting and occurred as a majority option only in the summer, and fruit pit planting, which occurred as a minority option in the fall. One might speculate how the process of annual incipient agriculture, which saw a shift from seed collecting to seed planting, began as people returned seasonally to some seed or fruit areas each year. This work would have led to some clearing, enrichment, and improvement of the habitat of the seeds and fruits, which, with selection of larger seeds for food, would have led to changes in the seed and fruit population, some of them possibly genetic. Eventually the process may have led to the use of the domesticates (genetically changed food plants) and finally to some planting of individual seeds (amaranth, chile, mixta squash) or pits (avocado) in some kind of plots or gardens (horticulture) (MacNeish 1978).

As I have indicated above, this general process seems to have continued into Coxcatlan times, when corn became first cultivated and then domesticated. Also in Coxcatlan we have some evidence that a similar process was involved in the cultivation of chupandilla fruit trees. However, the really new information that came out of Coxcatlan was that about half of the domesticated plants, white and black sapote, gourds, moschata squash, and common beans, were not domesticated in the Tehuacan regions. Thus, there were multiple origins of domesticated plants, not only in different places within the then ill-defined Mesoamerican boundaries, but also at different times.

Population pressure and environmental factors are not sufficient conditions for plant domestication, but cultural factors, such as scheduling and diffusion, are. However, our Coxcatlan data do give us some glimpse of how a more sedentary life and population, as well as other culture changes, may have taken place. It was my impression that locally developed horticulture, "coupled with the introduction of other domesticates from other regions, must have led to longer residence at the halting places and to rescheduling of macroband activities. Perhaps, macrobands came to collect some seeds in the spring along the *barrancas*, as well as planting some seeds and fruits. These latter plants reached fruition in the summer rainy seasons, thereby allowing the bands to be in the same spot for two seasons. This then became a base for hunting and collecting camps in other regions in the leaner seasons. This process again would gradually result in some

technological advances, greater populations and new changes in their social system" (MacNeish 1971:312).

This process led to more and more sedentarism and continued into Abejas times. Of it I wrote: "The planting of the same Coxcatlan plants plus tepary beans in gardens was only slightly more popular in the spring, summer, and perhaps fall than it was in Coxcatlan times. Now, however, there was an increasing emphasis on planting new, more productive corn types of hybrids. Some large concentrations of corn in certain activity areas, in association with digging sticks, plus the occurrence of many of the larger sites near the fertile flats, suggest that crops were beginning to be sown in fields (*barranca* agriculture). Also, cache and storage pits suggest that some seasonal surpluses were grown in order to have longer periods of occupancy of sites, as well as to allow greater security" (MacNeish 1978:153).

Here, at last, we see the beginning of a positive feedback situation between population pressure and improving "means of production," and we are now talking about the so-called Neolithic revolution, which, since it took place over four or five millennia, was obviously a Neolithic evolution instead. To further emphasize the point, let me note that the traditional conception of the Neolithic revolution before the Tehuacan Project was that pottery, ground stone tools, plant domestication, agriculture, and village life suddenly came together at roughly the same time and led to a whole new way of life and culture. In the Tehuacan sequence, ground stone started 10,000 years ago, plant domestication 8,000 years ago, agriculture 5,000 years ago, and pottery 4,500 years ago in highland Mexico. I believe there is some reason for Mesoamerican archaeologists to alter their basic conceptions about this cultural development and, I hope, to do away with the traditional concept of the Neolithic revolution.

These conclusions, coupled with the data about the first village from the coastal region of Veracruz, which we first found in company with Jim Ford on weekend trips from Tehuacan, should also indicate that, while agriculture may precede village life in one part of a pristine center of plant domestication such as Tehuacan, in another part, village life may well precede plant domestication and agriculture. In other words, there were multilinear evolutions, not unilinear revolutions, in the pristine centers of domestications. While we may have changed some basic conceptions due to our Tehuacan finds, this concept, the Marxists' or cultural materialists' "Neolithic revolution," seems in many cases unaltered among many Mesoamericanists. Perhaps, the next Tehuacan Project will make more progress in this realm than did our previous one.

The accomplishments noted above are, I hope, the basic contributions of the Tehuacan endeavors. However, we also uncovered data that have a bearing on other more recent developmental problems, although these were not the main concern of our project.

The growth of village or tribal life into towns or the chiefdom type of society is an important step in the rise of early pristine civilization, and one we do not understand very well. When one attempts to discern the causes or conditions that brought forth pristine chiefdoms, or priestdoms, a number of factors are usually mentioned (both before and after our Tehuacan endeavors); namely, population; changes in food production, such as irrigation or hydraulic factors; social stratification or social differentiation; division of labor, or the development of a number of full-time specialists; and the degree of centralization and complexity of the political and/or religious organization. The question became: Did our Tehuacan data give us any sequential data about how the above are related and suggest which of these were causes and which effects?

Obviously, since we excavated few large ruins, our relevant data come mainly from foodstuffs in caves, our reconnaissance, and Eva Hunt's (1972) and Woodbury and Neely's (1972) studies of irrigation. One thing is clear from our Purron Dam data: The use of irriga-

tion and the resultant increase in food production and energetic efficiency preceded population growth as well as the shift from a two-tiered social organization to a stratified one, with many full-time specialists and centralized social and political organization. While the steps to civilization or statehood may not be exactly as Wittfogel described them in his *Oriental Despotism* (1957), there can be no doubt that in this area of pristine civilization, the hydraulic factor was a crucial cause for tribal or village life to evolve into life on the chiefdom level. Our survey clearly shows that not only in the Purron Dam area, but in the valley as a whole, populations jumped noticeably after irrigation agriculture came into being, not before it. Further studies of burials, settlement patterns, house types, and manufacture of artifacts show that after the population-irrigation-agriculture positive-feedback syndrome was established, the numbers of full-time specialists increased dramatically and there developed a stratified society with an elite, specialists, and lower classes (farmers and peasants).

While our data seem not to have altered the basic conception of all Mesoamerican archaeologists on this matter, they should have. Our analysis of Tehuacan information on the above matter did not come to many definite conclusions or new theories, but it did suggest the directions future research should take and what factors must be considered. Like it or not, irrigation was one of them, and, needless to say, some of the more recent researches, both in highland and lowland regions, recognize this fact.

Somewhat the same may be said of the problem of the origin of the state as seen in the light of our accomplishments in Tehuacan. Fortunately, with our Postclassic Venta Salada materials, not only did we have good survey and cave materials, but we also tested a couple of sites, one of which was Coxcatlan Viejo, the capital of a city-state, and we had some ethnographic studies made of our region. In fact, as noted above, one of these even turned up with a sixteenth-century map of the *señorío* of Tehuacan, with all its tribute villages and the tribute noted. A later survey by Edward B. Sisson, in the Coxcatlan project that grew out of our Tehuacan endeavors, showed that we had found most of the ruins of these tribute towns, as well as many of the capitals and tribute towns of the other four or five *señorios* of our area, namely, Teotitlan del Camino, Tecomavaca and/or Quiotepec, Zapotitlan, and Tehuacan (Sisson 1973–1974). In fact, we even had evidence that the *Codex Leal* had references to specific towns of our valley and that the Borgia group of codices, if not written by our ancient Tehuacaneros, was at least pertinent to the Postclassic way of life of the people of the Tehuacan Valley. As with the previous problem, we uncovered sufficient data to initiate a project pertinent to this problem of the origin of the state but actually established few hypotheses or theories concerning the solution of this problem.

However, unlike our few conclusions or suggestions about the origin of chiefdoms, which were relatively positive, those about the origin of the state were of a more negative nature. It would seem that population pressures and surplus from food production from various kinds of irrigation agriculture that occurred in Palo Blanco, the phase preceding the state stage of Venta Salada, were among the necessary conditions for states to arise, not the triggering sufficient conditions. Further, when one looked at our site distributions in the late period, there were many empty spaces between them, and perhaps even evidence that population was diminishing in late Palo Blanco. A positive feedback between circumscribed territory, population, and diminishing food production did not seem to be a factor leading to our Venta Salada state.

On the positive side, the fact that some Palo Blanco sites were fortified and many were in fortifiable positions on the tops of mesas or hills, the large numbers of projectile points associated with certain structures (guard houses or garrisons), Venta Salada related codices with many scenes of warfare, and the occasional skeleton showing that

death had been violent, all suggest that warfare and militarism of one sort or another were crucial factors in the rise of our Tehuacan states. There also was evidence of major trade or exchange systems for this period, both in the documents and in the archaeological record, and everywhere we had evidence of increasing numbers of full-time specialists connected with manufacturing industries such as salt, mold-made pottery, weaving, flint knapping, metallurgy, and so forth. Some of our burials (tombs), structures, and settlement pattern data also suggested changing information flow and social organization as well as changing political and economic institutions. Although we never worked out exactly how these factors were related systemically, we felt that they were somehow the sufficient conditions for change. At least among ourselves at Tehuacan, we changed our basic conceptions of why the Mesoamerican prehistoric state developed, from the previously held simplistic, materialistic, Marxist, and population ones, to what we hope are better, even if more complex, models. Again, I don't know whether other archaeologists working in the area followed suit or not.

## METHODOLOGICAL ACHIEVEMENTS

Thus, basically we have seen in this very brief review that not only did our Tehuacan accomplishments bring forth new "facts" and hypotheses, but they also changed (at least our) basic conceptions concerning major problems of prehistoric Mesoamerican development. Yet, in a way, this may not have been the most important accomplishment of the Tehuacan Archaeological-Botanical Project. In fact, talking it over with many of my companions in this undertaking, more important than what we did was how we did it. Of course, our approach (or methodology) was based upon rather specific data collection techniques and methods of analyzing data (MacNeish 1967a).

However, before discussing the latter, I should explain our interdisciplinary approach, which I believe was the key to our whole undertaking, not only to our findings and our altering of basic conceptions, but even to our techniques and methods. This general approach has at least three basic assumptions. One is that a number of differing fields or disciplines brought to bear on a single problem will be more likely to adequately solve the problem than any one alone. Second, the interdisciplinary approach, with a number of different scientists (or scientific fields), often with rather different techniques and methods, working together on the same problem will have an interstimulating effect on each one of them. Finally, the barriers between many disciplines and fields are relatively arbitrary, so the differing assumptions, techniques, analyses, and methods of one or more can often be applied to another with beneficial results (MacNeish 1978).

In practice, our use of the interdisciplinary approach, once our original problem of the origin of agriculture and concomitant development of village life was defined, was incorporated into our basic plans and made part of our initial grant proposal. Thanks to long experience developing this approach in Tamaulipas and elsewhere, we not only knew roughly what other disciplines were pertinent to the solution of this problem, but we at the Peabody Foundation even knew many of the experts in these varied fields (MacNeish 1958). Thus, a lot of ground work was done informing them of our problem and asking how they would and could contribute to its solution. Their responses, after further discussion, went into our preliminary plans, and we started the project with everybody from every related field well informed about what the problem was and how and when they might attack it. Everybody knew what everybody else was doing and why.

In fact, though we scheduled our visiting interdisciplinary scientists so that they rarely overlapped because of our limited facilities, interdisciplinary studies began as early as any of the data-collecting archaeological activities. Their pattern was also always

roughly the same. First, the scientists came to our Tehuacan region to collect their own kind of related data. We provided every facility possible and little by little, by one means or another, also allowed the visiting scientists to get to know our techniques and methods of data collecting and analysis. Obviously, we learned the same about their fields. Thus, once we had attained a basic familiarity with each other, we could turn to attacking our common problem with data derived from their and our methods, and sometimes with new methods or techniques developed from the stimulation we gave to each other. The other thing that happened was that we, the organizers of the project, also became the liaison between one field or scientist and others, for they were scheduled to work with us one after another collecting their respective kinds of data. Later, we would turn to descriptive analysis and they, in turn, would be analyzing the appropriate data we had collected for them by our archaeological techniques.

Thus, interdisciplinary data collecting was going hand in hand with archaeological data collecting, although the major effort was in the latter field. The archaeological field work had two basic parts, reconnaissance and excavation. Although I found Coxcatlan Cave by myself after a brief survey, to start our investigation in Tehuacan, reconnaissance, generally speaking, preceded excavation, although it did overlap with some of the latter; for a period of time we had some archaeologists working in both endeavors, and, further, some of the reconnaissance for settlement pattern and population purposes was dependent upon chronological data derived from excavation. Thus, in part, our survey had two objectives: (1) to find sites (initially stratified) for excavations; and (2) to give an adequate sample of settlement pattern and population data. Although good hard work, walking over region after region, occurred, and we used black and white aerial photographs and even infrared and false-color aerial photographs to make the survey, our finding of the best stratified site came about because of our lab, which was doing initial typology and seriation as the survey proceeded, as well as testing our settlement pattern hypothesis by actual stratitests. Later, after we knew our sequence, we went back and resurveyed and mapped to solve specific problems of population settlement pattern and demography with their obvious social and political organization. Whether this method of survey altered anybody's basic conceptions, I don't know, for more and more survey in Mesoamerica has become dependent on statistical sampling techniques, with the surprising result that fewer and fewer preceramic sites have been discovered since our endeavors in Tehuacan.

However, the real basic data for Tehuacan came from the sites excavated, not from the survey. While we used good digging and recording techniques in these excavations, which were a cut above what often is done in Mesoamerica, there were no big breakthroughs in this line. We just dug and recorded as well and as carefully as we could and hoped that everybody after Tehuacan might do the same.

I do, however, believe that what we did with this well-found, exhumed, and recorded information was a little different from what had often been done previously in Mesoamerica. Our chronology was basically built on good, solid stratigraphy from nine major excavations and about twice as many tests or smaller excavations of stratified sites. A million artifacts and ecofacts came out of these chronological endeavors, and many of them were classifiable into types that were good time markers and permitted the definition of nine sequential cultural phases. Furthermore, about 120 radiocarbon determinations were made on the last eight phases for the last 9,000 years. In addition, cross-dating studies from the well-defined Tehuacan sequence allowed us to align sequences in most of the major cultural regions of Mesoamerica. This chronology has been improved and supplemented since our initial Tehuacan endeavors, but never before had it been done on such a comprehensive scale for such a long period. Further, we also derived chronological data about the environment from our interdisciplinary studies—data that supplemented and augmented our cultural developmental information. All in all, it was an accomplishment that altered basic conceptions of prehistoric Mesoamerican chronology, even if many archaeologists never recognized it as such.

Going hand in glove with these chronological descriptive studies were contextual descriptive studies that led to the reconstruction of the way of life of our various occupations and cultural phases. Again, we were heavily dependent on interdisciplinary studies in biology, zoology, and coprotology to reconstruct ancient subsistence and sustenance systems in a new and different way. Further, these types of studies, taken in conjunction with others, gave us data on the seasonality of the above activities, as well as demographic and settlement data and information on the changing ecosystems. However, archaeological analysis was vital to any reconstruction of subsistence systems, for it was the flora and fauna in conjunction with definite artifact types that indicated what the type of subsistence activity was and what food preparation techniques were utilized. Thus, the study of California computer line plots of artifacts and ecofacts on specific floors, or with seemingly specific occupations, was a technique we used to study ancient activities. These nonrandom spatial associations, taken in conjunction with ethnographic analogy, were our main basis for reconstructing ancient activities. Although our specific techniques for doing and describing these were new, there was nothing very new about the general methodology. However, we did occasionally add a new method, for in the case of grinding stones we experimented with modern ones and compared the evidence of our use-wear with the archaeological specimens: experimental analogy, if you will. While S. A. Semenov and others may have used this technique before the sixties, nothing similar had ever been attempted for Mesoamerica. Unfortunately, we never had the time or money to expand this technique into our studies of the technology whose reconstruction, I might add, was again dependent on archaeological associations and ethnographic analogies. A somewhat similar methodology was used in reconstructing ancient social systems and value systems, and again, from this standpoint, while we were "with the New Archaeology" we were not quite "of it."

This was also true on the higher level of cultural-historical integrations of Tehuacan. We had well-defined cultural phases which we often neatly summarized, but the full reconstruction of the way of life of each phase for this more than 12,000-year sequence has still not been published: there is nothing new about this kind of behavior by Mesoamerican archaeologists. On a still higher

level of methodology, we were, however, trying to move toward theory by analyzing the life spans of our phases to derive hypotheses about how and why cultures change. This was a deductive approach rarely applied to prehistoric Mesoamerican developmental data before the sixties. While we were not very successful in testing these Tehuacan hypotheses with comparative data to make generalizations of laws of cultural change, at least we tried.

Thus, our endeavors in Tehuacan tried to bring the science of archaeology to Mesoamerica. Whether this can be rated as an accomplishment or whether it has altered any archaeologists' basic conceptions of methodology to be applied to prehistoric Mesoamerican developments, I do not know, but I hope it has!

# 3. The Preceramic and Formative of the Valley of Oaxaca

*KENT V. FLANNERY, JOYCE MARCUS, and STEPHEN A. KOWALEWSKI*

## INTRODUCTION

THE VALLEY OF OAXACA lies in the southern highlands of Mexico at a mean elevation of 1,550 m. Semiarid and semitropical, with an annual precipitation of 500–700 mm, the valley contains some 700 sq km of relatively flat land. Much of this is the present and former alluvium of the Rio Atoyac and its tributary, the Rio Salado, whose drainage patterns have produced a river valley shaped like a Y or three-pointed star. The three major arms of this star are the northwestern, or Etla, subvalley; the eastern, or Tlacolula, subvalley; and the southern "Valle Grande," or Zaachila-Zimatlan–Ocotlan subvalley (Fig. 3-1). In the Central district of the valley, where the three arms converge, the mountaintop city of Monte Alban rises 400 m above the alluvium. Surrounding the valley floor is a zone of rolling piedmont, and beyond this a series of forested mountains which rise to 3,000 m.

The Valley of Oaxaca was one of the most heavily populated areas in Precolumbian Mexico and has yielded evidence for some of the earliest agriculture, public architecture, social ranking, hieroglyphic writing, urbanization, state formation, and militarism in Mesoamerica. The valley's population was supported, despite the fact that evaporation exceeds precipitation throughout most of the year, by a complex series of agricultural strategies including dry farming, high-water-table farming, well irrigation, canal irrigation, terracing, and floodwater farming (Kirkby 1973). All these social, political, economic, and technological achievements seem to have been the work of the Zapotec Indians, whose descendants still occupy the valley today (Nader 1969).

### Oaxaca Archaeology, 1965–1979

Fourteen years have now passed since the archaeology of the Valley of Oaxaca was synthesized in Volume 3 of the *Handbook of Middle American Indians* (Wauchope and Willey 1965). The nine well-written chapters (31–39) of that synthesis were by Ignacio Bernal, Jorge R. Acosta, Alfonso Caso, and Ronald Spores, four of our most outstanding Mesoamerican anthropologists; all are worth rereading today. However, the last fourteen

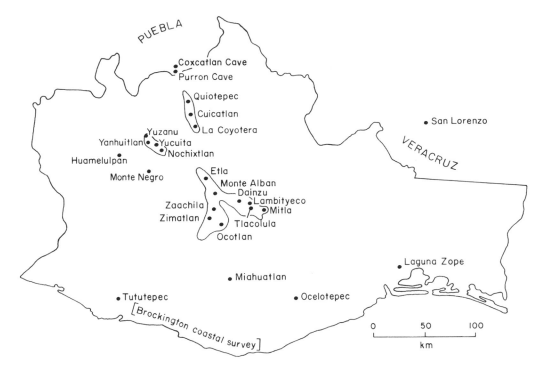

FIGURE 3-1. The state of Oaxaca, showing areas of intensive survey, modern towns, and archaeological sites mentioned in the text.

years have seen such intense research activity in Oaxaca that there is now a great deal to add to this synthesis (and that of Paddock 1966). Some of this research has been by two of the original *Handbook* authors: Bernal (1968a) excavated for years at the important site of Dainzu in the Valley of Oaxaca, while Spores (1972, 1974) spent more than a decade carrying out settlement pattern surveys, excavations, and ethnohistoric studies in the Nochixtlan Valley of the Mixteca Alta. Other major projects of recent years include Donald L. Brockington's surveys of Miahuatlan and coastal Oaxaca (Brockington 1973; Brockington, Jorrín, and Long 1974; Brockington and Long 1974), John Paddock's work at Lambityeco (Paddock, Mogor, and Lind 1968), Margarita Gaxiola González' (1976) work at Huamelulpan in the Mixteca, and Robert and Judith Zeitlin's work at Laguna Zope (R. Zeitlin 1978; J. Zeitlin 1978). Finally, there are two interrelated, long-term projects we have been asked to report on in this volume:

(1) an intensive settlement pattern survey of the Valley of Oaxaca and the Precolumbian city of Monte Alban by Richard E. Blanton (1978) and his associates (Kowalewski 1976; Feinman and Kowalewski 1979; Varner 1974) and (2) an interdisciplinary project entitled "The Prehistory and Human Ecology of the Valley of Oaxaca" (Flannery et al. 1970; Flannery and Marcus 1976a, 1976b; Kirkby 1973; Lees 1973; Schoenwetter 1974; Pires-Ferreira 1975; Drennan 1976a, 1976b; C. E. Smith 1978; Messer 1978).

*The Valley of Oaxaca in 1965*

Perhaps the easiest way to put in perspective the archaeological discoveries of the last fourteen years is to consider what was said about the Valley of Oaxaca in Volume 3 of the *Handbook*. To begin with, Monte Alban, now considered a candidate for Mesoamerica's earliest city, had no apparent roots. Although 39 sites of the Monte Alban I period

49

had been found, they had no antecedents. "It seems extraordinary," Bernal (1965: 796–797) pointed out, "that such a favorable area for human development as the valley of Oaxaca was apparently not inhabited until so late. We have no reliable data which could allow us to speak of preceramic cultures there. . . . Even more extraordinary than the paucity of information about preceramic man in Oaxaca is the lack of it for the earlier Preclassic subperiods." Authors of the early 1960s explained this lack of early cultures by reference to a giant lake, rooted in Zapotec legend, which was believed to have filled the valley prior to Monte Alban I. According to one view, Monte Alban I culture had developed at Monte Negro, a mountaintop center near Tilantongo in the Mixteca Alta, and spread into the Valley of Oaxaca after an earthquake opened an outlet for the lake and drained the valley. Some supporters of this view saw the famous *danzantes* of period I as "swimmers" rather than "dancers."

For those who didn't believe in a Mixtec origin for Monte Alban I, there were the Olmecs. For Caso (1965:854–855), "the sculpture of this first Monte Alban period has close connections with the Olmec style of La Venta and Tres Zapotes, but it is still an individual and characteristic style which should not be confused with the southern style of Veracruz and Tabasco." For Bernal (1965: 799), the early Oaxacan cultures were "rooted in this Olmec tradition and are Olmecoid," yet without being "a simple copy or product of the archaeological Olmecs." Michael D. Coe's (1968) later discovery that the Olmec style flourished between 1200 and 900 B.C. in no way undermined this notion; since nothing earlier than Monte Alban I was known from Oaxaca, the starting date for that horizon could be (and frequently was) pushed back to 600, 800, or even 1000 B.C.

While various authors debated whether Monte Alban I was Mixtec or Olmec, most agreed that Monte Alban II was Maya in origin; "the most probable homeland of the bearers of the Monte Alban II culture was Chiapas or the Guatemalan highlands" (Ber-

nal 1965:801). Moreover, Monte Alban II was seen as a kind of "site unit intrusion" whose bearers were "an aristocracy of rulers or priests" who lived at "relatively few sites in the valley" and "imposed their own ideas but did not constitute a majority capable of obliterating the old culture, which survived among the bulk of the population" (ibid.: 800). This was a reasonable conclusion, based on the frequency of waxy red and orange pottery and vaulted-roof tombs during Monte Alban II, coupled with the smaller number of known period II sites (24) when compared with period I. Not until the Monte Alban IIIA period did most Oaxaca archaeologists feel they were dealing with "Zapotec culture" (ibid.: 789).

Such was the accepted picture of early Oaxaca in 1965, and it would still be the accepted picture today were it not for the curiosity and enthusiasm of Ignacio Bernal, John Paddock, Richard S. MacNeish, and José Luis Lorenzo. None were content with the accepted picture, and all were aware of intriguing leads that remained to be followed up. "MacNeish thinks that some flints collected near Mitla belong to late preceramic horizons," wrote Bernal (1965:797). MacNeish and Paddock also felt that some figurine heads collected near Etla could belong to an undiscovered Early Formative horizon. Lorenzo (1960) had found no geological evidence for a lake in the Valley of Oaxaca, and he had already singled out some rockshelters near Mitla as possible preceramic sites (Lorenzo and Messmacher 1963). More than anyone else, these four colleagues were responsible for launching "The Prehistory and Human Ecology of the Valley of Oaxaca." In an act of characteristic generosity, Bernal provided Flannery with a list of 251 sites already located by his unpublished survey (Bernal 1965:795), and Lorenzo made available his preceramic surface collections for study. Paddock took Flannery on a guided tour of Lorenzo's rockshelters, and MacNeish helped him trace some of the enigmatic figurine heads back to the Etla sites where they had been collected years before. If ever a project had a "board of directors," it was this one.

## The Importance of a Long-Term Survey/Excavation Approach

Before discussing the specific research designs used on the preceramic and Formative periods of the Valley of Oaxaca, there are a few general points that should be made. First, the importance of long-term work in an area (on the order of ten to fifteen years) cannot be overstressed. No matter how well-thought-out the research design may be, one's perspective on an area changes considerably through time, as the result of an increasing familiarity for which there is no substitute.

Second, in any serious long-term study, survey and excavation must proceed hand in hand. Each has its strengths and weaknesses, its insights and blind spots. Excavators who feel they can really document their site's "rise to prominence as a regional center" without including settlement pattern survey are deluding themselves; settlement pattern specialists who feel their survey techniques are so powerful that they can "find out whatever they want without ever putting a shovel in the ground" are equally self-deceptive. Those who only excavate all too often make the simplifying assumption that their one site (or one pit!) "typifies" a phase for a whole region; in fact, they have no idea whether their site is typical, atypical, larger, smaller, or located differently from others. Those who only survey gain a necessary regional perspective, but all too often forget that their raw data amount to surface collections—manipulated in ingenious and scholarly ways, perhaps, but only through simplifying assumptions about the relationship between surface and subsurface remains which excavation may prove to be fallacious. Thus, excavators speak of "population growth" without being able to document it, while surveyors speak of "mounded constructions" at sites without knowing what any of them are. It is not merely a matter of scale: excavation

has as much to tell us about the regional integration of a valley as survey does, and intensive surface collection has as much to tell us about the internal layout of a site as excavation does.

Third, where ethnohistoric data are available, they can provide us with an interpretive framework for both settlement patterns and excavation results. In the case of the Valley of Oaxaca, were it not for ethnohistoric data on Zapotec institutions, archaeologists could make serious errors based on the use of geographic or locational techniques originally worked out for Western societies. Our notion of palaces as "residences" and of temples as "nonresidential" breaks down in Oaxaca: major areas of the Zapotec palace (*quihuitao*) were used for "assemblies of lords" or for conducting the business of the state, while some priests actually resided in the back room of the Zapotec temple (*yohopèe*), "hardly ever leaving it" (Marcus 1978).

In this chapter, we have tried to combine settlement pattern surveys by Blanton and Kowalewski, excavations by Flannery and his associates, and ethnohistoric studies by Marcus into one overall synthetic framework. Sometimes these three lines of evidence yield contradictory results, as in the case of site size estimates based on surface survey data versus excavation data. We do not take such contradictions to be discouraging, because the different approaches are simply measuring different variables; the resolution of such contradictions will provide still another source of information.

In the Valley of Oaxaca, survey has provided insight into the development of an administrative hierarchy, demographic growth, important reorganizations of the countryside's population, deviations from expected rank-size relationships which are of political significance, and the relationship between population and agricultural potential. Excavation, on the other hand, has established the presence or absence of institutions such as long-distance exchange, the pooling and redistribution of traded goods, hereditary ranking and the ways in which it was expressed, the formation of Zapotec state religion and its temple staff, the different social strata and how their members lived, and the specific techniques of agriculture used in different periods. To give only one example in which settlement patterns, excavations, and ethnohistory can be combined, let us consider the four-tiered hierarchy of settlements that had arisen by the Terminal Formative (or "Protoclassic") Monte Alban II period. We can now propose that a "great lord" like the Zapotec *coquitao* resided in a "great palace" at Monte Alban; that "lords" like the Zapotec *coqui* lived in smaller palaces at second-order centers, but evidently not at third-order centers; that temples staffed by full-time priests were present at first-, second-, and third-order centers; and that fourth-order sites were hamlets without administrative functions.

Finally, our work in Oaxaca builds on the studies reported in the original *Handbook*. Both Blanton and Kowalewski's surveys and Flannery and Marcus' excavations began with the 251 sites already discovered by Bernal. San Jose Mogote, the largest community in the valley prior to the founding of Monte Alban, is the site called "Cacique" by Bernal (1965: Fig. 1). At the time of Bernal's survey there were still no ceramic reports from Chiapa de Corzo or Tehuacan, and many surface sherds which we would now recognize as pre–Monte Alban were most likely interpreted as trade items. It is interesting to speculate on how different Oaxaca archaeology might have been, had Bernal and Paddock decided to excavate "Cacique" instead of Yagul in 1954.

## THE PRECERAMIC ERA
### Research Design

The goals of our research on the preceramic period were to recover the principles of adaptation for the hunting-gathering stage, the adaptive context in which early attempts at plant domestication took place, and the processes which led to an expansion of agriculture at the expense of other procurement systems. Our model was one in which adaptation was viewed as a series of problem-solving processes (Holland 1975) which, over a long period of time, made continual minor but cumulative changes in a complex set of interacting subsystems (Flannery 1968a).

The first stage of research was a reconnaissance for caves and preceramic open-air sites. Out of a sample of more than 60 sites, about 10 were selected for testing, and on the basis of test results 4 of these were selected for excavation. All occurred within 5 km of Mitla. They were Guila Naquitz (Fig. 3-2), a small dry cave with 6 preceramic living floors and superb plant preservation (excavated by Flannery); Cueva Blanca (Fig. 3-3), a larger cave with 3 preceramic living floors overlying a level with Pleistocene fauna (excavated by Flannery and Frank Hole); Martinez Rockshelter, a multiple-occupation site without clearly defined living floors (excavated by Flannery); and Gheo-Shih (Fig. 3-4), a preceramic open-air site with activity areas, features, and traces of "architecture" (excavated by Hole).

In the case of Gheo-Shih, a total surface pickup employing 5 × 5 m units preceded the actual excavation, the latter carried out by 1 × 1 m squares within each 25 sq m unit. In the case of the caves, all work utilized a 1 × 1 m grid. Excavation adhered to "natural" or "cultural" strata wherever present, with all plant remains, animal bones, and flint debitage recorded by squares within a living floor; all retouched flints, bone or wooden tools, knots, nets (Fig. 3-5), string, ground stone, and other artifacts were piece-plotted. The cave matrix was passed through two sizes of screens, and flotation samples were saved from each square to check on the rate of recovery by the smaller screens; pollen and radiocarbon samples were taken from squares which had no intrusive pits or rodent burrows.

The analysis of Guila Naquitz can serve as an example of the next stage of research. First, Charles S. Spencer (n.d.) converted the raw counts of plant species, animal species, and debitage into a series of contour maps showing the density and distribution of

FIGURE 3-2. Guila Naquitz Cave.

FIGURE 3-3. Cueva Blanca.

FIGURE 3-4. Gheo-Shih. The two parallel rows of boulders outline an artifact-free area which may represent some kind of public or ritual space. In the background is a dense cluster of stones and artifacts.

these items across each living floor. Some gross patterns emerged by inspection at this stage, but these were still unverified by statistical measures of association, and we now know that they masked a whole series of significant patterns which were undetectable to the naked eye. Using 2 × 4 m blocks (8 adjacent 1 × 1 m squares) as his units of analysis, Robert Whallon, Jr., brought out some of these patterns with an ordered matrix of Pearson's *r* values showing the associations among the 18 most commonly recovered classes of items on each living floor; this stage of analysis seems to recover associations at the level of the individual collecting trips upslope or downslope from the cave (Whallon 1973).

Next, using the original 1 × 1 m squares as his units of analysis, Robert Reynolds (n.d.) ran two further associational analyses on each living floor. The first, a Q-mode analysis, uses a Partition-Distance program to compare the 1 × 1 m cells with respect to presence/absence of the same 18 variables used

by Whallon. The second, an R-mode analysis, uses a Minissa program to compare the frequencies of the 18 variables as they are distributed among the 1 × 1 m cells. The second program brings out linear relationships; the first, nonlinear relationships. Both matrices produced were then subjected to multidimensional scaling to 2–4 dimensions and the results plotted on a diagram of the cave floor. In contrast to Whallon's program, Reynolds' focused at the level of the processing of foodstuffs, i.e., at the level of the activity area, feature, and activity pathway within each cave floor. Both the Q-mode and R-mode analyses separated plant and animal components and showed the activity paths; the latter showed the paths less clearly than the former, but it also separated seasonally available plants from those available year-round. Eventually, the results of Whallon's and Reynolds' programs were combined into a single model for the sequence of hunting, collecting, processing, cooking, and discarding of resources on each living floor and the way these activities changed through time (Reynolds n.d.).

The final stage of analysis is a computer simulation of the development of wild plant collecting and incipient agriculture over the period 8000–5000 B.C. in the eastern Valley of Oaxaca (Reynolds 1979). The first step was to establish the relevance of today's environment to the environment of the preceramic. This was done by a comparison of preceramic and modern pollen spectra (carried out by James Schoenwetter), a comparison of preceramic and modern flora (carried out by C. Earle Smith, Jr.), and a comparison of preceramic and modern rodent species from owl pellets (carried out by Flannery and Jane C. Wheeler). Next, density and distribution studies of the wild vegetation from the vicinity of Guila Naquitz were carried out at all seasons of the year for most of a decade (1966–1976) which included average years, dry years, and wet years; harvested wild plants were frozen, flown to Michigan, and analyzed by nutritionists John Robson and James Konlande. Reynolds' simulation, resembling that of David II. Thomas (1971, 1972, 1973) in some of its aspects, uses the environmental and nutritional data to generate a preceramic collecting strategy which predicts (and duplicates) our sequence of living floors with uncanny accuracy.

It is only at this stage of our research that we approach the goals set forth in the first paragraph of this section. While we do not want to anticipate the results which will be spelled out in the final report on Guila Naquitz (Flannery n.d.), it is already clear that the Oaxacan agricultural revolution can be simulated without resorting to population pressure, environmental change, or any of the major "prime movers" sometimes relied on. All that is required is a set of relatively simple policies which result in a resilient, diversified strategy for coping with an unpredictable succession of wet, dry, and average years—a strategy which evaluates its own procurement efficiency on an annual basis and modifies itself bit by bit by selecting from a limited series of alternative moves.

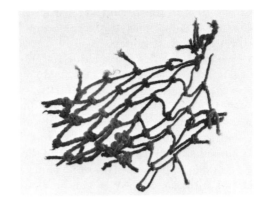

FIGURE 3-5. Knotted net from zone B3, Guila Naquitz Cave. Width of specimen 5 cm; this specimen is now in the Museo de Antropología, Oaxaca City.

It should be noted that this stage was reached only after thirteen years of excavations, analyses, and environmental studies. It should also be noted that our goals were achieved with a verbal model based on adaptive systems theory and a computer simulation based on mathematical systems theory. This is somewhat ironic in view of the fact that James Doran (1970) and Merrilee H. Salmon (1978) have recently suggested that systems approaches have little to offer archaeology. On closer inspection, however, it becomes clear that their observations are most relevant to General Systems Theory, or the more formal systems approaches of such fields as electrical engineering, which have never been (and probably never will be) used by archaeologists. In fact, the systems approaches used by archaeologists have come largely from ecology and developmental biology and have long been part of the biologist's standard arsenal for the analysis of living systems.

### The Paleoindian Period

Almost nothing is known of the Paleoindian period in the state of Oaxaca. There have been occasional discoveries of mammoth remains in the valleys of Tamazulapan and Nochixtlan, but none had associated artifacts.

Our best clue to this period so far is a small collection of fauna from stratigraphic zone F at Cueva Blanca (Flannery et al. 1970:17). This zone was a layer of indurated sand which at first appeared to be a sterile deposit at the base of the cave, but on further investigation yielded several lenses of animal bones which show definite evidence of burning and some signs of deliberate fracture. It was immediately apparent that some of these animals differed from the Holocene fauna associated with zones E–A at Cueva Blanca; unfortunately, no artifacts were found in any of the zone F lenses. Radiocarbon dates for zone E (which overlay F) ranged between 9050 and 8100 B.C.; zone F could thus be older than 10,000 B.C.

One of the first animals which came to light in zone F was the Texas gopher tortoise, *Gopherus* cf. *berlandieri*. This large land tortoise frequents the plains of south Texas and northeast Mexico today. Another significant member of the zone F fauna was a fox whose bones were too large and rugose to be those of the gray fox (*Urocyon*) native to Oaxaca today. They would appear to belong to the genus *Vulpes* (red foxes), and may well be those of *Vulpes macrotis*, the kit fox, which today inhabits Durango and Coahuila in northern Mexico. Neither the gopher tortoise nor the kit fox occurs anywhere near Oaxaca today, but zone F also includes genera which are native to both Oaxaca and northern Mexico. Particularly common in this category are cottontails (*Sylvilagus* spp.), jackrabbits (*Lepus* spp.), and wood rats (*Neotoma* spp.). Deer of the genus *Odocoileus* (probably the white-tailed deer *O. virginianus*, although the sample is small) are also present. The Pleistocene fauna which most closely resembles that from Cueva Blanca F is the Early Ajuereado phase fauna from zones XXV–XXVIII of Coxcatlan Cave in the Tehuacan Valley (Flannery 1967:140–144).

According to Schoenwetter (personal communication), pollen samples from Cueva Blanca F reflect a climate somewhat cooler than today's. Pine pollen dominates the sample, and there are occasional grains of spruce, fir, and elm. However, pollen of mesquite, columnar cacti, agave, and other thorn forest plants is much more common than that of spruce or fir, and suggests that a thorn forest like today's occurred not far from the cave. Perhaps the cooler winter temperatures of the Pleistocene merely lowered the altitude at which the various Oaxacan vegetation zones occurred.

### The Archaic Period

C. Earle Smith, Jr. (1978) has reconstructed the post-Pleistocene Valley of Oaxaca as an area originally covered by forest, brush, or low *monte*—not the open, grassy valley we see today, which is a product of agricultural land clearance. Along the Rio Atoyac and its major tributaries he sees a riverine forest of alder, willow, *ahuehuete*, fig, and *anona*. On the alluvium, where the subsurface water lies between 3 and 6 m below the surface, there would have been a lower forest of mesquite, acacia, and members of the Burseraceae, Malvaceae, and Euphorbiaceae. The piedmont (from the 6 m water table zone up onto the lower slopes of the mountains) would have had a thorn-scrub-cactus forest, of which patches survive near Guila Naquitz; prickly pear, organ cactus, leguminous trees, yucca, and maguey characterize this community. In the higher mountains grew a forest of oak, pine, manzanita, and madroño, now greatly thinned.

There are four lines of evidence which can be used to produce a tentative Archaic chronology for the Valley of Oaxaca. The first is the stratigraphic relationship of the various living floors in our sites. The second is the radiocarbon dates for those living floors. The third is the sequence of diagnostic artifacts, especially projectile point types. The fourth is a pollen chronology worked out by Schoenwetter and his associates for preceramic sites in the Mitla area (Schoenwetter and Smith n.d.).

THE NAQUITZ PHASE. The earliest phase is based on a series of 7 living floors, including Cueva Blanca E and Guila Naquitz E, D, C,

TABLE 3-1. Tentative Chronological Phases for the Oaxaca Preceramic, with Characteristic Projectile Points, Flora, and Settlement Type for Each Component

| Tentative Phases | Site and Level | Projectile Point Types | Important Flora | Type of Settlement and Season |
|---|---|---|---|---|
| Martinez (± 2000 B.C.) | Yuzanu | None | | MRC (microband), dry? |
| | Martinez Rock Shelter, Upper B | Virtually none | | Multiple short-term occupations |
| Blanca (3300–2800 B.C.) | Cueva Blanca C | Coxcatlan, La Mina, Trinidad, Hidalgo | | HCC (microband), winter |
| | Cueva Blanca D | Tilapa, La Mina, Trinidad, San Nicolas | | HCC (microband), winter |
| Jicaras (5000–4000 B.C.) | Gheo-Shih A, B | Pedernales, La Mina, Trinidad, San Nicolas | ↑ Zea pollen | OAC (macroband), summer? |
| Naquitz (early) (8900–6700 B.C.) | Guila Naquitz B | Pedernales | Cucurbit seeds   Zea pollen | Family microband, fall |
| | Guila Naquitz C | None | | Family microband, fall |
| | Guila Naquitz D | None | ↓             ↓ | Family microband, fall |
| Naquitz (late) (9100–8900 B.C.) | Guila Naquitz E | Unfinished Lerma? | | Family microband, fall |
| | Cueva Blanca E | Very few | | HCC (microband), winter? |
| Late Pleistocene (10,000 B.C.?) | Cueva Blanca F | None | | Burned, broken Pleistocene fauna |

HCC: hunting camp (in cave).
MRC: maguey-roasting camp.
OAC: open-air camp.
SOURCE: Adapted from Flannery and Marcus in press.

and B (with subdivisions B3, B2, and B1). Considering the available radiocarbon dates, a span of 9100–6700 B.C. would not be unreasonable for the phase. Projectile points are rare, with a possible unfinished Lerma point from Guila Naquitz E and a single Pedernales point from Guila Naquitz B. Utilized flakes and one-hand manos are typical artifacts. This phase is significant because Guila Naquitz D (8750–7840 B.C.) contains our oldest "pepo-like" cucurbit seed; Guila Naquitz C and B (7450–6670 B.C.) contain 14 seeds and peduncles identified as *Cucurbita pepo*, as well as pollen grains of *Zea* cf. *mexicana* or teosinte (Flannery 1973: Table 2; Schoenwetter 1974; Whitaker n.d.; Fig. 3-6, this volume).

According to Schoenwetter (1974: 298),

The vegetation pattern at Guilá Naquitz during the 6000–8000 B.C. period was responsive to a generally cooler yet more xeric climate. At Guilá Naquitz, this environment was neither as frigid as occurs in the valley today at extreme elevation, nor as xeric as occurs today in the valley's arid sec-

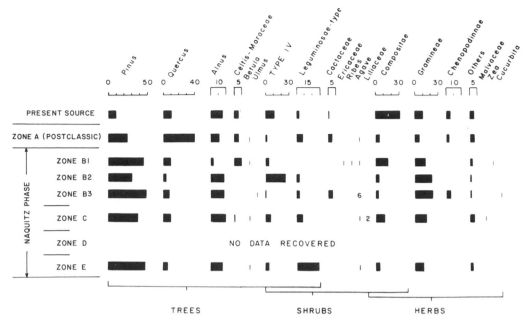

FIGURE 3-6. Pollen diagram from Guila Naquitz Cave. Redrawn with modifications from Schoenwetter 1974: Fig. 2.

tions. It was not sufficiently different to drastically change the character of ecological relations among plants nor to introduce plant types that are not palynologically represented there today. In consideration of these conclusions, my opinion is that the vegetation pattern at Guilá Naquitz throughout the preceramic period was that of a pine savanna, similar in its structure to pine, oak, and juniper savannas which occur today in many of the more temperate portions of highland Mexico. *The plant resources available at Guilá Naquitz today, with the addition of pinyon, would have been available throughout the preceramic period in sufficient quantity to support human populations of the size evidenced by the archaeological record.*

A representative component of the Naquitz phase was zone C at Guila Naquitz, the living floor selected by Whallon for a dimensional analysis of variance which appeared in *American Antiquity* (Whallon 1973: Table 2). Zone C represented the single encampment of a small band of people made during the September–November period. Acorns, piñon nuts, maguey quids, hackberry seeds, and other wild plants were represented. It looked as if the group had begun the occupa-

tion by covering the floor of the cave with oak leaves and grass as bedding. Later, this bedding (as well as some accumulated plant material above it) had caught fire and smoldered. Seeds of *Cucurbita pepo* were present and have been identified by Thomas Whitaker; Lawrence Kaplan has identified wild runner beans from zone C. Also in this level, Schoenwetter (1974) has identified *Zea* pollen which is in the size range for teosinte, the putative ancestor of cultivated maize, according to the view of George W. Beadle (1977) and others.

Whallon's dimensional analysis of variance revealed several groups of plants or animals with high mutual Pearson's *r* values. His interpretation of these is as follows:

In group 1 we find a series of plant items which come from the Lower Thorn Forest of the piedmont. The 2 tree legumes *Acacia* and Prosopis or mesquite, the leaf (or stem section) of *Opuntia* the prickly pear (nopal), and the leaves and chewed quids of *Agave* the century plant or maguey are all items which are well known to occur in the Lower Thorn Forest and which can easily be gathered at the same time on a collecting

58

trip. They are highly associated spatially within the occupation area and seem to have been processed together as the products of one type of gathering activity. Chewing maguey while working seems to have been common, judging by the quids and their strong association with this group. All these items show little or no correlation with other items.

Included in this group we find also a wild *Cucurbita*. It was previously suspected that this plant was collected from the Lower Thorn Forest, but there was no proof that it actually did come from this environment zone. Now, on the basis of the strong association of this cucurbit with the other plants collected strictly from this zone, this suspicion is strengthened, if not substantiated.

Group 2 is composed of the fruit of *Malpighia*, the West Indian cherry or nanche. Nanches come from the Upper Oak Woodland, but fruit somewhat earlier than the other items which are gathered from this zone and which form group 3b. Group 2 perhaps represents earlier collecting trips into this zone.

The plants in group 3a, *Leucaena/Lysiloma* (pods of 2 tree legumes, both known as guajes) and *Jatropha* or susí nuts, come from the Lower Thorn Forest. They tend to cluster a bit upslope on the piedmont, however, and may be best collected on special gathering forays.

Group 3b comprises acorns, pine nuts (pinyon), the small fruit *Celtis* or hackberry, and *Phaseolus*, wild runner beans. All these items are from the Upper Oak Woodlands, the wild beans being found in the underbrush.

Chipped stone waste flakes form group 3c. They are correlated both with the items in groups 3a and b and with those in group 4. These simple flakes clearly have multiple functions and are used in both plant processing and in butchering game. Their low correlation with groups 1 and 2, however, shows that they are used for only some types of plant processing.

The 3 animals hunted (deer, turtle, and rabbit) are not naturally found together but nevertheless appear to have been butchered or processed together. The deer come from the Upper Oak Woodlands, the turtle from ponds on the valley floor, and rabbits are ubiquitous. We have here perhaps an indication of an activity or activities differentiated from others not so much by the environmental zone being exploited or the time of exploitation, but by the composition of the work group involved. Hunting and butchering would

seem to be, on comparative grounds, primarily an activity of the men of the group, while the gathering of plant products would more likely have been done by a group of both sexes or by a women's group. (Whallon 1973:275–277)

THE JICARAS PHASE. The single Pedernales point from Guila Naquitz B belongs to a type which reached its greatest popularity during the phase we have called Jicaras. Palynological data and artifactual evidence place Gheo-Shih somewhere between Guila Naquitz B1 (6670 B.C.?) and Cueva Blanca D (3000 B.C.?). We have accordingly selected a date of 5000–4000 B.C. for Gheo-Shih, but cannot accurately date the beginning or end of the Jicaras phase.

Jicaras is the first phase in the Oaxaca sequence in which projectile points occur in any abundance and variety. The Pedernales type is a large-bladed *atlatl* point with moderate shoulders or barbs and a short, broad stem with a characteristically concave base (Fig. 3-7*a*). These points were evidently made by the hundreds in the eastern Valley of Oaxaca, but were never numerous in Tehuacan. MacNeish recovered a single Pedernales point (listed as an "aberrant" specimen) at the level 4–3 transition in El Riego Cave West, "a component of the Coxcatlan phase" (MacNeish, Nelken-Terner, and Johnson 1967:78).

Other projectile points from Gheo-Shih include the contracting-stem types Trinidad and San Nicolas and the straight-stemmed type La Mina (Fig. 3-7). All three types are well represented during the 5000–4000 B.C. period in Tehuacan. The Jicaras phase remains also included metates and manos of various types, bifaces, choppers, scrapers of various kinds, stone ornaments, and utilized flakes (Hole n.d.).

Because Gheo-Shih is one of the few open-air Archaic sites excavated in Mexico, it merits discussion in a bit more detail. The site occupies an area of about 1.5 ha and appears to be an example of what MacNeish (1964a) has called a "seasonal macroband camp." Excavations revealed oval concentrations of ar-

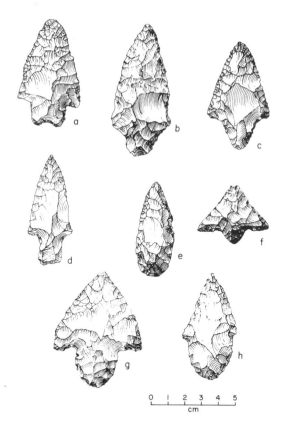

FIGURE 3-7. Projectile points from the Oaxaca Archaic: *a*, Pedernales; *b*, San Nicolas; *c*, Trinidad; *d*, La Mina; *e*, Abasolo; *f*, Coxcatlan; *g*, Tilapa; *h*, Hidalgo.

tifacts and accumulated stones which may mark the localities of impermanent shelters of some kind. In the center of the site occurred an unusual feature, which consisted of two parallel rows of boulders about 20 m long (Fig. 3-4). The space between them, which was 7 m wide, was swept clean and contained virtually no artifacts. To either side of the parallel lines of boulders, however, artifacts were abundant. The boulder lines ended without turning a corner, and their function is unknown. What they most resemble are the borders of a cleared "dance ground," such as characterized macroband camps of some Great Basin hunting-gathering Indian groups (see Flannery and Marcus 1976a: Fig. 10.1; Drennan 1976b: Fig. 11.11). One other area of Gheo-Shih, to the north, was of interest because it had an unusually high con-

centration of tools for hunting and butchering, and yielded a number of ornaments of drilled stone (mostly pendants). The making of pendants from flat river pebbles may have been one localized activity on the site.

Pollen was present at Gheo-Shih. Although Schoenwetter's study is not yet complete, the study so far shows pollen of maize or teosinte type. The location of Gheo-Shih is one that would be appropriate for rainy-season cultivation along the river floodplain, combined with the collection of mesquite beans and other plant foods available on the alluvium during the summer.

THE BLANCA PHASE. Two levels at Cueva Blanca, zones D and C, are sufficiently similar to be included within a tentative Blanca phase. Zone D has produced radiocarbon dates in the 3295–2800 B.C. time range, coeval with the early-to-middle Abejas phase in the Tehuacan Valley. All the projectile point types from Cueva Blanca D and C are shared with Abejas sites in Tehuacan, though the frequencies are different. In Tehuacan, the distinctive Coxcatlan point is the most common type in the Abejas phase, while Trinidad, San Nicolas, and La Mina are less common. At Cueva Blanca, the proportions are reversed: San Nicolas, Trinidad, and La Mina are common, while Coxcatlan points are rare. Two other types from the Blanca phase, Tilapa and Hidalgo, have so far not been found in the earlier Jicaras phase (Fig. 3-7).

A representative component of the Blanca phase would be zone D of Cueva Blanca. Zone D was a layer of tan-gray or salmon-colored ash which (originally) filled the entire excavated area of the cave and reached a thickness of 25–40 cm. This was probably the remains of the relatively long-term (winter, deer-hunting?) camp by a group of 5–8 persons. White-tailed deer were butchered in the northeast quadrant of the cave, and 9 projectile points and hundreds of flint chips accompanied them. A hearth, Feature 18, intrusive into zone E, evidently was dug down from D; it gave a C14 date of 3295 B.C. Charcoal from elsewhere in zone D gave a date of 2800 B.C.

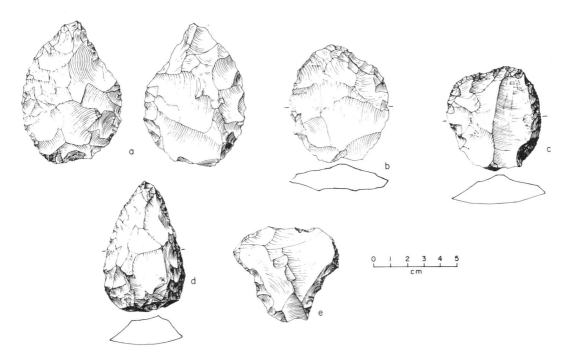

FIGURE 3-8. Chipped stone tools from the Oaxaca Archaic I: *a*, "Martinez biface" (dorsal and ventral views); *b*, Type B biface (dorsal view and cross-section); *c*, end scraper (dorsal view and cross-section); *d*, ovoid (convergent) scraper (dorsal view and cross-section); *e*, notched flake.

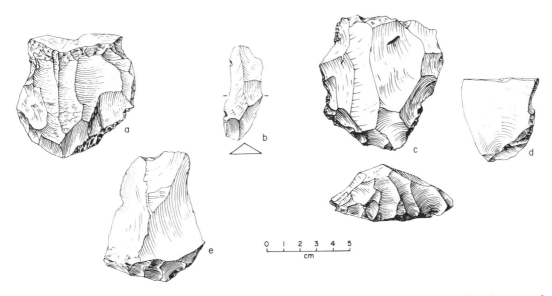

FIGURE 3-9. Chipped stone tools from the Oaxaca Archaic II: *a*, core; *b*, crude blade (dorsal view and cross-section); *c*, steep denticulate scraper ("scraper plane"), dorsal and lateral views; *d*, burin; *e*, flake with sheen (the stippled area on the upper left edge of *e* indicates an area of polish analogous to "sickle sheen," believed on the basis of circumstantial evidence to be caused by trimming off the tough, dirty leaf bases from a maguey heart).

Finally, we should note that there are suggestions of Blanca phase occupation elsewhere in the state of Oaxaca, including a Coxcatlan point from the Nochixtlan Valley (Spores, personal communication) and a Trinidad point from the Valley of Miahuatlan (Brockington 1973:15).

THE MARTINEZ PHASE. We come now to the latest, least-securely dated, and most tentative phase in the preceramic sequence. The Martinez phase is represented only by material from the upper 10 cm of zone B at the Martinez Rockshelter, which we have tentatively grouped with the Yuzanu material from the Yanhuitlan-Nochixtlan Valley (Lorenzo 1958). Yuzanu has produced radiocarbon dates of 2100–2000 B.C. (±200), but the material could easily go back to the 2300 B.C. date arbitrarily selected by Johnson and MacNeish (1972:24) for terminal Abejas.

The Martinez Rockshelter does contain crude stone "bowls" (and/or mortars) which may be related to late Abejas phase specimens from Tehuacan. However, dating is severely handicapped by the near absence of projectile points from the Martinez Rockshelter and their total absence at Yuzanu. A single La Mina point from the talus slope of the Martinez Rockshelter suggests continuity from the Blanca phase, but by this time projectile points were becoming rare in Oaxaca.

ARCHAIC SETTLEMENT PATTERNS. MacNeish (1964a, 1972) originally distinguished two kinds of settlements in Tehuacan: "macroband" camps, occupied for a season or more by 15–25 persons, and "microband" camps, occupied by 2–5 individuals for any period from a day or two to most of a season. Since even microband camps may contain both men's and women's tools, the inference is that they were produced by "family collecting bands" like those of the Paiute or Shoshone (Steward 1955); macroband camps would then represent places where several families coalesced during a time of abundant resources. These settlements can be further divided by site function to produce a wider range of site types: hunting camps, plant-collecting camps, maguey-roasting camps, and so on.

Gheo-Shih would be an example of a macroband camp in the Valley of Oaxaca; the site covers 1.5 ha and might have been occupied by 25 persons, probably during June–July–August when the surrounding mesquite groves would have been heavy with pods (180–200 kg of edible portion per ha), and when rainy-season cultivation of early domestic plants could take place. There are oval concentrations of rocks and tools which may indicate residence in small shelters; if so, these were apparently without postholes, and their floors were not excavated into the ground. We have already mentioned the boulder-lined "dance ground" in the center of the site and the ornament-making area. This suggests that certain rituals and craft activities may have been deferred until the local group was united in a macroband camp.

With the breakup of a macroband camp like Gheo-Shih, individual families evidently spread out over the countryside to engage in a wide range of activities. Zones E–B at Guila Naquitz would be examples of another settlement type, the microband camp whose primary purpose was for wild plant collecting. Guila Naquitz was probably occupied by only 3–5 persons, beginning at the end of the mesquite harvest season (September?) and lasting until the end of the acorn harvest (December?). Other microband camps seem to have been oriented more strongly toward hunting, although this was probably a difference of degree rather than kind. Zones D–C at Cueva Blanca may reflect this kind of microband occupation, with projectile points and deer bones relatively well represented and grinding implements rare.

In the heart of the dry season (February) there are too few plants available in the Guila Naquitz area to keep a family alive, and often the deer have moved up to the higher mountains where the lower evapotranspiration provides them with more to browse on. One of the activities of this season is the roasting of agave hearts, which are available year-round. We believe that one example of a maguey-roasting camp would be Yuzanu near Yanhuitlan in the Mixteca Alta (Lorenzo 1958: Fig. 17), while the Martinez Rockshelter may be another. We expect most (but not all) maguey-roasting camps to date to the dry season, and to be found most frequently at elevations above the valley floor.

THE ORIGINS OF AGRICULTURE IN OAXACA. Sometime between the end of the Pleistocene and 5000 B.C., the first steps toward agriculture were taken in Oaxaca and neighboring areas. Donald Lathrap (personal communication) has suggested that the bottle gourd (*Lagenaria*) may have been the first New World plant domesticated because of its obvious utility to preceramic food collectors. Bottle gourd rinds do occur in zones C–B of Guila Naquitz Cave (7450–6670 B.C.) in association with 14 seeds and peduncles of *Cucurbita pepo*. It may be that squashes were originally domesticated by hunter-gatherers who already knew and cultivated the bottle gourd, and who therefore instantly recognized these other members of the cucurbit family as potentially useful when they ran across them (Flannery 1973:301). Between 5000 and 3000 B.C., two more cucurbits, *C. mixta* and *C. moschata*, appeared in Tehuacan Valley sites (ibid.). Both Guila Naquitz and El Riego Cave also included specimens of the wild coyote melon, *Apodanthera* sp. Since cucurbits which become "tolerated weed associate[s] of man prior to the practice of agriculture" may already show "an increase in seed size over most wild species" (Cutler and Whitaker 1967:219), we may never know the exact date of domestication for each species.

Hundreds of small wild black runner beans were harvested by the occupants of Guila Naquitz between 8700 and 6700 B.C., but the species (which still grows near the cave) is one which has never been domesticated (Lawrence Kaplan, personal communication). Common beans (*Phaseolus vulgaris*) are not known from Tehuacan until 4000–

3000 B.C. levels, while tepary beans (*Phaseolus acutifolius*) are abundant by 3000 B.C. (Kaplan 1967); neither appears at Guila Naquitz.

Pollen grains of the genus *Zea*, in the size range of those of teosinte (*Z. mexicana*), occur in 7400–6700 B.C. levels at Guila Naquitz (Schoenwetter 1974). The outstanding recent genetic and anatomical research of Walton Galinat (1970, 1971) suggests that maize is ultimately derived from teosinte, a view shared by George Beadle, Jack Harlan, and others; Paul Mangelsdorf (1974) still disagrees. By the time of the Abejas phase in the Tehuacan Valley (3400–2300 B.C.) and the Blanca phase in the Valley of Oaxaca (3295–2800 B.C.), domesticated corn was probably as widespread in the area as Coxcatlan projectile points.

THE EARLY AND MIDDLE
FORMATIVE PERIODS
*Research Design*

With regard to the Formative period, our research goals were to identify the processes leading to the establishment of sedentary life; the rise of societies with hereditary ranking; and the eventual evolution of stratified, class-endogamous societies and the Zapotec state. We knew that the village was the key to many of the social, political, and economic processes of the Formative, and we hoped to work out ways of dealing with Formative sites as villages rather than as stratified heaps of potsherds. Once again, it has taken more than a decade even to approach these goals.

Valley-wide settlement patterns for the Formative were established by Blanton, Kowalewski, and their associates, using the intensive survey methods originally pioneered in the Valley of Mexico, and adding techniques adapted from locational geography. Patterns of settlement within each village were established by a series of excavations in which the units of analysis were houses, storage pits, activity areas, burials, and other features, rather than "levels" within "pits" or "trenches." These villages included San Jose Mogote (excavated by Flannery and Marcus), Barrio del Rosario Huitzo (excavated by Flannery and others), Fabrica San Jose (excavated by Robert D. Drennan), and Tierras Largas (excavated by Marcus C. Winter), all in the Etla region; San Sebastian Abasolo (excavated by Flannery), Santo Domingo Tomaltepec (excavated by Michael E. Whalen), and Mitla (briefly tested by Richard J. Orlandini and Schoenwetter), all in the Tlacolula region; Hierve el Agua in the mountains east of Mitla (excavated by James A. Neely); and La Coyotera in the nearby Cañada de Cuicatlan (excavated by Charles S. Spencer and Elsa M. Redmond).

Subsistence was studied through the flotation of carbonized seeds from ash deposits, with subsequent analysis by C. Earle Smith, Jr., Richard I. Ford, and Judith Smith; through pollen analysis by Schoenwetter and Suzanne K. Fish; by double-screening for animal bones, with subsequent analysis by Flannery and others; through site catchment analysis; and through a study of local dry-farming and irrigation systems by Anne V. T. Kirkby (1973), Susan H. Lees (1973), and James A. Neely (1967). Division of labor was studied by comparing the contents of activity areas, features, and house floors with an eye to establishing male and female work areas, common household activities, and craft specialization (by household, residential ward, village, or region).

Several methods were used to elicit data on social organization, all of them guided either by generalized models for pre-state societies proposed by Elman R. Service (1962), Morton H. Fried (1967), and Marshall D. Sahlins (1972), or by a model for the operation of the Zapotec state derived from ethnohistory (Flannery and Marcus 1976b; Whitecotton 1977). Residences from all periods were compared with regard to a series of standard criteria in an effort to detect emerging differences in access to imported materials and sumptuary goods which might reflect differences in status; for the Terminal For-

mative, we can document early versions of the minor palaces (*quehui*) or major palaces (*quihuitao*) in which the later Zapotec royalty and nobility are known to have lived. Burials of all periods were also compared in an effort to detect variations in treatment which might reflect status differences, as well as similarities in treatment which might reflect groupings within society. We noted whether burials were treated as individuals, as members of husband-wife pairs, or as members of a multiple interment. Designations of age and sex by physical anthropologist Richard G. Wilkinson made it possible to determine which offerings went with men versus women, or young adults versus elders; for example, analyses made it clear that vessels with Olmec designs like the "fire-serpent" and "were-jaguar" occurred primarily with males. In the Late and Terminal Formative, we could see the evolution of the masonry tomb from the earlier slab-lined grave and observe the eventual evolution of the Zapotec royal tomb with its elaborate funerary sculpture. Studies of the use of figurines by Drennan (1976b) and the nature of funerary urns by Marcus (n.d.) suggest that the ancestors figured prominently in both religion and the ideology of descent for much of Zapotec prehistory (Flannery and Marcus 1976b; Marcus 1978).

Design element studies by Stephen Plog (1976) suggest that as complex regional networks of sites developed, certain groups of hamlets shared the services of a local civic-ceremonial center. Public buildings at such centers were studied in order to document the growth of various Zapotec state institutions out of the more generalized institutions of earlier times. By the Terminal Formative, the standard Zapotec two-room temple (*yohopèe*) had appeared, as had the standardized I-shaped ballcourt and other architectural manifestations of state institutions and their professional staffs. Studies of early Zapotec hieroglyphic writing seem to document the placement of historically important events in the framework of a 260-day ritual calendar (Marcus 1976c).

Three variables frequently cited in the evolutionary studies of ancient high cultures are long-distance trade, local exchange, and warfare. Trade and exchange were studied by the tracing of raw materials to their sources, by analysis of the contexts in which such materials occurred within the village, and by quantitative comparisons of the amounts in various households (Pires-Ferreira 1975). The results showed that mechanisms such as reciprocity, pooling, and redistribution could be detected archaeologically for some materials (Pires-Ferreira 1976b; Winter and Pires-Ferreira 1976), and that each commodity had to be understood in its own right: obsidian was available to every household, marine shell exchange involved a small number of craftsmen, and magnetite mirrors may have been exchanged as gifts between elites. As for armed conflict, it may be represented as early as the Middle Formative in the form of monumental carvings of sacrificed captives; actual warfare and military conquest may be reflected in the Late Formative defensive walls of Monte Alban (Blanton 1978) and the Terminal Formative subjugation of places called Cuicatlan, Miahuatlan, Tututepec, and Ocelotepec by the Zapotec state (Marcus 1976b).

Finally, we have tried to reconstruct the evolution of Formative religion using (1) Roy A. Rappaport's model for the operation of ritual and religion (Rappaport 1968, 1969, 1971a, 1971b), (2) ethnohistoric data on sixteenth-century Zapotec religion (Marcus 1978), and (3) a contextual analysis of the ritual paraphernalia in Formative villages (Flannery 1976d). One can see in dim outline the gradual evolution of Zapotec religion—with its temple staff, ritual bloodletting, human and animal sacrifice, ancestor worship, costumed dancers, and sacred divination—out of a Formative pattern which was already complex.

## The Early Formative

THE ESPIRIDION COMPLEX. The oldest ceramics thus far recovered from the Valley of Oaxaca come from San Jose Mogote and have been assigned to the Espiridion complex. They were associated with the remains of a small wattle-and-daub house which may have been one of the first built there, its wall posts having been set in bedrock. The small sample of sherds is entirely without paint, slip, or plastic decoration. It includes a series of jar rims, jar shoulders, and body sherds virtually indistinguishable from those of Purron Plain (MacNeish, Peterson, and Flannery 1970:22), and hence assigned by us to that type. It also features a previously undescribed type, consisting entirely of hemispherical bowls whose walls are no more than 2–2.5 mm thick. The best represented type, however, is a burnished plain ware, the collection made up of undecorated jars and hemispherical bowls (Fig. 3-10a). The entire sample of sherds is irregularly fired, and grades in color from buff or tan to pinkish or mahogany brown; there is also one small figurine head which seems to represent a feline.

The Espiridion complex finds its closest parallels with the Purron complex ceramics from levels K and K[1] at Purron Cave in the Tehuacan Valley, but there are minor differences which discourage us from lumping the two complexes together. Future work could clarify their relationship and perhaps escalate them to the status of a true "phase."

THE TIERRAS LARGAS PHASE. The first period in our sequence to be characterized by a widespread ceramic complex was the Tierras Largas phase (1400–1150 B.C.). The principal vessel shapes were jars and hemispherical bowls, with tecomates and flat-based, outleaned-wall bowls constituting minor elements (Fig. 3-10b, c). While some vessels are undecorated, many hemispherical bowls had a red band at the rim, red parallel stripes, or red chevrons. Another form of decoration was zoned, dentate rocker-stamping on tecomates or outleaned-wall bowls.

Tierras Largas phase sites occur throughout the Valley of Oaxaca, and when intensive surveys are completed the total may well have reached 20 hamlets or villages, plus a

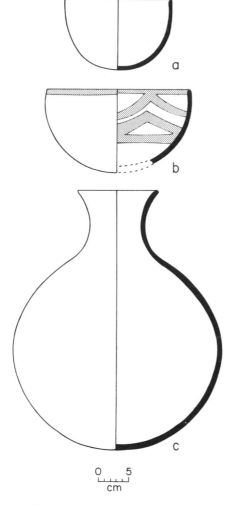

FIGURE 3-10. Pottery of the Espiridion complex and the Tierras Largas phase: *a*, reconstruction of the most common vessel shape of the Espiridion complex; *b*, red-on-buff hemispherical bowl, Tierras Largas phase; *c*, burnished plain jar, Tierras Largas phase.

few brief occupations in caves such as Cueva Blanca (Fig. 3-11). With the single notable exception of San Jose Mogote, all known sites are smaller than 3 ha, and most of them probably consisted of 10 households or less. The salt spring at Fabrica San Jose was also visited at this time, though there is no evidence of permanent occupation (Drennan 1976a).

Most densely occupied of the areas so far intensively surveyed was the Etla region, with 6 Tierras Largas phase communities lo-cated in a 200 sq km area. Five of these settlements were smaller than 3 ha, with the sixth community—San Jose Mogote—being the largest in the valley. Surface remains at the latter site consist of 10 discrete scatters of Tierras Largas phase sherds, varying between 0.1 and 1.6 ha each, and totaling 7.8 ha (Fisch 1978). Four of these scatters fall within the area excavated during seven field seasons by Flannery and Marcus, estimated by Fisch at 2.0 ha and by Marcus (1976d: Table 3.9) at 2–3 ha; this area contains the only known Tierras Largas phase public buildings, none of which were visible on the surface. Five of the 6 remaining surface scatters lie in areas never excavated. While the area with Tierras Largas phase surface sherds has almost certainly been increased through the use of early fill in later buildings, not all of the remaining scatters can be explained in this way. San Jose Mogote at this period is therefore reconstructed as a community with an estimated 147 persons (Fisch 1978) occupying 10 small residential areas, strung out over a horseshoe-shaped area of piedmont spur and sharing a public building. Thus, while the residential pattern is "dispersed" at the household level, it shows "clustering" relative to the rest of the valley, and suggests the rise of San Jose Mogote as a center of regional significance as early as 1150 B.C.

In the 801 sq km Central and Zaachila-Zimatlan regions, intensive survey showed only 9 small, dispersed occupations (plus a tenth just across the Rio Atoyac in the Ocotlan region). The size of the sites (based on surface sherds) ranges from 0.1 to 1.5 ha, and it seems likely that all were hamlets of only 3–10 households each. The mean population estimate for these two regions combined is 125 persons, suggesting a density of roughly 0.16 persons per sq km (Feinman and Kowalewski 1979). This brings the total population of the western part of the Valley of Oaxaca (Etla, Central, and Zaachila-Zimatlan survey areas) to a mean estimate of approximately 425 persons; no estimates are yet available for the eastern part of the valley.

Most of the Tierras Largas phase settle-

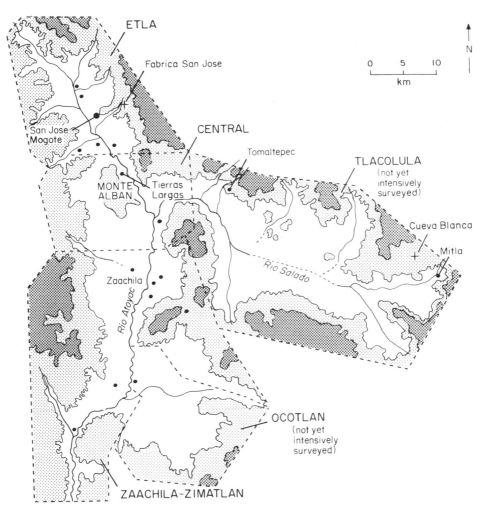

FIGURE 3-11. Tierras Largas phase sites in the Valley of Oaxaca as of 1979. Black circles are villages or hamlets; plus signs are camps or ephemeral occupations.

ments were located on low, well-drained piedmont spurs adjacent to the main river and the productive high alluvium zone. However, several sites were found both on the high alluvium itself and on higher ground in the middle piedmont, where tributary streams could have been tapped for irrigation. For the Central and Zaachila-Zimatlan areas, Margaret E. Curran (1978) compared Kirkby's (1973) estimates of potential maize productivity with the survey estimates of population. She found that the population of those regions was well below what the land

could have supported during this phase. In fact, according to Kirkby's estimates for the Tierras Largas phase, the total estimated population of the Etla, Central, and Zaachila-Zimatlan survey areas would have required less than 15 percent of the potential maize harvest from the Central and Zaachila-Zimatlan regions alone.

To the north, the earliest known stage of the Cruz phase in the Yanhuitlan-Nochixtlan Valley is very similar to Tierras Largas. Sherds from area K203 on the site of Yucuita, excavated by Spores (1972), are so similar as to suggest near-identity with samples from the Etla region. Farther away, the early Ajalpan phase of the Tehuacan Valley (MacNeish, Peterson, and Flannery 1970) and the Lagunita phase of the Isthmus of Tehuantepec (R. Zeitlin 1978) show similarities.

The basic unit of residence during the Tierras Largas phase was the nuclear family, manifested archaeologically by the remains of a 3 × 5 m house of pine posts, cane walls daubed with clay, and a thatched roof. Houses were usually accompanied by an assemblage of features outside, such as dooryards, lean-tos, subterranean storage pits, earth ovens, garbage middens, areas of craft activity, and sometimes burials. Each household within a hamlet was separated from its nearest neighbor by 30–40 m of open space. Neither in the household patterns nor in the burials do we find evidence for ranking or social inequality. The burials occur around households and are generally of single individuals; no elaborate offerings, group burials, or spatially segregated cemeteries have yet been found for this period. We conclude that the Tierras Largas phase was a time of egalitarian social organization.

During the transition from the Espiridion complex to the early Tierras Largas phase, a feature vaguely similar to the cleared and boulder-lined area at Gheo-Shih was constructed at San Jose Mogote. The evidence consists of an open area (perhaps 7 m wide from west to east), set apart from the residential areas of the hamlet by a double line of staggered posts. In some places, this double line of posts was reinforced by a row of heavy stone slabs set on edge. The orientation of this enclosure, which contained no architecture and was nearly free of artifacts, was slightly west of true north (Flannery and Marcus 1976a: Fig. 10.2).

Very soon after the abandonment of this structure in early Tierras Largas phase times, a different type of "public" construction was built at San Jose Mogote. This was a limeplastered, one-room public building of which 8 examples are known, although there is no evidence that more than one was in use at any time. The best preserved was Structure 6 (Flannery and Marcus 1976a: Fig. 10.3), which was roughly 4.4 × 5.4 m in extent and oriented north-south (Fig. 3-12). The walls had a core of upright pine posts (perhaps 20 in the entire structure), with bundles of canes lashed into the spaces between the posts and clay daubed over the walls. The floor was of lime stucco over a platform-like foundation of crushed bedrock, clay, lime, and sand; where preservation was good, the lower 40 cm of the wall appeared to have been expanded into a low bench which ran around the inside of the room. Two features occurred in these buildings with great regularity. Set against the south wall was a low rectangular platform, possibly a step, but more likely an altar of some kind. Directly north of this altar appeared a storage pit, incorporated into the original floor of the room and lined with the same stucco.

In 3 cases, these pits were filled with powdered lime (Flannery and Marcus 1976a: 211), which we originally described as being "of the very type used for the plastering and replastering of the room." While this may be true, in retrospect the amount of lime which could be stored in these small features seems insufficient for such a task. We now prefer Michael Coe's suggestion (personal communication) that these pits may have been used to store powdered lime for ritual purposes, such as mixing with narcotics like tobacco. The use of tobacco was widespread among the Zapotec, being mentioned in the sixteenth-century *relaciones* from Macuilxochitl, Miahuatlan, Nejapa, and other places in Oaxaca (Paso y Troncoso 1905).

THE SAN JOSE PHASE. One of the most striking events of the transition from the Tierras Largas phase to the San Jose phase (1150–850 B.C.) was the growth of San Jose Mogote. While there is no question about the impressive nature of this growth, estimates of it differ according to whether they are based on excavation or on settlement pattern survey. The results of seven seasons of excavation, combined with an intensive surface pickup by 5 m circles (Flannery

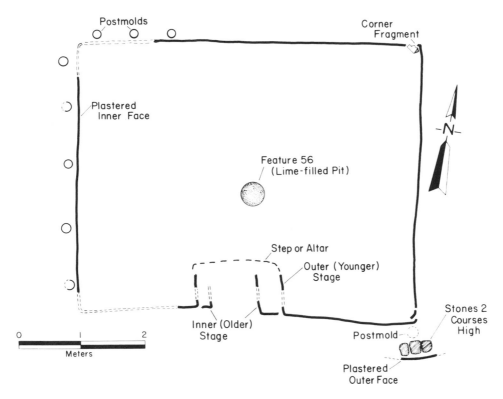

FIGURE 3-12. Structure 6 at San Jose Mogote, a Tierras Largas phase public building.

1976a: Fig. 3.4), suggest to Flannery and Marcus that the main residential area of San Jose Mogote covered about 20 ha at 900 B.C. with a population estimated at 80–120 households (400–600 persons?) (Marcus 1976d: Table 3.10). However, there is another area of San Jose phase occupation which lies several hundred m to the east, and which Flannery and Marcus have never included in their calculations because they were uncertain whether it represented (1) an outlying *barrio* of San Jose Mogote which should be included with the latter or (2) a separate community. The intervening area, although occasionally yielding San Jose phase sherds, is a strip of annually flooded stream alluvium which test excavations show to contain no in situ deposits. When the whole of this area was examined as part of Blanton and Kowalewski's survey, however, the zone over which San Jose phase pottery could be

picked up was determined to be 70 ha, with an estimated population of 700 persons (Fisch 1978). This figure would represent "greater San Jose Mogote" and is based on the assumption that the aforementioned outlying areas are indeed all part of one very large site.

In contrast to the situation at San Jose Mogote, most of the other previously occupied settlements in the valley remained the same size. There was a net increase of 1 site in the Zaachila-Zimatlan region (and one just across the Rio Atoyac in the Ocotlan region); 2 sites in the Central region; and 7 sites in the Etla region (Fig. 3-13). At least 23 of the known San Jose phase sites in the intensively surveyed parts of the valley remained in the 0.1–2.0 ha size range. The Tlacolula region has as yet not been intensively surveyed, but the known sites there, such as Tomaltepec, Abasolo, and Mitla, are

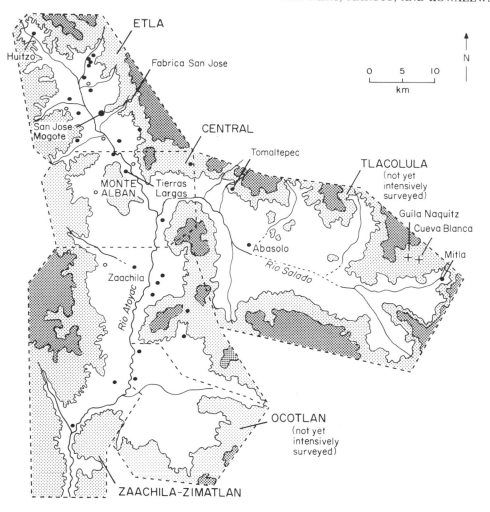

FIGURE 3-13. San Jose and Guadalupe phase sites in the Valley of Oaxaca as of 1979. Black circles are villages or hamlets; plus signs are camps or ephemeral occupations. White circles represent sites which appear to have been first founded in the Guadalupe phase; all other sites were founded prior to that phase. The lone Guadalupe site in the Zaachila-Zimatlan area may yet turn out to be San Jose phase.

also small. Brief occupations at Guila Naquitz Cave and Cueva Blanca also date to the San Jose phase.

It is significant that population growth in the valley during the San Jose phase did not correspond to the predicted pattern of growth based on the valley's agricultural potential. During the San Jose phase, an increment in corncob size made possible a doubling of the potentially productive farm land in the Valley of Oaxaca (Kirkby 1973:131).

Since the Zaachila-Zimatlan region had twice as much productive land as the Etla region, Kirkby's estimates for Etla (9 sites) and Zaachila-Zimatlan (16 sites) reflect their differential productive capacity.

The survey data indicate that the actual distribution of settlements was quite different: the Etla region had more sites and a much greater population, despite having only half the agricultural land. Population grew primarily in and around San Jose Mogote. It seems likely, therefore, that most growth was associated with organizational differences among the various arms of the valley, rather than with the distribution of arable land. The different rates of population growth may have been a consequence of San Jose Mogote's increased demands for agricultural support, tribute, and/or corvée labor for the maintenance of public buildings, demands that most likely were placed on the population of the Etla arm adjacent to that large settlement. In return, San Jose Mogote may have provided more services for that population.

The functional differences between San Jose Mogote and other sites were also more striking by this time; several different types of public buildings have been found at the site (see below). In contrast, the earliest public structures so far found at other settlements do not date until the close of the San Jose phase or the outset of the succeeding Guadalupe phase. In addition, San Jose Mogote apparently served as a center of specialized production and distribution that both mediated exchange relationships among the small agricultural communities in the Etla region and served to tie the region into a wider Mesoamerican exchange sphere (Flannery 1968b; Pires-Ferreira 1975; Winter and Pires-Ferreira 1976; Drennan 1976b).

One-room public buildings were still constructed during the early San Jose phase, but they were soon joined by public buildings of other types. Near the eastern limits of San Jose Mogote, a gentle slope was converted into a series of stepped terraces, faced with stones set in hard puddled adobe clay. The westernmost terrace rose in two stages to a height of 3 m; the easternmost was lower, but had 2 small stairways made from stone slabs on its downhill face. Below it were found 2 carved stones, Monuments 1 and 2, which may originally have been set in an upper tier of the terrace. Tentatively, Monument 1 seems to depict the head of a jaguar or other feline, while Monument 2 represents a raptorial bird; neither is stylistically "Olmec" (Marcus 1976b: Figs. 26, 27).

Residential patterns of the San Jose phase offer some insight into the social organization of that period. The data suggest that there were emerging status differences, but that these took the form of a continuum from relatively higher to relatively lower status, without a true division into social classes such as took place in later periods. The simplest and most common kind of residence at San Jose Mogote itself is typified by House 13, excavated by Marcus in 1974—a rectangular wattle-and-daub house 3 × 5 to 4 × 6 m in extent, with a clay floor surfaced with river sand, one doorway on the longer side, and a series of upright pine posts 10–15 cm in diameter (Flannery 1976a: Fig. 2.3). A somewhat better-made type of house, also fairly common, is represented by House 2 (ibid.: Fig. 2.15). This had a partial foundation of field stones, posts 15–20 cm in diameter (including large corner posts), and a layer of whitewash over the daub. Such houses tend to have a higher concentration of marine shell ornaments, shell debris, mica, and high quality Matadamas chert, suggesting that greater access to exotic raw materials was one of the ways in which relatively higher status was expressed.

Another example of a higher-status household was the House 16–17 complex (ibid.: Fig. 2.10). Here the actual whitewashed house (House 17) was accompanied by an additional structure (possibly a kitchen, shed, or outbuilding), forming an L-shaped unit facing onto a small patio. Through the patio (and between the two structures) ran a small drainage canal which was connected to a large cistern excavated in bedrock. In addition to large quantities of Matadamas chert, this house produced a "true" stingray spine (one from an actual ray, rather than a whittled deer bone imitation) and a set of figurines arranged in a scene, buried beneath the floor of the outbuilding (ibid.: Fig. 11.9).

Perhaps the highest-status residence found so far is Structure 16 in area A at San Jose Mogote. While the house itself was not unusual in size, posthole pattern, or wattle-and-daub construction, it rested on a 1 m high

71

platform of puddled adobe with a coating of lime plaster. Although smaller than the platform of Structure 11 at Tomaltepec (see below), this construction showed some similarities to the latter; its associated debris (including a metate and a mano) suggested a residence rather than a public building. Area A produced more than 500 fragments of magnetite and related iron ores, plus the bulk of the magnetite mirrors (see Fig. 3-14) and all the mirror-working activity areas so far found at the site. Hence, one possible interpretation of Structure 16 would be that it was the residence of the most important family occupying the magnetite-working *barrio* of the village during the San Jose phase. Mirrors of Oaxaca magnetite, perhaps made in this *barrio*, reached San Lorenzo in the Olmec area (Pires-Ferreira 1975).

Such impressive residences were not common, but neither were they restricted to the largest site in the area. A similar building can be seen in Structure 11 at Tomaltepec, a hamlet of only 5–8 households (Whalen n.d.). Structure 11, a platform roughly 4 × 8 m in extent and 1 m high, was built on large foundation stones, above which the construction was of puddled adobe, fist-size stones, and plano-convex adobes. No stairway was found, but the structure did have one unusual feature: beneath its floor was an adobe-plastered storage cell with a volume of 9 cu m, approximately six times the capacity of the average bell-shaped pit of that period. Although the building had an orientation of about 8° west of north, the debris in the storage cell (and the refuse associated with the rest of Structure 11) suggested a residence rather than a public building; there was also no associated lime plaster. The debris included large numbers of deer and rabbit bones; quantities of pine charcoal; abundant mica and marine shell, including some evidence for shellworking; carbonized maize, teosinte, and avocado; and more than 50 percent of the total Early Formative obsidian recovered on the site.

This relatively higher status residence may be contrasted with House 4 in Early San Jose

FIGURE 3-14. Magnetite mirrors from Area A, San Jose Mogote, San Jose phase. Width of lower specimen 1.3 cm.

phase Household Unit 2 at Tomaltepec (see Flannery 1976a:20, Fig. 2.5), a relatively lower-status household. This ordinary wattle-and-daub house had no platform, much less animal bone, much less obsidian, virtually no marine shell, and a chipped stone sample composed mostly of low-quality chert (Whalen n.d.). Thus, as at San Jose Mogote, relatively higher status seems to have been reflected in greater access to nonlocal products and deer meat, greater involvement in ornament production, and a more elaborate residence, although one not beyond the construction capacity of a single family.

Burials of the San Jose phase also show a continuum from simple (individuals buried with no offerings) to more elaborate (individuals buried with jade labrets and earspools, well-made pottery, shell or magnetite ornaments). There is a tendency for gray or white vessels bearing Olmec designs to occur with male burials, suggesting that some men may have belonged to descent lines with the "fire-serpent" or "were-jaguar" as the apical ancestor (Pyne 1976; Flannery and Marcus 1976b); infant burials with such vessels at Abasolo (Fig. 3-15) suggest that the association with the "fire-serpent" may have been there from

72

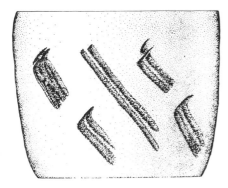

FIGURE 3-15. Gray cylindrical bowl with excised "fire-serpent" motif, found with Burial 4, a San Jose phase infant, at San Sebastian Abasolo. Height of vessel 8.2 cm.

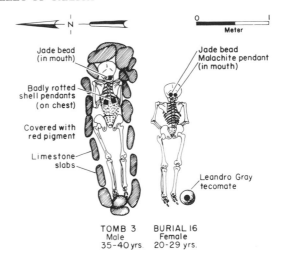

FIGURE 3-16. Tomb 3 and Burial 16 from San Jose Mogote. This male (in a slab-lined grave) and female, probably a marital pair, were found in a small San Jose phase cemetery.

birth. While most Early Formative burials were individual, through time there was an increase in (1) double burials involving a man and woman (perhaps a marital pair) and (2) cases where secondary burials were added to the primary burial of an adult male (perhaps a household head). From the San Jose phase onward, some skulls (most often those of women) show the tabular deformation which was considered a sign of beauty and high status in later periods. We still do not know why some individuals were buried near the houses, while others (primarily adults) were buried in cemeteries set apart from the residences; nor do we know why certain individuals were accompanied by dog burials. Finally, certain Early Formative adults were buried in graves lined with stone slabs (Fig. 3-16), perhaps a forerunner of the later stone masonry tomb.

At Tomaltepec, Whalen (n.d.) discovered a San Jose phase cemetery outside the limits of the village as defined by surface ceramics (Fig. 3-17). His excavations yielded more than 60 burials, amounting to the remains of some 80 individuals, 55 of whom could be aged and sexed by physical anthropologist Richard G. Wilkinson. There were no infants in the cemetery (babies apparently were buried near the house, as at Abasolo), and only 1 child. All the remaining burials were

those of adults, or of adolescents old enough to have passed through puberty (i.e., the "initiated" members of the community); the oldest were over 50 years old.

There were virtually equal numbers of males and females in the cemetery, but most females had died at 20–29 years, while most males had survived until 30–39. All burials were face down, and almost all had their heads to the east; while a few males were flexed, most burials were fully extended. Most of the secondary burials at the site occurred with the flexed group, i.e., they had been added to the burial of a flexed male.

Although the flexed males constituted only 12.7 percent of the cemetery, they received 50 percent of the burial vessels with carved "fire-serpent" designs and 88 percent of the jade beads; 66 percent of the burials covered by stone slabs also fell in this flexed-male group (Whalen n.d.). One 20–29-year-old male with a cylindrical "fire-serpent" vessel was accompanied by a 20–29-year-old female with a magnetite ornament in the shape of an Olmec "U-motif"; this couple may represent a husband-wife pair (Whalen n.d.).

A smaller cemetery, perhaps serving a sin-

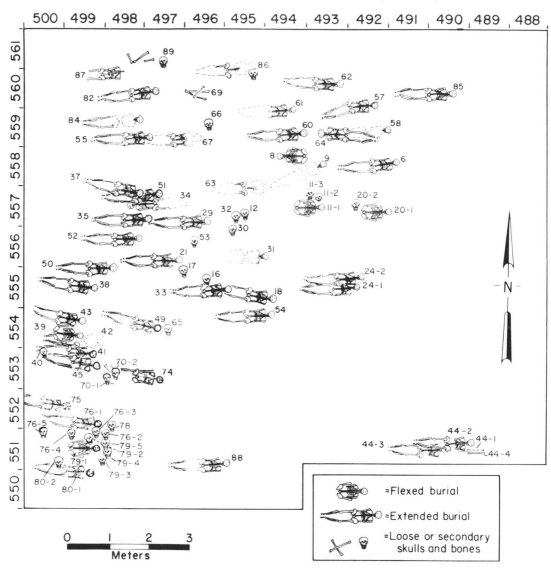

FIGURE 3-17. San Jose phase cemetery from Santo Domingo Tomaltepec. Offerings not shown. Courtesy Michael E. Whalen.

gle residential ward rather than an entire village, was found at San Jose Mogote. Like the burials from Tomaltepec, both sexes are represented and most skeletons are adults, buried face down and fully extended. Some burials are oriented east-west, others north-south. Almost all have at least one jade bead in the mouth and one or more pottery vessels; as is the case with burials at Tomaltepec and Tierras Largas (Winter 1972), vessels

with "fire-serpent" designs occur only with males.

The simplest San Jose phase burials have no beads and no offerings, and some may be stuffed into abandoned storage pits. One of the most elegant burials found so far was that of a middle-aged woman apparently associated with House 16–17; she had two fine jade earspools and a jade labret.

74

## The Middle Formative

During the Middle Formative, the Valley of Oaxaca witnessed the evolution of a possible three-tiered site hierarchy. At the top was San Jose Mogote, a "first-order" site more than ten times as large as the second largest site known. In the second tier of the hierarchy were sites like Barrio del Rosario Huitzo, a 3 ha Guadalupe phase settlement with substantial public buildings, and Santo Domingo Tomaltepec, a 2–3 ha Rosario phase community with modest public architecture. Finally, there were many "third-order" sites like Fabrica San Jose and Abasolo, with no apparent public buildings and only 1–3 ha in size.

We cannot as yet demonstrate that an *administrative* hierarchy accompanied this site typology; indeed, there is some reason to believe that the relationship between second-order sites like Huitzo and our one first-order site, San Jose Mogote, was competitive rather than subordinate. Plog (1976) compared the decorated Atoyac Yellow-white pottery of 5 San Jose/Guadalupe phase villages by means of a gravity model, based on the assumption that the degree of interaction between two communities is directly proportional to their size and inversely proportional to the distance between them. Several third-order sites shared a high frequency of decorative motifs with San Jose Mogote, suggesting that the latter may have served as a regional civic-ceremonial center for a whole series of hamlets without public architecture of their own. On the other hand, San Jose Mogote shared many fewer motifs with Huitzo than would have been predicted from their proximity, suggesting they may have been competing centers.

By the end of the Middle Formative, most of the farming techniques recorded ethnohistorically for the Zapotec had come into use. In addition to dry farming, the Zapotec practiced several kinds of irrigation. On land where the water table lies only 3 m below the surface, they still draw water from shallow wells to irrigate by hand. We have found prehistoric wells in archaeological deposits dating to 1000 B.C., and by 600 B.C. there were specialized jars that may have served for such irrigation (Flannery et al. 1970). Well-irrigation is a labor-intensive farming technique, and one in which children can play an important role. More than half the watering in well-irrigation villages like Abasolo today is done by boys between 8 and 18 years old. Once well-irrigation had begun, therefore, there may have been an increased selective advantage for families with large numbers of children; this in turn may have been one factor contributing to the explosive growth of population during the Early and Middle Formative periods.

Still another form of irrigation is to draw water from streams by means of small diversion dams and carry it to the fields in gravity-flow canals. Such canal systems can be securely demonstrated by 400 B.C. (Blanton 1978:54), and village rain-runoff canals which may have served as their prototypes go back as far as 1000 B.C. (Flannery 1976a: Fig 2.10). Perhaps the most spectacular example of Zapotec irrigation is the prehistoric site of Hierve el Agua, in the mountains to the east of the Valley of Oaxaca. Here excavations by Neely (1967) revealed 0.5 sq km of artificially terraced hillside, served by a complex series of canals which led from a group of permanent springs. The quantity of calcium carbonate in the water is so great that the canals have literally turned to stone from travertine deposition, thereby "fossilizing" an irrigation system used between 400 B.C. and A.D. 1300 (Flannery and Marcus 1976b: Fig. 2).

Some Middle Formative evidence for economic specialization on the hamlet level comes from Fabrica San Jose, where salt was produced from saline springs at the site (Drennan 1976a). The salt thus produced was presumably used at other communities in the valley, as well as at Fabrica San Jose. At the same time, salt production seems to have been a part-time specialty engaged in by households which were also agricultural; it represents the focusing of productive effort

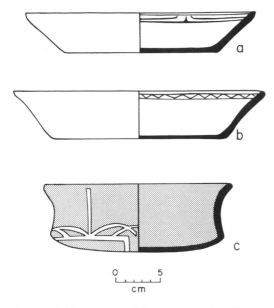

FIGURE 3-18. Pottery of the San Jose, Guadalupe, and Rosario phases: *a*, white monochrome bowl with double-line-break motif typical of the San Jose phase; *b*, white monochrome bowl with motif typical of the Guadalupe phase; *c*, gray composite silhouette bowl with "negative" white motif typical of the Rosario phase.

FIGURE 3-19. Gray bird-effigy vessel from Feature 105, Tierras Largas, Guadalupe phase. Height of specimen 12.8 cm. M. Winter excavation.

by many (or all) households in a single hamlet on a product which could be produced particularly advantageously at that locality.

THE GUADALUPE PHASE. The Guadalupe phase (850–700? B.C.) was originally defined on the basis of materials from Huitzo and San José Mogote in the Etla region of the valley (Flannery 1968b; Flannery et al. 1970). More recent surveys and excavations suggest that some of the most important ceramics and figurine types used to define the phase may not extend far beyond the Etla region; we have not yet been able to produce incontrovertible evidence that the Zaachila-Zimatlan and Tlacolula regions of the valley went through a comparable "Guadalupe phase." The most likely explanation is that the specific ceramic types involved originated at Huitzo, where they are most heavily represented. It is not yet clear what takes the place of the Guadalupe phase in the other parts of the valley, but one possibility is that the Rosario phase ceramic complex there grows out of a later variant of the San Jose phase ceramic complex. Throughout the valley, the period 850–700 B.C. is characterized by white monochrome pottery with incised double-line-break designs like those of the Dili phase at Chiapa de Corzo II and the early Santa Maria phase in Tehuacan (Fig. 3-18). The Guadalupe phase also includes gray monochrome pottery, usually in the form of bowls but sometimes as animal effigies (Fig. 3-19).

During the Guadalupe phase, Huitzo was a village of at least 3 ha which subsisted on maize, beans, cucurbits, chiles, avocados, prickly pear and organ cactus fruit, acorns, hackberries, and the fruit of the *cuajilote* (*Parmentiera* sp.). Near the start of the phase the villagers constructed a pyramidal platform (Platform 4) which rose in tiers with a sloping outer wall, and was oriented 8° west of true north. Although the outside presented a boulder or cobble facing set in hard clay, the interior was of earthen fill, stabilized by retaining walls made of plano-convex adobes. Above Platform 4 we found traces of a building which might once have

FIGURE 3-20. Artist's reconstruction of Platform 3, Barrio del Rosario Huitzo, Guadalupe phase. Drawing by N. Hansen.

stood on the platform; these remains included part of a plastered patio floor and the lower part of a lime-plastered stairway leading up from it.

Platform 3 was the best preserved Guadalupe phase public building found at Huitzo (Flannery and Marcus 1976a: Fig. 10.6). This was a platform roughly 1.3 m high and 11.5 m long east-west. The north-south width could not be determined because so much of the platform had been removed by modern adobe-makers; what remained was the northernmost 3.5 m, which included a stairway 7.6 m wide. There were 3 steps to the stairway, and all of them, as well as the northern façade of the platform, were heavily plastered with lime. The whole platform was oriented 8° west of true north, and the collapsed remains of the building above indicated that it had been a heavy structure of wattle-and-daub, square-cornered, with a thick coating of adobe clay, also surfaced with white plaster (Fig. 3-20).

In general, the Guadalupe phase may have witnessed an increase of 7 sites in the Etla and Central regions, where the ceramic complex is best represented (Fig. 3-13).

THE ROSARIO PHASE. The Rosario phase, which may have begun as early as 700–650 B.C., ended by 500–450 B.C. with the founding of Monte Alban, the great urban center described by Blanton and Kowalewski in Chapter 4 of this volume. During this phase, San Jose Mogote grew to be the political and ceremonial center for a network of some 18–20 villages in the northwestern part of the valley, serving a population estimated by Kowalewski at roughly 1,300–1,400 persons. The actual number of villages linked to San Jose Mogote cannot be specified until we know the limits of influence of Huitzo, a smaller (but presumably competitive) center still farther to the northwest.

Although populations elsewhere were increasing, the Etla region continued to be the most heavily occupied region of the valley. There were 25 settlements in the 801 sq km Central and Zaachila-Zimatlan survey areas (plus 1 more just across the river in the Ocotlan region), but their total population is estimated by Gary Feinman and Kowalewski (1979) to have been less than that of San Jose Mogote alone. The central area of settlement at the latter site had now exceeded 40 ha, with an estimated population of 100–140 households (Marcus 1976d: Table 3.11); if all possible outlying *barrios* are added to this, the total area of Rosario phase occupation is estimated by Eva Fisch at 61.9 ha, with a mean population of 1,000 persons. At the very least, San Jose Mogote was the largest community in the valley prior to the founding of Monte Alban.

The map of Rosario phase settlements (Fig. 3-21) suggests two concentrations of villages—in the Etla and Zaachila-Zimatlan areas—with the Central region more sparsely populated. If a third concentration shows up when the Tlacolula area is intensively surveyed, it will lend support to Blanton's (1978) model which postulates the founding of Monte Alban by three previously autonomous polities from different areas of the valley.

Despite the presence of more than 40 Rosario phase villages in the western part of the valley alone, the estimated population of the intensively surveyed parts of the valley remained substantially below Kirkby's (1973) predictions of the population that could theoretically have been supported by the maize of that period (Curran 1978). Moreover, demographic growth during the Rosario phase was not a simple response to agricultural expansion, as maize increased in size, and more and more land became potentially productive; the Central and Zaachila-Zimatlan areas still lagged behind Etla in total population, suggesting that some of the same sociopolitical factors which had placed the demographic center of gravity for the valley near Etla were still operating. These factors were not to change until the founding of Monte Alban brought about a shift of population to the Central survey region (Chapter 4, this volume).

The discovery of the Rosario phase effectively ended speculation on the cultural roots of Monte Alban I, whose pottery, art, architecture, and writing can now be shown to have arisen within the Valley of Oaxaca. For example, the pottery of the Rosario phase evolves directly into Monte Alban Ia

pottery through a series of gradual steps, many of which have already been outlined by Drennan (1976a: 56–57). Drennan has divided Socorro Fine Gray outleaned-wall bowl rims into 12 rim forms, 4 of which are restricted to the Rosario phase and 8 of which carry over into Monte Alban Ia gray ware; he has further defined 7 forms of rim eccentricities, 5 of which are restricted to the Rosario phase and 2 of which carry over (in modified form) into Monte Alban Ia. Incised designs on the rims of these bowls show a similar series of gradual changes. Early in the Rosario phase, the designs include crescents, double-line-breaks, and a motif like a pennant or naval flag. By the end of the Rosario phase, pennants are virtually absent, and during the transition to Monte Alban Ia, bands of fine-line crosshatching and complex scallops come to the fore. During period Ia, crescents and pennants are absent; only the most elaborate versions of the double-line-break survive; and swirling clouds, sine curves, and triangular areas of opposed hachure come to dominate. These are the familiar G15 and G16 types of the Caso, Bernal, and Acosta (1967) typology.

Two other attributes on Socorro bowls are restricted to the Rosario phase. One is a form of pattern burnishing between incised lines, called "zoned toning" in the Tehuacan Valley (MacNeish, Peterson, and Flannery 1970). The other is the use of "negative" or "resist" white painting (Fig. 3-18c) to produce crescents, double-line-breaks, or pennants on gray bowl rims. It appears that "negative" painting, "zoned toning," and "pennant incising" all died out before Monte Alban was founded, and we have therefore used their disappearance as the dividing line between Rosario and Monte Alban Ia.

The stone masonry architecture of the Rosario phase also leads directly into the architecture of Monte Alban I. During Rosario times, the focus of public building at San Jose Mogote had shifted to the top of Mound 1, a natural hill towering 15 m above the rest of the village. Perhaps the largest Rosario phase building was Structure 19, 22 × 28 m

78

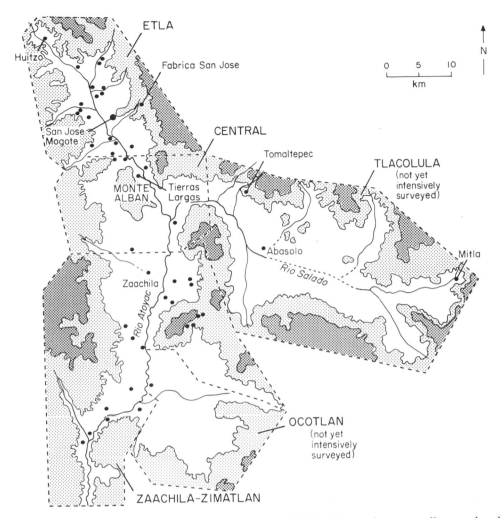

FIGURE 3-21. Rosario phase sites in the Valley of Oaxaca as of 1979. All sites shown are villages or hamlets..

in extent and standing up to 2 m high in places, built of limestone blocks which often weigh more than a ton. These rough-hewn blocks come from the Matadamas quarry to the west of San Jose Mogote; to reach the area of Structure 19, they had to be brought across 5 km of valley and the Rio Atoyac, then dragged to the top of a 15 m hill. Structure 19 shares its stairway with a still earlier building, Structure 19A, which represents an almost equally impressive building stage within Structure 19 (Fig. 3-22); both structures seem to have been the stone-faced platforms which supported a series of buildings made of rectangular adobes and surfaced with lime plaster.

Strong similarities can be seen between Structure 19/19A at San Jose Mogote, Building L at Monte Alban, and Buildings T and X at Monte Negro. The outer wall of Structure 19 features a series of huge slabs up to 1 m high and 40 cm thick, set upright in the manner of orthostats. The irregular gaps between these orthostats are filled with smaller, rectangular limestone blocks, set one above the other as if in a vertical column. This Rosario phase construction is strikingly similar to that of Building L (the so-called Building of

79

FIGURE 3-22. Structures 19 and 19A, Mound 1, San Jose Mogote. The stairway in the foreground belongs to Structure 19A; the outer wall of Structure 19 turns back to meet 19A behind the workman with the stadia rod. Rosario phase.

the *Danzantes*) at Monte Alban, which dates to period Ia (see Acosta 1965: Fig. 3). The orthostats on Structure 19 are plain, while those on Building L are carved; however, there is a carved stone—Monument 3, just outside the northeast corner of Structure 19 (see below)—which is stylistically similar to those on Building L. The Structure 19/19A stairway from San Jose Mogote also resembles that of Building T at Monte Negro (compare Acosta 1965: Fig. 28 with Fig. 3-22, this chapter): both are composed of large, irregular blocks of limestone without balustrades. In both wall construction and stairway construction, the intent appears to be to impress the viewer with the size of the stones used rather than the workmanship.

Structure 14, to the north of Structure 19, is incompletely explored but seems to have a Rosario phase stage as well; it is made of better-trimmed limestone blocks, and rises in places to a height of 3 m. In one angle of the south wall of the building is a huge altar

(Altar 1) composed of 2 multi-ton blocks of limestone. A narrow corridor separates Structures 14 and 19, and serving as the threshold for this corridor is a carved stone, Monument 3 (Fig. 3-23). Anyone entering or leaving the corridor would tread on the body of the person depicted: a naked individual with his eyes closed and mouth partly open, sprawled awkwardly in the manner of the so-called *danzantes* of Monte Alban. Elsewhere, Marcus (1976b, 1976c) has interpreted this as the depiction of a slain or sacrificed individual. A complex scroll covers his chest, possibly depicting blood issuing from an open wound such as that made for removal of the heart; a ribbon-like stream extends from this scroll to the edge of the stone, where we find two motifs whose carving wraps around the east edge of the monument. Carved between the individual's feet are two hieroglyphs which probably represent a name taken from the Zapotec 260-day ritual calendar. The ornate dot, below, represents the number 1; the other glyph, above, is *xoo*, or 'earthquake" ("motion"), the seventeenth day in the Zapotec list of 20 day names (Córdova 1578). At the moment, this inscription, 1 Earthquake, is our oldest evidence for the 260-day calendar and, perhaps, for the Zapotec custom of naming individuals for the day of their birth. It may also indicate that the custom of recording the sacrifices of named individuals had begun by this time. Ethnohistorically, such individuals were usually captives taken in warfare, a fact which may have some significance for the Rosario and subsequent Monte Alban I phases.

In addition to San Jose Mogote, there are a number of Rosario phase sites in the 2–3 ha range which had public buildings and apparently functioned as local civic-ceremonial centers. Both Huitzo and Tomaltepec belong to this second tier of the hierarchy.

Platform 2 at Huitzo dated from late in the Rosario phase. This was a large earthen platform with retaining walls of stone and adobe, and a possible stairway on the extreme west side; it was more than 20 m long. The retaining walls were oriented roughly 8° west of true north, and showed the earliest use of rectangular adobes in the Huitzo sequence. Under one of the retaining walls appeared the skeleton of a male 35–40 years old, head pointing north, body oriented with the long axis of the wall and squashed by the weight of the adobe bricks. Called Burial 3, this individual may represent a "dedication" or "sacrifice" as part of the construction of the platform, as in the case of Burial 55 in Structure 26 at San Jose Mogote (see below).

Platform 1 was the latest major building found at Huitzo. It seemed to fall right at the transition from the Rosario phase to Monte Alban Ia, and was composed of stone masonry walls several courses high, running 8° north of east for at least 20 m. The main north wall was flanked by a series of smaller walls which may constitute either supports for a porch of some kind or a row of small (1.5 × 1.5 m) rooms. A series of plaster floors extended north from the main wall and passed under the small "rooms"; none of the debris on these floors necessarily suggested that the building was of ceremonial function, but this does not prove it was a residence, since we know that in later times Zapotec priests lived in one room of the temple (Marcus 1978).

Rosario phase Tomaltepec was a community of 10–15 households with at least 1 public building of modest proportions; this was Structure 12, an adobe platform more than 3 m high (Whalen n.d.). It was founded on a series of stone slabs up to 1 m long, and its fill was earth and rock rubble. As in the case of Platform 2 at Huitzo, there were burials included in the structure—1 adult male of about 40 years and 3 females aged about 14, 30, and 40 years. Unfortunately, the full dimensions of this public building could not be investigated, but it seems to have continued in use into Monte Alban Ia, at which time some new floors were laid down on its surface.

During the course of the Rosario phase, a significant event took place on Mound 1 at San Jose Mogote. Structure 28 (and hence also its supporting platform, Structure 19) ceased to function as a public building. Not

FIGURE 3-23. Monument 3, San Jose Mogote. Between the feet of the sprawled figure is the date or day-name "One Earthquake." Rosario phase. Maximum length of stone 145 cm.

long after this, its flat upper surface was chosen as the locus where a series of adobe residential compounds were built. These residences would have been reached by ascending the same monumental staircase built for Structure 19A; they overlook the village from a height of 15 m; and they have as their platform a former public building whose construction required considerable corvée labor. This gives us reason to suspect we are dealing with families of quite high status within Rosario society.

The best-preserved such compound was the one belonging to stratigraphic zone B (Fig. 3-24), which consisted of a puddled-adobe patio with a large tomb, surrounded by remains of adobe residences. Structure 26 was the most complete building of the group, with walls of rectangular adobes over a foundation of field stones. Room 2 measured just over 1 m in width, and under one of its walls was an adult skeleton, Burial 55, apparently incorporated into the building at the time of its founding; it is similar to the "sacrificed"

81

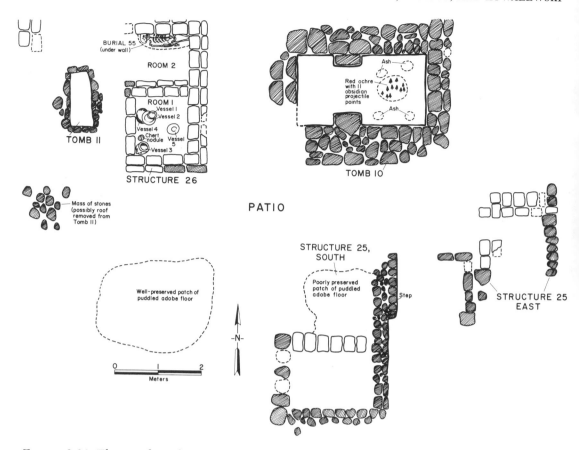

FIGURE 3-24. Elite residential compound from Mound 1, San Jose Mogote, showing houses, patio, and tombs, Rosario phase.

individual crushed under the retaining wall of Platform 2 at Huitzo (see above). Room 1 of Structure 26 (1.2 × 1.4 m) was apparently a storage unit of some kind, for it continued 1.0–1.2 m below the floor of the building and contained 5 whole vessels. Because we do not know the height of the roof we cannot estimate the storage capacity of Room 1, but its subfloor area alone had a volume of close to 2 cu m. Assuming the roof was at least as tall as the average adult skeleton of the period, this room would have had a storage capacity four or five times that of the average bell-shaped pit.

Tomb 10, in the center of the patio, appears to be a Rosario phase forerunner of the stone masonry tombs of Monte Alban. It was 3 m long and 1.7 m wide, divided by short

wall stubs into a main chamber and an antechamber with a floor of flagstones, covered by a layer of adobe plaster on the floor and walls. It appears to have been emptied prior to the Monte Alban I period, with only a human patella and a few ribs left behind to indicate the former presence of a skeleton. Also left was a large deposit of red ocher with 11 obsidian projectile points, the only remaining offering.

In addition to this higher-status residence, several residences of lower-status families were discovered in area A, to the east of Mound 1 and 15 m lower. While badly robbed for their building stones by later settlers, these Rosario phase residences seem to be like those found by Drennan (1976a) at the smaller nearby site of Fabrica San Jose. All were apparently of rectangular adobes over a foundation of field stones.

From the standpoint of political evolution, it is interesting to note that even the most elaborate Rosario phase residences so far discovered could have been built by the members of one family; they needed no corvée labor, such as was required by the later palaces of Monte Alban II. The compound which included Structures 25 and 26 at San Jose Mogote is most reminiscent of an "elite residential compound" found by Spencer and Redmond (n.d.a) at La Coyotera in the Cuicatlan area just northeast of the Valley of Oaxaca. La Coyotera, which is broadly contemporary with the Rosario and/or Monte Alban Ia phases, was organized into a series of large residential compounds, each measuring about 30–40 m on a side and separated from the others by at least 25–35 m of unoccupied space (Fig. 3-25). Spencer and Redmond were able to excavate one compound consisting of 18 structures arranged around 3 patios, the westernmost of which appears to have been where the highest-ranking family resided. House 7, the principal elite residence (56 sq m), was accompanied by a large tomb (Fig. 3-26) which featured an adult (probably male) individual in an extended supine position with his head to the north. The body had been painted with red pigment prior to burial, and was accompanied by 30 ceramic vessels and several shell ornaments, including a necklace.

## LATER FORMATIVE DEVELOPMENTS

The major events of the Late Formative (Monte Alban I) and Terminal Formative (Monte Alban II) periods in the Valley of Oaxaca centered around the rise of Monte Alban as the urban capital of a Zapotec state. The urbanization of Monte Alban and the development of settlement patterns in the Valley of Oaxaca are covered by Blanton and Kowalewski in Chapter 4 of this volume; what we will discuss here are the additional data on Monte Alban I and II developments which have resulted from recent excavations

FIGURE 3-25. Aerial view of Middle Formative community at La Coyotera, Oaxaca. The elite residence and tomb are near the right edge of the excavated area. Courtesy Charles S. Spencer and Elsa M. Redmond.

by Flannery, Marcus, Drennan, Whalen, Spencer, and Redmond, and which serve to complement the studies of Blanton and Kowalewski.

Settlement patterns reveal that there was a four-tiered site hierarchy during Monte Alban II, with a capital city (Monte Alban) at the head of a network of secondary regional centers (like San Jose Mogote and Cuilapan), small tertiary sites with one public building (like Tomaltepec and Fabrica San Jose), and hamlets with no public architecture. Excavations at these secondary, tertiary, and quaternary sites tell us that palaces suitable for Zapotec *coqui* or hereditary "lords" occur only at Monte Alban and at secondary centers; on the other hand, temples suitable for Zapotec *bigaña* or "priests" occur at every level from the capital down to tertiary centers.

### Zapotec State Institutions

One contribution that excavation can make is the definition of specific types of buildings which are the architectural manifestations of certain social or political institutions—in this

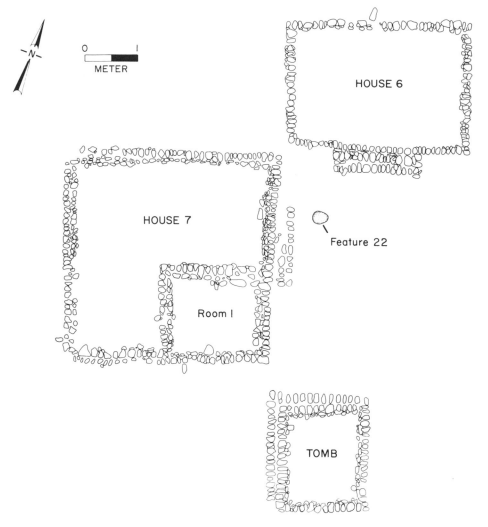

FIGURE 3-26. Stone foundations from elite residence and tomb from La Coyotera, Oaxaca. Middle Formative, contemporary with Rosario/Monte Alban Ia. Courtesy Charles S. Spencer and Elsa M. Redmond.

case, the institutions of the Zapotec state. In our research we have followed the definition of the state as a type of very strong, usually highly centralized government, with a professional ruling class, largely divorced from any bonds of kinship with the common people. The state also can wage war and draft soldiers, levy taxes, and exact tribute. States have public buildings, works, and services of various sorts, usually implemented through professional architects, engineers, and bureaucrats. Among these will usually appear public works of a religious nature, attended by full-time specialists maintaining a state religion (Flannery 1972a:403).

Based on the above definition, Flannery and Marcus (n.d.) have phrased the chronology of state formation in Oaxaca as follows. For the Rosario phase, they see no archaeological evidence for state institutions. For Monte Alban II, they consider the evidence for statehood to be clear and unmistakable. This throws the spotlight on Monte Alban I as the crucial 300-year period during which the state must have formed. As so often happens, the evidence from Monte Alban I is so fragmentary as to be ambiguous. Nowhere is this more true than at Monte Alban itself, where not a single elite residence of period I has been located.

Following William T. Sanders (1974:109), one archaeological clue to the rise of a "professional ruling class" should be the appearance of the true palace, a monumental structure consisting of both habitation areas and audience halls, and requiring corvée labor beyond the capabilities of even an extended family. Such palaces are clearly present in Monte Alban II, even at secondary centers like San Jose Mogote. The palace at San Jose Mogote, Structure 17 on Mound 8, resembles palaces at Monte Alban. Its exact dimensions cannot be recovered because of subsequent destruction and erosion, but it was greater than 30 m on its longest side, and its façade included limestone orthostats weighing a ton or more. On its south side, facing San Jose Mogote's Main Plaza, was a porch with massive columns. The rooms inside had stucco floors, and there was at least one sunken patio (Fig. 3-27).

San Jose Mogote also yields evidence for the public buildings, works, and services of the state as well as public works of a religious nature; the arrangement of these works, in fact, suggests a second-order imitation of Monte Alban. The Main Plaza at San Jose Mogote, laid out north-south, has almost the same dimensions as the Main Plaza at Monte Alban: 300 m north-south, roughly 150 m east-west. Mound 1 on its southern border, like the South Platform at Monte Alban, supported a series of temples; we have already seen that Mound 8 on its northern border, like the North Platform at Monte Alban, supported a palace. As at Monte Alban, there was an I-shaped ballcourt on one side (Fig. 3-28). However, the ballcourt at San Jose Mogote is on the west side of the Main Plaza, while the main ballcourt at Monte Alban is on the east. Also like Monte Alban, San Jose Mogote has important structures built over bedrock outcrops inside its Main Plaza.

The period II temples on Mound 1 at San Jose Mogote, like the two-room temples in Mound X at Monte Alban (Acosta 1965:Fig. 8), are rectangular structures with an inner chamber, an outer chamber, and columns to either side of the doorways. Structures 13 and 21 can serve as examples. Although poorly preserved, Structure 13 appears to be half again as large as its Mound X counterpart—perhaps because it was a major temple at San Jose Mogote, while Mound X was peripheral to the main temples at Monte Alban. Assuming that Structure 13 was symmetrical and had roughly the same proportions as the Mound X temple, it would have been at least $15 \times 8$ m in size. In addition to its greater size, Structure 13 had pairs of columns to either side of the vestibule doorway. Like the temple on Mound X at Monte Alban, it was oriented to the cardinal points. Structure 21, even more poorly preserved than 13, is similar in plan (Fig. 3-29).

Marcus' epigraphic research and the excavations by Spencer and Redmond (n.d.b) have yielded some data on the early Zapotec state's ability to wage war, draft soldiers, and exact tribute. These studies complement Blanton's (1978) discovery of some 3 km of defensive walls up to 4 m high at Monte Alban, dating to periods Ic–II.

One of the major public buildings erected in the Main Plaza at Monte Alban during this period was Building J, an unusual structure with an arrowhead-shaped ground plan (Acosta 1965:Figs. 10, 11). Into the wall of Building J were set more than 40 carved stones, believed by Alfonso Caso (1947) to represent places subjugated by Monte Alban during period II. These so-called "conquest slabs" contain the following elements:

1. A "hill" glyph, which signifies "the place of" and which is a constant on each stone.

2. A glyph, or combination of glyphs, which varies from stone to stone and represents the name of the "place" or "hill" below it. "Hill of the Rabbit," "Hill of the Bird," and "Hill of the Chile Plants" are but a few of the glyphs.

3. A human head, upside down, below the "hill" glyph, its headdress varying from

85

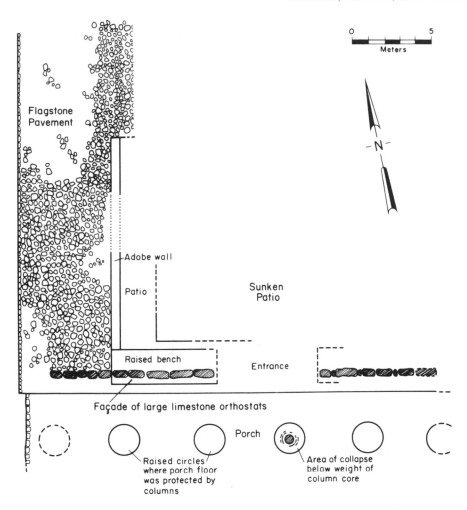

0          5

Meters

-N-

Flagstone
Pavement

Adobe wall

Patio

Sunken
Patio

Raised bench

Entrance

Façade of large limestone orthostats

Porch

Raised circles
where porch floor
was protected by
columns

Area of collapse
below weight of
column core

FIGURE 3-27. Eroded remains of Structure 17, a Monte Alban II palace on Mound 8, San Jose Mogote. The sunken patio and colonnaded porch are typical of the period.

stone to stone. Caso regarded these as the dead rulers of subjugated places, with the headdress perhaps regionally distinct and therefore reinforcing the place-name identifications.

4. Occasionally, a hieroglyphic text which in its most complete form includes a year, month, and day, plus noncalendric glyphs—perhaps relating to the date when certain places were subjugated.

In 1976, Marcus suggested that a few of these might be identified by comparison with the *Codex Mendoza*, a sixteenth-cen-

tury document that lists 35 places in Oaxaca which were then paying tribute to the Aztecs (Marcus 1976b). The Aztec documents use a series of place glyphs which she felt might simply be the Aztec translations of the Zapotec place names. So far, she has found four cases in which a *Codex Mendoza* place glyph closely resembles a Building J place glyph. These are as shown in Figure 3-31 and Table 3-2.

Since such a suggestion presupposes 1,500 years of continuity in place names, it is obviously only a model to be confirmed or rejected by future work. If it is confirmed, one might expect all four areas to show evidence of Monte Alban II occupation. Three of them—Miahuatlan, Tututepec, and Cuicatlan—are already known to have this. And of all these, the most exciting data relevant to this model may soon emerge from the Cuicatlan area. There Spencer and Redmond (n.d.b) investigated what may be a fortified Zapotec center guarding the main pass between the Cañada de Cuicatlan and the Tehuacan Valley. To the south of this fortified center, sites have Monte Alban style pottery; to the north, sites have Tehuacan Valley ceramics. Two sites, Quiotepec and La Coyotera, may provide evidence for Zapotec domination of the region recorded on Monte Alban's Building J as "The Place of Song." At Quiotepec, the period II Zapotec fortified a mountaintop which closed off the main route between Oaxaca and Tehuacan. At La Coyotera, they seem to have conquered a local agricultural settlement and erected a *tzompantli* or "skull rack" with the crania of some 60 of the defenders. Now it remains to check out this model for Tututepec and Miahuatlan—both of which are known to have substantial Monte Alban II settlements—and to identify more of the 40 places on Building J.

## Zapotec State Origins

Formative excavations in the Valley of Oaxaca over the last fourteen years support, and expand on, the model for the formation of the Zapotec state proposed by Blanton (1978). In this model, Monte Alban was selected as an administrative center precisely because it was on unoccupied, politically neutral (though possibly sacred) ground in the "no man's land" between the various arms of the valley. Its founding, around 500 B.C., might therefore be seen as the result of a confederacy among previously autonomous (perhaps even competitive) "chiefdoms" from various parts of the valley. This model is supported by an apparent cessation of monumental construction at competing centers like San Jose Mogote and Huitzo at roughly

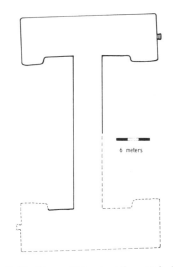

FIGURE 3-28. Plan of Monte Alban II ballcourt in Mound 7-south, San Jose Mogote. After Flannery and Marcus 1976a: Fig. 10.10.

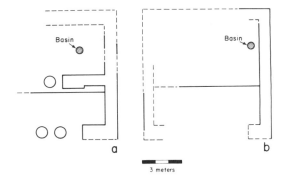

FIGURE 3-29. Eroded remains of two-room temples of the Monte Alban II Period, Mound 1, San Jose Mogote: *a*, Structure 13; *b*, Structure 21. The white circles are column bases; the shaded circles are shallow basins set in the floor.

the time that Monte Alban was founded. It is supported by continuities between the architecture, monument carving, and ceramics of the Rosario phase and those of Monte Alban Ia. It is also supported by the fact that Monte Alban, in its first stage, seems to have consisted of three discrete areas of settlement, possibly reflecting populations from three major areas of the valley (Blanton 1978).

FIGURE 3-30. Effigy brazier from a dedicatory cache below the floor of an eroded Monte Alban II temple, Mound 1, San Jose Mogote. Maximum height 55 cm. This vessel is now in the Museo Regional, San Jose Mogote.

Let us consider the implications of such a confederacy. At first the founding elite would have consisted of chiefly individuals (for the sake of argument, let us say from Etla, Zaachila-Zimatlan, and Tlacolula) whose kin ties to their area of origin would have been strong. But Monte Alban was the first administrative center of valley-wide significance, considerably extending the authority of such an elite. Perhaps it was during the 300 years of the Monte Alban I period that the "Etla elite" and the "Zaachila elite" became escalated in status to "the lords of Monte Alban," a stratum of professional rulers whose kin ties to the commoners and lesser elite of their former regions had become attenuated.

As for the origins of Zapotec state religion, our first archaeological clue is the appearance of the standard two-room temple. By the time it appeared—almost simultaneously with the palace—it is a good bet that the Zapotec possessed full-time priests who had, in effect, taken a great deal of religion out of the hands of the commoners. People who could have sacrificed their own quail at 1000

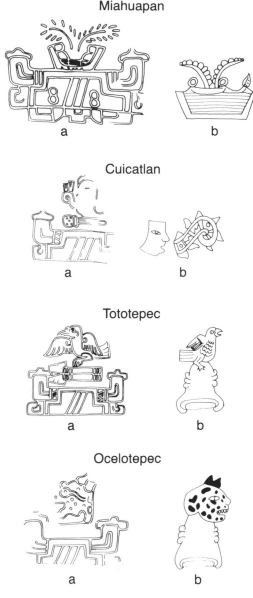

Miahuapan

a            b

Cuicatlan

a            b

Tototepec

a            b

Ocelotepec

a            b

FIGURE 3-31. A comparison of four place names from Building J, Monte Alban, to similar glyphs in the *Codex Mendoza*: a, place names carved on Building J; b, place names from the *Codex Mendoza*. (See Table 3-2.)

TABLE 3-2. Place Names from Monte Alban and *Codex Mendoza*

| Modern Town | Aztec and Zapotec Name | Glyph |
|---|---|---|
| Miahuatlan (Miahuapan) 85 km S of Oaxaca City | "In the Water of the Maize Tassels" | Maize tassels in an irrigation canal |
| Cuicatlan 85 km NE of Oaxaca City | "Place of Song" | Human head with feathered speech scroll emerging from mouth |
| Tututepec (Tototepec) 140 km SW of Oaxaca City | "Hill of the Bird" | Bird atop a hill |
| Ocelotepec 140 km SE of Oaxaca City | "Hill of the Jaguar" | Jaguar atop a hill |

B.C. probably had to bring it to the temple for professional sacrifice at 100 B.C. (Marcus 1978). It is also probably no coincidence that the small, hand-made figurines used for the construction of ritual scenes in households of the Early and Middle Formative had totally disappeared by Monte Alban II. The evolution of state religion may well have involved a mechanism called *linearization* (Flannery 1972a:413), in which a special-purpose arm (the priesthood) of a higher-order system (the state) takes over an activity (certain rituals) which was formerly performed by a lower-order system (the individual, family, or sodality).

## SUMMARY AND CONCLUSIONS

Let us now return to the topics we considered near the beginning of this chapter to see what modifications the last fourteen years have imposed on our synthesis of early Oaxaca.

There never was a giant lake in the Valley of Oaxaca; it has always been a river valley, occupied since the late Pleistocene. The Archaic portion of the preceramic sequence can be related to the Tehuacan caves, but has its own distinctive character and artifact inventory. The site of Gheo-Shih suggests that even preceramic sites may have had their own "public" space set aside, just as the Tehuacan caves suggest that ritual infanticide

was already practiced in the preceramic (MacNeish 1962:8–9).

Bottle gourds, *Apodanthera*, *Cucurbita pepo*, local runner beans, and pollen of the genus *Zea* (either teosinte or early maize) appear in dry cave remains dated between 7840 and 6910 B.C. While the *Cucurbita pepo* is regarded as having been phenotypically domestic by the latter date, it cannot be conclusively shown that the other plants were cultivated rather than collected in the wild.

In terms of the research goals mentioned at the beginning of the preceramic section, we are persuaded that the principles of adaptation during the hunting-gathering stage involved periodic evaluation and modification of a set of strategic priorities for wet, dry, and average years—priorities which included decisions about the vegetation zones used, the species used, the order of their use, and the area searched. The simulation by Robert G. Reynolds (1979) suggests that experiments with new species (including cultivars) most likely began in "wet" year strategies and were expanded to "dry" and "average" year strategies as they "proved themselves" by raising the overall efficiency of exploitation (calories and plant protein obtained versus search effort expended). Our survey results indicate that the population of the Valley of Oaxaca between 7840 and 6910 B.C. was far too low for "population pressure" to have been a factor in the origins of agriculture. As time went on, favorable genetic changes in the cultivars led to their being given increasingly higher priorities relative to some competing wild plants, until they had totally changed the system.

With regard to the research goals mentioned at the beginning of the Early and Middle Formative section, it has already been suggested that sedentary life began on the alluvium of the major local rivers once the productivity of maize had reached 200–250 kg per ha, making it worthwhile to clear away competing mesquite groves which yielded 160–180 kg per ha (Flannery 1973:299). The first villages appeared on piedmont spurs overlooking this alluvium, and between 1500 and 850 B.C. the western Valley of Oaxaca (Etla, Central, and Zaachila-Zimatlan areas) developed one of Mesoamerica's higher Early Formative site densities (at least 25 hamlets or villages in 1,000 sq km of intensively surveyed valley floor and piedmont). This density is particularly amazing in view of the fact that, as late as January 1966, we were not sure that the Valley of Oaxaca had *any* Early Formative sites.

The pottery of the period 1150–850 B.C. displays a number of Olmec motifs, supporting Caso's and Bernal's intuitive notions about Olmec themes in Oaxacan art, but moving it back 500 years: the truly "Olmec" period in Oaxaca is the San Jose phase, rather than Monte Alban I. At the same time, we should stress the fact that there is *no* evidence of actual Gulf Coast Olmec peoples in the Valley of Oaxaca. The specific "fire-serpent" and "were-jaguar" motifs used on San Jose pottery are actually more common in collections from San Jose Mogote than in collections from San Lorenzo (Pyne 1976); they are probably to be seen as Oaxacan variants of pan-Mesoamerican motifs whose widespread distribution (from Tlatilco to Tabasco) reflects shared iconographic conventions and underlying sacred propositions (Drennan 1976b). The fact that at least two mirrors made from Oaxacan magnetite reached San Lorenzo (Pires-Ferreira 1975) reinforces Flannery's (1968b) suspicion that

the two areas had an elite exchange relationship. Some ways in which the emerging Oaxacan elites expressed their status were in better-made residences and differential access to jade, *Spondylus* shell, pearl oyster, mica, stingray spines, and macaw plumes.

With regard to another of the goals discussed at the beginning of the Early and Middle Formative section, we would argue that the causes of hereditary ranking in Formative Oaxaca cannot simply be sought in Olmec influence; they must be sought within the valley itself. Oaxaca had public buildings by 1350 B.C. and developed the use of lime plaster, adobe brick, and stone masonry long before they appeared on the Gulf Coast. While Formative Oaxaca was supported by dry farming and several kinds of irrigation, the sources of ranking are not simply to be found in man-land relationships either. This is already clear during the San Jose phase (the first period for which any archaeological evidence of ranking can be detected), when the distribution of population deviated widely from Kirkby's (1973) predictions based on agricultural potential. Most of the absolute growth took place at one site, San Jose Mogote, and half of the villages in the intensively surveyed Rio Atoyac drainage occurred in the vicinity of the latter site. The decision-makers at San Jose Mogote appear to have provided ritual and religious leadership for these villages, pooled and redistributed obsidian, and monopolized certain kinds of craft specialization. In return for this leadership, satellite communities are presumed to have provided labor for the construction and maintenance of public buildings at San Jose Mogote, and the centripetal pull of this early ceremonial center overcame most centrifugal tendencies for agricultural dispersal. What we do not yet know is how this leadership became hereditary.

A major discovery of the last fourteen years is the fact that Monte Alban I was an in situ development within the Valley of Oaxaca, not a product of the Mixtec or Olmec. Its roots are to be found in the Rosario phase, a period in which San Jose Mogote became

TABLE 3-3. A Preceramic and Formative History of the Valley of Oaxaca

| | Phase or Complex | Inferred Events |
|---|---|---|
| 850 B.C. | San Jose | San Jose Mogote becomes a village with a residential core of 20 ha, and outlying *barrios* perhaps pushing the greater area of occupation to 70 ha (with an estimated 600–700 persons). The beginnings of hereditary ranking are seen in houses and burials. The Olmec "fire-serpent" and "were-jaguar" appear on pottery vessels with some male burials. Public buildings are accompanied by crude stone monuments, and ritual paraphernalia including conch shell trumpets, stingray spines, masks, and costume parts are widespread. Round adobes, possible irrigation wells, drainage ditches, and cemeteries appear. There is long-distance exchange of magnetite, obsidian, and marine shell. |
| 1150 B.C. | Tierras Largas | The first lime-plastered public buildings appear at San Jose Mogote, largest of a series of (20?) small villages. The basic unit of residence is a nuclear-family-size household with storage pits, burials, and work areas. Corn, teosinte, squash, avocados, and other plants were cultivated. In the Mixteca Alta, Yucuita is founded. |
| 1400 B.C. | Espiridion | The first wattle-and-daub house and the first simple monochrome ceramics appear at San Jose Mogote. |
| ±2000 B.C. | Martinez | Scattered, late preceramic occupations at Yuzanu in the Mixteca Alta and Martinez Rockshelter in the Valley of Oaxaca. Mortars, stone bowls, maguey-roasting pits. |
| 3300–2800 B.C. | Blanca | Occupation of Cueva Blanca; deer hunting with Coxcatlan, Tilapa, La Mina, Trinidad, Hidalgo, San Nicolas points; scattered finds at Nochixtlan and Miahuatlan. |
| 5000–4000 B.C. | Jicaras | Open-air macroband camp at Gheo-Shih with boulder-lined "dance ground" or public area; ephemeral shelters; ornament working. Grinding stones and *Zea* pollen present. Hunting with Pedernales, La Mina, Trinidad, San Nicolas points. |
| 8900–6700 B.C. | Naquitz | Occupation of Cueva Blanca E and Guila Naquitz E–B. Intensive collecting of acorns, piñon nuts, mesquite, hackberry, West Indian cherry, prickly pear, maguey, local runner beans, other plants; hunting with Lerma (?) and Pedernales points. Late in the phase, *Cucurbita pepo* seeds and *Zea* pollen appear. One-hand manos, nets, string, baskets, and fire-drills are used. |
| >10,000 B.C.? | Pleistocene | Burned, broken fauna in Cueva Blanca F, including species no longer present in Oaxaca. |

TABLE 3-3 Continued

| | | |
|---|---|---|
| A.D. 100 | Monte Alban II | Full-fledged Zapotec state with rulers living in palaces at both primary and secondary centers; temples staffed with priests at primary, secondary, and tertiary centers. Writing in multiple-column texts; list of > 40 places subjugated by Monte Alban. In the Mixteca Alta, the Ramos phase state forms at Yucuita, massive buildings with Zapotec glyphs appear at Huamelulpan, and Monte Negro begins to decline. |
| —0— | | |
| 200 B.C. | | |
| | Monte Alban I | The Zapotec state gradually forms. Monte Alban grows to 10,000–20,000 persons; over 300 *danzantes* are carved; valley floor population increases rapidly, and evidence for small-scale irrigation is widespread. Late in the period, Monte Alban erects 3 km of defensive walls; in the Mixteca Alta, Monte Negro is founded. |
| 500 B.C. | | Monte Alban founded. |
| | Rosario | San Jose Mogote reaches its peak development as a chiefly center serving an estimated 1,300–1,400 persons occupying 18–20 villages in the Etla region. An acropolis of public buildings on large stone masonry platforms is accompanied by stone monument carving and evidence for human sacrifice and the 260-day calendar. At the end of the phase, an elite family at San Jose Mogote (and possibly Huitzo as well) preempts the top of the largest public building for its residence. San Jose Mogote goes into decline as Monte Alban is founded. |
| 700 B.C. | | |
| | Guadalupe (Etla region)  > ? | In the Guadalupe phase, large public buildings on adobe platforms are built at Huitzo and San Jose Mogote. Male-female burial pairs and the pooling and redistribution of obsidian become widespread. |
| 850 B.C. | | |

the center of the most highly developed pre-state society in the valley. This phase has produced Mesoamerica's earliest evidence for hieroglyphic writing and the 260-day calendar, as well as providing a clear precursor for the *danzante* carvings of Monte Alban I. If such carvings are accepted as slain or sacrificed captives, we can propose that armed conflict was already present in the Rosario phase and escalated during Monte Alban I and II, with the construction of defensive walls and the recording of as many as 40 subjugated places on Building J at Monte Alban.

To comment on the last of the research goals in the Later Formative section, we follow Blanton (1978) in concluding that Monte Alban was founded by people from San Jose Mogote and elsewhere in the valley, and we propose that the Zapotec state arose during Monte Alban I, when the city's rulers allowed kin ties to their places of origin to wither, becoming a class-endogamous professional ruling stratum of valley-wide significance. Based on the research of the last decade, Monte Alban II may be seen not as an elite intrusion from Chiapas but as a full-fledged Zapotec militaristic state with colon-naded palaces, standardized temples, I-shaped ballcourts, and hieroglyphic records of conquest.

## ACKNOWLEDGMENTS

Flannery's work on the preceramic and Formative was supported by National Science Foundation grants GS-1616 and GS-2121. Flannery and Marcus' work at San Jose Mogote was supported by National Science Foundation grants GS-42568 and BNS-7805829. Marcus' work on ethnohistory and early Zapotec writing was supported by research grant RO-21433-75 from the National Endowment for the Humanities. Kowalewski's synthesis of Formative settlement patterns draws on data produced by National Science Foundation grant BNS-7619640 to Blanton.

Several artists worked on the illustrations, and we wish to thank Nancy Hansen (Figs. 3-7–3-9 and 3-20), Jane Mariouw (Figs. 3-12, 3-16, 3-17, 3-24, 3-26–3-29, and 3-31), Mark Orsen (Fig. 3-23), Susan Payne (Figs. 3-15 and 3-19), and Margaret Van Bolt (Figs. 3-1, 3-6, 3-10, 3-11, 3-13, 3-18, and 3-21). Photos used in Figs. 3-2–3-5 and 3-14 are by Chris L. Moser. Various stages of the manuscript were typed by Linda Krakker and Simone Taylor. Many archaeologists shared with us their unpublished data, and we are especially indebted in this regard to Richard Blanton, Frank Hole, Elsa Redmond, Charles Spencer, Ronald Spores, Dudley Varner, and Michael Whalen.

Finally, we are grateful to Mexico's Instituto Nacional de Antropología e Historia for permission to do this work. In Mexico City, Ignacio Bernal and José Luis Lorenzo were particularly helpful. In Oaxaca, we owe a great debt to the I.N.A.H. Centro Regional and its director, Manuel Esparza, for his aid, advice, and friendship.

# 4. Monte Alban and After in the Valley of Oaxaca

*RICHARD E. BLANTON and STEPHEN A. KOWALEWSKI*

THE VALLEY OF OAXACA has become one of the best-known areas in Mesoamerica for the understanding of Precolumbian sociocultural change. As shown in Chapter 3 of this volume, the Valley of Oaxaca has contributed greatly to the present level of knowledge about the origins of agriculture and the evolution of settled village life. The beginnings of urbanism and state-level political organization in the valley now seem at once clearer and yet more intricate. Recent work in the Valley of Oaxaca shows that the ups and downs and the reorganizations of an urbanized, state-level regional system may be as puzzling and as inherently interesting as the system's primitive beginnings. Normally when one thinks about the Postclassic in Oaxaca the Mixteca Alta comes most quickly to mind, but it now seems uncontestable that the valley retained its demographic and economic power after the fall of the Monte Alban state, until the arrival of the Spanish.

In these respects the Valley of Oaxaca is yielding information generally regarded as having more-than-local scholarly value. However, we must issue a warning—not to

our Oaxaca colleagues, for they know it as well as we, or better, they often say—that what we now know about Precolumbian times in the valley is only an outline of past events and processes. When we begin to have the sophistication to see the inner structures and the details, the outlines may take on new meaning. That is precisely what has happened in archaeological research in Oaxaca since the last "Archaeological Synthesis" (Bernal 1965) was written. Vague outlines had been drawn. The research since that time has generally confirmed the original, pioneering work, adding new patterns. Previous observations and conclusions have not been thrown out, but reinterpreted and given new behavioral significance. It is to be hoped that those of us who have done research since 1965 will be found to have made as few errors as those who preceded by the time the next synthesis is written.

## RESEARCH DESIGNS

Do the advances in our knowledge about the Precolumbian Valley of Oaxaca have to do with changes in research design? Have advances in theories about sociocultural change been responsible for whatever increment of understanding we have gained? Are archaeological projects more efficient and productive because of shifts in method and theory? It is clear that since 1965 Oaxaca specialists have asked—have been able to ask—questions, and generate partial answers, concerning demographic, economic, political, and social variables. There is generally more attention paid to environmental/human interactions. Written, peer-reviewed research proposals have become the rule. In this way research in the Valley of Oaxaca has reflected advances in method and theory in anthropology in general, just as it has contributed to those advances.

But we are hesitant to attribute whatever progress has been made in archaeological investigations solely to changes in the intellectual climate, when the hard fact is that since 1961 much more money has been spent on archaeology than in earlier years. Not including restoration or museum support, we estimate that between 1930 and 1960 the total amount spent on archaeological research in the Valley of Oaxaca may have been as low as $70,000. Between 1961 and 1979 the figure is close to $700,000. Most of this increase has provided for the enlistment of many more paid, well-trained project personnel for field and laboratory tasks. Gone are the projects where one archaeologist tried to supervise fifty or a hundred workers. There are now projects in which there are virtually no positions for the archaeologically unskilled. We also note that research in the valley has benefited ever since the projects of Alfonso Caso from sustained, long-term commitments to the area.

On one subject the culture-historical approach has not been proven productive in the Valley of Oaxaca. This is in the attribution of ethnicity to specific artifact complexes and stylistic traditions, especially in ceramics. The most controversial instance has been the debate over the contemporaneity of the "Mixtec" and "Zapotec" pottery traditions in the Postclassic and even as early as the Classic. Some investigators (Paddock 1966:213; Caso, Bernal, and Acosta 1967: 447) suggested that in a sense Monte Alban V, the Mixtec tradition, was contemporaneous with or earlier than Monte Alban IV, the Zapotec tradition. Donald L. Brockington (1973), using stratigraphic test pit samples from Miahuatlan, 40 km south of the valley, elaborates on this in considerable detail. Others, including Blanton (1978:27), have proceeded on the premise that one can't have more than one phase at the same time in the same place. Thus far in the survey coverage of the valley (Blanton et al. n.d.) we have not encountered a separate Zapotec ceramic complex coeval with the Monte Alban V of ca. A.D. 1000 on. Zaachila, believed to be an important Zapotec center in the Late Postclassic, has a clearly period V artifact assemblage (Gallegos 1962, 1963), but its most abundant pottery dates from Monte Alban IIIa and IIIb (Blanton et al. n.d.). The major Postclassic sites examined in the Tlacolula arm of the valley—Mitla and Yagul—have IV and V in stratigraphic order (Bernal 1966a: 346, 350; Bernal and Gamio 1974:91). The simplest interpretation of this evidence is that Monte Alban IV and V are not contemporary, and that V follows IV. The G-3M style (consisting of thin, hard, well-burnished gray bowls and jars) characteristic of period V begins in low frequency in the Classic and is more frequent in IV. What the settlement pattern project surveys can add is the existence of local variants within this wider trend (Blanton et al. n.d.; see also Paddock, Mogor, and Lind 1968).

While the chronological difficulties that may have arisen in part from the desire to identify ethnic groups now appear to have been resolved, there is still no agreement on the general feasibility or utility of making ethnic assignments. The issue is discussed by several participants in the *Cloud People* volume (Flannery and Marcus n.d.), and there are relevant interpretations in the Valle Grande–Central area survey report (Blanton et al. n.d.).

1. Huitzo
2. Etla
3. San Jose Mogote
4. Cerro de Atzompa
5. Tierras Largas
6. El Mirador
7. San Pedro Ixtlahuaca
8. Monte Alban
9. Oaxaca City
10. San Felipe del Agua
11. San Luis Beltran
12. San Andres Huayapan
13. Santa Cruz Amilpas
14. Loma de la Montura
15. Dainzu
16. Lambityeco
17. Tlacolula
18. Yagul
19. Mitla
20. Xoxocatlan
21. Hacienda Experimental
22. San Agustin de las Juntas
23. Cuilapan
24. Animas Trujano
25. Noriega
26. Coyotepec
27. Zaachila
28. Trinidad de Zaachila
29. Roalo
30. La Soledad
31. 3-7-44
32. Zimatlan
33. San Martin Tilcajete
34. Jalieza
35. Santa Cruz Mixtepec
36. 3-6-104
37. Santa Ines Yatzeche
38. Ocotlan
39. El Trapiche de Santa Cruz
40. Valdeflores
41. Tejas de Morelos
42. Santa Ana Tlapacoyan
43. El Choco
44. Santa Maria Ayoquesco

FIGURE 4-1. The Valley of Oaxaca, showing places mentioned in the text.

## PERIOD-BY-PERIOD SYNTHESIS

In this discussion we will synthesize what has been learned about the Precolumbian sequence in the Valley of Oaxaca since the publication of the last *Handbook* overview, beginning with Monte Alban I. The origins of Monte Alban and the development of the Terminal Formative (M.A. II) state have been discussed in the previous chapter, and for those periods we confine ourselves to reviewing the major features of the regional settlement patterns.

Comprehensive settlement pattern data exist for Monte Alban and for the Central and Valle Grande (Zaachila-Zimatlan) survey areas (see Figure 3-11). (Since this writing we have

completed the total survey of the valley, but we are just beginning the coding and analyses of these new data.) This means that virtually 100 percent of the visible archaeological sites have been mapped and described. The occupied areas of each component have been measured and dated. Local environmental features, including elevation, environmental zone, slope, topographic position, soils, erosion, alluviation, nearest water source, and water table depth, are recorded. Also noted are modern land use data, such as irrigation and drainage facilities, that are sometimes helpful in reconstructing past agricultural techniques. Obsidian, chipped stone, ground stone, adobes, building stone, plaster floors, burned daub, carved stone, tombs, burials, and other artifacts and features have been searched for and noted. Evidence for "workshops," or places where there is material evidence for the manufacture or use of commodities such as pottery, metates, shell, or obsidian has been carefully sought and recorded. Measurements and drawings of each of the roughly 500 pyramid mounds found are included in the survey data.

Potentially one of the most interesting data sets consists of systematic information on each of the more than 6,000 residential terraces mapped thus far. Of these, 2,073 are at Monte Alban, a few more than that number were mapped at Jalieza, and the rest were located at a score of smaller sites. Including the 1,700 settlement pattern project collections from Monte Alban, there are now over 3,000 pottery collections from different sites, or distinct areas of large sites (Feinman n.d.a, n.d.b). These have been coded by site and type for ease in distributional studies, as have the lithic samples (Appel n.d.a). Thus we now have the above particulars on each of the 2,300 sites in the Valle Grande and Central survey areas. (For Monte Alban, see Blanton 1978; for the Valle Grande and Central areas, see Kowalewski 1976 and Blanton et al. 1979, n.d.; for Etla there is a preliminary survey [Varner 1974], and there are more comprehensive settlement pattern data for Etla to be published with the projected report on the Tlacolula arm of the valley.) In the following discussion, the data presented without citation come from the settlement pattern project and are available, along with the project's full bibliography, in Blanton 1978 and Blanton et al. n.d.

## Monte Alban Early I (ca. 500–300 b.c.)

As noted in the previous chapter, the founding of the new regional capital at Monte Alban was the major feature of an entire reorganization of the Valley of Oaxaca settlement hierarchy. In the earlier Formative phases, settlements were centered more than one would expect around San Jose Mogote. In Monte Alban Early I the region became

Monte Alban–centered. For the Central and Valle Grande areas, about two-thirds of the increase in occupied area, and presumably population, occurred within 20 km of Monte Alban, and this does not include the roughly 5,000 people living at Monte Alban. Beyond 30 km from Monte Alban, site densities were little changed from the Rosario phase.

Monte Alban may thus have had about half of the valley's total population in Early I. From the beginning the city's inhabitants were living on residential terraces high up on the hill. Three fairly distinct, densely occupied areas are found in Early I, to the east, west, and south of the Main Plaza. On the north slope, densities of Early I artifacts are lower, indicating less dense habitation than in the three core areas, or occupation later in the phase. On the top of the mountain in the no-man's-land between these three residential wards was the principal public area. Apparently this plaza did have a few nonresidential buildings. It was not physically closed off to the public as it was in later times.

Below the level of Monte Alban in the settlement hierarchy were secondary administrative centers, evenly spaced and serving as the administrative head towns for districts. The prominent features of these secondary centers were their large size and the presence of public architecture. Four are known thus far, and several others are suspected in the Etla and Tlacolula survey areas. Those that have been mapped have 10–13 ha of occupied area, perhaps meaning populations of around 200 people. The buildings which we suspect had "administrative" functions are visible as mound-groups with internal, fairly closed plazas or courts (Fig. 4-2).

Apparently an area extending 6 km from Monte Alban was administered directly from the primary center. There are no secondary or tertiary administrative centers here, even though there are settlements that had relatively large populations. A tentative notion of what the district boundaries may have looked like was arrived at by constructing

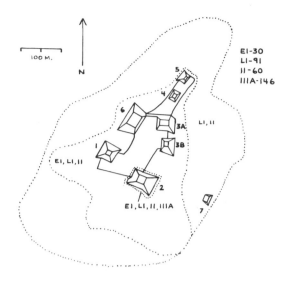

EI-30
LI-91
II-60
IIIA-146

LI, II

EI, LI, II

EI, LI, II, IIIA

FIGURE 4-2. Example of an Early I secondary center. Although later periods of occupation are present, we feel the site first reached the status of local center during Early I.

weighted Thiessen polygons around the secondary administrative centers. It is interesting that several of these internal boundaries fall along the major rivers and ridges. For example, the district headed by San Agustín de las Juntas probably had its common boundary with Monte Albán's district along the Rio Atoyac, as did the Zaachila district to the west of the Atoyac and the Ocotlan district east of the river in the Valle Grande.

There is some evidence suggesting a level of tertiary administrative centers, smaller in size and with less impressive formal architecture. Below this level were many smaller sites with less than 150 people. In the Valle Grande and Central areas these rural villages and hamlets number 92—66 of which are 1 ha or smaller in size. A third of the rural sites may be small enough to represent isolated residences.

One Early I settlement in the Valle Grande may well have been a market center. It is located roughly equidistant from 3 secondary administrative centers, on the boundary between their districts, 19 km south of Monte Alban. It covers almost 15 ha, a large area for an Early I settlement, and of all the large sites of its period, it is the best located in

terms of distances to other large centers. The site covers a low hill near the Rio Atoyac at Zimatlan. On the top of the hill is a 55 × 38 m artificial terrace, buttressed by large boulders. This unusual public architectural feature may have been a marketplace. Also in evidence at the site, and unusual for sites of this period, are signs of utilitarian pottery-making and production involving quartz quarrying and reduction.

### Monte Alban Late I (300–200 B.C.)

The latter part of period I saw continued growth within essentially the same pattern seen in Early I. The total number of sites in the Valle Grande and Central areas increased from 103 to 307, and the total occupied area expanded as well, so that the mean estimated population grew from 8,500 to 30,000. Similar growth most probably took place in the other two arms of the valley. It is interesting that virtually all of this growth was internal—the Valley of Oaxaca system did not expand the limits of its directly administered area beyond those established in Early I. No special sites or features that could be interpreted as having boundary maintenance functions are known from Early I. By Late I, however, there may be such a site (3-6-104) in the southern Valle Grande, 29 km from Monte Alban, near the edge of the administered area. The site consists of 8 ha of Late I habitation debris spread over the ridgetop of the highest mountain on the edge of the valley. Clearly the commanding view far to the south and back up the Rio Mixtepec tributary valley had some role in the site's function.

The internal growth within the same settlement structure established in Early I occurred along three dimensions. First, the system became even more Monte Alban–centered. The nearer to Monte Alban, the greater the expansion of population, in general. Second, there was greater occupation in certain selected piedmont areas, especially those near Monte Alban. Third, disproportionately the most expansion occurred in settlements that had administrative functions, as opposed to those that did not.

These trends can be illustrated by examining what happened from Early to Late I in each of the administrative districts. Monte Alban itself increased in size, from 5,000 to a median estimate of 16,000 people, covering all of Monte Alban proper and the El Gallo hill to the northwest. Additional energy was invested in Main Plaza construction. It appears that the Early I three-*barrio* internal structure was superceded in Late I, and there is evidence suggestive of something like the site subdivisions identifiable in Monte Alban IIIb. Without additional study the early history of the site subdivisions will remain unclear.

The rural area administered directly by Monte Alban underwent substantial population increase in Late I, but there was only one administrative site apart from Monte Alban, and that probably had only the lowest-level functions. Late I saw substantial growth on the low piedmont apron around Monte Alban, including the settlement discussed by Mason et al. (1977) west of Xoxocotlan, and Tierras Largas (Winter 1972), in Late I one of the larger rural settlements with over 30 ha of occupation. Two other Monte Alban district sites had populations in the 300–600 range, and these were also in the low piedmont.

The San Agustin district, in the southeastern part of the Central area and the northeastern Valle Grande, was oriented toward piedmont agriculture. Its capital, the same site as in Early I, increased to over 37 ha. Cuilapan, not a large site at all in Early I, grew substantially in Late I as it became the administrative center for a considerable piedmont expansion in the northwestern Valle Grande. The ceramic collections from the public buildings at San Agustin may indicate that that district, like Cuilapan's, did not exist from the beginning of period I. It is interesting that the Cuilapan and Zaachila districts, being relatively close to Monte Alban, had very few smaller administrative centers below the level of the district capital, while

the northern Ocotlan district, farther east and on the other side of the main river, and the southern district headed by Santa Ines Yatzeche, even farther away, each had a number of smaller administrative centers. The Ocotlan district capital grew substantially in size, as did the district's rural, mainly piedmont, population. In the southern district, however, most of the settlements were on the alluvium. Overall the population size does not seem to have changed much since Early I in the southern district.

Consistent with these patterns is a rather simple but effective measure of differential access to pottery—the number of types, on a presence/absence basis, per site. The survey collections, even though they are far from statistically adequate samples, unmistakably show that the number of types per site (1) declines with distance from Monte Alban, (2) is higher in sites with administrative functions than in nonadministrative sites, even if the nonadministrative sites are large, and (3) for administrative sites varies positively with level in the administrative hierarchy.

We may now identify several determining processes behind the formation of the early state in the Valley of Oaxaca. The increasing need for control and regularization of interregional interaction led to the creation of a larger-scale, central institution for dealing with cross-boundary flows. This process, as discussed in the previous chapter, is the essential motivator in Blanton's model for the origins of Monte Alban (Blanton 1976c, 1978, 1980). Funding and support for the new central institution were channeled through the administrative hierarchy set up in Early I. Previously autonomous units in the three arms of the valley became districts in the new structure. Increased demands for time and surplus production are evident between Rosario, Early I, and Late I. Higher demand for labor led to greater rates of household formation, probably involving in-migration and increased fertility. Piedmont areas nearest the sources of demand for food (especially Monte Alban) were agriculturally exploited.

This mode of production required extensive population dispersal, partly to minimize risk, and this in turn required further administrative investment. Thus almost from the very beginning the provisioning of Monte Alban and its administrative apparatus became an important central-place function as the new valley-wide integration was achieved.

### Monte Alban II (200 B.C.–A.D. 250)

The areas thus far surveyed show a decline in population from Late I to II (30,000 to 20,000). Etla may have held its own, and the population of Tlacolula is still not known, but a general decline within the valley is quite possible. The decrease may have been related to the apparent expansion of the Monte Alban state beyond the limits of the valley (see the discussion in the previous chapter). In the far southern Valle Grande, period II occupations were more numerous than those of Late I; and the possible Late I boundary site did not last into Monte Alban II, a fact consistent with the idea of expanding valley frontiers.

In the Central and Valle Grande areas the total number of Monte Alban II occupations shrank to 129. Nucleation is apparent, as mean site size increased from 5.6 ha in Late I to 9 ha in II. Small sites did exist, however, with 47 sites of 1 ha or less, perhaps 20 of which may have been isolated residences. The Central survey area was virtually abandoned during period II. Only 23 small Monte Alban II settlements were found there, down from 154 sites in Late I. Like the Valle Grande, the Etla arm's pattern may have been more nucleated in period II. In Tlacolula, Yagul (Bernal and Gamio 1974) and Dainzu (Bernal 1967, 1968b) are known to have been fairly important centers during the phase. Monte Alban itself was only slightly smaller than in Late I (down from 16,000 to 14,500), and major construction continued on and around the Main Plaza. Sometime near the end of Late I or the beginning of II an earthen wall was built around Monte Alban. Along with the nuclea-

tion of settlements, it would appear that a greater proportion of the population lived in sites with administrative functions. But there is evidence that administration was less centralized, less directly controlled by Monte Alban, in period II. Except for the abandonment of the previous San Agustin district, the old district structure changed rather little.

In the northern Ocotlan district, the capital in existence since the Rosario phase was moved to a new location (3-7-44) about 1 km away, on the top of a high hill commanding the pass between the northeastern Valle Grande and Ocotlan. The view is better than that at the prior, mid-slope site, and defensive considerations are not ruled out. At 54.3 ha, the site is one of the largest period II centers in the valley. The relatively formal layout and the buildings and plazas closed to casual traffic are typical of Valley of Oaxaca administrative centers.

The settlement pattern data, the epigraphic evidence discussed in the previous chapter, and the ceramic type distributions all point not only to less centralized control in period II, but also to less interaction, at least along certain behavioral dimensions, between different parts of the valley. This is most striking in the complementary distribution of A-9 bowls, found mainly in the northern Valle Grande, especially around Roalo, versus C-11/C-12 bowls, far more numerous in the Etla arm. Both types are found at Monte Alban.

The lesser amount of internal interaction and control was concurrent with an abandonment of the piedmont strategy for producing surplus. It may well be that a significant share of the revenues for the support of the state administration was generated by the mini-imperial adventures outside the valley noted in the previous chapter.

### Monte Alban IIIa (A.D. 250–450)

In the intensively surveyed areas of the valley, the Early Classic appears to have been a period of substantial population increase.

What is known of the Etla and Tlacolula areas suggests a decline from Terminal Formative levels. In the Central and Valle Grande areas combined, including Monte Alban, the estimated population increase was almost threefold (from 20,000 in II to 55,000 in IIIa). The number of sites grew from 129 to 357. Most of this growth occurred in the southern Valle Grande. Indeed, the far southern portion of the valley accounted for 70 percent of the total II to IIIa increment—nearly 30,000 people. In contrast, the Central survey area, with the exception of the large site at Xoxocotlan, continued to have only a few small settlements as in period II.

Monte Alban itself is estimated to have grown by 2,000 people, to about 16,500. An extended discussion of the new information provided by the settlement pattern project on Monte Alban at its Classic period zenith is included in the following section on Monte Alban IIIb. We may here note several features of the IIIa city. In the Early Classic we find the first substantial occupation of the Cerro de Atzompa, the northernmost hill at Monte Alban. The occupation at Atzompa was mainly on the top of the hill on the north slope. Apparently the densest IIIa occupation at Monte Alban was on the east and south sides of the Main Plaza—the part of Monte Alban located closest to the heavily populated Valle Grande. A new *barrio* (site subdivision 12), with roughly 700 people, was founded in this period. It had a close, possibly commercial, relationship to the Valle Grande. Construction on the Main Plaza continued in IIIa with the addition of the South Platform. There is little doubt that Monte Alban retained its status as the preeminent political center for the valley in IIIa.

The picture emerging from the settlement pattern data, at least in the Valle Grande, is one of more administrative control in the Early Classic, but most of the control was being exerted at the middle and lower levels. Monte Alban may have actually had less to do with internal valley affairs in IIIa than it did in Late I, confining itself perhaps to interregional problems such as those created by the expansion of Teotihuacan. In the endeavor to maintain the integrity of the valley system, the Monte Alban state must have been fairly successful. Continuing investigation in the valley (Paddock 1978:51; the settlement pattern surveys) has only reinforced the original view of Bernal that Oaxaca was not "part of a possible Teotihuacan empire" (Bernal 1965:802).

Monte Alban's own rural administrative district was neither large nor populous in IIIa. About 5 km southeast of the Main Plaza, the site of Xoxocotlan probably rose to the status of district capital. Zaachila and Cuilapan continued to function as district capitals, as did Santa Ines Yatzeche. Cuilapan and Santa Ines reached their maximum sizes in Monte Alban IIIa. Cuilapan covers 45 ha and consists of a nonmounded habitation area, a number of single mounds or loose mound clusters that were probably elite residences, and a more closed, "palace" complex, that is, buildings serving administrative, elite residential, and possibly ceremonial functions.

Jalieza became not only the new Ocotlan district capital but also the most prominent center in the Valle Grande in Monte Alban IIIa. Its large size (see Fig. 4-3)—it had roughly 12,000 people, occupying more than 4 sq km, and almost 700 residential terraces—suggests that it may have been a commercial center as well as an administrative capital with functions beyond its own district. The most distinctive IIIa ceramic type, the G-23 (Bernal 1949), is found in its greatest frequency in the Valle Grande, with Jalieza the probable center of distribution. The Early Classic was the first time that any community in the valley approached the size of Monte Alban, yet Jalieza was clearly subordinate politically, having few carved stone monuments and only one-fifteenth the mounded architecture volume of Monte Alban.

A new administrative district was created to handle the large population engaged in piedmont agriculture in the far southern Valle Grande. The probable administrative center of the district was at Tejas de Morelos.

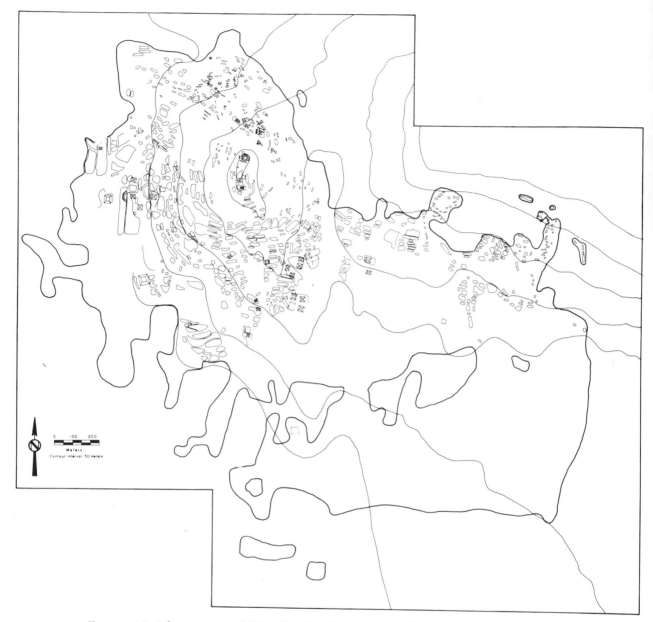

FIGURE 4-3. Jalieza in period IIIa. The dark line indicates the maximum limits of sherd scatter. The lighter features are the residential terraces and mounded buildings.

102

There were, however, several other large sites, indicating several levels and internal divisions, making this district perhaps the most heavily administered. Among the more important centers were Tlapacoyan (50 ha, 900 people) and Santa Cruz Mixtepec (400 residential terraces, roughly 3,200 people). Another kind of settlement that was important in the far southern Valle Grande was the small, hilltop terraced site, such as those at El Trapiche (Fig. 4-4), Tlapacoyan, and east of Ayoquesco. Located on isolated high piedmont hills, these sites have between 10 and 150 small, residential terraces arranged in concentric rings around the top of the hill, with 1–4 small mounds and several plazas on top. All of these settlements are short occupations within the IIIa phase.

Continuity, stability, and tradition in alluvial zone settlement, as opposed to discontinuity, oscillation, and cycles of development in piedmont settlement, was an enduring dynamic feature in the evolution of the valley sociocultural system. At no time can the differences between alluvial and piedmont communities be seen more clearly than during IIIa in the Valle Grande. The estimated increase in population living on the alluvium in the Valle Grande was from about 2,500 to 9,000; for the piedmont the growth was from 3,000 to 29,000. The large alluvial zone sites such as Xoxocotlan, Cuilapan, Zaachila, Roalo, and Santa Ines Yatzeche were all occupied continuously from at least Monte Alban I. The site of Tlapacoyan is technically in the piedmont, but it is immediately adjacent to the largest extent of alluvium in the far southern part of the valley, and, like Santa Ines, Zaachila, Tierras Largas, San Jose Mogote, and other sites, it was probably continuously occupied from Early Formative times.

The multi-component nature of the alluvium-oriented sites contrasts with the relatively short occupations of the piedmont. The capital of the ancient Ocotlan district (almost all of which is piedmont) was moved in every phase from Monte Alban I through V. The hill above La Soledad was occupied only in Late I and IIIa. Santa Cruz Mixtepec has little evidence of settlement until IIIa, when it became very large, but it has no obvious IIIb; it was reused in IV and in V (see also Winter 1978 for Santa Cruz). Tejas de Morelos was big in IIIa and IIIb, but never before or after. El Trapiche and scores of other piedmont sites in the southern Valle Grande were essentially single-phase IIIa settlements.

Alluvial sites have much more mounded architecture of all kinds than do piedmont sites. Xoxocotlan has 15 pyramid mounds over 1 m in height, totaling nearly 90,000 cu m of construction. Among sites with 20 or more pyramid mounds, Cuilapan has over 120,000 cu m of mounded architecture; Trinidad has 93,000 cu m; Santa Ines Yatzeche, very roughly 82,000 cu m; and Tejas de Morelos, 59,000 cu m. Activities at all of these settlements were probably oriented toward the alluvium. In each case, with only a few exceptions, IIIa was the period of greatest construction activity and also the last phase of major construction.

Piedmont sites have much smaller pyramid mounds. For example, Jalieza in the Early Classic had perhaps 12,000 inhabitants, five to ten times the number of people in any of the alluvial sites mentioned, but it had only 45,000 cu m of mounded construction. The hilltop site above El Trapiche, with roughly 1,200 people, had only 1,000 cu m, divided between 2 low mounds. The hilltop site above Tlapacoyan had 4 mounds and 1,200 cu m, with an estimated population of over 800. The construction at the piedmont sites used as examples here dates exclusively to IIIa. Similar results can be found in earlier periods.

One difference between piedmont and alluvial construction is building material. Local materials were generally used: adobe and earth in alluvial areas, and rock, gravel, and earth in the piedmont. It is doubtful that this would account for the great variation in mound size. After all, Monte Alban's inhabitants were not deterred from building over 600,000 cu m of pyramid mounds, and they used piedmont materials. Nor is population

103

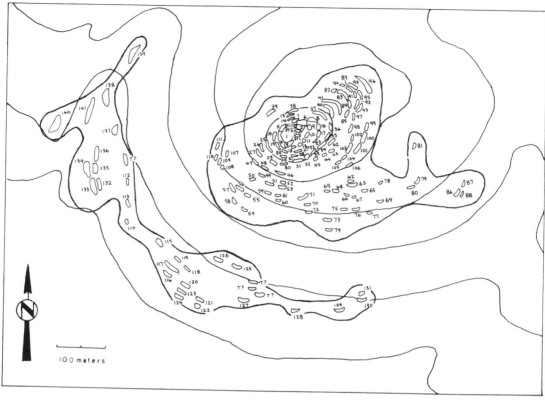

FIGURE 4-4. El Trapiche, a small terraced period IIIa site.

size a good predictor of mounded architecture volume, since there are more than a few
examples, like Roalo, of fairly small sites
with many large mounds, and large sites with
small amounts of construction. Instead, investment in mounded architecture may be
related to the organization of the local, agricultural work force. Efficient agriculture on
the alluvium requires comparatively large-
scale irrigation and drainage facilities and,
consequently, greater coordination and massed
labor than that available to a nuclear family
household. The agricultural work is seasonal,
though, and perhaps sporadic from year to
year. Mound building would be one activity
that would allow managers to regularize employment during slack periods—with a minimum of supervision, and with little in the
way of special skills required of workers. Regularization of employment would be of inter-

est to both owners and their laborers. There
very well may have been many ways in which
social strata in the alluvial districts were
bound to each other as they maintained their
traditional integrity against the more volatile
elements represented on the piedmont. To
this must be added the competitive-display
aspect of pyramid building. Most of the
mounds were elaborate residences of local
lords or perhaps "yeomen farmers," for
whom a large, highly visible house undoubtedly signaled status.

Piedmont agriculture, on the other hand,
requires relatively little regular organization
of labor above the nuclear family level. To be
sure, access to land and water needs to be
understood, and there must be an apparatus
for adjudicating disputes (Lees 1973). These
needs call for political administration, and
there is evidence of a great deal of this dur-

104

ing times of expanded piedmont development (e.g., Late I, IIIa). But the work itself—clearing, burning, cultivating, building small check dams and narrow, short canals—requires minimal overall coordination. On the piedmont there is thus far less benefit to elite or to laborers in occupying time by monumental house building. It may have even proved disruptive.

These interpretations about differences between traditional, alluvial zone communities and less traditional piedmont communities in the Late and Terminal Formative and Classic in the Valley of Oaxaca certainly need testing by intensive collection and excavation. In fact very little excavation has been done at Postformative sites. The settlement pattern survey has generated many such interesting relationships that can now be studied with forethought. It is a situation in which greater than usual returns can be expected from excavation. We hope that more researchers will take advantage of these opportunities in the Valley of Oaxaca.

## Monte Alban IIIb (A.D. 450–700)

The dating of IIIb has been discussed recently by Paddock (1978). In the settlement pattern surveys, Monte Alban IIIb pottery is considered to be like that of the Cerro de Atzompa, an almost pure IIIb context. The distinctive markers of Monte Alban IIIa and IV, though occurring in small percentages, are spread throughout the valley, so that at least with large collections fairly consistent phase assignments can be made. IIIa and IIIb thus can normally be separated from IV. The form, paste, and finish criteria for doing so are discussed in Blanton et al. n.d.

The extent of occupation dramatically declined in the Valle Grande. South of Zaachila the depopulation amounted to about 39,000 people. The Central area west of Monte Alban was extensively populated, however, as was Etla. Monte Alban achieved its maximum size of roughly 24,000 people. The density of settlement in the Tlacolula Valley is still unknown, but it may be that growth in the valley's northern and central areas canceled out the loss of population in the south. The contraction of the boundaries of the system and the drawing of activity toward the center are unmistakable.

Zaachila may have become the major administrative center for the entire southern arm of the valley. The IIIb settlement was apparently dispersed, and much of it may have been covered by the modern town, but our best estimate is that it reached its maximum size of about 2,000 people in this phase. Roberto Gallegos (1962, 1963) has published a sketch map of the mounded constructions, which have IIIb as their principal construction phase. Another district capital was San Pedro Ixtlahuaca, controlling the area west of Monte Alban. The Cerro de Atzompa, with considerable administrative architecture and a large population, may have served as a district capital for part or all of the Etla region. Below the level of these sites were third-rank centers, represented by El Mirador in the high mountains west of San Pedro Ixtlahuaca (see Fig. 4-5), Cuilapan, Noriega, and, virtually isolated in the south, Tejas de Morelos. The major Early Classic centers at El Choco, Santa Cruz Mixtepec, and Jalieza may have had IIIb occupations, but if so they were so small that their remains were swamped by the large IIIa and IV settlements.

The urban nature of Monte Alban has been recognized for some time by those who were familiar with the site (Bernal 1965:804–805; Paddock 1966:149–174). There has been substantial publication, based on excavations, on the urns (Caso and Bernal 1952), pottery (Caso, Bernal, and Acosta 1967), and the first 7 of the over 170 excavated tombs (Caso 1969). The architectural studies have not yet been published. New information has been provided by Blanton's (1978) detailed survey and mapping of the entire city (Fig. 4-6). Winter's excavations (Winter 1974; Winter and Payne 1976) unquestionably demonstrate the residential character of Monte Alban's terraces.

Analysis of the traffic patterns in the vicin-

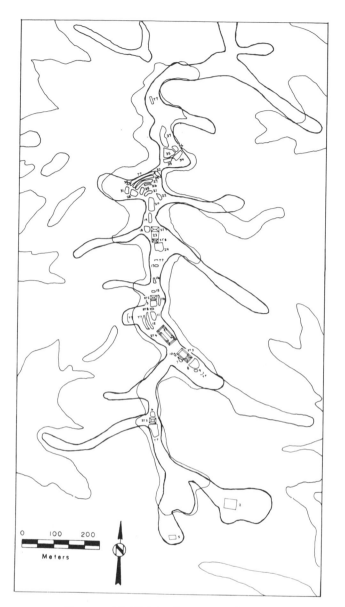

FIGURE 4-5. El Mirador in period IIIb.

Occupation away from the Main Plaza is not homogeneous, but it tends to cluster around fairly evenly spaced elite residence and plaza groups. There are 15 of these "site subdivisions" in IIIb. They vary in numbers of residential terraces, from 16 to 467; and, interestingly, the amount of mounded architecture in each is correlated with the subdivision's non-elite population size. The purpose of these units, and their possible relationship to outlying districts, remains unknown.

Craft production involving pottery-making, obsidian, shell, manos, metates, and other lithic objects may have occupied perhaps 10–15 percent of the city's population. Marketing may have been an important activity, since aside from the site subdivision plazas, there is evidence of a possible central market near the base of the north slope of Monte Alban. In essence, however, we believe that the city's reason for being was always "administrative." Its primary function was to regulate interregional matters. Derivative functions had to do with insuring logistical support for the city. Aside from these general statements, however, little is understood about exactly what so many people were doing at Monte Alban. Several directions for future research are indicated by the work of Marcus on the writing system (1976b, 1976c, 1980), and it should be noted that the published Monte Alban survey information still contains a good deal of unanalyzed data.

## Monte Alban IV (A.D. 700–1000)

At the time that Bernal wrote the summary of Oaxaca archaeology for the original *Handbook*, no one knew what a pure, full Monte Alban IV complex would look like. But in 1961 John Paddock and his associates began the excavations at Lambityeco that provided exactly what was missing (Paddock, Mogor, and Lind 1968; Paddock n.d.). Work at Lambityeco continued for more than ten years, producing an invaluable and truly massive amount of detailed architectural data and artifactual materials. More of these long-term

ity of the Main Plaza shows that as the political system became more centralized after period I, the plaza became more and more secluded. By IIIb it was entirely closed to casual traffic. Elsewhere on the site there is a network of roads serving the residential areas of the city, but none of these provides access to the central, administrative zone.

A major result of the mapping project relates to the settlement's internal structure.

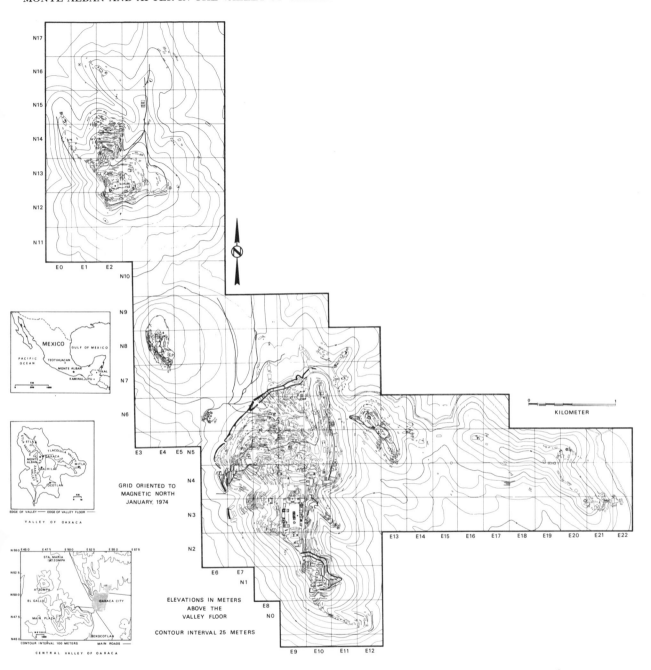

FIGURE 4-6. Monte Alban, as it would have looked in period IIIb, when all of the terraces were occupied: archaeological and topographical map. Map drafted by Jill Appel. See Blanton 1978 for a larger version of map with key to different types of structures.

investigations are needed, especially in the later periods.

Lambityeco's artifact complex as a whole is distinct from the IIIb materials at Monte Alban. The period IV remains are securely dated by an unusually tight cluster of radiocarbon dates to within a few decades of A.D. 700 (Rabin 1970:14–15). These dates are generally congruent with the ceramic cross-dates using Lambityeco's convincing imitations of Altar-Balancan Fine Orange and Puuc Slate (Paddock n.d.). (The chronological sequence, including period IV problems, is also addressed by Daniel Wolfman [1973], who has paleo-magnetic dates; Robert D. Drennan [n.d.], who reviews the available radiocarbon dates; Paddock [1978]; and Blanton et al. [n.d.].)

Aspects of Lambityeco's architecture are reported by Horst Hartung (1970) and Rosemary Sharp (1970, 1978). Emily Rabin (1970) discusses Lambityeco and period IV epigraphy, noting that the late monuments tend to emphasize "family" scenes, "possibly indicating a hereditary elite with a stress on lineage" (p. 12; see Marcus 1980). Ceramic production may have been an important activity at Lambityeco (Payne 1970; Swasey 1973; see also Kowalewski and Truell 1970). Salt production, described in detail by David Andrew Peterson (1976), was carried out on a large scale at Lambityeco during Monte Alban IV.

In the larger context of the region, Lambityeco was one of perhaps 10 or 12 communities that were formed in the valley after the breakup of the centralized state. Each consisted of one or more nucleated towns and several smaller villages, for a total population of several thousand. They appear to have been politically autonomous, petty states, separated from one another by unoccupied territory, and each with its own administrative facilities. Examples of these Monte Alban IV towns that have been mapped include Loma de la Montura (see Fig. 4-7), El Choco (Fig. 4-8), Santa Cruz Mixtepec, and Animas Trujano. A small rural population lived in the area around Zaachila. Monte Alban may have

been simply another of these petty states. The loss of its valley-wide sovereignty may have been accompanied by security threats, since the site has precincts defended by walls dating to this time, and since the occupation was confined to the area within the main defensive wall. A very rough estimate of 4,000 people for Monte Alban in period IV may be suggested, based on the area over which period IV artifacts are found.

Other sites previously suggested as being important in Monte Alban IV deserve mention. Mitla has some IV occupation, but, as with Yagul, its extent is not yet known. Yagul's period IV may be late, post-Lambityeco, probably coeval with Loma de la Montura. San Luis Beltran, tested by Bernal, has some apparently Monte Alban IIIb–IV public architecture, but virtually no evidence of a resident population (though Late I, II, IIIa, and V are represented). Possibly the site was being built as a new administrative district capital when the Monte Alban state collapsed. Noriega is mainly a IIIa and IIIb site, and Cuilapan's Monte Alban IV is of no great extent, especially compared to its IIIa component.

Jalieza (Fig. 4-9) reached its maximum size (534 ha, over 1,100 residential terraces, more than 16,000 inhabitants), and became the largest center in the valley, in period IV. At this time most of the valley's population was living in the Tlacolula and Valle Grande wings, so that Jalieza, strategically situated on the pass between those two areas, was also near the valley's period IV demographic center of gravity. Jalieza shows no evidence of being a central, political, or administrative capital, as Monte Alban had been. The city had no central plaza surrounded by "public" buildings. Instead, there were several isolated elite residences or palaces, located at some distance from one another along the main ridge, suggesting a highly decentralized, but still socially stratified, system. Jalieza may have functioned as a commercial central place, but another Monte Alban it was not.

These conclusions should be considered

108

FIGURE 4-7. Loma de la Montura in period IV.

provisional, for the problems surrounding the creation of the Postclassic world are by no means resolved. Hypothesis testing with intensive surface collections and excavations has scarcely begun. Little is known even about basic subsistence, household activities, or social organization. There is a good possibility that these subjects can now be very successfully studied in the Valley of Oaxaca, but more research and more long-term commitments are needed.

The collapse of Monte Alban and the onset of the Postclassic present us with a set of questions for which we have few final answers. We are fortunate, however, in having the intensive settlement pattern survey data to draw on in forming and testing hypotheses, and some pertinent information has come from excavations (Paddock 1978). These issues are discussed at some length in Blanton et al. n.d.; because of their complexity, only the briefest of summaries is possible here. The end of the Classic was not simply an event whose occurrence is explicable in simple terms. Instead, it can be understood only by reference to the dynamic properties

109

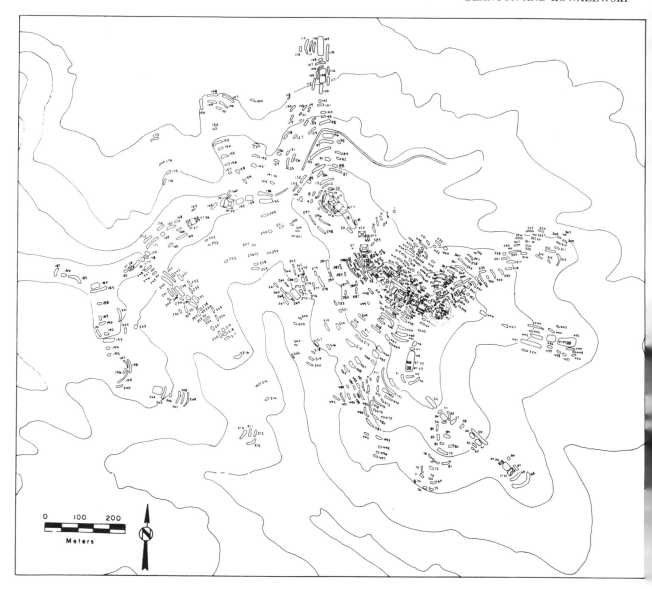

FIGURE 4-8. El Choco. The bulk of these terraces were occupied during period IV.

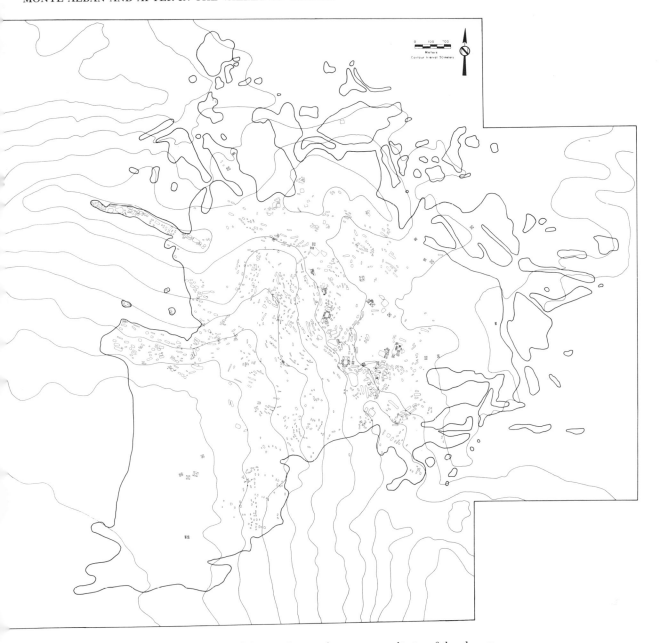

FIGURE 4-9. Jalieza in period IV. The dark line indicates the maximum limits of sherd scatter.

of the regional system in the Valley of Oaxaca and the nature of societal interactions in the Mesoamerican world-system. As we have noted, several times after the formation of Monte Alban the regional system was in a "growth cycle" (periods I, IIIa, and, on a smaller scale, IIIb), evidently instigated by the elite at Monte Alban. Each of these periods of growth was characterized by population expansion, administered piedmont agricultural development, more centralized regional government, and increased levels of governmental "meddling" in production and distribution.

In each of these cases, as the systems grew, we think that certain kinds of constraints came into play and problems were encountered that eventually became so serious that reorganization was the result (involving population declines, less centralized regional government, discontinuation of piedmont development, and reduced governmental "meddling" in production and distribution). As we see it, the early stages of a growth cycle were highly successful viewed from the perspective of the elite at Monte Alban. Virgin piedmont soils were no doubt initially highly productive, and population growth meant more households as taxpayers. As growth continued, however, desirable places for farming would have become scarcer, as would water for irrigation, and so disputes would have increased in frequency and ardor. Administrative costs would have increased as a result. Eventually, the fragile piedmont soils would have begun to show signs of wear and tear, and production would have declined. Furthermore, piedmont agriculture, while highly productive in some years, is risky. As piedmont populations grew, the state would have had increasingly more difficulty supplying farmers who had suffered deficits. At any rate, and for several reasons, we feel that costs of government would have been on the increase at the same time that productivity was on the decline. Breakdown is the result. After periods I and IIIa, though, Monte Alban managed to hang on as the capital center in spite of reductions in its regional

system—why was IIIb different? One factor to consider is that, especially during the Classic, it was necessary to maintain a costly, powerful, centralized government in the region to manage interregional affairs—especially, no doubt, in the light of Teotihuacan's threat. After Teotihuacan's demise no comparable empires developed. Considering the extremely high costs of maintaining a "growth cycle" administrative apparatus, people must have decided, sometime during IIIb, to end their support of the capital, opting for smaller and more locally autonomous governmental arrangements. So the demise of the great Zapotec capital was due to a combination of local problems and a fundamental change in the organization of the Mesoamerican world-system.

## Monte Alban V (A.D. 1000–1500)

The basic characteristics of the Late Postclassic regional system in the Valley of Oaxaca are the following: (1) as in Monte Alban IV, the valley continued to be politically fragmented, or "balkanized"; (2) population grew substantially, in the surveyed areas from 32,000 in period IV to 51,000 in V; (3) this growth took place within a highly dispersed settlement pattern, as opposed to the nucleated pattern of period IV (there are 867 sites in the surveyed areas, and the mean size is only about 3 ha); (4) late in the phase, but prior to the arrival of the Spaniards, population again began to agglomerate in the Monte Alban–Cuilapan area, forming the valley's largest community with roughly 13,500 people; (5) there was more economic specialization and region-wide commercial integration; and (6) political, social, ethnic, and economic ties linked valley communities into strong regional networks that transcended the limits of the physiographic province.

Monte Alban V is defined by the appearance of a ceramic complex dominated by G-3M bowls in a series of standardized forms. In some assemblages, especially in the northern and western parts of the valley, Huitzo Polished Cream (Paddock 1966:208) occurs together with probably Early V gray wares. The beginning dates for this ceramic type and its termination in the Valley of Oaxaca are not known. Plumbate and X Fine Orange vessel forms are extremely rare in the Valley of Oaxaca. They seem to tie into the local sequence at the very end of IV or the beginning of V. A convenient end date for V has not yet been determined. As Ronald Spores notes for Nochixtlan (1974), native material culture persisted for some time into the Colonial period. Monte Alban V versus Colonial assignments in the settlement pattern work have been made by the presence or absence of non-native pottery and certain changes in vessel form in the native gray and cream wares. Internal subdivision of period V along the lines proposed by Donald L. Brockington (1973) and by Ignacio Bernal and Lorenzo Gamio (1974) remains a distinct possibility, which will be tested when the local variants over the whole valley have been collected by the settlement pattern project.

Monte Alban V features—tombs, pits, houses, trash deposits—have been encountered at virtually every site that has been excavated in the Valley of Oaxaca. Two period V tombs have been salvaged and reported (Winter, Deraga, and Fernández 1975, 1977), and Chris L. Moser (1969) published another from Huitzo. Gallegos has carried out excavations of major tombs at Zaachila (1962, 1963). There has also been interest in locating the Aztec garrison in Oaxaca (see the discussions in several numbers of the *Boletín del Centro Regional de Oaxaca, I.N.A.H.* 1975). Since the study of the Yagul palaces in the 1950s (Bernal and Gamio 1974) there have been, lamentably, no excavations expressly designed to investigate Monte Alban V sites in a systematic contextual way.

Figure 4-10 shows the Monte Alban V settlement patterns in the Monte Alban, Central, and Valle Grande areas. Note the clusters of settlements in the mountains west of San Pedro Ixtlahuaca, at Monte Alban–Cuilapan, San Felipe–San Luis Beltran, Hueyapan, Santa Cruz Amilpas, Hacienda Experimental–San Agustin de las Juntas,

Coyotepec, Jalieza, and Valdeflores-Tlapacoyan. Other clusters in the valley are important—such as the major buildup in the Mitla area—but as of this writing we are just beginning to work with those data. Interestingly, the populations around Zaachila and Zimatlan were located up in the piedmont west of those modern pueblos, lending support to the idea that Zaachila was a symbolic, political capital, not a major population center. Work on relating the ethnohistorical descriptions of the valley's population to the archaeological settlement patterns is in progress (Appel n.d.b). It may eventually be possible to document continuity and change in *municipio* and district boundaries from Monte Alban V to the present.

Monte Alban V was not a time of great pyramid construction. Mounded architecture volumes, per unit of habitation area, are lower than in any other phase. We take this to mean that the period V elite could not control massed corvée labor in the way the elite of earlier periods could. The well-built palaces at Mitla, and a few other places in the Tlacolula arm of the valley, are clearly the exception, not the rule. Labor, like the settlements themselves, was probably dispersed in space and in its organization, in order to take advantage of very local resources and social circumstances. Certainly piedmont agriculture was a factor. The alluvium-based, traditional communities of the Classic disappeared in the Postclassic. Their decline was probably hastened by the importation of labor from the Mixteca. (Monte Alban V was incidentally not the first time in which there was such an influx of people—it may have happened in Monte Alban I and IIIa, too.) Households and villages, perhaps aided by improved market integration, were able to develop a more intensive degree of agricultural and craft specialization. Trade networks were more developed in the Late Postclassic, attested to by the wide distribution of obsidian, which must be imported from outside the valley (the exact sources have never been identified, but much of it may come from the Valley of Mexico). Obsi-

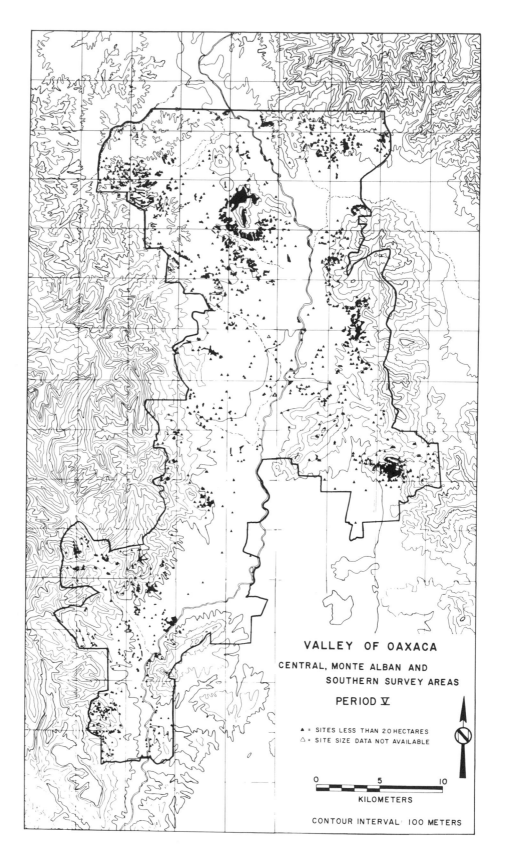

VALLEY OF OAXACA

CENTRAL, MONTE ALBAN AND
SOUTHERN SURVEY AREAS

PERIOD Ⅴ

▲ = SITES LESS THAN 20 HECTARES
△ = SITE SIZE DATA NOT AVAILABLE

0          5          10

KILOMETERS

CONTOUR INTERVAL: 100 METERS

114

dian frequencies are higher in period V than in any other period, and even the hamlets and isolated residences, especially near the center of the valley, typically have obsidian blades.

These and other lines of evidence suggest to us that regional integration was provided by economic links to a much greater extent in the Postclassic than in previous phases. Earlier, centralized, administrative decision-making institutions had governed the course of events in the valley. But with the increasing dependence of households on specialized products, exchange networks independent of centralized, political control began to emerge, probably because of their greater efficiency at high demand levels. This process, which was happening more or less simultaneously all over Mesoamerica, doomed ponderous, costly old centers like Monte Alban. Political balkanization was the result—a decline, some might say, but an arrangement that was far more complex and flexible than the Classic system.

## CROSS-PERIOD STUDIES

The use of pottery data for behavioral, nonchronological inferences has proven very informative. In addition to the pottery-making places identified through excavations at Lambityeco and Monte Alban (see also Houston and Wainer 1971), nearly 40 pottery workshops have been located on the settlement pattern survey. The locations and positions in the settlement hierarchy of places making different kinds of pottery tell us a great deal about the organization of production and exchange.

Gary Feinman (n.d.a, n.d.b) has been able to convincingly account for why the Oaxacan ceramics seem so plain in some phases and so fancy in others. Design simplicity and mass techniques are favored by highly centralized, administratively and monopolistically con-

trolled production and distribution. Design complexity and a high input of energy per pot are favored by less centralized, more competitive systems. Thus, Early I pottery shows great decorative variation, which declines in Late I, re-emerges in II, disappears with the plain pottery of the Classic, and comes back again in V. These ceramic shifts are neatly paralleled by our reconstruction of changes in the degree of administrative control in the regional system.

Detailed studies of the relationship between human settlements and the land and water resources on which Oaxaqueños depend have begun (Kirkby 1973; Curran 1978; Kowalewski 1980, n.d.; Fisch n.d.). These investigations, still somewhat exploratory in nature, tend to show that in the trajectory of the valley's human system, human/environmental relationships do not on the whole appear to be central causative agents. Human/human relationships seem to be much more centrally or directly involved in causing the system to change. More population/resource studies are planned.

## CONCLUSION

We have attempted to synthesize what has been learned since 1965 about the post–500 B.C. prehistory of the Valley of Oaxaca. Except for the Lambityeco work, there have been no sustained excavation efforts; however, much has been learned from the regional settlement pattern surveys. Indeed, the interpretation possibilities offered by the presently available data are too numerous and too complex to be adequately handled in an article of this length. Undoubtedly that is a sign that progress is being made.

## ACKNOWLEDGMENTS

Support for the Valley of Oaxaca Settlement Pattern Project was provided for by NSF (GS-28547, GS-38030, and BNS 76-19640). The Instituto Nacional de Antropología e Historia and the Centro Regional de Oaxaca have encouraged and facilitated every single

FIGURE 4-10. Settlement patterns of period V.

study mentioned in this article. The authors thank all those Oaxaca specialists whose studies have provided the content of this article, and Dr. Gregory Johnson, who contributed to the passage on corvée labor and mound building. We sincerely thank Linda Adams, who typed the manuscript. We take sole responsibility for any errors.

## BIBLIOGRAPHIC NOTE

The Centro Regional de Oaxaca has published an extremely useful bibliography of anthropology in the State of Oaxaca (Romero Frizzi 1974), and a partial listing of archaeological localities in the state, published in the *Cuadernos de los Centros* series.

# 5. San Lorenzo Tenochtitlan

*MICHAEL D. COE*

*MICHAEL D. COE*

## INTRODUCTION

S AN LORENZO TENOCHTITLAN is a complex of three sites (San Lorenzo, Tenochtitlan, and Potrero Nuevo) discovered in 1945 by Matthew W. and Marion
Stirling (Stirling 1955), and excavated by
them and Philip Drucker in 1946. During
those two years, the Stirling party uncovered
the largest and finest collection of Olmec
monumental sculpture known to that time,
but their stratigraphic research was never
published and thus the age of these stones
remained unknown. When I prepared two
articles on the Olmec area for the *Handbook
of Middle American Indians* (M. Coe 1965a,
1965b), I believed that the climax of Olmec
civilization had been reached in the Middle
Formative period, between 800 and 400
B.C., according to the radiocarbon dates on
La Venta, and that San Lorenzo Tenochtitlan
would be roughly contemporary with that
site. However, in the absence of archaeological data, this was uncertain, and one histo-
rian of art was able to suggest that the colossal heads of San Lorenzo belonged to the
Early Classic (Kubler 1962:67).

It was my conviction, however, that the

key to understanding the origin and *floruit* of
Olmec civilization might well be found at
San Lorenzo Tenochtitlan, for it lies closer to
the center of the Olmec heartland than La
Venta, in the midst of apparently fertile agricultural land. Accordingly, a Yale University
archaeological-ecological project was started
at San Lorenzo Tenochtitlan in 1966 and continued through 1968 (Coe and Diehl 1980),
supported by the National Science Foundation and coordinated with the Instituto Nacional de Antropología e Historia (INAH). In
1969 and 1970, INAH conducted its own
investigations at San Lorenzo, for the express purpose of finding new monuments by
means of the cesium magnetometer. The result of this research is that San Lorenzo Tenochtitlan has been established as one of
the oldest civilized communities in Mesoamerica, if not *the* oldest.

The site complex is located in the middle
part of the Coatzacoalcos drainage (Fig. 5-1),
close to the Rio Chiquito, a side branch of
the Coatzacoalcos (the river splitting to form
Tacamichapa Island). Geologically, this is a
region of eroded hills of Tertiary origin rising
above Recent flood plains; clay is in abundance, but, locally, there is no rock which

117

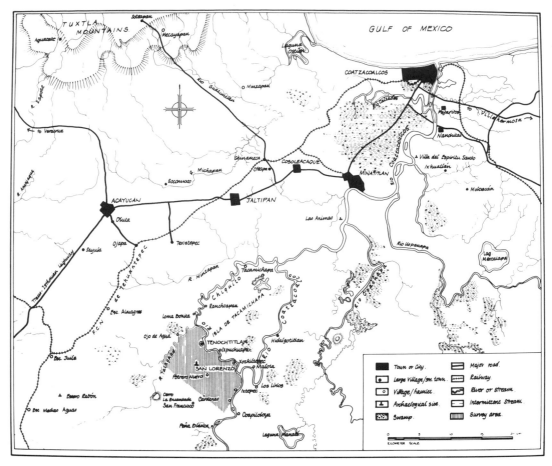

FIGURE 5-1. Map of the Coatzacoalcos Basin, with location of San Lorenzo Tenochtitlan. The shaded area was surveyed by the Yale expedition.

could have found use in construction or for carving. Thus, whatever rocks were used in ancient times all had to be imported. The most striking of these imports is basalt; the source for this is the Cerro Cintepec in the Tuxtla Mountains, about 50 km north-north-west of San Lorenzo Tenochtitlan.

Rainfall is high, most of it coming during the summer rainy season, but winter northers bring in many days of rain and mist during the rest of the year, so that there is no strongly marked dry season; crops can therefore be raised throughout the year. The rivers become swollen with the heavy summer rains and overflow their banks, flooding all of the land below the 28 m contour. As the so-called dry season progresses, the waters

recede, leaving only old oxbow lakes and ponds in the midst of grass-covered *potreros*; these have been important sources of fish protein for both the ancient and the modern inhabitants of the zone. Most significantly, the falling waters leave a rich deposit of silt along the natural levees which flank the rivers and streams, a point that will be examined later.

### THE SITES
#### San Lorenzo

San Lorenzo (Fig. 5-2) is by far the most important and imposing of the three sites, and in Olmec times the other two were probably little more than dependencies of it. It is

118

basically a plateau which rises up about 50 m above the surrounding countryside. It virtually dominates the landscape of this part of the middle Rio Coatzacoalcos, as it can be seen from many kilometers away. The plateau is about 1,200 m long in a north-south direction and covers 52.9 ha (Rossman 1976), making this the largest Early Formative settlement known to date.

When Matthew Stirling was investigating San Lorenzo, he thought that the ravines which cut into the plateau, in which many of the monuments were found, were simply the result of erosion, and that the stones had been tumbled into them by conquerors. However, our detailed mapping and extensive excavations have shown that the ravines were formed by the construction of finger-like ridges which jut out from the plateau on the north, west, and south sides. These display a degree of mirror symmetry, with matched pairs being the Group C and Group D ridges on the west, and the Southwest and Southeast ridges. It is my belief that the entire plateau is some kind of effigy mound, perhaps a gigantic bird flying east, but that the plan was never completed. Of course, the impression must not be left that all 50 m of the plateau is artificial: San Lorenzo is largely a natural eminence consisting of Tertiary clays and bentonites, but covered with up to 7 m of artificial fill.

There are about 200 mounds on the surface of San Lorenzo, most of which were domestic, so that we estimate an ancient population of about 1,000. Some of the mounds are large and obviously ceremonial: Group A, in the center of the site, takes on the typical "Olmec" layout with long north-south mounds flanking courts and with a central pyramid. However, house mounds are seen over a much wider area than the plateau top, extending, for instance, all over the Loma del Zapote which extends south of the Southeast Ridge, so that it is virtually impossible at the present time to estimate the Olmec occupation of this and other sites.

Other notable features of the San Lorenzo site are the 20 depressions which we called *lagunas*. Some of these certainly originated as borrow pits, and most are formless, though all hold water in the dry season. On the other hand, several have a geometric shape and are lined with bentonite, showing that they were planned pools, perhaps for ceremonial bathing. Similar ritual use of water on a very large scale can be seen in the stone aqueduct which was uncovered in the southwestern part of the site during the 1967 and 1968 seasons; this consists of U-shaped trough stones laid end to end and fitted with slab covers (Fig. 5-3). The main line, which falls at a 2 percent slope, is 170 m long; it is joined by three feeder lines, and the entire system contains some 30 tons of basalt, all imported from the Cerro Cintepec. Constructed in San Lorenzo B times, this remarkable example of Olmec engineering ability probably drained a large ceremonial *laguna* now covered by later fill. Loose drain covers eroding from the surface suggest that there was a matching system in the southeastern portion of San Lorenzo.

## Tenochtitlan

Originally called "Rio Chiquito" by Stirling (1955), Tenochtitlan is a large mound site underlying the modern village of that name. The ancient architects took advantage of a natural elevation lying near the Rio Chiquito to construct two groups of long, low mounds flanking plazas, with larger "pyramids" at one or both ends; our excavations, however, showed that while the original layout might be ascribed to the Olmec of the San Lorenzo phase, much of the site had been rebuilt in the Villa Alta phase, almost two millennia later.

About 700 m north of Tenochtitlan, the river bank has been undercut by the Rio Chiquito, exposing a deeply buried but extensive layer of village material belonging to the San Lorenzo phase, and more of the same material once could be seen further downstream on the opposite bank; the meandering river has probably cut through what was quite a large Olmec village.

119

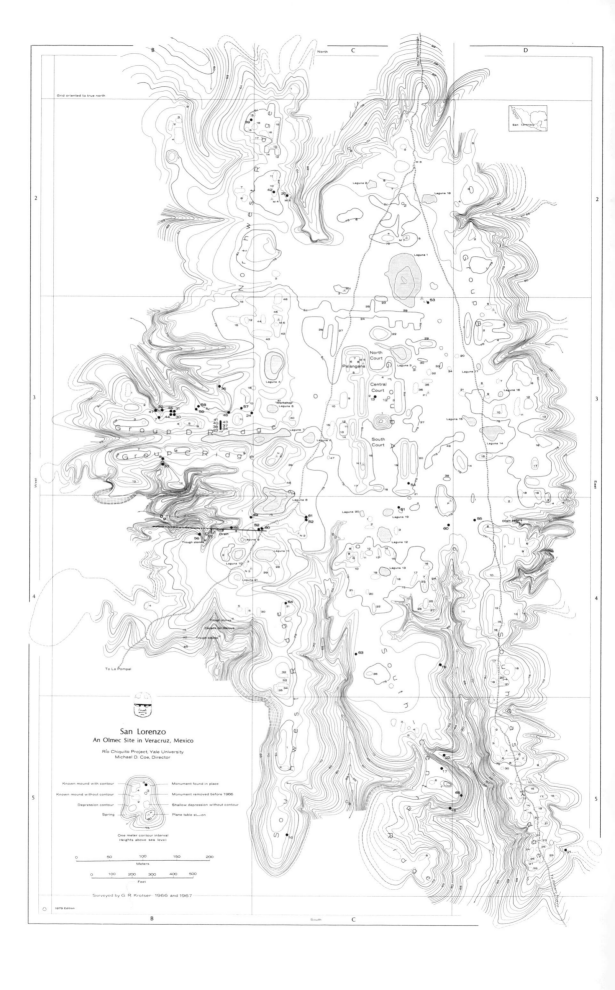

## San Lorenzo
### An Olmec Site in Veracruz, Mexico

Río Chiquito Project, Yale University
Michael D. Coe, Director

Known mound with contour · Monument found in place
Known mound without contour · Monument removed before 1966
Depression contour · Shallow depression without contour
Spring · Plane table station

One meter contour interval
Heights above sea level

0    50    100    150    200
Meters

0   100   200   300   400   500
Feet

Surveyed by G. R. Krotser  1966 and 1967

1979 Edition

FIGURE 5-3. Aqueduct on the southwestern side of San Lorenzo.

## Potrero Nuevo

The modern hamlet of Potrero Nuevo is situated 2.7 km east-southeast of San Lorenzo, and is built on top of a restricted group of small mounds. Excavations by Stirling and Drucker produced largely Villa Alta materials, with some sherds from the Nacaste phase (Middle Formative), and if it were not for the ascription by Stirling of 4 monuments to the site, we would have little justification in calling it "Olmec." Actually, 2 of these monuments (Potrero Nuevo Monuments 2 and 3) were found near or on the Loma del Zapote, and probably all of them originated at San Lorenzo.

## ARCHAEOLOGICAL SEQUENCE AND CHRONOLOGY[1]

San Lorenzo Tenochtitlan has had a very long and complex prehistory, of which the Olmec

FIGURE 5-2. Contour map of San Lorenzo, with the location of monuments discovered before 1969.

occupation of ca. 1150–900 B.C. was the most important. Important parts of the archaeological sequence are fixed through radiocarbon analysis, while others are crossdated with sequences elsewhere through stylistic comparison (Table 5-1).

## The Ojochi Phase

The Ojochi phase is the first occupation which we have been able to detect for San Lorenzo Tenochtitlan. Judging from its stratigraphic position underneath deposits of the Bajio phase and its obvious cultural ties with the Barra and Ocos phases of the Pacific Coast of Guatemala and Chiapas (Green and Lowe 1967:97–106; M. Coe 1961a), Ojochi probably began shortly after 1500 B.C. and lasted until about 1350 B.C. We have found Ojochi materials only at San Lorenzo itself, and even there they are highly localized, being pretty much confined to the center of the site, although an important deposit was found below Monument 20 on the edge of the Northwest Ridge. As far as can be seen, the Ojochi colonizers established a small set-

121

TABLE 5-1. The San Lorenzo Tenochtitlan Sequence and Mesoamerica

| | | San Lorenzo Tenochtitlan | La Venta | Central Chiapas | Guatemala–Chiapas Coast | Oaxaca |
|---|---|---|---|---|---|---|
| Early Post-classic | A.D.<br>1200<br>1100<br><br>900 | Villa Alta | | Ruiz (Chiapa XI) | | Monte Alban IV (?) |
| Late For-ma-tive | 300<br>0<br><br>400 | Remplas<br>——?—— | | Guanacaste (Chiapa V) | Crucero | |
| Middle For-ma-tive | 500<br>600<br><br>700<br><br>800<br>900 | Palangana<br>————<br>————<br>(Hiatus)<br>————<br><br>Nacaste | Phase IV<br><br>Phase III<br><br>Phase II | Francesa (Chiapa IV)<br><br>Escalera (Chiapa III)<br><br>Dili (Chiapa II) | Conchas II<br><br>Conchas I | Monte Alban I<br><br>Guadalupe |
| Early For-ma-tive | 1000<br><br>1200<br><br>1300<br><br>1400<br>1500<br>B.C. | San Lorenzo B<br>------------ Phase I<br>San Lorenzo A<br>————<br>Chicharras<br>————<br>Bajio<br>————<br>Ojochi<br>——?—— | | Cotorra (Chiapa I) | Jocotal<br><br>Cuadros<br><br><br>Ocos<br><br>Barra<br>↓<br>? | San Jose<br><br>Tierras Largas |

tlement on top of the sterile yellow, orange, and red stratified sands that underlie all cultural deposits on the San Lorenzo plateau, but did not significantly alter its shape by any large-scale construction.

Thin-walled tecomates are the dominant pottery shape, but flat-bottomed bowls with outflaring sides and narrow-necked bottles also occur. As in Ocos, the most striking ware is slipped in a deep hematite red which may be specular; red tecomates often are fluted, while on the bowls extensive gadrooning may occur. Other wares include red on burnished buff, the red being confined to zoned bands on rim and body; red-on-cream, with red bands appearing on the neck and body of bottles; plain burnished; and a burnished flesh-colored pottery. Quite frequent are coarse tecomates with red rims and red-striped exteriors.

The very important Camaño Coarse is a tecomate type which starts with Ojochi, where it is generally thin-walled and seldom brushed, and continues with various modifications until the Middle Formative Nacaste phase. That this is a utility ware can be seen by the charred food material (perhaps overcooked corn dough) which occurs on many interiors.

The whole feeling of Ojochi pottery is so close to that of Ocos that it must be a kind of country cousin of that more spectacular culture. However, many Ocos decorative techniques—such as iridescent painting and cord-marking—seem to be absent. Only one worn, shell-edge rocker-stamped sherd was found, in contrast to the fully developed stamping complex shown in Ocos. The corpus of Ojochi decoration is restricted to fluting, gadrooning, fingernail-gouging, stick-punching, zoning, and stick-burnishing in vertical lines or latticework patterns.

The artifact sample is small. A few pottery figurine fragments, both solid and hollow, were recovered, one showing the lower part of a person seated tailor fashion. Stone bowls and metates were manufactured from basalt, and ferrous pieces of laminar sandstone were used as grinding or lapidary tools. Grey obsidian was imported, but only small flakes and chips were found; the absence of blades is a striking feature of Early Formative lowland sites that has been noted elsewhere. Red hematite pigment was also imported, perhaps from deposits in the Isthmian region.

There is obviously nothing very Olmec about Ojochi. Its closest affiliations seem to be with the Pacific Coast of Chiapas and Guatemala. There may be a widespread occupation of both coasts of Mesoamerica which is of this type.

## The Bajio Phase

Radiocarbon dates suggest a placement for the subsequent Bajio phase at 1350–1250 B.C. However, in attempting to correlate Bajio with other ceramic complexes in Mesoamerica we are faced with some real quandaries which will be mentioned later. It was a particularly important occupation for the site of San Lorenzo, for we know that at this time vast quantities of fill were added to level off the top of the plateau and, more particularly, to begin construction of the long ridges which jut out from it on the west side; perhaps all the ridges were initiated in Bajio times. If so, this is indeed strange, for since we have been able to show bilateral mirror symmetry in the ridges, it follows that San Lorenzo as a center was planned as far back as the fourteenth century B.C.

It is not unreasonable to suppose that this ceremonial building activity resulted in the construction of temple mounds; none have been found, perhaps because of their destruction for fill by later occupants. But we discovered, deep in an excavation on the Group D Ridge, traces of a red sand platform that rose in a series of undulating steps to a height of at least 2 m.

The ceramic complex (Fig. 5-4) is strikingly different from that of Ojochi, although certain types of decorative modes continue. Most unusual are the large numbers of bottles which appear in Bajio, with bodies which are either fluted or deeply gadrooned to resemble gourds or squashes; necks are straight or slightly constricted toward the mouth. In addition, a very strange shape appears, one which is hardly Mesoamerican: flat-bottomed pots with constricted upper walls and enormous, outflaring rims. In wares, there is an overall drop in fine, burnished red pottery. Pottery which has been differentially fired to produce black and white areas makes its appearance. In the repertory of ceramic decoration, fluting and gadrooning continue, the gadrooning on bowl exteriors now greatly exaggerated, producing a series of swellings along rims. There is a great variety of punctation, mostly on the outside of flat-bottomed bowls with outflaring rims: semicircular (using the edge of a reed), stick, short linear, and fingernail-gouging. Some punctation is zoned in curvilinear bands and triangles. Plain bold rocker-stamping is present on the exteriors of deep, thick-walled bowls with specular red interiors. More rare is shell-back and shell-edge rocker-stamping. The culinary tecomate type, Camaño Coarse, is common, but walls are gradually becoming heavier, with increasing use of brushing to roughen the pot, perhaps for ease in holding.

All of the artifact types of Ojochi continue into Bajio, including stone bowls, footless metates, and grey obsidian confined to small flakes and chips. Lumps of untempered fired clay are quite frequent, possibly used in boiling. One rounded lump of asphalt was found, showing that the use of this material, so important to the Olmec, began in the Bajio phase.

More significant than any of these, however, are the pottery figurines. Both solid and hollow types were made. One fragment of a face, decorated with red pigment, comes from a hollow figure. Another is really astonishing, for it is the left leg with attached hand of a hollow, spraddle-legged baby identical in form to those usually considered typical of Olmec culture (Fig. 5-5). It is unfortunate that the head of this baby is missing, for

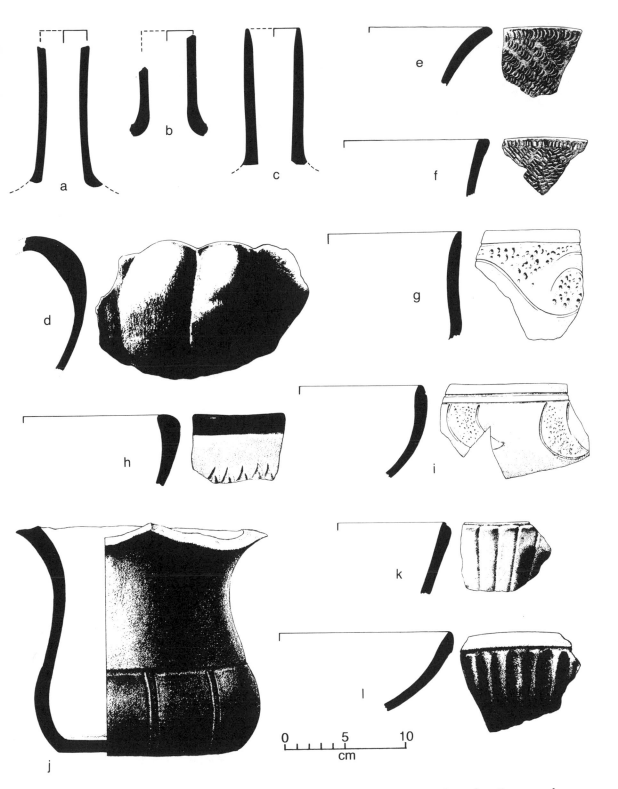

FIGURE 5-4. Bajio phase, selected ceramics: *a–d*, bottles; *e–f*, punctate; *g*, *i*, Embarcadero Punctate; *h*, plain rocker-stamping; *j*, Rosas Burnished; *k–l*, gadrooning and fluting.

FIGURE 5-5. Hollow pottery figurine fragment, Bajio phase.

it would be interesting to see if the Olmec artistic convention in faces had been developed this early.

It is difficult to relate Bajio to other more-or-less contemporary cultures in Mesoamerica, mainly because we are unsure just what might be on the same time level. There are, however, many links to the Pellicer phase of the Tabascan Chontalpa (Sisson 1976).

### The Chicharras Phase

Although there are a few continuities from Bajio into the Chicharras phase, especially in utility wares, a host of new types and modes suggests that a significant influx of ideas and/or people joined the previous population at San Lorenzo at about 1250 B.C., when, according to radiocarbon dates, Chicharras began. The most important aspect of Chicharras, however, is that it definitely foreshadows the thoroughly Olmec San Lorenzo phase, which followed on its heels at around 1150 B.C.

There is a tremendous increase in white-black pottery, especially white-rimmed black ware. Most of this is quite thin and extremely fine-paste, with strikingly black cores, although a coarser sand-tempered type is also frequent. Four white types also appear, all of which, along with the white-black pottery, continue into San Lorenzo. One of these, Ixtepec White, is fine-paste with black cores, while another, Xochiltepec White, is the so-called "white-clear-through" or "kaolin" ware often associated with the Olmec in the Central Highlands. Tatagapa Red also makes its appearance, confined to large, pure hematite-slipped tecomates; the decoration of the exteriors of these is pure incision in parallel lines, zoned crosshatching, or the very odd "false rocker-stamping," which is really incised rather than stamped. New shapes include the necked jar, "paint dishes" (which often do contain hematite pigment), thickened-rim bowls, and heavy bowls with greatly bolstered rims.

Although "false rocker-stamping" is dominant, there is some bold plain rocker-stamping; zoned plain rocker and shell-back rocker are very rare.

In Camaño Coarse, there is a further increase in tecomate thickness and in the frequency and degree of coarseness in brushing; interior-finger-punching in these is new. Composite incensarios, the form of which is not perfectly known, appear for this type. However, a large fragment of three-pronged incensario in a plain ware is known for Chicharras.

Hollow, white-slipped figurines, often with white-black firing, are known from fragments. But Chicharras produced the first solid figurines which seem to be Olmec; these are fine-paste and "white clear through." A few heads have vaguely Olmec features. The finest depicts a seated pregnant female, unfortunately headless. Other types were being made as well, including one which always shows a hunch-backed dwarf.

The artifact complex differs in no great way from that of Ojochi or Bajio, although two-footed metates are new. We also have the first celt, of a fine-grained greenish rock,

126

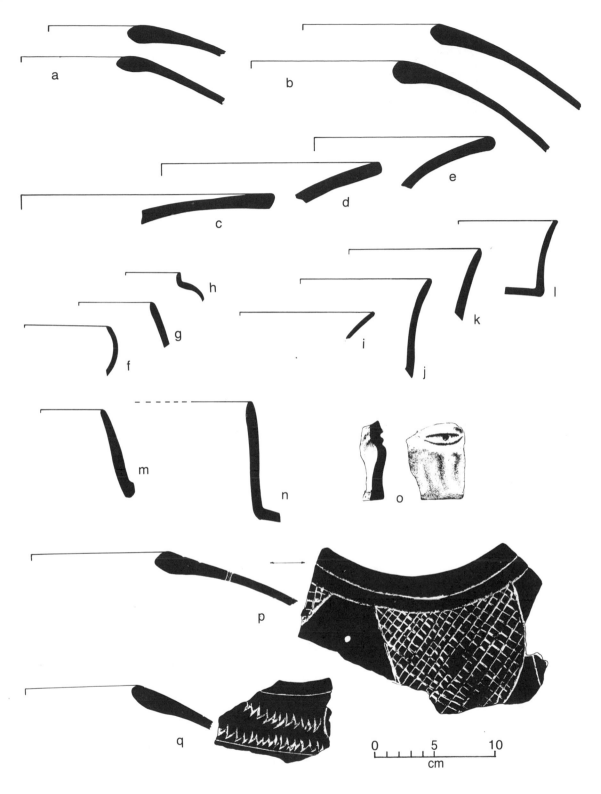

FIGURE 5-6. Chicharras phase, selected ceramics: *a–b*, Camaño Coarse; *c–e*, El Tigre White; *f–o*, Ixtepec White; *p–q*, Tatagapa Red.

FIGURE 5-7. Fragment of monument, Chicharras phase.

than 1200, and lasted until 900 B.C. During this span, most of the monuments were carved; the San Lorenzo site took on something of its present appearance (although most San Lorenzo phase mounds seem to have been demolished at a later date and used as fill); and population reached an all-time high that was not to be attained again until the Early Postclassic. Unusual engineering projects were carried out, such as the system of stone drains on the west side of San Lorenzo and the complex of artificial ponds which seem to have been controlled by such drains.

The ceramic markers for the phase are two pottery types which can only be called Olmec. Calzadas Carved largely consists of flat-bottomed bowls with outslanting or nearly vertical sides; the rims may be plain, bolstered on the exterior, or slightly everted. Exteriors were carved when leather-hard in broad gouges with sharp edges, the ends of the gouges either squared, or curved and tapered to resemble claws. The motifs on Calzadas Carved vessels show familiar Olmec elements like crossed-bands, jaguar-paw-wing, flame brows, and fire-serpent jaws. Red hematite once filled the gouges and roughened areas associated with them. Calzadas Carved varies from tan to grey to black in color, with some white-rimming through differential firing.

The other pottery marker is Limon Carved-Incised. In shapes, color, and firing it is identical with Calzadas Carved, but the grooved or incised designs are pretty much restricted to the opposed rotated scrolls known as the *ilhuitl* motif.

I suspect that these decorative modes and probably even the types themselves have a very wide distribution among Olmec-influenced sites from the latter part of the Early Formative. In particular, pottery decorated like Calzadas Carved is known for Cuadros on the Pacific Coast (Coe and Flannery 1967: Fig. 39a, b), in the San Jose phase of Oaxaca (Flannery, personal communication), and at Tlatilco and Las Bocas in the Central Highlands (M. Coe 1965c: Figs. 22–34); clos-

and a green stone pendant. A lucky chance of preservation of bone material in the otherwise acid soils of San Lorenzo has produced an awl and a piece of cut turtle carapace.

The real question for Chicharras, granted its status as a foreshadower of the San Lorenzo phase, is whether these people were carving stone monuments. The answer is an unequivocal "yes." Basalt chips and lumps occur throughout Chicharras levels, though this is not conclusive. However, in a buried Chicharras deposit in the Group D Ridge, we hit upon a basalt fragment (Fig. 5-7), which must have been broken from a monument, depicting a portion of a rope-like ornament exactly like those which appear on the helmets of San Lorenzo Monuments 3 and 4, both colossal heads. The outer surface of the original sculpture has been covered with red hematite. Whatever the form of the original monument, my own feeling is that the origins of the Olmec sculptural style will be found to be at least as early as Chicharras.

### The San Lorenzo Phase

A preliminary description of the San Lorenzo phase and its dating has already appeared (Coe, Diehl, and Stuiver 1967; M. Coe 1968); since this phase marks the height of Olmec civilization in the area, the subject is of some importance. Additional radiocarbon dates from San Lorenzo itself suggest that the phase began about 1150 B.C., rather

128

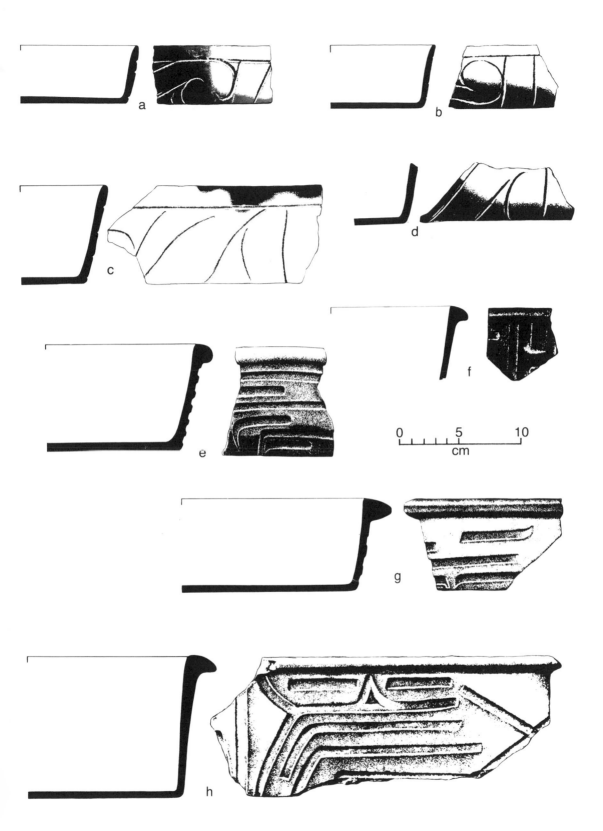

FIGURE 5-8. San Lorenzo phase, diagnostic ceramics: *a–d*, Limon Carved-Incised; *e–h*, Calzadas Carved.

er to home, it is well represented at El Tra-piche in central Veracruz (García Payón 1966: Pl. 23, 4–5; Pls. 24, 25). It should also be pointed out that decoration similar to that on Calzadas Carved is found on Monuments 6 and 7 at San Lorenzo, Monument 2 at Po-trero Nuevo, Altar I at La Venta, and on a monument from Laguna de los Cerros (M. Coe 1965c: Fig. 8), indicating a close identifi-cation with Olmec ceremonial life.

Most of the other pottery types of the San Lorenzo phase are a continuation of those known for Chicharras, but there are minor changes of mode and popularity among them. In Camaño Coarse, for instance, there is some stick-gouging in patterns like those known for Guamuchal Brushed of the Cua-dros phase (Coe and Flannery 1967: 28–30); the fine-paste, white-black types show a great decrease in frequency, with the coarser-paste types rising.

Not only Olmec pottery, but unequivocally Olmec figurines (Fig. 5-9) are common in San Lorenzo phase refuse. The best of these are fine-white paste, either solid or hollow, often retouched with red pigment, and depict men and women as well as the typical baby-faces. Other Olmec figurines are fashioned from a coarse, orange-brown paste, or a medium buff paste; many are seated tailor fashion and in stance and costume recall the monuments. Certain solid figurines are definitely ball-players, with heavy belts, and wear concave objects on the chest; they are usually daubed with asphalt and stand up by means of a sup-port at the back. Closely related to them are grotesque figurine heads, often with asphalt decoration, sometimes depicting the so-called one-eyed god, and it is entirely possi-ble that these are actually the heads for the ballplayers.

The artifact complex is rich and varied. In bone, we have a needle, an antler-tine husker, and bone tubes. Two-footed metates, plano-convex manos, and stone bowls of basalt are characteristic, as well as a kind of bowl with shallow, pecked depression of un-known use. Small sandstone slabs were used for lapidary work and for grinding hematite

pigment, which was brought in in quantity. Other mineral imports were asphalt, mica, and some serpentine (no jade is known for San Lorenzo). Ilmenite, magnetite, and hematite artifacts are particularly important, in the form of multidrilled beads and mir-rors, at least one of which was concave. A magnetite sliver with a groove running down one surface could easily have acted as a com-pass if floated on water by means of balsa wood in a gourd bowl; detailed experiments on this artifact are described by John B. Carl-son (1975).

In the obsidian and chipped stone indus-try, prismatic blades appear for the first time, as well as scrapers. Other innovations are projectile points, both flint and obsidian, of Shumla and Tlatilco types.

It was found possible to divide San Lo-renzo into A and B subphases. San Lorenzo A has all the things described above. To these, San Lorenzo B adds many new ele-ments. There is a great increase in soft-paste orange ware and in grey bowls with widely everted rims; scored rather than brushed tecomates appear; and there are many sherds from thick, mortar-like vessels of unknown function. Most significant, San Lorenzo B shows much greater involvement with other regions in Mesoamerica, most likely through increased trade contacts necessitated by the sharp production rise in local industries. Several new types of projectile points are in-troduced, and there is an influx of exotic ob-sidians, such as green, mottled red, and brown, some of which probably originated in the Central Highlands. We discovered not only extensive workshop areas for obsidian and brown flint, but also evidence for a stepped-up lapidary industry, which pro-duced ear spools and beads of serpentine, schist, and other exotic materials. In fact in San Lorenzo B refuse there is much more serpentine and schist than before.

In line with this new cosmopolitanism, for-eign figurine types appear, some of them with features vaguely reminiscent of Type C heads from the Valley of Mexico.

130

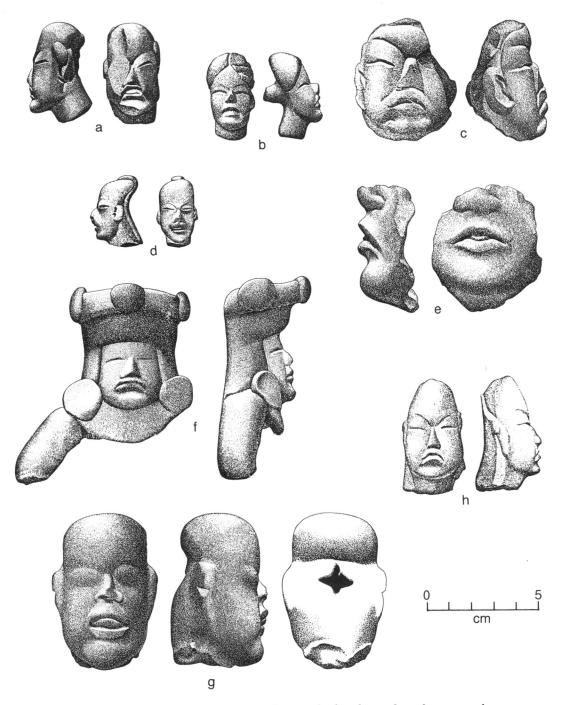

FIGURE 5-9. Olmec-style figurines, San Lorenzo phase: *a*, *b*, *d*, and *g* are fine white paste, the rest coarse orange. Scale in cms.

## The Nacaste Phase

The Nacaste phase saw no major formal constructional activity at San Lorenzo that we can detect, though house mounds were built on the Northwest Ridge, and there was a major domestic settlement in the southern part of Tenochtitlan. Nevertheless, there is some evidence that the building up of the ridges enclosing the monuments, sometimes with the addition of long, low mounds on top, was the work of what may be presumed to be Nacaste invaders.

With Nacaste there is a virtual disappearance of all previous pottery types except the coarse tecomates and soft orange ware, and a replacement of them with several kinds of very hard pottery fired at much higher temperatures (Fig. 5-10). One of these types, Camalote White, has a poor white slip on one surface, while the other type (Tacamichapa Hard) is unslipped. The obvious affiliation of this pottery is with initial Middle Formative phases such as Chiapa II or Dili (Dixon 1959), Conchas I (M. Coe 1961a), and Guadalupe (Flannery 1968b); accordingly, a dating of 900 to around 700 B.C. is suggested. Single and double-line breaks are found incised on rims of flat-bottomed bowls with outslanting sides, and there are cuspidors with thickened and sometimes everted rims, below which are incised parallel diagonals on vertical zones. Large tecomates may be very heavy and have bold freehand incising combined with scraped-away bands; the thinner Camaño Coarse specimens occasionally have small horizontal handles combined with interior finger-punching, as in Chiapa II (Dixon 1959: Fig. 54a, b).

This disappearance of older Olmec patterns can also be seen in Nacaste figurines, which have the large, punched eyes characteristic of the Middle Formative in southern Mesoamerica and show no Olmec features (Fig. 5-11). Nevertheless, some Olmec influence is implied by a few of the stone artifacts, perhaps reflecting the augmented importance of La Venta as a bastion of Olmec culture. One of these pieces is a tiny green

stone pendant incised with the face of a were-jaguar God II in the scheme of P. David Joralemon (1971). Another is a fragmentary serpentine "stiletto." Actually, some continuity of population from San Lorenzo times is suggested not only by the survival of the culinary pottery types but also by the artifact complex, which is very similar to that of the San Lorenzo B subphase. For instance, the same lapidary industry with the same tools occurs within Nacaste, including the related importation of much serpentine and green schist. Green and mottled red obsidians were also being brought in, as well as brown flint and small iron-ore mirrors. A final continuity is the presence of stone projectile points, including the Tortugas, Coxcatlan, and Garyito types.

## The Palangana Phase

There must be a hiatus between Nacaste and the Palangana phase which replaces it, since all of the Palangana pottery complex is completely new. Stylistic considerations lead me to equate Palangana with Chiapa IV or Francesa (Agrinier 1964:10–33), with a time range of perhaps 600 to 400 B.C., i.e., toward the end of the Middle Formative.

The Palangana reoccupation was principally concerned with the central part of the San Lorenzo site, where all previous inhabitants must have concentrated their ceremonial activity; unfortunately, only a part of the Central Group itself is Palangana in date, but this includes especially the four-sided court flanked with mounds, lying just northwest of the principal mound, which we have called the Palangana and believe to have been a ballcourt, probably the earliest known for Mesoamerica.

Palangana pottery (Fig. 5-12) is identical with much of that from the stratigraphic tests made by Drucker at La Venta (P. Drucker 1952: Fig. 34a, b; Fig. 38f; Pl. 20a), as well as with some of the ceramics of Tres Zapotes (P. Drucker 1943: Figs. 20, 22, 23). Thus, the reoccupation could have come from either area. Of overwhelming frequency are open,

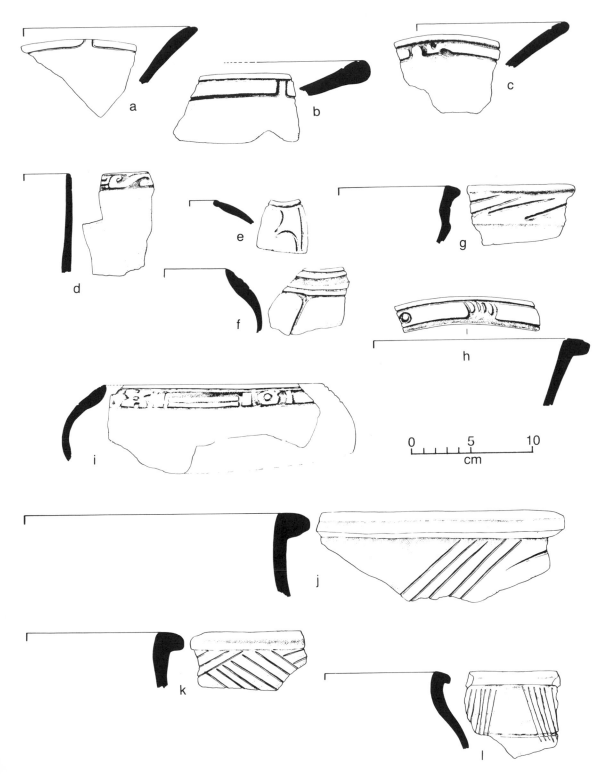

FIGURE 5-10. Nacaste phase ceramics: *a–i*, Camalote White; *j–l*, Tacamichapa Hard.

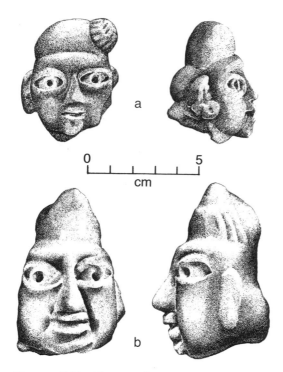

a

0        5
└─┴─┴─┴─┴─┘
cm

b

FIGURE 5-11. Nacaste phase figurines.

composite-silhouette bowls in tan, brown, or black; incising occurs on the angled zone of the exterior, usually zones of diagonal parallel lines enclosing areas outlined by sigmoid curves. Rim interiors sometimes have single, double, and triple lines with superior rather than inferior "breaks." Rocker-stamping, white-rimming, and other unusual forms of decoration are absent.

The interesting find of one Mars Orange trade sherd suggests a connection with the Maya Lowlands during the Mamom phase; I have found several other Mars Orange sherds in Drucker's La Venta material (now at the U.S. National Museum).

There is an impoverishment of the artifact complex, although serpentine ornaments and plaques are present. One green schist mask-like fragment recalls the Central Highlands or Guerrero more than it does Veracruz, while a tiny rock crystal fragment recalls the offerings of La Venta. Projectile points were still in use, one example resembling the Shumla type. The only known sculpture consists of tiny, crude turtle effigies of basalt.

Most Palangana figurines are solid, female, with peculiar triple-punched eyes. However, a few definitely Olmec heads, not like those of San Lorenzo, were recovered, suggesting once again the connections with La Venta.

## The Remplas Phase

A recent examination of some ceramic material from San Lorenzo Tenochtitlan shows that there is an additional cultural phase present in the area, which has been named Remplas.

Remplas pottery so far is confined to the site of Tenochtitlan. An excavation made by Francisco Beverido in 1966 in one of the small mound plazas of that site had produced pottery that I had recognized as Formative, but different from any of the Formative complexes known to me thus far. Because the amount of diagnostic material was so little, I set it aside for further study.

However, I have gone through all of the pottery excavated by Drucker in the 1946 season at San Lorenzo Tenochtitlan. Trenches 11 and 12, although nonstratigraphic, produced quantities of the same Formative material, along with Villa Alta and San Lorenzo sherds that could be easily factored out. These two trenches were cut into the north plaza of the principal mound group at the site. Thus, there is now sufficient material for a definition of Remplas.

Most characteristic of Remplas is a type which I am calling Ixpuchuapa Black Incised. While there is one necked jar, forms are mainly composite-silhouette bowls with S-angles. The surface is polished black. Decoration is pure incision, emphasizing inverted triangles filled with parallel diagonals, often with a line extending beyond the triangle apex; single or multiple horizontal rows of scalloping; diagonal parallel lines; and curvilinear areas filled with crosshatching. Red pigment has sometimes been rubbed into the lines.

There is also a coarse ware, confined to necked jars and tecomates. The temper is coarse, rounded sand, and firing tempera-

134

FIGURE 5-12. Palangana phase ceramics, all Macayas Tan-to-Black.

tures were probably quite low. The surface is smoothed, but rather bumpy and with a peculiar "leathery" feeling to the touch. Some jar necks have a horizontal rib at the rim which is painted red.

Red-slipped ware also occurs, apparently only in the form of squat, necked jars. The slip may be over the entire exterior, but also may be restricted to the lower body. There is crude post-slip incising in parallel lines, occasionally alternating with dashed lines. The overall texture and appearance of this ware is like that of coarse ware.

The only other ware identified as Remplas is white-rimmed black, quite well made. Some of this has almost chalky-white rims, while on some other examples the rimming is quite orange in color.

As for artifacts, only a single figurine body—solid, of a pregnant female—has been identified as Remplas.

The decorated pottery bears some resemblance to that of the Palangana phase, but may be easily distinguished from it. Ixpuchuapa Black Incised is much closer to the so-called *cerámica esgrafiada* from El Trapiche (García Payón 1966: Pls. 14, 15), which is undoubtedly Late Formative in date. It is also similar in its decorative motifs—but not in form—to some pottery which I have placed in a Cerro de las Mesas II phase and in a Tres Zapotes II phase—both with a possible Protoclassic affiliation (M. Coe 1965a: Figs. 14a, b, 17). Although it is difficult to be very exact about its placement, due to the limited material for study, I believe that Remplas is Late Formative, about equivalent in time to Guanacaste (Chiapa V), and it may follow directly on the heels of the Palangana phase.

Thus, there is no Late Formative hiatus, at least at Tenochtitlan, and it is possible that part of the mound complex at that site was constructed in Remplas times.

### The Villa Alta Phase

For some unknown reason, the entire San Lorenzo Tenochtitlan area was abandoned to the forest after the close of the Remplas phase and continued in that condition for centuries. About 900 A.D., following the usual correlations, a great wave of people came in to recolonize it, in the Early Postclassic phase called Villa Alta. Since practically all villages along the Rio Chiquito today are Nahuat-speaking, it is possible that the language of Villa Alta times was also Nahuat.

The ceramic complex (Fig. 5-13) is totally dominated by Campamento Fine Orange, which somewhat resembles X Fine Orange. This ware, which intergrades with a thin, fine grey pottery, usually centers upon flat-bottomed bowls with composite silhouettes and everted rims, supported by bulbous or slab-shaped hollow feet. It is much worn, but occasionally a red slip can be detected. This is accompanied by a small amount of Tohil Plumbate. Incensarios, both spiked and ladle, are very frequent.

Mold-made spindle whorls, mold-made figurines, hollow earspools, double-chambered whistles, and a number of other pottery artifacts were fashioned from the same fine orange clay (Fig. 5-14). These people picked up and reused many artifacts from earlier occupations—especially mirror fragments—but there are some Villa Alta specializations in stone tools, such as nutstones, the use of which can be inferred from the many finds of charred palm nuts in household debris. The obsidian industry, which utilized a good deal of green Pachuca obsidian as well as the usual grey variety, focused on blade production from cores which often had the ground striking platform typical of the Postclassic; from these blades they fashioned small gravers which occasionally resemble the well-known Tula points.

The massiveness of this occupation cannot be overrated. Not only was the principal mound at San Lorenzo a Villa Alta product, but major parts of Tenochtitlan were constructed by these people. At times, as in the latter site, Villa Alta planners took advantage of earlier, Olmec arrangements to construct their temples, so that a place like Tenochtitlan took on the linear appearance of bona

136

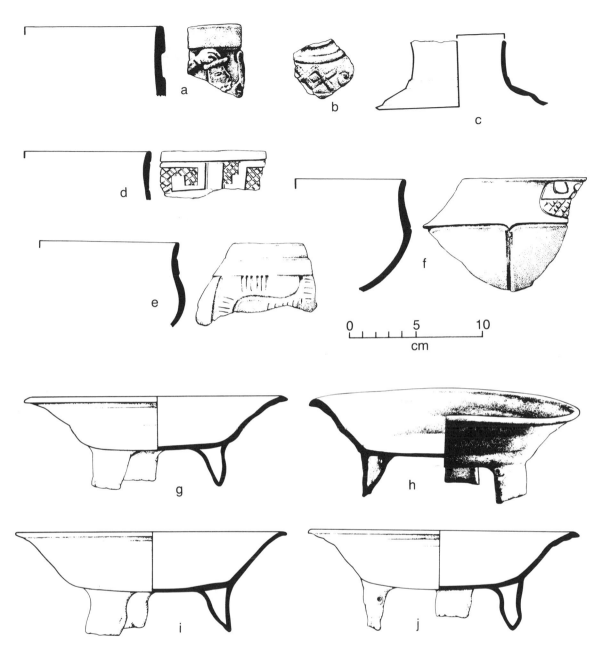

FIGURE 5-13. Villa Alta phase, selected ceramics: *a–b, d–f,* incised, carved, and mold-made sherds in Campamento Fine Orange and Zapote Fine Orange-to-Gray; *e,* Tohil Plumbate; *g–j,* Campamento Fine Orange.

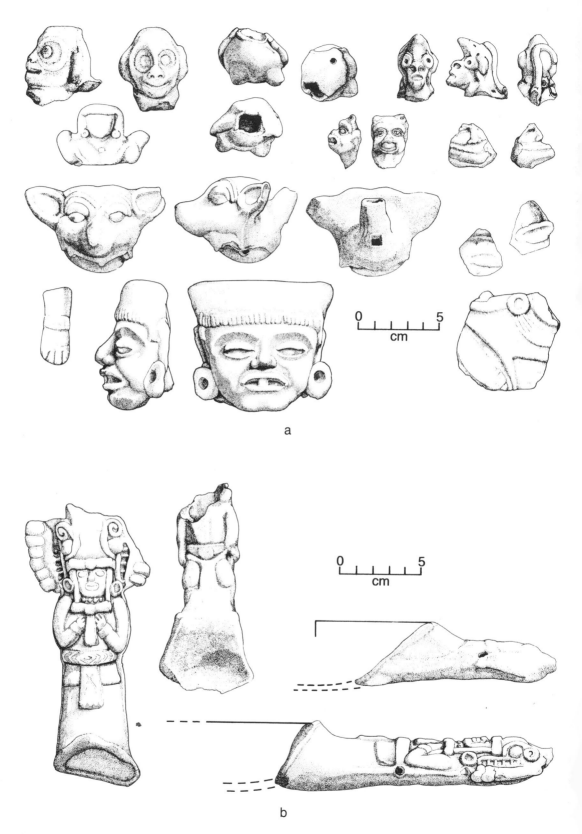

a

b

FIGURE 5-14. Pottery artifacts, Villa Alta phase: *a*, figurines; *b*, hollow handles for ladle censers.

138

fide Olmec centers like La Venta. Luckily for us, the major Villa Alta occupation of·San Lorenzo consists of only a thin veneer of debris over earlier strata. During the Villa Alta phase, some great pits were dug down into older plazas for the placement of offerings (including Campamento Fine Orange vessels and pyrite-encrusted mirrors), but we do not yet know the full extent of Villa Alta construction at Tenochtitlan.

## MONUMENTS
### Chronology

One of the major goals of the Yale 1966–1968 expedition was to date the monuments of San Lorenzo Tenochtitlan and to associate them with one or more cultural phases. It was therefore necessary to discover them in situ, which would have been impossible if all had been pushed into ravines by invaders. However, a lucky discovery during the 1967 season made it possible to place a *terminus ad quem* on their manufacture (M. Coe 1967). A line of intentionally buried monuments was found in the Group D Ridge, laid out across the ridge in a north-south direction over a specially prepared floor (Fig. 5-15); all of the monuments had been mutilated or destroyed before being so placed. Since the fill surrounding and covering the monuments contained no sherds later than San Lorenzo B, and since the stratum immediately above the fill contained Nacaste materials, it can be concluded that this act of destruction had occurred at the very end of San Lorenzo B, around 900 B.C. Similar lines are found elsewhere in the Group D Ridge. In fact, almost every monument dug by us or INAH had identical stratigraphic associations. Thus, practically all of the monuments of San Lorenzo Tenochtitlan predate 900 B.C., and stylistic similarities between the monuments on the one hand, and pottery and figurines, on the other, lead us to believe that most of them were carved in·the San Lorenzo phase.

Certain of the San Lorenzo monuments, however, may actually be earlier. The find of a basalt fragment showing parallel ropes in a Chicharras stratum on the Group D Ridge indicates that colossal heads may already have been manufactured in the Chicharras phase. Monument 42 of San Lorenzo (Fig. 5-16) was found in a very early San Lorenzo A stratum on the Northwest Ridge; this is a fragmentary column with a very simple relief carving of an arm. In my opinion, it bears a strong stylistic resemblance to Monument 41 (Fig. 5-17), a large column with a relief figure of a were-jaguar with one arm held by an oversize left hand. Both may well be anterior to the full-fledged Olmec style. Another relief figure which may be equally ancient is Monument 21 at San Lorenzo, with San Lorenzo A stratigraphic associations; this is a running dog or coyote in an archaic style.

### Categories

Thus far, 64 monuments have been discovered at San Lorenzo, 4 at or near Potrero Nuevo, and 6 at Tenochtitlan. We have treated as "monuments" all carved stones, no matter how fragmentary, which are not obviously utilitarian artifacts or which were treated by the destroyers of San Lorenzo as monuments, i.e., by being placed in lines with other monuments. There is reason to believe that very few of them, as discovered, were in their original positions.

In classifying these monuments, we have followed the categories defined by C. William Clewlow, Jr. (1974), with some modifications. The most obvious of these categories is that of the colossal heads (Fig. 5-18). There are 8 of these known for San Lorenzo, plus several other fragments which probably represent destroyed heads. There is general agreement among scholars that they are portraits of Olmec rulers of the San Lorenzo phase, especially as the helmet-like headgear for each bears distinctive insignia, and the faces exhibit no supernatural traits. Almost as impressive are the "altars," a misnamed category since David C. Grove (1973) has demonstrated that these table-top blocks were more likely thrones for the rulers. Two examples from San Lorenzo show on the

139

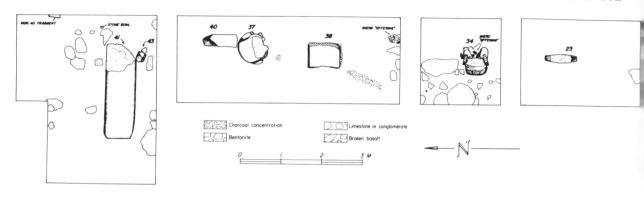

FIGURE 5-15. Line of buried monuments in Group D Ridge, San Lorenzo.

front side rulers seated within niches; in the case of Monument 14, the ruler holds a rope binding two captive figures on the side, and on Monument 20 (Fig. 5-19), he bears a were-jaguar baby in his arms, demonstrating respectively the Olmec themes of conquest and descent.

Similarly striking sculptures in other categories were excavated in the 1966–1968 campaign. Monument 34 (Fig. 5-20), found in the north-south alignment within the Group D Ridge, is a decapitated, half-kneeling figure which once had movable arms, now lost; it must have been a ballplayer. One of the very few stelae known for San Lorenzo is Monument 30 (Fig. 5-21), with a low-relief figure of a were-jaguar "dragon," also from the Group D Ridge. Those interested in knowing the full range of the San Lorenzo Tenochtitlan sculptural tradition should consult Coe and Diehl 1980 or the fine catalogue of Olmec monuments by Beatriz de la Fuente (1973).

The studies of Olmec iconography by Joralemon (1971, 1976) make it clear that many deities are represented in this sculptural art. One of his best-defined categories is that of God IV, whom both he and I consider the Olmec rain god. It is significant that Monument 52 (Fig. 5-22), an excellent example of God IV, was found buried at the head of the drain system and is hollowed out at the back like a trough stone. We were also able to establish that Stirling had encountered Monument 9, a hollowed-out duck figure with water symbols, at the lower terminus of the drain, and that a drain stone would fit perfectly into a U-shaped opening on one side of the duck.

## Magnetometry

During the 1968 season, Froelich G. Rainey of the University Museum (University of Pennsylvania) suggested that the cesium magnetometer might be employed to prospect for additional buried monuments at San Lorenzo, and a joint project was carried out with us after it was determined that the monuments were quite magnetic, and the surrounding matrix hardly magnetic at all. During this and the next season, the instrument was used in both "search" and "survey" modes, the latter producing a contour map of magnetic anomalies over most of the San Lorenzo surface (Breiner and Coe 1972). The project was a resounding success, with a number of archaeologically significant new sculptures discovered both by our expedition (including Monument 52) and by the incoming INAH team.

## Sources and Transport

Only one monument from San Lorenzo Tenochtitlan (Monument 16, a chlorite schist altar probably of Nacaste date) is not made of basalt. The remainder, as determined by a

FIGURE 5 16. Monument 42, San Lorenzo.

FIGURE 5-17. Monument 41, San Lorenzo.

petrographic analysis carried out by Louis Fernandez, are of Cerro Cintepec basalt, from an outwash fan on the sides of a volcano in the Tuxtla Mountains. The technical expertise required to get these stones from their source to the San Lorenzo plateau must have been mind-boggling. They would have to have been dragged down to the nearest navigable stream or river, loaded on very large rafts, and perhaps even floated out to sea before being poled up the Rio Coatzacoalcos. There is evidence from aerial photographs that the latter flowed much closer to the plateau than it does today, but it is still clear that monuments weighing in some cases over 20 tons would have to have been pulled on rollers through a vertical distance of some 50 m. Almost certainly this involved the coerced or inveigled labor of hundreds or perhaps even thousands of laborers.

We never found any evidence that the monuments had been fashioned in the San

Lorenzo Tenochtitlan area: no waste chips, no debitage, no hammering or pounding tools sufficient to have done the job. The ancient atelier for these Olmec sculptures is yet to be discovered, probably at the base of the Tuxtla range. Surely it would have been more economical to have removed as much weight from the stones as possible before their transport.

*Mutilation and Destruction*

Perhaps just as awe-inspiring as the creation and transport of these monuments is their mutilation and destruction at the close of the

141

FIGURE 5-18. Monument 17, San Lorenzo, one of the smaller colossal heads from this site (1.67 m high).

San Lorenzo phase, prior to their intentional burial. This includes fracture, the breaking away of huge pieces of the sculptures, particularly heads from figures; slotting, the careful cutting out of oblong compartments in the surface; pounding, especially of facial features; pitting, usually in pairs with nipple-like cavities at the bottom, producing what we have called "negative breasts"; and sharpening grooves. Very few of the Olmec sculptures of San Lorenzo Tenochtitlan are free from such disfiguration, surely a mark of the iconoclastic fury which was visited upon these symbols of the Olmec elite at the end of the Early Formative.

## ECOLOGY AND THE RISE OF THE SAN LORENZO OLMEC

Hand-in-hand with the archaeological research carried out by the Yale expedition went a fine-scale ecological analysis of the San Lorenzo Tenochtitlan environment, taking a 75 sq km area as a sample (M. Coe

FIGURE 5-19. Monument 20, an "altar" with a figure in a niche holding a were-jaguar baby.

142

1974). We conducted a very detailed survey of modern-day agricultural, hunting, and fishing practices in the zone, backed up by photogrammetric mapping. At the same time, we were able to establish through identification of faunal and macrofloral remains that the modern San Lorenzo Tenochtitlan environment is not very different from that of 3,000 years ago. Thus, what we have found out about present-day human adaptations is directly applicable to the Olmec situation.

The key to the understanding of peasant life along the middle Coatzacoalcos is the annual rise and fall of the rivers. As described previously, when the really heavy rains of the so-called wet season arrive, in June, the rivers and streams swell and overflow their banks, and the local landscape becomes a world afloat. At this time, only the land above the 28 m contour can be cultivated. Thus, in the higher elevations, there are two crops a year, thanks to the winter mists and rains. On the other hand, the local villagers are well aware that the best soils (*tierra de primera*) are those that lie along the annually inundated river levees, in spite of the fact that these yield crops only in the dry season when the water level drops. The uplands were communally owned in our time, but the prized river levee lands, with huge yields of corn, tended to be privately held. (Today, with the conversion of the entire area to a cattle economy, none of the land is communally owned.)

We were able to observe directly a process of increasing inequality based upon access to these prized lands which strikingly confirms Robert Carneiro's 1970 "circumscription theory" for the origin of the pristine state. According to Carneiro, coercion through military conflict over resources limited by geographical or social boundaries is the only valid causal factor in the rise of highly stratified societies or states. He describes the ethnohistoric situation along the middle Amazon, where stratified chiefdoms of some complexity arose as a result of rivalries to control primarily the rich levee lands along

FIGURE 5-20. Monument 34, San Lorenzo, a figure which once had movable arms, of either wood or stone.

FIGURE 5-21. Monument 30, San Lorenzo.

143

FIGURE 5-22. Monument 52, San Lorenzo, representing God IV in the Olmec pantheon.

the river, and secondarily the fish and reptile resources of the river itself. In the last twenty years, in the San Lorenzo Tenochtitlan area, one ambitious family in an otherwise egalitarian society has managed to consolidate its economic, political, and social control of the whole area through systematic aquisition of the levee lands, eventually attaining the not undeserved title of *caciques* ("bosses").

It would be difficult if not impossible to fully document such a process of increasing social and economic inequality in the time period just prior to the San Lorenzo phase—Chicharras—but the Carneiro theory seems to fit most parsimoniously with the known facts. Of course, the ancient Olmec did not

live by corn alone, and rich protein resources were available from the fish and turtles which abound in the rivers, streams, and ox-bow lakes and ponds. Faunal analysis by Elizabeth S. Wing has shown that snook and turtles were the major sources of animal protein, and abundant cannibalized human remains indicate that captives probably also played their part in the Olmec food chain. At any rate, this was an environment not unlike that of the ancient Nile Valley, with similar possibilities for the rise of a complex state.

## MESOAMERICA AND THE SAN LORENZO OLMEC

The San Lorenzo Olmec were by no means isolated within their Coatzacoalcos realm. The Olmec elite of San Lorenzo Tenochtitlan needed raw materials from elsewhere to support their religious, sociopolitical, and economic needs, and were able to export desired products in return. William L. Rathje (1971) has developed a model that is probably applicable to this process: in the absence of desired and necessary raw materials (and there are few in the Olmec heartland), crystallizing elites will develop prestige items that can be exported to the "boondocks" for the materials which they desperately need. He therefore views the rise of the lowland state as a response to resource deprivation rather than to riches.

In a way, the hypothesis put forward by Kent Flannery (1968b) is a corollary of Rathje's: diffusion of Olmec traits and even objects from the heartland to Oaxaca and the Central Mexican Highlands may have been a result not of military conquest and religious conversion, but of emulation by extra-Olmec elites of a more prestigious sociopolitical entity, expressed in trade networks which involved such items as iron-ore mirrors (said to have been produced in the Valley of Oaxaca). This hypothesis more or less rules out the Olmec, whoever they may have been, as a culture-producing, culture-diffusing entity in Mesoamerica.

The archaeological evidence cannot yet an-

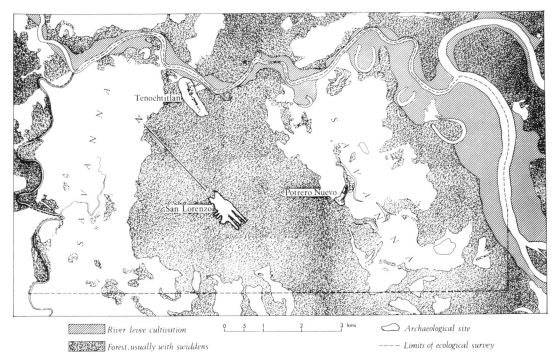

River levee cultivation     0   .5   1    2     3 kms     Archaeological site

Forest, usually with swiddens                   ---- Limits of ecological survey

FIGURE 5-23. Distribution of microenvironments in the San Lorenzo Tenochtitlan survey area.

swer these questions. Certainly the San Lorenzo Olmec needed basalt in quantity, for monuments, drain stones, and metates and manos, and surely they were able to control the Cerro Cintepec source from which this substance came. Bitumen, red hematite, and yellow ocher were available within the Coatzacoalcos drainage, and thus trade relationships need not be invoked for these. But schist, serpentine, and iron ore (for mirrors and other elite artifacts) would have to have come from metamorphic regions of southern Mesoamerica, especially the Isthmus of Tehuantepec and nearby areas of Oaxaca.

Trace element analysis has revealed the extent to which the San Lorenzo Olmec were dependent upon distant sources of obsidian, a substance as vital to their tool kit as steel is to ours (Cobean et al. 1971). There is no naturally occurring obsidian anywhere within the Olmec heartland, so all would have had to be imported. As early as Ojochi times, four different sources were being exploited, including the Guadalupe Victoria flow of the

Orizaba region of Veracruz and the great El Chayal outcrop in Guatemala (which eventually became the prime Classic Maya fount of this material). The total number of separate obsidian quarries increased until San Lorenzo B times, when it is clear that the Olmec elite commanded a trading or procurement network covering much of Mesoamerica, including the Valley of Mexico and Teotihuacan.

What did they send in the other direction? According to the Rathje hypothesis they would have sent prestige items, and it is true that Calzadas Carved and perhaps Limon Carved-Incised pottery was widely distributed through many parts of Mesoamerica on the 1150–900 B.C. time level, all replete with Olmec iconographic significance. Quite probably most of the large, hollow, white-slipped "baby" figurines found at Tlatilco, Las Bocas, Tlapacoya, and other Olmec-influenced sites in highland Mexico were actually manufactured at San Lorenzo. Of perishable items, one can only guess at painted

145

textiles, books, wooden "idols," and other paraphernalia suitable for Olmec worship.

The greatest single puzzle, which might be solved by future excavation, is the nature of San Lorenzo's involvement with other sites in the Olmec heartland. First, was La Venta the politico-religious successor to San Lorenzo Tenochtitlan, and did it have something to do with the latter's demise about 900 B.C.? Second, what was the relationship between San Lorenzo and Laguna de los Cerros, a site of equal size, replete with monuments, and apparently of the same age (Bove 1978)? Were San Lorenzo and this site dual capitals, in an ancient Mesoamerican tradition (i.e., Tula and Chichen Itza, or Teotihuacan and Cholula)? And lastly, how many other contemporary ceremonial and civic centers were there in the Olmec heartland during San Lorenzo times and later, and how was San Lorenzo involved with these? Increasing land clearance for sugar cane and cattle raising has revealed a number of obviously Olmec sites which can be seen from the air, particularly near the Tuxtla Mountains (Francisco Beverido, personal communication), and these may prove to contain answers to old questions as well as new puzzles for *olmequista* archaeologists.

NOTE

1. The section on archaeological sequence and chronology is an updated and expanded version of a paper originally published in the University of California Archaeological Research Facility Series.

# 6. Ecological Adaptation in the Basin of Mexico: 23,000 B.C. to the Present

WILLIAM T. SANDERS

## INTRODUCTION

THIS CHAPTER is a summary of the results of the Basin of Mexico Settlement Survey Project. It is also a summary of a recent book, *The Basin of Mexico: Ecological Processes and the Evolution of a Civilization* (Sanders, Parsons, and Santley 1979), which presents a much more detailed description of the project. The book is structured in terms of four levels in the research process—methodology; data presentation on the natural environment and the settlement history; a more analytical treatment of the settlement data, involving a reconstruction of changing ecological relationships through time; and a theoretical section on the broad implications of the project, in terms of anthropological theory as a whole. In this introductory section I will summarize the methodology, and the rest of the chapter will analyze linkages between settlement patterns, population history, resource exploitation, and sociopolitical evolution. I have eliminated the theoretical discussion which appears in the book version. For all of the topics treated in this brief summary the reader is referred to the more expanded discussion in the original study.

I designed the basic structure and objectives of the Basin of Mexico project in 1960, and they were then applied to the Teotihuacan Valley portion of the basin. The Teotihuacan Valley was surveyed under my direction in 1960–1964. This initial phase was particularly time-consuming, since most of the energy of the project was diverted into excavations, the purpose of which is discussed below. In 1966, Jeffrey R. Parsons, who had worked with the Teotihuacan Valley project as a graduate student, returned to the valley and surveyed a number of areas that had been overlooked in the original survey. Parsons then surveyed the Texcoco region in 1967, the Chalco region in 1969, the Xochimilco region in 1972, and the Zumpango region in 1973 (see Fig. 6-1). I returned to the area in 1972 to conduct a study of contemporary peasant agriculture in the Texcoco region. I completed the archaeological surveys of the Cuautitlan region during 1974 and the Temascalapa region in 1975. Richard E. Blanton, who had worked on Parson's Texcoco project, surveyed the Ixtapalapa region in 1969.

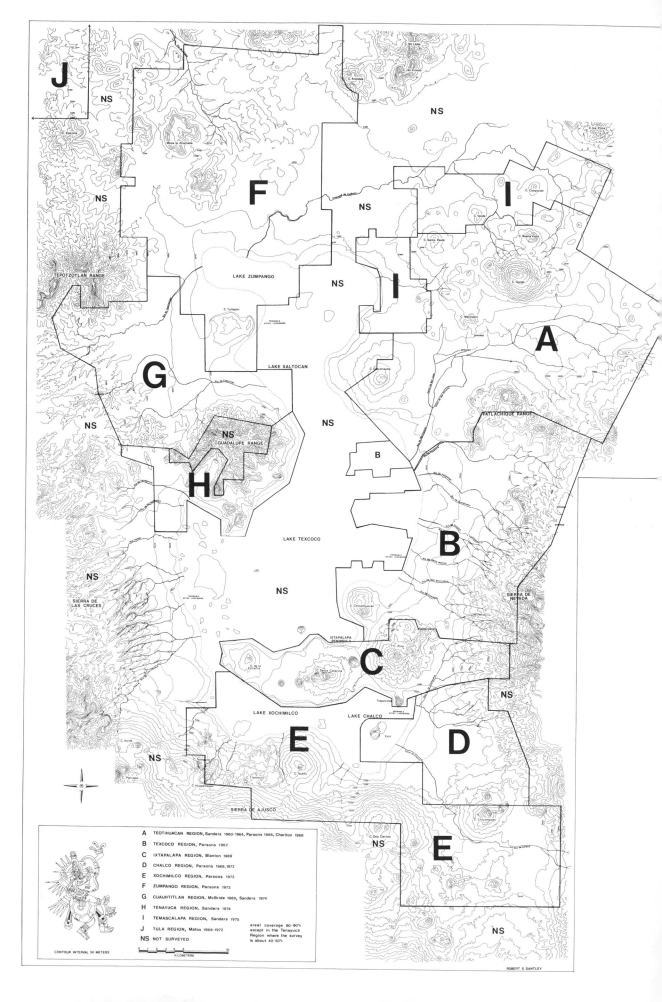

NS

**J**

C. Epazote

NS

Mesa la Ahumada

**F**

NS

TEPOTZOTLAN RANGE

LAKE ZUMPANGO

C. Tultepec

PROBABLE AZTEC LAKESHORE

LAKE XALTOCAN

**G**

NS

GUADALUPE RANGE

NS

**H**

NS

**I**

C. Coayucan

Verde

C. Santa Paula

C. Buena Vista

C. Gordo

C. Malinalco

SPRINGS

**A**

C. Chiconautla

PATLACHIQUE RANGE

**B**

las Lajas

las Cruces

C. Arandas

C. los Pitos

NS

NS

NS

**B**

PROBABLE AZTEC LAKESHORE

LAKE TEXCOCO

NS

SIERRA DE LAS CRUCES

PROBABLE AZTEC LAKESHORE

C. Chimalhuacan

SIERRA DE NEVADA

IXTAPALAPA PENINSULA

C. de la Estrella

C. Santa Catarina

**C**

C. Pino

Tlapacoya

NS

NS

C. Xictle

LAKE XOCHIMILCO

LAKE CHALCO

PROBABLE AZTEC LAKESHORE

**E**

Xico

**D**

C. Panzapa

C. Tlamaco

C. Teuhtli

C. Huixactepec

SIERRA DE AJUSCO

C. Chiconquiac

NS

C. Dos Cerros

**E**

NS

N

CONTOUR INTERVAL 50 METERS

0 1 2 3 4 5 10
KILOMETERS

A TEOTIHUACAN REGION, Sanders 1960-1964, Parsons 1966, Charlton 1968

B TEXCOCO REGION, Parsons 1967

C IXTAPALAPA REGION, Blanton 1969

D CHALCO REGION, Parsons 1969, 1972

E XOCHIMILCO REGION, Parsons 1972

F ZUMPANGO REGION, Parsons 1973

G CUAUHTITLAN REGION, McBride 1969, Sanders 1974

H TENAYUCA REGION, Sanders 1974

I TEMASCALAPA REGION, Sanders 1975

J TULA REGION, Matos 1968-1972

NS NOT SURVEYED

areal coverage 80-90%
except in the Tenayuca
Region where the survey
is about 40-50%

ROBERT S. SANTLEY

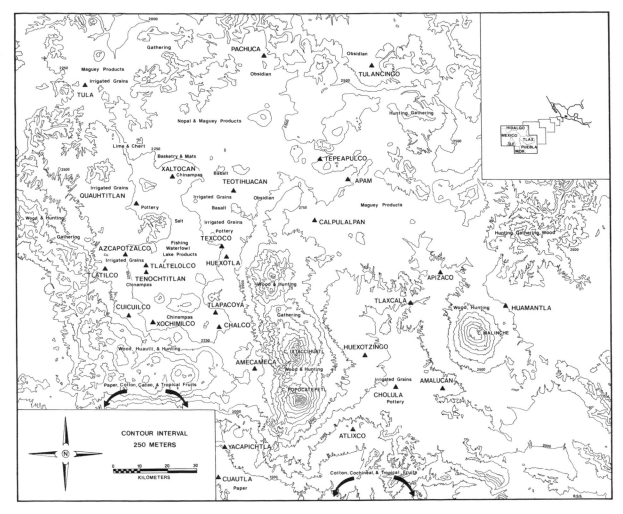

Figure 6-2. Central Mexican symbiotic region resource utilization. Reprinted from *The Basin of Mexico: Ecological Processes in the Evolution of a Civilization*. Copyright © 1979, by Academic Press, Inc.

Figure 6-1. Basin of Mexico: survey regions. Reprinted from *The Basin of Mexico: Ecological Processes in the Evolution of a Civilization*. Copyright © 1979, by Academic Press, Inc.

149

## Research Strategy

The primary research strategy was to conduct a 100 percent ground survey of all portions of the basin not covered by modern urban occupation, mapping the distribution of all Prehispanic remains. Black and white vertical aerial photographs, at a scale of 1:5,000, were used as a mapping technique. Visible divisions on the aerial photographs that reflected present-day cultural utilization of the landscape, such as house lots and agricultural fields, were examined as survey units. In areas of eroded, mostly hilly terrain, we either used natural features, such as *barrancas* or streams, as borders for our survey units, or arbitrarily divided up areas for such analysis. Prehispanic remains were plotted directly on the aerial photographs. We also recorded, using a formal schedule, all archaeological remains, primarily involving a subjective evaluation of the density of artifactual debris and a description of structures (which in this area consist primarily of earth and rock mounds). A qualitative scale was used to estimate the density of artifactual debris (primarily potsherds), ranging from scanty to heavy. We also recorded any unusual concentration of particular types of artifacts that might indicate specialized activities, differences in social status, or differentiation of structures into residential and other functions. Surface samples of sherds were taken to control the date of the occupation.

On the basis of these data, approximately 3,800 residential sites were defined, ranging in size from single-family hamlets to cities of over 100,000 inhabitants. In general, site borders were based upon a relatively continuous scatter of artifactual debris of a particular time component. This approach proved reasonably easy, with the exception of the Late Horizon, when rural settlement was dispersed and almost continuous over huge areas of the valley, making site definition almost impossible without more sophisticated statistical techniques of analysis (see the discussion below).

For a variety of reasons we did not actually achieve our 100 percent survey. Of the 7,000 sq km that make up the surface area of the basin, 1,000 sq km, consisting of high mountain slopes (which, on the basis of the sixteenth-century documentary literature and contemporary patterns of land utilization, were clearly not an agricultural resource), were not surveyed at all; 1,000 sq km occupied by the lakes were only partially surveyed, including those areas where, on the basis of sixteenth-century data, there were *chinampas* (floating gardens). This leaves an area of approximately 5,000 sq km. We actually surveyed about 3,500 sq km of this remaining area. Of the balance, about 500–600 sq km underlie contemporary Mexico City and its extensive suburbs, where surveys were impossible; and the remaining area includes small areas of alluvial plain, where, for a variety of reasons, surveys were impractical, and a large block of land in the northeast corner of the basin, where no surveys as yet have been conducted.

During the five years of the Teotihuacan Valley project much of our energy was devoted to excavations. There were a number of objectives in these excavations, all related essentially to problems encountered in the survey. First, we needed a much more refined relative chronology than that which was found in previously published studies. Most of these earlier studies were deficient, in that entire phases were undescribed, or only partially described, and, even in those cases, much of the existing chronology was based upon grave furniture. Second, we had virtually no information on rural or even urban domestic architecture for many of the phases, and hence needed excavation data to help us interpret the architectural remains.

Along with excavations, a number of intensive studies of the sixteenth-century literature were conducted, with two objectives: to flesh out our reconstruction of the Aztec or Late Horizon ecology and settlement, and to provide us with analogies for projection into the earlier phases.

Finally, data were collected on the contemporary cultural geography of the region, based on published studies plus follow-up studies that Thomas H. Charlton and I conducted during the course of the project (Charlton 1970a, 1970b). Palynological studies were conducted by Anton J. Kovar to ascertain possible patterns of change in the climate of the area (Kovar 1970).

## Data Analysis

A broad theoretical orientation for the project was the relationship between population pressure and sociocultural evolution. In order to investigate this relationship we needed to design a method of ascertaining, at some useful level of accuracy, the size and distribution of population during the various phases of the history of the basin. Demographic data were also very useful for other reasons, primarily in the realm of sociocultural reconstruction. For example, it was very important for us to be able to estimate such things as the ratio of rural to urban population, the relative population sizes of political groupings, and the distribution of population by ecological zones—the last in order to give us some understanding of the relative significance of various resource areas.

The reconstruction of population, in an absolute sense, from archaeological remains is obviously a difficult and complex process, but we felt relatively sure that useful results could be obtained within an acceptable range of error. The first step was to reconstruct the population in 1519, by a careful analysis of the Spanish tax data from the sixteenth century, as a control for our archaeological estimates. On the basis of this study, we estimated the population of the Basin of Mexico, including the Tula region (just outside the basin to the northwest), at 800,000–1,200,000 people. We then planned to compare the residential areas of the Aztec or Late Horizon sites found in our surveys with those of the pre–Late Horizon phases, in order to get a relative ratio of population for the earlier phases. In order to carefully con-

trol this type of comparison we attempted to establish a chronology that was divided into roughly comparable time units, of about 200 years each. One immediate difficulty in the simple application of this method was presented with respect to those Aztec sites where architectural preservation was good. In rural Aztec sites we found a variation in house density remains ranging from 1 or 2 per hectare up to 20. This meant that simply measuring the surface area covered by a site would not give us comparability in population from site to site. In contrast, virtually all of the sites from the Teotihuacan period are densely nucleated settlements, comparable to the densest of the Aztec sites that we surveyed.

In our studies of contemporary villages in the basin we also noted a similar range of house density within the villages, with a range from only 1 or 2 houses per ha up to 25 houses per ha. The correlation between the house densities on rural Aztec sites and the density of houses, or population, in contemporary villages seemed so close that we felt relatively safe in making rough equations between communities of the two time periods. In pre-Aztec sites, where the residential remains were equally well preserved, we could then correlate the house densities with those on Aztec sites and the modern communities to get reasonably accurate population estimates. In sites where residential remains were poorly preserved or not preserved at all, we used the density of sherd refuse and other artifacts on the surface, which, we had previously noted, correlated very closely with house densities on Aztec sites.

Finally we made one correction in our population estimates for the Late Horizon, as well as the earlier periods. My comparison of the population sizes of specific regions within the basin, with our reconstructed estimates from the archaeological remains of the Late Horizon, indicated that our minimum population figures from the ethnohistoric sources were still 20 percent higher than our maximum figures from the archaeological remains. This is probably due

151

to basic errors in the method of reconstruction of population, lack of preservation of some sites, or availability of sites for survey. We have therefore applied a 20 percent correction formula for all of our estimates of Prehispanic populations that were generated directly from the archaeological data. Our general feeling is that this reconstruction may be in error as much as 20 or 30 percent, but probably not more than this, and the margin of error makes these calculations still useful for our purposes.

On the basis of status, population density, and population size, we developed a typology of the residential archaeological sites. These are sites whose primary function was residence and which either were occupied continuously throughout the year, and from year to year, or at least were occupied for prolonged seasons of the year. The classification runs as follows:

1. *Rural sites*: residential sites in which the population was involved primarily in subsistence or some other extractive activity, and where there is little evidence of status differentiation among the residents (for example differences based on occupation, wealth, or political power).
   a. *Hamlets*: rural communities with a population of less than 100. One of the things we did not do in our site classification, but which would be useful, would be to break this down into suprafamily and single-family hamlets.
   b. *Small villages*: rural communities with populations of 100–500. We also divided these into two basic subtypes, those with a density of 5–20 people per ha, which we referred to as dispersed villages, and those with densities of 20–100 people per ha, which we referred to as nucleated villages.
   c. *Large villages*: rural sites with populations generally between 500 and 1,000. During the Middle Formative a number of villages exceeded this figure. Large villages were also divided into dispersed and nucleated.

2. *Local centers*: residential sites where there is some evidence of nonsubsistence activities, including occupational specialization; where we saw some indications of significant differences in wealth and political power, as expressed in variations in the size and quality of residences, and of associated artifact debris; and where there was clear evidence of the expression of political power, in the form of substantial ceremonial architecture. In general, all communities classified as centers had populations exceeding 1,000. Most of them had estimated populations of 2,000–5,000, but a number had populations exceeding this figure, up to a maximum of 40,000 in the case of Teotihuacan during First Intermediate phase 3. We also divided this type into two subtypes, regional centers and provincial centers. Regional centers occurred during those periods when our evidence suggests that the basin was politically fragmented, whereas provincial centers occurred during the phases when we had reason to believe that it was politically centralized.

3. *Supra-regional centers*: Three times in the history of the basin we have convincing evidence that it was politically unified under a single, very large center: Teotihuacan during First Intermediate phases 4–5 and the Middle Horizon; Tula during Second Intermediate phase 2; and Tenochtitlan and Texcoco during the Late Horizon. Tula is estimated by Richard A. Diehl (1974) as having a maximum population of 60,000; Teotihuacan, by René Millon (1973), as having a mean population of 125,000 and a maximum of 200,000; Texcoco, by Parsons, as having 20,000–30,000; and Tenochtitlan, by Edward Calnek (1970), as having 150,000–200,000. Of these sites only Texcoco was surveyed by the Basin of Mexico Settlement Survey Project.

*Chronology: Period and Stage*

In this study we will use a new chronological system, first presented at a symposium on

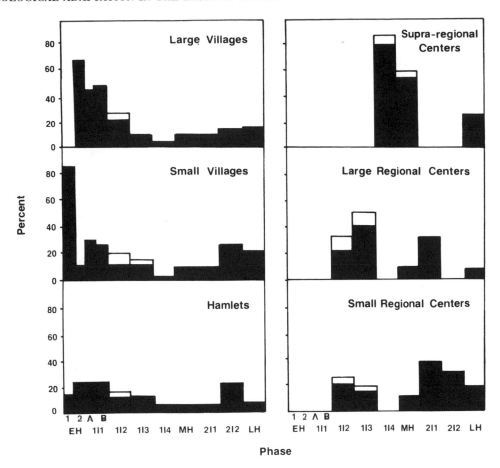

FIGURE 6-3. Histogram of population distribution by settlement type and phase in the Basin of Mexico. Reprinted from *The Basin of Mexico: Ecological Processes in the Evolution of a Civilization.* Copyright © 1979, by Academic Press, Inc.

the Basin of Mexico at the School of American Research in 1972 (Wolf 1976a). It is modeled after John H. Rowe's chronology for the Central Andes (Rowe 1960) and is an attempt to avoid the confusion presented by chronological systems that use terms that have both period and stage connotations. It includes the following periods: Lithic (30,000– 2500 B.C.), with three phases, 1 (30,000– 12,000 B.C.), 2 (12,000–5000 B.C.), and 3 (5000–2500 B.C.); Initial Ceramic (2500– 1500 B.C.); Early Horizon (1500–1150 B.C.), with two phases, 1 (1500–1300 B.C.) and 2 (1300–1150 B.C.); First Intermediate (1150

B.C.–A.D. 300), with five phases, 1 (1150– 650 B.C.), 2 (650–300 B.C.), 3 (300–100 B.C.), 4 (100 B.C.–A.D. 100), and 5 (A.D. 100–300); Middle Horizon (A.D. 300–750); Second Intermediate (A.D. 750–1350), with three phases, 1 (A.D. 750–950), 2 (A.D. 950–1150), 3 (A.D. 1150–1350); and Late Horizon (A.D. 1350–1519) (see Fig. 6-5).

In addition to this system we will also use a sequence of stages of ecological adaptation. Stage I is chronologically comparable to Lithic phases 1 and 2; Stage II extends from Lithic phase 3 through the Initial Ceramic, the Early Horizon, and the first half of First

153

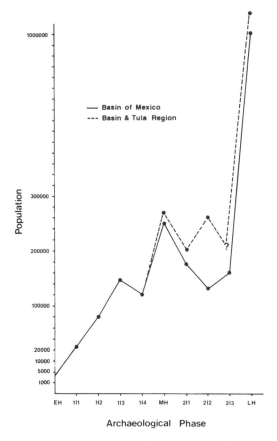

FIGURE 6-4. Population history of the Basin of Mexico. Reprinted from *The Basin of Mexico: Ecological Processes in the Evolution of a Civilization*. Copyright © 1979, by Academic Press, Inc.

## The Natural Environment

The fundamental characteristics of the Basin of Mexico as a habitat for a food-producing population, whose staple crop was maize, may be summarized as follows. The basin floor is at an elevation of 2,236 m above sea level. In Mesoamerica, elevations above 2,000 m are characterized by a frost season that runs normally from mid-October to mid-March, with occasional frosts as late as May and as early as the beginning of September. Maize is not frost-tolerant, and neither were any of the cultigens used by the Prehispanic population, so that the growing season did not exceed six months. The frosts also vary in their intensity, date of inception, and duration according to elevations within the basin. Because of the high elevation and the surrounding mountains, rainfall values are only moderate and vary considerably from year to year, particularly in the drier portions. Annual rainfall is highest in the southwest, lowest in the northeast, with a range of 900–450 mm on the plain. Values upslope are approximately 50 percent higher at each local station and reach their maximum in the upper piedmont zone (see Fig. 6-6). Regardless of the amount, however, rainfall is sharply seasonal, falling from May to September in most years, with maximal readings during the summer months. The amount of precipitation, date of inception, and closure of the rainy season vary considerably from year to year and this, combined with the fact that the frost season also varies from year to year, presents a major problem for successful maize agriculture in the basin, if based upon rainfall alone.

In comparison to highland basins in Mesoamerica as a whole, the Basin of Mexico is of considerable size (approximately 7,000 sq km), a fact of great importance for understanding its unique role in the overall history of the culture area. For example, it is nearly three times the size of the Valley of Oaxaca, the largest topographic unit in the Southern Highlands. Topographically it is also an enclosed basin, in which all of the drainage flows toward the center. At the time of the

Intermediate phase 1; Stage III includes the last half of First Intermediate phase 1 and extends through First Intermediate phases 2 and 3; Stage IV includes First Intermediate phases 4–5, the Middle Horizon, and all of the Second Intermediate; Stage V includes the Late Horizon. Stages VI–VIII are Postconquest stages and represent changes in ecological adaptation from the time of the Spanish Conquest to the present. Stage VI includes the years 1519–1650; Stage VII, 1650–1920; and Stage VIII, 1920–present. The definition of these stages is related to our reconstruction of the ecological systems and is based primarily upon resource utilization and its relationship to population.

154

TABLE 6-1. Basin of Mexico: Number of Sites by Type and Phase

| Period | Hamlet | Small Nucleated Village | Small Dispersed Village | Large Nucleated Village | Large Dispersed Village | Small Center | Large Center | Indeterminate | Salt Site | Quarry | Tezoyuca | Supra-regional Center | Small Ceremonial Precinct | Large Ceremonial Precinct | Total |
|---|---|---|---|---|---|---|---|---|---|---|---|---|---|---|---|
| EH1 | 5 | 4 | 0 | 0 | 0 | 0 | 0 | 2 | | 1 | | | | | 12 |
| EH2 | 12 | 1 | 0 | 2 | 0 | 0 | 0 | 2 | | 1 | | | | | 18 |
| FI1a | 17 | 2 | 4 | 2 | 0 | 0 | 0 | 3 | | 1 | | | | | 29 |
| FI1b | 47 | 6 | 6 | 6 | 0 | 0 | 0 | 5 | 2 | 1 | | | | | 73 |
| FI2 | 105 | 11 | 18 | 14 | 2 | 4 | 1 | 3 | | 1 | | | 1 | | 160 |
| FI3 | 135 | 10 | 27 | 3 | 7 | 10 | 2 | 0 | | 1 | 13 | | 4 | | 212 |
| FI4 | 130 | 1 | 2 | 0 | 2 | 0 | 0 | 1 | | 1 | | 1 | | 1 | 139 |
| FI5 | | | | | | | | | | | | | | | |
| MH | 149 | 55 | 22 | 15 | 2 | 9 | 1 | 4 | 2 | 2 | | 1 | 9 | 2 | 273 |
| SI1 | 128 | 18 | 22 | 12 | 3 | 14 | 1 | 1 | 2 | 1 | | | 2 | 1 | 205 |
| SI2 | 555 | 27 | 83 | 9 | 10 | 10 | 0 | 2 | 5 | 1 | | 1 | 5 | | 708 |
| SI3 | 258 | 4 | 11 | 2 | 2 | 14 | 0 | 105 | | 1 | | | 1 | | 398 |
| LH | 986 | 31 | 234 | 10 | 79 | 37 | 4 | 137 | 56 | 1 | | 2 | 54 | 5 | 1,636 |
| | 2,527 | 170 | 429 | 75 | 107 | 99 | 9 | 265 | 67 | 13 | 13 | 5 | 76 | 9 | 3,864 |

| | Totals | | |
|---|---|---|---|
| | Late Horizon | Pre-Late Horizon | All Phases |
| Hamlet | 986 | 1,541 | 2,527 |
| Small village | 265 | 334 | 599 |
| Large village | 89 | 93 | 182 |
| Regional-provincial center | 41 | 67 | 108 |
| Indeterminate | 137 | 128 | 265 |
| Special use | 57 | 23 | 80 |
| Supra-regional center | 2 | 3 | 5 |
| Ceremonial precinct | 59 | 26 | 85 |
| Tezoyuca sites | 0 | 13 | 13 |
| | 1,636 | 2,228 | 3,864 |

SOURCE: Sanders, Parsons, and Santley 1979.

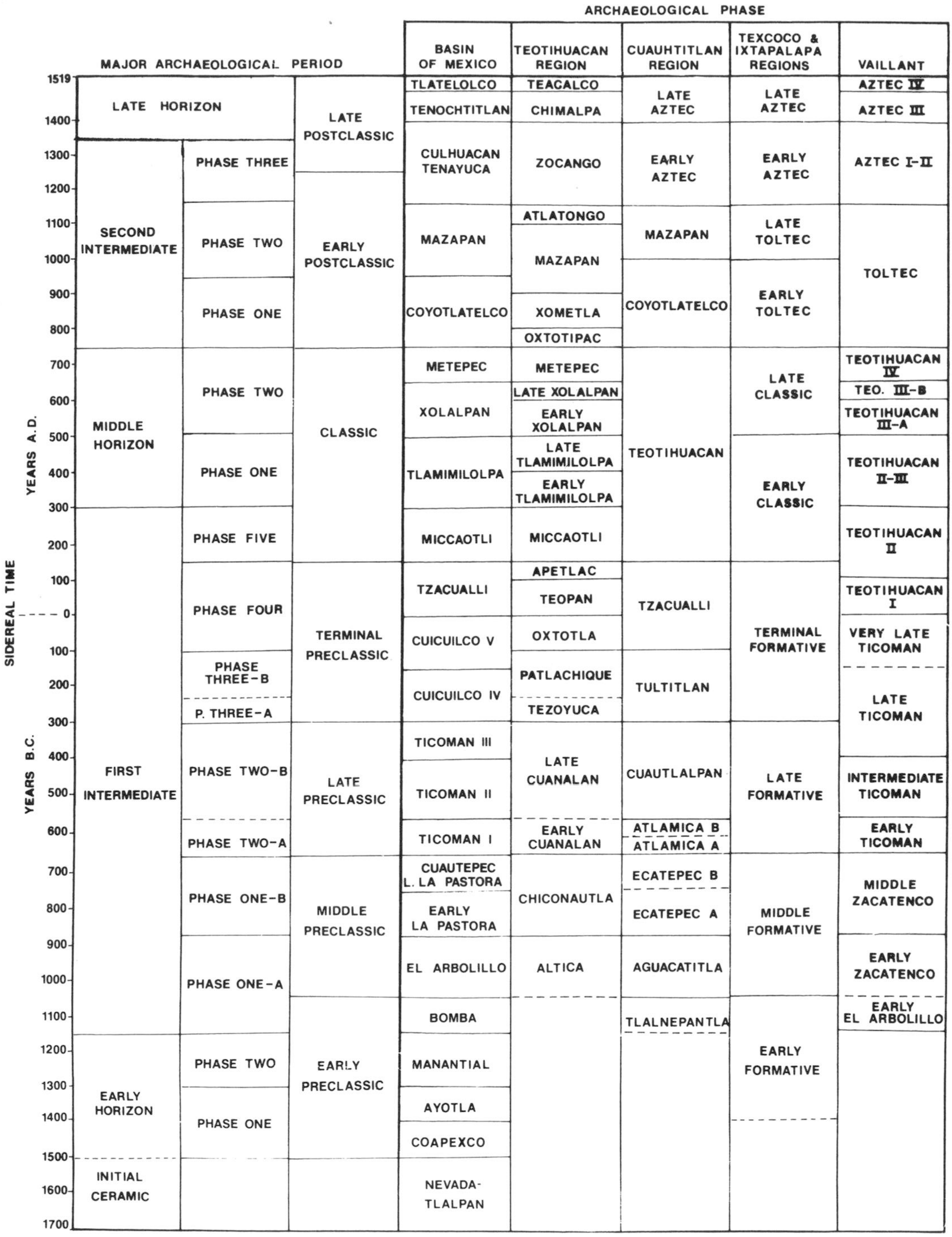

ARCHAEOLOGICAL PHASE

| Years | Major Archaeological Period | | Period | Basin of Mexico | Teotihuacan Region | Cuauhtitlan Region | Texcoco & Ixtapalapa Regions | Vaillant |
|---|---|---|---|---|---|---|---|---|
| 1519 | LATE HORIZON | | LATE POSTCLASSIC | TLATELOLCO | TEACALCO | LATE AZTEC | LATE AZTEC | AZTEC IV |
| 1400 | | | | TENOCHTITLAN | CHIMALPA | | | AZTEC III |
| 1300 | SECOND INTERMEDIATE | PHASE THREE | EARLY POSTCLASSIC | CULHUACAN TENAYUCA | ZOCANGO | EARLY AZTEC | EARLY AZTEC | AZTEC I-II |
| 1200 | | | | | | | | |
| 1100 | | PHASE TWO | | MAZAPAN | ATLATONGO | MAZAPAN | LATE TOLTEC | TOLTEC |
| 1000 | | | | | MAZAPAN | | | |
| 900 | | PHASE ONE | | COYOTLATELCO | XOMETLA | COYOTLATELCO | EARLY TOLTEC | |
| 800 | | | | | OXTOTIPAC | | | |
| 700 | MIDDLE HORIZON | PHASE TWO | CLASSIC | METEPEC | METEPEC | TEOTIHUACAN | LATE CLASSIC | TEOTIHUACAN IV |
| 600 | | | | XOLALPAN | LATE XOLALPAN | | | TEO. III-B |
| 500 | | | | | EARLY XOLALPAN | | | TEOTIHUACAN III-A |
| 400 | | PHASE ONE | | TLAMIMILOLPA | LATE TLAMIMILOLPA | | EARLY CLASSIC | TEOTIHUACAN II-III |
| 300 | | | | | EARLY TLAMIMILOLPA | | | |
| 200 | | PHASE FIVE | | MICCAOTLI | MICCAOTLI | | | TEOTIHUACAN II |
| 100 | | PHASE FOUR | TERMINAL PRECLASSIC | TZACUALLI | APETLAC | TZACUALLI | TERMINAL FORMATIVE | TEOTIHUACAN I |
| 0 | | | | | TEOPAN | | | |
| 100 | | | | CUICUILCO V | OXTOTLA | | | VERY LATE TICOMAN |
| 200 | | PHASE THREE-B | | CUICUILCO IV | PATLACHIQUE | TULTITLAN | | LATE TICOMAN |
| 300 | | P. THREE-A | | | TEZOYUCA | | | |
| 400 | FIRST INTERMEDIATE | PHASE TWO-B | LATE PRECLASSIC | TICOMAN III | LATE CUANALAN | CUAUTLALPAN | LATE FORMATIVE | INTERMEDIATE TICOMAN |
| 500 | | | | TICOMAN II | | | | |
| 600 | | PHASE TWO-A | | TICOMAN I | EARLY CUANALAN | ATLAMICA B | | EARLY TICOMAN |
| 700 | | PHASE ONE-B | MIDDLE PRECLASSIC | CUAUTEPEC L. LA PASTORA | CHICONAUTLA | ATLAMICA A | | MIDDLE ZACATENCO |
| 800 | | | | EARLY LA PASTORA | | ECATEPEC B | MIDDLE FORMATIVE | |
| 900 | | PHASE ONE-A | | EL ARBOLILLO | ALTICA | ECATEPEC A | | EARLY ZACATENCO |
| 1000 | | | | | | AGUACATITLA | | |
| 1100 | | | | BOMBA | | TLALNEPANTLA | | EARLY EL ARBOLILLO |
| 1200 | EARLY HORIZON | PHASE TWO | EARLY PRECLASSIC | MANANTIAL | | | EARLY FORMATIVE | |
| 1300 | | | | | | | | |
| 1400 | | PHASE ONE | | AYOTLA | | | | |
| 1500 | | | | COAPEXCO | | | | |
| 1600 | INITIAL CERAMIC | | | NEVADA-TLALPAN | | | | |
| 1700 | | | | | | | | |

(Left axis: SIDEREAL TIME — YEARS A.D. / YEARS B.C.)

FIGURE 6-5. Chronological concordances for the Basin of Mexico.

TABLE 6-2. Basin of Mexico: Population by Phase and Region

| | EH | 1I1 | 1I2 | 1I3 | 1I4 | MH | 2I1 | 2I2 | 2I3 | LH (Survey) | LH (Documentary) |
|---|---|---|---|---|---|---|---|---|---|---|---|
| Chalco-Xochimilco | 650 | 6,600 | 29,100 | 23,500 | Very small | 5,800 | 11,800 | 9,650 | 67,100 | 89,600 | (125,000) |
| Ixtapalapa | 480 | 855 | 9,864 | 8,886 | Small | 5,528 | 7,539 | 2,154 | 4,923 | 16,040 | (22,000) |
| Texcoco | 0 | 2,520 | 10,800 | 24,150 | Small | 4,850 | 38,200 | 7,938 | Subs. | 140,520 | (140,000) |
| Teotihuacan (1) | 0 | 683 | 3,994 | 43,601 | 93,792 | 147,807 | 39,262 | 33,001 | Subs. | 110,000 | (115,000) |
| Teotihuacan (2) | | | | | | 10,163 | | | | | |
| Temascalapa (1) | 0 | 0 | 0 | 0 | 675 | 6,648 | 3,198 | 5,779 | Uninh. | 15,939 | |
| Temascalapa (2) | | | | | | 19,292 | | | | | |
| Teotihuacan (3) | | | | | | 12,644 | | | | | |
| Tenayuca-Cuauhtitlan | 173 | 4,088 | 6,222 | 4,060 | 1,368 | 15,422 | 12,010 | 15,900 | Subs. | 61,717 | (85,000) |
| Zumpango | | 5,000 | 30 | ?900 | ?900 | 6,400 | 5,500 | 16,000 | 5,000 | 41,000 | (110,000) |
| Cuicuilco | (?)2,500 | 5,000 | 10,000 | 20,000 | 5,000 | | | | | | |
| Tacuba | Small | Small | Small | ? | Very small | Moderate | Moderate | ? | Moderate | | (350,000) |
| Pachuca | | | | | ? | Small | Very small | Moderate | Very small | | (100,000) |
| Tula | | | Small | ? | ? | Moderate | Moderate | 120,000 | ? | | (110,000) |

Subs.: substantial; Uninh.: uninhabited.
SOURCE: Sanders, Parsons, and Santley 1979.

157

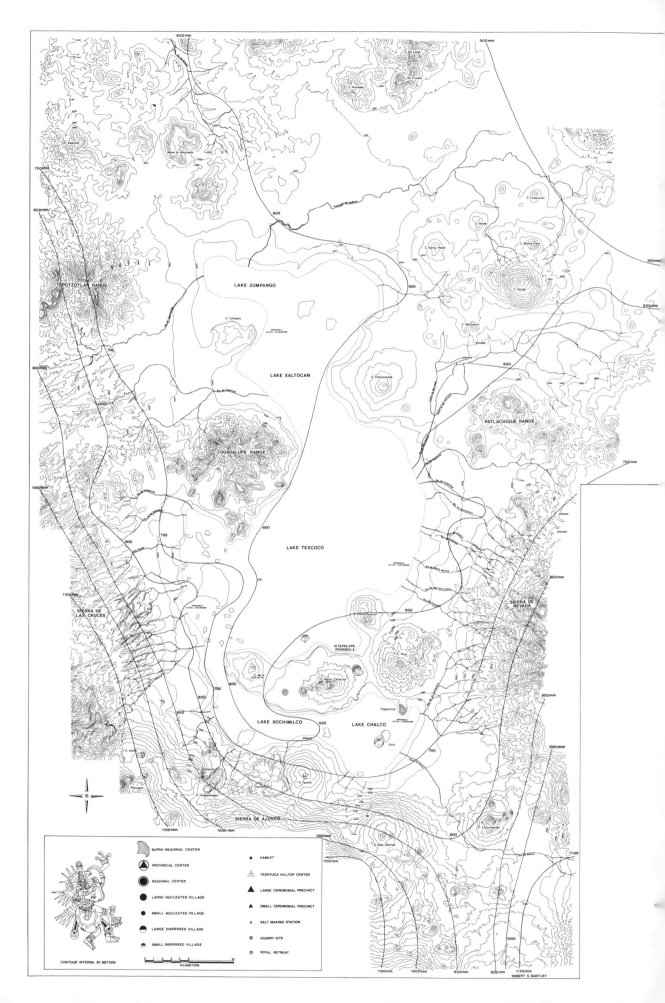

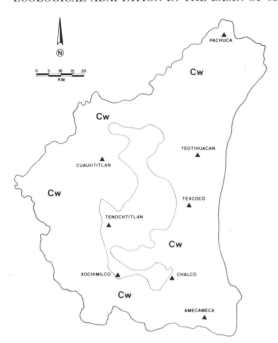

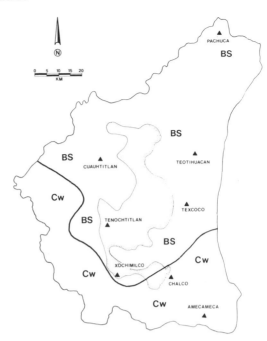

FIGURE 6-7. Basin of Mexico: C-B climatic boundary during wet year. Reprinted from *The Basin of Mexico: Ecological Processes in the Evolution of a Civilization.* Copyright © 1979, by Academic Press, Inc.

FIGURE 6-8. Basin of Mexico: C-B climatic boundary during dry year. Reprinted from *The Basin of Mexico: Ecological Processes in the Evolution of a Civilization.* Copyright © 1979, by Academic Press, Inc.

Conquest this drainage formed a chain of lakes and marshes that covered 1,000 sq km. Of these lakes, Xaltocan, Zumpango, and Texcoco were saline, and Lake Chalco-Xochimilco was a fresh water lake. The lakes were a valuable resource with respect to protein foods and transportation. In comparison to other highland regions of Mesoamerica, the level plains of the basin are quite extensive, but nevertheless there is a substantial area of agriculturally utilizable land on sloping terrain, and in those areas erosion was a serious problem.

FIGURE 6-6. The Basin of Mexico: rainfall. Reprinted from *The Basin of Mexico: Ecological Processes in the Evolution of a Civilization.* Copyright © 1979, by Academic Press, Inc.

The basin is a very young region geologically; much of the present topography is of volcanic origin and dates from the final phases of the Cenozoic and the Pleistocene. These two features of the geology have combined to produce an unusually favorable situation with respect to soil. A very substantial percentage of the basin is covered by a soil mantle which, prior to agricultural utilization, was relatively deep, with an ideal texture for agriculture, falling primarily into the sandy-loam, loam-clay, and loam categories, and characterized by extremely high fertility. Such soils also have high water-retention qualities, making them unusually favorable in this area of moderate rainfall.

On the basis of the variables discussed above we (Sanders, Parsons, and Santley 1979) have divided the basin into a number of ecological zones. Table 6-4 provides an eval-

159

TABLE 6-3. Basin of Mexico: Population Density by Phase and Region

| | EH | I11 | I12 | I13 | I14 | I15/MH | 2I1 | 2I2 | 2I3 | LH | Area (sq km) |
|---|---|---|---|---|---|---|---|---|---|---|---|
| Chalco-Xochimilco | 1.0 | 10.15 | 44.77 | 36.15 | Inap. | 8.92 | 18.15 | 14.85 | 103.23 | 137.85 | 650 |
| Ixtapalapa | 2.4 | 4.27 | 49.36 | 44.43 | Inap. | 27.64 | 37.69 | 10.77 | 24.61 | 79.69 | 200 |
| Texcoco | | 4.20 | 18.0 | 40.25 | Inap. | 8.0 | 63.8 | 13.23 | Medium | 234.20 | 600 |
| Teotihuacan | | 1.14 | 6.66 | 72.67 | 156.32 | 246.34 | 65.44 | 55.50 | Medium | 183.3 | 600 |
| Teotihuacan Valley (rural) | | | | | | 50.80 | | | | | |
| Temascalapa | | | | | 3.37 | 33.24 | 15.99 | 28.89 | Uninh. | 79.69 | 200 |
| Temascalapa and N. Periphery, Teotihuacan | | | | | | 59.36 | | | | | |
| Teotihuacan, N. Periphery | | | | | | 101.14 | | | | | |
| Tenayuca-Cuautitlan | .43 | 10.22 | 15.55 | 10.15 | 3.42 | 38.55 | 30.02 | 39.75 | Medium | 154.44 | 400 |
| Zumpango | | | .0005 | 1.5 | 1.5 | 13.0 | 9.16 | 32.50 | 8.25 | 70.00 | 600 |
| Cuicuilco | Very low | 12.5 | 50.0 | 100.0 | 25.0 | Low | | | | | 200 |
| Tacuba | Low | Low | Low | | ? | Medium | Medium | ? | Medium | (800) | 400 |
| Pachuca | | | | | Very low | Low | Uninh. | Medium | Uninh. | | 1,000 |
| Tula | | | Low | ? | ? | Medium | Medium | 120. | ? | Heavy | 1,000 |
| Sierra | | No permanent population | | | | | | | | | 1,000 |
| Saline lakebed | | Scanty resident population | | | | | | | | | 800 |
| | | | | | | | | | | | 7,650 |

Inap.: inappreciable; Uninh.: uninhabited.
SOURCE: Sanders, Parsons, and Santley 1979.

TABLE 6-4. Agricultural Quality of Ecological Zones of the Basin of Mexico

| Ecological Zone | Elevation | Quantity of Rainfall | Frost Risk | Soil | | | Susceptibility to Erosion | Drainage | Special Problems |
|---|---|---|---|---|---|---|---|---|---|
| | | | | Texture | Fertility | Depth | | | |
| Saline lakes | 2,236–2,242 | Low | Low | Clay | Very low | Deep | None | Very poor | Salinization, drainage |
| Fresh water lakes | 2,236–2,242 | Low | Low | Clay | Very high | Deep | None | Very poor | Drainage |
| Deep soil plain | 2,238–2,300 | Low | | | | | | | |
| Salinized | 2,238–2,244 | | Low | Clay | Very low | Deep | Low | Poor to good | Salinization, drainage |
| Inner | 2,240–2,250 | | Moderate | Loam | High | Deep | Low | Poor to good | Drainage |
| Outer | 2,240–2,260 | | Severe | Loam | High | Deep | Low | Good | Frost-rainfall |
| Thin soil plain | 2,240–2,300 | Low | Severe | Loam | Moderate | Moderate | Low | Good | Frost-rainfall Shallow soil |
| Upland alluvium | 2,450–2,600 | High | Moderate | Loam | Moderate | Deep | Low | Good | Frost |
| Lower piedmont | 2,250–2,350 | Moderate | Moderate | Sandy loam | Moderate | Moderate | Moderate | Very good | None |
| Middle piedmont | 2,350–2,500 | Moderate | Moderate | Sandy loam | Moderate | Moderate | Moderate | Excellent | Erosion |
| Upper piedmont | 2,500–2,700 | High | Severe | Clay | Low | Shallow | High | Excellent | Soil texture, fertility, erosion |
| Sierra | 2,700–5,700 | High to moderate | Very severe | Loam clay | Low | Very shallow | Very high | Excellent | Too high for agriculture |

161

uation of the characteristics of these zones in terms of their suitability for agricultural exploitation, and Figure 6-9 indicates their distribution.

## ECOLOGICAL ADAPTATION
### Stages I–II (23,000–900 B.C.)

A major deficiency of our survey was that we did not make a specific search for preceramic sites. The possibility of finding an isolated preceramic site, i.e., an occupational site where there were no ceramics, was remote, considering the very heavy Late Horizon occupation of the basin, but a detailed study of surface collections of lithic materials probably would have resulted in the definition of a number of preceramic components, mixed with those of later sites. Since this was not done, we have no clear picture of what the population density and distribution was prior to the earliest phase of agricultural utilization. Also, based upon the evidence from Richard S. MacNeish's Tehuacan project (MacNeish 1964a), it is likely that there was a long preceramic period in the history of the basin, when some agriculture was practiced along with hunting and gathering. The discussion that follows is based almost entirely upon excavated data from the Tlapacoya site.

Tlapacoya is a large, complex site at the base of the eastern slope of Cerro Tlapacoya in the Ixtapalapa region. Besides the Aztec village, the site has the following ceramic components: Early Horizon, First Intermediate 1, First Intermediate 2, and First Intermediate 3. These components were isolated and described in our Basin of Mexico surface survey. Excavations by the National Institute of Anthropology, Division of Prehistory, under the direction of José Luis Lorenzo, have revealed a long sequence of preceramic occupation going back to 23,000 B.C. (Lorenzo 1975).

The earliest phase has not yet been named or described in any detail in the literature. We will refer to it as the Tlapacoya phase, and it runs from 23,000 to 6000 B.C. Besides the Tlapacoya site, a number of mammoth kills (for example at Tepexpan and Ixtapan) also date from this phase. All of these sites, including the mammoth kills, are on the lake shore, but Tlapacoya is the only residential community known. The artifact inventory would suggest hunting of large game and generalized collection of wild plants. The absence of grinding stones would indicate that nuts and seeds were not processed, so only a fraction of the available food from plants was apparently utilized by this early hunting and gathering population. The paucity of known residential sites of this phase may be partly due to a lacustrine tendency for their location; most of them may be buried under extensive lake sediments. Theoretically the population of the basin during this phase was rather small, because of the limitations of the plant-collecting sector of the economy. Seed- and nut-producing plants are extremely abundant in the basin and would have added enormously to the food supply if they had been utilized. Stage I of ecological adaptation, then, involves a relatively generalized approach to the use of wild resources and probably a very small population, perhaps not more than a few thousand.

Stage II runs from 6000 to approximately 900 B.C. Christine Niederberger (1975, 1979) defines two major preceramic phases that belong to this overall stage: the Playa phase, lasting from 6000 to 4500 B.C., and the Zohapilco phase, from 3000 to 2000 B.C.

The Playa phase is described by Niederberger as one of climatic optimum, with an annual rainfall estimated at 1,400 mm and a mean annual temperature of 20° C. The rainfall was approximately double that of the same area today and the temperature was 6° warmer, comparable to the frost-free band on the Morelos Escarpment at an elevation of 1,600–1,800 m. The economy was essen-

FIGURE 6-9. Basin of Mexico: ecological zones. Reprinted from *The Basin of Mexico: Ecological Processes in the Evolution of a Civilization.* Copyright © 1979, by Academic Press, Inc.

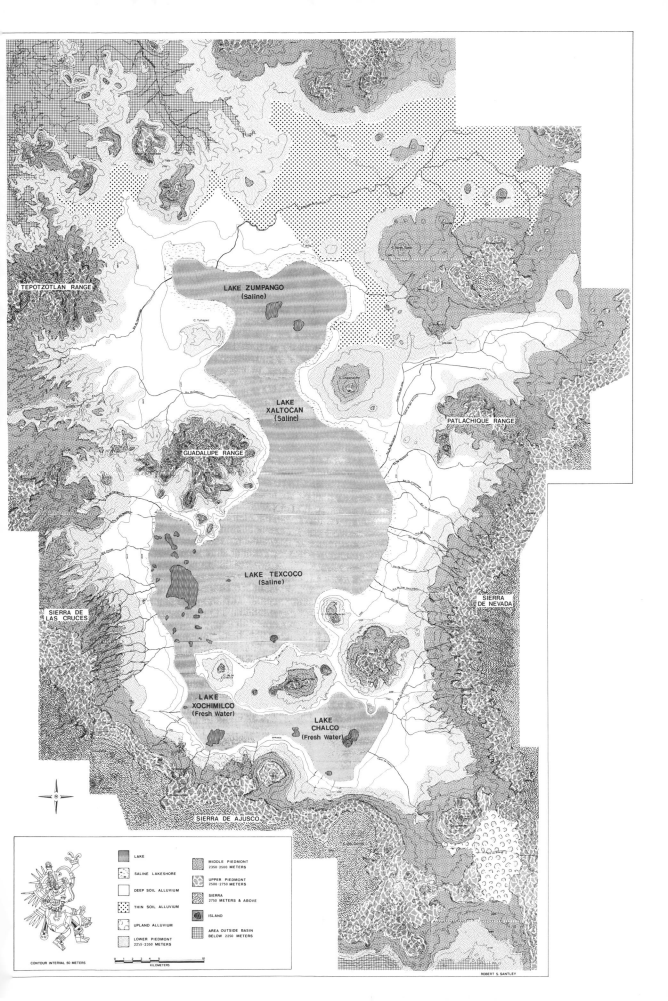

TEPOTZOTLAN RANGE

LAKE ZUMPANGO
(Saline)

C. Tultepec

LAKE
XALTOCAN
(Saline)

PATLACHIQUE RANGE

GUADALUPE RANGE

LAKE TEXCOCO
(Saline)

SIERRA
DE NEVADA

SIERRA DE
LAS CRUCES

LAKE
XOCHIMILCO
(Fresh Water)

LAKE
CHALCO
(Fresh Water)

SIERRA DE AJUSCO

LAKE

SALINE LAKESHORE

DEEP SOIL ALLUVIUM

THIN SOIL ALLUVIUM

UPLAND ALLUVIUM

LOWER PIEDMONT
2255-2350 METERS

MIDDLE PIEDMONT
2350-2500 METERS

UPPER PIEDMONT
2500-2750 METERS

SIERRA
2750 METERS & ABOVE

ISLAND

AREA OUTSIDE BASIN
BELOW 2250 METERS

CONTOUR INTERVAL 50 METERS

0 1 2 3 4 5        10
KILOMETERS

ROBERT S. SANTLEY

tially a food-collecting one, with a strong lacustrine orientation. Some of the plants collected, such as physalis, amaranth, chenopodium, various cucurbits, portulaca, and maize, particularly the last, were probably cultivated. It is clear however that agricultural products made up only a small proportion of the diet of the population, so that it still had essentially a hunting and gathering economy. Toward the end of the Playa phase there were a series of devastating volcanic eruptions that caused a general impoverishment of the flora of the area, but by the beginning of the Zohapilco phase there was a substantial recovery. This latter phase apparently witnessed an increased use of cultigens (for example maize pollen grains increased in size, suggesting further domestication), but even with the addition of chile peppers and chayotes, the economy is assessed by Niederberger as still essentially a food-collecting one. In relationship to the increase in the significance of agricultural seed crops, there is a development of a grinding tool complex.

In the absence of regional surveys we have made some rough calculations of the carrying capacity of the basin, based on a food-collecting economy (Sanders, Parsons, and Santley 1979). These estimates are based upon the faunal and floral remains recovered from a variety of excavations, and upon analogic reasoning based on data from recent food-gathering economies. We estimate the absolute carrying capacity at perhaps 16,000 people, or a little more than 2 people per sq km. This density approximates the more productive portions of California in aboriginal times. On the basis of the demographic behavior of recent hunters and gatherers, we further estimate that the actual population during the Zohapilco phase was probably in the neighborhood of 8,000, that is, somewhere around 50 percent of carrying capacity.

For the succeeding ceramic phases, where we have extensive surveys, we estimate the numbers of settlements in the survey area for Early Horizon phases 1 and 2 and First Intermediate phase 1 as shown in Table 6-5. As

can be noted in the table, there is little evidence of significant population growth on these ceramic sites during the period 1300–900 B.C. Furthermore, the data from the ceramic sites would suggest only a minor growth of population from the Zohapilco phase.

Our data on regional settlement from the period of time running from 1300 to 900 B.C. are based entirely on those sites where ceramics were present. There is an implication from both Niederberger's data on the preceramic phases at Tlapacoya and the data from these early ceramic sites that these communities were sedentary settlements. There is a good possibility that, at the same time that the ceramic-bearing sites were occupied, there were hunting and gathering campsites in the northern half of the valley, occupied by more nomadic groups, but we have no data at present on this aspect of the settlement of the basin.

At any rate, in the Early Horizon, sedentary settlement was clearly limited to the southern and western portions of the basin, and we have no ceramic sites north of a diagonal line from Azcapotzalco to Chimalhuacan during phase 1. During phase 2 of the Early Horizon there were 3 hamlets north of this line: at Loma Torremote and El Arbolillo on the west side of the basin, and another in the upper Papalotla Basin in the eastern part of the Basin of Mexico. In terms of ecological zones, sites occur on the lake shore and piedmont areas. Surprising is the occurrence of 2 small villages near Amecameca, at the edge of the upland alluvium, at an elevation of nearly 2,500 m. Perhaps this points to the relatively low significance of agriculture in the economy of these early ceramic sites, since this is not a very favorable zone for the domestication of early varieties of maize but would be a highly favorable habitat for wild nuts and seeds. This basic pattern continues during First Intermediate subphase 1a, except that two hamlets appear on the north slope of the Patlachique range, in the Teotihuacan survey region, the first time that ceramic sites appear in that portion of the

TABLE 6-5. Population History during the Early Horizon–First Intermediate Phase 1

|  | Early Horizon 1 | Early Horizon 2 | First Intermediate 1a | First Intermediate 1b |
|---|---|---|---|---|
| Large villages | 1 or 2 small | 2 | 2 | 6 |
| Small villages | 2 | 1 | 6 | 12 |
| Hamlets | 5 | 12 | 17 | 47 |
| Indeterminate | 2 | 2 | 3 | 5 |
| Population | 2,000 | 4,000 | 6,000 | 20,000 |

SOURCE: Adapted from Sanders, Parsons, and Santley 1979.

basin. In conclusion, the period from 6000 to 900 B.C. was one of ecological and demographic stability, and agriculture probably remained as an adjunct to a basic hunting and gathering economy, even during the early ceramic phases.

## Stage III (900–100 B.C.)

Stage III in the history of the basin is an extraordinarily dynamic one. It is a period of sustained rapid population growth, of colonization of over two-thirds of the basin by a food-producing, ceramic-manufacturing population, and of striking changes in the organizational aspects of the population. In our opinion this remarkable population growth is the product of a shift to food production as the primary subsistence base, particularly a shift to intensive use of stored seeds like beans, amaranth, and maize. The sociopolitical evolution that we recorded in our survey is clearly the direct result of substantial population growth based upon this new resource procurement strategy.

SETTLEMENT TYPES. The stage comprises three phases, First Intermediate 1b, First Intermediate 2, and First Intermediate 3. Table 6-1 provides a classification of sites by type and phase. Seventy residential localities were occupied during phase 1b, including 47 hamlets, 6 small nucleated villages, 6 small dispersed villages, 6 large nucleated villages, and 5 residential sites of indeterminate sta-

tus, but undoubtedly falling within the village category. During phase 2 the number of hamlets increased to 105, small villages to 29 (11 nucleated, 18 dispersed), large villages to 16 (14 nucleated, 2 dispersed). Along with these sites there are 3 residential sites of indeterminate category, but probably classifiable as villages. A new settlement type emerged, the regional center, of which our survey located 5, 4 of which are classified as small, i.e., with populations of only a few thousand, and 1 (Cuicuilco) large, with an estimated population of 10,000. A total of 158 residential sites were occupied during phase 2.

Finally, during phase 3, the number of hamlets increased to 135, and small villages to 37 (10 nucleated, 27 dispersed). The number of large villages declined somewhat to 10, primarily because the small centers increased in number to 10 (that is, large villages, in several cases, evolved into centers). Cuicuilco increased in size to its maximum population of 20,000. The most extraordinary event, however, was the meteoric rise of Teotihuacan as a large regional center, with an estimated population of 40,000. Besides the 10 small centers, there were 13 small hilltop residential sites, with ceremonial architecture, in the central portion of the basin, sites we refer to as Tezoyuca hilltop centers. The chronological relationship of these sites to the 2 large centers and the other small centers is still a problematical one.

POPULATION HISTORY. The overall population of the basin at the end of First Intermediate subphase 1b was approximately 20,000. This increased to 80,000 by the end of phase 2 and to 140,000 by the end of phase 3. Although we cannot, at this time, divide phases 2 and 3 into subphases, what evidence we have suggests that this was a period of sustained, continuous population growth with a net annual increase of 3 per 1,000 or, in terms of percentages, a .3 percent annual increase. This amounts to a doubling rate of every 200 years, a remarkable growth rate for a preindustrial population.

GEOGRAPHIC PATTERNING OF SETTLEMENT. With respect to the geographic pattern of settlement during the stage, the following summary can be made (see Figs. 6-11–6-13). Approximately 90 percent of the population of the basin was distributed south and west of a diagonal line from Ecatepec to Chimalhuacan during phase 1b. Overall population density in the area of substantial settlement was 10–20 per sq km. More specifically, sites tend to be located on the lower edge of the lower piedmont, directly above the alluvial plain, a location which provided easy access to the deep soil of the alluvial plain, to the adjacent piedmont, and to the nearby lakeshore. Several settlements were within the plain, while a few were located well up on the lower piedmont (all of these are in the Tacuba region, including the large village of Tlatilco). All settlements were located in the vicinity of major streams, probably in response to the use of water as a resource, and possibly because of the effects of flooding on the soil texture in the immediate vicinity of such streams. On the basis of the actual distribution of occupational sites, more specific patternings can be observed. First, there was a continuous strip of very densely settled terrain, running from Ecatepec to Cuicuilco, which was the demographic heart of the basin during phase 1b and had a population density at least several times the overall figure. Besides this demographic core there were two major zones of sparser, pioneer population. One of these includes the Texcoco region and the Patlachique range, which had a total population of 1,500, virtually all residing in hamlets. Much of this settlement was on the alluvial plain adjacent to the Rio Papalotla. The second concentration was along the middle courses of the Cuautitlan-Tepoztlan basins. All of the settlements in this area were located on the edge of the lower piedmont, overlooking the plain, and we estimate the total population at about 1,000. The entire northern half of the basin was still unoccupied and presumably was still utilized by nomadic hunting and gathering bands.

Phase 2 was essentially an extension of the pattern described above. Of the total estimated population of 80,000 in the basin during this phase, approximately 60,000 were still located west and south of the Ecatepec-Chimalhuacan line. Major changes were the appearance of a substantial concentration of population well up on the piedmont, around Tlalmanalco in the Xochimilco region, and a general increase of population in the Chalco-Xochimilco region, in contrast to the former heavy focus on the Tenayuca and Tacuba regions, although the latter area was still well populated. The overall population density was in the neighborhood of 40–50 per sq km, which means that the effective density in the well-settled areas was well over 100 per sq km.

The Texcoco and Teotihuacan regions were now well populated, compared to their tiny First Intermediate 1 populations, and their inhabitants resided in small and large villages and even a regional center, as well as a number of hamlets. The focus of population was on the Lower and Middle Piedmont, where settlement was almost continuous. The total population was approximately 15,000, about ten times that of First Intermediate 1b. The Cuautitlan and Tenayuca regions, on the

FIGURE 6-10. Basin of Mexico: Early Horizon. Reprinted from *The Basin of Mexico: Ecological Processes in the Evolution of a Civilization.* Copyright © 1979, by Academic Press, Inc.

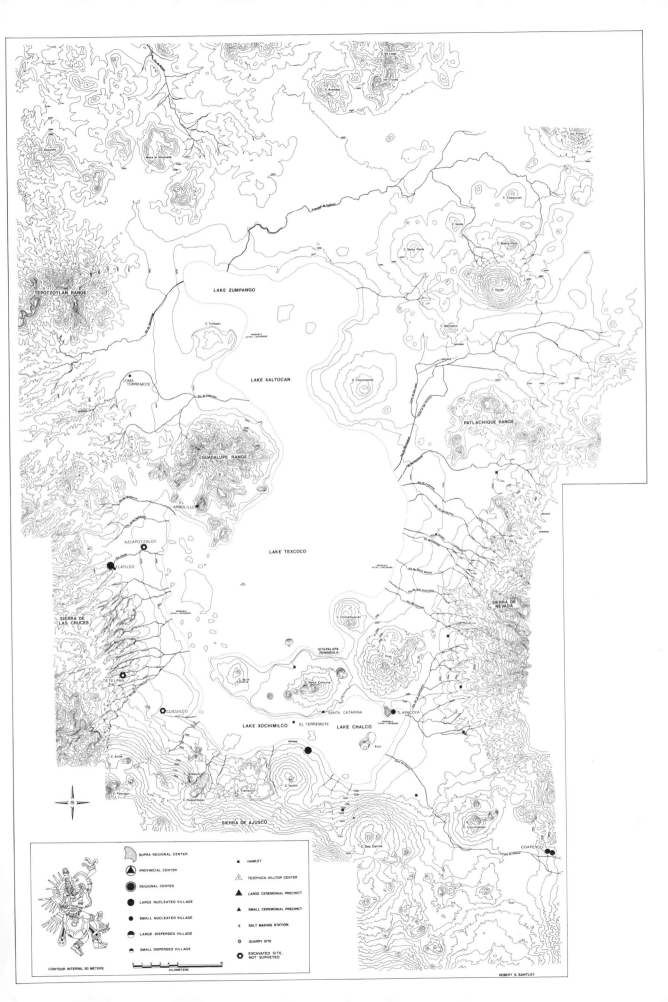

LAKE ZUMPANGO

LAKE XALTOCAN

LAKE TEXCOCO

LAKE XOCHIMILCO    LAKE CHALCO

TEPOTZOTLAN RANGE

C. Epazote

Mesa la Ahumada

LOMA
TORREMOTE

C. Tultepec

C. Chiconautla

GUADALUPE RANGE

PATLACHIQUE RANGE

EL
ARBOLILLO

C. Arandas

C. Coyucan

C. Verde

C. Santa Paula

C. Buena Vista

C. Gordo

C. Malinalco

SIERRA DE
LAS CRUCES

AZCAPOTZALCO

TLATILCO

C. Chimalhuacan

C. Pino

SIERRA DE
NEVADA

TETELPAN

CUICUILCO

IXTAPALAPA
PENINSULA

C. de la
Estrella

C. Santa Catarina

SANTA CATARINA

TLAPACOYA

EL TERREMOTE

Xico

C. Xotla

SPRINGS

C. Tepalcapa

C. Teuhtli

C. Pipicapa

C. Huapaltepec

SIERRA DE AJUSCO

C. Chicomoztoc

C. Dos Cerros

COAPEXCO

ROBERT S. SANTLEY

SUPRA-REGIONAL CENTER

PROVINCIAL CENTER

REGIONAL CENTER

LARGE NUCLEATED VILLAGE

SMALL NUCLEATED VILLAGE

LARGE DISPERSED VILLAGE

SMALL DISPERSED VILLAGE

HAMLET

TEZOYUCA HILLTOP CENTER

LARGE CEREMONIAL PRECINCT

SMALL CEREMONIAL PRECINCT

SALT MAKING STATION

QUARRY SITE

EXCAVATED SITE,
NOT SURVEYED

CONTOUR INTERVAL 50 METERS

KILOMETERS

other hand, had a population approximately comparable to that of the preceding phase.

During phase 3 a number of major changes can be seen in the settlement pattern of the basin, some of which represent intensification of trends that occurred during phase 2. First, the Lake Chalco-Xochimilco basin remained a well-populated region, but its total population was virtually the same as during phase 2; i.e., this region was in a phase of population stabilization. The Tenayuca and Tacuba regions underwent a rapid process of population decline, possibly related to the increasing size of Cuicuilco. In the Cuautitlan region there was a substantial population reduction, and the remnants of this population were nucleated at a single small regional center near Cuautitlan.

The most important event was the emergence of the Teotihuacan and Texcoco regions as a major focus of population. About 65,000 people, or nearly half the population of the basin, resided there at this time. Population density in the Texcoco region in phase 3 was equivalent to that in the south, and the density in the Teotihuacan Valley exceeded it. With respect to the specific location of population in the Texcoco and Teotihuacan regions, the pattern was similar to that of phase 2 except for the dramatic rise and concentration of population around the future city of Teotihuacan, on the edge of the alluvial plain of the Teotihuacan Valley, where some 40,000 people resided.

There was also for the first time a scattering of hamlets in the northern basin, a new frontier for the expanding agricultural population.

RESOURCE PROCUREMENT. As noted in the introduction, much of our reconstruction of resource utilization is really a hypothesis, since it is based primarily on indirect data from settlement location and population distribution; direct evidence for resource utilization is still spotty. The focus of this discussion will be food procurement, but I will briefly mention the utilization of other resources as well. Our reconstruction is based on the settlement and population data and

the acceptance of two theoretical principles in terms of decision-making among farming populations, i.e., the law of least effort and the law of minimization of risk.

Perhaps another way of putting it is that individual farmers or groups of farmers were playing a game of strategy against the natural environment. To recapitulate the general discussion of the natural environment and the problems of agricultural adaptation, the significant variables are water, temperature, and soil texture. Water supply in the basin is highly variable. First, the annual precipitation, as has been noted, follows a gradient of diminishing rainfall from southwest to northeast. Rainfall also increases moving upslope from the lakeshore. Water also varies in terms of availability of permanent sources in the form of springs, natural ground-water seepage, and sporadic flows in the thousands of temporary streams or *barrancas*. In portions of the plain, unusually high water table conditions produced a pattern of swamps and water-logged soils that can be utilized only when large drainage projects are undertaken.

With respect to temperature, the critical variable is the fall frosts, and these vary in duration, frequency, time of inception, and severity from year to year. They also vary with elevation, with the most severe conditions in the Sierra (where agriculture based upon maize is not possible), moderately severe on the upper piedmont and outer plain, least severe on the inner plain and the lower-middle piedmont.

Soil texture must be considered in conjunction with rainfall. In the better-watered areas, sandy loams would seem to present ideal conditions for cultivation, in terms of the twin problems of moisture retention and workability; in the drier areas some labor in-

FIGURE 6-11. Basin of Mexico: First Intermediate phase 1. Reprinted from *The Basin of Mexico: Ecological Processes in the Evolution of a Civilization.* Copyright © 1979, by Academic Press, Inc.

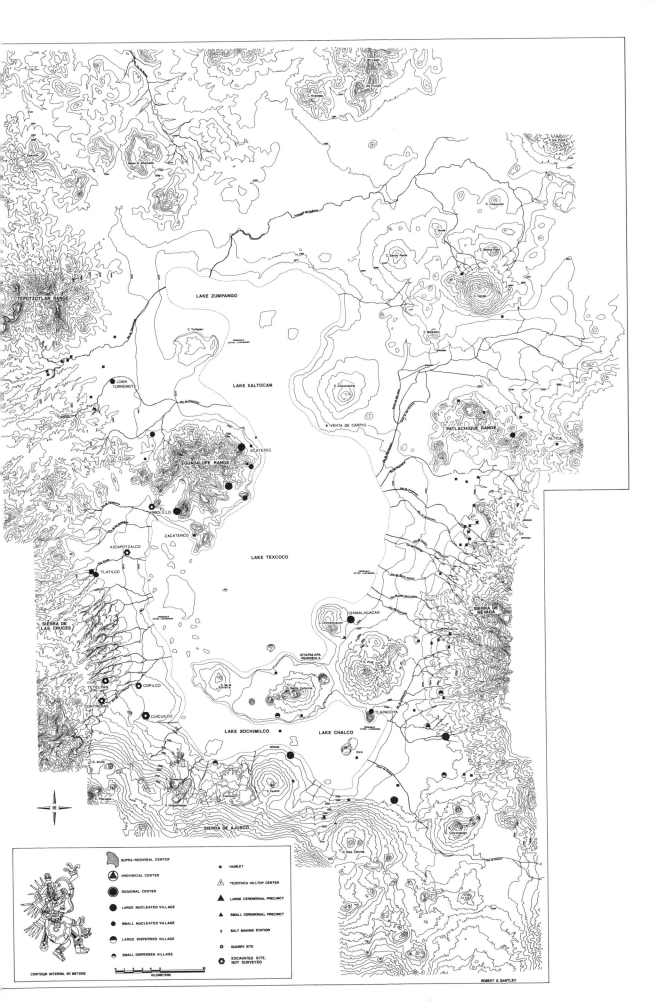

LAKE ZUMPANGO

LAKE XALTOCAN

TEPOTZOTLAN RANGE

C. Tultepec

PROBABLE AZTEC LAKESHORE

LOMA TORREMOTE

C. Chiconautla

C. Arandas

Ixo Cruces

C. lste Lagos

Mesa la Ahumada

C. Epazote

C. Santa Paula

C. Verde

C. Buena Vista

C. Cinayucan

C. Gordo

C. Maravicio

PATLACHIQUE RANGE

ALTICA

ECATEPEC

GUADALUPE RANGE

EL ARBOLILLO

ZACATENCO

AZCAPOTZALCO

TLATILCO

LAKE TEXCOCO

VENTA DE CARPIO

PROBABLE AZTEC LAKESHORE

SIERRA DE LAS CRUCES

SIERRA DE NEVADA

CHIMALHUACAN

C. Chimalhuacan

IXTAPALAPA PENINSULA

C. Pino

TETELPAN

COPILCO

CONTRERAS

CUICUILCO

C. de la Estrella

C. Santa Catarina

TLAPACOYA

C. Xicte

LAKE XOCHIMILCO

LAKE CHALCO

Xico

Huopalapan

C. Tlamanaco

C. Teuhtli

SIERRA DE AJUSCO

C. Dos Cerros

C. Larumbonio

CONTOUR INTERVAL 50 METERS

0 1 2 3 4 5          10
KILOMETERS

ROBERT S. SANTLEY

SUPRA-REGIONAL CENTER

PROVINCIAL CENTER

REGIONAL CENTER

LARGE NUCLEATED VILLAGE

SMALL NUCLEATED VILLAGE

LARGE DISPERSED VILLAGE

SMALL DISPERSED VILLAGE

HAMLET

TEZOYUCA HILLTOP CENTER

LARGE CEREMONIAL PRECINCT

SMALL CEREMONIAL PRECINCT

SALT MAKING STATION

QUARRY SITE

EXCAVATED SITE, NOT SURVEYED

put would have to be sacrificed in order to use soils with a higher water-retention ability, but heavier texture, i.e., loams and clay loams. One of the situations in the basin that would have presented an unusually favorable picture for hand cultivators in Prehispanic times is the fact that only a very small percentage has soils classified as clays, primarily found in a few places in the plains and on a relatively small stretch of upper piedmont. Finally, a serious problem in the area with respect to soils is that of physical erosion, since a substantial percentage of the basin does include land in sloping terrain.

The only good direct data on food resources for this long period of time come from excavations at Loma Torremote (Santley 1977), which had its primary occupation during the first half of First Intermediate phase 2. Even these data are only partially analyzed, and we can only present a very general picture. What the data indicate is that maize was of the pre-Chapalote-Naltel-Toluqueño type, i.e., with small ears and kernels, and it probably required a short growing season. It is also clear that agriculture was the main source of food, and the great number of storage pits associated with the house compounds indicates that seed storage was an important part of the subsistence strategy. Along with maize, amaranth was common; two species of beans were cultivated (*P. vulgaris* and *P. lunatus*); nopal, squash, chile peppers, chia, and sechia were all utilized and probably cultivated. Hunted and gathered resources were very similar to those obtained during First Intermediate phase 1, but with a definite reduction in the contribution of deer to the diet, probably the result of the much more substantial population residing in the basin at this time. It is estimated that deer contributed no more than .9 percent of the food supply during First Intermediate phase 2.

Although we cannot prove this from direct evidence, the sudden increase in population in the middle of First Intermediate phase 1 probably relates to the new food procurement system, i.e., the shift from hunting and gathering as a primary source of food to agriculture. The only other additional data we have, in terms of actual botanical remains, come from the phase 2b site of Cuanalan, where recent excavations have revealed that the maize was still of the small-eared pre-Toluqueño variety. By way of extrapolation we would argue that Toluqueño maize probably appeared during the succeeding phase 3 (see discussion below of the food procurement system during First Intermediate phases 4–5 and the Middle Horizon).

If Esther Boserup's (1965) theoretical paradigm of the process of agricultural intensification is applied to the Basin of Mexico, then most of the cultivation during the First Intermediate 1–2–3 continuum would have been extensive, most particularly during phase 1, and in the frontier areas during phases 2 and 3. As noted above, however, some areas had unusually high population densities. In these areas the population density exceeded the carrying capacity of an extensive approach to land use even during phase 1.

More direct evidence of this process of intensification can be found in the data from a few excavated sites and from surface samples. One line of evidence consists of basalt hoes, which appear in the southern basin by phase 2. They should appear in areas like the Ecatepec-Tacuba area by phase 1 and in the Texcoco and Teotihuacan regions by phase 3, but we lack excavated data to justify this reconstruction. The presence of hoes is good evidence for the intensification process, since grasses, the type of vegetation which occupies fallowed fields the first few years, could not be effectively controlled without soil-turning techniques. Other evidence from excavations indicates that floodwater irrigation dates from phase 1 in the Tenayuca

FIGURE 6-12. Basin of Mexico: First Intermediate phase 2. Reprinted from *The Basin of Mexico: Ecological Processes in the Evolution of a Civilization.* Copyright © 1979, by Academic Press, Inc.

170

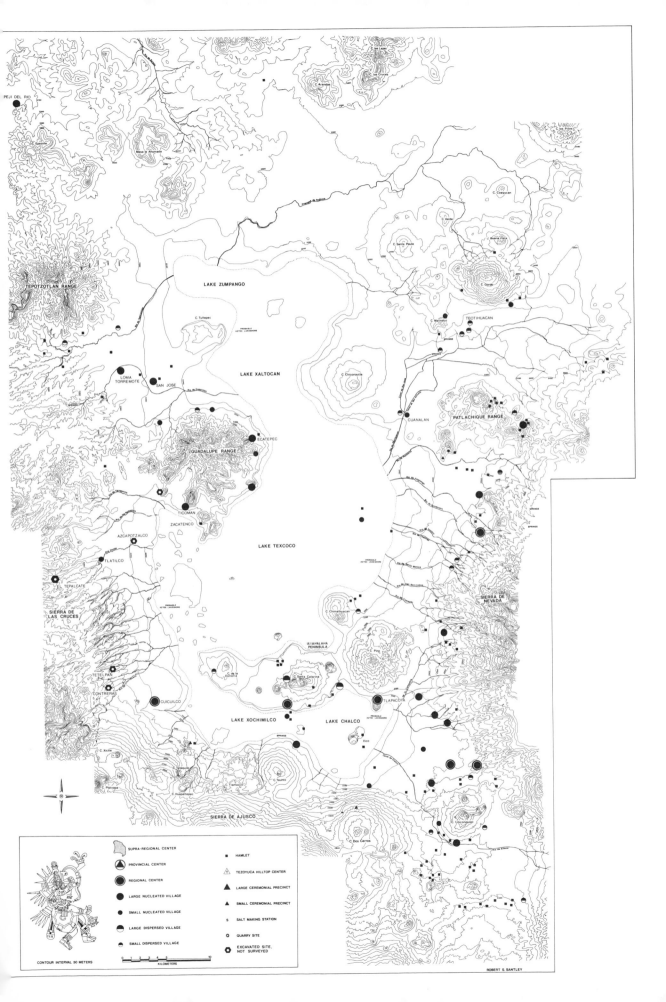

region (at Santa Clara), and terracing, based on survey data, is well established in a number of First Intermediate 3 villages and regional centers in the Texcoco region; both techniques indicate a more intensive agricultural regime. What we suggest, and we clearly need more data to support this reconstruction, is a pattern of small areas of intensively cultivated agricultural land around most of the large villages and regional centers, with larger areas of extensive cultivation around these zones or on the frontier. In such areas hamlets were the dominant settlement type. The close spacing of large communities in some areas would mean that there was a fairly extensive zone of continuously and intensively cultivated land.

In summary, our data indicate a process of increasing pressure on food resources produced by the continuously rising population. The response to this was increasing population density in prime agricultural regions, i.e., the better-watered areas, accompanied by intensification of agricultural utilization of such areas and population fissioning into marginal areas, where there were rainfall-frost problems. As a corollary of this process, by phase 3, indirect evidence from settlement locations and pollen profiles indicates that there was a substantial development of small-scale drainage agriculture and spring-based irrigation systems in the climatically marginal Teotihuacan and Texcoco regions. This response was so successful that the demographic and political superiority of the better-endowed areas of the basin began to fade by the conclusion of the phase, and the stage was set for the dramatic events of ecological Stage IV, described below.

SOCIOPOLITICAL EVOLUTION. One of the most interesting results of our demographic analysis is the striking tendency of populations in all phases to be concentrated in a few large sites. During phase 1 the largest communities were large villages, and 50 percent of the population was located in such communities; during phase 2, 30 percent of the population was located at Cuicuilco, an additional 20 percent resided in smaller regional

centers, and 20 percent in large villages, or 70 percent in communities exceeding 500 people; during phase 3, 40–50 percent resided at either Cuicuilco or Teotihuacan, 15–20 percent in small regional centers, and 10 percent in large villages; 65–80 percent therefore lived in settlements with populations exceeding 500, 55–70 percent in settlements with over 1,000 people. We believe, although more data are needed to substantiate this argument, that the tendency for population to concentrate in larger settlements is related to a combination of processes, some political, e.g., competition among the various political groupings, and some economic, e.g., intensive use of the land, accompanied in the drier sections of the basin by hydraulic techniques of cultivation.

With respect to the general process of sociocultural evolution, there is no evidence of community stratification during phase 1, and the relatively even spacing of large and small villages in the more densely settled areas of the basin would suggest a series of independent tribelets. The same pattern applies to hamlets in the more marginal areas of the valley, but here it appears that clusters of hamlets probably formed small tribal units. The contrast, then, is between nucleated and dispersed tribes, with nucleated tribes living in the more intensively cultivated, densely populated parts of the basin and dispersed tribes residing in the frontier areas. Evidence from burials at sites like Tlatilco, El Arbolillo, and Zacatenco suggests ranking patterns within the larger settlements, and there may have been some small-scale ceremonial architecture at the site of Tlatilco.

During phase 2 the appearance of small centers in the south and the presence of 1 small center in the Texcoco region, all with ceremonial architecture, would indicate an

FIGURE 6-13. Basin of Mexico: First Intermediate phase 3. Reprinted from *The Basin of Mexico: Ecological Processes in the Evolution of a Civilization.* Copyright © 1979, by Academic Press, Inc.

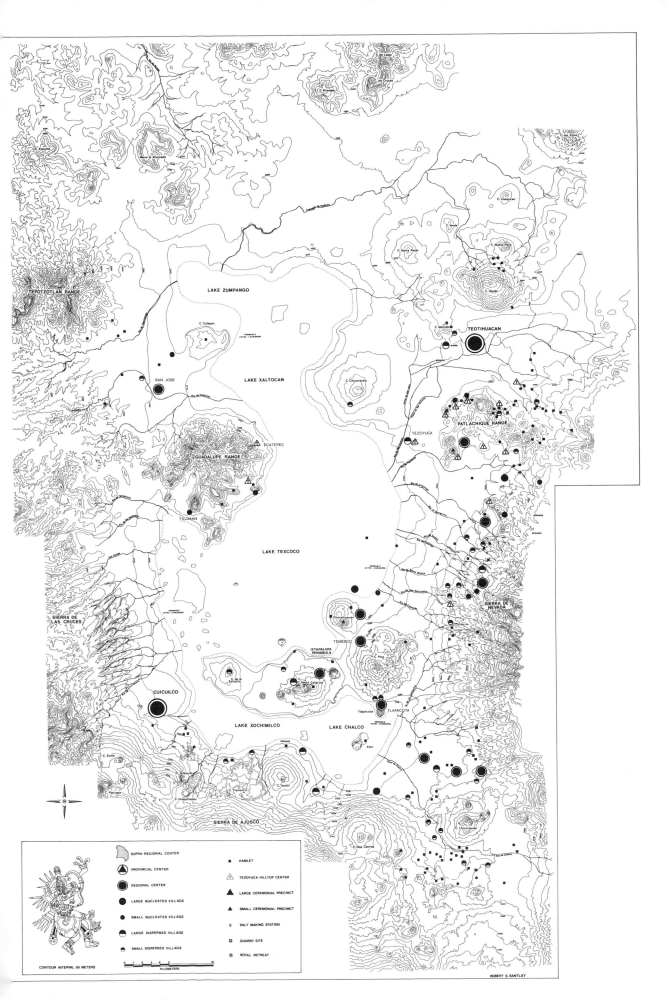

LAKE ZUMPANGO

C. Tultepec

PROBABLE
AZTEC LAKESHORE

SAN JOSE

LAKE XALTOCAN

TEPOTZOTLAN RANGE

Mesa la Ahumada

C. Epazoyo

TEOTIHUACAN

C. Coayucan

C. Verde

C. Santa Paula

C. Buena Vista

C. Gordo

C. Malinalco

C. Chiconautla

TEZOYUCA

PATLACHIQUE RANGE

ECATEPEC

GUADALUPE RANGE

TICOMAN

LAKE TEXCOCO

PROBABLE
AZTEC LAKESHORE

SIERRA DE
NEVADA

SIERRA DE
LAS CRUCES

PROBABLE
AZTEC LAKESHORE

Chimalhuacan

TEMESCO

IXTAPALAPA
PENINSULA

C. Pino

C. de la
Estrella

Santa Catarina

CUICUILCO

Tlapacoya

TLAPACOYA

Xico

LAKE XOCHIMILCO

LAKE CHALCO

PROBABLE
AZTEC LAKESHORE

SPRING

C. Xictle

C. Teuhtli

Tetecuilo

C. Huapalapan

Tlamanalco

C. Chiconquiac

Pipizapa

SIERRA DE AJUSCO

C. Dos Cerros

N

| | SUPRA-REGIONAL CENTER | | ■ | HAMLET |
| △ | PROVINCIAL CENTER | | ⚠ | TEZOYUCA HILLTOP CENTER |
| ◉ | REGIONAL CENTER | | ▲ | LARGE CEREMONIAL PRECINCT |
| ● | LARGE NUCLEATED VILLAGE | | ▲ | SMALL CEREMONIAL PRECINCT |
| • | SMALL NUCLEATED VILLAGE | | S | SALT MAKING STATION |
| ◖ | LARGE DISPERSED VILLAGE | | ⊕ | QUARRY SITE |
| ◞ | SMALL DISPERSED VILLAGE | | Ⓡ | ROYAL RETREAT |

CONTOUR INTERVAL 50 METERS

0 1 2 3 4 5    10
KILOMETERS

ROBERT S. SANTLEY

intensification of ranking and some centralization of political authority, but still a highly fragmented political situation. The spacing of such settlements with respect to each other and to large villages in the same region would argue for the existence of a great number of political groupings of various sizes. Elsewhere, in the Cuautitlan, Tenayuca, and Teotihuacan regions, the pattern was probably similar to that of the preceding phase 1, i.e., a series of small tribelets with only slight development of ranking and with a population primarily concentrated in small and large villages.

One exception to this overall patterning is the large center (estimated population 10,000) at Cuicuilco in the southwest corner of the basin. The major problem at Cuicuilco is the internal chronology of the site; it is certain that some ceremonial architecture does date from this phase, but the scale of such construction is not clear. In all probability, the large, well-known pyramid, with its 60,000 cu m of volume, dates from the succeeding phase. Whatever the nature of the site, it clearly was the largest settlement and the center of the largest political grouping in the basin at this time, and it may have had some level of political control over some of the smaller centers in the same general portion of the basin. What we are suggesting here is that some kind of paramount chiefdom may have existed, centered at Cuicuilco, during phase 2; but it seems more probable that this kind of development occurred in the succeeding phase.

Phase 3 was an exciting one with respect to sociopolitical evolution. Cuicuilco increased in size to a town of 20,000 people. There is evidence of a massive ceremonial center, a possible grid pattern of house compounds and streets, and overall planning (Florencia Muller, personal communication). With two exceptions (Tlapacoya and IX-TF4; see Blanton 1972b), all of the centers in the southeastern portion of the basin went through a process of population decline and an apparent reduction of ceremonial construction, suggesting that this area may have been po-

litically integrated under the control of Cuicuilco at this time. In other words the paramount chiefdom, which we suggested as possibly beginning in phase 2, was well established at this time. The dramatic reduction of population in the western half of the Ixtapalapa peninsula and the overall reduction of population in the Tacuba and Tenayuca regions may be related to a process of migration of people in those areas to Cuicuilco. We should consider those areas as a kind of direct agricultural hinterland to a population resident at the center. If this, in fact, is what occurred, then we have a small-scale version of the process of population nucleation that surely occurred in the succeeding phase (First Intermediate 4) at Teotihuacan. The population of the Cuautitlan region was concentrated in a single small regional center at San Jose, possibly as a defensive posture in reaction to the expansion of Cuicuilco's political power.

Another major political event was the emergence of a large center at Teotihuacan with an estimated population of 40,000 at that time (R. Millon 1973). At least 90 percent of the population of the Teotihuacan Valley was concentrated at this one locality. If we had a more refined phasing of First Intermediate phase 3 we might possibly show that virtually all the population resided in the city by the end of the phase. The Texcoco region and the eastern half of the Ixtapalapa region seem to have served as a kind of buffer area of small chiefdoms between these 2 large centers. In that area were 4 small regional centers and their supporting populations, each with an estimated total of 7,000–8,000 people.

With respect to the economic aspects of settlement, the patterning and spacing would indicate that even the largest communities were essentially agrarian settlements. In the case of Teotihuacan, where virtually the entire population of the region was nucleated into a single large community, this reconstruction would seem certain. If our reconstruction of the agricultural system that maintained the town is correct, then virtually the entire population could have been supported within a radius of 10–15 km. Population profiles from the springs and excavations of floodwater irrigation canals near Otumba would seem to justify this model.

Final support for this reconstruction is derived from Michael W. Spence's analysis of the obsidian industry at Teotihuacan, where he estimates that only 1 percent of the population was involved in this craft during this stage and further argues that much of the specialization was part-time (Spence 1974a). This is in sharp contrast to the 11 percent which he estimates were dedicated to obsidian working at the peak of Teotihuacan's growth in Middle Horizon times. While we would not deny the significance of craft production and trade in increasing the political power of the ruling class at Middle Horizon Teotihuacan, these factors were relatively insignificant during First Intermediate phase 3.

The reduction of population within a comparable radius of Cuicuilco during phase 3 probably involved a similar process of political and agricultural evolution. The spacing of small regional centers and large villages in the southeastern part of the basin and in the Texcoco region also indicates that these centers and larger villages were essentially agrarian settlements.

A corollary of this pattern of political fragmentation and nucleation in a few large settlements is the tendency of the large settlements to be located in areas of prime agricultural land, but within easy access of a variety of other resources as well. In the Texcoco region, for example, the bulk of the population was concentrated in a few communities on the middle piedmont, with access to adjacent areas of the lower piedmont, upper piedmont, alluvial plain, and lakeshore as well. In the south the same pattern is characteristic, i.e., each of the large communities had access to all areas, but was located on either the plain or the lower piedmont. Cuicuilco, San Jose, and Teotihuacan were all located on the edge of, or within, the alluvial plain, but within easy access of all the nearby ecological zones, excepting the

lakeshore in the last two cases. The only resource that would not be within reach of each of the territorial groupings was obsidian, and the special development of obsidian specialization at Teotihuacan was undoubtedly a response to this situation; i.e., Teotihuacan was the only community physically proximate to the obsidian resources. This fact undoubtedly was of considerable significance in the later development of the city.

### Stage IV (100 B.C.–A.D. 1350)

During Stage IV, a period of time almost double the length of Stage III, a number of processes and factors, the operation of which is not yet well understood, led to a stabilization of population. In fact, the stage is marked by a series of phases of minor population growth and decline; the major point, however, is that there was no overall tendency to either decline or increase. It was also a stage of cycling of political centralization and fragmentation, which correlate positively with the phases of moderate growth and decline, respectively.

SETTLEMENT TYPES. With respect to settlement types, by phase, the pattern can be quickly appreciated by a glance at Fig. 6-3. During First Intermediate phase 4 the survey recorded 137 residential localities: 1 supra-regional center (Teotihuacan itself); 2 large villages, both dispersed; 3 small villages, 1 nucleated, 2 dispersed; and 130 hamlets, a pattern which was accompanied by the establishment of a single political system in the basin, centered at Teotihuacan. By the Middle Horizon, when Teotihuacan's political and economic power reached its zenith, the pattern had shifted to include the following residential communities: the city, 9 provincial centers, 17 large villages (15 nucleated, 2 dispersed), 77 small villages (55 nucleated, 22 dispersed), and 149 hamlets.

Following the decline of Teotihuacan as a major city, there was a phase of political fragmentation, in which the residential settlement hierarchy was as follows: 1 large regional center (Teotihuacan), 14 small re-

175

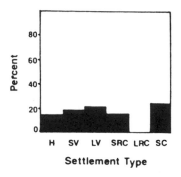

FIGURE 6-14. Histogram of population distribution by settlement type in the Basin of Mexico and the Tula region during Second Intermediate phase 2. Reprinted from *The Basin of Mexico: Ecological Processes in the Evolution of a Civilization.* Copyright © 1979, by Academic Press, Inc.

gional centers, 15 large villages (12 nucleated, 3 dispersed), 40 small villages (18 nucleated, 22 dispersed), and 128 hamlets.

During Second Intermediate phase 2 the basin was again politically unified, under the hegemony of Tula, and the settlement hierarchy included a supra-regional center (Tula), which however lies outside the basin proper in the Tula region. If we were to include only our Basin of Mexico settlement data then the site listing would include 10 provincial centers, 19 large villages (9 nucleated, 10 dispersed), 120 small villages (83 dispersed, 37 nucleated), and 555 hamlets. Including settlements in the Tula region as well, an additional area of 1,000 sq km (Mastache de Escobar and Crespo 1976), then the total site number would include the city, 10 provincial centers, 58 large villages (36 dispersed, 22 nucleated), 196 small villages (101 dispersed, 95 nucleated), and 590 hamlets (see Table 6-6). A phase of political fragmentation (Second Intermediate phase 3) followed the demise of Tula, and our incomplete sample includes 14 small regional centers, 4 large villages, 14 small villages, 258 hamlets, and an additional 105 unclassified residential sites (most of these last were probably hamlets or small villages).

POPULATION HISTORY. As has been noted, this is a period of minor cycling of population

but with overall stability. During First Intermediate phase 4 the population declined from its phase 3 peak of 140,000 to approximately 100,000–120,000, rose to a peak of about 230,000 during the Middle Horizon, declined to 180,000 during Second Intermediate phase 1, declined further to 120,000, if we include only the population within the basin itself, and rose again to 160,000 during phase 3. If we add the population of the Tula region to these values, then Second Intermediate phase 2 was a phase of population growth, to approximately the level of the Middle Horizon population (which we estimate at about 260,000, including the Tula region). Considering the fact that the Basin of Mexico was a rural sustaining area for Tula, such an addition is a reasonable way to manipulate the data. If we were to add the population of the Tula region to that of the Basin of Mexico during the two phases of political fragmentation, this would raise the values for those periods somewhat, but not by more than a factor of 20 percent, so that there is a clear correlation of population maxima during the phases of political centralization and population minima during the phases of political fragmentation.

The reasons for the initial decline between phases 3 and 4 are not clearly understood but are probably related to a combination of the effects of the military conflicts among the various polities of phase 3, just prior to the unification of the basin, and possibly also to the process of massive relocation of 90 percent of the population of the basin at Teotihuacan during the first few decades of phase 4. As for the decline of population during the periods of political fragmentation, it was probably the product of conflicts among the various polities during these phases.

The *apparently* slower population growth, compared to Stage III, during the periods of peace and growth of political power of Teotihuacan and Tula could, in fact, be the product of the expansion of these centers in foreign affairs, with possible attendant migration involved in the establishment of military and commercial colonies, but we have no

TABLE 6-6. A Comparison of Sites of the Basin of Mexico and the Tula Region in Second Intermediate Phase 2

| | Basin of Mexico (Surveyed Area: 3,500 sq km) | Tula Region (Surveyed Area: 1,000 sq km) |
|---|---|---|
| Supra-regional center (est. population 60,000) | 0 | 1 |
| Provincial centers | 10 | 0 |
| Large villages | | |
| Dispersed | 10 | 26 |
| Nucleated | 9 | 13 |
| Small villages | | |
| Dispersed | 83 | 18 |
| Nucleated | 37 | 58 |
| Hamlets | 555 | 35 |
| Small ceremonial centers | 2 | 1 |
| Salt-making stations | 5 | 0 |
| Indeterminate | 2 | 0 |

SOURCE: Sanders, Parsons, and Santley 1979.

way of knowing what the scale of this type of migration was. If the growth rates of Stage III had been sustained during the phase of the growth of Teotihuacan in Stage IV, by A.D. 700 the population of the basin would have been approximately double that which our figures would suggest. This means that at least the population number that we ascertain as residing in the basin would have to have been residing in foreign areas as the product of such a migration. This would seem rather extreme, and we suggest that, in fact, there was a real slowdown in population growth rates during the overall period of Teotihuacan's rise.

GEOGRAPHIC PATTERNING OF SETTLEMENT. In contrast to the overall pattern of relative demographic stability and minor cycling, the period was one of extraordinary variety in regional settlement (see Figs. 6-15–6-19). It began with the dramatic, and apparently rapid, process of nucleation of virtually the entire population of the basin at Teotihuacan. The most recent estimate of the population of the city is about 90,000 during this phase; our total rural population did not exceed 15,000. Furthermore about half of this "rural population" resided within a 10-km radius of Teotihuacan itself!

During the succeeding First Intermediate phase 5 and Middle Horizon there was a modest return to the countryside, but a return that resulted in a pattern of settlement so distinct and different from that of First Intermediate phase 3 that we are convinced that it was the product of a process of planning, engineered by the rulers of Teotihuacan in response to the needs of the city. The population of our survey area doubled from First Intermediate phase 4 to the Middle Horizon, and virtually all of this growth occurred in the countryside. In comparison to phase 3 there was a major shift in geographic distribution of population. The overwhelming percentage of the Middle Horizon population resided in climatically marginal portions of the basin (see Figs. 6-6, 6-16).

More specifically, most of the population was concentrated in a diagonal band 25 km wide and 60 km long that runs from Otumba in the northeast to Azcapotzalco in the southwest. Within this area of approximately 1,500 sq km resided about 85–90 percent of the total population of the Basin of Mexico, with

177

an average density of about 125 people per sq km. The rural component of this population was distributed primarily in large and small villages, 6 small provincial centers, and 1 large provincial center (Azcapotzalco). Geographically the communities were concentrated around the periphery of the Teotihuacan Valley, particularly on the northern periphery, in what we have called the Temascalapa survey region, along the Tepoztlan-Cuautitlan river systems, and along the northwest shore of Lake Texcoco. Northwest and southeast of this demographic center the rural population was sparse and distributed primarily in hamlets and small nucleated villages. This pattern probably evolved gradually through the various phases in the history of the city, although we currently lack the tight chronological control to present an exact sequence of events.

During Second Intermediate phase 1 there were major changes in settlement distribution, although some of the features clearly reflect the persistence of Middle Horizon patterns of settlement. First, the largest settlement, although with a drastically reduced population (from 125,000 to 40,000), remained at Teotihuacan. Second, about two-thirds of the population remained in the Otumba-Azcapotzalco band described above as the heartland of the Middle Horizon population. Nearly all of the remainder resided in a series of large settlements, primarily regional centers, in the southeastern portion of the basin. Finally, there were a few small centers in the northwest. The northwestern population was roughly comparable in size to that of the population of the same area in Middle Horizon times, theoretically representing a continuation of the same population. The most significant change was in the south, a demographically marginal region during the history of the growth of Teotihuacan. Historically, Second Intermediate phase 1 was a phase of rapid decline of Teotihuacan, resulting in political fragmentation, yet with a certain stability of population and cultural traditions.

By phase 2, the pattern had altered significantly, although one can still detect a persistence of the Middle Horizon patterning. For example, the old Middle Horizon demographic heartland was still a well-populated region; in fact its overall population was roughly comparable to that during phase 1. Its specific distribution, however, was quite different, with the bulk of the population residing in hamlets and small villages, and Teotihuacan itself had declined in status to a town of 10,000 people.

The southern part of the region reverted to demographic marginality, with the population residing almost entirely in hamlets, a pattern similar to that during the Middle Horizon. The most interesting change was in the northwest, where the population was much denser than in any previous phase and resided in a large number of small villages. The overall pattern is one of a northwest to southeast gradient of population, with the northwest being the most densely settled portion of the basin. Spot surveys also indicate that the unsurveyed northeast part of the basin was well settled—for the first time.

If we include in our assessment the 1,000 sq km surveyed by Alba Guadalupe Mastache de Escobar and Ana María Crespo in the Tula region, we find a continuation of the above pattern, with the densest population of all located within a relatively short radius of Tula itself. The population of the city is estimated at about 60,000, and a rough estimate of the population residing in the outlying settlements, within the Tula region, is an additional 60,000. This total of 120,000 residing in an area of 1,000 sq km is comparable to the entire population of the much larger Basin of Mexico.

During First Intermediate phase 4, with a return to political fragmentation, there was an equally dramatic shift of population in

FIGURE 6-15. Basin of Mexico: First Intermediate phase 4. Reprinted from *The Basin of Mexico: Ecological Processes in the Evolution of a Civilization.* Copyright © 1979, by Academic Press, Inc.

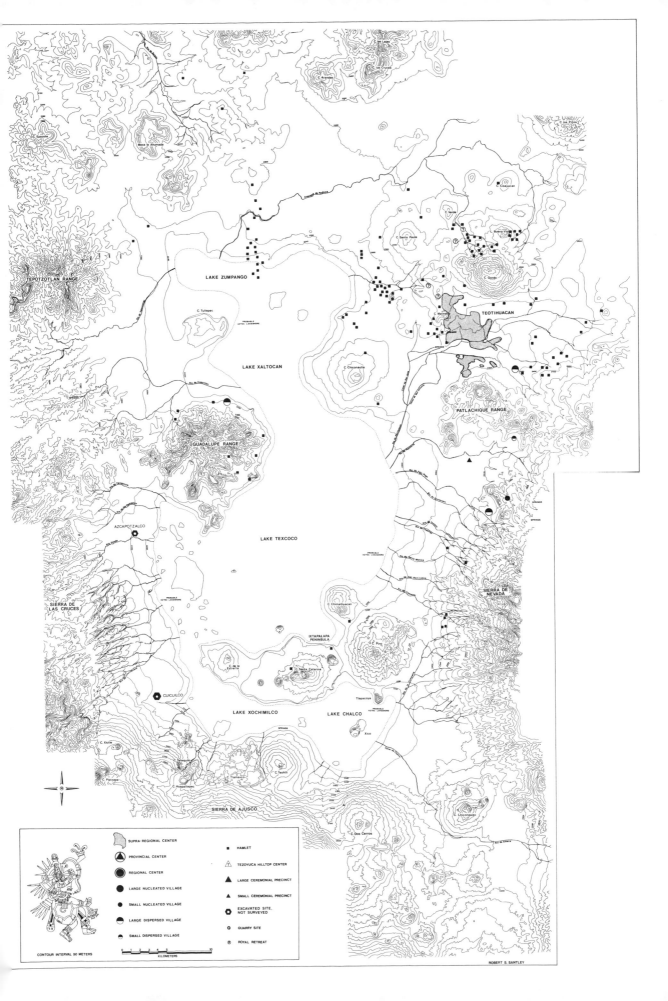

LAKE ZUMPANGO

LAKE XALTOCAN

C. Tultepec

PROBABLE
AZTEC LAKESHORE

C. Chiconautla

TEPOTZOTLAN RANGE

C. Coayucan

C. Verde

Buena Vista

C. Santa Paula

C. Gordo

C. Mainalco

TEOTIHUACAN

PATLACHIQUE RANGE

GUADALUPE RANGE

AZCAPOTZALCO

LAKE TEXCOCO

PROBABLE
AZTEC LAKESHORE

SIERRA DE
NEVADA

SIERRA DE
LAS CRUCES

PROBABLE
AZTEC LAKESHORE

C. Chimalhuacan

IXTAPALAPA
PENINSULA

C. de la
Estrella

C. Santa Catarina

CUICUILCO

Tlapacoya

PROBABLE
AZTEC LAKESHORE

LAKE XOCHIMILCO

LAKE CHALCO

Xico

C. Xictle

C. Teuhtli

C. Pipixaipa

Tlapacoya

C. Huepaltepec

C. Dos Cerros

SIERRA DE AJUSCO

C. Chiconquiac

## Legend

- SUPRA-REGIONAL CENTER
- ▲ PROVINCIAL CENTER
- ◔ REGIONAL CENTER
- ● LARGE NUCLEATED VILLAGE
- ● SMALL NUCLEATED VILLAGE
- ◖ LARGE DISPERSED VILLAGE
- ◡ SMALL DISPERSED VILLAGE

- ■ HAMLET
- △ TEZOYUCA HILLTOP CENTER
- ▲ LARGE CEREMONIAL PRECINCT
- ▲ SMALL CEREMONIAL PRECINCT
- ⊕ EXCAVATED SITE, NOT SURVEYED
- ◇ QUARRY SITE
- ⊗ ROYAL RETREAT

CONTOUR INTERVAL 50 METERS

KILOMETERS

ROBERT S. SANTLEY

space. The overall pattern was very similar to that of First Intermediate phase 1, with most of the population living in large settlements, primarily regional centers, and with a definite concentration of population in the central and southern portions of the basin. The northern portion was virtually deserted during this phase.

RESOURCE PROCUREMENT. The following reconstruction is admittedly based primarily on the indirect evidence of settlement history, with only occasional hard data with respect to subsistence, but I feel that it provides a convincing explanation of the major shifts in population during the various phases. I believe that the dramatic changes in settlement and political organization between Stages III and IV of ecological adaptation are essentially related to the development of hydraulic agriculture, i.e., small-scale swamp reclamation around the springs of San Juan, and permanent irrigation, based upon various spring sources, on a large scale. The strongest argument in favor of this reconstruction is the abrupt and dramatic shift of population to the climatically deprived areas of the basin, where the rainfall-frost problem is most acute. These are also areas where the soils are characteristically fertile and well drained and have great moisture storage potential, so that the various techniques of water control would have had dramatic effects in terms of the support of a dense population.

This process is essentially a development from earlier experimentation with the same basic pattern of land utilization around the centers in the Papalotla-Teotihuacan basins during ecological Stage III. Approximately 55,000 people were living in these two areas by the end of First Intermediate phase 3. All of the caloric requirements of this population could have been met by a combination of small-scale *chinampa* agriculture at the springs of San Juan and large-scale utilization of the spring resources of the Teotihuacan-Papalotla irrigation systems. Our estimate of the carrying capacity of the irrigated land at this time, assuming a lower-producing vari-

ety of maize (with an average yield of about 1,000 kg per ha), 100 percent of the irrigable land planted in maize, and a population deriving 65 percent of its caloric minima from this resource, is 80,000. Our hard data indicate that the Teotihuacan irrigation system was in use during this phase but probably not on that scale. In this model it will be assumed that these water resources were utilized and that there were major areas of canal irrigation in the Teotihuacan Valley and a series of smaller areas directly associated with the small regional centers along the Papalotla.

During First Intermediate phase 4 the nucleation of much of the population of the Basin of Mexico at Teotihuacan would have put tremendous economic pressures on further development of irrigation in the Teotihuacan-Papalotla basins. In fact, it would have required maximal utilization, if the city derived most of its food supply from these lands. Energetically, this would make sense, since it would achieve two objectives: a primary food supply from a relatively short radius, and a marked improvement in crop security in this somewhat marginal environment.

The exploitation pattern, by Middle Horizon times, presents a more complex picture (see Fig. 6-12). On the basis of the settlement pattern described in the previous section, three major zones may be defined in terms of the relationship of the population to resources: the inner core, the outer core, and the periphery. The inner core included the alluvial plains and the adjacent piedmont of the Teotihuacan Valley, an area of approximately 300 sq km. In the center of it was the city, with its estimated 125,000 people. In light of our settlement data, it seems that this region was directly cultivated by people re-

FIGURE 6-16. Basin of Mexico: Middle Horizon resource utilization. Reprinted from *The Basin of Mexico: Ecological Processes in the Evolution of a Civilization.* Copyright © 1979, by Academic Press, Inc.

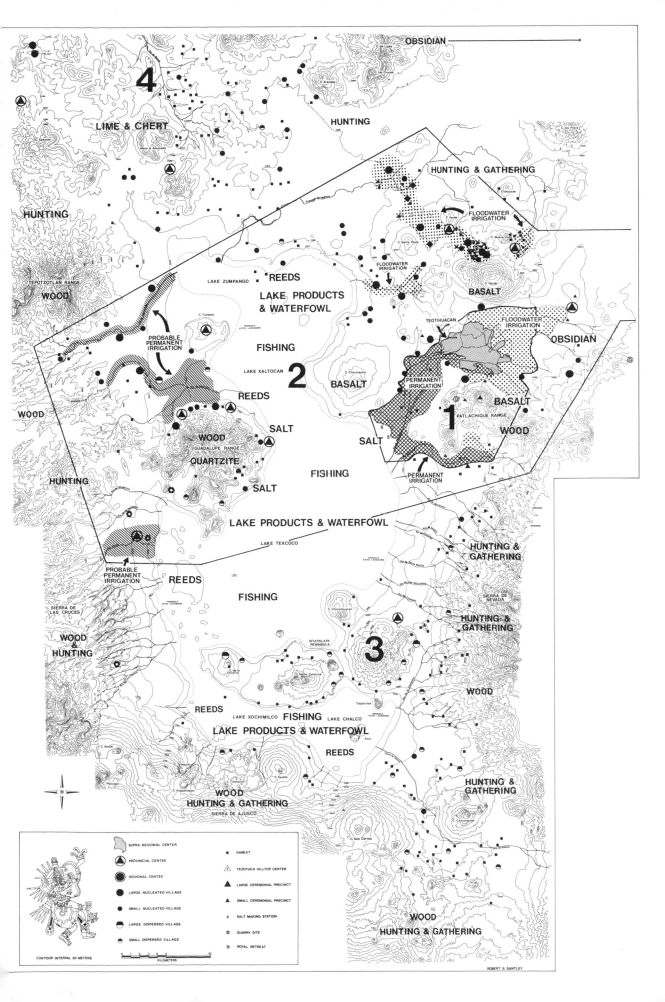

OBSIDIAN

4

LIME & CHERT

HUNTING

HUNTING & GATHERING

HUNTING

Floodwater
Irrigation

REEDS

Tepotzotlan Range

WOOD

LAKE ZUMPANGO

LAKE PRODUCTS
& WATERFOWL

Floodwater
Irrigation

BASALT

C. Tultepec

PROBABLE
PERMANENT
IRRIGATION

LAKE XALTOCAN

FISHING

2

C. Chiconautla

BASALT

Floodwater
Irrigation

OBSIDIAN

TEOTIHUACAN

WOOD

REEDS

PERMANENT
IRRIGATION

BASALT

WOOD

SALT

1

PATLACHIQUE RANGE

WOOD
GUADALUPE RANGE

SALT

WOOD

QUARTZITE

SALT

PERMANENT
IRRIGATION

FISHING

LAKE PRODUCTS & WATERFOWL

SALT

PERMANENT
IRRIGATION

HUNTING

PROBABLE
PERMANENT
IRRIGATION

REEDS

LAKE TEXCOCO

HUNTING &
GATHERING

FISHING

SIERRA DE
LAS CRUCES

SIERRA DE
NEVADA

HUNTING &
GATHERING

WOOD
& HUNTING

IXTAPALAPA
PENINSULA

3

WOOD

C. Santa Catarina

C. de la
Estrella

Tlapacoya

REEDS

LAKE XOCHIMILCO  FISHING  LAKE CHALCO

Xico

LAKE PRODUCTS & WATERFOWL

REEDS

C. Xictle

HUNTING &
GATHERING

WOOD
HUNTING & GATHERING

SIERRA DE AJUSCO

C. Teuhtli

C. Dos Cerros

C. Chiconquiac

WOOD
HUNTING & GATHERING

SUPRA-REGIONAL CENTER

PROVINCIAL CENTER          HAMLET

REGIONAL CENTER           TEZOYUCA HILLTOP CENTER

LARGE NUCLEATED VILLAGE    LARGE CEREMONIAL PRECINCT

SMALL NUCLEATED VILLAGE    SMALL CEREMONIAL PRECINCT

LARGE DISPERSED VILLAGE  S  SALT MAKING STATION

SMALL DISPERSED VILLAGE  Q  QUARRY SITE

                         R  ROYAL RETREAT

CONTOUR INTERVAL 50 METERS

KILOMETERS

ROBERT S. SANTLEY

siding in the city. The inner core also included a large area of permanently irrigated land below the city and a somewhat smaller, but still extensive, floodwater-irrigated plain above the city. We would also include in this core the Papalotla drainage basin, an additional 100 sq km, even though it is separated from the Teotihuacan Valley by the rugged Patlachique range. Including the range itself, the total size of the inner core was 500 sq km. Included within the inner core was a total area of 9,700 ha of permanently irrigated land and 2,300 ha of floodwater-irrigated plain, or a total of 12,000 ha of prime agricultural land. We estimate the carrying capacity of the plains at approximately 140,000 people or substantially higher than the same area during First Intermediate phase 3. This calculation makes the assumptions that the productivity level of the maize was comparable to that of the modern peasant maize used in the area, that all of the land was planted in either maize or some equivalent basic grain like amaranth, and finally that 65 percent of the calories consumed by the population were based upon this crop. There is evidence supporting the argument that the maize at this time was of comparable productivity to that used today. This evidence is in the form of sampled plant remains from a number of excavations, collected under Millon's Teotihuacan mapping project and analyzed by Emily McClung de Tapia (1977). What the samples indicate is that Toluqueño maize, a specialized type of maize adapted to the high plateau areas of Mesoamerica, with a short growing season of three to four months, was known at this time, and furthermore that Conico, a hybrid type which is the product of a mixture of Toluqueño with a Columbian maize, was also present. Conico inherited the 3–4 month growing season characteristic of Toluqueño, but with a considerably higher productivity, and is the major type of maize grown in the Teotihuacan Valley today.

The outer core consisted of a zone of settlement measuring approximately 1,000 sq km that ran from northeast to southwest and contained most of the rural population of the basin. These settlements can be sorted into four groups. One consisted of a string of settlements located well up on the piedmont of the Teotihuacan Valley proper, probably with an agricultural system based on rainfall and floodwater irrigation. The population utilizing this area was approximately 10,000. Second, on the north flank of the Teotihuacan Valley some 20,000 villagers resided in an area of gently sloping terrain, in close association with several major drainage basins that provided floodwater irrigation and flowed northwest toward the northern lakes. This is also an area of recent volcanic activity and extremely fertile soils. Confirming evidence, in the form of canals and artificial *barrancas*, in close proximity to the zones of Middle Horizon occupation and in some cases directly related spatially to these settlements, suggests that this was an area of extensive floodwater irrigation. The third cluster of settlements included a set of villages aligned along the Tepoztlan and Cuautitlan rivers. Major springs occur in the upper courses of both streams, and the overall flow, as well as the available alluvial land that could have been irrigated from these sources, is comparable to that of the Teotihuacan-Papalotla system. A theoretical 10,000 ha of land could have been irrigated from these streams, but our resident Middle Horizon population was only about 12,000 people. The distribution of settlements does suggest the use of the streams for canal irrigation, but if the irrigated land was cultivated only by the resident population (it is remotely possible that some lands were cultivated by residents of the city, but the distance—25 km—makes this unreasonable), and based on our calculations of the energetic efficiency of irrigation agriculture, not more than 4,000–5,000 ha could have been

FIGURE 6-17. Basin of Mexico: Second Intermediate phase 1. Reprinted from *The Basin of Mexico: Ecological Processes in the Evolution of a Civilization*. Copyright © 1979, by Academic Press, Inc.

182

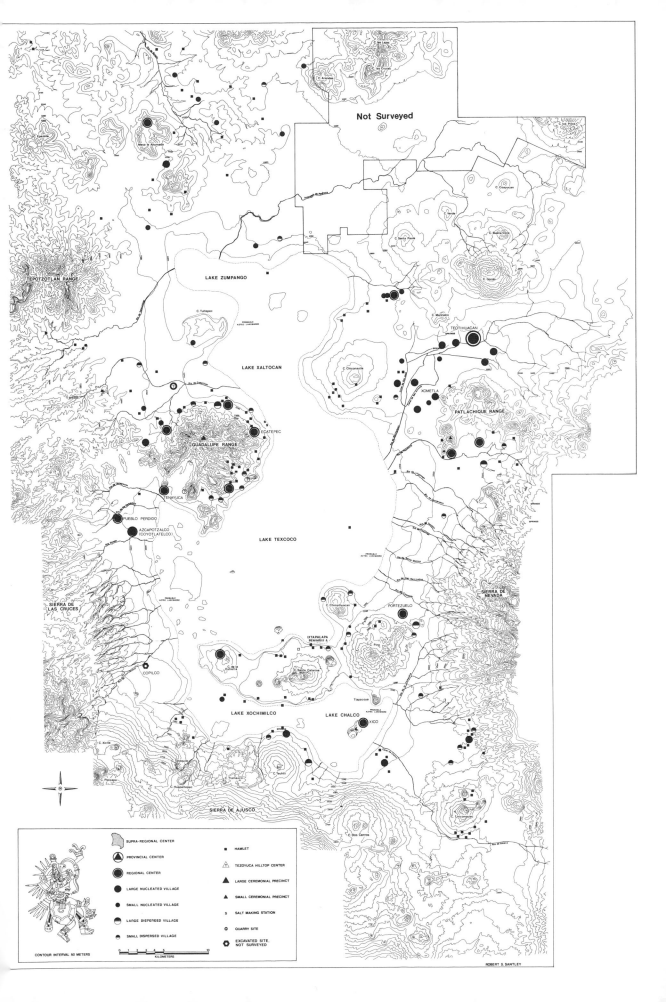

Not Surveyed

TEPOTZOTLAN RANGE

LAKE ZUMPANGO

C. Tultepec

PROBABLE
AZTEC LAKESHORE

LAKE XALTOCAN

C. Coyuacan

C. Verde

Buena Vista

C. Santa Paula

C. Gordo

C. Malinalco

TEOTIHUACAN

C. Chiconautla

XOMETLA

PATLACHIQUE RANGE

Mesa la Ahumada

C. Epazote

GUADALUPE RANGE

ECATEPEC

TENAYUCA

PUEBLO PERDIDO

AZCAPOTZALCO
(COYOTLATELCO)

LAKE TEXCOCO

PROBABLE
AZTEC LAKESHORE

SIERRA DE
LAS CRUCES

PROBABLE
AZTEC LAKESHORE

C. Chimalhuacan

PORTEZUELO

SIERRA DE
NEVADA

IXTAPALAPA
PENINSULA

C. Pino

COPILCO

C. de la
Estrella

C. Santa Catarina

Tlapacoya

PROBABLE
AZTEC LAKESHORE

LAKE XOCHIMILCO

LAKE CHALCO

XICO

C. Xicte

Tetecuta

C. Teuhtli

C. Pipsapa

Tlamaco

C. Huepaltepec

SIERRA DE AJUSCO

C. Chiconcuac

C. Dos Cerros

LEGEND

◖ SUPRA-REGIONAL CENTER

◭ PROVINCIAL CENTER

⬤ REGIONAL CENTER

● LARGE NUCLEATED VILLAGE

• SMALL NUCLEATED VILLAGE

◗ LARGE DISPERSED VILLAGE

◖ SMALL DISPERSED VILLAGE

■ HAMLET

⚠ TEZOYUCA HILLTOP CENTER

▲ LARGE CEREMONIAL PRECINCT

▲ SMALL CEREMONIAL PRECINCT

S SALT MAKING STATION

✧ QUARRY SITE

⬡ EXCAVATED SITE,
NOT SURVEYED

CONTOUR INTERVAL 50 METERS

0 1 2 3 4 5        10
KILOMETERS

ROBERT S. SANTLEY

brought under cultivation, half the capacity of the system. The surpluses generated by the cultivation of this much land, however, would have provided for an additional 24,000 urban residents at Teotihuacan, a substantial contribution to the support of the city. The fourth cluster of settlements lay along the western lakeshore of Lake Texcoco in an area of substantial hydraulic potential (i.e., an area where there is juxtaposition of large areas of sloping terrain, which would provide abundant runoff, and small areas of alluvial lakeshore plain, which could have been irrigated from this runoff). Permanent irrigation was also feasible in the drainage of the Remedios and Hondo rivers.

The periphery lay to the northwest and southeast of the outer core and was occupied by a widely dispersed population, residing primarily in hamlets and small villages, at a very low overall population density. We suggest that this occupation was the product of colonization, planned by the rulers of the city to obtain other than basic food resources (i.e., lake products, lime, obsidian, wood, reeds, etc.).

Second Intermediate phase 1 can be easily summarized. The stability of the Middle Horizon inner-outer core area during this phase is surely a reflection of the persistence of the same basic patterns of land use. The virtual absence of population in the upper Teotihuacan Valley, the north periphery of the Teotihuacan Valley, and the Tepoztlan Valley reflects the general population decline that characterized the basin as a whole, and the remaining population apparently retrenched around the areas of abundant perennial water resources. Another change was the establishment of a number of large nucleated settlements in close spatial relationship to the irrigable land of the lower Teotihuacan Valley and the middle Papalotla Valley. What this undoubtedly reflects is a shift of residence of cultivators who once lived at Teotihuacan to localities closer to their land resources.

The reasons for the return of a substantial population to the southern basin, a climatically favorable area, are not clear, but the close association of a large number of sites to the lacustrine habitat could be interpreted as related to the development of small areas of *chinampa* cultivation. At this time we have no direct support for this argument, but it would be rather difficult to explain the substantial Second Intermediate phase 1 community on Xico Island otherwise.

The First Intermediate phase 2 pattern of agricultural exploitation includes the following features: substantial occupation of the Teotihuacan Valley alluvial plain, of the Cuautitlan-Tepoztlan basins, and of the Tula-Salado basins, the latter the region of densest settlement of all. The three permanent irrigation systems, i.e., the Cuautitlan-Tepoztlan, Teotihuacan-Papalotla, and Tula-Salado systems, all have very comparable spring flows, sufficient to irrigate approximately 10,000 ha of land each. The data would suggest that the Teotihuacan (but not the Papalotla segment) and the Tula-Salado systems were fully utilized, but that only a fraction of the Cuautitlan (comparable perhaps to that of the Middle Horizon) was utilized. Tula, then, seems to have received its major food supply from a substantial area of hydraulic agriculture located within easy access of the city. The balance of the Basin of Mexico was occupied by a great number of hamlets with overall low population densities.

As has been pointed out, the phase 4 population distribution was almost a reproduction of that of phase 1, suggesting very comparable patterns of land use. There was an even heavier concentration of population, however, along the southern lakes, on the shore and offshore islands, suggesting that *chinampa* agriculture was substantially developed at this time. There is also direct evidence of *chinampa* cultivation in the northern lake of

FIGURE 6-18. Basin of Mexico: Second Intermediate phase 2. Reprinted from *The Basin of Mexico: Ecological Processes in the Evolution of a Civilization.* Copyright © 1979, by Academic Press, Inc.

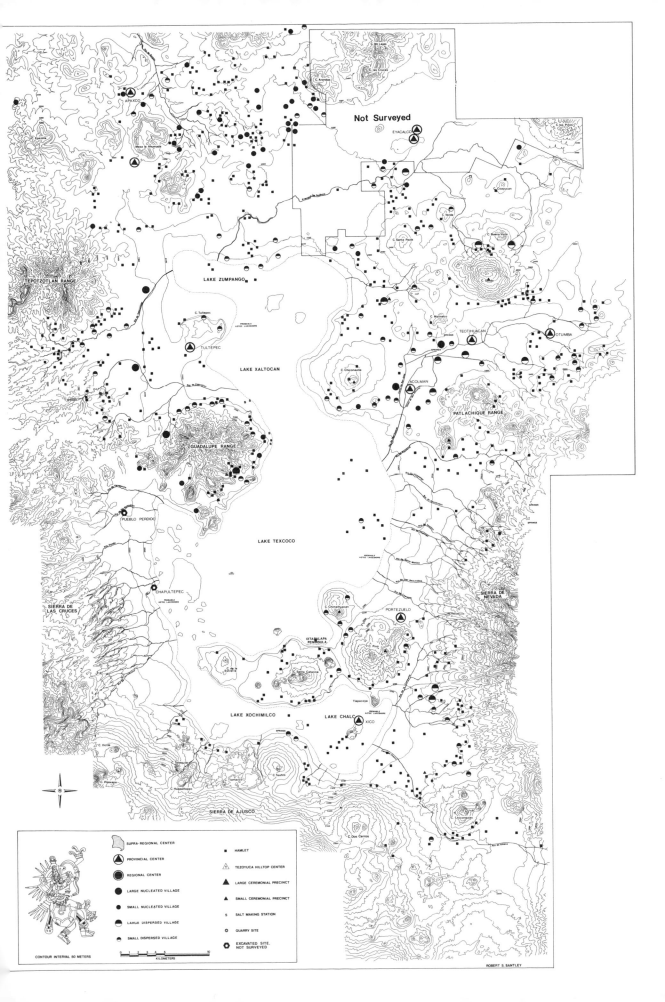

**Not Surveyed**

APAXCO

C. Arandas

EYACALCO

Cixayucan

C. Verde

C. Santa Paula

C. Buena Vista

Coxla

TEPOTZOTLAN RANGE

LAKE ZUMPANGO

C. Tultepec

C. Malinalco

TEOTIHUACAN

OTUMBA

TULTEPEC

LAKE XALTOCAN

C. Chiconautla

ACOLMAN

PATLACHIQUE RANGE

GUADALUPE RANGE

PUEBLO PERDIDO

LAKE TEXCOCO

SIERRA DE
LAS CRUCES

CHAPULTEPEC

SIERRA DE
NEVADA

C. Chimalhuacan

PORTEZUELO

IXTAPALAPA
PENINSULA

Pino

C. de la
Estrella

C. Santa Catarina

Tlapacoya

LAKE XOCHIMILCO

LAKE CHALCO

XICO

C. Xicte

C. Tlamanco

C. Teuhtli

SIERRA DE AJUSCO

C. Dos Cerros

**Legend:**

- SUPRA-REGIONAL CENTER
- PROVINCIAL CENTER
- REGIONAL CENTER
- LARGE NUCLEATED VILLAGE
- SMALL NUCLEATED VILLAGE
- LARGE DISPERSED VILLAGE
- SMALL DISPERSED VILLAGE
- ■ HAMLET
- TEZOYUCA HILLTOP CENTER
- LARGE CEREMONIAL PRECINCT
- SMALL CEREMONIAL PRECINCT
- S SALT MAKING STATION
- QUARRY SITE
- EXCAVATED SITE, NOT SURVEYED

CONTOUR INTERVAL 50 METERS

0 1 2 3 4 5 10
KILOMETERS

ROBERT S. SANTLEY

Xaltocan, around Xaltocan Island, associated with a large phase 4 regional center.

SOCIOPOLITICAL EVOLUTION. The sociopolitical history of the period includes an initial phase that lasted approximately 850 years and was characterized by political and economic centralization, followed by a short period of 200 years of political fragmentation, a subsequent period of 200 years of political centralization, and another 200 years of fragmentation. During the two periods of political integration the center was a large, compact, nucleated community. Teotihuacan's mean population during the Middle Horizon is estimated at 125,000, with a range of 75,000–200,000. In our reconstruction of the food production system of Teotihuacan, we suggested that the land of the inner core (i.e., the alluvial plains in the immediate vicinity of the city) was cultivated not by villagers living in rural settlements, but by a population residing at Teotihuacan itself, an unusual but by no means unique pattern. René Millon's surveys and excavations by a number of people indicate that the residents lived in large compounds that had populations of 30–100 each (R. Millon 1973). Ethnographic analogy, the internal plan of the compounds, the occupational structure, and data from burials suggest that the residents of the large house compound formed a close-knit corporate group, based in many cases on kinship. Surface samples imply that approximately 25 percent of the 2,000 compounds occupied during the Middle Horizon were inhabited by occupational specialists, predominantly obsidian workers. To this total should be added religious, political, and perhaps military specialists. Possibly two-thirds of the population of the city were farmers, cultivating the lands of the inner core. It is possible that some, if not many, of the economic specialists of the city held some agricultural land, and therefore were part-time rather than full-time specialists. At any rate Teotihuacan was obviously a large agrarian settlement as well as an urban center. During phase 4, when the city increased from its phase 3 level of 40,000 to 90,000 people,

186

much of the gain was apparently produced by migration of people from farming settlements into the city, and the data we have on occupational specialization indicate that perhaps 80–90 percent of the residents of the city were farmers.

Tula's relationship to its core was quite different (see Fig. 6-20). The city itself was only half the size of Teotihuacan, but there were an additional 60,000 people residing in nearby villages within the Tula region. It is interesting that the total population of Tula and its nearby rural settlements is approximately equivalent to that of Teotihuacan, and that the total population of the Tula region and that of the entire Basin of Mexico are almost identical, 240,000–260,000. A reasonable reconstruction, based on the settlement pattern, is that most of the people who lived in the city of Tula were not farmers. This argument is substantiated by direct evidence of large-scale occupational specialization, particularly in obsidian working, based on Diehl's survey (Diehl 1974). In other words, the urban population was roughly comparable to that of Teotihuacan in size; the difference between the two was that in the case of the Middle Horizon city, there were extensive suburbs around the urban core, occupied by farmers, whereas in Second Intermediate phase 2, such farmers lived in discrete rural settlements.

The larger size of the centers, the larger population politically integrated under these centers, the evidence of palace construction, the monumental scale of religious architecture, and striking differences in housing and burials, indicating differences in wealth, all argue for much more marked levels of social stratification than in ecological Stage III. There is also conclusive evidence of very widespread external trade and political relationships.

FIGURE 6-19. Basin of Mexico: Second Intermediate phase 3. Reprinted from *The Basin of Mexico: Ecological Processes in the Evolution of a Civilization.* Copyright © 1979, by Academic Press, Inc.

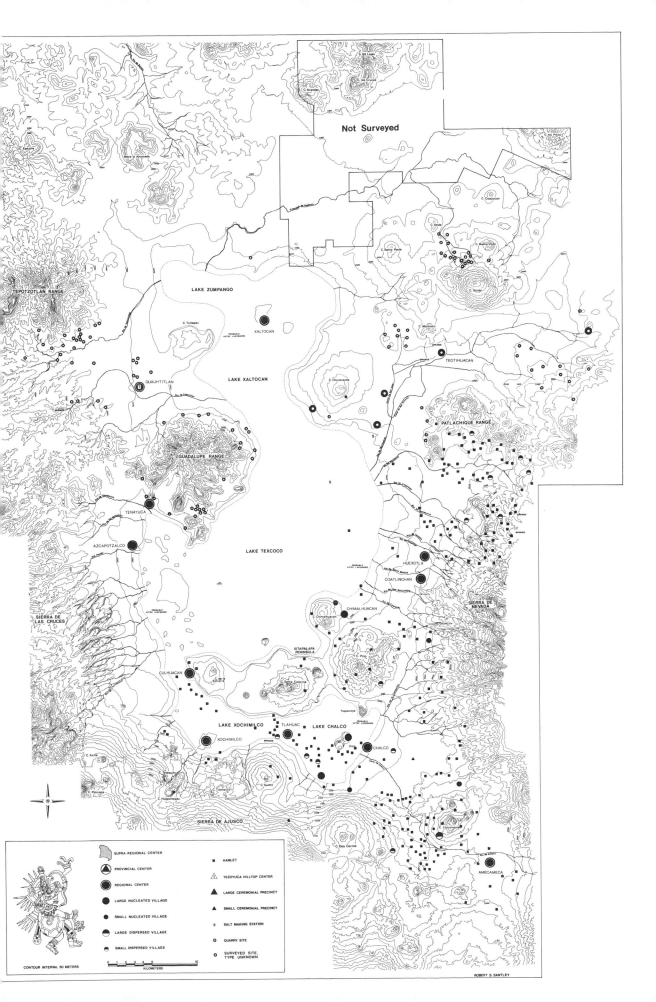

**Not Surveyed**

TEPOTZOTLAN RANGE

Epazoba

Mesa la Ahumada

LAKE ZUMPANGO

C. Tultepec

XALTOCAN

C. Arandas
las Cruces

C. Coayucan

C. Verde

C. Santa Paula

C. Buena Vista

C. Gordo

C. Macinalco

TEOTIHUACAN

QUAUHTITLAN

LAKE XALTOCAN

PROBABLE
AZTEC LAKESHORE

C. Chiconautla

PATLACHIQUE RANGE

GUADALUPE RANGE

TENAYUCA

AZCAPOTZALCO

LAKE TEXCOCO

PROBABLE
AZTEC LAKESHORE

HUEXOTLA

COATLINCHAN

SIERRA DE
NEVADA

SIERRA DE
LAS CRUCES

C. Chimalhuacan

CHIMALHUACAN

CULHUACAN

C. de la
Estrella

IXTAPALAPA
PENINSULA

C. Pino

C. Santa Catarina

C. Xictli

Tlapacoya

PROBABLE
AZTEC LAKESHORE

LAKE XOCHIMILCO

TLAHUAC

LAKE CHALCO

CHALCO

XOCHIMILCO

SPRINGS

Tetequilco

C. Huepallepec

Pipixapa

C. Teuhtli

Tlamimilolpa

C. Dos Cerros

AMECAMECA

SIERRA DE AJUSCO

**Legend**

- SUPRA-REGIONAL CENTER
- PROVINCIAL CENTER
- REGIONAL CENTER
- LARGE NUCLEATED VILLAGE
- SMALL NUCLEATED VILLAGE
- LARGE DISPERSED VILLAGE
- SMALL DISPERSED VILLAGE

- ■ HAMLET
- △ TEZOYUCA HILLTOP CENTER
- ▲ LARGE CEREMONIAL PRECINCT
- ▲ SMALL CEREMONIAL PRECINCT
- S SALT MAKING STATION
- ⊙ QUARRY SITE
- ⊙ SURVEYED SITE, TYPE UNKNOWN

CONTOUR INTERVAL 50 METERS

0 1 2 3 4 5    10
KILOMETERS

ROBERT S. SANTLEY

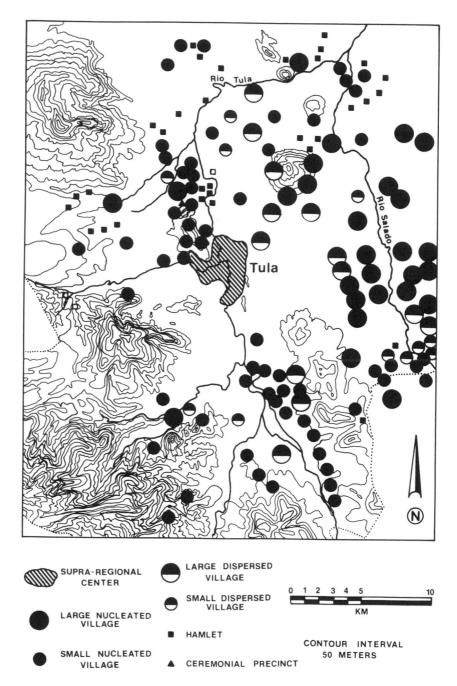

SUPRA-REGIONAL
CENTER

LARGE NUCLEATED
VILLAGE

SMALL NUCLEATED
VILLAGE

LARGE DISPERSED
VILLAGE

SMALL DISPERSED
VILLAGE

HAMLET

CEREMONIAL PRECINCT

0 1 2 3 4 5                    10
KM

CONTOUR  INTERVAL
50 METERS

FIGURE 6-20. The Tula region, showing the distribution of Second Intermediate phase 2 occupation. Reprinted from *The Basin of Mexico: Ecological Processes in the Evolution of a Civilization*. Copyright © 1979, by Academic Press, Inc.

*Stage V (A.D. 1350–1519)*

The final phase of the Prehispanic period represents the climax of occupation of the basin, in terms of population size and density, intensity of land use, urban and political evolution, and remodeling of the geographic landscape. Of the 3,864 sites that we defined in the survey, 1,636, or approximately 40 percent, date from this short period of less than 200 years. It is difficult to find a contemporary houselot or agricultural field that does not have some Aztec III or IV ceramics in it.

It is also a time period for which it is hard to define sites and to characterize them in terms of the typology discussed previously. Much of the rural population lived in highly dispersed settlements, which tended, in some cases, to merge physically and make site or community definition exceedingly difficult. Most rural aggregates of residential structures had small ceremonial precincts associated with them that served as centers of political, economic, and religious integration. We have often used the spacing of such precincts as a guide, and have drawn rather arbitrary borders between the zones of associated residences.

SETTLEMENT TYPES. Rural settlements tend to conform very closely to topographic features. For example, in the linearly shaped lower and middle Teotihuacan Valley, the alluvial plain is flanked by narrow, gently sloping piedmont on both sides, and the piedmont, in turn, abuts on the steep slopes of nearby hills and ranges. Rural settlements tend to have a markedly linear form, with individual clusters like beads on a string. The upper section of the same valley, however, is fan-shaped, with a wide piedmont surrounding a small alluvial plain and traversed by a radial network of streams. Houses tend to be almost evenly distributed on the interfluves between these various streams. This last pattern is approximated on the wide Texcoco piedmont. In the southern survey regions and the Cuautitlan region, rural Aztec sites tend to be predominantly in the form of rather closely spaced, but physically dis-

crete, dispersed hamlets and small villages. In the *chinampa* zone, within Lake Chalco-Xochimilco, each house tends to be associated with a small square of *chinampas*, so we have a completely dispersed settlement in that area.

Bearing in mind the problems of site definition discussed above, our Late Horizon rural settlements are classified as follows: 986 hamlets, 265 small villages (31 nucleated, 234 dispersed), and 89 large villages (10 nucleated, 79 dispersed). Besides these we have definite ethnographic references to 137 other communities, primarily in the Tacuba region, that undoubtedly would fit into the village status if we had the settlement data. During this phase there were numerous nonresidential sites as well, including 56 definite salt-making sites (but we know of great numbers of these that have been destroyed by the recent urban growth of Mexico City, on the west shore of Lake Texcoco) and 59 hilltop ceremonial precincts, probably local shrines dedicated to the rain god Tlaloc.

On the basis of documentary accounts, we know that the basin, in 1519, was divided up into approximately 60–65 principalities, each ruled by a hereditary lord or *tlatoani* (Gibson 1964). Prior to political manipulations by the Culhua-Mexica and Acolhua dynasties, each *tlatoani* domain was originally territorially discrete and included a small center and its outlying settlements. In a number of cases several *tlatoani* shared the same physical center, each controlling a ward of that center, along with outlying settlements. If these are combined and only physically discrete communities considered as centers, the number of centers is perhaps 45–50. In terms of population many of these centers fell into two classes, one with a population of 3,000–4,000 and the other with 5,000–6,000. Several centers were considerably larger, including Texcoco, Ixtapalapa, Tlacopan, and Xochimilco, which had populations between 10,000 and 30,000. Many of these centers are occupied today by densely settled and nucleated towns and large villages, so that only a few of them were available for our settlement survey. In those cases where we do have data, they indicate that the pattern consisted of a series of concentric zones, including a very densely nucleated inner core, where the houses seem to have been virtually continuous and separated only by alleys; an outer core of less dense settlement, but in which the houselots were still relatively small (a settlement density comparable to that of nucleated villages today); and a rural fringe of dispersed settlement (where settlement density approximated present-day scattered villages).

At the top of this settlement hierarchy was the twin city of Tenochtitlan-Tlatelolco, which had a core area of 12–15 sq km and an estimated population, following Calnek (1970), of 150,000–200,000—the largest urban concentration in the history of Mesoamerica.

POPULATION HISTORY. The most significant demographic event of Stage V is the abrupt change from a pattern of relative stability for 1,250 years to a brief period of extraordinary growth, with a final population estimated conservatively at 800,000, and more probably at 1,200,000. Taking an average of these two figures, this is roughly four times the previous peak, which occurred during the climax of Teotihuacan and Tula. The annual growth rate, if we assume that this was entirely an internal process and that it started perhaps a little earlier than the period actually began, would be about .7 percent, which is twice the rate of the period of dynamic growth during ecological Stage III. Our settlement survey suggests that there were only a few unoccupied areas left by 1519.

GEOGRAPHIC PATTERNING OF SETTLEMENT. As the population data suggest, the basin was densely settled in 1519, with an average of almost 200 people per sq km. In terms of areas actually settled, i.e., excluding the high sierra, large stretches of saline marsh, and the middle and upper piedmont of the Cuautitlan region, which were not settled, the effective agricultural density was probably closer to 300 people per sq km.

Such densities had been achieved only in highly localized, small areas during the preceding stages. The major geographic areas of population expansion may be summarized as follows: (1) dense settlement of the upper piedmont, over virtually all of the basin; this territory had been virtually unused during all previous periods; (2) an enormous expansion of cultivation of the alluvial plains; prior to this period only a few selected areas had been fully utilized, primarily the Teotihuacan Valley plains; (3) a large-scale colonization of the southern lakes by the process of *chinampa* cultivation; and (4) a substantial colonization, for the first time, of the upper and middle piedmont around Milpa Alta (see Fig. 6-21).

Although population was dense throughout the Basin of Mexico, there was still a particular area that stood out as a demographic core. This area included the western portions of Lakes Xochimilco and Texcoco and the adjacent lower piedmont and alluvial plain, a total area of 600 sq km, where 40 percent of the total population of the basin resided in 1521. Of this total, nearly half lived in the twin cities of Tenochtitlan-Tlatelolco.

RESOURCE PROCUREMENT. During the long period from 1000 B.C. to A.D. 1350, a variety of basic agricultural techniques were developed, i.e., drainage agriculture, permanent irrigation, floodwater irrigation, and terracing—techniques that went hand in hand with a process of intensification of land use. During the earliest phases, such techniques of cultivation were applied over relatively small areas, and much of the basin was apparently still using extensive techniques of cultivation. The major event of the Late Horizon is the generalization of intensive agriculture over the entire surface of the basin. Virtually none of the techniques used in the

FIGURE 6-21. Basin of Mexico: Late Horizon. Reprinted from *The Basin of Mexico: Ecological Processes in the Evolution of a Civilization.* Copyright © 1979, by Academic Press, Inc.

Not Surveyed

TEPOTZOTLAN RANGE

GUADALUPE RANGE

PATLACHIQUE RANGE

LAKE ZUMPANGO

LAKE XALTOCAN

LAKE TEXCOCO

SIERRA DE NEVADA

SIERRA DE LAS CRUCES

TLATELOLCO

TENOCHTITLAN

IXTAPALAPA PENINSULA

LAKE XOCHIMILCO

LAKE CHALCO

SIERRA DE AJUSCO

CONTOUR INTERVAL 50 METERS

KILOMETERS

SUPRA-REGIONAL CENTER
PROVINCIAL CENTER
REGIONAL CENTER
LARGE NUCLEATED VILLAGE
SMALL NUCLEATED VILLAGE
LARGE DISPERSED VILLAGE
SMALL DISPERSED VILLAGE

HAMLET
ETHNOHISTORIC SITE, NOT SURVEYED
LARGE CEREMONIAL PRECINCT
SMALL CEREMONIAL PRECINCT
SALT MAKING STATION
QUARRY SITE
ROYAL RETREAT
CAUSEWAY

ROBERT S. SANTLEY

Late Horizon were invented or developed during that period; it is the scale of their application then that is unique.

A major process of intensification was the development of drainage agriculture on the alluvial plains, particularly the lower and middle section of the Cuautitlan plain, the Chalco plain, the plains around the middle and lower course of the Avenida Pachuca, and the lakeshore plain of the Texcoco region. All the regions were lightly or sporadically utilized until this period, when for the first time a large-scale intensive agricultural approach, involving drainage agriculture, permanent irrigation, and floodwater irrigation, was applied. This process reached its most dramatic aspect with the colonization of the southern fresh water lakes and swamps of Chalco and Xochimilco by the technique of drainage cultivation referred to in the literature as *chinampa* agriculture (Armillas 1971). The final phase of this process involved the development of an elaborate network of sluice gates and dikes that converted parts of saline Lake Texcoco into a fresh water lake for *chinampa* colonization (Palerm 1973). Briefly, *chinampas* are artificial islands, either constructed by hand from lake sediments or produced by a process of large-scale ditching. Characteristic of this system of cultivation is intensive land use, including the use of green fertilizers and mulches, pot irrigation, and successive planting by the use of seedbeds.

The basic techniques of permanent canal irrigation had been developed by the Middle Horizon but had been applied broadly only in the Teotihuacan-Papalotla drainage. The Late Horizon witnessed a final and full expansion of the use of all permanent hydraulic resources. Another major development was floodwater irrigation, which, for the first time, was generalized over an enormous area.

In terms of the economic significance of this expansion of hydraulic agriculture, we make the following assessments. Approximately 12,000 ha of land were converted to *chinampa* agriculture, including about 10,000 in the fresh water lakes and approximately 2,000 in the saline lakes. We estimate that this amount of land could have supported approximately 228,000 people. The 20,000 ha of permanently irrigated land within the Basin of Mexico itself and the 10,000 ha in the Tula region could have sustained an additional 250,000 people (these calculations are based on a grain yield of 1,400 kg per ha, assuming that 80 percent of the caloric intake was derived from grain). When one adds to these figures an unknown amount of lakeshore terrain that was converted to drainage agriculture and a theoretical maximum of 40,000–50,000 ha that could have been brought under cultivation using floodwater irrigation, then the effects of the full development of the hydraulic potential of the Basin of Mexico can be brought into sharp focus.

Another technique that had been well developed during the earlier phases but limited to small areas was terracing. During the Late Horizon it became generalized over virtually all of the sloping terrain of the basin from the lower to the upper piedmont.

At least two basic types of terraces were utilized. One consists of the use of earth embankments, usually planted with a soil-retaining crop such as maguey. This type of terrace has been referred to as either a *metepantli* or a *bancal* and is generally found in gently sloping areas. During the nineteenth century, however, the large haciendas in the basin colonized even steeper slopes by planting maguey in closely spaced lines (1–2 m) parallel to the slope, in effect forming a series of sloping terraces which are also referred to as *metepantli*. It is not clear whether this type of land utilization is Prehispanic in origin. The second type of terrace involves the use of more solid construction (in its most highly developed form, consisting of roughly trimmed stone blocks; in its more rustic form, irregular chunks of stone or volcanic conglomerate) set in earth. This type is used in more rugged terrain. In some areas, particularly around Milpa Alta in the rugged upper and middle piedmont (where there is a high percentage of recent volcanic formations), such constructions are often above ground, forming an enclosure that serves the double function of soil retention and property definition.

Archaeological remains of Aztec terraces are particularly abundant in the Milpa Alta area, on the Texcoco piedmont, on the Ixtapalapa Peninsula, and throughout the sloping terrain of the Teotihuacan and Temascalapa regions. It should be noted, however, that these are also areas where the Late Horizon occupation occurred at the upper limit of maize cultivation and included considerable terrain with a substantial angle of slope. This setting required the use of more solid terrace construction, and therefore the remains of these terraces have survived. Definite evidence of terracing in the Cuautitlan region is sporadic, presumably because the Late Horizon occupation did not occur much above 2,300 m; hence terracing in this area would have been applied to gently sloping terrain, and would have been of the *metepantli* type, which is difficult to detect archaeologically.

One of the distinctive features of the Late Horizon pattern of utilization of resources other than basic foodstuffs (and in respect to food we would argue that most settlements were self-sufficient or nearly so) is intense, local, part-time specialization. Documentary and archaeological evidence demonstrates the existence of this type of specialization in obsidian mining, salt manufacturing, wood processing, fishing, hunting, lime processing, pottery-making, and reed processing. This development is clearly the product of the dense overall population, and consequent pressures on resources generally, in an environment which is essentially heterogeneous, with highly localized concentrations of natural resources. While similar patterns of local specialization may have occurred in earlier times (note the above discussion of the Middle Horizon), considering the spac-

ing and the location of settlements and the overall lower population density, it did not approximate the intensity that was achieved during the Late Horizon.

SOCIOPOLITICAL EVOLUTION. The data base on the subject of Late Horizon sociopolitical and economic organization is enormous, and it is clearly not possible to discuss all of the details and controversies involved. For this reason I will try to be as general as possible.

Aztec economy was a mixture of a number of components: the temple and the state, with access to surplus production, via the taxation system; a landed aristocracy; a professional commercial and craft production class; and a "free" peasantry, with communal land rights over specific tracts of agricultural land. Access to political and economic power was possible through inherited land rights; the holding of political offices, some of which were inherited and some acquired; trade; and, to a certain degree, skilled craftsmanship. Goods were obtained either by redistribution of taxes by the state or through a hierarchy of regional markets, focused on the great marketplace of Tlatelolco (Carrasco and Broada 1976; Carrasco 1978). Many of these patterns had apparently been present in earlier times, particularly during the two phases of political centralization at Teotihuacan and Tula, but the scale and complexity of the sociopolitical systems during the Late Horizon must have been considerably greater, because of the considerably larger population.

On the political side, there is a serious problem in comparing a center like Teotihuacan or Tula with Tenochtitlan, since we have much richer sources of information for the latest center, whereas we must derive our understanding of the earlier centers almost entirely from archaeological data. Nevertheless, on the basis of archaeological data from our region and other areas in Mesoamerica, it is my opinion that the direct political sphere of influence of Teotihuacan, i.e., the area that it could collect taxes from, was relatively small and probably did not include land outside of the central plateau, i.e., the highland basins of Toluca, Tula-Salado, Puebla-Tlaxcala, and the Amacusac. Teotihuacan influence outside this central plateau was probably based upon commercial ties, and it is believed that the Teotihuacanos had established a number of colonies of merchants, at Kaminaljuyu, Matacapan, Monte Alban, and probably other places as well. Tula's political domain was probably comparable in size but with a northwesterly bias. I do not believe that the political domains of these centers were comparable either in size or in extent to that of Tenochtitlan at the time of the Spanish Conquest, with its estimated 200,000 sq km of politically controlled area and an estimated population of 5–6 million.

Perhaps the clearest demonstration of this power lies in the spatial and physical dimensions of the metropolitan area of Tlatelolco-Tenochtitlan. (See Fig. 6-22 in connection with the following discussion.)

The city of Tlatelolco-Tenochtitlan was located on several islands and artificial ground in the western arm of Lake Texcoco. It had an estimated population of 150,000–200,000 concentrated in an area of 12–15 sq km, and it was occupied almost entirely by a non–food-producing population. The city was divided into 5 administrative wards, including Tlatelolco, and these, in turn, into a total of 80 smaller wards, each of which had specialized economic functions. Sahagún, for example, mentions 7 wards of merchants alone at the time of the Conquest. Surrounding the city were at least a dozen smaller settlements on natural or artificial islands in the lake and associated with outlying fringes of *chinampas*. The various zones of *chinampas* must have formed an almost continuous zone that occupied most of the western arm of Lake Texcoco and was coterminous with the much larger *chinampa* area to the south in Lake Chalco-Xochimilco. Crisscrossing the lake and extending through these fringe settlements from the city to the mainland was a network of dikes-causeways that served a double function of regulating the waterflow and providing access to the city from the lakeshore settlements. The adjacent lakeshore was densely settled by a concentration of towns and villages, four of which, Tacuba, Azcapotzalco, Ixtapalapa, and Xochimilco, had populations exceeding 10,000. Besides this a number of smaller towns, such as Tenayuca, Tacubaya, Mixcoac, Coyoacan, Mexicalcingo, Huitzilopochco, and Culhuacan, had populations of 3,000–6,000 each. In this zone of about 600 sq km, which we refer to as the metropolitan area, in 1519 there lived approximately 400,000 people, of whom at least 60 percent were non–food-producing specialists of various kinds. From the air, the denseness of settlement and the presence of the causeways would have given the impression of a single great settlement.

## Stages VI–VIII (A.D. 1519–Present)

Following the Spanish Conquest was a period of 131 years (ecological Stage VI) that can be best described as a time of ecological disaster. This was primarily a biological disaster, promoted by the introduction of a series of exotic epidemic diseases, such as chickenpox, smallpox, mumps, whooping cough, and measles. These biological disasters, however, brought on a series of geographic and cultural disasters. Between 1520 and 1597, 28 years were epidemic years. Most of these involved single epidemics, which I have called minor epidemics, but there were several times during this phase when, over a period of only a few years, multiple epidemics hit the area, such as in 1545–1548 and in 1576–1581. The native population (i.e., those classified by the Spaniards as Indians and subject to the royal and *encomienda* tax system) declined from a peak of 1 million people in 1519 to 400,000 by 1568, to 180,000 by 1585, to a nadir of 100,000 by the middle of the seven-

FIGURE 6-22. Greater Tenochtitlan. Reprinted from *The Basin of Mexico: Ecological Processes in the Evolution of a Civilization.* Copyright © 1979, by Academic Press, Inc.

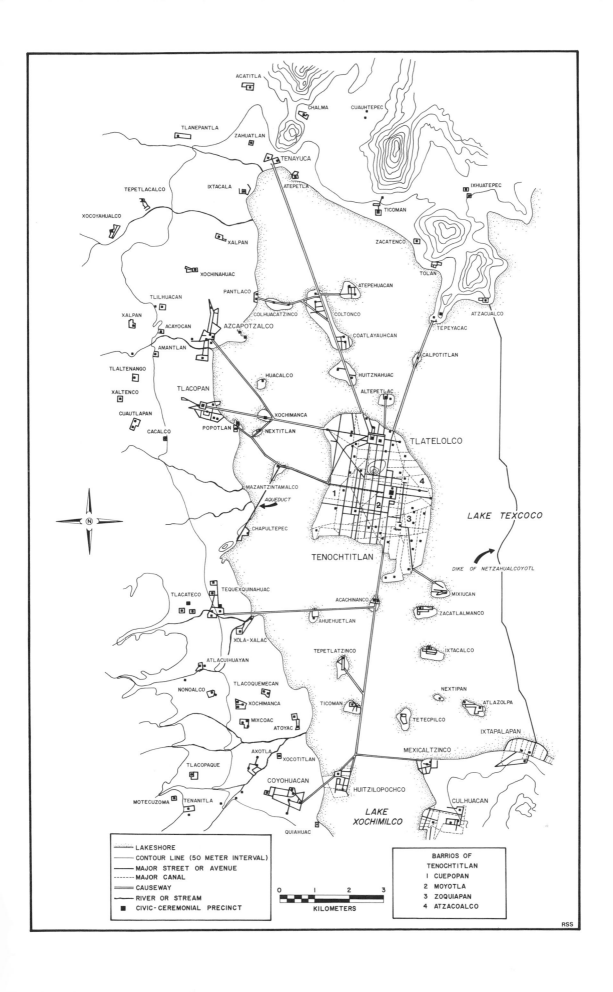

ACATITLA

CHALMA

CUAUHTEPEC

TLANEPANTLA

ZAHUATLAN

TENAYUCA

TEPETLACALCO

IXTACALA

ATEPETLA

IXHUATEPEC

TICOMAN

XOCOYAHUALCO

ZACATENCO

XALPAN

TOLAN

XOCHINAHUAC

PANTLACO

ATEPEHUACAN

TLILHUACAN

COLHUACATZINCO

COLTONCO

ATZACUALCO

XALPAN

ACAYOCAN

AZCAPOTZALCO

COATLAYAUHCAN

TEPEYACAC

AMANTLAN

HUITZNAHUAC

CALPOTITLAN

TLALTENANGO

HUACALCO

ALTEPETLAC

XALTENCO

TLACOPAN

CUAUTLAPAN

XOCHIMANCA

CACALCO

POPOTLAN

NEXTITLAN

TLATELOLCO

MAZANTZINTAMALCO

4

AQUEDUCT

1

LAKE TEXCOCO

CHAPULTEPEC

2

3

TENOCHTITLAN

DIKE OF NETZAHUALCOYOTL

TLACATECO

TEQUEXQUINAHUAC

ACACHINANCO

MIXIUCAN

AHUEHUETLAN

ZACATLALMANCO

XOLA-XALAC

TEPETLATZINCO

IXTACALCO

ATLACUIHUAYAN

TLACOQUEMECAN

NEXTIPAN

NONOALCO

ATLAZOLPA

XOCHIMANCA

TICOMAN

MIXCOAC

TETECPILCO

ATOYAC

IXTAPALAPAN

AXOTLA

XOCOTITLAN

MEXICALTZINCO

TLACOPAQUE

COYOHUACAN

HUITZILOPOCHCO

CULHUACAN

MOTECUZOMA

TENANITLA

LAKE
XOCHIMILCO

QUIAHUAC

LAKESHORE

CONTOUR LINE (50 METER INTERVAL)

MAJOR STREET OR AVENUE

MAJOR CANAL

CAUSEWAY

RIVER OR STREAM

CIVIC-CEREMONIAL PRECINCT

BARRIOS OF
TENOCHTITLAN

1 CUEPOPAN

2 MOYOTLA

3 ZOQUIAPAN

4 ATZACOALCO

0    1    2    3

KILOMETERS

N

RSS

teenth century. This latter figure is slightly higher than that of the population of the basin during First Intermediate phase 2 and slightly below that of First Intermediate phase 4.

Combined with this demographic disaster was a policy of periodic relocation of population into fewer settlements, called *congregaciones*, to facilitate taxation and religious conversion. Residents of smaller, peripheral rural communities, of the type I have called hamlets and small villages, were resettled in the large villages and provincial centers. Since most of the centers were located in areas of flat terrain, in effect, this meant abandonment of intensively cultivated terraces in piedmont areas. With the massive reduction of population, such land went out of cultivation. This abandonment was necessary because the Indians continued using hand techniques of cultivation during this period, and thus could not maintain these lands in production; furthermore, the urban markets did not generate sufficient demand to absorb the surpluses that could have been obtained from such lands. The vacant lands were either taken over by the Spaniards for stock grazing or utilized by the Indian villages for the same purpose. The result was a process of accelerated erosion, and large zones of highly productive terrace systems became *tepetate* wastelands within a few decades.

While the Spaniards clearly altered the political superstructure of native society at the higher levels, there were few changes in the sociopolitical organization on the village level. Major changes in religious behavior affected the native culture more profoundly. Technological and economic changes were relatively slight, except that the surplus labor of the peasant population was undoubtedly much more heavily utilized than it had been during the Late Horizon.

The period 1650–1920 (ecological Stage VII) was one of a gradual demographic recovery, as the native population adapted, either through a natural process of partial immunization or by racial mixture with the Span-

iards, to the new disease vectors. By 1900 the population of the basin and the Tula region had reached 1 million, or roughly that of the Late Horizon. Of this population, however, only about 400,000 resided in agricultural communities or small towns, and the balance resided in the metropolitan area of Mexico City. This means that the proportion of the population that we would classify as urban was considerably higher than it had been in the Late Horizon, and the metropolitan area was supported by agricultural production from an area much larger than the Basin of Mexico. The rural component of this population was only about half that of the Late Horizon. The system of resource exploitation included intensive cultivation of areas close to the settlements and extensive cultivation on the degraded soils of the sloping areas, combined with some attempts at reclamation of these areas for terraced agriculture. In terms of the two components, urban and rural, the urban population of the basin increased from approximately 80,000 in 1650 to 600,000 by 1900, while the rural component increased from 100,000 to 400,000.

During this period there was a gradual process of Hispanization of the native population, involving the introduction of Spanish agricultural and craft technology, increased use of livestock, and a final disintegration of the old native system of political organization and social stratification, all of this correlated with and functionally related to the rapid growth of the haciendas in the area. For example in the lower Teotihuacan Valley in 1920, 7 families owned approximately 90 percent of 10,000 ha of agricultural land; the remainder was distributed in smaller holdings among 400 peasant families. The balance of the population, 1,200 families, had no direct access to land. At this time the villagers were forced to make ends meet by a combination of growing a small percentage of their food supply on their small holdings, working seasonally for the haciendas, and migrating on a seasonal basis to the coastal areas, where they worked on the coffee plantations. This process had reached such a serious level

196

by 1911 that it resulted in the agrarian revolution.

The period from 1920 to the present (what we are referring to as ecological Stage VIII) is an extremely dynamic one, in which the industrial revolution and agrarian reform produced major alterations in the lifestyle and economy of the basin.

I can only briefly sketch some of these processes. With respect to population, it has been a period of spectacular growth, primarily the product of migration from the entire national territory to the metropolitan area. Internal growth in the small settlements, however, has been rapid as well, with many of the rural municipios having doubled or tripled their population since 1910. Most of the people who still live in the old peasant villages now have an economy based upon some agriculture, but primarily on urban occupations. They are commuters who go to Mexico City daily to perform urban work.

The decline of food production in the economy has resulted from several processes, including ecological degradation, the major cause of which is the gradual lowering of the water table in the deep soil plains because of the drainage of the lakes, perforation of deep wells, and the capture of springs for urban use. The overall process since 1519 has been one of steady degradation of the agricultural resource through the process of erosion on sloping terrain and the progressive desiccation of the basin floor.

The period is characterized by mass transportation and mass education, and there have been more significant changes in the traditional village culture of the area during the past 50 years than during the 400 years from 1519 until 1920. Urban occupations, with their promise of increased income and accessibility to consumer goods, have also impeded the agricultural recovery of the area.

# 7. Teotihuacan: City, State, and Civilization

*RENÉ MILLON*

## INTRODUCTION

ARCHAEOLOGISTS HAVE RECOGNIZED for decades that people from Teotihuacan, located in the Valley of Mexico in the Central Mexican Highlands, near Mexico City, had an extensive network of relationships, direct or indirect, with many peoples in other parts of Middle America during the middle centuries of the first millennium A.D. The character of these relationships and the role of Teotihuacan have been the subject of much discussion and little agreement. But there has been increasing recognition that at its height Teotihuacan's role was of exceptional importance.

In recent decades we have witnessed growing recognition of the extent of the archaeological remains around Teotihuacan's major monuments and a growing disposition to identify them as urban (e.g., Armillas 1950:37, 68–69; Marquina 1951:58; Sanders 1956:123–125; R. Millon 1957, 1960, 1961). But existing evidence still led some to depict Teotihuacan as a "ceremonial center" with a relatively small permanent population (e.g., Mayer-Oakes 1959:369). Differences of

opinion could not be resolved conclusively, given what was known. Writing in 1961, shortly after his Teotihuacan Valley Project was under way, William T. Sanders (1971:34) argued that Teotihuacan was "a true city," based on its estimated size, its hypothesized population density, direct evidence of social differentiation, and its dominant cultural position. While his argument was persuasive, it could not be definitive (Sanders 1971: 34–40); it had to be taken largely on faith.[1]

That is no longer the case. Few now question that Teotihuacan was a truly major urban center, whatever definition of nonindustrialized city is used (cf. Dumond 1972). More than this, Teotihuacan now is widely recognized as a far more complex urban society than previously postulated by its most partisan advocates. How did this come about?

From 1960 to 1964 the Mexican government's Instituto Nacional de Antropología e Historia (INAH), directed by Ignacio Bernal, carried out an extensive program of excavations on the city's major avenue, the "Street of the Dead," uncovering most of the previously unexcavated temples, public buildings, and "palaces" for a distance of 2 km (Fig

FIGURE 7-1. Teotihuacan. Pyramid of the Moon, foreground, Pyramid of the Sun, left; Ciudadela, left, and Great Compound, right, in middle distance. The "Street of the Dead," excavated for 2 km from the Moon Plaza south to the Ciudadela, continues unexcavated to the south for more than 3 km (see map, Fig. 7-3).

7-1) (Bernal 1963; Acosta 1964b; Sociedad Mexicana de Antropología 1966, 1972; Lorenzo 1968a). Meanwhile, beginning in 1962 a related project which I directed, together with Bruce Drewitt and George L. Cowgill,[2] involved a detailed surface survey of the entire area of the ancient city, with a photogrammetric map as its baseline, and with associated small-scale excavations, to produce a detailed map of its archaeological remains (Figs. 7-2, 7-3) (R. Millon 1964, 1966b, 1968a, 1970b, 1973, 1976; Millon, Drewitt, and Cowgill 1973). Much of the information from the mapping survey and the surface collections of objects made during the survey has been coded and incorporated in a data file prepared under Cowgill's direc-

tion (Cowgill 1968, 1974). It includes 291 items of information on each of 5,047 "sites" at Teotihuacan. Each site is an architectural unit, a structurally related space, such as a plaza or street, or some other space of social or cultural significance, such as a cemetery.

Evidence for 20 sq km (8 sq mi) of construction, most of it residential, was found and located on the map. Surface remains yielded evidence for hundreds of craft workshops—most devoted to obsidian working, but also including more than 200 ceramic workshops and a more modest number of other workshops (lapidary, shell, figurine). The new evidence for economic, social, political, and cultural complexity has dramatically changed earlier views of the kind of city Teo-

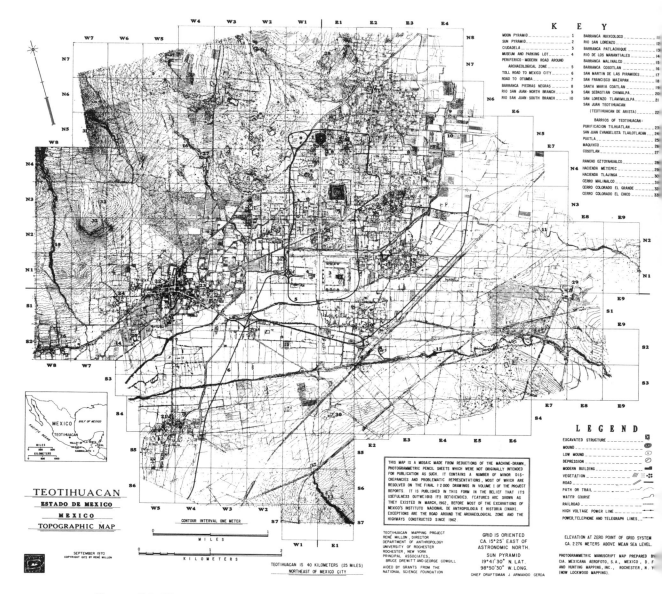

FIGURE 7-2. Photogrammetric map of the region of ancient Teotihuacan, prepared from a reduced mosaic of the topographic sheets used in the field to produce Fig. 7-3. The grid system of 500 m squares is oriented to the "Street of the Dead," the north-south axis of the ancient city (ca. 15°25' east of north).

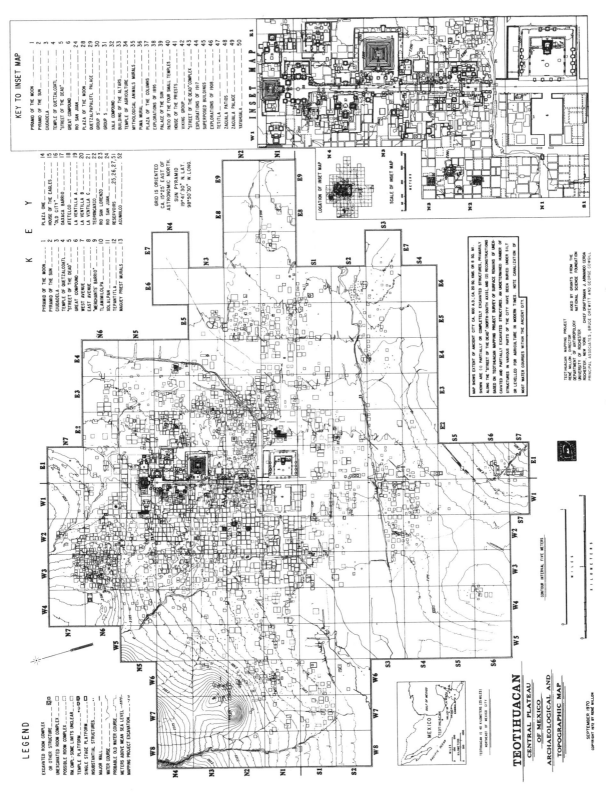

FIGURE 7-3. Ancient Teotihuacan. Most buildings shown are unexcavated apartment compounds.

tihuacan was. These findings, together with the Valley of Mexico surface surveys of Sanders, Jeffrey R. Parsons, Richard E. Blanton, and their associates (Sanders 1965; Sanders et al. 1975; J. Parsons 1968, 1971, 1974a, 1977; Blanton 1972a, 1972b; Wolf 1976a: Pt. 2:31–201), have transformed past conceptions of city and valley, carrying discussion to a different level of discourse, posing new questions about such problems as urbanization, urbanism, city and state, city and region, craft specialization, exchange systems and markets, internal and external social and political relations, demographic change, population movements, population resettlement, and urban-rural relations.

In addition, recent work in the regions surrounding the Valley of Mexico has helped to provide a better understanding of the context in which Teotihuacan came to play its unique role—to the northwest, in the region of Tula and beyond (e.g., Cobean 1978; Crespo and Mastache de Escobar 1976; Davies 1977; Diehl 1974, 1976; Diehl and Benfer 1975; Healan 1974a, 1974b, 1977; Mastache de Escobar 1976; Mastache de Escobar and Crespo 1974; Matos Moctezuma 1974a, 1976; Yadeún Angulo 1975); to the east, northeast and southeast, in Hidalgo, Tlaxcala, and Puebla (e.g., Aguilera 1974; Charlton 1978b, 1979b; Contreras S. 1965; Dumond 1972, 1976; Dumond and Muller 1972; Fundación Alemana para la Investigación Científica 1973; García Cook 1973a, 1974a, 1976a, 1976e, 1978; García Cook, Arias, and Abascal 1976; García Cook and Merino 1977; García Cook and Mora López 1974; García Cook and Rodríguez 1975; García Cook and Trejo 1977; Hirth and Swezey 1976; Marquina 1970a, 1970b; Muller 1970; D. Snow 1969; M. and E. Snow 1969, 1970); to the south, in Morelos (e.g., Charlton, Grove, and Hopke 1978; Cook de Leonard 1956; Grove et al. 1976; Hirth 1974, 1978a, 1978b; Litvak King 1970, 1972, 1973, 1974); and to the west, in the Valley of Toluca (e.g., Piña Chan 1972, 1974b). As a result we now can raise questions and formulate hypotheses that were not even recognizable issues as recently as 1960.

The transformation in our knowledge has been accompanied by major discoveries and advances in the Maya area, both in the lowlands and in the highlands, bearing on the relation of Teotihuacan to a number of Maya cities and regions, especially to Tikal and Kaminaljuyu (e.g., R. E. W. Adams 1977; Ball 1974; Brown 1975; Cheek 1976; W. Coe 1965c, 1972; Coggins 1975, 1979a, 1979b, 1979c, 1980; Culbert 1973a; Greene and Moholy-Nagy 1966; Haviland 1977; Hellmuth 1975, 1978; Lee and Navarrete 1978; L. Parsons 1969, 1978; Pasztory 1978a, 1978b, 1978c; Pendergast 1971; Quirarte 1973; Rattray 1978a; Sanders 1978; Sanders and Michels 1977; Wetherington 1978). Among these discoveries are stelae at Tikal apparently relating directly or indirectly to Teotihuacan (W. Coe 1965c:33, 35; 1972; Coggins 1975, 1979a, 1979b, 1979c). Recent breakthroughs in deciphering Maya hieroglyphs (Berlin 1958; Proskouriakoff 1960; Jones 1977:28) are playing a crucial role in making historical data in the texts on one of these stelae increasingly accessible (e.g., Coggins 1975, 1979a, 1979b, 1979c; Haviland 1977).

The discovery of a Oaxacan enclave in Teotihuacan during the mapping (Fig. 7-3, no. 17) has strengthened already existing evidence at Monte Alban for a special relation between these two great urban centers (R. Millon 1973:41–42; 1974:349–353; Acosta 1958–1959, 1965; Bernal 1965; Blanton 1978:57; Caso 1938; Caso, Bernal, and Acosta 1967).

In what follows I have been asked to concentrate on what I believe are some of the significant accomplishments of the Teotihuacan Mapping Project to date. Given this objective and space limitations, what follows is highly selective. At the outset the major point to emphasize is the unique perspective our intensive study of Teotihuacan has given us, a perspective we still are only beginning to exploit.

Our survey demonstrated the importance of planning in the layout and building of the city (Drewitt 1966, 1969; R. Millon 1973: 42–44).[3] At its height in the fifth, sixth, and seventh centuries A.D., Teotihuacan was an immense city for its time, with a very different plan from what previously had been known. The great Ciudadela or "Citadel" precinct (Fig. 7-3, inset, no. 3) was at the city's center, not at or near the city's southern end. With a companion precinct of great size, the Great Compound, discovered in our survey, the two structures formed a massive architectural unit at the intersection of the main north-south axis, the "Street of the Dead," and a subordinate east-west axis, East Avenue and West Avenue, also discovered in our survey, effectively dividing the city into quadrants (Fig. 7-3, inset). The long-known "Street of the Dead" (its Aztec name), oriented 15°25′ east of north,[4] with its immense pyramids and gigantic precincts, was found to have many distinctive three-temple complexes among its more than 75 temples. We found that most of the rest of the city's area was covered by more than 2,000 residential compounds. Because of their size and internal layouts, I have called them apartment compounds (Figs. 7-3, 7-4, 7-6).

## THE TEOTIHUACAN APARTMENT COMPOUND

Apartment compounds were one-story, surrounded by high, windowless stone walls, surfaced with a locally distinctive concrete without lime content[5] and covered with a thin coat of lime plaster.[6] Fifty to sixty meters square was a common size; many were several times larger, still others a fraction of that size (Fig. 7-3). The interiors were divided into rooms, porticos, patios, and passageways, usually grouped into definable subunits that I have interpreted as apartments. Each compound has one or more temple platforms of varying size, often set in a prominently placed courtyard. Our excavations uncovered many kitchen floors of earth with shallow hearths. Many such floors probably went unrecognized in previous excavations. Cooking probably also occurred on portable ceramic stoves with three-prongs (three-pronged "burners") placed directly on plaster

floors. The compounds evidently were occupied for hundreds of years, and many of them were rebuilt three, four, or more times, with successive building levels often a meter or more above those they supplanted. Where we have evidence, later building level layouts seem to replicate earlier ones, with relatively minor modifications (Séjourné 1966a: Fig. 22; Linné 1942: 110–111). Interior walls were made of stone and/or other durable building materials, or sometimes of adobe, surfaced with concrete and faced with plaster. Floors were surfaced with the same materials. Patios had drains to carry off excess rainwater, and networks of drains, often stone-lined, running beneath the floors, carried this water outside the compounds into the streets, or sometimes into storage reservoirs within compounds. The drain networks were laid out and constructed before the floors of concrete and plaster that covered them.

The compound was planned, laid out, and completely built in a single operation. The plans of all compounds so far excavated differ from each other (Figs. 7-4, 7-5); no single plan was replicated. Each compound was built to a distinctive plan that we must hypothesize corresponded to perceived needs of the person(s) for whom the compound was built. Except for minor modifications, layouts appear to have been maintained for 100 years or more. Thus, whatever the increase or decrease in numbers of its occupants, or their changing needs over the years, they would have had to adjust to the internal layout of apartments and to the compound as a whole.

The apartment compound was obviously a relatively inflexible unit. This has yet to be fully appreciated (Séjourné 1966a: Fig. 22; R. Millon 1976: 218), in part because excavated compounds are few (Fig. 7-4) and had no city-wide context before we mapped the city, and in part because not until 1961 were the first complete apartment compounds excavated (Séjourné 1966a: 12–13) (Fig. 7-4, top; Fig. 7-6). Enough of Xolalpan had been excavated earlier to suggest a rectangular

203

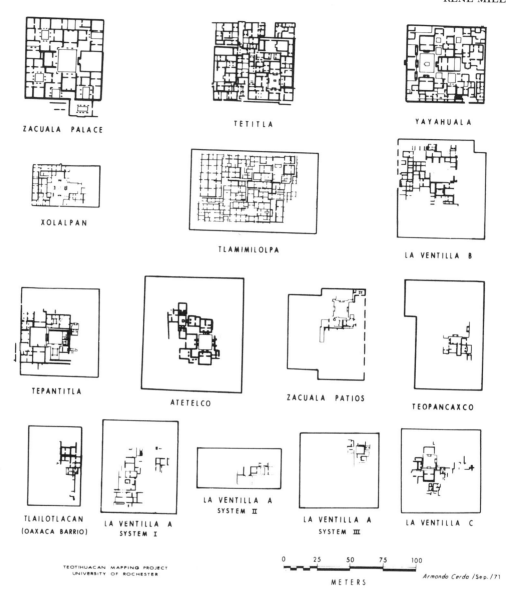

ZACUALA PALACE        TETITLA        YAYAHUALA

XOLALPAN        TLAMIMILOLPA        LA VENTILLA B

TEPANTITLA        ATETELCO        ZACUALA PATIOS        TEOPANCAXCO

TLAILOTLACAN
(OAXACA BARRIO)        LA VENTILLA A
SYSTEM I        LA VENTILLA A
SYSTEM II        LA VENTILLA A
SYSTEM III        LA VENTILLA C

TEOTIHUACAN MAPPING PROJECT
UNIVERSITY OF ROCHESTER

0    25    50    75    100

METERS

Armando Cerda /Sep./71

FIGURE 7-4. Plans of excavated or partly excavated apartment compounds in Teotihuacan, all drawn to the same scale. In the case of partly excavated compounds, the locations of most exterior walls are approximate.

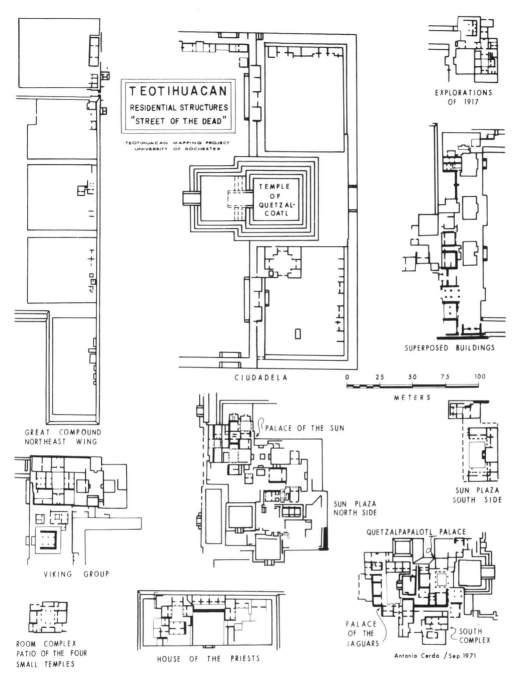

FIGURE 7-5. Plans of excavated or partly excavated residential structures on the "Street of the Dead" drawn to the same scale as the apartment compounds in Fig. 7-4.

205

FIGURE 7-6. Excavated apartment compounds in squares N2W2 and N3W2, foreground; at top, Ciudadela, left, and Great Compound (Fig. 7-3, inset, nos. 3, 6). The three excavated compounds visible are Yayahuala, bottom right; Zacuala Palace, center right; and Tetitla, right (Fig. 7-3, inset, nos. 50, 49, 47).

walled compound of the size indicated in Fig. 7-4 (Linné 1934), but it existed in isolation. No one knew that the compounds numbered in the thousands and were the standard residential unit for the average Teotihuacano (e.g., Kidder, Jennings, and Shook 1946:249). Sanders (1971:37) thought that Tlamimilolpa (Fig. 7-4) was not a "building" but rather part of "an extensive urban ward" with "small clusters of rooms separated by alleys." We now know that Tlamimilolpa was a large, relatively isolated apartment compound in a sparsely built-up section on the eastern edge of the city and that its "alleys" were interior passageways (Fig. 7-3, no. 10; Fig. 7-4).

Extrapolating from the number of enclosed rooms in the plans of excavated apartment compounds, I estimated that a compound 60 m on a side would have housed at least 60 and probably 100 or more people, living in a number of different households (R. Millon 1970b:1079–1080; 1973:45). We found from stratigraphic and other evidence that the apartment compound became the standard residential unit many years after Teotihuacan had become a city. One excavated compound dates to the Early Tlamimilolpa phase (ca. A.D. 200–300) (Fig. 7-7); most date to the Late Tlamimilolpa phase (ca. A.D. 300–400) and some to the Early Xolalpan phase (ca. A.D. 400–550).[7] By the fifth century A.D., early in the Xolalpan phase, apartment compounds were everywhere. The building of apartment compounds was *not* accompanied or immediately

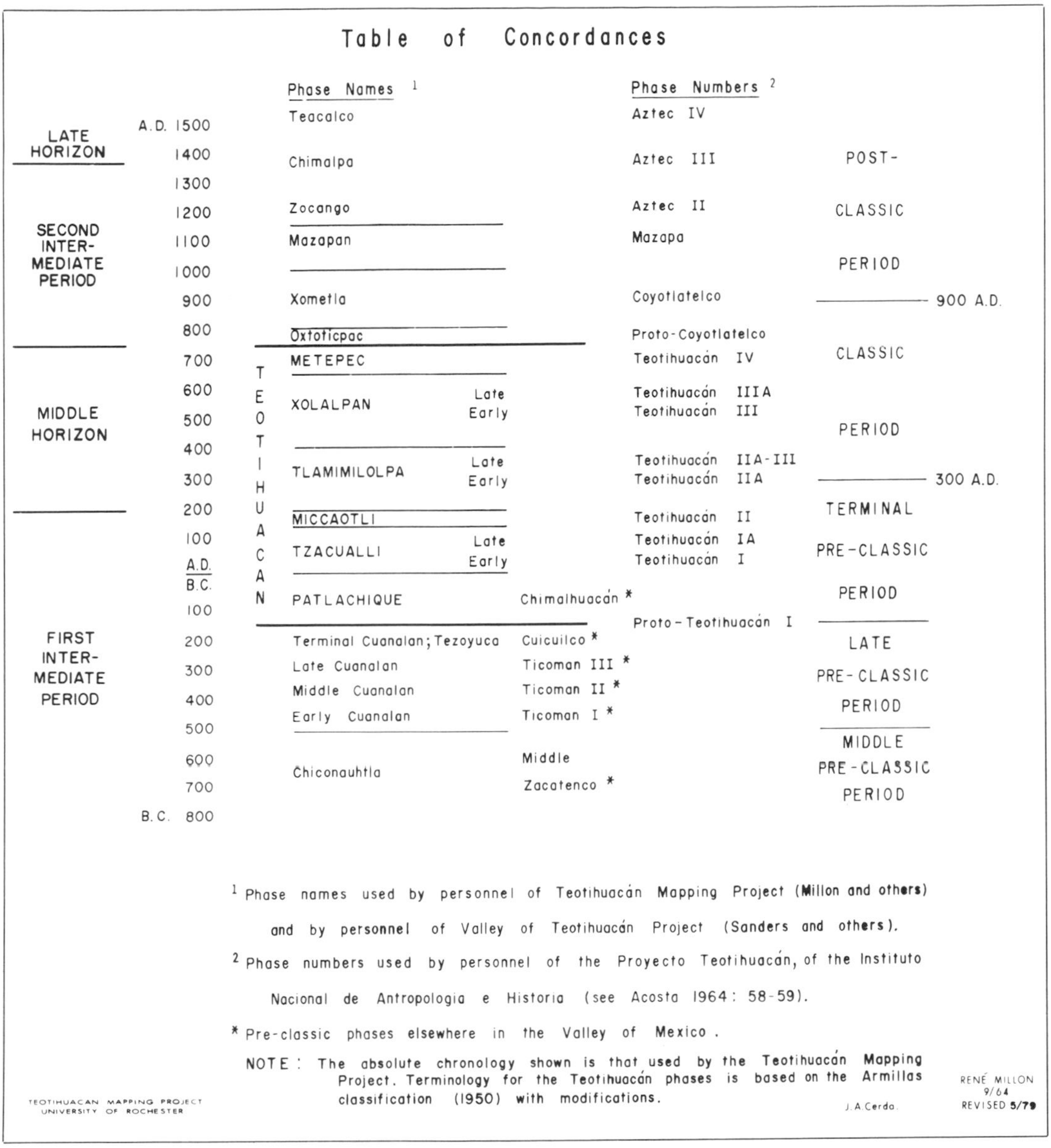

Table of Concordances

| | | Phase Names [1] | | Phase Numbers [2] | | |
|---|---|---|---|---|---|---|
| LATE HORIZON | A.D. 1500 | Teacalco | | Aztec IV | | |
| | 1400 | Chimalpa | | Aztec III | POST- | |
| | 1300 | | | | | |
| | 1200 | Zocango | | Aztec II | CLASSIC | |
| SECOND INTERMEDIATE PERIOD | 1100 | Mazapan | | Mazapa | | |
| | 1000 | | | | PERIOD | |
| | 900 | Xometla | | Coyotlatelco | | ——— 900 A.D. |
| | 800 | Oxtoticpac | | Proto-Coyotlatelco | | |
| | 700 | METEPEC | | Teotihuacán IV | CLASSIC | |
| | 600 | XOLALPAN | Late | Teotihuacán IIIA | | |
| MIDDLE HORIZON | 500 | | Early | Teotihuacán III | | |
| | 400 | | | | PERIOD | |
| | 300 | TLAMIMILOLPA | Late Early | Teotihuacán IIA-III Teotihuacán IIA | | ——— 300 A.D. |
| | 200 | MICCAOTLI | | Teotihuacán II | TERMINAL | |
| | 100 | TZACUALLI | Late Early | Teotihuacán IA Teotihuacán I | PRE-CLASSIC | |
| | A.D. B.C. | | | | | |
| | 100 | PATLACHIQUE | Chimalhuacán * | | PERIOD | |
| | 200 | Terminal Cuanalan; Tezoyuca | Cuicuilco * | Proto-Teotihuacán I | LATE | |
| FIRST INTERMEDIATE PERIOD | 300 | Late Cuanalan | Ticoman III * | | PRE-CLASSIC | |
| | 400 | Middle Cuanalan | Ticoman II * | | PERIOD | |
| | 500 | Early Cuanalan | Ticoman I * | | | |
| | 600 | | Middle | | MIDDLE PRE-CLASSIC | |
| | 700 | Chiconauhtla | Zacatenco * | | PERIOD | |
| | B.C. 800 | | | | | |

(The word TEOTIHUACAN is printed vertically down the center of the table.)

[1] Phase names used by personnel of Teotihuacán Mapping Project (Millon and others) and by personnel of Valley of Teotihuacán Project (Sanders and others).

[2] Phase numbers used by personnel of the Proyecto Teotihuacán, of the Instituto Nacional de Antropologia e Historia (see Acosta 1964: 58-59).

* Pre-classic phases elsewhere in the Valley of Mexico.

NOTE: The absolute chronology shown is that used by the Teotihuacán Mapping Project. Terminology for the Teotihuacán phases is based on the Armillas classification (1950) with modifications.

TEOTIHUACAN MAPPING PROJECT
UNIVERSITY OF ROCHESTER

RENÉ MILLON
9/64
J.A.Cerda.
REVISED 5/79

FIGURE 7-7. Chronological chart for the Teotihuacan Valley, with new period and horizon terminology at left and traditional period terminology at right. The absolute dates for Teotihuacan shown at left represent my views on how conflicting radiocarbon dates from the ancient city best can be reconciled. In Paul Tolstoy's revised terminology for the Valley of Mexico, the phase shown above as Middle Zacatenco has been subdivided into at least four phases.

preceded by major increases in population. Teotihuacan's population increased very rapidly early in its history, then leveled off "on a long plateau" (Cowgill 1979a, 1979b). A major part of the early population increase (in the first century A.D.) came from the deliberate concentration of rural populations in the city, as discussed below (Economy and Polity section).

Using the area of each of the apartment compounds plotted on the map for a building-by-building population estimate, I have calculated a probable population of 125,000 for the city as a whole, with a distinct possibility that it reached more than 200,000 at its maximum (R. Millon 1970b:1079–1080; 1973:45). It was the sixth largest city in the world in A.D. 600 (Chandler and Fox 1974: 368).

The combined evidence from INAH excavations and our survey suggested common compound involvement in ritual and economic activities and the presence of units with corporate qualities, possibly bound by kinship (R. Millon 1966c:151; 1967a:43; 1968a:113–114; 1970b:1079; 1973:40; 1976: 216; see also Sanders 1965:173; 1966:125– 129; Séjourné 1966a:191–192; Séjourné and Salicrup 1965:6). How do we test hypotheses about the internal composition of the apartment compound population stimulated by our accumulated evidence? Michael W. Spence[8] analyzed one line of evidence— human skeletal remains (1971, 1974b, 1976, 1979a), centered for the most part on statistical studies of genetically based characteristics by means of discrete trait analysis, to explore possible residential practices. Analyses of skeletal evidence from adult burials in La Ventilla B (Fig. 7-4) were interpreted as indicating that the compound was occupied "by a number of males with fairly close biological links, while the females of the compound were genetically more diverse" (Spence 1979a; see also 1974b). The most reasonable explanation appeared to be that the compound occupants practiced virilocal residence, the men tending to remain after

marriage to women from other compounds. An exception seems to have occurred in a sector in the northwest part of the compound, where women seem to have married men who were outsiders. Analyses of more fragmentary evidence from other compounds seem to fit the virilocal residence interpretation. We do not know, of course, whether the apparent tendency to virilocal residence was formally recognized as preferential. Spence's evidence is biological, not social.

Another possible line of evidence is comparative. Comparative archaeological, historic, and ethnographic evidence suggests that the "inflexible" Teotihuacan apartment compound was a most unusual structure for the standard residential unit in a large nonindustrialized city (R. Millon 1976:221–222 n. 7). What kind of a social unit occupied these compounds? Edward Calnek (1974b, 1979) has argued for the existence of cognatic descent among the Aztecs, associating it with the household compound he believes was the characteristic residential unit in the Aztec capital and contrasting it with the Teotihuacan apartment compound (Calnek 1976: 299–300). Susan M. Kellogg, analyzing evidence for cognatic descent units in the Aztec capital, suggested a further possibility that could be tested—the existence of cognatic kin groups in Teotihuacan apartment compounds. She points out that cognatic kin groups provide for a wide range of choices because the number of kin to whom one "can try to mobilize an attachment" is doubled "when compared to a unilineal system" (Kellogg 1979:187).[9]

Cognatic descent units with an agnatic bias would be consonant with the evidence from La Ventilla B and would also provide a relatively flexible and resilient kin unit as the core population of the apartment compound. If the residents of an apartment compound formed a cohesive unit around a core of cognatic kin capable of adjusting to relatively rapid changes in size, this might have helped to create a favorable environment for the rapid expansion of the diversified craft economy that was disclosed in our survey. Furthermore, from the standpoint of the individual, internal differentiation and any tendencies to stratification within and among units of cognatic kin would have been tempered by the existence of alternatives, with opportunities to choose to activate the most advantageous ties possible. Such an availability of choices to individuals for social and/or occupational advancement would have had obvious advantages for the well-being of the society as a whole.

But the relative size and inflexibility of the large apartment compound, when occupied over many generations of demographic vicissitudes, suggest that it still would have been necessary at predictably recurring low points in a demographic cycle to recruit personnel on other bases than kinship (patron-client, for example), with ties so established perhaps phrased in terms of putative or fictive kinship. This is a simpler model than I put forward several years ago (R. Millon 1976: 221), yet still accommodates the archaeological evidence for internal differentiation and differences in status within compounds. It is subject to testing in different ways in future excavations of apartment compounds, provided they are carried out with sufficient care and control to recover contextual data from floors (R. Millon 1976:222; Flannery and Winter 1976:41–44). Statistical analyses of skeletal material from future burials would test Spence's findings and place them in a broader context (R. Millon 1976:222–223). If future compound excavations yield the data we anticipate, testing necessarily would involve statistical analyses similar to those of Cowgill, Altschul, Ester, Freedman, M. Smith, Sload and others on surface materials, discussed below.

We have only fragmentary evidence of the antecedents of the apartment compound (R. Millon 1973:52, 56, 63; 1976:221). Since the plans of the admittedly small sample of excavated apartment compounds differ from each other (Fig. 7-4), they do not look like structures built by the state to a uniform internal plan. At the same time, however it came into existence, the apartment compound, as a potential organizational level between household and neighborhood, would have provided an ideal unit for administration, taxation, labor recruitment, social control, and other state requirements.

Apartment compound layouts would have made life more livable in a crowded urban environment, where density of construction was high and compounds were very close, separated only by narrow streets. Yet on the peripheries of the city, where limitations of urban space are not obviously involved, compounds apparently were built in the same way.

As the evidence accumulates, from our work and that of others, answers, if only partial, begin to suggest themselves for what began as an unknown and emerged as an enigma: the existence of the apartment compound as a standard architectural unit for the great majority of the city's population. Despite differences in internal layout and size, the compounds conform to sufficient criteria to imply the existence of a general model. There is also some evidence of experimentation with the form. Founders' burials may also be associated with the building of a compound and thus serve as a clue to the particular circumstances under which specific compounds came to be built.[10]

The timing of the beginning of the construction of apartment compounds coincided internally with a great expansion of craft production and externally with expansion of the Teotihuacan state beyond the Valley of Mexico, as discussed below. All the evidence taken together points to a powerful state apparatus, capable of making bold, long-range plans and carrying them out. The tradition of planning and venturous practice went back to Tzacualli times. The later decision to reconstruct the urban landscape as a long-term undertaking in "urban renewal" must have come from those vested with ultimate decision-making power. It may represent the urban dimension of the process whereby population and settlements in the Valley of Mexico continued to be planned, regulated, and controlled, as discussed below (Economy and Polity section).

By the Early Tlamimilolpa phase, the heterogeneous population brought together during the Tzacualli phase (first century A.D.) had achieved sufficient stability and prosperity to begin to be resettled again, this time in apartment compounds, probably easing or solving emerging internal problems for the state, perhaps providing a more secure base for the expansion occurring beyond the Valley of Mexico. The increasing flow of produce, raw materials, and goods from newly incorporated regions would have supported such a plan. The diverse populations had been urbanized and "Teotihuacanized." However much social units differed from each other originally, after so many generations of living in the city, a measure of social and cultural uniformity would have resulted. The apartment compound as an architectural form would have been suited admirably to ensuring city-wide uniformity while at the same time making possible the preservation of whatever particular customs and beliefs its occupants may have continued to maintain, for which there is considerable evidence.

Cognatic descent units may have emerged from the initial heterogeneity. Perhaps the state developed to its fullest extent in the process of "shaking down" initial diversity.

The Teotihuacan apartment compound as a standard residential unit did not survive the fall of Teotihuacan. This may be an important clue to the negative side of compound life. But, more fundamentally, it may point to the indivisible bond between the architectural unit, the social unit inhabiting it, and the character of the state that fostered it.

Testing hypotheses relating to the apartment compound and its occupants should yield understanding of its weaknesses as well as its strengths (R. Millon 1973, 1976). But, clearly, its strengths outweighed its weaknesses through most of its history.

## BARRIOS

The more than 600 craft workshops discovered in our survey tended to cluster in neighborhoods or *barrios*. An ethnic group from Oaxaca lived in a *barrio* in the western part of the city (Fig. 7-3, no. 17). We found a *barrio* on the eastern periphery where merchants may have lived (Fig. 7-3, no. 9). Other apartment compound groupings were so sharply set off from their immediate surroundings that *barrio* boundaries seem self-evident. The Tepantitla compound is on the southern edge of such a *barrio* (Fig. 7-3, no. 12). The clustering of compounds into *barrios* does not necessarily imply that *barrios* were formally or even informally recognized as entities. But it does raise the question that they may have been corporate entities, forming an organizational level of great importance for state administration and control, and for local organization of activities. *Barrios* did exist in the Aztec capital and were used by the state for purposes of administration and control (Calnek 1976:295). They have also been isolated at Monte Alban by Blanton (1978:37–39, 66–93). There is a suggestion in Spence's skeletal comparison of Zacuala Palace and Zacuala Patios that males from apartment compounds within a *barrio* were more closely related to each other than to males in nearby *barrios* (Spence 1974b, 1979a).

The questions concerning the corporate qualities of apartment compound demographic units may be relevant on the *barrio* level, and deserve exploration and testing. Cognatic descent units again may have formed the core of a *barrio* and served as the focal point for *barrio*-oriented ritual performed in *barrio* temples. *Barrios* may have been enduring social units and, especially when occupied by craftsmen over long periods of time, may have had strongly corporate qualities. Spence (1974a, 1979b) argues for such units and suggests that they may have played an important role in the obsidian production system and its beginnings.

Because of the importance of this question, we wondered whether *barrios* could be distinguished in all parts of Teotihuacan. It became clear from examining the contexts of excavated apartment compounds that there were significant differences in the status of occupants of adjoining compounds clearly belonging to the same *barrio* (Zacuala Palace and Zacuala Patios) (Fig. 7-3, inset, nos. 48, 49; Fig. 7-4), and still greater differences between adjoining *barrios* (the two Zacuala compounds and Yayahuala) (Fig. 7-3, inset, nos. 48–50; Fig. 7-4). This and other evidence from our data pointed to abrupt disjunctions in status between *barrios*, rather than to any simple gradient in status from highest in the city center to lowest on the periphery.

In some places, free-standing temples seemed to be associated with compound clusters, but this was clearly not the case in most. Instead, *barrio* temples tended to be located *within* apartment compounds, perhaps within the compound of the *barrio* leader. Laurette Séjourné and Graciela Salicrup (1965) suggest that the Yayahuala compound housed a *barrio* temple complex; the case for this seems to me to be persuasive. Yayahuala, unlike Xolalpan, La Ventilla B, or Tetitla, has a public entrance, approached from street level by a six-step staircase (Séjourné 1966a: 199, Lám. 104). The staircase is on the west and opens onto the large main patio, on three sides of which are relatively large temples. The patio and temples occupy a larger proportion of the compound area than do the main temples in other excavated apartment compounds. It stands out as important in a ritual sense, yet is otherwise crowded and tenement-like. The relatively large apartment immediately north of the main (east) temple may be where the *barrio* leader lived, but this would be difficult to determine now.

Thus, a case can be made for the division of Teotihuacan into *barrios*, and, using our map, I prepared a tentative *barrio* plan. It has never been published, but some parts have been subjected to statistical testing by investigators working at Brandeis University

with Cowgill, using the Teotihuacan Mapping Project Data File, discussed above. This work was begun by Matthew S. Freedman (1976) and has been refined and extended by Jeffrey H. Altschul, who is now investigating this and related problems. Using twenty-five artifact categories, he selected a sample of 102 free-standing temples and apartment compounds, selecting apartment compounds representative of the *barrios* where the temples were found, yet not so close to the temples as to include possible residences of temple personnel. Evidence for such an association had been found earlier by Michael E. Smith (1975, 1976). Using an "average linkage" cluster analysis, the purpose was to test whether outlying temples would tend to be more closely associated with the *barrios* around them or with state temples and pyramids on the "Street of the Dead," as suggested by an earlier analysis of Michael R. Ester (1976).

Two preliminary results are of interest. In the northwest the analysis singled out a group of apartment compounds and two possible cemeteries, but the cluster included no temples, suggesting that on the northwestern periphery of what I have called the "Old City" (Fig. 7-3, no. 16) (R. Millon 1973:38–39), several *barrios* had no associated free-standing temple(s). These *barrios* may have also shared other socially or culturally distinctive beliefs and practices in funerary customs and related ritual observances.

In the same area, temples that formed parts of three-temple complexes clustered with structures on the "Street of the Dead." Further examination of three-temple complexes in squares N5W2 (Plaza 1) (Fig. 7-3, no. 14) and N6W3 (Fig. 7-3) suggests that specific activities were associated with different parts of three-temple complexes, and that these activities involved the inhabitants of a small number of apartment compounds in different *barrios* in this part of the city (Altschul, personal communication, 1979). This will be pursued further. But at this point it poses the intriguing possibilities (1) that some of the activities carried on by personnel associated with three-temple complexes were internally differentiated (associated with different cults and administrative responsibilities?) and (2) that these activities—ritual and/or administrative—crosscut *barrio* lines, involving some people from different, adjoining *barrios*. This and other evidence suggests that outlying temples played an important role in the internal administration of the city, administering several *barrios* in an administrative hierarchy at least two tiers below the top. Such complex crosscutting ties—across compound, *barrio*, and occupational boundaries—would have served to strengthen the fabric of the society and to diminish the potential for divisiveness and social isolation of residential complexes symbolized by the high, windowless compound walls.

The problem of *barrio* identification is far from solved. But Altschul's continued research through a variety of statistical approaches looks very promising.

## STATUS AND STRATIFICATION

Teotihuacan must have been a highly stratified society. The more than 2 km of monumental construction on the northern part of the "Street of the Dead," which we see now in spare, skeletal form, seems designed to overwhelm the viewer by sheer size, scale, and number (Fig. 7-1).[11] The immensity of the Pyramid of the Sun and the Pyramid of the Moon (their Aztec names and possibly not misnomers), the vastness of the Ciudadela precinct, the multiplicity of temples and public buildings, all contribute to an overpowering effect. To this must be added the grandiose proportions of a plan that encompassed the building of such structures over a span of almost a mile and a half on an avenue equal to this scale. The bold self-confidence manifest in the planning and execution of this grand design points to an authority, be it individual or collective, that had unchallenged prestige, with an ability to motivate masses of people and the power to mobilize and direct workers and resources on a scale that un-

til then was without precedent in Middle America. The imposition of monumentality of this magnitude on the city's vital central avenue represents a spectacular realization in stone of the values and goals of its builders, no less than the monumental use of public space in imperial Peking, ancient Rome, Paris, Versailles, Washington, or the contemporary Manhattan skyline. In trying to understand what has been uncovered, we are trying to learn many things—among them, how these values and goals came to take on such importance as to be effectively internalized, what institutions were used to implement them and how, and what processes of social and cultural change strengthened or subverted them and how.

A vast gulf must have separated the strata at the apex of Teotihuacan society and those at its base. The gulf is not dramatically expressed in art, as it is among the Lowland Maya and in the Valley of Oaxaca, where subjugated individuals are shown in graphic images, principally on carved stone monuments (for instance, bound or dead, or at or beneath the feet of another figure) (e.g., Marcus 1974, 1976b, 1978; Flannery and Marcus 1976b). Teotihuacan's principal art form was the painting of murals, of which several hundred are known (e.g., Villagra Caleti 1951, 1955, 1971; Séjourné 1959, 1962, 1966a; Hall [Millon] 1962; C. Millon 1972b, 1973; Kubler 1967; A. G. Miller 1973b; Pasztory 1973, 1974, 1976). Most murals appear to be concerned with religious and mythical themes, with fertility and abundance, and with ritual practices and practitioners. Explicit representations of subjugation and forcible domination of one individual over another are absent from murals and are unusual in other art forms such as decorated vessels (C. Millon 1978).

Levels of subordination clearly exist. In various murals the placement or size of figures in relation to each other implies subordination of some to others, whether supernatural or human. Major differences in status are implied by differences in dress. Sumptuously dressed figures engaging in ritual activities, often in procession, are believed, with reason, to be priests. Other figures are dressed modestly, often only in loincloths. They are depicted infrequently and usually are miniature in scale. But one individual is not shown subservient to another. Men in loincloths do not serve others in rich apparel. No one has his foot on another man's neck (C. Millon 1978).

While there is evidence of human sacrifice, whatever the status of the victim, such sacrifices are not represented explicitly in art. For example, human sacrifices have been reported from the Pyramid of the Sun, the corners of the Temple of Quetzalcoatl in the Ciudadela (Fig. 7-3, inset, no. 4), and, probably, La Ventilla B, where infants may have been sacrificed in the building of altars (Batres 1906:22, [40]; Armillas 1950:44; Vidarte de Linares 1964:18–24). We found a skeleton of an apparently sacrificed victim (an adult male) in an excavation in the southeast corner of the Pyramid of the Sun (TE 16B) (R. Millon 1970a:23; Spence 1979a). In art, representations interpreted as human hearts, sometimes impaled on knives, are common (Séjourné 1960:119–126; 1966a: Figs. 82, 83; Villagra Caleti 1971:Figs. 14, 19–21; A. G. Miller 1973b:Figs. 129, 132, 216–219, 341; R. Millon 1973:Fig. 20a). So, too, is blood in various contexts. But artists avoided explicit representations of human sacrifice. We have no equivalent to the heart sacrifice scene at El Tajin (Kampen 1972: Fig. 23). The only explicit representation of sacrifice in the mural art shows the sacrifice of a bird, almost certainly a quail, on an upper wall; figures on the lower wall hold the "human heart" representations impaled on knives (Villagra Caleti 1971:Fig. 21; A. G. Miller 1973b:Fig. 343). Representations of armed figures illustrate the same point. While the military must have played an important role from very early times, military figures are not represented in murals, figurines, and pottery until late in Teotihuacan's history (R. Millon 1976:240). Even then, armed figures

are not shown in combat (C. Millon 1978; see also Pasztory 1976: 196–199).[12]

We are confronted with cultural constraints and artistic conventions that govern what may be represented and how it may be represented. As the major art form, mural art must have been an important channel of communication in the city's information network. Since so much is found on public buildings, temples, and shrines, it may be considered the official graphic medium for transmitting ideas and beliefs considered ideologically acceptable and desirable. But while the hierarchical nature of social relations and the structure of power, authority, and domination were expressed dramatically and "resonate to the point of overstatement in architecture, the graphic arts seem to be tuned to a different key" (C. Millon 1978).

If we cannot find evidence in the graphic art for the lowest rung on the social ladder, no more can we point to the highest. All available evidence indicates that the religious system and the polity were associated closely. Temple and polity probably were not differentiated conceptually (C. Millon 1973). The iconography is still obscure, and the religiosity of the art may be deceptive. But we cannot point to any identifiable, recognizable portraits or idealized representations of the individuals at the very top, such as the Maya produced. Some of the small clay figurines may represent local leaders, particularly those shown seated. But figurines probably were personal or household objects in contrast to the public or semipublic mural art.

We do not know what bearing, if any, this has on the relationship of ruler and ruled. But the seeming absence of representations makes it more difficult to determine the character of the relationship and to develop testable hypotheses. For the present, the rulers appear as remote as the summit of their greatest pyramid, more impersonal than the supernaturals who flourish on the city's walls. It would not be surprising if such near invisibility were a true measure of social distance and of the kind of mystique that may have informed the official ideology. Our ideas may change with further study (C. Millon 1978).

I have argued that there is evidence for the existence of six or more status levels (R. Millon 1976:227–228). At least two are found in the residential compounds on the "Street of the Dead." Those at the apex probably lived in the twin palaces in the Ciudadela (Fig. 7-5). The second highest stratum, probably numbering several thousand, undoubtedly consisted of distinct levels, for it includes most of the priestly and administrative hierarchy, except for those in outlying temples and temple complexes. Many of them probably lived in apartment compounds on the Great Compound (Fig. 7-3, inset), opposite the Ciudadela, for these two immense enclosures seem to have formed the political, religious, administrative, and, probably, military center of the city.

I envisage a major gap between the highest strata and those below them. There is evidence for at least three levels of status in an intermediate grouping, and for at least one level below that (R. Millon 1976:227–228). (I explicitly avoid the term "middle class" because of the inevitable connotations it carries in its association with modern industrialized societies.)

The evidence from our survey suggested that people of lowest status did not live in apartment compounds, but in small, insubstantial one- or two-room adobe structures, unsurfaced by concrete or plaster (what today are called *chozas* by local people). These structures appear in conventional form on our map throughout the city, their specific locations being arbitrary for the most part (R. Millon 1973:23–24), and were not included in my population estimates. I thought of them as comprising a few thousand people. To put it another way, there does not seem to me to be evidence for a significantly large pauperized group. Nor, it is argued, does public health seem to have been a significant problem (Somolinos-D'Ardois 1968). Large-scale nutritional studies are needed to test these assumptions.

In research still in progress, Rebecca Sload has taken coded categories involving insubstantial structures and other assumptions in the data file concerning status and subjected them to preliminary statistical analyses. We made only gross status distinctions in residential architecture for coding purposes in our field lab. We interpreted all insubstantial structures as places where people of low status had lived, while "room complexes"— apartment compounds and smaller residential compounds (R. Millon 1973:5, 23)— were divided into only two categories. The first included compounds on or near the "Street of the Dead" and exceptional or outstanding remains elsewhere, interpreted as occupied by people of high status. The second category subsumed all other compounds in an "intermediate" grouping.

Sload's objective was the refinement of coding categories relating to status. Her method was the multivariate statistical technique of discriminant analysis (Gottscho [Sload] 1977). Her sample included 80 apartment compounds and 82 insubstantial structures. One of her aims was to try to determine if insubstantial structures close to apartment compounds differed from those at some distance from them. Fourteen variables, all artifact categories, were used in the analysis.

While her results are not conclusive, it appears that many of the close insubstantial structures were outbuildings associated with apartment compounds, rather than residences. Not surprisingly, the residual "intermediate" status category seems to include some apartment compounds whose residents were of low status. Sload's analyses are continuing and look very promising.

## CITY AND REGION

Teotihuacan cannot be considered apart from its immediate region, the Teotihuacan Valley, nor from the Valley of Mexico, the larger region. This proposition was basic to the research recommendations made at the Valley of Mexico conference in Chicago in 1960 (Wolf 1976b:5).

I should make explicit how I use such terms as "city," "urbanism," and "urbanization." My principal concern is that these terms have heuristic value. If facilitation and clarification of research is the goal, a research strategy with an open-ended, relatively unrestricted conception of what constitutes a city seems most useful. Paul Wheatley (1971: 388), drawing on central-place theory in geography, writes of "the city as an instrument for the organization of dependent territory, . . . as a principle of regional integration, as a generator of effective space." The "effective space" concept (Friedmann 1961:92) involves the social transformation of the area around a city through the influence of urban institutions (see Wheatley 1972:614 n. 75). It forces the investigator to adopt a regional approach (Blanton 1976a, 1976c; G. Johnson 1977; R. McC. Adams 1965; 1966:18–19, 63; 1972:735–736, 747–748; R. McC. Adams and Nissen 1972:8–33, 85–94; Flannery 1972a; Hammond 1972, 1974; Marcus 1973, 1976a, 1976b; Hirth 1974; Skinner 1964, 1965, 1977; Ginsburg 1979; Sanders 1956; Palerm and Wolf 1957). Using Wheatley's statement as a point of departure rather than a definition, I find it most useful to leave open the lower limits of what constitutes a city in a given region, subject to inquiry along varying lines of evidence in each case. This means considering evidence for such questions as size of settlement; kinds of relationships with other settlements in the region; density of population; degree of stratification; extent of craft specialization; existence of state institutions; relationship of institutions, beliefs, and practices to the state; degree of involvement of others, both within and beyond the region, with ritual, myths, beliefs, and cult practices in the center; importance of marketplace trade, foreign trade, and other forms of internal, regional, and long-distance exchange; and other evidence of how the center and region were re-

organized and integrated. Basic evidence for the regional context of the center are the size, number, disposition, and degree of differentiation within and among other communities in the region; the quality, intensity, number, and kind of relationships their populations have with the center; the ways in which regional resources are exploited; and the wider setting of the region itself. Whether or not a particular center was a city as well as what kind of a city it was depends on the degree to which it manifested such characteristics and relationships as these, and on the extent to which, or the intensity with which, they were manifested (Hardoy 1973:xxii–xxiii). This makes it possible to consider not only different degrees of urbanism but also different kinds of urbanism. The same is true of the urbanization process within a single community or among several communities in a regional hierarchy. I find that analysis is facilitated and comparisons sharpened in this open-ended conception of the city.

I will also comment briefly on how I use the term "state." For Wheatley, "the city was the organizing principle of the state," and cities whose urban form was not imposed "were in their earlier phases city-states" (1971:8, 398). City and state coincide by definition. For me they do not. How Teotihuacan became a city and how the Teotihuacan state came into being are, as we shall see, inextricable dimensions of the same transformational process, but analytically separable nonetheless. The city, the physical locus of the power of the state, is at the same time a community, however large or small, a center of social activity, a religious and cultural center. When we consider the state, the focus shifts to stratification, to control over people and resources, and to the centralization of authority that comes into existence and maintains that control through political institutions. The city is the source of organization for both region and center; but it is from the legitimately constituted institution of the state and those who control it that the actual exercise of authority flows, and it is hierarchically ordered state institutions that organize, administer, and control both city and region.

Robert McC. Adams (1975:454–455) sees "the propensity for increased social stratification and political centralization as constituting the vital, central axis of development toward statehood." The evidence from Teotihuacan accords with this. But Adams goes on to say that his concerns lead him to a research strategy in which "substantial emphasis" is placed "on the distribution of wealth" in "tombs, private houses, and ritual contexts." We have little such evidence from Teotihuacan during the Patlachique and Tzacualli phases because, except for the work of Darlena K. Blucher (1971), we know little about residences of those phases and have few burials from them. Adams contrasts his approach to the development of the state with that of Henry T. Wright and Gregory A. Johnson, who identify the state "with the emergence of an apparent three-tiered hierarchy" (R. McC. Adams 1975:455; see Wright and Johnson 1975:267, 273, 274; G. Johnson 1973:2, 3, 15; Wright 1977:383; see also Flannery 1972a). Teotihuacan headed such a hierarchy from the beginning of the Tzacualli phase or earlier.

The Wright and Johnson formulation, Adams continues, places the advent of the state "a minimum of several centuries earlier than a primary concern for a stratified social order with 'disembedded' political institutions allows me to do." He notes that their differences "probably touch on differing assessments of the core processes by which civilizations came into being or of how they are to be distinguished from all lesser levels of sociocultural integration" and identifies "disembedded" political institutions with the ability of rulers to pursue "autonomous goals, with a sufficient level of 'free-floating,' potentially mobilizable resources. . . . Neither of these features can be identified before the emergence of the militaristic Mesopotamian urban polities in the Early Dynastic Period" in the first half of the third millennium B.C.

Instead, he argues, "earlier patterns of control, at least in that region, . . . tend to be identified . . . by their theocratic overtones and the apparent absence of a secularized elite" (R. McC. Adams 1975:455). This is a distinction Adams had made earlier when he wrote of "the transformation of essentially theocratic authority into political rule" (1966:138). In discussing the former, he comments: ". . . the probability of a primarily religious focus to social life at the outset of the Urban Revolution . . . appears to be the decidedly most reasonable reconstruction of the available evidence. Why should this have been so? Part of the answer may lie with the necessity for providing an intelligible moral framework of organization for society as it increased cumulatively in scale and complexity . . ." (R. McC. Adams 1966:121).

The evidence from Teotihuacan accords with this interpretation but at the same time accords with an interpretation involving the early appearance of state institutions. At Teotihuacan, a strong religious focus was integral to the transformation process itself, as state institutions were coming into being. Yet, for Adams, "theocratic authority" is not transformed "into political rule" until a "secularized elite" comes into existence (cf. Wright 1977:386). Part of the problem at issue seems to be the association of a "secularized elite" with clear evidence of control over critical resources in the society (e.g., Friedman and Rowlands 1978:275n.66). There is considerable evidence for such control at Teotihuacan without evidence for a "secularized elite." Here again it seems to me that the necessary focus on the social relations of production and distribution, on social stratification and political centralization (Cancian 1976), should not require us to ignore evidence for significant differences in the ordering of social relations between two areas as different as early Mesopotamia and Prehispanic central Mexico (cf. R. McC. Adams 1966:111–119). At Teotihuacan, evidence for the pursuit of "autonomous goals" by those at the top is not accompanied by evidence of secularization. But it is accompanied by a radical restructur-

216

ing of the settlement hierarchy with all that that implies, in accordance with the pursuit of those goals. The very top levels of the society may be priest-rulers and priest-administrators—even they appear to have been divided into two groups that may or may not have exercised different powers (R. Millon 1976:237)—but differentiation of institutions could and did exist at lower levels in Teotihuacan society with profound long-term consequences for everyone for centuries before artistic representations of military figures became prominent late in the city's history. As we shall see, there is strong evidence for the exercise of state power in the first century A.D., when Teotihuacan suddenly grew to several times its former size as a result of an apparently comprehensive plan for depopulating the countryside and resettlement in the city (J. Parsons 1977). Whatever else may have been involved in the formulation and execution of this plan, the transformation it represents could not have been carried out except through the exercise of legitimate authority centralized in an ultimate decision-making body with the power to use legitimate force, military or other, in the enforcement of that authority at a number of levels in the internal and regional administrative hierarchies. In this context military and policing functions would have played for some time a subordinate but critical role within the city and region and in external affairs. A measure of the power of the state is provided by the evidence for hierarchical control over people and resources locally and regionally at different points in its "trajectory," as we shall see (Cowgill 1979a).

Teotihuacan's sacralized polity would have been subject to constraints and limitations that would not have affected a secularized state with "disembedded" political institutions. But this should not blind us to the transformational change in social relations that already must have occurred before the decision to concentrate the valley's population was made and carried out. This argues for gradations in the kinds of states we distinguish, gradations from relatively weak to relatively strong within sacralized polities themselves, as well as a range from weakly developed states with circumscribed powers in the least differentiated polities to stronger states with "disembedded" political institutions and greater autonomy in secularized polities. This makes it possible to consider different degrees in the development of state power and different kinds of institutions for its exercise. It also facilitates comparisons, without losing the difference in kind between states and all other polities.

*Teotihuacan and Its Region: Setting, Resources*

The Teotihuacan Valley (500 sq km), in the central part of which the ancient city was located, is a subvalley in the northwestern part of the Valley of Mexico (8,000 sq km), with an altitude of over 2,200 m (Sanders 1965:22; Lorenzo 1968b:66–69). Teotihuacan occupied a strategic location for passage to and from the Valley of Mexico, and for access to obsidian sources, permanent springs, a potentially rich, irrigable alluvial plain[13] and the Valley of Mexico's uniquely valuable lake system (see Chapter 6 of this volume for maps and discussion of the Valley of Mexico setting, climate, ecological zones, resources, irrigable lands, etc.; see also Sanders 1976a, 1976b; Logan and Sanders 1976; J. Parsons 1976; Sanders, Parsons, and Logan 1976; Blanton 1976b; 1976c; McClung de Tapia 1978, 1979; Starbuck 1975, 1977; Litvak King 1978).

At the east of the Teotihuacan Valley, beyond Otumba, there is unobstructed passage into the Plains of Apan, Tlaxcala, and the Valley of Puebla (see Fig. 6-2, this volume), and on to Veracruz and the Gulf Coast. In addition to its strategic location, Teotihuacan was also in a region of raw materials of great importance—"grey" obsidian in the middle and upper valley and in the adjoining region to the northeast, with the most prized "green" obsidian deposits in Central Mexico 50 km to the north. In the Valley of Mexico, salt was obtainable from Lake Texcoco, and valuable deposits of limestone lay to the northwest. Other resources included a variety of stone outcroppings, principally volcanic in origin, for building, domestic, and ritual use, and deposits of clay for ceramics— all in the context of a network of lakes that was a major source of food and that facilitated communication and transport (but concerning restrictions on the latter, see Litvak King 1978:116).

Clearly, there was something unique about the Valley of Mexico. Twice in less than 1,500 years, first Teotihuacan, then Tenochtitlan-Tlatelolco, the two most complex urban societies in Precolumbian America, arose in this remarkable setting.

Information we obtained from analysis of plant and animal remains from our excavations and those of others provides direct information on diet, and on flora and fauna used for other purposes. Emily McClung de Tapia (1977, 1979) carried out plant analyses; David R. Starbuck (1975, 1977), the study of animal remains. Most plant material analyzed comes from our excavations, largely from flotation of soil samples (McClung de Tapia 1979:107–116; Struever 1968). McClung de Tapia's material extends from Late Tzacualli to Metepec (ca. A.D. 100–750). A preliminary analysis of soil samples from kitchen floors from our excavation in Tetitla (TE 24) was made by Richard I. Ford and Joel N. Elias (1972) of the University of Michigan Museum of Anthropology. McClung de Tapia (1974) and Jorge Angulo V. (1972) also attempted to identify plants in Teotihuacan art.

Following are plant genera identified by McClung de Tapia (1979:103–229, 317–319) from carbonized remains from some of our excavations and from Séjourné's Burial 11 from Zacuala Patios: SEEDS—*Zea mays* (maize grains, cobs, cupules); *Phaseolus vulgaris* (*frijol*, common bean); *Phaseolus coccineus* (*ayacote*, runner bean); *Cucurbita* sp. (*calabaza*, squash, pumpkin); *Capsicum* spp. (chile); *Solanum* sp. (*papa*, wild tuber); *Physalis* sp. (*tomatl, tomate, tomatillo*, green husk tomato, ground cherry); *Opuntia* spp.

(*nopal*, prickly pear); *Persea americana* (*ahuacatl, aguacate*, avocado); *Amaranthus* sp. (*huauhtli, alegría*); *Chenopodium* spp. (*huauhtzontli, epazote*); *Spondias* sp. (*ciruela*, plum); *Portulaca* sp. (*verdolaga*, purslane); *Acacia* sp. (*huizache*); *Scirpus* sp. (*tule*, bullrush); *Argemone* sp. (*chicalote, amapola*, poppy); *Cissus* sp. (*temecate, Tripas de Judas, Molonqui*); other *Cactaceae* (other than *nopal*, possibly *Mammillaria* sp. and others); Family Cyperaceae (other than *tule*); Family Gramineae (other than maize and reed); Family Leguminosae (other than beans and *huizache*); Family Malvaceae (other than cotton); Family Solanaceae (other than chile and wild tuber); Family Rosaceae (other than "Mexican cherry" and "Mexican hawthorn"); Family Eleagnaceae; Family Cruciferae. FIBERS—*Gossypium* sp. (*algodon*, cotton); *Ficus* sp. (*amate*, bark paper); *Phragmites australis* (*carrizo*, reed); *Fucraea* sp.; Family Liliaceae (*izote*?). OTHER—*Lagenaria siceraria* (*jícara*, bottle gourd); *Selaginella* sp. (*Doradillo*, spike moss); *Juniperus* sp. (juniper).

McClung de Tapia was not able to identify three types of seeds that occurred throughout the samples in high frequencies. Ford and Elias (1972) found two plant species she did not—*Prunus capuli* (*capulín*, Mexican cherry) and *Cratageus mexicana* (*tejocote*, Mexican hawthorn) (McClung de Tapia 1979:172–173, 319).

Notably absent from McClung de Tapia's identifications is maguey (*Agave* spp.). "Probable" maguey fiber is reported from Burial 1 at Tlamimilolpa (Linné 1942:156–160, 180). The plant is represented in murals (e.g., R. Millon 1973:Fig. 48b) and is grown widely in the valley today. It is a plant of many uses, both today and in the Prehispanic past. Its absence from our samples is puzzling.

Maize cobs are small. *Cónico* and *Palomero toluqueño* were found. Both, as well as *Nal-Tel/Chapalote* complex recently have been identified at Cuanalan in the southern Teotihuacan Valley in First Intermediate period contexts by Carlos Alvarez del Castillo

218

from material excavated by Linda Manzanilla in a 1976 INAH excavation (McClung de Tapia 1979:187–188, Table 4). *Cónico* had been identified earlier from Manuel Gamio's (1922) Ciudadela excavations. Paul C. Mangelsdorf has identified a maize cob from Zacuala Patios Burial 11, now in the Harvard Botanical Museum, as belonging to the *Nal-Tel/Chapalote* complex (McClung de Tapia 1979:177). In one of our excavations in the "merchants' *barrio*" (TE 11) (Fig. 7-3, no. 9), we found on an earth floor the impression of a maize husk (McClung de Tapia 1979:199) that looked as though it had been steamed, possibly a discard from a *tamal* (tamale).

We do not yet have enough information to make judgments about the relative importance of the various plants in the Teotihuacan diet, or in the diet of people of differing status. A wide range of plants were exploited early in the city's history and continued to be exploited thereafter. Some must have been imported from warmer climates (e.g., avocado, cotton).

Faunal remains analyzed by Starbuck included material from our survey and excavations and his own excavation in Yayahuala (TE 26), from the northwest periphery of Patlachique phase Teotihuacan (Blucher 1971), from INAH "Street of the Dead" excavations, and from Laurette Séjourné's excavations (especially Tetitla). Fish bones were recovered in flotation; most of the rest were recovered in normal screening and sifting (Starbuck 1977:153). In addition to small fish obtainable in the area of the springs and of the permanent streams in the lower valley, the lakes to the south probably were exploited, because of the large number of bones of turtles and water fowl. Following are the most common species in his analyses (Starbuck 1977:154, 156, Table 1): *Odocoileus virginianus*, deer; *Canis famillaris*, dog; *Sylvilagus* sp., cottontail rabbit; *Lepus callotis*, jackrabbit; *Meleagris gallopavo*, turkey; Family Anatidae, ducks, geese; Family Phasianidae, quail, bobwhite.

Of these only the dog and the turkey were domesticated; together they totaled less than an estimated 10 percent of the meat consumed. Animal food was more important than had been realized previously, and its importance has been interpreted as continuing throughout the city's history through the expansion of the hunting area well beyond the Teotihuacan Valley (Starbuck 1977:158). Apparently, roughly the same balance was maintained between cultivated and wild species in both animals and plants over a period of centuries, probably through expanding the area in which resources were exploited (McClung de Tapia 1979:325–328). Plant and animal resources apparently exploited would have yielded a diet adequate to human requirements (McClung de Tapia 1979:295–304). Whether most city dwellers actually maintained or were able to maintain such a diet is quite another matter, about which we know little as yet.

## ECONOMY AND POLITY

As our mapping survey progressed, we were impressed increasingly with the scope of the planning and of the vision that created this urban design on so grand a scale, that provided an urban context to match the conception of its monumental center with its overpowering religious and public architecture, that imposed a deliberately skewed cruciform layout on the landscape to serve as the model for the orientation of all construction, residential as well as public, for hundreds of years (Drewitt 1966, 1969; R. Millon 1973: 42–44). What is even more remarkable is that the daring vision embodied in this grand urban design now appears to be only the most visible manifestation of a planning endeavor that was geopolitical in scope and that sought (1) to reorganize totally the management of the entire region and its resources, radically transforming its settlement hierarchy and the way its agricultural resources were exploited, an effort that involved large-scale and permanent relocation of people in the tens of thousands (J. Parsons 1977); (2) to develop, manage, and exploit the "inner hinterland" in the Valley of Mexico in accord

219

with this plan, while reorganizing and managing an "outer hinterland" in the semitropical Valley of Morelos to the south and in other regions to the northwest, northeast, east, and southeast, in accordance with another quite different plan involving the imposition of a radically different settlement hierarchy (Hirth 1978b); (3) to exploit the uses of, and to manage and monopolize the procurement and distribution of obsidian, the major regional resource, a critical raw material, apparently maintaining separate manufacturing centers and separate exchange systems for local and regional distribution, on the one hand, and foreign distribution, on the other (Charlton 1978b, 1979b; Spence 1974a, 1979b); (4) to develop similar means for the exploitation and distribution of other raw materials as finished goods (for example, Thin Orange ceramic ware, manufactured elsewhere but its distribution controlled by Teotihuacan); and (5) to exploit the appeal of those beliefs and rituals associated with Teotihuacan that transcended ethnic and cultural bounds to make the most of the religious and cultural attraction of the center, while validating and legitimating economic expansion under the aegis of Teotihuacan's sacralized polity.

We are only beginning to glimpse the outlines of this remarkable exercise in statecraft and what we see may be misleading. The farther removed we are geographically from Teotihuacan, the more difficult it is to judge the evidence—for example, Teotihuacan "presence" in the Valley of Guatemala or in the southern Maya Lowlands. Nevertheless, what is emerging from the combined researches of a number of archaeologists in Central Mexico is an almost bewilderingly complex model of the economy and polity of Teotihuacan. For reasons that should be clear, it is not possible to discuss one without the other. In what follows, I may be overstating the case for the many manifestations of planning that current research seems to be disclosing. At this point in our understanding, overstatement is heuristically preferable to understatement, if it serves both to

sharpen the focus and widen the scope of future research strategies.

We still know very little about the social relations of production in the cultivation of lands immediately surrounding Teotihuacan. We do not know who owned the land. This is a major concern, since I estimate that at least two-thirds of the urban population lived from cultivating land (R. Millon 1970b:1080; 1976:228). However owned, those who controlled the state institutions must have been directly involved in the way land was exploited. Early in the Tzacualli phase (first century A.D.) most of the inhabitants of the eastern and southern Valley of Mexico, and perhaps of other as yet unreported areas, were removed from, or otherwise convinced to leave, their lands and homes, and resettled in Teotihuacan (J. Parsons 1977:Map 1, Table 1; also 1968, 1971, 1974a, 1976) (see Fig. 6-15, this volume). That population was concentrated in the city, while the countryside was being depopulated, has been known since early in the Valley of Mexico surface surveys. What was not known was how long it took to occur. In discussing the interpretation of a similar population concentration at Uruk in southern Mesopotamia in Early Dynastic times, Robert McC. Adams (1972:747) points out that "choices between major processual alternatives often depend on the length of the time span with which a transformation like the emergence of cities occurs." This was the problem with interpreting the evidence from Teotihuacan and its countryside. It now appears that the process of concentration and resettlement took place early in the Tzacualli phase over a very short period of time. It was during the Tzacualli phase that Teotihuacan expanded explosively to cover an area of more than 20 sq km (R. Millon 1966b:71–72; 1973:52–54; 1976:212; Cowgill 1974:385–387). The earlier settlement (Patlachique phase) (150–1 B.C.), the first large settlement, covered 8 sq km, most of it in the northwest quadrant of the area occupied later (R. Millon 1973:51–52; Cowgill 1974:381–385).

Population estimates for the earlier phases

are difficult to make and subject to large margins of error. Cowgill (1974:383; 1977; 1979b: 55) estimates that by the end of the Patlachique phase, Teotihuacan had a population of at least 20,000 and perhaps as much as 40,000. It was already a settlement of sufficient size and complexity to provide demographic, political, economic, and sociocultural bases for the explosive expansion to follow. Prior settlement in the area of the later city was scattered, with total population not exceeding several thousand (R. Millon 1973:50; Cowgill 1974:378–381). Thus, the expansion of Patlachique phase Teotihuacan was itself a phenomenon of critical importance, about which we still know very little (Blucher 1971, 1972; also Winning 1976).

Sometime during the Patlachique phase or perhaps at the beginning of the Tzacualli phase, Teotihuacan may have been strongly "influenced" by peoples from the Puebla-Tlaxcala region. Cultural indebtedness to Cholula and to Cuicuilco in the Valley of Mexico, has been acknowledged for some time (e.g., R. Millon 1967a:38), but the scope of the possible indebtedness to other societies in the Puebla-Tlaxcala region has been emphasized only recently (e.g., in such realms as architectural planning, the form of temple architecture,[14] and religious doctrines and practices, including beliefs and conceptions relating to the "Rain God" (García Cook 1973a, 1978:175–176, Fig. 3; García Cook and Trejo 1977:64–65, 67).

The expansion of Patlachique phase Teotihuacan may have drawn on surrounding populations, but it does not appear to have involved massive demographic shifts. The Tzacualli phase expansion, on the other hand, affected a major part of the Teotihuacan Valley population (Sanders 1965; Sanders et al. 1975:184ff., Fig. 110), as well as most of the population from the eastern and southern Valley of Mexico (J. Parsons 1977: Map 1, Table 1; Logan and Sanders 1976: Map 1; see also Fig. 6-15, this volume).[15] Jeffrey Parsons estimates that the population of the Teotihuacan Valley had risen to 100,000, most of it in Teotihuacan (1977: Table 1). This suggests

that Cowgill's (1979b:55) recent, tentative estimate of 60,000–80,000 for the early city is, if anything, conservative. The population of Tzacualli phase Teotihuacan probably reached 80,000 or more very early in the Tzacualli phase, following the population concentration. After the initial resettlement, part of the population was later relocated in the valley during the Miccaotli and Tlamimilolpa phases, mostly not in previously occupied areas, but in small communities in prime zones for rainfall agriculture; the hierarchy of communities was reduced from what it had been before the resettlement by "two or three tiers in the local . . . settlement hierarchy" (J. Parsons 1977).

For 600 years or more, 85–90 percent of the inhabitants in the eastern and southern Valley of Mexico were concentrated in the Teotihuacan Valley, most of them in the city, with the other 10–15 percent dispersed more or less evenly in small settlements over the rest of the area (see Fig. 6-16, this volume). Total populations remained well below what they had been in the Patlachique phase throughout these centuries in the east and south (reduced by 80 percent and 65 percent respectively), while they increased substantially in the formerly marginal and sparsely settled Zumpango area to the northwest. If resettlement occurred rapidly, as the evidence now indicates, it is likely to have involved compulsion as well as persuasion. The Teotihuacan state must have come into being early in this process, if it had not already emerged when the relocation policy was decided.

Why did this concentration occur? What kind of leadership conceived it and directed it? How was it related to the massive building program in the city? to the rapidly growing obsidian production system? How and by whom were rights to land, water and other valued resources allocated among old and new settlers? How and by whom were conflicts created by the absorption process resolved?

The evidence that population concentration proceeded at a much faster pace than it

221

had been possible to argue previously pushes some of these questions into the Patlachique phase, where it will be even more difficult to explore them. The timing, of course, can be explored in the countryside in excavations that may also provide clues to the circumstances preceding the resettlements.

The population concentration also poses the question of why it persisted for so long. The advantages for the Teotihuacan hierarchy of having most of the population of the Valley of Mexico in the city are evident. Direct intervention in the agricultural sector would have been possible, and this potential was evidently exploited in a plan calling for the resettlement of a limited number of small farm communities in the most fertile areas. The plan seems to have been designed to maximize the advantages and minimize the dangers to the state—"the almost final solution" (R. Millon 1973:59) to the endless conflict between city and countryside.

Administration and control came directly from Teotihuacan itself and, in the eastern and southern Valley of Mexico, from secondary centers in the southeast (Portezuelo) and the western side of the lakes (Azcapotzalco) (see Fig. 6-16, this volume) (Blanton 1972b: 69, 79, 81, 213; J. Parsons 1976:87, Map 8). Teotihuacan was a "primate city," overwhelmingly dominating its settlement hierarchy, being at least twenty-five times larger than its "secondary centers" (Jefferson 1939; Blanton 1976a:255–257; 1976c:199–200; C. A. Smith 1976b:30–32). Nor are the secondary centers and other settlements so spaced as to form "any kind of coherent central place model" (M. Smith 1979:122).

### The Outer Hinterland

Control over the Valley of Mexico, its "inner hinterland" (Hirth 1978b:331), secured, the Teotihuacan state began a process of expansion, in the latter part of the Tlamimilolpa phase (fourth century A.D.) or earlier, into new areas, forming part of what Hirth calls its "outer hinterland." The Rio Amatzinac region in the eastern part of the subtropical Valley of Morelos was such an area (Hirth 1974:182–229, 242–256; 1978b). "These areas supplied regional commodities to support Teotihuacán's large population and provided regional markets for its burgeoning craft industries" (Hirth 1978b:331–332). Near the beginning of the Middle Horizon, with "agricultural intensification" as a major incentive, ". . . the valley was unified under a large administrative centre, population was relocated into rural areas, and controlled by a highly structured settlement hierarchy" (Hirth 1978b:332, Figs. 3, 4). Cotton may have been grown for Teotihuacan; this was one of the most important cotton-producing areas for the Aztecs (Hirth 1978b:328). We found cotton in our excavations (TE 2, TE 20) (McClung de Tapia 1979:139), as Linné did earlier (1942:155–160, 180, 191). Morelos seems most likely to be a major source (see also Litvak King 1978:120).

Hirth's evidence is subject to other interpretations. But data from two other regions, to the northwest and to the east and southeast, yield analogous evidence of domination and exploitation by the Teotihuacan state. In the region around Tula, a major Teotihuacan occupation lasted from the Late Tlamimilolpa through the Metepec phases (ca. A.D. 300–750) (Cobean 1978:81–82, 84). Alba Guadalupe Mastache de Escobar and Ana María Crespo (1974, 1976) postulate a process of colonization by people from Teotihuacan or with close ties to it that reached its peak in the Late Tlamimilolpa phase. Many settlements are located in lime-producing areas (Mastache de Escobar and Crespo 1976; Cobean 1978:82). Two locations in the lime-producing areas have connections with the Teotihuacan Oaxaca barrio (Crespo and Mastache de Escobar 1976; Cobean 1978: 84–85).

The Oaxaca barrio (Fig. 7-3, no. 17) was occupied by people from Oaxaca (fourth century A.D.), whose descendants lived there for centuries in standard Teotihuacan apartment compounds, while maintaining some of their old customs.[16] After its discovery in our survey, we and others excavated there (Fig. 7-4, lower left). The two Tula region sites have the same mixture of Oaxacan and Teotihuacan pottery types as the Oaxaca *barrio*, with the same long time span (Rattray n.d.; Cobean 1978:85).

The Teotihuacan state more closely managed and more actively exploited the Tula region than the "outer hinterland" in eastern Morelos. The settlement hierarchy included another tier with a provincial center (Chingu) three times the size of the primary Morelos center (ca. 2 sq km) and architecturally much more complex. The major resource must have been lime (Cobean 1978:84–85), used in vast quantities in construction and, almost certainly, domestically, to soften maize kernels for *masa*, maize dough (see Hilda Castañeda Saldaña's 1976 study of grinding implements from our survey).

To the east was the Plains of Apan region of southeastern Hidalgo and northern Tlaxcala (García Cook and Trejo 1977; García Cook and Merino C. 1977; see also Chapter 8, this volume). There are 5 large, highly structured settlement hierarchies in this "Teotihuacan Sphere" with major provincial centers of 100–200 ha or more, and with monumental civic-religious architecture (García Cook and Trejo 1977:57–68, Figs. 5, 6; cf. Dumond 1976). This densely settled area played a major role in provisioning Teotihuacan. The sites, as well as the "Teotihuacan Corridor" sites discussed below, seem to span the Late Tzacualli, Miccaotli, and Tlamimilolpa phases (ca. A.D. 100–400). Most continued to be occupied during the Xolalpan and Metepec phases (ca. A.D. 400–750), but seem to have assumed increasing autonomy late in this period and in so doing probably played a role in the fall of Teotihuacan, as the passage of goods through the "Teotihuacan Corridor" began to be impeded (García Cook and Trejo 1977:66–68; Hirth and Swezey 1976).

To the southeast is the "Teotihuacan Corridor." It passes through and divides an extensive area ("Cultura Tenanyecac"), independent of both Teotihuacan and Cholula, through Apizaco to Huamantla, following a linear, then a dendritic network of Teotihua-

can (as opposed to Tenanyecac or Cholula) sites with the same type of settlement hierarchy as the "Teotihuacan Sphere" (see Chapter 8, this volume). Between Apizaco and Huamantla, one linear arrangement of Teotihuacan sites turns toward the Gulf Coast, the other toward the Puebla Valley, in the direction of Tehuacan and Oaxaca (Litvak King 1978:120), with a branch splitting to the west toward Cholula (García Cook and Trejo 1977:65–66, Figs. 5, 6; García Cook and Merino C. 1977:71–76, Maps 3, 4). Another major "Teotihuacan Corridor," to the northeast, ran from Teotihuacan to Tepeapulco to Tulancingo (presumably with passage there to the Gulf Coast and El Tajin?) (García Cook and Merino C. 1977:76; Litvak King 1978:120). (More foreign pottery reached Teotihuacan from El Tajin than from any other single Gulf Coast center; Sayre and Harbottle 1979:Table 1; Rattray and Ruiz 1977.) The existence of a "corridor" to the northeast also is implied by Thomas H. Charlton's surveys northeast of Tepeapulco (1978b). Tepeapulco is a short distance northeast of the passage from the Teotihuacan Valley (20 km northeast of Otumba) and was an important obsidian production center subject to the Teotihuacan state (Charlton 1978b). Jaime Litvak King (1978:120) discusses a possible "flow of cacao from Guerrero" via a Rio "Balsas route" through western Morelos into the Valley of Mexico. (See also L. Parsons and Price 1971; Price 1978; R. E. W. Adams 1978; Hammond 1978; Rathje, Gregory, and Wiseman 1978.)

## Craft Production

Almost 400 obsidian workshops operated in the city at its height, most in apartment compounds. Some are isolated, but most are in clusters that we interpret as neighborhoods or *barrios*. Workshops also are associated with precincts within or adjoining major public buildings. There are two kinds of workshop areas, local and regional.

Local workshop areas produced the major artifact categories (blades, cores, scrapers, and bifacials), usually were on or near major avenues or streets, and served their own neighborhoods. Concentrations of obsidian debris are less intense than in regional areas, suggesting either part-time specialization or that not all adult males in a compound participated (Spence 1979b).

Workers in the six regional workshop areas produced obsidian artifacts for use throughout the city and beyond (Spence 1979b). Regional areas adjoin three of the largest public buildings—the Pyramid of the Moon, the Ciudadela, and the Great Compound. Precinct workshops also are associated with these structures. The Great Compound regional area (N1W2, both sides of West Avenue, Fig. 7-3) specialized in making cores and blades. In the Pyramid of the Moon regional area, northwest of the pyramid, north of the walled enclosures adjoining it, an area of workshops specialized in cores and blades; another produced cores, blades, and bifacials. The latter is also true of the Ciudadela regional area, east of the Ciudadela, north of East Avenue and south of the river (TE 13) (Spence 1979b).

One of the major and exclusive products of most regional areas was a blank with a pointed base not used locally (Spence 1967: Fig. 2a,b,c; 1979b). Michael W. Spence (personal communication, 1979) believes that the blanks were made for distribution outside the city, including such foreign areas as Oaxaca. This hypothesis will have to be tested, probably outside the Valley of Mexico.

Evidence on procurement and distribution from the Pyramid of the Moon precinct and its regional area, where all workshops within and north of the precinct were linked by proximity, common typology, and the use of blocks of grey obsidian, indicates that the raw material was brought into the precinct (TE 5) and distributed to directly controlled workshops within the precinct and to the associated workshops outside it (Spence 1979b: Table 1). Aside from this area the distribution of grey obsidian does not appear to have been centralized.

The fine green obsidian from Navajas,

Spence argues, was exploited, transported, and distributed uniformly to workshops within the city under the direction and control of the state by the Tlamimilolpa phase (Spence 1974a, 1979b; Spence and Kimberlin 1979). From then on 90 percent or more of the output of workshops in core/blade production was of green obsidian (Spence 1979b: Table 2; Spence and Kimberlin 1979). There are no major obsidian workshops to the south, in the Valley of Mexico or beyond.

The only other center of obsidian production, also under Teotihuacan control, known to have been importing green obsidian from Navajas, is Tepeapulco (Charlton 1978b: 1231–1234; 1979a). Large workshops there also produced implements of grey obsidian from Otumba and a major source to the northeast of Tepeapulco (Paredon) (Charlton 1978b:1233). Production appears to have been for export, much of it south and east through the "Teotihuacan Corridor"; none was destined for Teotihuacan or elsewhere in the Valley of Mexico (Charlton 1978b:1233–1235; 1979a).

The obsidian production system now appears to be associated with the very beginnings of Teotihuacan, supporting an earlier prediction (R. Millon 1973:51–52). A cluster of 9 obsidian workshops near the western periphery[17] of Patlachique phase Teotihuacan probably dates to that phase (Spence, personal communication, 1979).[18] At Tepeapulco two major obsidian workshops also date from this phase (Charlton 1978b: Fig. 4). A scattering of other obsidian workshops have been found in other parts of the Valley of Mexico dating from this period (ca. 150–1 B.C.) (Spence 1974a). Thereafter, apparently, none existed until after the fall of Teotihuacan—the control over the distribution of raw materials, grey and green, from the center was complete. The potential of the obsidian production system may have been evident to Teotihuacan's leaders early in the phase. Nine workshops are few in comparison to almost 400 several hundred years later. But they are an uncommon number for the time, and more craft workshops than are known from many important Middle American cities at any time.

The rapid and dramatic population increase in Tzacualli phase Teotihuacan (first century A.D.) was accompanied by an equally dramatic increase in the number of obsidian workshops to 48 or more (Spence 1974a; personal communication, 1979). Control over the distribution of obsidian throughout the Valley of Mexico and perhaps beyond, as raw material as well as finished objects, began in the Tzacualli phase and was aided by Teotihuacan's proximity to its major Central Mexican sources (Spence 1979b). The state was beginning to "monopolize" obsidian exploitation and distribution in Central Mexico, without directly organizing and controlling production in the city itself. The exploitation, transport, and distribution of Navajas obsidian within the city was not yet controlled, as it was from the Tlamimilolpa phase on (Spence 1979b; Charlton 1978b). Perhaps only the deposits themselves and the access route to them were under Teotihuacan control.

Ceramic workshops are found in all parts of the city, concentrated near the principal sources of clay and in areas with other craft workshops (TE 20) (Fig. 7-3, no. 22) (Krotser 1976b, 1979). They show a close association with high population concentrations during the Xolalpan and Metepec phases (Ester 1976:83). A cluster of several *barrios* in squares S3W1–W2 and S4W1–W2, with more than 30 workshops that specialized in the manufacture of a special kitchen ware (San Martin Orange) used throughout the city but rarely found much beyond it, may have had its own specialized marketplace in an enclosed plaza in the south of square S3W1 (Fig. 7-3), with the major access route a temple complex fronting the "Street of the Dead." With one or two other exceptions, pottery workshops are so distributed as to suggest that their location was of little concern to the state. This may be an important clue to an economic climate in the city relatively free of state interference during its period of greatest prosperity.

## Exchange

A primate city can be the "hub of . . . [a] 'solar' marketing system . . . where politics dominates commerce" (C. A. Smith 1976b: 36; 1976c:334; see also 1976b:28–32, 36–39, 44–51; 1976c:309–321, 338–345, Fig. 1, Tables 1, 2).[19] Data for such systems come from present-day societies in Middle America and elsewhere quite different from Teotihuacan in critically important ways (C. A. Smith 1976a:1:255–300, 1976b, 1976c); but they are thought to be relevant to urban origins and to large complex societies of the past (1976b:50–51; 1976c:344–345). The settlement hierarchy predicted for a region dominated by a primate center certainly seems relevant (C. A. Smith 1976b:30–32, 36–39). Most of the volume trade in a "solar" system flows into and out of the center, with state revenues coming from control of the exchange process. There is little exchange among communities at lower levels in the settlement hierarchy. Craft specialization is concentrated in the center or in areas under the control of the state.

Such a system would be consonant with what I have postulated in the past (R. Millon 1966c, 1976:241–242), but would structure it in a regional framework. Revenues from market trade would have contributed significantly to state income, but in a context that would have included major income from land, some temple- and state-owned, some taxed, and from a small number of state-directed craft workshops. Thus, there would have been some control over production, greater control over exchange, and direct control of some critical and highly valued raw materials needed by everyone (e.g., obsidian, lime). The state would have controlled large-scale movements to and from the center of raw materials, produce, and finished goods, receiving high revenues with relatively little intervention in the productive process. Most day-to-day economic activities in the city (and the hinterlands) would not have been supervised. Most of what was produced in fields or workshops would have been at the disposal of the producers, with varying amounts exchanged for other goods, produce, raw materials, or services in the marketplace, where vendors would have been taxed, or in the case of craft products destined for export, exchanged with and/or turned over to the appropriate official(s) in the hierarchy. It can be predicted that cultivators both in the city and in the hinterlands would have exchanged foodstuffs and other raw materials at temples for ritual services or paraphernalia or for raw materials and paraphernalia used in household and/or mortuary ritual (e.g., copal incense, bark paper) (Linné 1934:113; 1942:136, 147; McClung de Tapia 1979:138–139; Linné 1942:126, 132, 153, 155, 157, 160, 180–181, 188).

Marketplace exchange would have been facilitated by the use of media of exchange. Were cacao "beans" used, as they were in the Aztec capital (R. Millon 1955)? Cacao was known to the Teotihuacanos, and its acquisition may have been one motive for expansion to the Gulf Coast (e.g., Marquina 1951:Foto. 206; Kampen 1972:Fig. 5a; L. Parsons 1978: 34) and the Pacific coastal regions of Chiapas and Guatemala—the "cacao route" of Sanders and Price (1968:168; L. Parsons 1969: 160) (e.g., L. Parsons 1969:74; Coggins 1975:156–157; Hellmuth 1978:73, Fig. 3). Cacao pods hang from a tree on a Teotihuacan cylindrical vessel fragment showing tropical birds, possibly quetzales, and a hunter with a blowgun (Musée de l'Homme 82.17.72; Linné 1942:Fig. 175; M. Coe 1962:Fig. 28). I have seen *candeleros* in the shape of cacao pods; a cacao tree is probably represented on one of the Tlalocan murals at Tepantitla (e.g., Marquina 1951:Lám. 29, left of weeping figure).

The "Offering Scene" mural from the Temple of Agriculture on the "Street of the Dead" (Fig. 7-3, no. 34; A. G. Miller 1973b: Figs. 68–78; Villagra Caleti 1971:Fig. 5) may represent the complex institutional web of temple and market (R. Millon 1976:242). Marketplace exchange seems to take place in the upper part of the mural, and the individual on the right holds small objects in his ex-

tended hand, described as "seeds," that seem likely to be cacao "beans" (A. G. Miller 1973b:Figs. 68, 69, 75a, b). If so, cacao was being used as a medium of exchange in the Teotihuacan marketplace early in the Middle Horizon (Tlamimilolpa phase), for this is an early mural (C. Millon 1972a:86).

What was the role of merchants, especially in long distance trade (L. Parsons and Price 1971; Chapman 1971; Price 1978; Bittman and Sullivan 1978; Berdan 1978)? On the city's eastern edge we found exceptionally high concentrations of foreign pottery (primarily Gulf Coast but some Lowland Maya), on the surface and in excavation. I dubbed the area the "merchants' *barrio*," but the quotation marks are meant to indicate that this may be a misnomer. It does not appear to have been occupied by foreigners. The Gulf Coast sources have been confirmed by Sayre and Harbottle (1979:Table 1), and a Fine Orange ware with a "cut" white slip, of which we have many sherds, has just been identified as coming from Matacapan and the Tuxtlas region of southern Veracruz (Evelyn Rattray, personal communication, 1979), a possible region of Teotihuacan settlement "conveniently situated between highland Teotihuacan and its Kaminaljuyu outpost" (L. Parsons 1978:29). The building with the highest concentration of Gulf Coast and Maya pottery is a multi-room structure of adobe, possibly a warehouse or storage area (TE 4). This is not necessarily evidence of merchants operating independently of the state. But it raises the question of how freely merchants were able to move about within the city and beyond it. Even if linked to and partly controlled by the state, were merchants with entrepreneurial motivations involved in its expansion (R. McC. Adams 1974; Bittman and Sullivan 1978:212–213, 217)? We still have only fragmentary clues and, aside from the suggestive "merchants' *barrio*" evidence, little basis for making judgments.

Foreign goods and raw materials would have flowed into the city in large quantities, of which we see or are able to recognize only a tiny fraction. Some of them were destined for craft workshops. Lapidaries in a *barrio* in N3E5 (TE 18) (Fig. 7-3) worked in stone (e.g., jade and related stones, onyx) and in a single species of shell (*Isognomon alatus*, tree oyster) (Starbuck 1975:124, 150). There are two other possible areas of shell workshops—in the "Old City" (Fig. 7-3, no. 16) (*Spondylus*) and in the Oaxaca *barrio* (*Chama echinata*; its use was apparently confined to the *barrio*) (Starbuck 1975:150–151). Huge quantities of shell were imported both from the Gulf and from the Pacific, with Pacific varieties especially desired (Starbuck 1975:112–159). Shells were highly prized for ornamental uses and, above all, for their ritual value, especially *Spondylus*, *Pecten*, and conch shells (*Pleuroploca gigantea*, *Turbinella angulata*, *Strombus* [*Tricornis*] *gigas*).

Long distance trade in shells must have been a major concern of the state. Some kind of control of the shell trade from both coasts in Central Mexico and far beyond seems probable, and the fall of Teotihuacan probably had "a disruptive effect upon long distance shell trade throughout Mesoamerica" (Starbuck 1975:154–155).

Mica (especially "book" mica) obviously was highly prized and must have been imported in quantity (under state auspices?) (from Oaxaca?) (Walter Lombardo, personal communication, 1978) (e.g., Linné 1934:153; 1942:132, 136, 138, 146, 173; Armillas 1944:123–124, Fotos 3, 4). Its importance is reflected in our survey, especially by the frequency with which fragile fragments of "book" mica were found.

The possible existence of a northeasterly "Teotihuacan Corridor" to the El Tajin region of the Gulf Coast via the Tulancingo region has been mentioned previously. Northwest of the Tula region, evidence at San Juan del Rio suggests that another "corridor" may have existed to Queretaro. Cinnabar mines were exploited in the Sierra de Queretaro 200 km from Teotihuacan in what appears to have been another enterprise directly controlled by the Teotihuacan state late in its history. The area is barren and difficult to reach today, and all supplies for the support of the mine workers would have to have been brought into the area (Secretaría del Patrimonio Nacional 1970:49; Franco 1970a, 1970b; R. Millon 1973:61–62). Cinnabar was a highly prized substance in Mesoamerica from the time of the Olmec in the Early Horizon; these mines were first exploited by the Olmec in the first millennium B.C., how extensively is not known. Cinnabar was used at Teotihuacan to decorate fine pottery and in burial ritual (e.g., Spence 1976:131, 133–134, 137–138), and it probably had many other religious and secular uses. The Sierra de Queretaro mining enterprise is a dramatic example of the total support of a productive process by the state. Given what we now know of the other exploitative activities of the Teotihuacan state, this undertaking seems to carry the Teotihuacan stamp. But, given the nature of the evidence (largely ceramic), the possibility cannot be excluded that it was carried out by a polity based in central Veracruz.

Hundreds of kilometers farther to the northwest, extensive mining operations were undertaken in the Chalchihuites region of Zacatecas from ca. A.D. 250 to 500 (Weigand 1968; Kelley 1971; Weigand, Harbottle, and Sayre 1977; Holien and Pickering 1978). Because the mines yielded much more than possibly could have been consumed locally, Phil C. Weigand has suggested that their exploitation was related to Teotihuacan (Weigand 1968:45; Weigand, Harbottle, and Sayre 1977:16–20). "Blue-green mineral stones," "white jade," flint, cinnabar, and hematite (Weigand, Harbottle, and Sayre 1977:18; Weigand 1968:50) are the most likely of the minerals mined in the area to have been of interest to the Teotihuacanos. Hematite was a red pigment used in enormous quantities by the Teotihuacanos, in architectural decoration and as the main pigment in murals and in decorating ceramics. Turquoise from New Mexico (possibly from the Cerrillos zone) also may have been channeled through the Chalchihuites district before reaching Central Mexico (Weigand, Har-bottle, and Sayre 1977:16–20, 31). Minerals from these mines and turquoise from New Mexico probably reached Teotihuacan, but as yet there seems to be little direct evidence of a Teotihuacan· "presence" there (Weigand, Harbottle, and Sayre 1977:18–19; Charlton 1978b:1235). If Teotihuacan was directly in-volved in this exploitation process, it should be possible to determine the nature of its in-volvement in further research.

## THE TEOTIHUACAN DOMAIN

The regions in Central Mexico controlled from Teotihuacan form a compact domain of perhaps some 25,000 sq km or some 10,000 sq mi, an area comparable in size to Belgium or the Netherlands or the state of Massa-chusetts. The population in this core area of the Teotihuacan state is obviously very diffi-cult to estimate. A total population of per-haps 300,000–500,000 seems a reasonable approximation. How do we relate this mod-est area to the extraordinary impact Teoti-huacan had? The obvious answer is that this same area, albeit with much larger popula-tions, supported the military and economic expansion of the Aztecs. The area that Teoti-huacan dominated, while small, was extraor-dinarily rich in resources, more than ade-quate to have supported an empire (Bernal 1966b; Jiménez Moreno 1966; Blanton 1976c:200) extending far beyond this "key economic area" (Chi 1936).

I am not arguing that Teotihuacan was the seat of an empire. The Teotihuacan "pres-ence" in centers beyond the bounds of its core domain could be as overpowering as di-rect military control (see Davies 1978), or as remote as receiving something at third or fourth hand without necessarily knowing that such a place existed. Most instances, natu-rally, are far more complex and difficult to in-terpret. Military power, trade, and religion were involved in many of these instances in varying combinations and not necessarily in that order. Each case has to be analyzed in its own terms, for it is clear that a number of

different kinds of relationships are involved, from the most intense to the most casual.

Polity, economy, and ideology were linked inextricably not only within Teotihuacan's ur-ban society and the bounds of the state but also in foreign relations. Teotihuacan expan-sion, to the extent that it occurred, was not purely a commercial process, not purely an exercise in domination, nor purely the spread by whatever means of a system of re-ligious beliefs. It is easy enough to say this. The problems arise in the analysis of individ-ual instances, including negative cases. (For a recent examination of the problems involved in interpreting Teotihuacan's relationships with other parts of Middle America, see Pas-ztory 1978a, especially the contributions of Pasztory, L. Parsons, Sanders, and Hell-muth.)

## POLITY, RELIGION, AND IDEOLOGY

I use the term "civilization" not in any bounded sense based on boxlike categories, but in an intentionally open-ended sense that makes it possible to examine the myriad cul-tural dimensions of the complex societies that collectively formed Middle American civilization. In dealing with complex so-cieties at a moment of time or over the course of their histories, I do not believe it is possible to ignore the civilizational dimen-sion, though, obviously, it need not be desig-nated by this term. Nor am I suggesting that this dimension necessarily exists in all com-plex societies (e.g., Fallers 1961; R. Millon 1968b:209–210). I do insist, however, that, even though my discussion must be sum-mary and tangential, this dimension is indis-pensable to an understanding of Teotihuacan when it came into existence, when it was at its height, and when it fell. In what has gone before I have dealt several times with aspects of Teotihuacan civilization, which I shall not repeat here.

*Tablero-talud* façades appear on virtually all the platform structures now exposed on the "Street of the Dead" (Fig. 7-8). Since the *tablero-talud* convention long has been rec-

FIGURE 7-8. The Puma Mural Group on the east side of the "Street of the Dead." The Pyramid of the Sun is in the distance at right. Note the characteristic Teotihuacan temple architecture on all structures fronting the "Street of the Dead"—stepped platforms of one or more tiers, decorated with horizontal *tableros* (framed panels) and sloping *taludes* (basal aprons). Structures relating to the Puma Mural Group extend for more than 150 m to the east, to the main temple-pyramid of the group, in front of which we excavated in 1978 (TE 27) for contextual evidence dating to the time of the city's destruction ca. A.D. 750.

ognized as the symbol for temple in Teotihuacan, it is not strange that the platforms supporting the many temples on both sides of the avenue were so constructed. But the platform convention also is applied to the public buildings and residential compounds (Fig. 7-5; cf. Kubler 1973). The result is that the more than 2 km of continuous construction from the Ciudadela to the Pyramid of the Moon are built in the image of the temple (Fig. 7-1), however the platforms were used, or even when they supported no structures but served to fill in otherwise open areas.[20] Whatever the intent of the architects, the consequence of so building this long, closed avenue is to consecrate the entire avenue. Juan Vidarte de Linares (1968) has compared it to a great open-air cathedral. The result is the sacralization of the locus of secular activities. The most dramatic example of this is the Great Compound, which has a more secular appearance than any of the three other major structures. Yet for unbroken expanses of almost 250 m each, the façades of its north and south wings were covered by immense single-tiered *tablero-talud* construction. The Great Compound was probably the bureaucratic center and the locus of the principal marketplace. But its façade was that of a temple precinct. The sacralization of the polity was so pervasive that the most secular of the city's major public buildings bore a temple façade.

The shrines, temples, and rituals must have been powerful attractions to people near and far.[21] It obviously would have been advantageous to the hierarchy to encourage traffic for religious, cultural, and other reasons, including its great marketplace. Traffic of the kind and scale implied by the sheer

229

number of temples and the central location and immense size of the marketplace would have posed problems of social control. Temple and market may have played a critical integrative role in containing and regulating competing, clashing, and contradictory interests (R. Millon 1966c; 1976:241–242). In maintaining the "peace of the market," the importance of the sacralization of the marketplace becomes apparent. The sacred symbols and shared beliefs of the religion, with the beliefs, myths, and rituals attached to the site itself as a sacred place and cosmic symbol, would have provided an ideological basis for containing conflict in the marketplace. Agents of the state would have been present; but rather than rely on force alone, they would have been exercising authority to which all the prestige of Teotihuacan religion was attached.

Given the enormous impact of Teotihuacan in so many regions for so much of the Middle Horizon, did the religion of Teotihuacan involve a system of beliefs that transcended ethnic boundaries? (See, for example, Willey 1962.) Esther Pasztory (1978b:9) discusses whether the Teotihuacanos were the first in Middle America "to systematize religious belief," and, in another context, argues that "Teotihuacán had a more profound influence on cult imagery than the distribution of specific Teotihuacán motifs would indicate. Teotihuacán was . . . the first . . . in Mesoamerica to turn the agricultural fertility cult into a state cult" (Pasztory 1978c:131–132). While her case in its entirety may be overstated, the apparent contrast between religious beliefs and the iconography of power among the Zapotec and Maya on the one hand (Marcus 1974, 1976b, 1978) and at Teotihuacan on the other, suggests that the differences may have had a bearing on the extraordinary role played by Teotihuacan during its ascendancy.

In the cosmogony of the Teotihuacanos was Teotihuacan thought to be the place where the present cycle of human existence came into being, when the sun and the moon rose to the heavens from a fire into which two de-

ities had thrown themselves as sacrifices to end the darkness (e.g., Séjourné 1960:86; Vidarte de Linares 1968)? This was the belief of the Aztecs at the time of the Conquest (Sahagún 1953:4–7; Mendieta 1945:1:87; Heyden 1975:142). At least four paintings at Teotihuacan seem to have elements of the "Fifth Sun" creation myth (Aveleyra Arroyo de Anda 1963:Fig. 12; Edwards 1966:28, Pl. 15; A. G. Miller 1973b:Figs. 59, 89–96, 162, 195, 196; R. Millon 1973:Fig. 48a; Villagra Caleti 1951:Fig. 9, left; 1971:Figs. 22, 23; Vidarte de Linares 1968; C. Millon 1972b:7–8; 1978).

If this belief was espoused at Teotihuacan and related to "the day that 'time began'" (Malmstrom 1978:114), it could represent a crucial dimension of a system of beliefs and rituals that transformed the city's shrines and temples into great pilgrimage centers. Teotihuacan's distinctive east of north orientation would have commemorated *when* time began, because Teotihuacan would have been *where* time began.[22] Such beliefs, combined with ritual cycles designed to maintain the sun in the sky, might have been part of the early attraction of the city to outsiders and could have provided the basis for a cult transcending ethnic boundaries.

However such a system of beliefs might arise, it is not difficult to envisage some in the hierarchy who would come to realize the political and economic potential of the spread of the cult, who would begin to exploit it, to use it instrumentally, to manipulate it, to transform it into a state cult, so as to consolidate the position of the hierarchy and to facilitate the expansion of the Teotihuacan state. Such a process would be completely consonant with genuine belief in the particular and specific message of the cult. Belief and statecraft would reinforce each other.

A tradition of investiture of rulers at Teotihuacan (Heyden 1975) would have been an understandable outgrowth of the combination of sacredness of place and the prestige of the city's sacralized polity.

If Teotihuacan was a pilgrimage center on the scale I postulate, the state religion must have embodied a system of belief and ritual that had meaning and appeal not only to regional administrators and foreign rulers (Feuchtwang 1977), but to people in a wider range of statuses in the societies with which the Teotihuacanos were in contact. The deities of a systematized state religion of a successful, powerful, expanding state are readily perceived as responsible for and clothed with the power and the glory. There are many "rainmakers." But some are more equal than others. Teotihuacan's sacralized polity and its state religion are two aspects of the same phenomenon. The planners and architects of the "Street of the Dead" drove this message home to every visitor and pilgrim.

Is it possible to subject this network of hypotheses to testing? What has to be done is to subject all of the evidence—economic, social, political, and religious—in each of the reported instances of a major Teotihuacan "presence" to the kind of rigorous "contextual analysis" to which Flannery (1976c, 1976d) has subjected ritual paraphernalia from early Oaxacan villages of the first and second millennia B.C. Only in this way will it be possible to arrive at some judgment on the relative roles of commerce, kinship, marriage, other social ties, force, ritual, and ideology in a particular case. There appears to be a sufficient body of evidence from Tikal during the time of the two rulers who reigned from ca. A.D. 380 to 445 to make possible an evaluation of the nature of the relationship between Teotihuacan and Tikal (or Kaminaljuyu and Tikal) during that period. William R. Coe (1965c, 1972), Coggins (1975, 1979a, 1979b, 1979c), Proskouriakoff (personal communication, 1976), Haviland (1977), and others have made and are continuing to make major steps in that direction. In addition to the wealth of material involved, this is the only instance for which there is a text that specifically refers to the relationship (Stela 31). This is obviously the best test case we now have of the relationship or possible relationship of Teotihuacan to a major foreign center, in this case the greatest city in the southern Maya Lowlands.

## THE RISE OF TEOTIHUACAN

The economic and political dimensions of the spectacular rise of Teotihuacan provide us with a basis for understanding Teotihuacan, the economic center, and Teotihuacan, the political center. What evidence do we have for the rise of Teotihuacan, the sacred center? New evidence has come from the accidental discovery in 1971 or earlier of a cave 100 m long, running in an easterly direction 6 m beneath the Pyramid of the Sun. Its entrance is in the center of the pyramid's central staircase (Fig. 7-9), only the first three steps of which remain (Heyden 1973, 1975; Baker et al. 1974). The conclusion is inescapable that the pyramid is where it is because the cave is there. The cave is a natural formation within the lava flow (Heyden 1975:131), but its form was altered by the Teotihuacanos by constructions that, at several points, narrowed it to 1 m or less and by roofs of basalt slabs that simultaneously lowered its ceiling at several points to a height of 1.5 m, too low for most adults to stand erect. Because of these alterations the cave has a more sinuous appearance than it originally had. It ends some meters south and west of the center of the pyramid in a large chamber from which four smaller chambers branch. The present form of the chambers was created largely and perhaps entirely by the Teotihuacanos. The cave was extensively used throughout the Tzacualli phase near the end of the First Intermediate period (ca. A.D. 1–150), when the first great pyramid was built on the site. That pyramid was almost as high as the pyramid we see today (TE 22) (R. Millon 1973:Fig. 17b; Rattray 1973) and nearly as wide at the base (Millon, Drewitt, and Bennyhoff 1965:10, 20, 21, 29–31, 34, Figs. 18, 19, 82, 83, 120, 124).

Teotihuacan is riddled with caves, especially east of the Pyramid of the Sun and in the "Old City" (Fig. 7-3, no. 16), a region now called by the Nahuatl name Oztoyahualco, "in a circle of caves" (Heyden 1975:139). Caves had sacred attributes from the time of the Olmec in the Early Horizon, during the

FIGURE 7-9. Entrance to the cave beneath the Pyramid of the Sun. Note metal cover protecting the entrance, with a worker seated next to it on the remnants of the steps that originally led to the top of the three-tiered platform structure that is attached to the front of the pyramid (Plataforma Adosada). The metal cover is on the north side of the chamber giving access to the cave. The chamber itself lies beneath the center of the staircase, as does the entrance to the cave. The doorway to the right of the worker gives access to the tunnel system made by archaeologists over the years to explore the pyramid interior. The cave lies more than 6 m below the surface at the base of the staircase.

first and second millennia B.C. This may be one of the reasons the Patlachique phase Teotihuacanos built their settlement where they did, instead of on the northern edge of the alluvial plain, as suggested by Cowgill (1979a). But only *this* cave came to be endowed with such sacred attributes as to become the site for one of the world's largest pyramids.

What were the myths and beliefs central to Teotihuacan religion? What role did caves play in it? We shall be able to understand the significance, role, and undisputed evidence for the attraction of the religion only if we

are able to gain some comprehension, however limited, of its special "message"—a message repeatedly re-enacted in ritual performances and successful enough, even on present evidence, for multitudes to have gathered there to celebrate it. "Every living and healthy religion has a marked idiosyncrasy. Its power consists in its special and surprising message and in the bias which that revelation gives to life" (Santayana 1905–1906, as quoted in Geertz 1966:1). The problem we confront is to try to gain a "contextual" understanding of Teotihuacan religion (R. McC. Adams 1966:35) that must be based largely on archaeological evidence (Flannery 1976c, 1976d; Drennan 1976b; Flannery and Marcus 1976a, 1976b; Marcus 1978).[23] "The acceptance of authority that underlies the religious perspective that . . . ritual . . . embodies . . . flows from the enactment of the ritual itself" (Geertz 1966:34). "There are . . . definite organizations and defined occasions, such as a calendar of festivals, a system of local shrines, or an educational system, which are set apart particularly for the rehearsal and reproduction of the ideologies otherwise embedded in social activity" (Feuchtwang 1975:73). For the archaeologist working at Teotihuacan a major problem is how to gain sufficient contextual understanding of ritual performances to make possible the formulation of testable hypotheses about the extent to which the religion of Teotihuacan not only "described" or "reflected" the social order produced by the urbanization process but also helped to shape that process.

The principal language spoken at Teotihuacan probably was Nahua, the same language, in an earlier form, as that of the Aztecs (Jiménez Moreno 1974:10–12). Even if this was not the case, the argument for significant continuities in cultural traditions from the Olmec to Teotihuacan to Xochicalco, the Toltecs, and the Aztecs is a powerful one when "all relevant iconographic *contexts*" are analyzed (Nicholson 1976:170–171, emphasis in original; Caso 1966, 1967). The Aztec myth about the creation of the sun and the moon and the present cosmos (the Fifth Sun) at Teotihuacan has several variants. In one of them, as Gerónimo de Mendieta observed, in a history completed in 1596, "About the creation of the Moon, they say that when that (god) who threw himself into the fire turned into the Sun, another (god) went into a cave and came out as the Moon" (Mendieta 1945:1:87; translated in Heyden 1975:142). This suggests that in the Teotihuacan myth the world began when *both* the sun and the moon emerged from the cave. Such a myth and beliefs and ritual performances attending it over a period of years could have provided the ideological basis for the decision to build a great pyramid over the cave and to orient it and the "Street of the Dead" in front of it to the day the present cycle of time began, given a social and cultural milieu in which an enterprise of this scale could be contemplated and undertaken. The name of the Pyramid of the Sun comes from the Aztecs, but archaeological evidence uncovered in INAH excavations in the 1960s may support the attribution.[24]

We may never know whether there was evidence in the cave to support this hypothesis. Aside from the constructions mentioned earlier, there were 17 to 19 barriers or blockages across the cave, beginning near the inner chambers (Fig. 7-10). These were usually of stone with mud mortar, faced with standard Teotihuacan concrete but never plastered. When the cave was first entered, all these barriers were said to have been pierced previously at least once, presumably in Prehispanic times. Our excavations (TE 28)[25] support this interpretation, for the blockages seem to date either to the latter part of the Tzacualli phase (ca. A.D. 100–150) or to the Miccaotli phase (ca. A.D. 150–200) (analyses of this material are not completed). But later material was found between blockages and in the inner chambers, dating to the Late Tlamimilolpa phase and perhaps later. Fragments of two carved discs of slate or shale had been found in the inner chambers. Doris Heyden believes the discs were mirror backs for divination, suggesting that the cave may

FIGURE 7-10. Interior of the cave beneath the Pyramid of the Sun, more than 60 m from the entrance, looking east, with the remains of blockage 10 in the right foreground and of other blockages beyond, to the east. Two U-shaped stone drain channels are visible, one propped against a blockage on the north side of the cave, the other against a blockage on the south side (in front of the rod in middle distance). The number 8 refers to a survey station, not a blockage. This is a relatively straight 10 m stretch of the cave.

have housed an oracle since a 1580 *relación geográfica* refers to an oracle next to the pyramids (Heyden 1975:131, 142).

The inner chambers were completely excavated by Jorge R. Acosta, reportedly down to bedrock, 1.8 m below the cave floor at its deepest point (Baker et al. 1974:12). All the original floor in all the inner chambers was completely excavated. Acosta died before he was able to submit a report. His field notes are temporarily inaccessible. Before he excavated the inner chambers, the entire length of the cave was cleared of debris. So much was removed that a block and tackle was set up in the entrance; the workmen involved say that truckloads were hauled away for construction fill in various parts of the archaeological zone and that there was nothing "of importance" in it.

The roof of the central inner chamber, unlike the rest of the cave, is not of lava but of *tepetate* (the local hardpan subsoil) and is deeply, alarmingly cracked. The crack is not widening, however, and may be ancient. Pillars built between the chambers seem too frail to have been intended to support the cracked roof as George T. Baker suggests (Baker et al. 1974:12). The weight of the entire pyramid lies above this area. If the crack dates to the time the cave was in use, this may explain why it was finally abandoned. "Hundreds of pieces of varying-sized basalt slabs" were found in the inner chambers and may once have formed a floor (Baker et al. 1974:12). The slabs are the familiar *lajas* used to support *tableros* in *tablero-talud* architecture (Fig. 7-8). They are still stacked in the inner chambers. A striking feature of the cave is the presence of U-shaped channels of stone (Fig. 7-10) and stone drain covers. Stones of this shape are not normally used as drains in above-ground construction, and we now know from our excavations that water did not ever flow naturally in the cave, except from seepage near its entrance. The cave was not the source of a spring, as I and others had speculated (e.g., Heyden 1975: 141). This argues that water was brought into the cave and artificially made to flow through drain channels as part of the ritual performed there.

We were able only to excavate in five places within the cave, usually in two adjoining pits, separated by a baulk. Everywhere, except in the inner chambers previously excavated by Acosta, we found charcoal in great abundance, sometimes in fire pits, sometimes from small fires. The cave is, of course, totally dark a short distance from its entrance (and totally soundless). The Teotihuacanos used fires to provide light while they were in the cave; even so, the amount of carbon we found in our pits was surprising. The ceiling of the cave seems strangely free of soot, however, probably because torches normally were not used (we have no evidence of hand-held lamps, either) and fires on the cave floor provided light for ritual. Cave ritual involved the use of three pottery forms that do not occur commonly in quantity in other contexts (Rattray, personal communication, 1978). Nor have they been found associated in this way elsewhere. They seem peculiar to ritual in the cave. We have some idea of what some of those dishes and jars contained. In one of several large fire pits in the highest part of the cave, near its center and beneath a blockage, Jeffrey H. Altschul found offerings of fragments of iridescent shell surrounded by an enormous quantity of tiny fish bones. Altschul notes that "almost all the fish bones were spines with one vertebra . . . no otoliths or scales" (1978). They seem too frail and minute (2–5 cm) to have been used in blood-letting ritual, such as has been inferred from the contexts in which marine fish spines were found in early Oaxacan villages (Flannery 1976d:341–343; Flannery and Marcus 1976b:377–378). The bones were "in excellent condition," despite having been burned in the fire pit. There is no evidence of the utilitarian use of fire. All use of fire seems to have been ritual use, and fire itself seems to have been not only essential to the ritual but, together with water made to flow artificially, the most essential part of it, although differential preservation may be affecting our judgment. The union of fire and water may be symbolized by the burned offerings of fish bones and shell. The juxtaposition of symbols of fire and water is frequent and plays a prominent role in later Teotihuacan religion.

The narrowed areas with low ceilings begin near the entrance and alternate with open areas where the natural cave ceiling is usually much higher. Whoever entered the cave would have been forced into alternating between crouching or kneeling and standing (Altschul 1978). Everything that was done to the cave and in the cave proclaims ritual. To the uninitiated, it would have been a terrifying place. By its nature it never could have been accessible to more than scores, at most hundreds of people. Even when Teotihuacan was small and had only a population of 10,000–20,000, the cave would have been a mysterious and dangerous place to the vast majority. Given the amount of data we were able to collect in our small excavation pits, by troweling throughout, screening everything, and conserving soil for flotation, it is painfully obvious that an enormous amount of data had been irretrievably lost earlier. Unfortunately, we never may be able to say with more specificity what kinds of ritual performances were enacted, or what beliefs were inculcated and reaffirmed in those enactments. Nevertheless, the stubborn fact remains: the pyramid must be where it is and nowhere else because the cave below it was the most sacred of sacred places. Whether or not the Teotihuacanos believed that the sun and the moon had been created there, the rituals performed in the cave must have celebrated a system of myth and belief of transcendent importance. The guardians of the system, however they came to be such, would have had awesome prestige and the loyalty of the ordinary Teotihuacano, whether cultivator or craftsman. This differentiation alone could have provided a powerful lever for the acceptance of a growing system of stratification and at the same time granted legitimacy to the authority of those who were beginning to consolidate what would come to be the power of the state. In this view religion and ritual would have played a major role in the formation of Teotihuacan's hierarchical society and in the legitimation of the authority of the state.

Religion and ritual also could have played a critical role in the plan for the resettlement of the rural populations in the city. Such a sweeping transformation demanded a compelling motivation. It required the exercise of power, but power alone would not have been sufficient. If the system of belief and ritual centering about the cave was as powerful a motivating force as I suggest, the decision to build the pyramid may be what precipitated the decision to concentrate the population in the city—not because such a concentration was necessary for the undertak-

ing, but because the undertaking of this mammoth task would have had sufficient meaning so that participation would have justified disruption in daily life. The concentration may have been viewed and presented as temporary, until its advantages to the leadership became apparent after the fact. Force alone cannot explain this concentration, nor can the attraction of sacred symbols or the requirements of an expanding economy. Taken together they can and do. Just because the argument may be logically persuasive does not mean, of course, that this is what happened. The process I have outlined has to be subjected to testing and to survive such testing before it can be accepted. I believe, however, that the process of transformation involved in executing the plan for population concentration in the city is more understandable when viewed in the terms in which I have couched it.

## The Destruction of the City and the Collapse of the State

When the city was destroyed, it was not in an obvious condition of decline. This does not mean, however, that the state was not experiencing increasing difficulties (Cowgill 1979a). These difficulties may have been building slowly for some time (Hirth and Swezey 1976). Evidence comes from several regions—from the eastern Morelos hinterland (Hirth 1978b); from a more and more independent western Morelos, where an increasingly powerful and autonomous fortified Xochicalco was interrupting the flow of goods and materials from the south and the southwest (Litvak King 1970); from northern Tlaxcala and the "Teotihuacan Corridor" (García Cook and Trejo 1977:66–67). There is not space to review this evidence here, for it involves continued expansion in some directions as well as probable contraction in others and is not a simple process (R. Millon 1973:61–63; McClung de Tapia 1978, 1979). Stated briefly, the flow of goods in some parts of the city's exchange system may have been impeded well before the city's destruction,

235

and the cumulative effect of this may have played an ultimately critical role in the weakening of the Teotihuacan state (Hirth and Swezey 1976).

Cowgill (1979a), commenting on the arguments of Litvak King (1970) and Hirth and Swezey (1976), suggests that, when considering reasons for the weakening of the Teotihuacan state, it is useful to examine the "dynastic cycle" in Chinese history, a "process . . . in which ever larger and ever less efficient bureaucracy, higher taxes (especially for peasants), increasing diversion of tax revenues into the pockets of local officials, and decreasing availability of revenue for state purposes, all contribute in a positive feedback cycle to the eventual collapse of the state." Chinese society was far more complex than any Prehispanic society in the New World, its civilization much richer, its state much more centralized. Nevertheless, if this is recognized, the feedback cycle described could prove useful in a systematic examination both of what we know of the Teotihuacan state and of the city itself in their last centuries.

The military is most prominently represented at Teotihuacan in the Metepec phase (ca. A.D. 650–750). This may be both a symptom of difficulty and a cause of it.[26] Accumulating problems and conflicts, internal and external, may have been met by more exercise of force than customary, exacerbating existing tensions and creating new ones, and precipitating rapid, convulsive social and economic deterioration—so rapid that it is not manifest in what we see. For Teotihuacan to have been destroyed as it was, the state apparatus must have been in a condition of near impotence. Except for one *possible* reference by Leopoldo Batres (1906:15), there is no evidence that the city's inhabitants were slaughtered. The data available imply that the destruction was relatively bloodless, whether carried out from within or by invaders. This must mean that it occurred at a time of internal crisis. In the face of growing crisis, a split may have developed within the hierarchy over how to meet it. The ensuing factional dispute could have grown so deep and bitter as gradually to paralyze the power of the state and render it unable to act effectively when the onslaught came, from within or without.

All of this is hypothetical, but not beyond testing. Something much like this must have happened, since the evidence seems to show that the city was not destroyed in bitterly contested combat. In fact, it appears that most of the city was not destroyed at all. It was principally the center that was destroyed. This is why it makes more sense to postulate that the state itself must have been in a paralyzed condition of internal crisis before those who destroyed it came into the city's center.

Legendary Teotihuacan may have been born in the fiery creation of the sun and moon when "time began." If so, what was created in fire was destroyed by fire, abruptly, violently, cataclysmically.[27] The heart of the city was burned, but little else. The fire was very selective, something we can recognize only now, from the perspective of the city as a whole. It was confined largely to the monumental architecture on the "Street of the Dead" and to temples and associated buildings in the rest of the city. We have some 400 instances of burning in the little more than 2 sq km that comprise the area from the Ciudadela to the Pyramid of the Moon 500 m on each side of the "Street of the Dead." In the remaining 18 sq km of the city we have half that number, and many are temples, some with the apartment compounds associated with them. The principal targets of burning were pyramids, temples, and public buildings.

In considering the evidence for the total and deliberate destruction of the center of Teotihuacan through a coordinated series of planned acts of ritual destruction, it is important to realize that Teotihuacan was defensible, and to recall that it was not in an obvious state of decline (R. Millon 1973:39–40, 59, 63).

Destruction seems most often to have taken the form of burning in front of the staircase, on both its sides, on the top of a temple, and, where part of its floor was exposed, inside the temple itself, because the inside actually was burned or because material from a burning roof had fallen on the floor. In the Ciudadela, all temples have visible evidence of burning in them, as do most of the other structures, including the two palaces. Several of the temple platforms fronting the "Street of the Dead" also show signs of intense burning on their sides, as well as in the front and on both sides of the staircase. In the Great Compound, all but three of its unaltered (i.e., unleveled) apartment compounds show signs of burning.

The main temple of the Puma Mural Group (TE 27) was violently destroyed and burned. Building stones and building blocks of carved *tepetate* either were hurled or fell with such force that they bounced when hitting the plaza floor, the *tepetate* blocks leaving yellow smudges. One of the first acts seems to have been the smashing of a large green onyx sculpture, judging from the position of its fragments. The surface of the plaza floor was covered by a thin layer of ash (2–5 cm). Building material from the destruction of the temple seems to have fallen onto the plaza floor while an intense fire was burning on it (Sempowski 1979). The painted plaster on the *talud* at the base of the pyramid was discolored by a burning beam that had fallen across it. Part of the *tablero* on this *talud* collapsed.

The ritual destruction of monuments is a cultural tradition with deep roots in the Middle American past, dating back at least to Olmec civilization, in the Early Horizon, ca. 1000 B.C. (M. Coe 1968:47–55, 72–77). There was, as well, a tradition of ritual destruction by fire at Teotihuacan itself. During the Tlamimilolpa phase the front and both sides of the staircase of the Temple of Quetzalcoatl in the Ciudadela (Fig. 7-3, inset, no. 4) were subjected to a fire so intense that it cracked some stones and caused others to spall. This destruction was followed by renewal in the form of rebuilding in front and on top of what had been ritually destroyed

(the Plataforma Adosada, the four-tiered temple platform built in front of and partly over the destroyed central, lower part) (R. Millon 1973: Figs. 32b, 34).

The traditional interpretation of the fall of Teotihuacan is that it was destroyed by fire (Armillas 1950:69). Whether it was destroyed by invaders or because of internal collapse or both was not clear (R. Millon 1973:59; 63). Our evidence shows that the fires that destroyed the city center were deliberately and systematically set. The destruction was a ritual destruction and cannot be understood if thought of purely in terms of pillaging, looting, and burning. It must be seen in its cultural context. So viewed, the destruction of Teotihuacan's temples does not differ from planned acts of ritual destruction at other times and places in Middle America. Planned ritual destruction of monuments was sometimes followed by renewal and rebuilding, sometimes by abandonment of part or all of a Prehispanic center. For example, see Michael Coe's comments on San Lorenzo (1968:47–55) and William Coe's on the ritual destruction and rebuilding involving Stela 31 at Tikal (1965c:34). The placement of sculptures in the interior of Mound B at Tula may be another example (Dutton 1955:202).

What makes the burning of Teotihuacan stand out is the sheer magnitude of the destruction. Systematic data on which parts of Teotihuacan were burned, and which were not, were not available until all of the city was mapped. Thus, until recently it was impossible to formulate testable hypotheses concerning its fall, and whether and to what extent its ritual destruction had a structured, processual dimension that might be matched in other Middle American centers.[28]

The particular course taken by the fall of Teotihuacan was in one sense unique. To the extent that no other center was at once so large, so powerful, so influential, to that extent its fall and the consequences of it were unique. But it is not the unique aspects that concern me here.

The extent, intensity, and deliberateness of the destruction argue that while the form was ritual, its purpose was political. Again, this is not unique. At the time of the Spanish Conquest, the burning of a temple symbolized the subjugation of a political entity by its conquerors. Those who destroyed Teotihuacan, whether they were foreign or Teotihuacano, used existing cultural forms, customs, and practices to carry out this monumental sequence of acts of ritual destruction. Viewed contextually, the destruction of Teotihuacan becomes a special case of a recurrent process in Middle American history and prehistory.

To destroy Teotihuacan politically was itself a monumental undertaking, in some ways matching the energy that went into its building. Destroying it politically apparently required destroying it so thoroughly ritually that it never again could rise to a position of political preeminence. Those who burned it succeeded in their objective.

The problem of the identity of the victors is not solved; but it has been structured and the range of possibilities significantly narrowed. We have some slender evidence that the center of the city was destroyed by invaders, and outlying temples by Teotihuacanos, to whom the temples were the visible local symbols of state domination. If invaders were responsible, they must have been culturally closely related to the Teotihuacanos. This sensitizes us to evidence we might not otherwise notice. Only a people so related would have been motivated to carry out ritual destruction on the scale and with the scope and intensity I have described. The invaders had to have been so aware of Teotihuacan's systems of beliefs and values, of the symbolism with which the location was imbued, as to be convinced that only such total destruction in prescribed ritual form would destroy Teotihuacan forever as a great political center. Under such circumstances disaffected groups within the city, for factional or other reasons, could have acted with them or on their own to destroy outlying temples.

## AFTERMATH

Not long after the destruction of the city there were good-sized settlements to the east and west of the "Street of the Dead," perhaps forming a single community. But the "Street of the Dead" itself now lived up to its Aztec name and seems to have been avoided for the most part. There is no space to consider how much demographic and cultural continuity there was, what use was made of apartment compounds still standing, or many other questions on which there is information. It is enough to note that, large and complex as the post–Middle Horizon community may have been, it was a pale reflection of the great sacred city that had dominated its world for 400 years or more.

## ACKNOWLEDGMENTS

Research findings from many research projects are discussed in this chapter. Research that I directed was supported by National Science Foundation grants G23800, GS207, GS641, GS1222, GS2204, GS3137, and BNS77-08973. This research was carried out with successive permits from the Instituto Nacional de Antropología c Historia and the Secretaría de Educación Pública. These permits and concessions were facilitated by archaeologists in the Departamento de Monumentos Prehispánicos and the Consejo de Arqueología. I am particularly grateful for assistance over the years rendered by Ignacio Marquina, Ignacio Bernal, Eduardo Matos Moctezuma, the late Jorge R. Acosta, Ponciano Salazar, Florencia Muller, Eduardo Contreras S. and Román Piña Chan. I owe a special debt of gratitude to José Luis Lorenzo for his unfailing helpfulness and support.

From 1973 to 1979 our research facility at Teotihuacan was supported for varying periods by contributions from Brandeis University, the University of Rochester, the State University of New York at Buffalo, the University of Toronto, the University of Western Ontario, and the Ivey Foundation, London, Ontario, as well as by donations from individuals and corporations. The facility is currently receiving support from research grants to George Cowgill by the National Endowment for the Humanities and the Wenner-Gren Foundation for Anthropological Research. It is capably, efficiently, and skillfully supervised by Pedro Baños, with the reliable assistance of Ceferino Ortega.

This and an earlier version of this chapter were read by George Cowgill, who made many thoughtful critical comments and valuable suggestions, most of which I have tried to take into account. Arnold Green read the present version and made suggestions for its clarification and improvement that I have tried to follow. Helpful suggestions concerning the present version that were subsequently incorporated in the text were also made by Jeffrey H. Altschul, Sallie Brennan, Bruce Drewitt, R. David Drucker, Garman Harbottle, Susan M. Kellogg, Joyce Marcus, Evelyn Rattray, Jeremy A. Sabloff, Martha Sempowski, Rebecca Sload, Michael W. Spence, Margaret H. Turner and Phil C. Weigand. All versions of the text have been read by Clara Millon, whose critical comments were accompanied by numerous suggestions for substantive changes. The chapter could not have been completed without her contributions and assistance.

## NOTES

1. Sanders' article was not published for ten years. By the time it was, the question was no longer at issue.

2. Drewitt, who joined the project at its inception and directed most aspects of our field survey during its most critical period, from 1964 to 1966, also scrupulously supervised the preparation of our maps in the field lab. His high standards of consistency and his eye for crucial detail were largely responsible for the successful completion of that phase of our work. Cowgill, who joined the project in 1964, has played a major role in the development of mathematical analyses of archaeological data, both by example and as constructive critic. His skills and versatility were indispensable in the solution of manifold problems in the survey and in the supervision of the preparation of the maps themselves. His Teotihuacan Mapping Project Data File has been a major and continuing contribution to our work, and a model for others.

3. Drewitt (1969; personal communication, 1971) has made a strong case that the basic unit of measurement was .805 cm, a case greatly strengthened by R. D. Drucker (1974:129–143) (R. Millon 1976:218 n. 4) (cf. Harleston 1974; Tompkins 1976:238–281). Cowgill has also worked with long distance measurements in the valley.

4. East Avenue was discovered by Drewitt in our 1959 investigations (R. Millon 1961:Fig. 1; 1964:Fig. 1; 1973:34). Drewitt first observed that east-west orientations frequently are not perpendicular to the "Street of the Dead" but instead form angles with it that are 1° or 1°30′ from the perpendicular (e.g., East Avenue—91°, or the Ciudadela—91°30′) (Fig. 7-3 and inset) (Drewitt 1966:84). These orientations are deliberate (R. Millon 1973:29, 37–38); efforts have been made to explain them on the basis of stellar (Dow 1967) and solar observations (R. D. Drucker 1973). The problem posed by Teotihuacan's distinctive east of north orientation requires comment. Zelia Nuttall (1928) and Ola Apenes (1936) suggested that the 105-day difference between the 365-day vague year used in Prehispanic times and the ubiquitous 260-day Mesoamerican ritual calendar could be related to a latitudinal zone in the tropics that includes the Maya center of Copan where the zenith passage of the sun occurs twice a year—April 30 and August 13—at 105- and 260-day intervals, with the 105-day interval falling during a critical part of the agricultural year. These solar phenomena and time intervals, it was suggested, might have been the source of the time-span represented in the 260-day ritual calendar that, when permutated with the 365-day vague year, produced the famed 52-year calendar round. Drawing on the observations of Apenes, R. David Drucker (1973, 1974:168; 1977) has related Teotihuacan's basic north-south orientation (what we call "Teotihuacan north") to these 105, 260, and 365 day periods during the critically important early time in its history ca. A.D. 1. He calculated that at that time from the vantage point of the base of the center of the Pyramid of the Sun, the setting sun in the Teotihuacan Valley on August 12 was 15°27′ north of west, and 15°29′ north of west on April 29 (R. D. Drucker 1977:App. II). His dates are one day earlier than those of Nuttall and Apenes because of the required calculation for the

change in the earth's obliquity in A.D. 1. August 12 is 52 days after the summer solstice; April 30 begins the interval 52 days before it. These two 52-day periods plus a day for the solstice itself (52+1+52) total 105 days. Drucker (1973, 1974: 168; 1977) argued that Teotihuacan's basic east of north orientation was derived from the north of west orientation observable on August 12. At Teotihuacan's latitude, August 12 and April 29 do not coincide with the zenith passages of the sun. But Drucker argued that it was the time-span derived from the southern latitude and its perceived significance that was seen to be critical rather than the solar phenomenon from which it presumably was derived. Vincent H. Malmstrom (1978) subsequently argued that Teotihuacan's north-south orientation was related to Mesoamerican calendrical systems, including the Long Count and "the day that 'time began'" (1978:114). He related the east of north orientation of the western face of the Pyramid of the Sun to the present-day position of the setting sun in the Teotihuacan Valley on August 13, with August 13 presumably representing the legendary day "time began," ca. 3000 B.C. in the Middle American Long Count calendrical system. The relevant date for A.D. 1 actually would be August 12 because of the change in the earth's obliquity (Drucker 1977:App. II). The precise day is uncertain in any case because of correlation problems (Lounsbury 1978:760, 809–810, 815–816). Malmstrom (1973, 1978) relates the origin of calendrical systems based on the ritual calendar, the vague year, and the Long Count to the region of Izapa, rather than Copan, because, he argues, Izapa was the only known major ancient center in the latitude where such observations could be made at the times he believes they were made. (See also Dow 1967 and Aveni and Gibbs 1976.)

5. Edwin R. Littmann's "plaster" (1973:175–176, 177–180); Sanders' "stucco" (1966:137).

6. Littmann's "wash coat" (1973:175–186).

7. This dating is based on radiocarbon dates and on ceramic analyses carried out first by James A. Bennyhoff (1966), whose analytic ability and sensitivity to ceramic change provided us with our chronological baseline during the survey, and subsequently by Evelyn Rattray (1973, 1978b, n.d.), associated with the mapping project since 1967, who has substantially modified and refined Bennyhoff's chronology. Rattray's analyses include material from our excavations and from burials and offerings from our excavations and those of others. Fig. 7-7 shows the working chronology we have

been using for the mapping project (R. Millon 1966a:1). For various reasons, I now believe that the Early Xolalpan phase begins ca. A.D. 400, rather than A.D. 450, the date we have used in the past (e.g., R. Millon 1973:Fig. 12; 1976:Fig. 15). Rattray's study of ceramics and ceramic chronology (n.d.) is virtually completed and will be an invaluable contribution not only to our knowledge of Teotihuacan but also for its data and analyses on cross-ties with other regions. Her study has been aided enormously by the neutron activation analyses of local and foreign pottery from our survey and excavations and from the source regions of many of the foreign wares by Edward Sayre and Garman Harbottle (1979). For discussion of problems of absolute chronology see, e.g., R. Millon 1973:60–61 and Tolstoy 1978:260–264. Some of the comments of the latter attributed to me require modification, but there is no space for such discussion here. We hope to have additional radiocarbon samples analyzed in the near future. The new period terminology adopted at the Valley of Mexico conference in Santa Fe in 1972 (Wolf 1976a) and used in this and some other chapters in this volume is shown in the column at left. The traditional terminology is shown at right. The new terminology has been used by conference participants in subsequent work (e.g., Sanders, this volume) and also by Tolstoy (1978). It is not as free of problems as I thought it would be, but it is freer than is traditional terminology. As anticipated, its reception has been less than enthusiastic, being favored by some (e.g., Schwerin 1977:350), criticized by others (e.g., Flannery 1977:761; Kubler 1978:58–59; Bray 1978:127).

8. Spence, associated with the mapping project since 1964, has made two major contributions to the project: analyses of the obsidian production system, still in progress (Spence 1966, 1967, 1974a, 1979a, 1979b; Spence and Kimberlin 1979; Spence and Parsons 1972), and the work on skeletal material.

9. The same suggestion was made in 1976 by Martha Sempowski of the University of Rochester in an unpublished paper on the basis of the relative inflexibility of the very different types of residential compounds associated with cognatic descent in some Yoruba cities.

10. For example, Burial 1 at Xolalpan (Early Xolalpan phase) was placed in a small tomb of stone, the south wall of which was the base of the outer wall of the compound itself (Linné 1934: 54–59, Figs. 9, 10, 16, 21–25, 225, 297, 307,

240

315–317). (Burials 2–4 seem to follow it at brief intervals.) Linné's interpretation is different, but examination of his plans and cross-sections and the brief comments he makes on what he found and how he excavated make it clear that his interpretation does not follow from his own evidence (Linné 1934: 40–74, 216, Fig. 339). Most of the rooms Linné excavated were built only once, when the compound itself was built, and Burial 1 is associated with its construction. Most Teotihuacanos probably were buried without durable offerings and I suspect were cremated. This prediction can be tested in future excavations if carried out with sufficient care. In the one cremation area isolated in our survey (in square N4W3) (Spence 1979a), most burned bone fragments were tiny and stood out primarily because the concentration was so great.

11. The "Street of the Dead" was laid out in the Tzacualli phase (ca. A.D. 1–150). We found in excavation (Teotihuacan Mapping Project Test Excavation 22—hereafter in abbreviated form, TE 22) that an earlier Pyramid of the Sun almost as high as the one we see today was built in the early part of this phase (R. Millon 1973: Fig. 17b); the innermost Pyramid of the Moon also dates to this phase (Acosta 1966: 46–47); according to our survey, all three-temple complexes on the "Street of the Dead" date to this time period. Another excavation of ours (TE 19) disclosed that the Ciudadela precinct dates to the Miccaotli phase (ca. A.D. 150–200) (R. Millon 1973: 54–55; Rattray 1973) and may overlie earlier construction (R. Millon 1973: 52, 54–55; see also R. D. Drucker 1974). The Great Compound (TE 17) dates to the beginning of the Middle Horizon or earlier (R. Millon 1973: 57; Rattray 1973).

12. Rare exceptions occur, e.g., a vessel showing the "chase of a warrior and his sacrifice [sacrificial victim]" (Muller 1978: 177, Fig. 32b); a ceramic effigy whistle with tied legs, the figure's heart (?) and entrails (?) exposed (Burland 1948: Pl. 17). "Bound" figurines (see, e.g., Séjourné 1966b: Fig. 161; Artes de México 1965: 91, lower left) date to the Metepec phase (Barbour 1976: 96) and perhaps earlier. Séjourné suggests that they may represent wrapped corpses (1966b: [245]). Warren T. D. Barbour suggests that they are swaddled infants and, metaphorically perhaps, captives, citing Sahagún's description of a birth (Barbour 1976: 99, 134, 142 n. 1). Figurines of women carrying "bound" children (see, e.g., Séjourné 1966b: 211, Fig. 142; Artes de México

1965: 119, upper left) are the basis for terming the "bound" figurines infants. Evelyn Rattray (personal communication, 1979) reports finding a mold-impressed sherd (Metepec phase) representing a figure she believes to be in a submissive pose. A fragment from the Tetitla "Pinturas Realistas" paintings, apparently showing a seated figure borne by an individual, has been excluded from consideration. The overall foreign content of these paintings, in particular their Maya images and connections (Hall [Millon] 1962: 81–85; C. Millon 1972b: 11–12), serves, perhaps, to underscore the point at issue.

13. Elsewhere I have stated my reasons for not relating the rise of the Teotihuacan state to the presumed "managerial requirements" of the valley's irrigation system(s) (R. Millon 1973: 47–48; 1976: 244–245).

14. The characteristic temple architecture of Teotihuacan, the *tablero-talud*, is said to have been found earlier in Tlaxcala than it has been at Teotihuacan (García Cook 1973a). At the same time it should be realized that early temples that may incorporate interior structures dating to the Patlachique phase have not been excavated as yet at Teotihuacan.

15. Most Patlachique phase settlements were abandoned and not later reoccupied. There was little Tzacualli phase occupation in most of the Valley of Mexico, while Tzacualli phase Teotihuacan grew to more than 20 sq km. (It should be noted that this chapter was written before the publication of Sanders, Parsons, and Santley 1979.)

16. For example, in one of their apartment compounds (Fig. 7-4, lower left) they built a Oaxaca-style tomb, with antechamber and associated stela (TE 3A) (R. Millon 1973: 41–42, Fig. 60a, b; Spence 1976). They used Oaxaca-style funerary urns. An outstanding one was brought from Oaxaca (TE 3) (R. Millon 1967b, 1973: Figs. 58, 59; Sayre and Harbottle 1979: Table 1, no. 179); another, smaller and simpler, was made in the Oaxaca style from local Valley of Mexico clays (Rattray n.d.; Sayre and Harbottle 1979: Table 1, nos. 151, 202). They also made utilitarian and ritual vessels in Oaxaca forms from Valley of Mexico clays (Rattray n.d.; Sayre and Harbottle 1979: Table 1, nos. 22–26).

17. Rather than near the eastern periphery, which would have been closer to the source material.

18. See Charlton (1978a, 1979a) for earlier obsidian workshops in the Valley of Mexico.

19. I am indebted to Michael Spence for calling Smith's work to my attention.

20. Judging from stratigraphic evidence, the "Street of the Dead" underwent this transformation involving the placement of all structures on two-tiered platforms or one immense single-tiered platform during the Xolalpan phase or later. Cowgill's observation that most monumental construction at Teotihuacan was relatively early (pre-Xolalpan or earlier) is correct (R. Millon 1973:52–57) but does not take into account the magnitude of the construction effort that gave the "Street of the Dead" its present appearance (Cowgill 1979b: 53).

21. See general discussion of pilgrimages and of pilgrimage and commercial routes in T. Lee 1978:3–4.

22. See note 4 above.

23. In some of the works cited, Flannery and Drennan draw in part on the ecologically oriented work of Roy A. Rappaport (e.g., 1968, 1971b). I find a less limited stimulus in the work of such investigators as Clifford Geertz (e.g., 1957, 1963, 1964, 1966) and Stephen Feuchtwang (1974, 1975, 1977).

24. Antonio de Herrera y Tordesillas, in a work first published in 1601, writes of beliefs that the sun and the moon came out of a cave (1944:1:308; reported in Heyden 1975:134). If both the sun and the moon did emerge from the cave in Teotihuacan belief, it is also possible that the cave represented the earth (or underworld) to which the mythical sun was said to return at night, and from which he re-emerged at dawn (see Heyden 1975:141 for discussion in another context of caves as places of emergence and return).

25. Our excavations (TE 28A–D) were carried out with exceptional skill and judgment under most difficult conditions by Jeffrey H. Altschul in 1978. Rebecca Sload intensively analyzed, probed and photographed the cave. Stephanie Makseyn skillfully prepared critically important drawings. Walter Lombardo served as geological consultant. Bruce Drewitt's help, ideas, energy, and resourcefulness were indispensable. The published drawings of the cave are not accurate (Heyden 1973, 1975; Baker et al. 1974). We have had to prepare new drawings of all of it. To make this possible, the cave was surveyed in detail by G. R. Krotser and Darlena K. Blucher. Robert P. Millon also provided assistance for a brief period. John Sempowski aided in the resolution of surveying problems outside the cave at the base of the pyramid. Susan M. Kellogg and Martha Sempowski also worked briefly in the cave. C. Earle Smith provided critical assistance in several ways, including the identification of the in situ impression in dried mud of a wooden post in the middle of the ceiling at the eastern end of the cave passage, immediately before it opens into the chambers where the cave ends.

26. Most armed men depicted in artistic representations date to the Metepec phase; so far only one or possibly two are earlier than the Late Xolalpan phase. But Teotihuacan or Teotihuacan-related military figures are depicted in foreign contexts by local artists 100–200 years earlier (e.g., Tikal Stela 31 and scene from plano-relief cylindrical tripod, W. Coe 1965c:33, 36–37, top); the cylindrical tripod (Greene and Moholy-Nagy 1966) is made in Teotihuacan style but was not made at Teotihuacan, as James A. Bennyhoff (personal communication, 1966) was the first to notice; the shape of the tapering supports on the tripod suggests Cerro de las Mesas as a possible source.

27. See comments by Ignacio Bernal in Benson 1968:72–73. Our excavation (TE 27) in 1978 in and in front of the main (easternmost) temple-pyramid (73A:N4E1) in the Puma Mural Group (Fig. 7-3, inset, no. 36) yielded much in situ evidence of violent destruction (Sempowski 1979). This difficult excavation was very capably and rigorously carried out by Darlena K. Blucher. Martha Sempowski was her able assistant, aided by Walter Lombardo.

28. Many of us tend to fall unwittingly into methodological traps concerning the "growth" of civilizations that affect our investigations and analyses (see Yoffee 1979 for a recent critique). This is especially true when we try to examine a process like the cataclysmic destruction of Teotihuacan. If we are to understand processes of transformational change such as those involved in both the rise and the fall of Teotihuacan, we should not, in our concern with process, lose sight of the fact that "processes of social change are conceptual arrangeabilities of events" (Bock 1963:237). However consciously aware we may be of the methodological pitfalls posed by teleological models or by models of growth that derive change from the "nature" of the thing changing, in which phenomena of rise, florescence, and decline are taken for granted (Bock 1956, 1963, 1978), related assumptions (see, e.g., Rappaport 1978) all too often

tend to color our thinking because of the pervasiveness of "habits of thought." The uncritical "restoration of evolutionism" has led even its critics into methodological sinkholes where "differen[tia]tion in form and function and movement from the simple to the complex are re-presented as the fundamental processes of change" (Bock 1978:74; cf. Yoffee 1979:27). It is worth repeating what some students of human evolution say about the heuristic value of the concept of evolution in studies of human evolution: "The statement that we may study human biological history, human cultural history and the interrelations of the two should mean precisely the same thing as that we may study human biological and cultural evolution. Understanding comes from study of the data, and no information is added by using the word 'evolution' in preference to the word 'history'" (Washburn and Lancaster 1968:216). The anachronistic character of so many theoretical formulations today will continue to hamper research until the evolutionist assumptions on which they are based are subjected to a truly rigorous and "agonizing reappraisal" of their implications and consequences for the analysis of change. I make no claim to have done so here, nor to be free myself from many of these "habits of thought." I confine myself to calling attention to the problem.

# 8. The Historical Importance of Tlaxcala in the Cultural Development of the Central Highlands

ANGEL GARCÍA COOK

## INTRODUCTION

UNTIL RECENTLY all archaeological
work ignored the area of Tlaxcala
and relegated it to a secondary
place in the studies of cultural development
of the Central Highlands. At most, archaeologists acknowledged that Cholula, in the
Puebla Valley, had played a role of some importance, though under the control of Teotihuacan at one point and later of Tenochtitlan.
Eduardo Noguera's publications on the site of
Tizatlan (1925, 1927, 1934) and Sigvald
Linné's work on Calpulalpan (1942) provided
information on Tlaxcalan sites, but always
linking them to Teotihuacan and cultures of
the Basin of Mexico. Although the role Tlaxcala played as an ally of the Spanish during
the Conquest of Mexico was well known, the
importance of this region in prehistory has
been overlooked.

Studies in Tlaxcala and the Puebla Valley
during the 1970s have revealed that this region was important in the integration of the
"high cultures" of the Central Highlands—
Tezoquipan, Cholula, Teotihuacan, Tenochtitlan, etc.—as well as in their disintegration

or transformation. We know that a great
thrust of sedentary groups in this area preceded a complex, advanced Formative society which steadily exerted its influence
over other nascent cultures in the Basin of
Mexico. These grew into the cities of Teotihuacan and Cholula, which at their height
carried on continuous commerce with regions to the south and nearer the Gulf. Later,
those from the Tlaxcala-Puebla region, together with other groups from the fringes of
the Basin of Mexico, brought about the disintegration of these theocratic cultures, transforming them into societies that emphasized
secular and militaristic values more than religious ones. Even though the Tlaxcala-
Puebla region bordered on Tenochtitlan and
Tlatelolco, the most powerful of the late Pre-
columbian cities, it remained independent.
Kingdoms such as Tlaxcala, Atlangatepec,
Tliliuhquitepec, and Tecoac flourished, each
autonomous yet willing to band together for
protection against the menacing Aztec Empire. To eliminate forever the Mexica
threats, the Tlaxcalans allied themselves with
the Spanish conquerors.

I will describe briefly the cultural develop-

244

ment of the Tlaxcala-Puebla region, pausing to explore the evidence for the above statements. More than 100 anthropological and historical articles, most of which report research carried out in the past decade by the Fundación Alemana para la Investigación Científica in collaboration with the Mexican Instituto Nacional de Antropología e Historia, contain more detailed information than this summary permits. The cultural sequence for Tlaxcala is based on archaeological data from surface survey, stratigraphic tests, and more extensive excavations at selected sites. My conclusions draw on more than 100 C14 dates, including 65 from my own investigations (Figs. 8-1, 8-2).

Information about nomadic, preceramic, and preagricultural groups in this area abounds (García Cook 1976b; Lorenzo 1967; Mirambell 1974; Mora and García Cook 1975), but I will not discuss them in detail. Despite some regional variations, all preagricultural peoples here lived by gathering food, relying on what the temperate environment offered.

## TZOMPANTEPEC CULTURAL PHASE
### (1600–1200 B.C.)

In the Tlaxcala-Puebla area we know of 19 settled hamlets in existence 3,500 years ago, each occupied by a different group. Agricultural products constituted at least half of their economy. The inhabitants of these small settlements apparently came from regions to the south or southeast, to judge from their cultural remains, which show similarities to contemporaneous materials of the Ajalpan phase in the Tehuacan Valley (García Cook 1974a; MacNeish, Peterson, and Flannery 1970), the central Gulf Coast, and areas to the south in Chiapas and Guatemala. Eighteen of these hamlets are in the present state of Tlaxcala; only one is in Puebla, near San Martin Texmelucan. Although scattered over 2,000 sq km, these sites share a number of traits, including concentrated settlements, usually of 10 to 25 residences in a linear arrangement; similar pottery; houses situated

on terraces with agricultural lands nearby; similar religious beliefs, as indicated by ceramic representations; an economy based on hunting, gathering, and agriculture; and comparable technologies.

These similarities make it possible to postulate the beginnings of a local cultural development, called Tzompantepec, between 1600 and 1200 B.C. This culture includes the 18 sites in the southern half of the state of Tlaxcala (the Tlaxcala Block); the 1 site in the Puebla Valley exhibits closer ties to the few contemporaneous sites known in the southern portion of that valley and in the Basin of Mexico. (Although only 19 settlements have been found for the Tzompantepec phase, certainly a larger number exist. Excavations in sites of the succeeding Tlatempa phase would reveal the remains of additional Tzompantepec settlements and would also confirm the dramatic increase in the number of Tlatempa phase sites.)

## TLATEMPA CULTURAL PHASE
### (1200–800 B.C.)

By about 1200 B.C. it is possible to identify 150 settlements with a series of shared culture traits which constitute a new archaeological culture, called Tlatempa. Although the bulk of the population still lived in agricultural hamlets, several larger villages contained more impressive architectural remains. The presence of small platforms, substructures, and "altars" used for religious ceremonies or perhaps as elite residences indicates social differentiation, as the majority of homes lacked even stone foundations. Kilns for firing pottery and canals on terraces for controlling water have been found. Evidence for the rise of more elaborate cults includes figurines as well as vessels similar to censer covers or lids, with anthropomorphic or zoomorphic forms. These are called *tejones* and resemble vessels known as "duckpots."

An important feature in some of the settlements, both linear and circular, is sloping walls on both residential and agricultural ter-

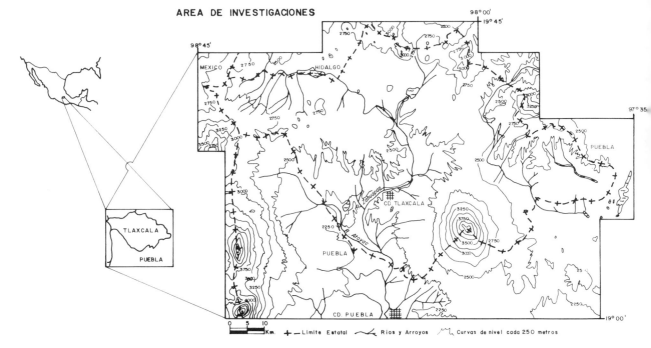

FIGURE 8-1. Map of the Tlaxcala-Puebla region.

races. The terraces are faced with cut stone or *tepetate* and are larger than Tzompantepec counterparts, measuring 60–150 m long, 6–15 m wide, and 1–1.5 m high. Sites actually surveyed average about 80 residences, although some settlements contain only 20, and a few are limited to about 10 houses. The largest villages include up to 200 dwellings. These features imply a more complex society with at least three groups dedicated to different activities: priests, farmers, and artisans.

The Tlatempa phase dates from 1200 to 800 B.C., exactly the years when Olmec culture flourished and exercised great influence in the Central Highlands. Evidence of Olmec influence appears at Tlapacoya (Ayotla and Justo subphases); at Tlatilco (Tolstoy and Paradis 1970); at Chalcatzingo (Grove 1974a); at Gualupita or in the vicinity of Atlihuayan, Morelos (Grennes-Ravitz and Coleman 1976); and in the south of Puebla, at Las Bocas and in the Tehuacan Valley. It occurs also at sites in Guerrero and in the Valley of

Oaxaca. In the Tlaxcala-Puebla region, however, the Olmec are poorly or scarcely represented.

Elements considered Olmec or a small amount of material with certain Olmec characteristics are found at three sites south of San Martin Texmelucan and at another three east of La Malinche. No Olmec or Olmecoid traits exist in the other settlements of the Tlaxcala Block or in the Sierra de la Caldera.

Perhaps one can talk of a horizon style, since similar decorative elements appear throughout a large area, but on locally made pottery, and in our case with local forms and workmanship. The characteristic pottery of this phase is a white ware, including such types as Tlatempa Blanca, Incised Tlatempa Blanca, Tlatempa Red-on-White, Tlatempa Red-on-White incised, and others. Forms are similar to those of Tilapa Red-on-White of Salinas La Blanca, Guatemala, and in surface finish they resemble Progreso Blanco of the Pavon and Ponce phases of the Huaxteca and Canoas White of the Tehuacan Valley (Mac-

246

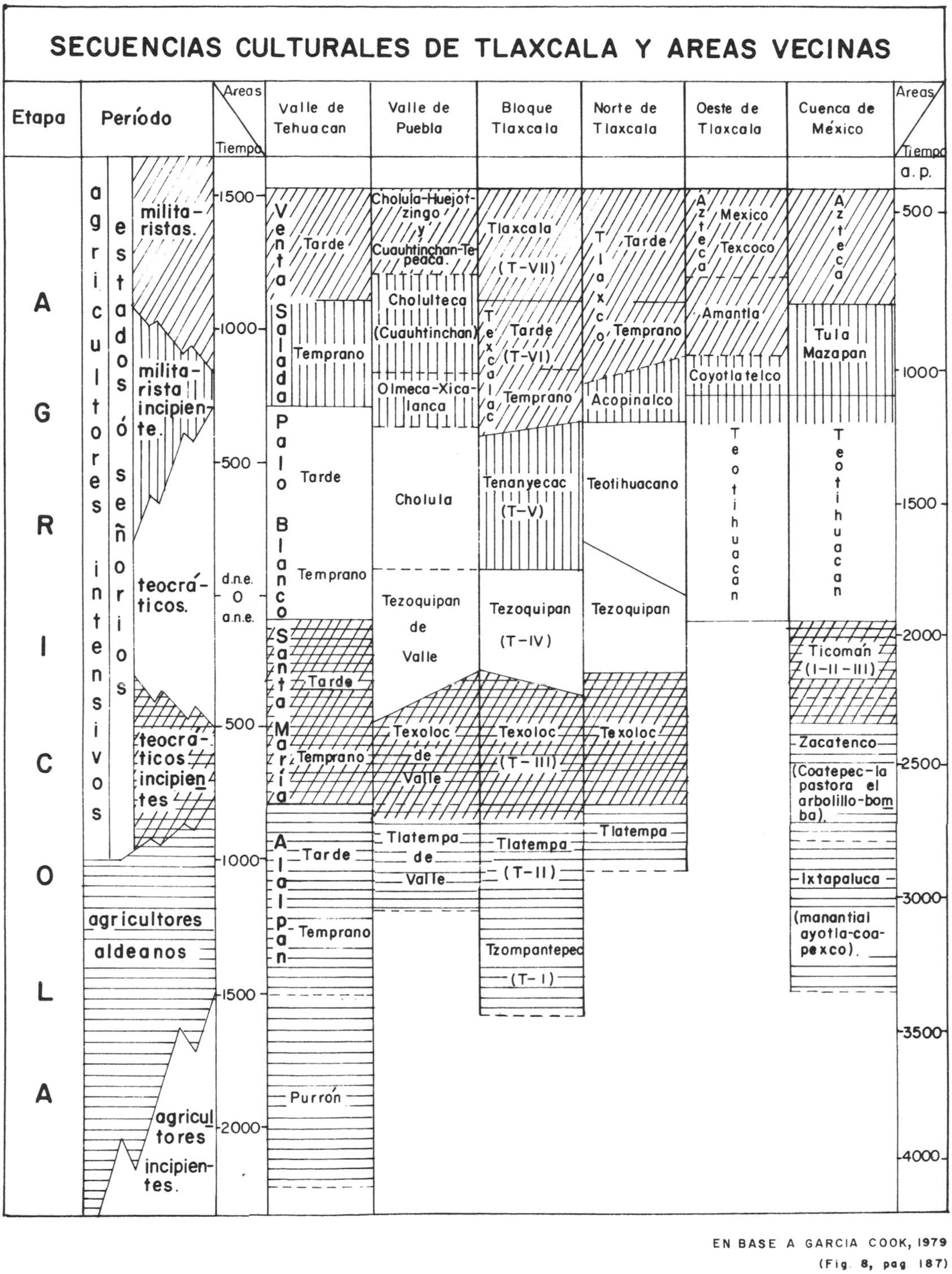

SECUENCIAS CULTURALES DE TLAXCALA Y AREAS VECINAS

EN BASE A GARCIA COOK, 1979
(Fig. 8, pag 187)

FIGURE 8-2. Chronological chart for the Tlaxcala-Puebla region.

Neish 1954; MacNeish, Peterson, and Flannery 1970; G. Ekholm 1944; García Cook 1973a; Rodríguez 1975). The same happens with ceramic figurines. The characteristic style is Type C1, which seems to be a local product beginning in the Tzompantepec phase. Other types of Tradition C are present (C6, C3, C10, CE), but there is only one artifact of Type D2 (Trejo Alvarado 1975).

Beginning with the Tlatempa phase, regional distinctions appeared. Evidence for this subdivision includes the presence— though often rare—or absence of surface Olmec elements; ceramic forms, dimensions, and finish; the location of sites in relation to topography; residential patterns within settlements; and relationships observed with other areas. Using these criteria, it is possible to delineate two culture areas: Tlatempa proper, covering 90 percent of the state of Tlaxcala, and Tlatempa de Valle, in the Puebla Valley and east of La Malinche (Fig. 8-3).

Tlatempa, represented by 100 sites, was more closely associated with groups near Tehuacan (perhaps as a result of local tradition), with Oaxaca, the Puebla Valley, and the central Gulf Coast. Tlatempa de Valle, on the other hand, had stronger relations with the Basin of Mexico, Morelos, and of course the Tlaxcala Block.

From the beginning of the phase, cultural exchanges between the Tlatempa groups and the Basin of Mexico and other surrounding regions are visible. Tlatempa traits found in the Basin of Mexico include the rare red-on-white pottery of Zacatenco, which probably derives from Tlaxcala, as well as a few figurines of Type C1 or of Tradition C. Tlatempa de Valle, in contrast, either received from or exchanged ceramic forms and figurines of Types D2 and C9 with the basin and shared several Olmec or Olmecoid elements with the basin and with Morelos. The differences in material culture and in external relations between the groups of the Tlaxcala Block, in south-central Tlaxcala, and those in the Puebla Valley and east of La Malinche pre-vailed during the entire cultural sequence of this region.

## TEXOLOC CULTURAL PHASE
### (800–400/300 B.C.)

During the next cultural phase the population increased dramatically, doubling that of Tlatempa. Settlements were fifteen times more numerous than during the Tzompantepec phase. Towns developed as a new and more elaborate type of settlement, with more complex social implications. The appearance of towns, as well as changes in ceramic types, architectural features, systems of terracing, techniques of irrigation and water control, and the distribution and size of settlements, marks the beginning of the Texoloc cultural phase, lasting from 800 to 400 or 300 B.C.

Improvements in technology permitted the Texoloc culture, building on Tlatempa advances, to construct a cultural landscape which differed markedly from the natural landscape the Tzompantepec group knew. During Texoloc, great advances in irrigation technology led to a sharp increase in agricultural production. Terraces were larger than those of earlier phases, and both sloping and vertical terrace walls were entirely covered with cut stone or *tepetate*. Terraces measured 60–300 m long, with horizontal surfaces 8–15 m wide and retaining walls .80–2.50 m high (Abascal and García Cook 1975). The majority of these terraces had canals to control water drainage or canals for both runoff and irrigation. Several Texoloc settlements had small ponds to hold and regulate water. Reservoirs dug into the *tepetate* and blocked at the lower end by a dam of cut *tepetate* and dirt took advantage of natural changes in the slope of the terrain. Drainage canals leading from the dams facilitated the irrigation of fields below.

In addition to canals on farming terraces, archaeological remains reveal systems of primary and secondary canals designed mainly as rainwater drainage controls, but also as irrigation channels. These systems indicate a

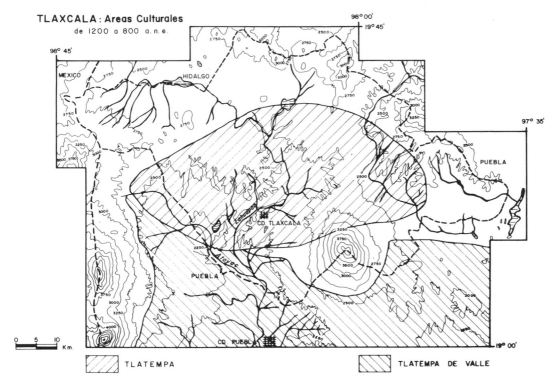

FIGURE 8-3. Early Formative period culture areas of the Tlaxcala-Puebla region.

great advance in erosion control. Several systems of primary and secondary irrigation canals have been located in the Puebla Valley and by aerial photographs in other areas (Abascal and García Cook 1975; Fowler 1968).

Polished stone hoes appeared for the first time in this phase. These have been considered agricultural tools, particularly for digging or cleaning canals (Tesch and Abascal M. 1974). Although these could have served as hoes, the Otomis until recently used similar instruments for pounding agave leaves to separate the fibers for textile making (Soustelle 1937). This interpretation is supported by the appearance of spindle whorls during the Texoloc phase. One recalls the Spanish conquerors' admiration of the magnificent clothes of maguey fiber worn by the Tlaxcalan women: it appears probable that this long tradition of processing fiber began in the Texoloc phase (Muñoz Camargo 1947; García Cook and Merino C. 1974; García Cook 1978).

The production of ceramics also increased sharply at this time. While white pottery continued, a characteristic brown ware appeared, which included a small amount of black, and later of red, pottery. This sometimes had thick incised lines on the rims, and in form and decoration it resembled Quachilco pottery from Tehuacan (MacNeish, Peterson, and Flannery 1970), of which I think Texoloc brown ware was the antecedent (García Cook 1976b; Rodríguez 1975). This ware had a wide distribution. A similar type, characterized by smaller vessels, finer paste, and better surface finish, appears in the Valley of Puebla, where it is known as Texoloc de Valle. In the south, Texoloc brown ware reached the Cuauhtinchan-Tepeaca region. Its northern and northwestern distribution

FIGURE 8-4. Huehueteotl effigy censer from Tlaxcala.

FIGURE 8-5. Side view of the Huehueteotl censer.

includes several parts of southern Hidalgo and Cuauhtitlan, in the state of Mexico, in addition to the influences on contemporaneous pottery in the rest of the Basin of Mexico (McBride 1975; Dávila 1974).

Kilns for firing pottery and many other ovens, possibly for cooking maguey stems,[1] multiplied in number during the Texoloc phase. If these ovens were important factors in the layout of settlements in the Tlatempa phase, during the succeeding period this tradition grew stronger, and we can even speak of settlements actually centered around such ovens. Were these possibly pottery towns?

Along with the characteristic brown ware and spindle whorls, *comales* for cooking tortillas appeared for the first time in the Texoloc phase (Trejo Alvarado and Ruiz Aguilar 1975). This ceramic form was common and widespread in the following phases. Also present for the first time were short earplugs, both solid and hollow, which seem to reflect a strong western influence (García Cook 1976d; García Cook and Merino C. 1974).

The Texoloc phase produced a great quantity of ceramic figurines of Types E, EH, and H, the last deriving from Western Mexico. Type G began in this phase, while Type C10 continued from the preceding period (Trejo Alvarado 1975). We suggest that the Tlaxcala-Puebla area transported Types E and C10 to the Basin of Mexico, where they seem to have begun later.

Ceramic censers were also numerous. The pedestal bases of some of them bear effigies of Huehueteotl (García Cook 1976b) and were decorated in a red, white, and yellow polychrome. Because representations of Huehueteotl appear at the beginning of the Texoloc phase in the Tlaxcala-Puebla region, they are considered antecedents of the Huehueteotl censers from Cuicuilco. Those from Cuicuilco resemble the early Tlaxcala censers but are more elaborate. At Cuicuilco the censer itself was less important than the effigy, while at Tlaxcala the vessel was the important element and the Huehueteotl effigy was adapted to the shape of the censer pedestal (Piña Chan 1960 and 1974a; García Cook 1976b; see Figs. 8-4, 8-5).

Ceramics provide information about technology, religion, social differentiation, and the activities of their producers—potters,

250

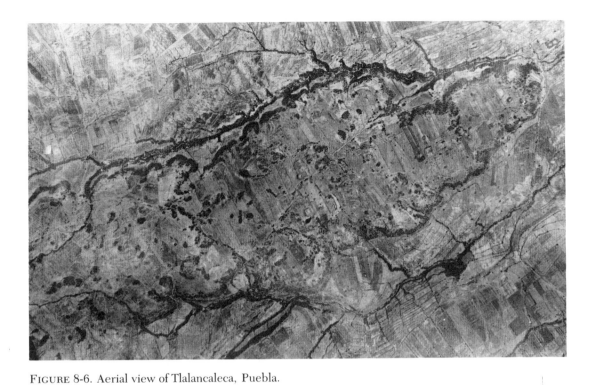

FIGURE 8-6. Aerial view of Tlalancaleca, Puebla.

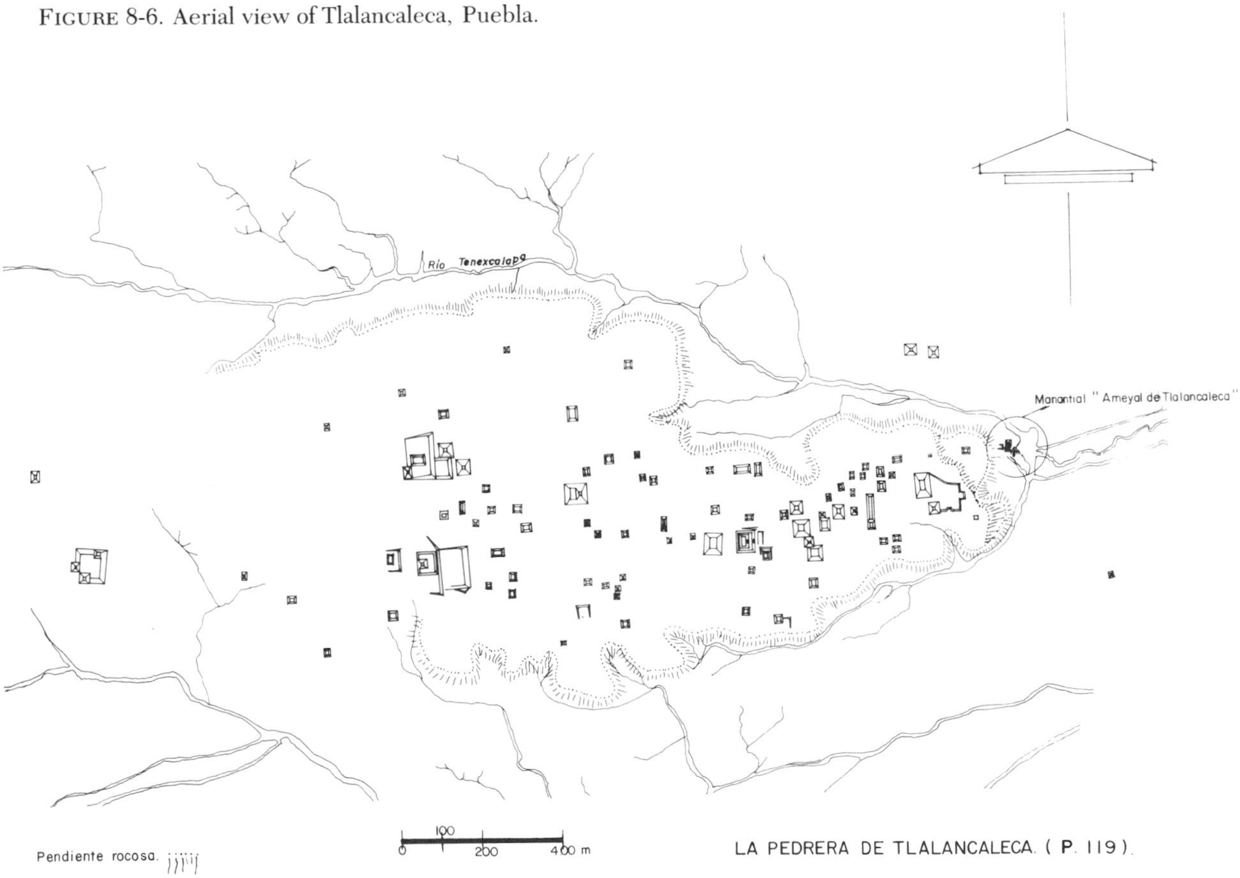

Pendiente rocosa. ﹔﹔﹔﹔﹔

LA PEDRERA DE TLALANCALECA. ( P. 119 ).

FIGURE 8-7. Model of Tlalancaleca, based on aerial photographs and surface explorations.

251

weavers, priests, and merchants. Additional information is provided by characteristics inherent in the settlements themselves.

The village, which began in the Tlatempa phase, continued during Texoloc to coexist with rural hamlets. In the villages resided both peasants' and people engaged in nonagricultural tasks such as the regulation of religion, water, production, and internal politics. These, in turn, were under the direction of authorities in the towns. Towns were permanent settlements with both a peasant population, seen archaeologically through the similarity and the simplicity of their houses, and (usually) a planned ceremonial, religious, and civic center with platforms, plazas, and pyramids (García Cook and Merino C. 1977).[2]

In the Texoloc cultural phase rural hamlets ranged in population from 100 to 500 people and were mainly clustered, although some were more dispersed. Villages and towns numbered more than 40. Some of these can be considered great towns or cities because they had large and dense populations of 2,000 or more, intricate layouts, plazas enclosed by high structures, internal streets, drainage systems in some of the buildings, and sculpture or stelae erected as an integral part of the settlement (García Cook and Merino C. 1977). Tlalancaleca is an example of this type of settlement.

Tlalancaleca, built on the flanks of the volcano Iztaccihuatl in the far northwest of the Puebla Valley, faces the Tlaxcala Block. Occupation of this large site began late in the Tzompantepec phase, around 1300 B.C., and was at its height in the Texoloc phase, 800–300 B.C. The nuclear settlement contained over 200 ha strategically located on an outcrop of the lava flow from the volcano and about 50 m above the surrounding land (García Cook 1973a; Noguera 1964). The city covered another 500 ha including the lower land, which had 2 villages and 2 hamlets dating to this phase as well as magnificent farming land (Figs. 8-6, 8-7).

Tlalancaleca had 24 raised structures, about 50 lower residential platforms, about

400 rural dwellings with no visible foundation, and about 50 terraces for homes and farming. The raised mounds attained measurements such as 30 × 30 × 8 m; 40 × 40 × 15 m; 60 × 60 × 12 m; 70 × 40 × 9 m; and 130 × 80 × 8 m. Sizes of low residential platforms include 10 × 15 × 1 m; 20 × 15 × 2 m; 30 × 30 × 1 m; and 60 × 20 × 2 m.

In Tlalancaleca, as in the other great towns, towns, and villages, stucco covered the pyramids and platforms. The stucco coating in general was coarse and solid, averaging 8 cm thick, though in some cases it was as much as 15 cm thick. The fill of buildings consisted of earth and stone or networks of adobe walls, and cut stone or *tepetate* faced the structures.

In Tlalancaleca large balustrades bordered stairways, and the use of the *talud-tablero* dates to the end of the Texoloc phase (Figs. 8-8, 8-9, 8-10). Two monolithic basins or sarcophagi from Tlalancaleca resemble one found inside a pyramidal structure at Totimehuacan, in the Puebla Valley (Fig. 8-11). They are similar also to those reported from La Venta and Tres Zapotes (García Cook 1973a; Noguera 1964; Spranz 1966, 1967, 1970).

Tlalancaleca shared ceramic types with both the Puebla Valley and the Tlaxcala Block and included elements from the Basin of Mexico and the west. Stone sculpture included a representation of Huehueteotl (García Moll 1976), several of Tlaloc, and a stela with an engraved person whom Carmen Aguilera (1974) identifies as Tlahuizcalpantecuhtli. There is also a smooth stela in the form of a vertical disc carved from a large rock outcrop of the mountain. This stela seems to have served as the base for establishing the settlement, or perhaps it was later carved just to the east of the group of monumental structures, where the flat land changes into the natural slope of the hill (García Cook 1973a; see Figs. 8-12–8-17).

At Tlalancaleca, archaeologists found another set of sculptures, of which two circular stones are noteworthy (Fig. 8-18). These had a central hole and a decoration of flowers with four petals radiating from a central circle. One stone bore 13 flowers and the other 9. In addition, the stones had a semicircle of incised punctates (5 on one stone and 7 on the other) which Noguera (1964) relates to the ballgame and the calendar. My explorations of Tlalancaleca uncovered a set of three smoothed rocks decorated with incised punctates forming a double-lined rectangle, crossed diagonally through the center by two intersecting lines of punctates (Fig. 8-19). The number of punctates on these three artifacts—116, 97, and 147—totals 360 (García Cook 1973a). Can we conclude that these stones also relate to keeping track of time?

Other culture traits observed at Tlalancaleca could be enumerated, but those already mentioned are palpable evidence of the great technological and cultural advances during the Texoloc phase. These became even more diverse during the succeeding Tezoquipan phase.

The number of sites with large structures and purposeful planning, the sarcophagi, the representations of gods in pottery and stone, the various calendrical elements, and the smooth stela show the enormous importance religion had acquired. The strength of the priestly class, located in these larger settlements and ruling the smaller surrounding sites, grew correspondingly. The formation of small, incipient theocratic states can be postulated at this time. These later gave way to regional theocratic states, which in turn were superceded by the largest theocratic state of all, Teotihuacan.

Because of the supremacy of some sites over others, groups selected land located strategically in terms of topography and regional placement. Towns needed to be visible from a distance, have easily controlled access, and lie on routes to other areas. Fully fortified sites, such as Gualupita Las Dalias or "Tlalancalequita" (García Cook and Rodríguez 1975; see Fig. 8-20) appeared at this time, especially in the late Texoloc phase (600–300 B.C.). Fortified sites later had a wide distribution in this area.

The above information allows us a glimpse

FIGURE 8-8. Balustraded stairway of a platform at Tlalancaleca.

FIGURE 8-9. Side view of a stairway with balustrade at Tlalancaleca.

FIGURE 8-10. *Talud-tablero* on a platform at Tlalancaleca, showing construction techniques.

FIGURE 8-12. A carved representation of Tlaloc from Tlalancaleca.

FIGURE 8-11. Stone basin or sarcophagus from Tlalancaleca.

of the complexity of Texoloc social organization and permits us to infer the existence of priests, shamans or medicine men, artisans, peasants, and the first merchants. People or groups differentiated among themselves according to their specialized social roles as well as the position they occupied in economic production. A ruling group maintained, or was based on, control of religion, government, and the economy. This control devolved on priests, who carried out cults of the gods, which had increased in number, and established the guidelines both for agricultural and handicraft (ceramics, weaving) production and for trade with other areas. The priest either was strongly tied to the merchant or was himself the merchant.

For food the Texoloc culture relied mainly on agricultural products, supplemented by hunting, fishing, and gathering. Other products were obtained by trade, which had reached active proportions, with groups near and far.

I have already mentioned Texoloc characteristics, mainly ceramic, found in the south

FIGURE 8-13. Stela with a depiction of the god Tlahuizcalpantecuhtli, Xolotl, or Mictlantecuhtli, found in the Ameyal at Tlalancaleca.

FIGURE 8-14. Front view (east side) of the Ameyal Stela, Tlalancaleca.

and in the Basin of Mexico. Texoloc groups also maintained relations with Tehuacan and the central Gulf Coast, and, as in the Tlatempa phase, a strong influence from Western Mexico accelerated the internal development of this area. The western influence is visible both in ceramics and in the infiltration of religious ideas. Pottery similar to Chupicuaro wares, figurines of Types H4 and H3, and short solid and hollow ceramic earplugs are found. It is probable that the representation of Huehueteotl comes from the west, along with the generalized use of truncated conical mounds and perhaps the utilization of stucco to cover buildings. In Tlaxcala the western influence is reflected in a large number of settlements, and three sites were occupied by western groups themselves. From one of these came the Huehueteotl censer and abundant short earplugs, and another was the fortified site of Gualupita Las Dalias, which had 15 pyramidal structures and numerous truncated conical mounds (García Cook and Rodríguez 1975; Guevara 1975).

Based on the strong presence of western cultural elements, the settlement types, regional pottery-making technology, lithics, stone facing on terraces, and other settlement features two Texoloc culture areas can be established: Texoloc and Texoloc de Valle (Fig. 8-21).

Texoloc occupied all the Tlaxcala Block and parts north and east of it, covering more than 2,500 sq km and encompassing about 300 separate settlements sharing the same culture. It maintained contacts with the Tehuacan area, the Puebla Valley, the central Gulf Coast and the Basin of Mexico, to which it seems to have exported more cultural traits than it received. Texoloc shared with the Basin of Mexico the strong influence and actual presence of groups from Western Mexico.

In the south, separated only by topography and cultural characteristics such as smaller ceramic vessel forms and the absence of hoes and spindle whorls, a cultural variant named Texoloc de Valle developed contemporaneously with Texoloc. Its major contacts were with the Basin of Mexico, Tehuacan,

255

FIGURE 8-15. Stela in its original position west of a structure beside the spring at the Ameyal, Tlalancaleca.

FIGURE 8-16. Front view of the plain stela found in the eastern part of Tlalancaleca.

FIGURE 8-17. South side of the plain stela from Tlalancaleca.

Morelos and, to a lesser extent, Western Mexico.

## TEZOQUIPAN CULTURAL PHASE
(400/300 B.C.–A.D. 100)

All the technological and intellectual changes that were accelerating during the Texoloc phase crystallized in the succeeding Tezoquipan phase (400 or 300 B.C.–A.D. 100). These developments—religion, the roles of priests and artisans, hydraulics, and construction—had been gestating during earlier phases. The Tezoquipan phase completely shaped the religious character of government, the enormous political and economic power of the priestly class, and the growth of the artisan class. In the main, artisans did not contribute to food production yet enjoyed a social status higher than that of the peasants, who were economically active in agriculture. Tezoquipan marked the climax of hydraulic systems, and agricultural technology therefore also reached its apogee during this phase. All this was the result of a marked technological transformation combined with

the great intellectual developments of the Texoloc phase.

In Tlaxcala, Tezoquipan was represented by more settlements than any other phase. Because of the number of large population centers and the scarcity or absence of dispersed occupational zones, it appears that it also was the time of greatest population density.

Tezoquipan settlements became more concentrated, and the few dispersed groups of the Texoloc phase disappeared. Large, nucleated hamlets and villages with 200–250 residences abounded. About 50 towns with civic

256

FIGURE 8-18. "Calendar stones" from Tlalancaleca, now in the wall of the church of San Matias Tlalancaleca.

FIGURE 8-19. Stone with incised punctates. Two similar stones were found at Tlalancaleca.

FIGURE 8-20. Aerial view of Tlalancalequita, or Gualupita Las Dalias, showing human modification of the landscape.

or ceremonial centers included at least 250–300 residences each. Great towns or cities numbered only 5 in Texoloc, but 20 in Tezoquipan. These and other large towns show marked advances in architectural arrangements and urban features, such as open plazas with architecture on three sides; location of raised structures according to regular linear or concentric patterns; buildings with superstructures; common use of blue, red, or white stucco; the *talud-tablero*; and the ball-game at one site, where its appearance seems to correspond to the end of the Texoloc phase. During Tezoquipan, 30 percent of all towns, great towns and villages contained raised structures.

The ballcourt at Capulac Concepcion (P-211), situated south of La Malinche in the region of Amozoc, Puebla, dates to the beginning of Tezoquipan (see Figs. 8-22, 8-23). For this period it was enormous, as the playing field measured 105 × 12 m, and the interior was raised an average of 2.5 m. The open ballcourt stood on a large platform in the north-central sector of the settlement, which was at its height during earlier phases. Its principal occupation ended with Tezoquipan (García Cook 1974b, 1976b).

The presence of cities or great towns sur-

257

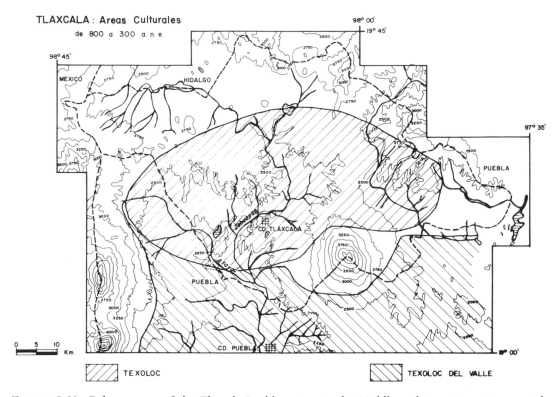

**TLAXCALA : Areas Culturales**
de 800 a 300 a.n.e.

TEXOLOC

TEXOLOC DEL VALLE

FIGURE 8-21. Culture areas of the Tlaxcala-Puebla region in the Middle and Late Formative periods (800–300 B.C.).

rounded by lesser towns, villages, and hamlets leads me to believe that these were certainly "city-states" with political, economic, and religious control over a considerable area around them. Tlalancaleca, because of its great size and complexity, the architectural features and artifacts mentioned above (ordered plazas, raised structures with several tiers, streets and access to the site, sculptural elements, common use of stucco, *talud-tableros*, balustraded stairways, drainage in some buildings, plain and carved stelae, and calendrical elements), and the presence of cultural traits from numerous places (the Tlaxcala Block, the Puebla Valley, the Basin of Mexico, Western Mexico, and distant regions) appears to represent not just a city-state but a regional theocratic state. As such it controlled a larger area—if not through the economy, then through religion.

Several "city-states" or small theocratic states in the Tlaxcala Block during Tezoquipan can be named. These include Gualupita Las Dalias (Tlalancalequita), occupied by groups from the west; Tecopilco; San Jose Tetel, west of Apizaco; Cuajimala; Xalpetlahuaya; San Dieguito; Quetzalcoapan; (T-13), one of Los Tetlas; and La Laguna, in the northeast. In the Puebla Valley, besides Tlalancaleca in the far north, there were Nopalucan; Atlantepec; Papalotla; San Jacinto; San Aparicio; Los Teteles de Gorozpe, important, like Capulac Concepcion, since the Texoloc phase; San Francisco Coapan, west of Cholula; Amalucan, east of Puebla; Los Teteles de San Miguel, in Cuauhtinchan, in the south of the Valley; and Totimehuacan.

As mentioned above, Tezoquipan is thought to mark the climax of hydraulic systems for agriculture and water control. This

258

idea is based on the presence of new and diverse instruments for farming. Like the preceding phase, Tezoquipan had agricultural terraces, extensive systems of primary and secondary canals for irrigation, and a greater number of reservoirs for controlling, storing, and distributing water, both from rain and feeder canals. New in this period were dikes to redirect river water and to form canals along the natural levees of these rivers. Another innovation was the use of fields near lakes and between or beside rivers to construct ridged fields or *chinampas* (Abascal and García Cook 1975; Dávila 1974). Furrowed agricultural fields were in existence (Seele 1973), and the number of stones used either as hoes or as pounding stones for separating agave fibers to weave into cloth increased.

During the Tezoquipan phase ceramic white ware tended to disappear and was used only in small censers, while brown ware was produced in lesser quantities, different forms, and smaller sizes than before. A red ware took their place. Surface treatment of this included: red interior and exterior; red interior and brown exterior; white-on-red; white and red bands on the natural brown of the clay; red incised and engraved; and white-on-red incised. Almost all vessels had a composite silhouette, and decoration, when it appeared, was a painted or incised step fret, large in the Tlaxcala Block and smaller in the Puebla Valley. Type E continued to predominate among figurines, along with Types H, principally H4 and H3, and G. At this point figurines known as Teotihuacan I (Trejo Alvarado 1975; Rodríguez 1975) appeared. The number of *comales*, short earplugs, and spindle whorls multiplied.

The evidence for recognizable deities grew. In addition to Huehueteotl, Tlaloc, and anthropomorphic or zoomorphic figures, a dual god of life and death appeared at the beginning of this phase. This may have been Mictlantecuhtli, Xolotl, Quetzalcoatl, or Tlahuizcalpantecuhtli. He was represented by carving on a block of stone (Stela or Object 7 of Tlalancaleca) placed by the west side of a

FIGURE 8-22. View from the southern end of the ballcourt at Capulac Concepcion, Puebla.

FIGURE 8-23. Excavations in the center of the ballcourt at Capulac Concepcion. View to the south-southwest.

259

pyramidal structure. This structure and two others were placed around a spring called Ameyal de la Pedrera Tlalancaleca, and the channeled water flowed around and between the structures (Aguilera 1974; García Cook 1973a, 1974a).

During the Tezoquipan phase, religion, as well as its representatives and executors, was fully integrated and institutionalized. It had reached its maturity, and the process which began during Tlatempa had taken definite form, attaining political and economic, as well as purely religious, control over Tezoquipan society.

Tezoquipan society was clearly divided into different classes. Priests or chiefs of the large sites occupied the highest level, followed by artisans and chiefs of smaller towns, villages, and hamlets. Last came the peasants, who were the majority of the population and provided its economic base. The merchant class, which arose during the Texoloc phase, also played a very important role. In conjunction with the priest or local chief, the merchants took charge of the distribution and trade of items produced by the populace. In exchange they acquired general necessities such as clothing, ornaments, and food that did not exist locally. They procured raw materials for manufacture by certain artisans when these materials came from sources—quarries, woods, clay banks, etc.—owned by neighboring groups sharing the same culture. They also obtained merchandise such as seashells, precious stones, feathers, dyes and paints, cotton, salt, and food by long distance trade.

These small theocratic states were based on exploitation by the leaders—priests, merchants, and, to a lesser extent, artisans—of the large population of the great towns and small suburban groups, which together formed protocities, and of the small towns, villages, and hamlets around them. The leaders were dependent on the services and tribute provided by the peasants. Besides producing surplus to feed the chiefs and priests, the specialized artisans (potters, weavers, lapidaries, stonecutters, and masons), and

perhaps the merchants, the peasants also had to contribute occasionally to communal tasks such as cleaning canals, constructing terraces and temples, cleaning and maintaining religious centers, and transporting and erecting monuments. In addition, they had to render individual services upon demand (García Cook 1976b).

All these Tezoquipan cultural elements (large populations, elaborate irrigation systems, and ceramic types) in fact came into existence in the second half of the Texoloc phase. Sites such as Tlalancaleca, Totimehuacan, Atlantepec, Nopalucan, Los Teteles de Gorozpe, Capulac Concepcion, Quetzalcoapan, San Jose Tetel, La Laguna, San Felipe Tezoquipan, and several others with Tezoquipan characteristics were in existence by 500 B.C., but not until 400 B.C. did these traits become common. By 300 B.C. Tezoquipan culture had spread throughout the area under discussion. About the time of Christ, settlements in some parts of this area took on a more rural character, and new groups sharing a proto-Teotihuacan culture (Tezoyuca and early Tzacualli-Patlachique) entered the region. Particularly in the Puebla Valley and among the first inhabitants of the far north and west of Tlaxcala the proto-Teotihuacan presence was felt (García Cook and Merino C. 1977), and by about A.D. 100 this cultural stagnation or regional ruralization was almost ubiquitous, although in some places elements of Tezoquipan culture persisted for even another century. The year A.D. 100, then, marks the end of Tezoquipan and the end of the cultural apogee of Puebla-Tlaxcala.

Tezoquipan advancements were of such a high level that it can be suggested that we are dealing with the "regional Classic period,"[3] defining "Classic" as the time of the greatest cultural and economic achievements in a given area. In addition, Tezoquipan fulfills all the requirements proposed for the "Classic" period or horizon: permanent agriculture, *chinampas* and ridged fields, irrigation, terraces, active commerce, hamlets built around ceremonial centers, some urban zones, religion as an integrating force, theocracy, and a cult of the water god (see Palerm and Wolf 1961; García Cook 1974a, 1974b). Besides this, it appears that members of Tezoquipan culture—at least the intellectuals and artisans—participated actively in the rise of Teotihuacan and Cholula.

Tezoquipan culture covered all the Tlaxcala Block north and east of the present state and the entire Puebla Valley. It was the period of greatest cultural unity in the Puebla-Tlaxcala zone, where more than 150 sites flourished. Nonetheless, to judge from the distribution and internal placement of settlements, the quality of culture features (ceramics, lithics, terrace systems, and forms of agriculture), relations with groups in other areas, and goods exchanged, it is possible to differentiate two variants of the same culture: Tezoquipan and Tezoquipan de Valle.

Tezoquipan culture was centered north of the Puebla-Tlaxcala Valley, embracing a large part of the state of Tlaxcala and all the Tlaxcala Block (north and east of the state); it maintained strong contacts with Western Mexico and the Gulf Coast. It included three sites occupied by Western Mexicans, present since the Texoloc phase, and of course shared many traits with the Puebla Valley, where the Tezoquipan de Valle subculture developed. Relations with Tehuacan and Oaxaca were almost nonexistent. There were ties with the Basin of Mexico, where Tezoquipan influence is seen in the use of stucco, figurines of Types E and C10, and architectural elements such as balustrades, *talud-tableros* (later), platforms, and enclosed plazas.

My investigations established all the boundaries for Tezoquipan, which occupied an area of about 3,000 sq km with over 300 different settlements, more than 100 of which had raised structures. This was the largest culture area in Prehispanic Tlaxcala.

Tezoquipan de Valle was located south of Tezoquipan proper, occupying all the Puebla Valley and the land east of La Malinche. Our explorations in the south and southeast of this area indicated that this culture covered a fairly wide zone in the south, perhaps extending as far as the Cordillera de Tentzo and north to Atlixco, and several known sites confirmed this. We surveyed only 30 percent of the region we consider Tezoquipan de Valle and found about 80 settlements, 25 of which had raised structures (Fig. 8-24). Tezoquipan de Valle showed a strong influence from the Tehuacan Valley and Oaxaca, major ties and trade with the Basin of Mexico, rare exchanges with the Gulf Coast, and none or very few with the west. Several decorative characteristics on pottery and figurines continued from the Texoloc phase, adapted to local forms and combined with foreign traits, especially those of the Basin of Mexico.

We suggest that Tezoquipan culture, including Tezoquipan de Valle, played an important role in the rise of the great theocratic cities which succeeded it, Cholula and Teotihuacan. This influence was noticeable both in regional (Cholula) and in extraregional (Teotihuacan) impact. The contemporaneous Ticoman phase in the Basin of Mexico, which included Cuicuilco (Tolstoy and Paradis 1970), lacked the architectural and hydraulic technology and the intellectual and religious solidarity necessary to establish a monumental city like Teotihuacan. Jeffrey R. Parsons' survey of the area (1969, 1971, 1973, 1974b, 1976) showed a significant population density in the basin at this time, with probably 250 settlements in this 8,000 sq km area. Nonetheless, only about 10 were major sites with important ceremonial centers; these included Tepalcate Chimalhuacan, Cuicuilco, Ticoman, Cerro del Tepalcate, Tezoyuca, Temesco, and Teotihuacan. Of these only Cuicuilco was very large; the rest were hamlets and small farming communities. Even if we assume that the number of villages and towns with civic or religious structures in the basin was five times greater than those known and that they cannot be seen because of later populations and constant depredations by Mexico City, then there would be perhaps 50. This is still a smaller number than the 150 sites in our area of only 6,000 sq km.

Proponents of a local origin for Teotihuacan (Dixon 1966, West 1965, R. Millon 1960,

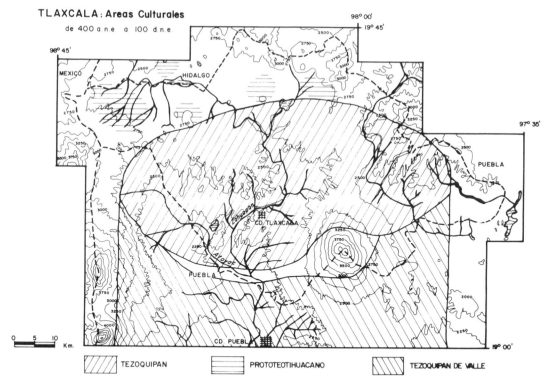

TLAXCALA: Areas Culturales

de 400 a.n.e. a 100 d.n.e.

| | | |
|---|---|---|
| //// TEZOQUIPAN | PROTOTEOTIHUACANO | \\\\ TEZOQUIPAN DE VALLE |

FIGURE 8-24. Culture areas of the Tlaxcala-Puebla region in the Tezoquipan cultural phase (400 or 300 B.C.–A.D. 100).

among others) base their argument on the fact that artifacts with Teotihuacan characteristics are not found in other areas. However, Tlaxcala-Puebla, besides its strong theocratic society, had features which appeared later at Teotihuacan and at Tlapacoya a little before that. Among them were balustrades, *talud-tablero* constructions, drainage in principal buildings, and the widespread and frequent use of architectural stucco. These were present in Tlaxcala by 900 B.C. Other traits present in Tlaxcala before the rise of Teotihuacan included highly elaborate centers with numerous ceremonial structures, plazas, and the ballgame; acquaintance with a calendric system; a pantheon of at least three gods (Huehueteotl, Tlaloc, and Mictlantecuhtli or Tlahuizcalpantecuhtli), stelae, stone sculpture, and complex systems of farming.

I believe that the peoples of the Ticoman phase in the Basin of Mexico possessed neither the technical nor the intellectual capacity to establish a metropolis like Teotihuacan, later the seat of a great theocratic state. Nor had the inhabitants of the Basin of Mexico developed a society sufficiently complex, with strong enough religious control, to make such a city possible. About A.D. 100, and beginning a century earlier, a depopulation and a ruralization of the Tlaxcala-Puebla area took place. This can be attributed to the emigration of the populace, especially the intellectuals and artisans, to the nascent Teotihuacan and Cholula (García Cook 1974b, 1976b).

262

## TENANYECAC CULTURAL PHASE
## (A.D. 100–650)

With the rise of Teotihuacan and Cholula, to the northwest and south of Tlaxcala respectively, the technical and cultural apogee reached during Tezoquipan in Tlaxcala and the northern part of the Puebla Valley had passed. The population became more rural, and a general cultural stagnation set in.

The Tenanyecac phase in Tlaxcala started at A.D. 100 and lasted until 650. The population declined from that of Tezoquipan. Occupation sites declined 30 percent in number, and small, dispersed hamlets reappeared, after their absence in the preceding phase. This implies strongly that fewer people inhabited the region. Settlements with civic or religious structures (great towns or cities, towns, and villages) became scarcer; 70 percent of them either had arisen during Tezoquipan and continued into the early part of this phase or appeared only at the end of Tenanyecac and persisted during the following phase. Only 25 percent of the major Tenanyecac sites show definite community planning, the presence of one or more plazas, and the use of drains. The *talud-tablero* was not used, and the terraces of most ceremonial structures were faced with simple *taludes* or with *taludes* capped by a low vertical molding. The common and widespread use of stucco to cover buildings was abandoned.

In Tenanyecac culture the strongly theocratic society of Tezoquipan was changing. Even though the priesthood continued to exercise some control, its enormous strength during Tezoquipan was debilitated by the appearance of new governing chiefs, for whom religion played a secondary role. These chiefs were primarily concerned with staying independent from the great urban centers arising in neighboring zones, Teotihuacan and Cholula, and thereby consolidating their military authority over the populace. Militarism arose not with the goal of conquering more territory or subjugating weaker groups; rather, everything seems to indicate that militarism became necessary in order to keep the groups independent and to enable them to avoid becoming tributaries of the new (expansionist?) states. It developed, then, as a necessity for self-defense and protection of self-interest.

In the first part of Tenanyecac—A.D. 100 to 250 or 300—the height of Tezoquipan cultural tradition persisted in some villages and towns. In the second part of the phase, A.D. 300–650, Tlaxcala and the northern Puebla Valley fell into complete decadence. The area contained mainly hamlets and farming villages. Only for the purpose of fighting to maintain their independence did settlements group into *cacicazgos* or kingdoms, surrounded by small populations to provide subsistence.

If it is indeed certain that Tenanyecac culture was stagnant in comparison with the rapid evolution of earlier phases and that its settlements had become more rural, especially more so than during the Tezoquipan phase, then a redistribution of the populace is also clear. The people gathered into kingdoms or *cacicazgos* and fortified themselves to stay independent of Teotihuacan and Cholula.

During the Tezoquipan phase, control of the populace had been distributed among more than 50 principal settlements, of which about 20 were prominent. In the Tenanyecac phase this number declined to only 10 cities, 3 of them fortified, 24 towns or primary centers, and approximately 60 villages or secondary centers. Large and small hamlets, both concentrated and dispersed, numbered slightly more than 100 (García Cook and Merino C. 1976; García Cook and Trejo 1977).

All these clusters or "blocks" of sites, which we associate with kingdoms or *cacicazgos*, exercised economic and political control and shared another important feature. Each had, in addition to civic or ceremonial structures, one or more settlements either fortified or strategically located. This indicates the change in the locus and nature of power and has led me to consider Tenanyecac a transition from the Classic to the Postclassic in this area (García Cook 1974b).

Along with the exit of a large number of people—intellectuals, artisans, and perhaps farmers—Tenanyecac witnessed the arrival of new groups, the Ñuiñe, who lived farther south, as Wigberto Jiménez Moreno and John Paddock (1966) have suggested. The immigrants included Otomis and later, during the second part of this phase, perhaps the Olmeca-Xicalanca.

We have identified several of these *cacicazgos* or kingdoms by the clustering of the sites that composed them. The Nativitas Block integrated the great towns of Xochitecatl, Cacaxtla, Atoyatenco, and Mixco, forming 12 farming hamlets, 3 minor towns, and 7 villages into a powerful unit. Mixco, Atoyatenco, and perhaps Xochitecatl, in the far northeast and southwest, were fortified. Los Contlas (Tlacatecpac, Tetepetla, and Tepenacas) created another block to avoid domination by Teotihuacan or Cholula. Tetepetla was fortified (García Cook and Mora López 1974). The Totolqueme Group was located on the hill of the same name, and the principal center of the Tenexyecac Group lay on a ridge of the Tlaxcala Block leading into the Puebla Valley. The Ocotitla Block, east of Tlaxcala, centered around the fortified cities of Ocotitla and Piedra del Padre, both strategically located and protected by defensive ditches. Other groups with strong local traditions also coalesced but adapted themselves to the power exercised by the emergent Teotihuacan. They maintained strong ties with and depended in large measure on Teotihuacan, as well as on each other and on additional sites named below. One of these blocks was Los Tetlas, with Chimalpa, Actipan, and El Santuario as primary centers which in turn controlled several minor hamlets (García Cook 1976b; see Figs. 8-25, 8-26).

The preceding paragraphs provide part of the evidence for cultural stagnation in the Tenanyecac phase: the population was distributed among fewer settlements, and the total number of people declined. But cultural "stagnation" does not necessarily imply technological backwardness, nor does it always signify a smaller yield in production. Rather, it simply refers in this instance to a different means of social control, based more on political and economic factors than on technological or religious sanctions.

Certain aspects of technological change may help explain this cultural stagnation. Ceramic technology suffered a marked decline. Most pottery was a red monochrome or a red and reddish-brown bichrome, very coarse and friable. During the first half of the Tenanyecac phase, figurines reflected a strong western influence, but they were all poorly made. Except for those from Teotihuacan and the rare examples from the Gulf Coast, the local figurines had a poorly finished surface (Trejo Alvarado 1975). The same happened with *comales*, easy to recognize by their coarseness. Solid or hollow earplugs were rare and crude; some were elongated and of poor quality. Only spindle whorls increased in number and variety. This might indicate a growth in textile making, as would the rise in the number of hoes, or agave pounders (García Cook and Merino C. 1974; Tesch and Abascal M. 1974).

Agricultural techniques had advanced considerably during the preceding phase, incorporating complete irrigation and water control systems. These hydraulic complexes and the intensive use of land continued. Agricultural production should have increased during Tenanyecac, because lands previously ignored were utilized, especially in the Puebla Valley, where ridged fields and *chinampas* attest to intense agricultural activity.

In lithics, although the number of "hoes" or agave pounders rose, grinding implements were cruder than during Tezoquipan. Basin metates outnumbered those with legs. An increase in projectile points indicates either the return of hunting to a position of highest importance or the occurrence of fights among these groups or against foreigners.

In general, no new or characteristic technological advances marked this phase. The only changes might be the placement of canals along the center of terraces, the use of

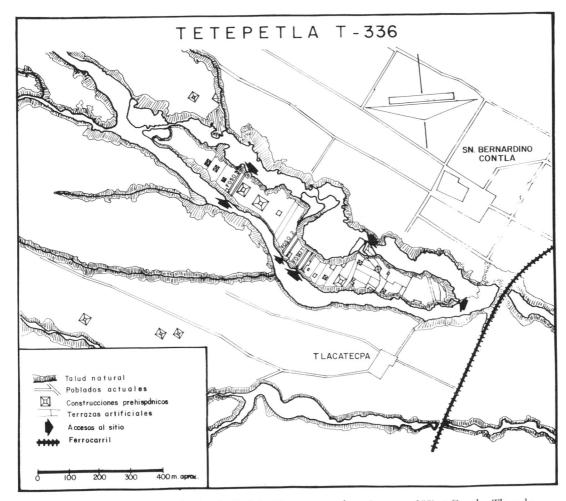

FIGURE 8-25. Fortified site of the first half of the Tenanyecac phase (ca. A.D. 300) at Contla, Tlaxcala.

irrigation trenches closed at both ends, and the decrease in enclosed kilns for firing pottery.

Trade and commerce declined sharply. This is logical, considering that the majority of inhabitants of the region were farmers in hamlets, while it was those in the villages and towns who imported artifacts from other areas, perhaps in exchange for farm products. Tenanyecac culture was developing just as commercial control in the Mexican Highlands was becoming centralized at Teotihuacan, with its system of commercial routes or networks for this purpose. Tlaxcala was not exempt from this commercial domination; on the contrary, it participated in it very actively and played a large part in the trade routes of Teotihuacan.

During the preceding Tezoquipan phase, the culture described above was not the only one developing in Tlaxcala. Rather, several settlements to the north, including Tezoyuca, Patlachique, and early Tzacualli, shared a proto-Teotihuacan culture. These people were contemporaneous with the occupants of the Teotihuacan Valley and other parts of the Basin of Mexico, and they had similar cultural features. South of Tlaxcala, in

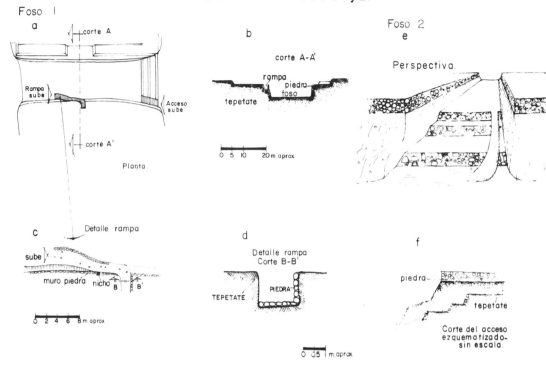

# TETEPETLA   T-336
## Detalles de los Fosos 1y2.

FIGURE 8-26. Details of some of the entrances to the fortified site of Contla.

the Puebla Valley, several elements characteristic of this proto-Teotihuacan culture indicate its amalgamation with contemporaneous Tezoquipan de Valle groups.

During the Tenanyecac phase (A.D. 100–650) there were also other cultures developing in the area. In the north, a well-defined area inhabited by Teotihuacan groups is considered to lie within the Teotihuacan Sphere (García Cook 1976b, 1976c, 1978), encompassing about 80 settlements, also grouped in blocks. In the west, the Calpulalpan Block had 16 settlements and 2 major centers (cities?), Calpulalpan and Tecoaque. The Chulco Block also comprised 16 sites and 2 macroregional centers, which were either provincial or primary, depending on how closely they were affiliated with Teotihuacan, and 1 town, plus villages and hamlets. The San Nicolas Block, with 9 settlements near the

mountain of the same name, had 1 governing city in the north. Another large group of over 20 sites occupied the north central area. In addition to Teotihuacan features, this area showed a strong influence from the Gulf Coast and included 1 site with settlers from El Tajin toward the end of the phase. A smaller group of 11 sites, with its large principal center at Cerritos de Guadalupe, also lay in the north just outside the Tenanyecac area, at the beginning of the Teotihuacan Corridor (discussed below). A last group, northeast of Tlaxcala, had 15 somewhat dispersed settlements and only 1 town (a primary provincial center), 2 villages, and hamlets (García Cook 1976b, 1976c; García Cook and Merino C. 1976, 1977; García Cook and Trejo 1977).

To the south, in the Puebla Valley, developed the Cholula culture, whose principal

266

centers of Cholula, Manzanilla, Flor del Bosque, San Mateo, and Chachapa shared a considerable number of features with Teotihuacan in the Basin of Mexico, Monte Alban in Oaxaca, and El Tajin on the Gulf Coast as well as with Tenanyecac. The rural sites, however, belonged to a Tenanyecac culture, and as they maintained ties with the areas mentioned, this culture has also been called Tenanyecac de Valle.

The Tlaxcala Block and the Sierra de la Caldera, locus of Tenanyecac culture, was divided north of La Malinche by a large chain of sites with Teotihuacan culture called the Teotihuacan Corridor. Crossing from the northwest to the southeast, this united the Teotihuacan Sphere (and, presumably, Teotihuacan itself) with Cholula, passing east and south of La Malinche, and with the Gulf Coast, by way of the Oriental Basin and the Sierra Blanca (García Cook 1974b, 1976b, 1976c). From Cholula, this route continued toward Oaxaca either via Tehuacan or else via Atlixco, Izucar, and Acatlan, all in Puebla. The latter route could have continued south of the Sierra Nevada to unite the Puebla Valley with Morelos and Guerrero, but this is only an inference from other works (see Fig. 8-27).

The Teotihuacan Corridor did not just link Teotihuacan with Oaxaca or the Gulf Coast. Rather, along it were transferred from region to region not only raw materials and manufactured objects, but also ideas and cultural advances. The corridor included site clusters with major centers and secondary settlements, such as Los Tetlas, north of Apizaco; Baquedano, on Quimicho Mountain; Col. Juarez, north of Huamantla; and El Pinal, on the mountain of the same name, east of La Malinche. In the Puebla Valley were Manzanilla, Chachapa, San Mateo, and Cuauhtinchan, although characteristics at these sites linked them more with Cholula than with Teotihuacan.[4]

Almost all the Teotihuacan—or Teotihuacanoid—settlements, whether in the sphere or in the corridor itself, were nucleated. Small, dispersed hamlets were very rare, and the few examples showed stronger ties to Tenanyecac culture. In Tlaxcala and the northern Puebla Valley were 11 cities, 10 towns, 15 villages, over 100 small compact and dispersed hamlets, and 3 military garrisons or lookouts (García Cook and Trejo 1977). Each city or great town occupied over 100 ha, and most covered 200 or more.

Seven of these larger settlements had more than 20 structures on high platforms. Los Cerritos de San Nicolas and Los Cerritos de Guadalupe included over 100 buildings each, with superstructures ranging in height from 1 m to (in more than 30 cases) 3.5–4.0 m. All these buildings bore stucco, although it was not of Tezoquipan quality. Absent were the *talud-tablero* and the characteristic orientation of Teotihuacan architecture. Here, buildings were aligned north-south or sometimes 8–10° east of north. Pottery of these sites was either very similar to or the same as Teotihuacan ceramics.

Tenanyecac culture in the Tlaxcala Block was thus the result of a regional tradition with which new settlers merged. The northern part of the state of Tlaxcala, below the Teotihuacan Sphere, was occupied by groups with Teotihuacan affiliations. To the east, the Teotihuacan Corridor crossed the Tenanyecac region and the lands east of La Malinche. To the south and southwest developed the Cholula culture (Tenanyecac de Valle) with strong Teotihuacan influence as well as culture traits and perhaps people from Oaxaca and the central Gulf Coast.

At this point Tlaxcala played a very important role in the Central Highlands. Tenanyecac groups, supposedly stagnating, were actually undergoing significant political changes.

Small theocratic states disappeared, especially during the middle of this phase, giving way to independent *cacicazgos* or kingdoms concerned more with political and economic control than with technological or religious matters. Economic power had passed from the hands of the priests to those of the military chief or chiefs, or else the priests had surrounded themselves with a military fac-

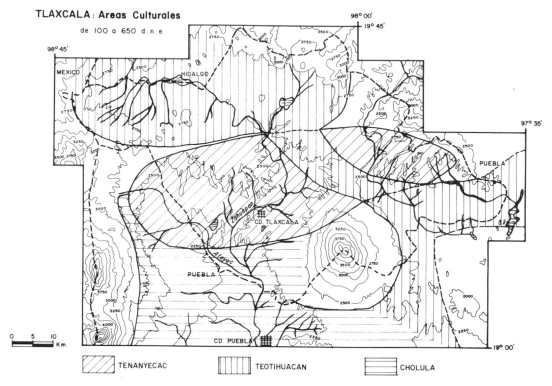

TLAXCALA: Areas Culturales
de 100 a 650 d.n.e.

TENANYECAC          TEOTIHUACAN          CHOLULA

FIGURE 8-27. Culture areas of the Tlaxcala-Puebla region in the Tenanyecac cultural phase.

tion or had acquired a bellicose character themselves. Society took on a different aspect, appearing as a result to share a certain cultural stagnation. Large pyramidal structures, imported or luxury items, and ornaments for the elite were all absent. But agricultural production increased notably through the exploitation of previously unused areas and especially through a system of intensive farming.

The social organization of Tenanyecac differed from that of its local predecessors. Peasants constituted the bulk of the population, followed by a small number of artisans, and very few merchants, perhaps found only in some kingdoms. Above all these were the *caciques* or lords who were warrior-priests or lords perhaps linked by family ties, as was seen later in kingdoms mentioned in historical documents, where power or the reigning house was hereditary. A military class or war-

rior group as such probably did not exist. Rather, the chiefs or leaders made defense plans and directed battles when they took place, and the peasant population served as the army. The strong and complex military organization in the area at the time of the Spaniards' arrival, on the other hand, suggests that there was indeed a small group of specialists in the martial arts who, together with the chiefs, designed defensive sites, organized military tactics, and directed the troops (García Cook 1976b).

In the Tlaxcala-Puebla region lived Tenanyecac groups as well as people related to Teotihuacan (in the north and in the Teotihuacan Corridor) and Cholula (in the south). These three great cultures played a large role in the Central Highlands. On one hand, the Tenanyecac groups brought together independent *cacicazgos* or kingdoms, giving strong direction to social development. On the

268

other hand, Teotihuacan groups living in western Tlaxcala played a more important part than did Teotihuacan groups in the south-central and western parts of the Basin of Mexico (Tlaxcala includes the eastern part of the Basin of Mexico). The Basin of Mexico was characterized by an increasingly rural populace, since more than half its total population—ignoring the east and the northeast—lived in Teotihuacan. About 3 major cities or towns west of the Sierra Nevada and south of Teotihuacan seem important; in the remainder of this part of the basin the population declined 25–50 percent from that of the preceding phase (J. Parsons 1976; Sanders, Parsons, and Santley 1979). In the west and the north were Azcapotzalco and 3 or 4 other important sites. In contrast, Tlaxcala had 21 cities and towns in the Teotihuacan Sphere and Corridor, and the population increased more than 350 percent, compared with the number of proto-Teotihuacan inhabitants. We think this unequal growth occurred because Teotihuacan recognized the importance of having commercial control over groups in the south and on the Gulf Coast (García Cook and Trejo 1977).

The Teotihuacan groups in Tlaxcala, once the city of Teotihuacan was consolidated, were important in the maintenance and permanence of the metropolis. As had been true during the rise of Teotihuacan, those in Tlaxcala played a more vital role than similar groups in the Basin of Mexico, because they controlled the principal commercial route to the Gulf, through Oaxaca, and perhaps Morelos and Guerrero (another route lay toward the eastern slopes of the Sierra Nevada). The subordination and cooperation of the Teotihuacan groups in Tlaxcala seems most effective during the first half of the Classic period at Teotihuacan. During the second half, several important cities or macroregional centers tried to gain autonomy. Teotihuacan centers in Tlaxcala or those with a Teotihuacan tradition figured large in the fall of Teotihuacan, since they dominated the major commercial route connecting the east and the south with the Basin of Mexico. It appears

that they selected which goods would pass through the region, fortifying themselves but blockading and weakening Teotihuacan (García Cook and Trejo 1977).

Tenanyecac groups also encouraged the fall of Teotihuacan because within the region developed a number of ethnically distinct kingdoms—Mixtec, Otomi, Chochopopoloca, and Olmeca-Xicalanca. Some of these became important, as will be shown, and overpowered the city of Cholula, thus contributing to the downfall of Teotihuacan.

Tenanyecac imparts an impression of instability, because it was hemmed in by Teotihuacan to the north and in the corridor and by Cholula to the south and southwest. But these external pressures gave rise to several internal kingdoms. About A.D. 650 a new set of changes and conflicts took place in the region, as the result of both the arrival of new groups and the resettlement and conquest of new lands by others.

## TEXCALAC CULTURAL PHASE
(A.D. 650–1100)

Everything seems to indicate that the Olmeca-Xicalanca, who had been in the area for at least half of Tenanyecac (since about A.D. 300), took over Cholula. Thus the apparent stability of this city and the commercial control it exercised in this zone for the benefit of Teotihuacan were disrupted. This was one of the causes of the fall of Teotihuacan. The Olmeca-Xicalanca established their capital at Cacaxtla, which as a result flourished. From there they controlled the part of the Puebla Valley from the Nativitas Block southward. The Tlaxcala Block and the center of the state benefited from the new status quo. An influx of people from the south merged with the Tenanyecac groups to form a new culture called Texcalac.

With the arrival of these new groups came a technological and cultural renaissance. The Teotihuacan Corridor was closed. Population increased, as did the number of hamlets, villages, and towns. Great secular towns arose, while ranches and dispersed hamlets multiplied. The increasingly scattered settlement pattern seems to indicate the arrival of many families, possibly from Teotihuacan or Cholula, who established dispersed residences; perhaps many of them were descendants of the old Tezoquipan or Tenanyecac settlers who had abandoned the region to take up residence in the cities. The pattern indicates also that political and economic problems prevented the settlers from establishing true cities, so that they could form only large settlements, some covering 8 sq km. Or possibly they chose isolated residences in order to find land which was less exhausted from intensive use during the preceding phases and more protected from erosion. At the same time, they may have tried to stay isolated from the intense military struggle constantly waged over political and economic control.

Fortified sites became more numerous, and strong military control of the populace led to a diminution of religious power. This we infer from the size and arrangement of pyramidal structures, present at only 50 sites, or a decrease of 50 percent from the preceding Tenanyecac phase. Rites associated with war arose. Perhaps the cult of Camaxtli made its appearance, like those of Xipe and Tezcatlipoca, to judge from figurine representations and from statements in documentary sources. The strength of secular or military chiefs grew and was reflected in the steadily rising number of residential structures in comparison with presumed ceremonial buildings. In addition, some of the representations on local figurines were possibly portraits of important personages.

The Texcalac phase is dated A.D. 650–1100, but the territory was not fully consolidated until about 850. During the first part of the phase (A.D. 650–850) internal strife for territorial and political hegemony was intense, and surrounding groups carried on continual struggles. In the last part of this phase (A.D. 850–1100) conditions stabilized with the arrival of new groups, among them the Teochichimecs or Toltec-Chichimecs, who settled in the central part of the Tlaxcala Block and fortified Tepeticpac. Boundaries

were laid out, and the kingdoms or small military states agreed to remain united, respecting each other's independence but cooperating as small confederated states, perhaps under the leadership of the strongest political and military group, which was located at Tepeticpac (García Cook 1976b).

During Early Texcalac (A.D. 650–850) the Olmeca-Xicalanca controlled the region southwest of Tlaxcala, with its principal headquarters in the Nativitas Block and its capital at Cacaxtla (see Fig. 8-28). South of La Malinche and in the southeast sector were groups with Mixtec affiliations. Although they show strong ties to the Olmeca-Xicalanca, we have grouped them under the rubric of Cuauhtinchan-Mixtec. Once Cholula disappeared, they took over that part of the Puebla Valley.

In the north, Early Texcalac also saw a fierce struggle for regional control among its neighbors. It seems that a large number of people with diverse cultural ties carried on continuous battles, while a few groups remained isolated and independent, perhaps often for only short periods. This time of chaos in the northern region of Tlaxcala we have named Acopinalco complex (García Cook and Merino C. 1979). Despite the great political and cultural instability, in the first half of Acopinalco (A.D. 650–750) the strongest groups, who exercised definite regional control, were those with Tajin affiliations (more than 70 percent of the sites show such evidence). They occupied several great towns and towns with certain characteristic traits of Tajin culture. During the second part of Acopinalco (A.D. 750–850) one detects greater control over the populace by the Mixtecs or the Olmeca-Xicalanca. Perhaps the latter group stayed only a short time during their journey to Zacatlan, where the historical sources say they took refuge after leaving southwestern Tlaxcala.

People with first Teotihuacan IV and then Coyotlatelco traditions occupied the northwest during Early Texcalac. These western Tlaxcalans had, since their earliest settlements, continuously maintained ties with the

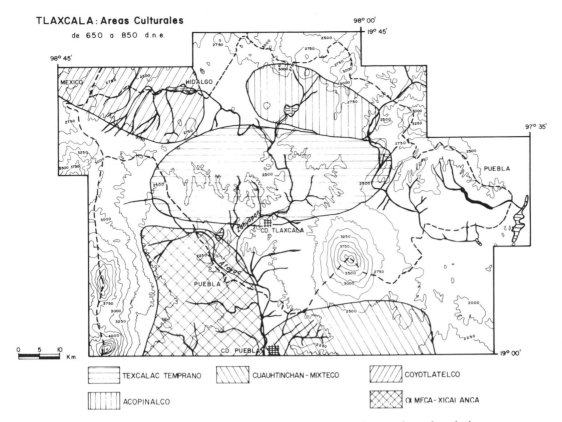

FIGURE 8-28. Culture areas of the Tlaxcala-Puebla region in the Early Texcalac cultural phase.

rest of the Basin of Mexico. They formed a part of the basin in terms of both physical geography and culture (García Cook and Merino C. 1977).

During Late Texcalac (A.D. 850–1100) this culture area was completely defined, its borders were clearly delimited, and the kingdoms or small military states maintained total independence from each other (Fig. 8-29). At the same time, they united to avoid conquest by the newly arriving groups or by residents of the northwest, west, and southwest, who were slowly gaining strength.

Late Texcalac marks the exit of the Olmeca-Xicalanca from the southwest. Perhaps they were expelled about A.D. 850 by the Poyauhteca Chichimecs, who took control and settled in Cholula, turning it back into an important regional capital. Thus the Puebla

Valley was occupied by the Cholulteca culture (ceramic phase Cholulteca II). South and southeast of La Malinche, Cuauhtinchantlaca groups reached their apogee, and even though they maintained ties with the Cholulteca they still had their own culture and were more closely allied with Mixtec groups further south.

A group different from those in the rest of the region gained strength in the north during the Late Texcalac phase. These were Huaxtecs or Otomis influenced by the Huaxtecs. They had been present, though in small numbers and scattered, since the end of Acopinalco, and by A.D. 850 or 900 they had delimited and consolidated their area (García Cook and Merino C. 1979). According to archaeological evidence and documentary sources for later stages, these groups main-

271

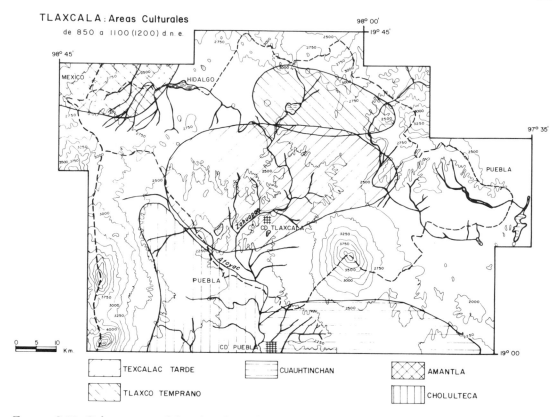

FIGURE 8-29. Culture areas of the Tlaxcala-Puebla region in the Late Texcalàc cultural phase.

tained strong ties with the Texcalac groups, and we think they remained united from this time on, especially for defense against enemy groups surrounding them.

These groups in northern Tlaxcala exhibited traits resembling or duplicating those of the Huaxtecs in northeastern Mexico, such as similar ceramic elements with identical decorative modes, burial patterns, the disposition of settlements, and farming techniques. Their cultural features also resembled those of Late Texcalac and, later, of Tlaxcala, but they had their own characteristics; for this reason and to circumscribe a space and definite time we consider them a local culture, named the Tlaxco culture (García Cook 1978; García Cook and Merino C. 1979; Merino C. 1980).

To the far northwest, completely separated

by a wide unoccupied zone, were groups tied to the Basin of Mexico. Even though they had many cultural features in common with other sites just to the west, such as Huexotla, we nonetheless think they were independent kingdoms. They alone controlled all the northwestern part of Tlaxcala, and we have labeled them the Amantla culture. This was the name of one of the most important settlements of this period (others were Palo Hueco and Mal Pais). From this point on these were bitter enemies of their neighbors to the southeast.

The Texcalac culture, surrounded by the groups mentioned above, kept up relations with groups south of Puebla—Huehuetlan, Izucar, and Tepexi—perhaps by way of Cuauhtinchan and Cholula. Contact was certain with the central Gulf Coast, very strong

272

with the Huaxtec area and the rest of the Puebla Valley, but very limited with the Basin of Mexico.

At the beginning, then, Texcalac culture was involved in a series of struggles, both internal and among its neighbors to the north and the south. During the middle part of the phase, additional changes and consolidation took place in the Tlaxco culture to the north. A large number of intellectuals and soldiers, the Olmeca-Xicalanca, left the region. Most of the important Tenanyecac sites, some of which had persisted during the first half of Texcalac, such as the Olmeca-Xicalanca sites in the Nativitas Block, suffered a massive depopulation. But a large number of people were arriving from the Basin of Mexico. First came the Poyauhteca Chichimecs, then the Teochichimecs or Toltec-Chichimecs, the Mixtecs from the Ñuiñe area and lands controlled by Cuauhtinchan in southern Puebla, and the Huaxtecs or Huaxtec-influenced Otomis from the north-central Gulf Coast. The Texcalac phase saw a new regional florescence with the arrival of these peoples, especially those from the south, who injected new culture into the area, and the Chichimecs, who consolidated and defined Texcalac culture proper. The population increased, making use of all available land for farming. All power lay in the hands of the military class, now fully defined. Settlements and major population centers increased and were now situated in inaccessible and easily defensible places. They were concentrated toward the center of the Tlaxcala Block, in the Cerros Blancos, where the completely fortified site of Tepeticpac was built. This played a large role in the following phase (García Cook 1976b; García Cook and Mora López 1974).

The Tlaxcala territory which the Spanish found when they arrived in 1519 originated during the Texcalac phase. Government was based on a confederation of small states or kingdoms, of which Tepeticpac was one of the most important.

## Tlaxcala Cultural Phase (A.D. 1100–1519)

By A.D. 1100 the Tlaxcala territory had taken the form it had in 1519, and we think the large Tlaxcalan kingdoms mentioned in the documents made their appearance from this time on, although Tepeticpac was well established a bit before. This final stage in the regional development of central Tlaxcala, dating from A.D. 1100 until 1519, when the Spaniards arrived and abruptly cut off local development, we have named Tlaxcala.

The Tlaxcala phase comprehends all the groups that lived in central Tlaxcala and developed the culture which the Spanish conquerors found upon their arrival. None of the names of individual kingdoms was used for this last phase, in order to avoid giving the impression that any one kingdom exercised hegemony over the others.

Documentary sources and several historians say that four kingdoms made up the Republic or Senate of Tlaxcala: Tepeticpac, Ocotelulco, Tizatlan, and Quiahuiztlan. We believe there were more, some mentioned in the sources themselves. Charles Gibson (1952:12–13) notes that neither the conquerors nor the earlier chroniclers indicated the presence of only four kingdoms; rather, this version was introduced a little over two decades later. Indeed, the first narratives, including those of Cortés, Bernal Díaz del Castillo, and Sahagún, listed others, such as Tepeyanco, Atlihuetzian, Hueyotlipan, Tecoac, and Tzompantzinco (Gibson 1952; Muñoz Camargo 1947; Davies 1968). The four well-known kingdoms appear to have played a very important role because of their geographic position, especially during the founding of the colonial city of Tlaxcala. Perhaps they were feared and respected as well because of their strategic location and because they possessed the fortification of Tepeticpac, where leaders could take refuge in case of attacks by the Mexicas or their allies. Archaeological remains corroborate the existence of the above sites and others: Xaltocan, Chiauhtempan, Huiloapan, Tlacocalpan, Xalpetlahuaya-Quimicho, Yauhquemecan, Xipe-tzingo, and Temetzontla. I deny neither the importance of Tepeticpac, Ocotelulco, Tizatlan, and Quiahuitzlan nor the definite connections among their ruling dynasties. I do want to clarify that archaeological studies indicate that other centers were of equal or greater importance.

The organization of Tlaxcalan culture probably resembled that of the Texcalac phase, based on a confederation of small military states or groups of kingdoms. These stayed in power by force of arms and controlled the bulk of the rural populace, as well as the artisans and merchants, who because of their profession enjoyed a better position than the rural majority. Documentary sources say that in at least three of the four best-known kingdoms rulership was hereditary. This was not so in others; in Quiahuitzlan, for example, accession to government office was through election (Muñoz Camargo 1947). We think that this pattern of attaining power by inheritance or voting was widespread among the other kingdoms, whose development we believe paralleled that of the four best known. Leadership was probably inherited in the majority of cases and acquired through voting in others. Quite possibly stronger kingdoms interfered when conflicts occurred during elections of leaders in smaller kingdoms. In the region of Cuauhtinchan, according to the documents (Reyes 1975), new chiefs or lords were invested with authority in Cholula, and later in Tenochtitlan. In central Tlaxcala, chiefs or governors and also knights could well have been sworn into office in several of the kingdoms that were stronger economically and politically, such as Ocotelulco or Tepeticpac.

The Tlaxcala culture occupied only the Tlaxcala Block, an area of 1,400 sq km in the center of the state of Tlaxcala (Fig. 8-30). The rest of the state, along with the Puebla Valley, remained inhabited by groups with different traditions, some in conflict with the people of the Tlaxcalan culture.

Just to the southwest, separated by an uninhabited corridor, a culture strongly linked with the Basin of Mexico developed alongside Tlaxcala, although it had its own characteristics. We have called this the Cholula-Huejotzingo culture because these two places were the principal centers of the area. Cholula-Huejotzingo culture interacted with the south and was strongly controlled by the Mexicas in the Basin of Mexico. It maintained contacts with Tlaxcalan groups and on various occasions joined them against the Mexicas. Cultural differences are visible, however, and most of the time the Cholula-Huejotzingo people served on the side of the Mexicas in attacks against Tlaxcala.

Groups ruled principally by Cuauhtinchan settled in the southeast. Despite their local traditions, they were always tied to the Mixtecs to the south. Tepeaca took over this zone when the Mexicas conquered the Mixtecs. Although these groups were closely bound to the Cholultecans and were later under the Mexicas, they were distinguished by their closer relations with groups immediately to the south.

In the northwest, again separated from the Tlaxcalans by a wide uninhabited zone, lived people who shared the culture of the rest of the Basin of Mexico, which first Texcoco and then the Mexicas themselves controlled. From the earliest occupation, this northwestern part of the state of Tlaxcala had the same culture as the basin, particularly the northeastern part of the basin, of which it formed a geographical as well as cultural part (García Cook and Merino C. 1977).

In northern Tlaxcala, groups of the Tlaxco culture were contiguous with the Tlaxcalans. These, as we have mentioned, were Huaxtec-influenced Otomis and seem to have belonged to what the documents call the Kingdom of Tliliuhquetepec (García Cook and Merino C. 1979). They maintained close relations with the Tlaxcalan groups, whom they frequently joined to oppose the Mexicas threatening to absorb them. They also observed strong ties with north-central Veracruz and the Huaxtecs in general.

During this final Prehispanic stage a small zone of ca. 50 sq km within the Tlaxco cul-

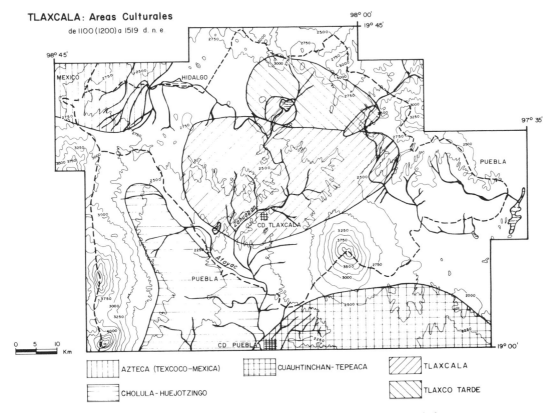

FIGURE 8-30. Culture areas of the Tlaxcala-Puebla region in the Tlaxcala cultural phase.

ture had a great number of Tlaxcala cultural elements. This area, we think, corresponded to the Kingdom of Atlangatepec, also mentioned in historical sources. In the far east of the Tlaxco region, merging with Tlaxcalan groups, was a small region with equal proportions of Tlaxco and Tlaxcala features. This we consider the Kingdom of Tecoac, occupied by Otomis and Tlaxcaltecs at the arrival of the Spanish conquerors.

In 1519 the groups just mentioned occupied the state of Tlaxcala and the northern part of the Puebla Valley. This region, above all the Tlaxcalans, played a very important role in the conquest of Mexico, as they cooperated with the newcomers in defeating the Mexicas and later in colonizing other regions of Mexico.

It can be seen, then, that the Tlaxcala area

played a strong part throughout the history of the Central Highlands. First developed the great Tezoquipan culture, whose technological knowledge and advances crystallized in the creation of Teotihuacan and Cholula. Later the Tlaxcala area participated in the overthrow of both cities and maintained control of the region. Finally, this area contributed to the defeat of the Mexicas at Tenochtitlan and, thus, to the beginning of a new culture, Mexico.

NOTES

1. Maguey stems, called *quiote*, are still prepared in the same manner.

2. Some "secular towns," especially during the late phases, had no monumental architecture. A certain distribution within residential areas, how-

ever, indicates a social difference between the urban and rural classes.

3. This is true especially for Tlaxcala at this time, since in the Puebla Valley, Cholula and sites such as Chachapa and Manzanilla flourished later.

4. A recent publication by William T. Sanders, Jeffrey R. Parsons, and Robert S. Santley (1979) included information from drawings prepared for a symposium on the archaeology of Central Mexico presented at the 1976 International Congress of Americanists in Paris. This information has been distorted, perhaps to justify the theoretical positions of these investigators.

Map 20 of their 1979 work, "Central Mexican Symbiotic Region: Middle Horizon Settlement," omits original information presented in Paris and modifies the legend as convenient (I have the original maps in my possession). This unscientific attitude ignores conclusions based on our intensive studies in the Puebla-Tlaxcala region.

Sanders, Parsons, and Santley excluded the following information: symbols for the regional centers; sites in strategic positions; fortified and unfortified macroregional centers; primary and secondary centers; military lookouts; garrisons and fortified hamlets. Thus, they present the completely false idea of a totally peaceful, symbiotic region. The authors eliminated both the "Teotihuacan Corridor," which my investigations established, and the idea of an unstable social environment. The abundance of defensive or strategically placed sites shows this instability, as does the non-participation of most settlements in Teotihuacan culture or political control.

# 9. Tula

*RICHARD A. DIEHL*

W HEN THERE THEY [the Tolteca] went—they went to live, to dwell on the banks of a river at Xicocotitlan, now called Tula. Because verily they resided together, they there dwelt, so also many are their traces which they produced. And they left behind that which today is there, which is to be seen, which they did not finish—the so-called serpent column, the round stone pillar made into a serpent. Its head rests on the ground; its tail, its rattles are above. And the Tolteca mountain is to be seen; and the Tolteca pyramids, the mounds, and the surfacing of Tolteca temples. And Tolteca potsherds are there to be seen. And Tolteca bowls, Tolteca ollas are taken from the earth. And many times Tolteca jewels—arm bands, esteemed green stones, emerald-green jade—are taken from the earth.

(Sahagún 1961: 165)

Bernardino de Sahagún's informants and other sixteenth-century chroniclers believed that the Toltecs had created Central Mexican civilization and that their capital, Tollan, had been located at Tula, Hidalgo. Archaeological investigations have shown that the first belief was mistaken and that complex cultures existed as long ago as the Formative period. Tula's claim as the Toltec capital, however, is accepted by most, though not all, modern writers. This "orthodox view" stems from Wigberto Jiménez Moreno's (1941) analysis of Colonial period documents, Jorge R. Acosta's twenty seasons of archaeological investigations at Tula, and Pedro Armillas's (1950) comparison of Teotihuacan and Tula. The most recent exhaustive treatment of the subject is by Nigel Davies (1977), who basically agrees with the orthodox view.

Not everyone is convinced, however. Enrique Palacios (1941), Laurette Séjourné (1954), and Robert Chadwick (1971b) have argued that Teotihuacan or even Tilantongo, Oaxaca, was the Tollan of Mexica legend. Although the research reported here has not produced data which can resolve the conflict, I believe the orthodox view is correct.

Although Désirée de Charnay and Antonio García Cubas had excavated at Tula in the nineteenth century, Acosta conducted the first modern archaeological investigations during an INAH project which lasted from 1940 until 1960 (Acosta 1940, 1941, 1945,

1956a, 1956b, 1956–1957, 1957, 1960, 1961a, 1961b, 1964a). Several articles in Volumes 10 and 11 of the *Handbook of Middle American Indians* discussed Acosta's work, and I refer the interested reader to them and to Acosta's original reports.

The INAH renewed research at Tula in 1968 under the direction of Eduardo Matos Moctezuma. This project has included settlement pattern surveys, large and small excavations, and ethnohistorical investigations. Some of the results have been published by Matos Moctezuma (1974a, 1976) and Juan Yadeún Angulo (1975). Although the following pages primarily deal with data collected by the University of Missouri-Columbia (UMC) Tula Archaeological Project, information from Matos Moctezuma's project will be mentioned where appropriate.

The research in the past decade has resulted in the introduction of several new terms for Tula archaeological features, and it seems best to define them at this point, since they may be unfamiliar to the reader.

Tula Grande is the area of the major civic-religious structures on the site. The principal buildings include Pyramids B and C, Ballcourts 1 and 2, the Palacio Quemado, the Palacio Quetzalcoatl, the Tzompantli, and the Adoratorio. The term Tula Grande was coined by the INAH project, and it replaces the term Main Ceremonial Precinct which I used in earlier publications.

Tula Chico is a group of medium-sized mounds located 1 km north of Tula Grande. The mound layout is similar to that of Tula Grande, but the complex was constructed early in the city's history and was not in use during the Tollan phase florescence.

The Acropolis is a large architectural macrocomplex located in the central part of the city; it includes Tula Grande and other architectural units. It is bounded by steeply sloping artificial faces on the north, east, and west sides and perhaps on the south as well.

Ballcourt 1 is a large I-shaped structure at the north edge of Tula Grande which was excavated and partially restored by Acosta.

Ballcourt 2 is a large I-shaped ballcourt located on the west edge of Tula Grande which Matos Moctezuma excavated and consolidated in 1969.

El Corral is a Tollan phase temple mound located about 2 km north of Tula Grande. It combines round and rectangular elements and probably was dedicated to the Ehecatl cult.

Toltec Small Stone Facing is a wall veneer constructed of small tabular limestone pieces laid horizontally and covered with stucco. It was used extensively in public buildings and occasionally in residences.

The Corral Locality is a room complex 30 m east of the El Corral temple excavated by the UMC project in 1970.

The Canal Locality is a series of residential complexes located several hundred meters southwest of the El Corral temple near the Endho Canal. It was excavated by the UMC Project between 1970 and 1972.

A House is a physically discrete series of contiguous and interconnected rooms which served as a residence for one or two nuclear families.

A House Group is a cluster of Houses which form a compound.

## History and Objectives of the UMC Tula Archaeological Project

The fieldwork phase of the UMC project lasted from 1970 until 1972; data and artifact analysis were finished by the end of 1979. I was the project director in 1970, and Robert A. Benfer has been codirector since 1971.

The project attempted to collect information on various topics which Acosta had either neglected or treated in a superficial fashion. These include chronology, settlement and community patterns, domestic architecture, economy, social and political organization, and religion (Diehl 1974:1). The basic aims were to (1) collect information on non-elite activities and (2) document the dynamic aspects of Toltec history and culture.

Excavation and survey were the primary data collection techniques. The excavations emphasized extensive horizontal clearing of residences at two places in a zone of dense surface debris near the northern edge of the city. In addition, stratigraphic test pits were dug in Tula Chico, El Cielito, an obsidian workshop area, and the El Tesoro site at Tepeji del Rio, Hidalgo. The major excavations were generally terminated at the floor levels of the uppermost well-defined structures, but test pits were excavated to bedrock to check for earlier remains. Descriptions of the excavation methodology can be found in Diehl, Benfer, and Healan 1974 and Healan 1974a.

Although a small regional survey was made in the area around Tula (Cobean 1974a), the main survey effort concentrated on the Tula urban zone. James Stoutamire conducted this survey in two stages: first he defined the outer boundaries of the ancient community; then he conducted a systematic surface collection of artifacts within those boundaries. The survey methodologies are described in Stoutamire 1974, 1975.

## THE RESULTS OF THE UMC TULA ARCHAEOLOGICAL PROJECT
### Chronology

I had several reservations about Acosta's chronology when the project began. In the first place, it was based on a small sample of test pits in the Tula Grande area of the site. I was also uneasy about the degree to which the chronology depended on ceramic cross-ties with poorly defined Basin of Mexico phases. Finally the absolute dates were derived from confused and often contradictory sixteenth-century legendary accounts. It is now apparent that Acosta's chronology was more valid than I anticipated, and in fact I now have a much higher opinion of his overall research at Tula than I did in 1970.

The new Tula chronology is a result of ceramic studies by Robert Cobean (1974b, 1978) and is aided by C14 assays. The ceramic samples he studied included materials from the Canal and Corral Locality excavations, the UMC urban zone survey, and the INAH test pits at Tula Chico. The occupa-

tional sequence is divided into seven ceramic phases; the earliest begins at ca. A.D. 700, and the latest extends into the Early Colonial period (Table 9-1).

PRADO PHASE (A.D. 700–800). The Prado phase is the earliest occupation the UMC project has data on, but Alba Guadalupe Mastache de Escobar and Ana María Crespo have recently discovered Formative and Classic remains under Tula de Allende. The absolute dates for the Prado phase are guesses based on equally problematic Basin of Mexico dates. The ceramics are similar to the Coyotlatelco complex (Tozzer 1921; Rattray 1966; Nichols 1975) in the basin, but the principal diagnostic types have closer ties with Late Classic materials in the Bajio of Queretaro, Guanajuato, and Michoacan than with basin Coyotlatelco types. The diagnostic types are Guadalupe Red-on-Brown Incised, Ana Maria Red-on-Brown, and Clara Luz Black Incised. Tripod cylindrical vases reminiscent of Teotihuacan examples are the most common form. Surface decoration emphasizes red painted "Coyotlatelco-like" designs and elaborate incised motifs.

The similarities to ceramics from the northern frontier suggest to Cobean (1978:627) that an elite group from the north or west established itself over the indigenous population of the area at this time. Prado phase materials have been found in excavations at Tula Chico and are present but rare in other parts of the urban zone and the surrounding settlements.

CORRAL PHASE (A.D. 800–900). The Corral phase marks the first substantial occupation at Tula. Cobean (1978:628) reports that "most Corral pottery is nearly identical to analogous Coyotlatelco sphere types in the Basin of Mexico" but suggests a continuation of ties with the Bajio and the general northern Mesoamerican frontier. The principal diagnostic types include Coyotlatelco Red-on-Brown and Rito Red-on-Cream. The surfaces are smoothed or polished, and Coyotlatelco-style red painted designs are the typical decoration. The monochrome wares are analogous to Basin of Mexico Coyotlatelco types;

TABLE 9-1. Chronology for the Tula Area

|  | Phases Tula Area | Phases Basin of Mexico | Periods |
|---|---|---|---|
| A.D. 1519–? | Tesoro | Aztec IV | Colonial |
| 1300–1519 | Palacio | Aztec III and IV | Late Horizon/Late Postclassic |
| 1150/1200–1300 | Fuego | Aztec II and III | Second Intermediate/Early Postclassic |
| 950–1150/1200 | Tollan | Mazapan | |
| 900–950 | Terminal Corral | Coyotlatelco | |
| 800–900 | Corral | | |
| 700–800 | Prado | | |

they include *ollas*, *comales*, and unfooted bowls. The Corral complex is a complete complex in that it contains all the functional types in use at the time, as opposed to the incomplete nature of the Prado phase complex as it is presently known. The Tula Chico mound complex appears to have been the major civic-religious zone at this time, but Tula Grande's possible importance cannot be ruled out until its early construction history is better understood.

TERMINAL CORRAL (A.D. 900–950). Terminal Corral is a poorly known provisional phase. The best evidence for it was found in Tula Chico and in subfloor fill at the Corral Locality.

Joroba Orange-on-Cream and Mazapa Red-on-Brown are the two major diagnostic types. The former has orange painted volutes on a cream background; the latter has wavy-line red painted designs. Hemispherical bowls and flat-bottomed dishes are the most frequent forms. As suggested above, the status of this phase is ambiguous. It has never been found in a clearly defined stratigraphic context, but the diagnostic types are rare or absent in the earlier Corral and later Tollan phases. Its importance in the social and political evolution of Tula is difficult to assess, but this was a critical time in the city's history because it immediately preceded Tula's emergence as a pan-Mesoamerican power center.

TOLLAN PHASE (A.D. 950–1150/1200). The Tollan phase was the time when Tula grew to its maximum size and importance. The Tula Chico complex was abandoned, a cult center to the foreign Huastec deity Ehecatl was established at the nearby El Corral complex, and Tula Grande became the sociopolitical center of the city.

I will not describe the Tollan phase ceramic complex at length (interested readers can consult Acosta 1956–1957; Chadwick 1971b; and Cobean 1974b for published descriptions and illustrations and Cobean 1978 for a detailed analysis of the materials). Suffice it to say that the complex emphasizes orange and cream wares but also contains red-on-brown types. The light-colored wares are part of a general Central Mexican transition from earlier red-on-browns to Postclassic oranges; however Cobean does not view the Tula orange wares as directly ancestral to Aztec orange ceramics. The virtual absence of Wavy-line Mazapan Red-on-Buff pottery is noteworthy; it has heretofore been considered a Tula-Toltec diagnostic, but our data show this is not true.

Seven carbonized wood samples from the Canal Locality excavations have been radiocarbon-dated by Professor Minze Stuiver of the University of Washington (Table 9-2). The samples came from two contexts, hearths and possible roof beam fragments. We hesitated to submit the possible beam

TABLE 9-2. Radiocarbon Dates for the Tollan Phase (processed by the University of Washington)

| Sample | UMC Project Identification Number | Date | Comments |
|--------|-----------------------------------|------|----------|
| QL-129 | 02092033 | Recent | Hearth, considered invalid |
| QL-130 | 03409030 | 1020 ± 50 (A.D. 900–1000) | Possible hearth or beam fragment, considered valid |
| QL-131 | 039140020 | Too small, insufficient yield | Associated with kiln, considered invalid |
| QL-132 | 03314020 | 1130 ± 70 (A.D. 900–1000) | Hearth, considered valid |
| QL-1020 | 0320840 | 1110 ± 40 (A.D. 900–1000) | Possible beam fragment, considered valid |
| QL-1021 | 06050080 | 1070 ± 70 (A.D. 900–1000) | Hearth, considered valid |
| QL-1022 | 06042070 | 360 ± 40 | Hearth or oven, considered invalid |

fragments in light of the problems sometimes associated with such samples (cf. R. Millon 1973:60–61; Kovar 1966) but did so because the absence of significantly older structures in the area decreased the possibility that they were from older, reused beams. Three samples (QL-129, QL-131, and QL-1022) did not provide useful dates for various reasons. The other four show that the houses and associated Tollan phase ceramics were in use between A.D. 900 and 1000 in calendric time. The MASCA correlation factors suggest that QL-1021 and QL-1022 are somewhat older than the calendric dates, but it seems best not to read too much into four samples. These samples do not provide beginning or ending dates for the Tollan phase; only a good sample series from earlier and later contexts can do that. However I suspect that the traditional date of ca. A.D. 1200 for the fall of Tula is at least a century too late because I believe the excavated structures were abandoned near or at the time of that event. Cobean (personal communication, 1979) accepts the A.D. 1200 date for Tula's fall. It is to be hoped that this reaffirms the old adage that two reasonable people can interpret the same facts in different ways; in any case it certainly demonstrates that the facts do not speak for themselves.

## The Urban Zone Survey

The urban zone survey had four basic objectives: (1) determination of the limits of the ancient occupied area; (2) definition of the community settlement patterns and their changes through time; (3) estimation of the population density and total population during the city's history; and (4) identification of special activity areas.

The data have not been completely analyzed, so some of the results are tentative. I am confident about the size of the total occupied area, the distribution of Tollan phase ceramics, and the distribution of total lithic remains, but the conclusions about pre– and post–Tollan phase occupations may change.

The survey field and laboratory techniques have been discussed by Stoutamire (1974, 1975) and will not be repeated here.

The Tula urban zone boundaries are shown in Fig. 9-1. They enclose 14 sq km, 13 of which show evidence of Prehispanic occupation. The other 1 sq km contains the El Salitre swamp, which was not occupied but probably provided water fowl, reeds, and other aquatic products and the name Tollan ("place of the *tule* reeds"). The outer boundaries of the 14 sq km mark the edge of continuous archaeological debris from two major periods of occupation, the Tollan and Palacios phases, but do not define the limits of a single community at one given point in time.

The archaeological site occupies a ridge overlooking the Rio Tula and the adjacent low-lying areas. The Rio Rosas joins the Tula inside the site limits, and another stream may have flowed north along the route of the now abandoned Endho Canal, which follows an obvious older natural drainage feature. Most of the site lies east of the Rio Tula, but it also covers the west banks on the lower edges of Cerro Mogone, the Rio Rosas, and Cerro La Malinche. The area under the town of Tula de Allende was occupied, but the remains are almost completely obliterated by modern construction.

Tula's major public buildings are concentrated in Tula Grande and Tula Chico. Tula Grande is located at the southern edge of the main ridge overlooking the confluence of the Tula and Rosas rivers. All the buildings investigated so far were erected during the Tollan phase but may contain earlier interior constructions. Tula Chico, as mentioned above, is a group of moderate-sized mounds located about 1 km north of Tula Grande (Matos Moctezuma 1974b). The complex was constructed, used, and abandoned prior to the Tollan phase. It is so devoid of Tollan phase debris that it apparently did not even serve as a garbage dump, suggesting that it had a very special significance to the Tollan phase people.

The total surface refuse is heaviest in the northeastern section of the site, the same general area with the longest occupational history. The heavy refuse is a result of dense Tollan phase habitation rather than the long occupation span per se. Since the preliminary-survey ceramic analysis was done before Cobean refined the ceramic sequence and the collections have not yet been reanalyzed, I will discuss the results in terms of three general phases; pre-Tollan (Prado, Corral, and Terminal Corral), Tollan, and Aztec (Fuego, Palacio, and Tesoro).

Pre–Tollan phase materials are only found north of a line connecting Tula Grande and El Salitre and east of the Rio Tula; the highest density is centered on Tula Chico. The areas south of the line and west of the river were apparently unoccupied at this time. Our survey procedures included collecting all the surface debris from selected 10 m squares in each grid unit on the site; counts of these ceramics show a maximum density of 1.5 sherds per collection unit, indicating a very light occupation at this time.

Tollan phase debris is by far the heaviest component on the site surface. The maximum density of Tollan phase sherds is 30 per collection unit, and most of the occupied area had at least 5 sherds per collection unit. The refuse density is greatest in the northeast, but the entire area east of the Rio Tula had at least moderate debris and the habitation area spread to the west bank of the Rio Tula. Thirteen sq km contain Tollan phase debris; 10.75 had minimum densities of 5 sherds per collection unit. The remaining 2.25 sq km were either very lightly occupied or not used for habitation.

Obsidian tools and debris occur in large quantities at various places on the site; unfortunately most of it cannot be unequivocally assigned to a specific phase in areas with multiple components. The raw counts show a peak of 50-plus pieces per collection unit east of El Salitre and decline as one moves away from that zone. The large quantities of cores, small chips, other manufacturing debris, and tools indicate the presence of workshops in a 1.5–2 sq km area.

Calculations of the total urban population

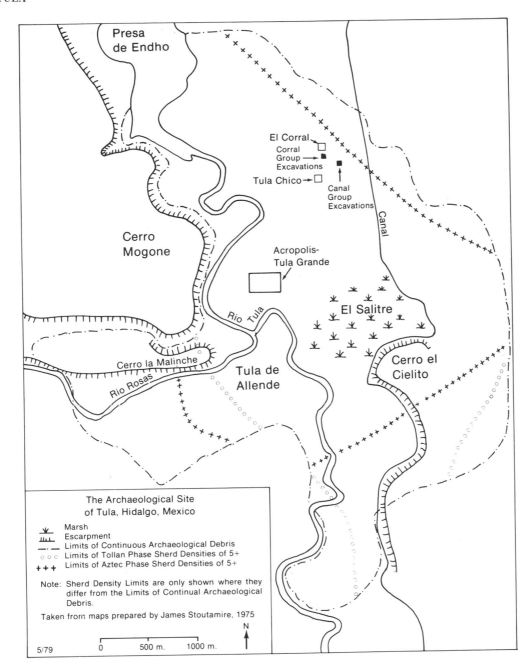

FIGURE 9-1. The archaeological site of Tula.

are difficult to make in the absence of population density figures. We have used an average of 5,000 people per sq km in the past (Diehl and Benfer 1975; Stoutamire 1975) and will do so here, but this is little more than a guess based upon ethnographic data from the Teotihuacan Valley (Sanders 1965; Diehl 1970). The variations in Tollan phase refuse density suggest similar variations in population density, and these must be taken into account before reasonably accurate population estimates can be made. Unfortunately our excavation data are not much help because it appears that our houses were more closely spaced than those in other parts of the site. If the 10.75 sq km Tollan phase core area had an average density of 5,000 people per sq km, the total population was about 53,000 people. I believe this figure is too high and that it should be reduced by 30 or 40 percent, leaving 32,000–37,000 inhabitants.

## Architecture

The Canal and Corral Locality excavations uncovered almost 2,000 sq m of architectural remains. Dan M. Healan has analyzed the Canal Locality excavations in detail, and much of the following section is based on his work (1974a, 1974b, 1977). The Canal Locality temple data come from Terrance L. Stocker's reports on his excavations (1974, n.d.) and the Corral Locality summary is based on a manuscript by Margaret Mandeville (n.d.).

Approximately 60 rooms, corridors, and courtyards were partially or totally excavated in the Canal Group (Fig. 9-2). Healan (1977) has grouped them into 15 multi-room Houses and 3 larger units called House Groups. The buildings consist of square or rectangular rooms with limestone block foundations, stone and adobe block walls, and flat roofs (Fig. 9-3). Most walls apparently lacked special facings, but a few had lime plaster facings or small tabular limestone façades covered with white plaster. These Toltec Small Stone Facings were primarily used on courtyard facings and altars in the courtyards. Most floors were simple compacted earth

surfaces, but a few had lime plaster coverings. Several kitchens were identified by the presence of hearths and food preparation and serving utensils. In situ metates in and around courtyards indicate that some food preparation prior to cooking was done outside when possible. Two hearth types were defined: simple floor-level affairs sometimes surrounded by stones, and stone-lined fireboxes sunk into floors. Six subfloor burials were found in the Canal Locality; more might have been located had we excavated more extensively in the subfloor areas. Although a few burials contained offerings, none were elaborate enough to indicate social status distinctions.

Special-function architectural features include courtyard altars, deep subfloor storage pits, and a kiln. Each courtyard had an altar or shrine in the center. Although all had been badly damaged by ancient looting, enough remained to show that they were low, rectangular or square platforms with sloping *talud* walls. At least one was decorated with tenoned carved stone human skulls. The looting and occasional human teeth and bones in the fill suggest that the altars contained well-stocked burials, perhaps of senior kinsmen.

Two adjacent rooms in House II contained rectangular storage pits excavated into the floors and lined with adobe blocks. One had a small stairway-like entrance and several adobe blocks on the floor which may have served as shelf supports. Nine exotic pottery vessels found behind one shelf support included four Central American Papagayo polychrome pieces and five Plumbate vessels (Diehl, Lomas, and Wynn 1974). The second pit was empty. Two pits in adjacent rooms indicate special activity involving large-scale storage.

The kiln was a rectangular affair constructed of unmodified rocks. The walls and floor were burned bright red, and some of the stones had vitrified surfaces. Large potsherds from many different vessels covered sections of the kiln; our workers, who are also potters, suggested that they were used to re-

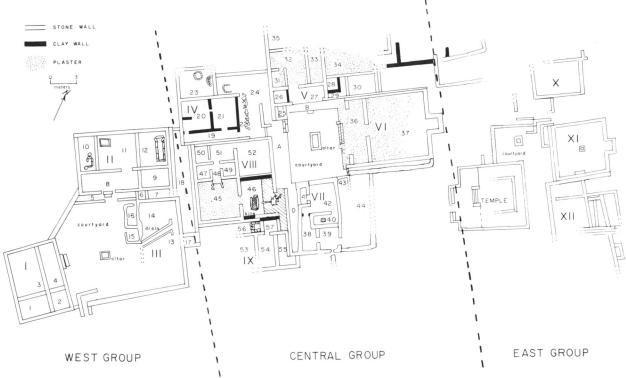

FIGURE 9-2. Ground plan of the Canal Locality architecture. Roman numerals designate Houses; arabic numerals designate rooms. The rectangular features in rooms 11 and 12 are subfloor storage pits. Drawn by Dan M. Healan.

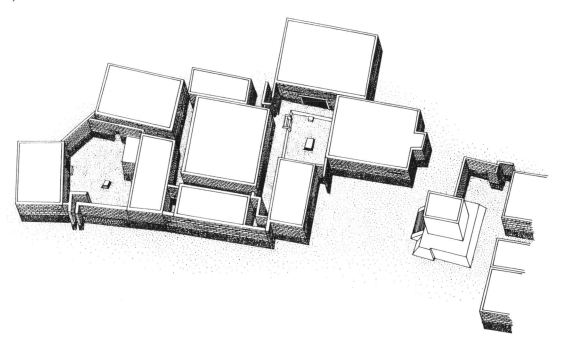

FIGURE 9-3. Reconstruction drawing of the Canal Locality Houses and Temple. Drawn by Dan M. Healan.

285

tain the heat. Debris from misfired or broken objects was not found, so we are not certain what was fired in the kiln, but a nearby pile of ceramic drain tubes may represent the kiln products. Identical tubes form an in situ drain system under the residences, and similar tubes apparently were placed in roofs to facilitate rainwater runoff. The absence of identifiable ceramic-working tools, molds, or raw clay in the Canal Locality Excavations may indicate that unfired pieces were brought in from elsewhere to be fired.

A small temple was found at the eastern edge of the Canal Locality. The rectangular platform had a stairway facing west, and superstructure wall and floor remnants were still visible. Stocker (1974) has defined four Tollan phase construction stages in the platform. Stage I, the earliest, measured 4.5 m east-west by 3.8 m north-south and 1 m high. The Stage I superstructure consisted of two tiny rooms with plaster floors sunk 40 cm below the platform surface. The Stage II platform was only slightly larger than its predecessor and appears to have used the same superstructure, although a new set of balustraded stairs were built over the old ones. In Stage III the north and east platform walls were not altered, but the south and west walls were enlarged and a new balustraded stairway was built. The Stage IV platform was considerably larger than its predecessors and included additions to all four sides. The final dimensions were 7.5 m north-south, 8.5 m east-west and 1.0 m high. The shape was altered by adding small "wings" or extensions to the north and south walls at the front or west side. The stairway was much wider than the earlier ones but lacked balustrades. The single-room Stage IV superstructure is represented by lime plaster floor fragments and adobe wall stubs; it measured 2.3 by 1.2 m and had an open porch leading to the stairs. Rough limestone blocks set in mud mortar were the basic construction materials for all phases, although remnants of Toltec Small Stone Facings were found with Stages I and IV. Numerous large Tlaloc-effigy incensario fragments suggest that the temple was dedi-

cated to this deity, although such incensarios may have been used in buildings and rituals associated with other gods and activities.

The Corral Locality excavations exposed seven complete rooms and portions of twelve others; unfortunately not enough was excavated to clarify the room arrangement. The structures were erected in the Tollan phase, but the subfloor fill contained Corral and Terminal Corral ceramics. The major weight-bearing walls were constructed of rough stone blocks laid in mud mortar; in some cases earth walls were added later to partition large rooms into smaller units. Two adjacent rooms each contained four column bases; these appear to have supported vertical wood columns which in turn supported the roofs. Other unusual architectural features were noted. One room had a small rectangular altar with a sloping *talud* and slightly overhanging cornice constructed against the south wall. The *talud* surface was made of broken potsherds laid horizontally in a manner imitating the Toltec Small Stone Facing style. A burial inside the altar contained the seated remains of an adult male minus his skull, which may have ended up on a *tzompantli*, and three nondescript pots. A small open box made of metate fragments was built into the floor north of the altar; it contained only soil.

The unusual architectural features and the artifact inventory all suggest that the Corral Locality was not an ordinary residence. The occupants may have been involved with the nearby El Corral temple; perhaps they were priests attached to it. Unfortunately we did not have the resources and time to expand the excavations further.

## The Economy

We have a considerable fund of data on economic matters in the Toltec city. The information is incomplete on every topic but is of interest in itself and provides relevant background material for future studies. In the following section I will combine the archaeological data with ethnohistorical information collected by Lawrence H. Feldman (1974a, 1974b).

AGRICULTURE. Although agriculture was obviously the mainstay of the Tula economy, the evidence for crops and techniques is still incomplete. Steven Armsey floated soil samples from the excavations to recover carbonized plant remains; these remains have been identified by Richard Ford at the University of Michigan Museum Paleobotanical Laboratory. The identified seed fragments include *Zea* sp. (maize), *Chenopodium* sp. (chenopodium), *Opuntia* sp. (*nopal*), *Amaranthus* sp. (amaranth), *Portulaca* sp. (*verdolaga*), *Prunus* sp. (*capulín*), *Diospyros* sp. (persimmon), and *Prosopis* sp. (mesquite).

According to Sahagún, the Toltecs grew maize (1961:169), squash, amaranth, chile, maguey for *pulque*, cotton, and cacao (1952: 14–17). The latter two items were almost certainly imported from lower, more temperate zones, although Feldman (1974b:Table 19) notes that two sixteenth-century towns near Ixmiquilpan grew cotton. Beans were not identified or mentioned by Sahagún, but since they grow in the area today, their absence in Prehispanic times is undoubtedly more apparent than real.

The wood fragments in the identified samples include *Pinus* sp. (pine), *Quercus* sp. (oak), *Juniperus* sp. (juniper), *Prosopis* sp. (mesquite), *Prunus* sp. (*capulín*), and *Agave* sp. (maguey). The first three may have been used for construction or firewood; the remainder were apparently used for firewood after their other economic uses had ended.

B. Miles Gilbert (n.d.) has identified the faunal remains found in the excavations. They indicate that the Toltecs ate virtually everything that moved in the Tula area (Table 9-3). As can be seen, deer and domestic dog account for almost 70 percent of the total identified bones.

Toltec agricultural techniques apparently included *temporal* or rainfall farming, terracing, and irrigation. Rainfall farming and terracing were almost certainly restricted to hillsides and other areas which could not be irrigated. Terrace remains are visible on Ce-rro Mogone across the river from the Tula ridge, but their function is not known. The evidence for Toltec irrigation systems in the Tula area is suggestive but scanty. Agustín Peña and María Carmen Rodríguez (1976) have identified possible garden canals in the Daini residential complex they excavated in the urban zone. Mastache de Escobar and Crespo's (Mastache de Escobar 1976) investigations of contemporary and historic irrigation systems in the region indicate the probable existence of river-fed systems in Toltec times. Documentary data do show that early sixteenth-century systems had Prehispanic origins (Feldman 1974a). In addition, Sahagún (1961:166) mentions irrigated lands when discussing Toltec structures at Tula.

Our excavations did not reveal garden areas in or near the houses, but the settlement density may have precluded them. However, Peña and Rodríguez do have circumstantial evidence for houselot gardens in less densely settled parts of the city. *Chinampa* or swamp cultivation has been suggested for the El Salitre area, but the soil and water are so saline that crops cannot be grown there today, and the same probably was true in the past.

NONAGRICULTURAL ECONOMICS. Recent research has shown that non-agrarian activities, such as resource procurement, manufacturing, and distribution of the finished products, were very important in the economies of Mesoamerican urban centers. The study of these activities was an important part of the project, but our research only scratched the surface of the topic. Many problems remain to be resolved; some may be resolved through future analyses of our data, while others will require new research.

MANUFACTURING. Sahagún alludes to manufacturing activities throughout his discussion of the Toltecs in Books 3 and 10 of the *Florentine Codex* (1952, 1961). Virtually all the craftsmen he discusses produced elite sumptuary goods; they included lapidaries, other stonecutters, metalworkers, woodcarvers, feather workers, scribes, potters, spinners, and weavers. The working of semiprecious green stones is particularly noted and emphasized. He also mentions raw-materials resource areas, for example, a turquoise source at Xiuhtzone Mountain near Tepoztlan, State of Mexico. The emphasis on elite goods is understandable, given the fact that Sahagún's informants were elite people. The scarcity of such items in the archaeological inventory is not surprising; many were perishable, and there is evidence for systematic looting of Tula in Aztec times.

The manufacture of *tecali* (travertine) vessels is the only elite craft for which we have archaeological evidence (Diehl and Stroh 1978). An unfinished bowl found on the surface (Tejera 1970) and a few pieces of reused manufacturing debris in our Houses prove that the craft was practiced during the Tollan phase, but workshops have not been identified.

The manufacture of everyday utilitarian objects was more important to Tula's economy than that of elite goods, and most of the archaeological data pertain to such mundane items.

Stoutamire's and Yadeun's surveys detected dense obsidian workshop debris in a 1.5–2 sq km area. A more recent intensive INAH survey of the area (Nalda and Pastrana 1976; Pastrana Cruz 1977) has produced considerable evidence, and it is obvious that obsidian processing was a very important economic activity at Tula. The survey data and Alice N. Benfer's analysis of obsidian tools and debris together provide considerable insight into the entire industry. Robert Cobean (1979) and Dan Healan (1979) have recently reviewed all the data on the Tollan phase obsidian industry, and the following discussion is based upon their reconstruction.

The obsidian workshop zone was covered with residences, and the processing apparently took place in the Houses rather than in specialized workshops. Although a variety of tools were made, polyhedral blade cores were the most common product. The workshops produced many more cores and tools than were needed to satisfy the local demand, and the excess production must have been distributed to nonlocal consumers via the market system or some other exchange mechanism. The consumers probably bought finished cores and struck off blades as they were needed.

Approximately 90 percent of the workshop area obsidian is green and presumably came from the Pachuca source, but black and grey obsidians also occur. The latter colors seem to be more prevalent than green in pre–Tollan phase contexts (Stoutamire 1975; Cobean 1979), suggesting that Tula did not gain direct control of the Pachuca sources until Tollan phase times. X-ray florescent spectroscopy trace element analyses have shown that Tollan phase obsidians came from Pachuca, Hidalgo (green); Zinapecuaro, Michoacan (grey); Otumba, State of Mexico; and possibly Altatongo, Veracruz (Hester, Jack, and Benfer 1973).

The quantity of ceramics on the site shows that ceramic manufacture was an important industry at Tula; pottery workshops have not been identified, but they must have existed. The sophistication of the Canal Locality kiln suggests a complex ceramic technology and perhaps full-time specialization. A possible figurine workshop with numerous mold fragments on the surface has been identified west of the Rio Tula; other such workshops must have existed, but the constant recovery of molds for modern reuse may be removing this element of the archaeological record from the site surface. The nature and importance of the Toltec ceramic industry will remain unclear until we can identify potters' tools, manufacturing steps, and the output of specific workshops. Paula H. Krotser's (1976a) studies of Classic period ceramic workshops at Teotihuacan should provide many useful insights into these matters.

The frequency of spindle whorls in our excavations indicates an important fiber processing industry associated with the living areas. If Mary H. Parsons (1972) is correct, the larger whorls were used for coarse fibers like *ixtle* and the smaller ones for finer threads such as cotton.

INTERREGIONAL EXCHANGE. The archae-

TABLE 9-3. Faunal Remains in the UMC Excavations at Tula (Identified by B. Miles Gilbert)

| Scientific Name | Common Name | Percentage of Total Sample |
|---|---|---|
| Odocoileus sp. | Deer | 45.2 |
| Canis familiaris | Domestic dog | 24.2 |
| Lepus californicus | Jackrabbit | 9.7 |
| Sylvilagus sp. | Cottontail rabbit | 6.5 |
| Cratogeomys castanops | Pocketgopher | 2.9 |
| Rana sp. | Frog | 2.6 |
| Neotoma sp. | Rat | 1.6 |
| Tayassu tajacu | Peccary | 1.0 |
| Meleagris gallopavo | Turkey | 1.0 |
| Dasypus cf novemcinctus | Armadillo | .6 |
| Anas sp. | Duck | .6 |
| Ardea sp. | Heron | .6 |
| Peromyscus sp. | Mouse | .6 |
| Passeriformes (order) | Small bird | .6 |
| Taxidea taxus | Badger | .3 |
| Terrapene sp. | Boxturtle | .3 |
| Ictiobus sp. | Fish | .3 |
| Buteo sp. | Hawk | .3 |
| Testudines (order) | Turtle | .3 |

ological record contains evidence of extensive interregional exchange networks involving both utilitarian and luxury products. The distances involved and the exotic nature of some of the imports suggest a Toltec *pochteca*-like trade organization, but more data are needed to confirm its existence.

Tula's proven imports include ceramics, raw obsidian, and shells; its probable imports include a few finished obsidian pieces, rubber, animal skins, feathers, semiprecious stones, cotton, and cacao. Tohil Plumbate is the most notable ceramic import; over 1,000 sherds and 5 complete vessels were found in the excavations, and 300 sherds were collected during the survey, more than were collected of some of the rare local pottery types. Virtually all the identifiable vessel shapes are drinking goblets. Since Plumbate was manufactured in the famous Xoconusco cacao zone of Chiapas and Guatemala, Diehl, Lomas, and Wynn (1974) suggested that the vessels arrived at Tula filled with cacao beans and were used for drinking chocolate and

other liquids. Central American Papagayo polychrome was another ceramic tradeware, and once again drinking-vessel forms predominate. Other tradewares include Isla de Sacrificios–like pottery from central Veracruz and Huasteca V pieces from the northern Gulf Coast. The complete absence of Fine Orange and related fine paste wares suggests a lack of significant ties between the Toltec capital and southern Veracruz and the western and northern Maya zones. This is particularly puzzling in light of the association of these ceramics with Tula-inspired Toltec architecture at Chichen Itza. Trade connections with North and West Mexico are indicated by a few Cloisonne sherds and Pacific Coast shells (identified by Feldman). Closer to home, Wavy-line Mazapan pottery is so rare at Tula that it may have been imported from Basin of Mexico production centers.

Tula's exports are difficult to identify because very little has been published on other Second Intermediate period sites in Mesoamerica. Tula almost certainly controlled the distribution of Pachuca and perhaps Zinapecuaro obsidian, and we know that Pachuca obsidian reached San Lorenzo Tenochtitlan during the Villa Alta phase (Cobean et al. 1971). Other possible exports include large Tlaloc incensarios, figurines, *tecali* vessels, and perhaps lime.

Some evidence suggests that Tula and sections of the central and northern Gulf Coast formed a symbiotic region (Sanders 1956). The Gulf Coast ceramics; the Ehecatl Temple; the ill-defined "Toltec influence" at Castillo de Teayo, El Tajin, Tuzapan, Chachalacas, and Cacahuatenco (García Payón 1971: 533–535); and vague ethnohistorical accounts from both areas (García Payón 1965; Sahagún 1961) all point in this direction. The Veracruz area could have provided Tula with maize and other foodstuffs in times of scarcity, as well as feathers, animal skins, rubber, and other tropical products; Tula may have reciprocated with obsidian, basalt products, and luxury craft goods (Diehl and Feldman 1974).

## Social Organization

Our excavations provide information on several basic levels of social organization in Toltec society. Healan (1977) has defined three social groups among the occupants of the excavated Houses: the nuclear family, the kindred or expanded family, and the neighborhood. Most of the Houses appear to have been nuclear family residences, as indicated by the presence of a single hearth and sufficient sleeping and storage space for a group that size. Larger Houses with two or more apparently contemporaneous hearths may have sheltered two or more nuclear families.

The House Groups contained several nuclear families which undoubtedly were related, but the filiation and descent rules are not clear; social and economic differentiation among kindred members is indicated by differences in House size and architectural elaborateness. The courtyard altars were a focus of kindred ritual, and the burials in them

may contain the remains of kindred founders.

The existence of neighborhood groups is problematical; the only reason for suggesting them is that the temple at the east edge of the Canal Group seems to have served more people than merely the residents of the excavated Houses. This large ritual group must have had spatial boundaries, constituent kin groups, and an internal hierarchy, but since nothing is known about these features, it seems rash to compare the group to the Aztec *calpulli* at this time.

Higher levels of organization must have existed in Toltec society (see Carrasco 1971: 373–374), but information is lacking.

## Political Organization

The archaeological data do not shed much light on the political structure of the Toltec state. The existence of only one large civic-religious precinct suggests centralization of power in the hands of a single elite. The significance of the shift to Tula Grande at the beginning of the Tollan phase may represent the ascendency of one group over another; if so, the Tula Chico party lost their former power and could not maintain their own ceremonial precinct. This sequence of events may relate to the Quetzalcoatl-Tezcatlipoca conflict saga and the flight of Quetzalcoatl and his followers, but this topic is too complex to be adequately dealt with here.

The boundaries of the Toltec state are completely conjectural. Feldman (1974b), Pedro Carrasco (1971), and others have suggested that Tula was involved in a triple alliance with Otampan and Culhuacan, but its date and nature are unclear. I believe that essential resource areas such as the Pachuca and Zinapecuaro obsidian mines had to be effectively controlled by Tula. Therefore, I would minimally define a Toltec state which extended from the Sierra Madre Oriental in the Pachuca area to eastern Michoacan. I doubt that much if any territory south of the Basin of Mexico was under direct control, although Kenneth G. Hirth (1977) suggests that Tula controlled the Rio Amatzinac drainage in

290

eastern Morelos. The northern section probably included the Bajío and the eastern foothills of the Sierra Madre Occidental as far north as La Quemada, Zacatecas. The political relationships between Tula and southern Mesoamerica, including Chichen Itza, remain as poorly understood as ever, despite the evidence for economic ties with southern Guatemala and Central America.

## Late Horizon Aztec Tula

Our research emphasized the Toltec phases of Tula, and we did not collect much information on later times. However we do have data which confirm Davies' contention that Tula remained "quite an important place" and that "perhaps it even enjoyed a privileged position, due to its sanctity and prestige" (Davies 1977:41–42). In the following paragraphs I will draw on these data, other archaeological information, and some of the documentary sources in an attempt to show that Davies is correct.

Cobean defines three Aztec phases at Tula: Fuego (Aztec II–III transition), Palacio (Prehispanic Aztec III and IV), and Tesoro (Aztec IV and other Early Colonial materials). Acosta found Fuego ceramics at Tula Grande, but only traces were recovered in the survey. The maximum sherd densities (.5 per collection unit) occur around the edge of El Salitre; they may represent temporary visitors who extracted marsh resources rather than permanent residents. Yadeún Angulo (1975:23) suggests that the Aztec II Fuego phase is not a distinct chronological unit but rather that Aztec II trade wares were contemporaneous with the end of the Tollan phase. I once accepted this interpretation but now doubt it for reasons too complex to go into here. In any case, more data are needed from Tula and especially from the Basin of Mexico before the issue can be resolved.

The combined Palacio and Tesoro occupations represent a community second in size only to that of the Tollan phase. Sherd densities of 5+ per collection unit occur over a 7–8 sq km area which includes the whole

Tollan phase settlement except its southern and western extensions. The highest densities (10+ per collection unit) are concentrated in the Acropolis–El Salitre zone. If all 8 sq km were occupied at a density of 5,000 people per sq km, the community contained 40,000 people. This seems too high, and I would provisionally lower it by 50 percent to 20,000. Yadeún Angulo (1975:24) suggests the Aztec population was between 20,500 and 37,460 inhabitants.

Acosta found impressive evidence of Aztec reuse, modification, and looting in every Tula Grande building he excavated. Pyramid C, the largest Toltec structure on the site, was so badly destroyed that he could not restore it. A large trench was found in the east or back side; it almost certainly served for the removal of Atlantean column roof supports. The stairway was so badly damaged that only the three lowest steps remained in place, and the facing stones were stripped from the entire mound surface. Since none of the finished stone was found in the debris, it presumably was removed to be used elsewhere. Several caches of flint "sacrificial knives" and Aztec pots were found on the ruined west surface of the mound, and a small rectangular platform was erected north of the stairway.

The Pyramid B Tlahuizcalpantecuhtli Temple was accorded the same treatment except that Aztec caches and platforms were not found. The looters did not succeed in removing all the Atlantean sculptures; dismembered sections of some were found in the trench dug into the north side of the mound. Virtually all the carved friezes were removed except those which had been covered up by Tollan phase construction.

The Palacio Quemado was both looted and reused. The looting involved removal of the sculptured tablets from most of the banquettes in the rooms. Aztec constructions in the ruined building included a rectangular platform in Sala 2 and a tomb built into the north portico floor.

The facing stones were stripped from Ballcourt 1, and a rectangular platform was built on the ruined playing field surface. Acosta

291

found several Toltec sculptures associated with Palacio phase debris in this ballcourt, demonstrating both the fact of the looting and its date. Ballcourt 2 received similar treatment: the surfacing stones were removed, and a *temascal* (sweat bath) was built on the edge of the ruined playing field. The Aztecs apparently reconstructed Ballcourt 2 and used it for a time (Matos Moctezuma, personal communication). The ruined condition in which Charnay found the Adoratorio in the center of the Tula Grande plaza suggests that it too suffered vandalism.

The ruined courtyard altars in the Canal Locality indicate that Aztec looters directed their attention to residential structures as well as public buildings. The date of this looting is unclear; it is not recent, but it did take place after debris began to accumulate on the abandoned courtyard surface. Thus I assume it was done in Aztec times.

Tula's destruction and looting is frequently associated with the final conquest of the city. I doubt this because the effort involved seems too great and too systematic to be the immediate aftermath of a conquest. Instead I think it was a planned, systematic treasure hunt directed by the rulers of Tenochtitlan or some other elite who claimed Toltec dynastic descent and attempted to validate it with bonafide Toltec art.

Several passages in Sahagún allude to these looting activities. The last two sentences in the quote at the beginning of this chapter are the clearest reference to it: "And Tolteca bowls, Tolteca ollas are taken from the earth. And many times Tolteca jewels—arm bands, esteemed green stones, emerald-green jade—are taken from the earth" (Sahagún 1961:165). Small wonder that Tula's yield of elite objects in recent times has been so disappointing, and how ironic that this intense Aztec activity has led Chadwick, Séjourné, and others to doubt that Tula was the Tollan of legend. Most of the Toltec artistic legacy probably lies buried beneath the streets of Mexico City!

Other aspects of Tula's unusual role in the Aztec world deserve mention. Its absence

from the *Codex Mendoza* tribute list while other nearby towns are included may mean that it was exempt from tribute payment or controlled directly by the Tenochtitlan dynasty. Davies (1977:42) reports marriage alliances between the ruling families of Tenochtitlan and Tula. One such marriage occurred in the time of Axayacatl; a later one involved Don Pedro Tlacahuepan, a son of Moctezuma II who became the Duque de Moctezuma de Tultengo after the Conquest. Don Pedro apparently lived in the palace Acosta excavated on El Cielito hill. This impressive structure is a Precolumbian building with a few Colonial architectural modifications and both Palacio and Tesoro ceramics. Recent looting in a large residential compound below El Cielito uncovered very elaborate Chalco-Cholula polychrome ceramics and other exotic trade wares which one might expect to find in a palace. Some of Don Pedro's descendents are prominent citizens in Tula de Allende today, and the Duque de Moctezuma de Tultengo title still exists (Davies 1977).

One last piece of information is of interest. R. C. Padden (1967:240–274) has shown that the idol of Huitzilopochtli was a focal point for Indian pagan revivalism in the mid-sixteenth century. It had been removed from the Templo Mayor during the Conquest but was hidden rather than destroyed as the Spaniards assumed. The Colonial authorities were never able to locate and confiscate it, but its last known location was in a cave somewhere near Tula. Perhaps the pagan backsliders felt that this historic and sacred area was also the safest for this Holy of Holies.

Clearly, Aztec Tula was not just another town in the realm. A great deal remains to be learned about its special significance for the Aztecs.

## DISCUSSION

The degree to which the UMC and INAH projects have changed our ideas about Tula and the Toltecs is evident when one compares the new information with the treatment given these topics in the older syntheses of Mesoamerica. Robert McC. Adams (1966), Ignacio Bernal (1959), Michael D. Coe (1962), William T. Sanders and Barbara J. Price (1968), Muriel Porter Weaver (1972), and Eric R. Wolf (1959) all emphasized legendary accounts of Tula's rise and fall, the Quetzalcoatl myth cycle, dynastic lists, and other facets of the documentary record. Their archaeological information consisted of building and artifact descriptions, coupled with observations to the effect that much remained to be learned about Tula and the Toltecs. This is part of a larger pattern in Mesoamerican studies in which archaeological information is increasingly de-emphasized as one approaches the Spanish Conquest and the documentary data become more plentiful. This is the fault of the researchers, not the synthesizers; until recently, Postclassic archaeology has been the neglected stepchild of Mesoamerican studies. Fortunately the situation is changing.

The new Tula chronology has resolved some problems and created others. It is now clear that Tula was not a causal factor in Teotihuacan's decline and collapse; in fact, it didn't exist at that time. Toltec Tula's growth was marked by two episodes of dramatic population increase. The first occurred during the Prado and Corral phases; the second resulted in the Tollan phase city. The rapidity of the growth suggests substantial immigration in both cases. Tula's ceramic ties with north and west Mexico indicate one source of immigrants, but the Basin of Mexico and particularly Teotihuacan must have provided substantial numbers. In his preliminary analysis of the UMC project skeletal remains, Robert A. Benfer (1974) noted that the individuals studied were taller than might be expected and speculated that they were more closely related biologically to northern Mexican than to central or southern Mexican populations. Unfortunately the ethnic identities, occupational skills, and socioeconomic statuses of the immigrants are not known; such information would provide many insights into the urbanization process. The large-scale immigra-

tion must have imposed a considerable strain on the Toltec social and political organization; one can imagine conflicts over land rights, taxation, access to economic resources, ethnic pride, etc. The manner in which these problems were handled by a northern-derived elite without experience in such matters is not known. Tula's short-lived florescence and rapid decline suggest that effective permanent solutions were not found and that the sociopolitical structure did not provide effective integration.

The new information on Toltec urban life fills a gap between the emerging pictures of urbanism at Teotihuacan (Bernal 1963; Cowgill 1974; R. Millon 1973, 1976) and Tenochtitlan (Calnek 1974a, 1976; Lombardo de Ruiz 1973). We now have partially comparable information on the three communities which determined much of Central Mexican culture history, and we can analyze the basic similarities and variations in a Central Mexican urban tradition. I will briefly describe some of these similarities and differences in the following paragraphs, but space limitation precludes a detailed analysis.

The total population sizes of the three cities differed substantially. René F. Millon (1970b) estimates that Teotihuacan had between 75,000 and 200,000 inhabitants, with 125,000 as the most probable figure. Tenochtitlan's total population size is a subject of much debate; Calnek (1974a:54) suggests a minimum of 150,000 and a possible figure twice as large. Tula's estimated 32,000–53,000 inhabitants is by far the lowest of the three. Many possible factors may account for these differences; different agricultural potentials, economic systems, areal settlement histories, competitive situations, and others, but I will refrain from speculating on them.

Urban planning is another area of considerable variation in the three cities. The Teotihuacan map demonstrates that it was the most systematically planned urban community in Precolumbian America. Tenochtitlan also exhibited a great deal of planning, though not to the same degree as Teotihuacan. Tula lacks any evidence of planning beyond that involved in the Acropolis. There is no physical evidence of a division into quarters analogous to the *campan* of Tenochtitlan or the quarters of Teotihuacan, or of public communication arteries such as streets and causeways. These differences are the result of several factors. Tula had a much shorter life span than Teotihuacan and may simply have lacked the time to go through the growth phases and organizational changes of its predecessor. Perhaps Tula should be compared with Tzacualli and Miccaotli phase Teotihuacan rather than the Metepec phase metropolis. Tenochtitlan's life span was comparable to Tula's, but its high degree of planning can be explained by the fact that most of the city was built on an artificially created land surface. Also, the causeway-aqueducts and canals which provided the skeleton of the city were absolutely essential for potable water and communication with the mainland. The mainland Aztec communities probably were more similar to Tula than to Tenochtitlan in matters of urban planning.

The three communities also show significant differences in the size and complexity of non-elite residential structures. The standard Teotihuacan residence was a 3,600 sq m apartment compound divided up into numerous subunits. Most of them contained temples which served the 60–100 or more residents (R. Millon 1976). The standard Tenochtitlan house was a walled compound, comparable in size and complexity to individual Teotihuacan apartments (Calnek 1976: 300). These compounds were occupied by joint bilateral families spanning several generations with a modal size of 10–15 people (Calnek 1972:111). The Tula House Groups are intermediate between Teotihuacan and Tenochtitlan in resident population and architectural complexity. Healan (1977:151) estimates that the two completely excavated House Groups sheltered 29 and 60 persons respectively. The above observations are based on small samples, but they suggest a decrease in basic resident group size through time; this may in turn indicate significant

changes in social organization and personal interaction patterns.

The number of contemporaneous urban centers differs significantly in each case. Settlement pattern surveys in the Basin of Mexico (J. Parsons 1976) and the Tula region (Mastache de Escobar and Crespo 1974) show that Teotihuacan and Tula were the only true urban centers in the immediate area during their respective florescences. The Late Horizon picture is quite different; at least twelve communities in the Texcoco, Chalco, and Xochimilco survey zones had 10,000 or more inhabitants (J. Parsons 1971, 1974a, 1976), and other cities existed on the west side of the basin. This indicates that Aztec society was more urbanized than its predecessors and that caution should be exercised when applying ethnohistorically derived Aztec models to older archaeological remains.

The three cities appear to have shared many non-agrarian economic characteristics. Raw material procurement, manufacturing, and trade were crucial elements in the economic well-being of all three centers. The importance of the obsidian industries is just beginning to be appreciated, and much remains to be learned about them. A word of caution is in order; the high visibility of obsidian in surveys should not lead us to overemphasize it at the expense of less visible but perhaps more important industries such as ceramics, woodworking, and weaving. René Millon and his colleagues have identified workshops of these industries at Teotihuacan; more intensive surveys at Tula and documentary research at Tenochtitlan might do the same.

The three cities also appear to have shared a basic policy of military aggression and political expansion as a means to economic ends. Raw materials, markets, exotic goods, and the elimination of economic competition seem to have been the primary goals behind Aztec, Toltec, and Teotihuacano military policy. While it is difficult, with purely archaeological data, to separate economic relationships conducted among equals from those carried out in a setting of military dominance, the documented Aztec practices probably were similar to those of their predecessors.

The above paragraphs touch on only a few of the topics which might be covered in this review. We will be able to say much more when our final reports are written. In the meantime the veil which has covered Toltec archaeology for so long has been partially lifted and the panorama is an exciting one.

### ACKNOWLEDGMENTS

The UMC Tula Archaeological Project has been financed by National Science Foundation grants GS-2814, GS-28119, and BNS-02752; and several grants from the University of Missouri Research Council. The research was conducted under Concesiones 3/70, 3/71, and 15/71 from the Instituto Nacional de Antropología e Historia; I extend thanks to the then Director de Monumentos Prehispánicos, Arqo. Ignacio Marquina, for his aid in arranging the permits.

The INAH Proyecto Tula personnel have been most helpful; I particularly want to thank Ana María Crespo, Clara Luz Díaz, Manuel Gándara, Carlos Hernández, Guadalupe Mastache de Escobar, René Ocaña, Alejandro Pastrana Cruz, and Juan Yadeún Angulo. Eduardo Matos Moctezuma provided help and encouragement in his dual roles as Sub-Director de Monumentos Prehispánicos and Director of the Proyecto Tula. Our project would not have existed without his unfailing support over the years.

The UMC Project has involved many people; some of their contributions are explicitly acknowledged in the text; others are not, but all deserve my sincere thanks. They include Ramón Arellanos M., Steven Armsey, Lourdes B. de Arellanos, Alice N. Benfer, Robert Cobean, Viola Ch. de Diehl, Lawrence H. Feldman, B. Miles Gilbert, Dan M. Healan, Roger Lomas, Margaret Mandeville, Terrance L. Stocker, James Stoutamire, Edward Stroh, Jr., and Jack T. Wynn. Finally I owe a very special thanks to project Codirector Robert A. Benfer for his help and patience since 1970. Although I have drawn on data collected by all the above people, they do not share the blame for any misinterpretations.

# 10. Tikal: An Outline of Its Field Study (1956-1970) and a Project Bibliography

𝄚𝄚𝄚𝄚𝄚𝄚𝄚𝄚𝄚𝄚𝄚𝄚𝄚𝄚𝄚𝄚𝄚𝄚𝄚𝄚𝄚𝄚𝄚𝄚𝄚𝄚𝄚𝄚𝄚𝄚𝄚𝄚

*CHRISTOPHER JONES, WILLIAM R. COE, and WILLIAM A. HAVILAND*

A FOURTEEN-YEAR PROGRAM of research and preservation in Tikal closed as 1970 began, and it did so in response to nothing so elegant as an appropriate sample achieved or for that matter the fulfillment of marvelously sound strategy. Instead what dictated an end to fieldwork was simply concern with the immense volume of data already registered and its mandatory processing toward publication. The Tikal Project, undertaken by the University Museum of the University of Pennsylvania, had intended to terminate work during 1965, and the additional enormously productive years principally were due to the sudden and generous subsidy of the project by the government of Guatemala. This support had a practical goal, namely, touristic development of Tikal; inevitably this wrought a great expansion of excavation in architectural settings, in the midst of which basic research interests stood uncompromised. Also a stimulus in those final years was the funding by the Ford Foundation of specialist student participation. Accordingly, these final, lengthy seasons not only allowed intensified work within the site's focal sector, but also decisively end-ed the project's decade-long confinement to a Tikal depicted on the Carr-Hazard map (1961). At least a spatial definition of Tikal as a whole then became feasible, although behind this objective lay the presumption of inherent demographic limits.

Not surprisingly, the factual inpouring in those last years at least doubled the "data mass" on hand from past study. No way occurs to express the project's magnitude except to pose certain realities: for example, an accumulation of nearly 60,000 photographic negatives, or a staff list of 113 individuals. More telling is an archive centered on some 13,000 field decisions to segregate either matrices or contexts and the material content they bear, whether purposefully or fortuitously present.

## PROGRAMS

Though never coherently designed and termed as such, the project split into a number of programs. Exemplifying this is the central mapping done from 1957 to 1960 and, afterward, the cruciform half-kilometer "strip" mapping and the recording of promi-

FIGURE 10-1. Commanding the eighth-century epicenter of Tikal, Temple I overlies a tomb identified as that of Ruler A. Courtesy Tikal Project, University Museum.

nent constructional clusters wherever located relative to the primary center of Tikal. A major part of the excavations done divided between a "small structure" program (read "housemounds") and another devoted to documenting from top to bottom the epicentral aggregates which tradition odiously dictated to be studded by "temples" and "palaces." Considerable digging came to be done in programs responding to patterns: so-called twin-pyramid groups; assemblages of structures marked in each case by a squarish, easterly fixed entity facing inward (e.g., Str. 5G-8); and east-west arrangements each centrally marked by a miniscule "mound" (e.g., Str. 6E-144). Functional considerations led to a ballcourt program and, moreover, to one neatly devoted to investigations of *chultuns*,

or underground storage chambers. Causeways as such were specially dissected, although a single season (1960) of concentrated digging probably was inadequate in view of the problems they pose. Likewise perhaps too restricted was a "mystery mound" program in which sheer curiosity as to makeup took us to excavate, and most rewardingly so, a scattering of small and large features lying beyond the scope of major central studies (this alone led us, for instance, to the colossal Str. 5D-54 of Late Preclassic age). Beginning in 1960, and a task common to most following seasons, was a ceramic test-pitting program, one understandably in search of significant deposits of long- and short-term origins lying principally within the central 9 sq km of Tikal. Wherever not caught up by excava-

297

tion, all still visible architecture underwent detailed recording in a program initiated in 1966. Also, and from the very start of the project, a monument recording program existed. It was in 1965 that, concerned with mapping sensitivity, we carried out what was termed a "vacant terrain" program of digging; basically guiding this was the question of "housemounds" of so little vertical prominence as to escape detection during conventional site mapping under in any case densely forested conditions. And concurrent with all these active interests were laboratory study programs which focused on standard categories of ceramics and artifacts (also "ecofacts") but with such components as censers and figurines independently treated.

PUBLICATION

*Tikal Report No. 11*, the last to be issued, appeared in 1961. With the report series adopted as the format for full statement, we nevertheless soon found it impossible to fashion topically integrated units for publication because of the ongoing field and laboratory programs which, as stated above, ended only at the close of 1969. Even had we previously been able to wrap up a particular major subject for *Tikal Report* release, its completion was dubious because of ever onerous, off-season processing of raw records. Moreover, original intentions unquestionably became deflected by the writing of numerous doctoral dissertations based on Tikal data. Today, nearly a decade after the project's close, a felicitous situation exists: of the twenty-eight reports scheduled, a half-dozen are in various stages of final editing. Totaling some 7,000 pages of typescript and a thousand-odd line illustrations, these represent major contributions to Tikal archaeology. It is to be hoped that their appearance in print will encouragingly hasten the completion of the entire series.

The University Museum will continue to publish the *Tikal Reports* in its Museum Monographs series. Following is a projected listing of report numbers, authors, and titles.

Since we are committing ourselves to the numeration by publishing *Tikal Report No. 33A* now, these are not likely to change. The authors and titles will remain subject to revision. For one thing, the untimely death of Dennis Puleston in 1978 has left us without a principal author for preparation of those volumes which he had not been able to complete.

Slated for first appearance are *Tikal Reports No. 12* and *No. 33A* (see below). The latter is being copy edited and will likely be out in 1981. Following this will be published *Tikal Report No. 14*, the largest and most central of the excavation reports, now complete with its massive set of illustrations and text. Also finished and ready for printing are *Reports No. 19*, *No. 20*, and *No. 22*. Although final illustration plates and much of the text have long been ready for *Reports No. 25*, *No. 27*, *No. 28*, *No. 29*, *No. 31*, and many of the excavation reports, we are reluctant to predict publication times for them until the first ones are out.

*Projected List of* Tikal Reports

*No. 12.* William R. Coe and William A. Haviland, *Introduction to the Archaeology of Tikal.*

*No. 13.* Dennis E. Puleston, *The Settlement Survey of Tikal.*

*No. 14.* William R. Coe, *Excavations in the Great Plaza, North Terrace, and North Acropolis of Tikal (Group 5D-2).*

*No. 15.* Peter D. Harrison, *Excavations in the Central Acropolis of Tikal (Group 5D-11).*

*No. 16.* Christopher Jones, *Excavations in the East Plaza of Tikal (Group 5D-3).*

*No. 17.* Peter D. Harrison, *Excavations in the West Plaza of Tikal (Group 5D-10).*

*No. 18.* Christopher Jones, *Excavations in the Twin-Pyramid Groups of Tikal (Groups 30-1 . . .).*

FIGURE 10-2. Deep trenching of the North Acropolis. Crew is working at various constructional stages dating to around A.D. 1. Courtesy Tikal Project, University Museum.

In regard to interpretations of Maya prehistory, the potentials of this series are great indeed. We will confine ourselves here to an outline of three areas of importance: the methodology of the project, and the implications for interpreting rulership and epigraphy, on the one hand, and demography and subsistence on the other. Details of the archaeological sequence can be found by consulting various publications listed in the bibliography, such as W. Coe 1965b, 1965c, and 1967.

## METHODOLOGY

Because of its unprecedented size, the Tikal Project developed its own elaborate set of explicitly stated systematics and standards, both in the accumulation of a field record and in the preparation of the final reports. The standards have since become widely known and have been adopted as models by other projects.

Perhaps the earliest and best-known set of standards to have emerged from the project are those of the Tikal map (*Tikal Report No. 11*, Carr and Hazard 1961). The insistence upon careful locational and horizontal controls, the use of elaborate surveying equipment in spite of difficult forest conditions, the specific rules for portraying structures and other features, and the persistent coverage of the entire huge area around the site have all left their mark on subsequent mapping projects.

In the same way, the drawings of the Tikal monument carving set a precedent for the modern art of depiction, especially in the insistence upon a full and varied set of controlled-lighting photographs as a base. Perhaps equally important was the firm distinction between reliable and questionable features, as represented by either solid or dotted lines, a convention continued by Ian Graham in the *Corpus of Maya Hieroglyphic Inscriptions* (1975:22–24).

The carefully-thought-out file card system of operation and lot cards, object catalog cards, and general index cards has proved to be more than adequate for handling the hundreds of thousands of artifacts found. It was planned in detail in advance, was simple enough to be learned by over a hundred new staff members, and forms an extremely workable and accessible tool for analysis. The file was begun before the age of the computer, yet its systematic organization would make it easily adaptable to computer tape.

The Tikal Project field drawing and drafting standards have also become famous, perhaps more than anything else for the large-scale and realistically drawn sections. Again, every aspect of these drawings and of their inking for final publication was carefully controlled by rules, so that all illustrations are comparable throughout the reports.

The detailed and realistic section drawing exemplifies the basic Tikal strategy of excavation, in that it focuses upon stratigraphy as the basis of control. A related aspect was the decision to write up the excavation reports as if each stratigraphically integrated architectural group were in itself an isolated entity (W. Coe 1962c:504–506; Culbert 1967:94). In that way, the temporal subdivisions (time spans) within the group came to depend primarily upon their internal stratigraphy rather than upon ceramic content, C14 determinations, architectural typology, art style, or epigraphic inscription. Within the report on a group, each structure or platform was described separately, generating its own time spans of construction, use, addition, renovation, and collapse. These were then collated to form the basis of group time spans guided by stratigraphic connectives. Thus, our descriptions were given in such narrow local perspective that the humble yet indisputable facts of abutment, run-under, union, and rip-out provide the primary considerations for relating any feature to any other. Everything within the group report speaks for itself. Of course, on the next level, when groups are to be compared to one another outside of their stratigraphic reach, then such syntheses will have to rely on typological and other correlative devices. Instead of trying to fit each structure or feature into a larger picture of Maya civilization, we have assembled a basic record from which writers (including ourselves) are free to make connectives beyond those which we know to be demonstrable.

Tikal "site phases" will emerge as a final stage of analysis and abstraction. In fact, it would not be surprising if each synthesizer felt free to subdivide Tikal development in a different way, whether by decades, katuns, reigns, constructional events, ceramic change, art styles, or whatever. What is important is that in the initial stages of analysis the stratigraphy was allowed to control the data as much as it could, independent of the other, broader temporal considerations.

Such a vast amount of specific data has been stratigraphically interrelated within

FIGURE 10-4. Detail of Stela 31, a major fifth-century monument shattered and buried in the late seventh century. Depicted is a profile portrait of "Stormy Sky," one of Tikal's most famous rulers. Courtesy Tikal Project, University Museum.

FIGURE 10-3. The text of Tikal Stela 29 records 8.12.14.8.15 (A.D. 292) in bar and dot numerals, the earliest such date encountered in the central Maya Lowlands. Courtesy Tikal Project, University Museum.

groups at Tikal—probably more than in any other Mesoamerican excavation—that the potentials are great for describing the development of the community in terms of very small periods of time. Out of such description should emerge a more meaningful understanding of cultural processes, the underlying economic and political causes, and even personal and conscious motives. For Tikal, these speculations will have the advantage of being based upon a huge and carefully controlled data base.

The carry-over in methodology from the Tikal Project to subsequent University Museum excavations has been virtually com-

plete, each time building upon the lessons of the previous excavation. The excavations in Tayasal, Guatemala, in 1971 were largely supervised by former Tikal excavators (Coe, H. Stanley Loten, Miguel Orrego) and followed the Tikal laboratory and field standards with little change. The records are presently being compiled and inked for publication according to Tikal conventions.

The Quirigua excavations from 1974 to 1979 utilized Tikal standards almost exclusively: the illustration scales and conventions, the complete card file, and so forth (Sharer and Coe 1979). Excavation strategies also reflected a Tikal background, emphasizing a strong combination of settlement pattern research and deep trenching. The basic goal of the complex Quirigua Acropolis excavation by Coe and Jones, for example, was to develop an internally controlled sequence of constructional activity which can be keyed into dynastic information from the monuments or data from the surrounding zone

(Jones, Ashmore, and Sharer in press). This application of the Tikal Project approach toward the data is again producing a reconstruction of the past by integrating distinct and independent data sets.

EPIGRAPHY AND RULERSHIP

During the project's years at Tikal, research on monuments and inscriptions focused on the formidable job of assembling a complete and precise record. New monuments were discovered in mapping and in excavation. They and the already-known stelae and altars were excavated for stratigraphic contexts, substela caches, and total stela form. Numerous photographs were taken of the carved surfaces of each stone monument and fragment, and Coe's scale drawings, based on this photographic record, are visual statements of what we are able to see in the carving. Together with photographs, notes, and commentary on the inscription, these will appear soon in *Tikal Report No. 33A*. Many of the new discoveries of monuments and inscriptions have been reported upon and illustrated in a preliminary way in earlier *Tikal Reports* and separate articles: *Tikal Reports No. 3, No. 4, No. 6, No. 8*; W. Coe 1958, 1959, 1962c, 1963b, 1965b, 1965c, 1967; Moholy-Nagy 1962; Satterthwaite 1956, 1958a, 1958b, 1963, 1964, 1967; Satterthwaite and Ralph 1960; Shook 1958b, 1960; Shook and Kidder 1961; Trik 1963.

The inscriptions of Tikal were slow to yield dynastic history, even though an "inaugural" date on Stela 4 and an "initial" date on Stela 23 were recognized by Tatiana Proskouriakoff as early as 1960 in her breakthrough article in *American Antiquity*. More recently, two studies, one by Christopher Jones and one by Clemency C. Coggins, have supplied the beginning of a preliminary synopsis of Tikal's dynastic history. Both rose out of work on the *Tikal Reports* and utilized the project's drawings as their principal sources of data.

Jones' paper (1977) was first written and circulated to colleagues in 1970. It stemmed from work on noncalendric glyphs for *Tikal Report No. 33*. In its first form, the study outlined epigraphic arguments for three inaugural statements in the Late Classic Tikal inscriptions and then identified the monuments and constructions of these sequent rulers (designated A, B, and C). Subsequently, name-glyphs of Rulers A and B were supplied by Proskouriakoff and Heinrich Berlin, and thus the revised paper was able to present a much fuller account of the reigns. One of the more important discoveries was that Burial 116, the famous tomb of Temple I, could positively be identified as that of Ruler A by the occurrence of name-glyphs on a jade mosaic vessel, on carved bone objects, and on a set of bone and shell tweezers. Another contribution was in the recognition that some of the inscriptions seemed to recite the direct parentage of the rulers.

Coggins' study drew upon the project illustrations which were sent to George Kubler's Tikal Art Seminar at Yale University (organized as a vehicle for the production of *Tikal Report No. 36, The Art of Tikal*). The subject of Coggins' dissertation (1975) was the painting and drawing styles, but, since burials are the principal sources for her material, she utilized dynastic inscriptions heavily in order to link specific interments to named rulers. For the Late Classic, she used Jones' work as a base, and for the Early Classic she built upon unpublished epigraphic studies by Proskouriakoff. Especially significant was the clarification of the lengthy and difficult text of Stela 31, in which the current ruler, Stormy Sky, mentioned his predecessors Curl Nose and Jaguar Paw. This is a striking example of how noncalendric decipherment can help place ambiguously written dates in a sequence of named rulers and dated reigns. Coggins also pointed to the possible identification of several occupants of Tikal tombs, arguing on the basis of a dated tomb inscription, name-glyphs on interred objects, proximity to a ruler's monuments, and seriation of painting and drawing style. Coggins' approach demonstrates above all that the great wealth of well-controlled excavational

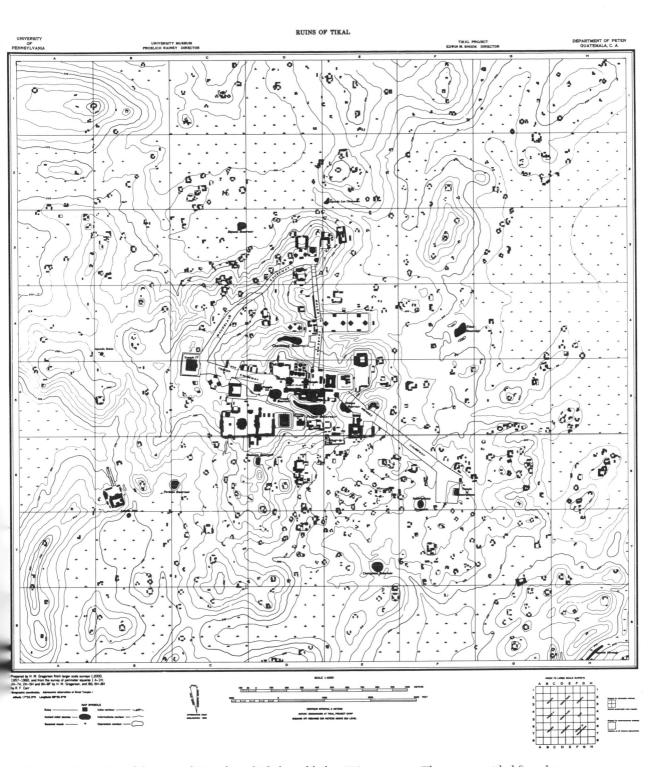

FIGURE 10-5. Map of the central 16 sq km of Tikal, gridded in 500 m squares. The map provided firm data for consideration of demography and subsistence. Courtesy Tikal Project, University Museum.

and epigraphic data from Tikal is an unparalleled data base for testable hypotheses. This opportunity for studying Maya art within archaeologically controlled contexts forms the basis for *Tikal Report No. 36, The Art of Tikal*, now being edited by Arthur G. Miller.

Research on Tikal rulership is now in a dynamic phase, in which basic contextual decipherments are being discovered and proven on a pan-Maya basis. These studies, though unpublished thus far, have been circulated privately among epigraphers in a generous desire for criticism. They include a study of parentage statements by Linda Schele, Peter Mathews, and Floyd Lounsbury and the numbered successor statements by Berthold Riese. A book on emblem glyphs by Joyce Marcus (1976a) is important for Tikal in that it cites epigraphic evidence that the site was the principal center of Maya cultural and political leadership through most of the Classic Period.

Although we should be wary of adopting a "great man" view of Maya history on the basis of our new concepts of rulership, we nevertheless must observe that the placement of such events as births, enthronements, successions, and deaths of rulers into our stratigraphic sequences, together with the powerful focus which Maya public art and epigraphy places on these personages, often supplies us with possible motives for observable phenomena. It furthermore causes us to be less willing than in the past to dismiss Classic Maya development as basically incomprehensible. In the same way, we are less content with an abstract reconstruction of the economic and political processes which underlie monument carving and temple building, as well as the location of the major centers, the steady spread of sites from the core area, and finally, the transition from the central Peten to the Yucatan.

## Demography and Subsistence

Between 1957 (Haviland 1981) and 1968 (Puleston 1973), the Tikal Project developed a corpus of survey and test pit data bearing on prehistoric settlement which, at the time, was unmatched by any other project in the Southern Lowlands (Haviland 1966a). Equally important, the project amassed a large body of detailed excavation data which proved essential for a reliable understanding of the survey and test pit data (for a case in point, see Haviland 1981). Even today, Tikal is one of the few sites in the Southern Lowlands where such a quantity of excavation records exist to supplement survey and test pit data.

Although the results of the Tikal Project's investigation of settlement patterns remain to be published fully, numerous articles and dissertations have dealt with one or another aspect of this work (Becker 1971, 1973b; Carr and Hazard 1961; Fry 1969, 1979; Fry and Cox 1974; Green 1970; Harrison 1970a, 1970b; Haviland 1963, 1965, 1969, 1970, 1972c, 1974, 1978, 1981; Haviland et al. 1967; D. Puleston 1965, 1968, 1971, 1973, 1974; O. Puleston 1969; D. Puleston and Callender 1967). These serve to alert scholars to the significance of the Tikal data, as well as to make available general information for which they would otherwise have had to wait until some time in the 1980s. On the other hand, both the factual base and our general understanding of prehistoric settlement at Tikal improved as time went on, and thus statements in earlier publications have often had to be corrected and revised in later ones. Those who make use of these publications should consider them as working papers rather than the final word, and the earlier ones should not be used without reference to the most

FIGURE 10-6. Map of the environs of Tikal. Note Tikal National Park boundaries, northern and southeastern earthworks, and so-called "satellite" sites. Centrally outlined is the area of the map in Figure 10-5. Cardinally radiating from the epicenter are .5 km wide, 12 km long survey strips which defined the limits of Tikal. Strip mapping was extended northward to Uaxactun. Courtesy Tikal Project, University Museum.

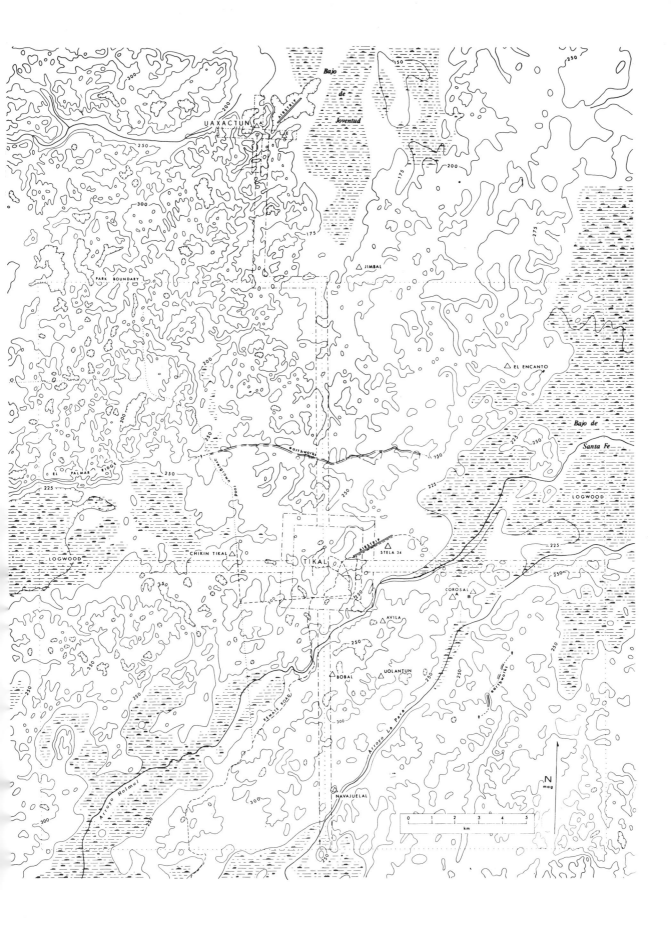

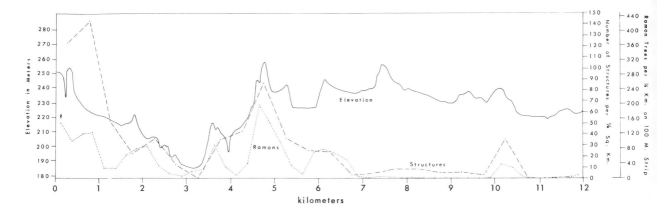

FIGURE 10-7. The south survey strip in Figure 10-6 plotted in terms of structures encountered as well as topographic elevation and occurrences of ramon trees, the latter posed anciently as a major food resource of Tikal. Courtesy Tikal Project, University Museum.

recent as well (see Haviland 1978 in this regard).

The work of the Tikal Project was instrumental in laying to rest the theory that the Maya, as swidden agriculturalists, could not have maintained populous, permanent settlements. Previously it was orthodoxly thought that sites such as Tikal must have been centers for ceremonial activity and inhabited by few, if any people, and, moreover, that the bulk of the population must have lived in houses widely dispersed over the countryside, with no discernible boundaries between communities. By contrast, Tikal was found to have covered an area of about 120.5 sq km between A.D. 480 and 830. It was bounded on the east and west by *bajos* and on the north and south by artificially constructed earthworks running between the *bajos*. There is a direct and significant correlation between these boundaries and settlement density; inside, there are roughly 112 structures per sq km; in the countryside beyond, roughly 39 per sq km. At the approximate center of the 120.5 sq km area is a clearly distinguishable nucleus consisting of Tikal's Great Plaza and contiguous monumental architecture.

The crucial point is this: the amount of cultivable land available per structure at Tikal is 0.59–0.82 ha, insufficient for more than

kitchen gardens. These, combined with intensive drainage agriculture carried out in the *bajos*, and perhaps some swidden agriculture carried out at some distance from Tikal, provided food for the numerically high and fully sedentary population.

## CONCLUSION

To summarize, the past two decades have seen sweeping changes in our understanding of the Classic Maya, and the publications from the Tikal Project have been extremely instrumental in effecting many of these transformations. Every major synthesis or analysis of Mesoamerican civilization since that of William T. Sanders and Barbara Price (1968) has relied heavily upon the project information in describing the nature of the Classic Maya community and in comparing it with those of Central Mexico and the rest of the world. As we have mentioned, the Tikal maps destroyed forever the old model of an aloof temple center and we began to see the site as a functioning multi-activities "city." At the same time, the North Acropolis excavations (W. Coe 1965a) shattered any arguments that Classic Maya civilization was imported wholesale from a highland setting. The huge scale of Haviland and Puleston's peripheral settlement survey provided ar-

306

chaeology with much firmer population estimates and total site definition. Haviland's preliminary skeletal studies suggested that Tikal suffered from improper nutrition during the Late Classic period. The ecological studies by Puleston and others at Tikal were the first to free us from the mistaken notion that the Maya relied exclusively on swidden agriculture, and the finding of the Tikal earthworks finished off our romantic images of the peaceful Maya. The discoveries of new monuments, inscriptions, and tombs at Tikal, set within their full stratigraphic contexts, have left no doubt in anyone's mind that authority focused powerfully upon personal rule and that political motive affected the art and architecture at least as strongly as did religious and aesthetic sensibilities. Finally, the excavation of a probable marketplace and other architectural groups unique to Tikal has brought us to ponder whether or not Tikal might have dominated a major trade route from the southeast through to Central Mexico. The importance of trade in the planning of Late Classic Tikal and the strategic nature of its location might therefore provide us with a plausible economic reason for its early and long-lived dominance over the rest of the Classic Maya area.

The restoration of Tikal, originally undertaken by the Tikal Project as part of its long-range goals and now continued on a grand scale by the Guatemalan Government, has made the site one of the most renowned and photographed archaeological sites in the world. This fame has surely aided in placing Tikal in the public mind as the example *par excellence* of a Maya center. Thus it is fortunate that the data from the Tikal Project years are such a suitable match to the site itself, so broad in scope and so rich in detail. Perhaps no other Maya site has been investigated with such prolonged intensity and care, and conceivably none ever will be. It is hoped that the accompanying bibliography can serve as a record of the project's early publication effort and be an introduction to the appearance of the final reports.

To conclude, it is important to recognize that highly productive studies have continued at Tikal under former project members, Carlos Rudy Larios and Miguel Orrego of the Institute of Anthropology and History of Guatemala. A major excavation within what Sylvanus G. Morley termed Group G (Str. 5E-58, etc.) is being prepared for publication in a special series. This is true as well for vast materials recouped from scores of devastating looters' digs so saddeningly situated within the confines of Tikal.

## THE BIBLIOGRAPHY

Concluding this synopsis of the Tikal Project is what we believe to be its complete, current bibliography, here arranged in standard alphabetical order. To merit inclusion, entries are authored by actual project members and by subsequent affiliates and, furthermore, wholly or significantly concern Tikal. Theses and dissertations are appropriately listed. The topical range is ample, from single "new find" contributions and yearly factual reviews to both bounded and broad interim syntheses of interpretive quality. A majority of titles adequately convey content.

This is hardly the place to search the array of factors which have and seemingly continue to promote so much divulgation outside the *Tikal Report* series. No policy guides such, and in its lieu haphazardness and individual inclination prevail. An exception does exist in the generally annual summaries of project undertakings and to some extent of progress as well. The reader fresh to Tikal might indeed usefully turn to the following items, arranged chronologically: Shook 1957 (1956 season); Shook 1958a (1956 and 1957 seasons); W. Coe 1959 (1959 season); W. Coe 1963a, 1963b (1962 season); W. Coe 1962c and Shook 1964 (reviews of 1956–1962 seasons); W. Coe 1964 (1963 season); W. Coe 1965a (1964 season); Lowe 1966 (1965 season); Lowe 1967a (1966 season, incomplete); Lowe 1968 (1967 season); and Lowe 1969 (1968 season). There are regrettable final gaps in reporting, although to a degree W. Coe 1971 corrects for this. One should add that a comprehensive statement of 1966 "sustaining area" studies is provided by Haviland et al. 1969, widely distributed in mimeographed form.

BIBLIOGRAPHY OF THE TIKAL PROJECT, 1956–1979

ADAMS, RICHARD E. W., AND AUBREY S. TRIK
1961  *Tikal Report No. 7: Temple I (Str. 5D-1): Post-constructional Activities.* Museum Monographs, The University Museum. Philadelphia: University of Pennsylvania.

BAILEY, J. W.
1972  A Preliminary Investigation of the Formal and Interpretive Histories of Monumental Relief Sculpture from Tikal, Guatemala: Pre-, Early and Middle Classic Periods. Ph.D. dissertation, Department of Anthropology, Yale University. Ann Arbor: University Microfilms.

BECKER, MARSHALL JOSEPH
1971  The Identification of a Second Plaza Plan at Tikal, Guatemala, and Its Implications for Ancient Maya Social Complexity. Ph.D. dissertation, Department of Anthropology, University of Pennsylvania. Ann Arbor: University Microfilms (BWH71-25982).
1973a  The Evidence for Complex Exchange Systems among the Ancient Maya. *American Antiquity* 38:222–223.
1973b  Archaeological Evidence for Occupational Specialization among the Classic Period Maya at Tikal, Guatemala. *American Antiquity* 38:396–406.

BRONSON, BENNET
1978  Angkor, Anuradhapura, Prambanan, Tikal: Maya Subsistence in an Asian Perspective. In *Pre-Hispanic Maya Agriculture,* edited by Peter D. Harrison and B. L. Turner II, pp. 255–300. Albuquerque: University of New Mexico Press.

CARR, ROBERT F., AND JAMES E. HAZARD
1961  *Tikal Report No. 11: Map of the Ruins of Tikal, El Peten, Guatemala.* Museum Monographs, The University Museum. Philadelphia: University of Pennsylvania.

COE, WILLIAM R.
1958  Two Carved Lintels from Tikal. *Archaeology* 11:75–80.
1959  Tikal 1959. *Expedition* 1(4):7–11.
1962a  Maya Mystery in Tikal. *Natural History* 71:10–12, 44–53.
1962b  Priestly Power and Peasant Corn: Excavations and Reconstructions at Tikal. *Illustrated London News* 240:103–106, 135–137.
1962c  A Summary of Excavation and Research at Tikal, Guatemala: 1956–1961. *American Antiquity* 27:479–507.
1963a  Current Research (Tikal). *American Antiquity* 28:417–419.
1963b  A Summary of Excavation and Research at Tikal, Guatemala: 1962. *Estudios de Cultura Maya* 3:41–64.
1964  Current Research (Tikal). *American Antiquity* 29:411–413.
1965a  Current Research (Tikal). *American Antiquity* 30:379–383.
1965b  Tikal, Guatemala, and Emergent Maya Civilization. *Science* 147:1401–1419.
1965c  Tikal: Ten Years of Study of a Maya Ruin in the Lowlands of Guatemala. *Expedition* 8(1):5–56.
1967  *Tikal: A Handbook of the Ancient Maya Ruins.* Philadelphia: The University Museum, University of Pennsylvania. (Spanish version, 1971, Asociación Tikal, Guatemala.)
1968  Tikal: In Search of the Maya Past. *The World Book Year Book,* pp. 160–176. Chicago.
1971  El Proyecto Tikal: 1956–1970. *Anales de La Sociedad de Geografía e Historia de Guatemala* 42:185–202. (Bears 1969 dateline.)
1972  Cultural Contact between the Lowland Maya and Teotihuacan as Seen from Tikal, Peten, Guatemala. In *Teotihuacán: XI Mesa Redonda* 2:257–271. Mexico City: Sociedad Mexicana de Antropología.
1975  Resurrecting the Grandeur of Tikal. *National Geographic* 148:792–795.

COE, WILLIAM R., AND VIVIAN L. BROMAN
1958  *Tikal Report No. 2: Excavations in the Stela 23 Group.* Museum Monographs, The University Museum. Philadelphia: University of Pennsylvania.

COE, WILLIAM R., AND J. J. McGINN
1963  Tikal: The North Acropolis and an Early Tomb. *Expedition* 5(2):24–32.

COE, WILLIAM R., EDWIN M. SHOOK, AND LINTON SATTERTHWAITE
1961  *Tikal Report No. 6: The Carved Wooden Lintels of Tikal.* Museum Monographs, The University Museum. Philadelphia: University of Pennsylvania.

COGGINS, CLEMENCY C.

1975 Painting and Drawing Styles at Tikal: An Historical and Iconographic Reconstruction. Ph.D. dissertation, Department of Fine Arts, Harvard University. Ann Arbor: University Microfilms (BWH76-03783).

1979b A New Order and the Role of the Calendar: Some Characteristics of the Middle Classic Period at Tikal. In *Maya Archaeology and Ethnohistory*, edited by Norman Hammond and Gordon R. Willey, pp. 38–50. Austin: University of Texas Press.

CULBERT, T. PATRICK

1963 Ceramic Research at Tikal, Guatemala. *Cerámica de Cultura Maya* 1(2–3):34–42.

1967 Preliminary Report of the Conference on the Prehistoric Ceramics of the Maya Lowlands (1965). *Estudios de Cultura Maya* 6:81–109.

1973b The Maya Downfall at Tikal. In *The Classic Maya Collapse*, edited by T. Patrick Culbert, pp. 63–92. Albuquerque: University of New Mexico Press.

1974 *The Lost Civilization: The Story of the Classic Maya*. New York: Harper and Row.

1977 Early Maya Development at Tikal, Guatemala. In *The Origins of Maya Civilization*, edited by Richard E. W. Adams, pp. 27–43. Albuquerque: University of New Mexico Press.

DAHLIN, BRUCE H.

1976 An Anthropologist Looks at the Pyramids: A Late Classic Revitalization Movement at Tikal, Guatemala. Ph.D. dissertation, Department of Anthropology, Temple University. Ann Arbor: University Microfilms (BWH76-22086).

DYSON, ROBERT H., JR.

1962 The Tikal Project—1962. *Archaeology* 15:131–132.

FERREE, LISA

1970 The Pottery Censers of Tikal, Guatemala. Ph.D. dissertation, Department of Anthropology, Southern Illinois University. Ann Arbor: University Microfilms (BWH73-06203).

FRY, ROBERT E.

1969 Ceramics and Settlement in the Periphery of Tikal, Guatemala. Ph.D. dissertation, Department of Anthropology, University of Arizona. Ann Arbor: University Microfilms (BWH70-05245).

1972 Manually Operated Post-Hole Diggers as Sampling Instruments. *American Antiquity* 37:259–261.

1979 The Economics of Pottery at Tikal, Guatemala: Models of Exchange for Serving Vessels. *American Antiquity* 44:494–512.

FRY, ROBERT E., AND S. C. COX

1973 *Late Classic Pottery Manufacture and Distribution at Tikal, Guatemala*. Working Paper No. 70. Institute for the Study of Social Change, Purdue University.

1974 The Structure of Ceramic Exchange at Tikal, Guatemala. *World Archaeology* 6:209–225.

GREEN, ERNESTENE L.

1970 The Archaeology of Navajuelal, Tikal, Guatemala, and a Test of Interpretive Method. Ph.D. dissertation, Department of Anthropology, University of Pennsylvania. Ann Arbor: University Microfilms (BWH71-19229).

GREENE, VIRGINIA, AND HATTULA MOHOLY-NAGY

1966 A Teotihuacán-Style Vessel from Tikal: A Correction. *American Antiquity* 31:432–434.

GUILLEMIN, GEORGE F.

1967 Tikal: Formación y evolución del centro ceremonial. *Anales de la Sociedad de Geografía e Historia de Guatemala* 40(3,4):203–223.

1968a Development and Function of the Tikal Ceremonial Center. *Ethnos* 33:1–39.

1968b Un "Yugo" de madera para el juego de pelota. *Antropología e Historia de Guatemala* 20:25–33.

1970a Some Aspects of Function and Symbolism at the Ceremonial Centers of Tikal and Copan. In *Verhandlungen des XXXVIII. Internationalen Amerikanistenkongress* (Stuttgart-Munich, 1968) 1:173–174. Munich.

1970b Artefactos de madera en un entierro clásico tardío de Tikal. In *Verhandlungen des XXXVIII. Internationalen Amerikanistenkongress* (Stuttgart-Munich, 1968) 1:175–178. Munich.

1970c Notas sobre restauración y reconstrucción en los sitios de Tikal e Iximche, Guatemala. In *Verhandlungen des XXXVIII. Internationalen Amerikanistenkongress* (Stuttgart-Munich, 1968) 2:119–123. Munich.

HARRISON, PETER D.

1963 A Jade Pendant from Tikal. *Expedition* 5(2):12–13.

1970a  The Central Acropolis, Tikal, Guatemala: A Preliminary Study of the Functions of Its Structural Components during the Late Classic Period. Ph.D. dissertation, Department of Anthropology, University of Pennsylvania. Ann Arbor: University Microfilms (BWH71-19235).

1970b  Form and Function in a Maya "Palace" Group. In *Verhandlungen des XXXVIII. Internationalen Amerikanistenkongress* (Stuttgart-Munich, 1968) 1 : 165–172. Munich.

HAVILAND, WILLIAM A.

1962  A "Miniature Stela" from Tikal. *Expedition* 4(3) : 2–3.

1963  Excavation of Small Structures in the Northeast Quadrant of Tikal, Guatemala. Ph.D. dissertation, Department of Anthropology, University of Pennsylvania. Ann Arbor: University Microfilms (BWH63-07050).

1965  Prehistoric Settlement at Tikal, Guatemala. *Expedition* 7(3) : 14–23.

1966a  Maya Settlement Patterns: A Critical Review. In *Archaeological Studies in Middle America*. Middle American Research Institute, Tulane University, Pub. 26 : 21–47. New Orleans.

1966b  Social Integration and the Classic Maya. *American Antiquity* 31 : 625–631.

1967  Stature at Tikal, Guatemala: Implications for Ancient Maya Demography and Social Organization. *American Antiquity* 32 : 316–325.

1969  A New Population Estimate for Tikal, Guatemala. *American Antiquity* 34 : 429–433.

1970  Tikal, Guatemala, and Mesoamerican Urbanism. *World Archaeology* 2 : 186–198.

1972a  Family Size, Prehistoric Population Estimates, and the Ancient Maya. *American Antiquity* 37 : 135–139.

1972b  Estimates of Maya Population: Comments on Thompson's Comments. *American Antiquity* 37 : 261–262.

1972c  A New Look at Classic Maya Social Organization at Tikal. *Cerámica de Cultura Maya* 8 : 1–16.

1974  Occupational Specialization at Tikal, Guatemala: Stoneworking–Monument Carving. *American Antiquity* 39 : 494–496.

1975  Tikal Report No. 22: Excavations in Residential Areas of Tikal: Group 7E-1, an Elite Residential Group. MS, University Museum, University of Pennsylvania.

1977  Dynastic Genealogies from Tikal, Guatemala: Implications for Descent and Political Organization. *American Antiquity* 42 : 61–67.

1978  On Price's Presentation of Data from Tikal. *Current Anthropology* 19 : 180–181.

1981  Dower Houses and Minor Centers at Tikal, Guatemala: An Investigation into the Identification of Valid Units in Settlement Hierarchies. In *Lowland Maya Settlement Patterns*, edited by Wendy Ashmore. Albuquerque: University of New Mexico Press.

HAVILAND, WILLIAM A., D. E. PULESTON, R. E. FRY, AND E. GREEN

1967  The Tikal Sustaining Area: Preliminary Report on the 1967 Season. MS, University Museum, University of Pennsylvania.

JONES, CHRISTOPHER

1969  The Twin-Pyramid Group Pattern: A Classic Maya Architectural Assemblage at Tikal, Guatemala. Ph.D. dissertation, Department of Anthropology, University of Pennsylvania. Ann Arbor: University Microfilms (BWH69-21375).

1977  Inauguration Dates of Three Late Classic Rulers of Tikal, Guatemala. *American Antiquity* 42 : 28–60.

in press  Tikal as a Trading Center: Why It Rose and Fell. *Acts, 43rd International Congress of Americanists* (Vancouver, 1979).

LEONE, M. P.

1971  Late Classic Burial Ceramics from Tikal, Guatemala. Master's thesis, University of Arizona.

LOTEN, H. STANLEY

1970  The Maya Architecture of Tikal, Guatemala: A Preliminary Seriation of Vaulted Building Plans. Ph.D. dissertation, Department of Anthropology, University of Pennsylvania. Ann Arbor: University Microfilms (BWH70-25686).

LOWE, GARETH W.

1966  (ed.) Current Research (Tikal). *American Antiquity* 31 : 460–463.

1967a  (ed.) Current Research (Tikal). *American Antiquity* 32 : 137.

1968  (ed.) Current Research (Tikal). *American Antiquity* 33 : 418–420.

1969  (ed.) Current Research (Tikal). *American Antiquity* 34 : 354.

MILLER, ARTHUR G.

1973a  Architectural Sculpture at Tikal, Guatemala: The Roof-Comb Sculpture on Temple I and Temple IV. In *Actas del 22nd Congreso Internacional de Historia del Arte* (Granada), pp. 177–183.

1978 A Brief Outline of the Artistic Evidence for Classic Period Cultural Contact between Maya Lowlands and Central Mexican Highlands. In *Middle Classic Mesoamerica: A.D. 400–700*, edited by Esther Pasztory, pp. 63–70. New York: Columbia University Press.

MOHOLY-NAGY, HATTULA

1962 A Tlaloc Stela from Tikal. *Expedition* 4(2): 27.

1963a The Field Laboratory at Tikal. *Expedition* 5(3): 12–17.

1963b Shells and Other Marine Material from Tikal. *Estudios de Cultura Maya* 3:65–83.

1966 Mosaic Figures from Tikal. *Archaeology* 19(2):84–89.

1976 Spatial Distribution of Flint and Obsidian Artifacts at Tikal, Guatemala. In *Maya Lithic Studies: Papers from the 1976 Belize Field Symposium*, edited by Thomas R. Hester and Norman Hammond. Special Report, Center for Archaeological Research, University of Texas at San Antonio 4:91–108.

1978 The Utilization of *Pomacea* Snails at Tikal, Guatemala. *American Antiquity* 43:65–73.

OLSON, G. W.

1969 Descriptions and Data on Soils of Tikal, El Peten, Guatemala, Central America. *Cornell Agronomy News* 69(2). Ithaca, N.Y.

PULESTON, DENNIS E.

1965 The Chultuns of Tikal. *Expedition* 7(3):24–29.

1968 *Brosimium Alicastrum* as a Subsistence Alternative for Classic Maya of the Central Southern Lowlands. Master's thesis, Department of Anthropology, University of Pennsylvania.

1971 An Experimental Approach to the Function of Classic Maya Chultuns. *American Antiquity* 36:322–335.

1973 Ancient Maya Settlement Patterns and Environment at Tikal, Guatemala: Implications for Subsistence Models. Ph.D. dissertation, Department of Anthropology, University of Pennsylvania. Ann Arbor: University Microfilms (BWH74-14128).

1974 Intersite Areas in the Vicinity of Tikal and Uaxactun. In *Mesoamerican Archaeology: New Approaches*, edited by Norman Ham-

mond, pp. 303–311. Austin: University of Texas Press.

1978 Terracing, Raised Fields, and Tree Cropping in the Maya Lowlands: A New Perspective on the Geography of Power. In *Pre-Hispanic Maya Agriculture*, edited by Peter D. Harrison and B. L. Turner II, pp. 225–245. Albuquerque: University of New Mexico Press.

PULESTON, DENNIS E., AND DONALD W. CALLENDER, JR.

1967 Defensive Earthworks at Tikal. *Expedition* 9(3):40–48.

PULESTON, DENNIS E., AND G. W. OLSON

1970 Examples of Ancient and Modern Use and Abuse of Soils. In *New York's Food and Life Sciences*, pp. 27–29.

PULESTON, DENNIS E., AND OLGA S. PULESTON

1971 An Ecological Approach to the Origins of Maya Civilization. *Archaeology* 24:330–337.

PULESTON, OLGA S.

1969 Functional Analysis of a Workshop Tool Kit from Tikal. Master's thesis, Department of Anthropology, University of Pennsylvania.

RAINEY, FROELICH G.

1956 The Tikal Project. *University Museum Bulletin* 20(4):2–24. Philadelphia: University of Pennsylvania.

1970 Tikal: A Fourteen Year Program Now Completed. *Expedition* 12(2):2–9.

RALPH, ELIZABETH K.

1965 Review of Radiocarbon Dates from Tikal and the Maya Correlation Problem. *American Antiquity* 30:421–427.

SATTERTHWAITE, LINTON

1956 Maya Dates on Stelae in Tikal "Enclosures." *University Museum Bulletin* 20(4):25–40. Philadelphia: University of Pennsylvania.

1958a *Tikal Report No. 3: The Problem of Abnormal Stela Placements at Tikal and Elsewhere.* Museum Monographs, The University Museum. Philadelphia: University of Pennsylvania.

1958b *Tikal Report No. 4: Five Newly Discovered Carved Monuments at Tikal and New Data on Four Others.* Museum Monographs, The University Museum. Philadelphia: University of Pennsylvania.

1960 Maya "Long Count" Numbers. *Expedition* 2(2):36–37.

1963 Note on Hieroglyphs on Bone from the

Tomb below Temple I, Tikal. *Expedition* 6(1):18–19.

1964 Dates in a New Tikal Hieroglyphic Text as Katun-Baktun Anniversaries. *Estudios de Cultura Maya* 4:203–222.

1967 Radiocarbon and Maya Long Count Dating of "Structure 10" (Str. 5D-52, First Story), Tikal. *Revista Mexicana de Estudios Antropológicos* 21:225–249.

SATTERTHWAITE, LINTON, VIVIAN L. BROMAN, AND WILLIAM A. HAVILAND

1961 *Tikal Report No. 8: Miscellaneoı Investigations: Excavation near Fragı ent 1 of Stela 17, with Observations on Stela P34 and Miscellaneous Stone 25; Excavation of Stela 25, Fragment 1; Excavation of Stela 27; Excavation of Stela 28, Fràgment 1.* Museum Monographs, The University Museum. Philadelphia: University of Pennsylvania.

SATTERTHWAITE, LINTON, AND WILLIAM R. COE

1968 The Maya-Christian Calendrical Correlation and the Archaeology of the Peten. In *XXXVII Congreso Internacional de Americanistas: Actas y Memorias* (Buenos Aires, 1966) 3:3–21.

SATTERTHWAITE, LINTON, AND ELIZABETH K. RALPH

1960 New Radiocarbon Dates and the Maya Correlation Problems. *American Antiquity* 26:165–184.

SHOOK, EDWIN M.

1957 The Tikal Project. *University Museum Bulletin* 21(3):36–52. Philadelphia: University of Pennsylvania.

1958a *Tikal Report No. 1: Field Director's Report: The 1956 and 1957 Seasons.* Museum Monographs, The University Museum. Philadelphia: University of Pennsylvania.

1958b The Temple of the Red Stela. *Expedition* 1(1):26–33. (Spanish translation, 1958, *Antropología e Historia de Guatemala* 11:7–14.)

1960 Tikal Stela 29. *Expedition* 2(2):28–35.

1962 Tikal: Problems of a Field Director. *Expedition* 4(2):11–26.

1964 Archaeological Investigations in Tikal, Peten, Guatemala. In *XXXV Congreso Internacional de Americanistas: Actas y Memorias* (Mexico, 1962) 1:379–386. Mexico City.

SHOOK, EDWIN M., AND WILLIAM R. COE

1961 *Tikal Report No. 5: Tikal: Numeration, Terminology, and Objectives.* Museum Monographs, The University Museum. Philadelphia: University of Pennsylvania.

SHOOK, EDWIN M., AND ALFRED KIDDER II

1961 The Painted Tomb at Tikal. *Expedition* 4(1):2–7. (Spanish translation, 1962, *Antropología e Historia de Guatemala* 14:5–10.)

STUCKENRATH, ROBERT, JR., WILLIAM R. COE, AND ELIZABETH K. RALPH

1966 University of Pennsylvania Radiocarbon Dates IX: Tikal Series. *Radiocarbon* 8:371–385.

TRIK, AUBREY S.

1963 The Splendid Tomb of Temple I at Tikal, Guatemala. *Expedition* 6(1):2–18.

WEBSTER, HELEN T.

1963 Tikal Graffiti. *Expedition* 6(1):36–47.

# 11. Dzibilchaltun

*E. WYLLYS ANDREWS V*

DZIBILCHALTUN is a large Maya site about 20 km from the Gulf of Mexico and 14 km north of the center of Merida, northwest Yucatan. The region is a flat limestone plateau, only about 5 m above sea level. The climate is semiarid, and the vegetation today consists of patches of scrubby thorn forest mixed with sisal fields. The site receives only about 700 mm of rain a year, and precipitation diminishes rapidly to the north. Few archaeological sites are known between Dzibilchaltun and the shore. Most of those reported are relatively small and lie within the 10 km zone north of Dzibilchaltun.

The site was reported in 1942 (E. W. Andrews IV 1942; Brainerd 1942, 1958:15–18). Major excavations, directed by E. Wyllys Andrews IV of the Middle American Research Institute at Tulane University, began in early 1957 and continued until 1965 (Andrews IV 1959, 1960, 1961, 1962, 1965a, 1965b, 1968, 1969, 1972). The project included research at 2 Formative sites that lie west and north of Dzibilchaltun proper, called Komchen and the Mirador Group. Goals foremost in 1957 included the docu-

mentation of a long and if possible complete sequence at a northern site (no such sequence was available), the definition of the earliest communities in the area and their pottery, a settlement pattern study, and stratigraphic evidence that would elucidate the chronological and developmental relationship of Puuc (Florescent) architecture to an earlier block-wall and slab-vault style (Early period II).

The project has provided a sequence running from about 800 B.C.[1] until after the Spanish Conquest of Yucatan, although the site was at times not heavily occupied. The other goals were attained, at least in large part, and some of the final analyses of data exceed in richness the results that could have been expected in 1957 or even in 1965, when field research ended.[2]

From January to June 1980 the Middle American Research Institute studied settlement patterns at the large Formative site of Komchen, 6 km northwest of the center of Classic Dzibilchaltun. Some of the preliminary results of this project at Komchen, which was first investigated by Tulane in 1959–1960 and 1961–1962 (Andrews IV

313

| GREGORIAN CALENDAR | NORTHERN MAYA LOWLANDS CULTURE PERIODS | DZIBILCHALTUN CERAMIC COMPLEXES | G. W. BRAINERD CERAMIC STAGES (1958) | R. E. SMITH CERAMIC COMPLEXES (1971) | TIKAL | PALENQUE | MAYA LONG COUNT |
|---|---|---|---|---|---|---|---|
| 1600 | COLONIAL | | COLONIAL | CHAUACA | | | 12. 0.0.0.0 |
| 1500 | | | | CHIKINCHEL | | | 11.15.0.0.0 |
| 1400 | DECADENT | CHECHEM | LATE | TASES | | | 11.10.0.0.0 |
| 1300 | (LATE POSTCLASSIC) | | (MAYAPAN) | | | | 11. 5.0.0.0 |
| 1200 | | | MEXICAN MIDDLE | HOCABA | | | 11. 0.0.0.0 |
| 1100 | MODIFIED FLORESCENT (EARLY POSTCLASSIC) | 2 ZIPCHE 1 | EARLY (TOLTEC CHICHEN) | SOTUTA | ? CABAN | ? POST-BALUNTE | 10.15.0.0.0 |
| 1000 | Puuc Coast-East PURE | 2 COPO | (PUUC) | CEHPECH | | | 10.10.0.0.0 |
| 900 | FLORESCENT (TERMINAL CLASSIC) North | | | | | BALUNTE | 10. 5.0.0.0 |
| 800 | Puuc | 1 | FLORESCENT | (TEPEU 2) MOTUL | EZNAB IMIX | MURCIELAGOS | 10. 0.0.0.0 |
| 700 | EARLY PERIOD II (LATE CLASSIC) | | (CHENES) | (TEPEU 1) | IK | OTOLUM | 9.15.0.0.0 |
| 600 | | | | | | | 9.10.0.0.0 |
| 500 | EARLY PERIOD I | PIIM | REGIONAL | COCHUAH | MANIK | MOTIEPA | 9. 5.0.0.0 |
| 400 | (EARLY CLASSIC) | | | (TZAKOL) | | | 9. 0.0.0.0 |
| 300 | | | | | | PICOTA | 8.15.0.0.0 |
| 200 | | 2 | ? | CIMI | | | 8.10.0.0.0 |
| 100 A.D. | LATE FORMATIVE | | FORMATIVE | | CAUAC | PRE-PICOTA | |
| 0 B.C. | | XCULUL | | | | ? | |
| 100 | | | | TIHOSUCO | | | |
| 200 | | 1 | | (CHICANEL) | CHUEN | | |
| 300 | | | | | | | |
| 400 | MIDDLE | 3 | | | TZEC | | |
| 500 | FORMATIVE | 2 NABANCHE | | | | | |
| 600 | | | | | EB | | |
| 700 | | 1 | | | | | |
| 800 | | | | | | | |

FIGURE 11-1. Chronological chart for the Northern Maya Lowlands. The chart follows an 11.16.0.0.0 correlation of Maya and Christian calendars and uses the terminology established by E. W. Andrews IV for Northern Maya Lowland cultural periods. In this scheme, which I believe is useful primarily for the northern plains in the state of Yucatan and for the Puuc region of Yucatan and northern Campeche, Early period I corresponds to the general Mesoamerican Early Classic, Early period II to the Late Classic, the Pure Florescent to the Terminal Classic, the Modified Florescent to the Early Postclassic, and the Decadent period to the Late Postclassic. A difference between this chart and that prepared by Andrews IV (1965a:289, Table 1, especially the left column) for his article in Volume 2 of the *Handbook of Middle American Indians* is the deletion of long transitions between the Early period and the Pure Florescent and between the Modified Florescent and the Decadent periods. These changes, based on my own judgments and those of Michael P. Simmons, of the architectural sequence, in the first case, and of the ceramic sequence, in the second, have the effect of shortening the sequence by about 250 years (see Ball and Andrews V 1975; Andrews V 1978; Andrews IV and Andrews V 1980). The Formative sequence also reflects major changes that result from the 1980 project at Komchen, notably the deletion of the Komchen phase and the beginning of the Late Formative Xculul phase at 300 B.C. (see note 3). The base of the Middle Formative Nabanche phase is left intentionally vague in this chart. The columns illustrating the Tikal and Palenque sequences were drawn after consultation with Joseph W. Ball.

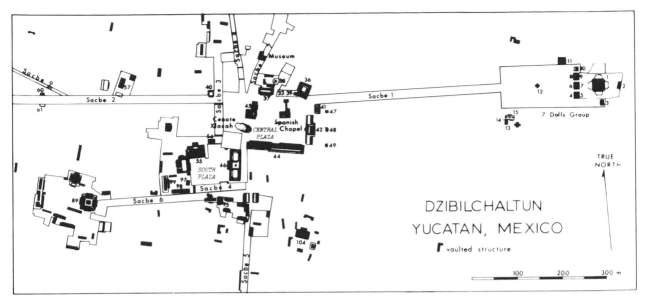

FIGURE 11-2. Map of the central portion of Dzibilchaltun. This simplified map omits most of the small structures. The complete site map appears as Middle American Research Institute Pub. 47 (Stuart et al. 1979).

1962, 1965b), are included in the following pages, although analysis of the 1980 data is still in its early stages at the time of writing.[3]

## MIDDLE FORMATIVE VILLAGES AND TOWNS (NABANCHE 1–2, CA. 800–400 B.C.)

The Nabanche phase at Dzibilchaltun contains the earliest ceramics so far excavated in the Northern Maya Lowlands, with the exceptions of the lowest pottery from Loltun Cave, some of which probably dates to the Early Formative period (Norberto González and Ricardo Velásquez, personal communications, 1978, 1980), and very likely the pattern burnished monochrome ceramics from Mani Cenote (Brainerd 1958:24). Formative ceramics are scattered over the entire site (Kurjack 1974:Fig. 3), but no important settlement seems to have existed near Cenote Xlacah, at the center of Dzibilchaltun. Nabanche architectural remains are known from the Mirador Group and from Komchen. The Mirador Group, 7.4 km south-southwest of Cenote Xlacah, includes more than 30 large to medium mounds, all of which were occupied during the Formative period. This group was badly sacked in 1978. Its center

consisted of 6 mounds that faced onto an open plaza (Fig. 11-4). It is not certain, however, that this central arrangement was so focused before the late Nabanche phase.

Structure 605, a low mound on the south side of the plaza, contained remains dating from the beginning of Nabanche to the Xculul phase. The earliest structures under this platform included a low, rectangular, 60 sq m platform faced with a thick wall of mud and gravel covered by lime plaster. This platform faced south onto a low, paved terrace of about the same dimensions. Remains of several single-room oval dwellings averaging about 2 × 3 m lay just above bedrock to the south of the terrace (Fig. 11-5).

Structure 605 expanded to the south, east, and west during Nabanche 2, and several small superstructures of various shapes were built atop the growing platform. A round structure, 4 m in diameter, had walls of four courses of poorly shaped stones that rose to about 60 cm. Beside it was a slightly smaller rectangular room with a doorway facing west. A further structure had three straight sides, rectangular rear corners, and a rounded front side with a doorway.

The latest Formative room at Structure

315

FIGURE 11-3. Map of the Maya area showing sites referred to in the text.

316

FIGURE 11-4. Structures 601–606 in the Mirador Group, Dzibilchaltun, about 7 km west of the center of the Classic site. The drawing shows the plaza at about the end of the Late Formative period. The small shrines on these platforms date to the Decadent period, and the two oval rooms in the plaza are probably Colonial. Structure 605, which was intensively excavated, is at upper right.

605 was probably an oval sweat house, built on bedrock against the main platform retaining wall (Fig. 11-7). Walls were at least 110 cm high and were presumably roofed with poles and thatch. A plaster floor covered most of the interior but in one area was replaced by a zone of burned stones and nested sherds. A stairway led down from the main platform into the room. Beside the steps was a rectangular, plaster- and stone-lined trough, perhaps for storing water.

By the end of Nabanche 2, Structure 605 encompassed about 600 sq m, and all earlier superstructures had been covered by fill. The platform in later periods apparently supported no permanent buildings, although perishable superstructures may have been present. The original platform, oriented to the south, had become a U-shaped structure, facing north onto the open plaza. The other five platforms around this plaza, one of which attained a height of 3.5 m before the end of the Formative period, all had attained considerable size by the end of Nabanche 1–2.

Most of the other tested structures in the Mirador Group contained Nabanche 1–2 sherds, indicating that before the end of the Middle Formative the group possessed a presumably ceremonial core surrounded by a small village.

Komchen, 6 km northwest of the center of Dzibilchaltun, was far larger than the Mirador Group. Occupation at this heavily looted site was concentrated in the Middle and Late Formative periods, although several portions of it, especially near the center, were reoccupied in the Late Classic. These late inhabitants built a number of perishable dwellings on ruined Formative platforms but rarely added significantly to the size of earlier constructions.

The extent of Komchen during the Nabanche phase has not yet been determined. A limited analysis of the sherds obtained in the course of the 1980 investigations indicates that settlement was widespread, perhaps covering as much as 1 sq km, but with what density is not known. Most of the very big

317

FIGURE 11-5. Nabanche 1 house in Structure 605, Mirador Group, Dzibilchaltun: a small single-room oval house measuring 3 × 3.8 m, with a lime plaster floor and a wall of unshaped stones set in mud mortar. The original height of the wall is unknown.

FIGURE 11-6. Nabanche 2 house in Structure 605, Mirador Group, Dzibilchaltun: rectangular house with rounded corners.

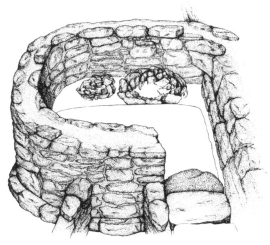

FIGURE 11-7. A Nabanche 2 sweat house in Structure 605, Dzibilchaltun. This room was attached to the west wall of the main platform. Steps lead down from the platform surface; a rectangular masonry-lined enclosure, possibly for water storage, is to the left. At the far side of the room are two fire-blackened concentrations of nested sherds and stones.

platforms near the site center date to the Late Formative, but at least two major constructions predate 300 B.C. The fact that these are the only two investigated in detail leads me to believe that other large platforms may contain sizable remains of the Middle Formative.

Structure 450, one of the most extensive building complexes, consisted of a pyramidal platform facing south onto a large raised plaza (Andrews IV and Andrews V 1980: Figs. 28–41). Its earliest construction dates to Nabanche 2, with Nabanche 1 sherds underlying this fill in pockets. A 1.3 m high, four-step platform fronted on a rectangular terrace that covered approximately 1,400 sq m to a depth of as much as 1 m. Walls over 1 m high enclosed this probably empty plaza on three sides; at its southern end these walls were replaced by two long, rectangular platforms, which also stood at least 1 m high and limited access to the plaza. It is not known whether any of the platforms bore superstructures.

Structure 500, one of the four largest platforms at the center of Komchen, appears to have been started in late Nabanche 1–2 or perhaps earlier; by about A.D. 250 or 300, when construction ceased, it covered close to 70 × 75 m at a height of about 2.5 m and supported a large pyramidal structure at its south end that rose to a total height of more than 7 m (Andrews IV and Andrews V 1980:Fig. 44). Like all other big platforms near the core of Komchen, Structure 500 was extensively looted for stone in the early 1950s, and only portions of the huge platform and even less of the pyramid remain today. Remnants of the earliest construction periods are very limited.

The first major construction inside Structure 500, probably dating to late Nabanche 1–2, consisted of a platform or terrace, about 50 cm high, of undetermined extent, on which was built a further platform with regularly coursed, battered walls that rose at least 3 m. Its size is unknown, but one side was about 22 m long. This wall and the floor on which it rests were covered with lime plaster. No other features can be assigned definitely to this period, although several extensions and low adjacent platforms are probably roughly contemporary.

These early platforms at Structures 450 and 500 were clearly different from the more modest residential constructions that surround the core of Komchen. Before 400 B.C. both Komchen and the Mirador Group provide sure evidence of public architecture in formal arrangements concentrated near the centers of villages or towns.

The Nabanche 1–2 ceramic complex is assigned peripheral membership in the Mamom ceramic sphere (J. W. Ball, personal communications), but important characteristics distinguish it from contemporary complexes of the Southern Maya Lowlands. Some major southern groups are common in Nabanche 1–2, including Achiotes Unslipped, Sapote Striated, and Joventud Red; Pital Cream and Muxanal Red-on-Cream are present in small quantities. A Dzudzuquil Buff group appears to be a local development, as

does Ucu Black, although the latter sometimes approaches the southern Chunhinta Black slips. Nabanche Joventud Red includes rare vessels with an opaque, consistent bright orange slip that may be related to southern Middle Preclassic orange pottery. Slips on Nabanche pottery, including Joventud Red, are generally hard, opaque, and glossy, in contrast to coeval waxy slips to the south.

The origins of the Nabanche complex are far from clear. Joseph W. Ball suggests ties with southern Middle Formative complexes, the Acachen complex of Becan, closer complexes such as Edzna I and Dzibilnocac I, and Lopez Mamom in northern Belize. It also appears to share traits with early Isthmian complexes, especially in the local black and buff groups, and Ball believes that a portion of the initial colonization of northwest Yucatan may have been from the Gulf Coastal Lowlands (see also Joesink-Mandeville 1970; Joesink-Mandeville and Meluzin 1976).

Ball and I currently prefer a beginning date of about 800 B.C. for the Nabanche phase. Hearth charcoal from an early Nabanche deposit in the Mirador Group is dated by C14 to 975 B.C. ± 340 (LJ-505). Given the uncertainty about the origins of the Nabanche complex and the paucity of early C14 dates, we should best regard the 800 B.C. estimate with caution.

Five of the seven Nabanche burials were simple interments in platform fill; the other two were urn burials containing a child and an infant. Most were secondary interments. Pottery vessels constituted the only furniture, and these were found only with the urn burials.

Long distance trade was limited in Nabanche 1–2. No jade securely dates to this span, although a few pieces in later fill may be early or middle Nabanche. Only four fragmentary obsidian blades, one dating to Nabanche 1, are assigned to this period. The chert was local and of poor quality, and grinding implements were of coarse local limestone (Rovner 1975:142–146).

Evidence for subsistence, as in other periods at Dzibilchaltun, is mostly indirect. Numerous limestone metates and a few crude manos suggest maize agriculture, and quantities of shell in middens and fill indicate extensive marine gathering. Remains of large game animals, especially white-tailed deer, brocket, peccary, and dog, are more common in Formative levels than in the Classic, suggesting possible overhunting by a much larger population in the latter period, or perhaps expansion of agricultural lands with a concomitant reduction of the subsistence base for large fauna.

These and other data suggest that during early Nabanche 1-2 settlements in northwest Yucatan were small farming villages, scattered regularly over the landscape. Formal arrangements of probably nonresidential, public architecture appeared sometime during late Nabanche 1-2, probably as early as 500 B.C., in the Mirador Group, at Komchen, and presumably at other Formative sites in this area. This development coincided with an increase in population that reached a peak in the Late Formative period.

## The Growth and Decline of Formative Complex Society (Nabanche 3 and Xculul Phases, ca. 400 b.c.–a.d. 250)

Komchen remained the largest settlement in this part of northwestern Yucatan during the late Middle Formative and Late Formative. Structure 500, perhaps the most important focus of civic and religious activity during Nabanche 3 (ca. 400–300 B.C.), is at present the only investigated platform showing major activity during this span. It approached its final size during these last years of the Middle Formative. The main rubble-filled platform was raised to an average height of about 2.5 m and covered about 70 m north-south by more than 40 m east-west. Lower rectangular platforms, definitely complete by this time, and perhaps considerably earlier, extended east and west from the south end of the platform, bringing the east-west length of the T-shaped complex to about 75 m. The pyramidal structure at its south end was also enlarged, reaching a height of at least 3 m by the end of this phase and covering about 30 × 30 m. Its central stairway, enlarged several times, faced north; symmetrically-placed ramps and stairways provided access to the southeast and southwest corners of the huge building. Although destruction through looting prevents more than a sketchy reconstruction of this building phase, Structure 500 was as large as or larger than any currently recorded Middle Formative platform in the Maya Lowlands.

Construction techniques, associated pottery, and C14 dates lead us to place this building in the late Middle Formative, rather than later. Battered platform walls of roughly shaped blocks set with long, thin spalls in regular courses are identical to those of Nabanche 1-2 and different from walls of the Late Formative Xculul phase.

Nabanche 3 ceramics, recovered for the first time in quantity during the 1980 season, derive directly from those of Nabanche 1-2, which they resemble more closely than they do those of the Xculul complex. Achiotes Unslipped and Sapote Striated remain major groups, indistinguishable from those of Nabanche 1-2. Ucu Black continues, but tends somewhat more to opaque, less waxy slips than earlier. Nabanche 3 black pottery also shows a slightly different range of forms. A Tamanche Variegated Buff group developed directly from the Nabanche 1-2 Dzudzuquil Buff, which it more closely resembles than it does the Late Formative Percebes Buff. The Sierra Red ceramics of Nabanche 3 form a continuum with Nabanche 1-2 Joventud Red; the Kayal variety of the Sierra group continues with little change in slip characteristics through the Late Formative. Other Late Formative red types do not appear in Nabanche 3, however. The complex marks the end of a local tradition, with little influence from other regions.

Two C14 dates for Xculul 1, 250 ± 90 B.C. (LJ-279) and 320 ± 80 B.C. (I-171), set an end date for Nabanche 3 no later than about 300

B.C. The estimated beginning date of 400 B.C. relies on the presence of Sierra Red and certain form attributes.

The extent of Nabanche 3 settlement at Komchen should be defined by current research, but the size of Structure 500 alone bespeaks a respectable community. Good-quality jade in building fill provides our best evidence for long distance trade. No obsidian was found in Nabanche 3 deposits.

The greatest community size and density at Komchen was reached in the Late Formative period, possibly by the end of Xculul 1 (ca. A.D. 150). At its peak, the town covered about 2 sq km, with perhaps 900–1,000 individual structures. About five huge platforms cover 5 ha around a central plaza measuring 100 × 150 m. Hundreds of large, low residential platforms ranging from 10 to 30 m on a side spread out 500–700 m from the core in all directions; these probably bore more than one perishable superstructure each and could in many cases have housed substantial extended families. Scattered among these are smaller structures, probably also house platforms, that tend to be more numerous toward the outer edge of the site.

The largest platforms at Komchen are as massive as some of the great structures at Classic Dzibilchaltun. Two, facing each other across the plaza, measure about 25 × 80 m; another is about 60 × 65 m; and Structure 500 covers 70 × 75 m. All four originally rose at least 8 m and possibly much more, but looting has destroyed all traces of superstructures on them.

Komchen was not arranged in groups or in clusters of the kind found at Dzibilchaltun, and at many other large Classic settlements. Structures were evenly distributed, except near the borders of the site, where they thinned out rapidly, and the community was relatively dense. Concentric zoning is apparent in the concentration of massive ruins at the site core and in the tendency for large residential platforms to be more numerous and larger as one approaches the center, but this latter tendency is not marked. The absence of abrupt changes indicates that the site grew gradually, by accretion, from the center out.

The small Nabanche 2 platform inside Structure 450 was enlarged several times in Xculul 1. By late Xculul 1 the platform had grown to a height of 3.5 m above the adjacent terrace. The south side consisted of a broad inset stairway flanked by 4 m wide sloping balustrades bordered by recessed panels. It could not be determined whether Structure 450 bore a masonry superstructure.

The large enclosed Nabanche plaza in front of Structure 450 was buried sometime in late Xculul 1 or Xculul 2 by a larger terrace about 1 m higher. This new terrace was extended around the east and west sides of Structure 450, but stone-robbing had destroyed its form here. No ceramics from this complex postdate the Formative period.

From the south side of Structure 450 a 6.7 m wide causeway, oriented 33° east of true north, runs 230–250 m southwest to abut the southeast corner of the larger Structure 500. The 1 m high road was built in Xculul 1.

Structure 500, for reasons unknown, was abandoned for a short period at the beginning of the Late Formative. The rebuilding of the badly decayed walls and several new additions coincided approximately with the appearance of the Xculul 1 ceramic complex. A number of early walls were shored up or covered by new ones, the main north stairway was completely rebuilt, and the low southern wing platforms of Nabanche 3 were broadened, raised to the height of the main platform, and joined to it. A new stairway on the east side of the pyramid faced the southern terminus of the new causeway. The Xculul phase pyramid now exceeds 7 m in height but was probably much higher before the mound was looted.

During Xculul 2 the lower portion of the massive north stairs was covered by a set of five or more gradual steps with broad treads. The last datable additions to Structure 500, pairs of broad rectangular projections beside the latest steps, are placed at A.D. 250–300.

Structure 605, in the Mirador Group, was enlarged in the Xculul phase to the east, west, and south. The original Nabanche 1 platform, on the north side, remained a courtyard surrounded by higher surfaces that were accessible from it by short stairways. Construction of a broad stairway along the north side of the structure emphasized the reorientation of the platform in this direction, facing the large, open plaza defined by Structures 601–606. The final enlargements to Structure 605 produced a one-level platform covering about 750 sq m, still oriented to the north. Structure 603, the largest platform in this group, was far smaller than any of the major buildings at Komchen.

Sometime near the end of Xculul, construction ceased at both sites, and after the Formative period both were effectively abandoned for a time. The only known group of platforms that dates exclusively to the terminal phase of the Formative period is the Xculul Group, 2.6 km west of Cenote Xlacah. This group, now destroyed, included about a dozen residential platforms, similar to those at Komchen, that were enlarged continuously throughout Xculul 2 (Andrews IV and Andrews V 1980: Figs. 48–55). They were probably abandoned at the end of this period but, like many structures at Komchen and the Mirador Group, were reoccupied during the Late Classic period.

Architectural ties between Dzibilchaltun and other Lowland Maya sites in the Late Formative are limited. The excavated buildings show only general similarities to known structures in the Central and Southern Lowlands and suggest a local development that owed relatively little to foreign architectural traditions.

Those resemblances that do emerge, however, indicate contacts with areas whose connections with northwest Yucatan may have been by coastal routes, rather than overland. Structures 450 and 500 were huge, single-level platforms with a pyramidal structure at one end. This arrangement is also characteristic of Late Formative sites in northern Belize, including Structure 34 at Cuello (Hammond 1977: 81), Structure 29 at Cerros (Freidel 1978: 256–257; personal communi-

cation, 1978), and others, but it is not a Southern Lowland feature. The presence of Late Formative masonry causeways at Komchen and Cerros (Freidel, personal communication, 1978) may also reflect a special relationship between these sites. Structure 29 at Cerros is connected to a smaller structure by a 120 m long causeway oriented 31° east of true north, remarkably similar to the 33° orientation of the Komchen road. Architectural and sculptural features at these northern Belize sites, however, are far more like Southern Lowland than Northern examples.

The Xculul 1 balustrades flanking the stairway of Structure 450 are without contemporaneous parallel in the Maya Lowlands, but they are very similar to Protoclassic Horcones balustrades at Chiapa de Corzo (Lowe and Agrinier 1960: 20–22; Lowe 1962: 9–10). At both sites balustrades must have been present no later than A.D. 1, and at Komchen their presence by 100 B.C. or earlier is likely. The nature of the contact implied is far from clear.

Xculul ceramics are related to the Chicanel ceramic sphere, although a number of important types are local. A few groups continue with minor changes from Nabanche, such as Achiotes Unslipped, Sapote Striated (now rare), and Sierra Red, but most groups are new. Percebes Buff, an extremely variable group, is probably related to the Nabanche 3 Chacah Variegated Buff. Xanaba Red, a widespread northern Yucatan group, is distinguished from Sierra Red by its flaky slip. The common Unto Preslip-Striated Black has no clear antecedents and is apparently a localized type. Polvero Black, also limited to Xculul, is frequent. Less important complex members include San Felipe Brown, Flor Cream, a burnished gray pottery, and an early orange and red-on-orange glossy ware (the last limited to Xculul 2). Resist trickle decoration is increasingly frequent during Xculul, especially on red and on buff slips. This mode can be traced back to a few Nabanche 3 examples.

Ball believes the closest ties of the Xculul

complex are to the Late Formative Cienaga sphere of northeast Yucatan and to contemporaneous pottery in northern Belize. The direction of these links argues strongly for maritime contacts.

Two burials are dated to early Xculul 1, both from Structure 450 and both quite different from Nabanche interments. They are simple burials situated on or near the north-south axial line of the platform. The first, in fill, consisted of the flexed legs and pelvis of an adult, without accompanying furnishings. The second, placed in construction fill of a later enlargement of the platform, contained a mature male, a younger female, parts of a child aged 3–6, and artifacts of shell, jade, and sherd. The male was extended, and both adults lacked skulls. In place of the man's skull was a dish.

Both burials were probably dedicatory. The partial skeleton in the first and the missing heads in the second also raise the possibility of sacrificial interments.

Three probable early Xculul 1 burials were found in Structure 605. All were simple. One contained the scattered remains of three adults accompanied by a bone needle, some shell beads, five jade beads, and a jade pendant. Seven or eight burials date later in the Xculul phase. All were simple primary or secondary interments without exotic furnishings.

Jade artifacts appear with some regularity in early Xculul burials and caches. About ten beads and pendants derive from offerings, and another ten or so pieces, including portions of ear-flare assemblies, were encountered in Xculul 1 fill. Late Xculul burials and caches contained no jade, nor did the fill of Structure 226, and it is likely that jade imports to Komchen and other sites in the Dzibilchaltun area dropped off sharply after Xculul 1. Obsidian was even rarer in the Late Formative than in the Nabanche phase. Only one fragmentary blade from the 1959–1962 excavations can be dated with certainty to Xculul 1, and not one is sure to pertain to Xculul 2.

Ground and chipped stone artifacts continued to be made of local, poor-quality stone; the good chert and limestone of later periods were not imported during the Formative. This circumstance leads Irwin Rovner (personal communication, 1978) to suggest that the impetus for formal, long distance trade was related to external factors, rather than being an expansion of local trading activities. It also might indicate that trade in exotic materials was largely a maritime phenomenon.

Komchen has several hallmarks of Classic sites in this area, including a core of massive buildings enclosing a large plaza, a densely inhabited and concentrically zoned residential area covering 2 sq km, a raised masonry causeway identical to those of later periods, and evidence of long distance trade, notably in jade. The community at its peak must have included several thousand persons, and its emergence during the late Middle Formative surely coincided with the rise of hierarchical political structures and social stratification in northwest Yucatan. The existence of this huge early community raises questions regarding its origin and its role in the development of Lowland Maya civilization.

Two generally opposed points of view characterize the recent literature on this topic. William T. Sanders (1977), Joseph W. Ball (1977c), and David L. Webster (1977) regard the development of complex, stratified societies as a response primarily to local conditions. In somewhat different ways, they see conflict over decreasing quantities of arable land leading to the establishment of institutionalized elites throughout the Maya Lowlands. Ball suggests that the Maya of northwest Yucatan, living on relatively poor agricultural land along the Gulf of Mexico, were subject to intense environmental circumscription and that the development of large Late Formative centers such as Komchen can best be explained by a need to control and protect the farming land necessary to support a growing population.

William L. Rathje (1971) and David A. Freidel (1978, 1979) have argued that control of regional trade was in some instances a more important mechanism than local pressures in the rise of stratified sociopolitical structures. Here their arguments diverge, however, for Rathje views this process as emanating from a "core" area in the Peten, whereas Freidel, drawing on evidence of changing settlement patterns at the large Formative site of Cerros, argues that complex societies developed more or less simultaneously in various parts of the lowlands in response to increasing participation in regional trade networks, or interaction spheres.

The case of Komchen seems to support Freidel's interpretation. The site is 19 km from the Gulf Coast and about 15 km south of the salt marshes that lie behind the present barrier beaches. Most of the land north of the site is not suitable for farming, and rainfall, which averages only 600–800 mm per year at the center of Dzibilchaltun, several kilometers south of Komchen, drops off drastically toward the coast. This area in historic times provided large quantities of salt for export (Roys 1957; A. Andrews 1980a, 1980b), and several authors have argued in recent years that this resource was exploited by the Classic period (for example, Andrews IV 1968) or earlier (A. Andrews 1980a:253–255). Jack D. Eaton (1978:62–63) has suggested that salt production was a function of some of the small Late Formative coastal sites situated in the nearby salt marshes. With the growth of large Late Formative towns in the Maya Lowlands, the need for salt would have increased, and sites like Komchen were ideally situated to exploit and export this commodity. Salt trade to many parts of the lowlands would have been far easier along the coast and subsequently by inland waterways than along inland routes, and it seems certain that Komchen was involved in a trading network extending in both directions around the coast of the peninsula. Its phenomenal growth in the Late Formative probably derived in part from the resultant commercial stimulation.

The limited archaeological data that bear on the question appear to offer no conflict. Long distance trade in jade began about the time Komchen was becoming a powerful center, and external relationships in both architectural style and ceramics argue that maritime rather than inland interaction was paramount in linking this site to other centers in southern Mesoamerica. The distinct form taken by this early complex society in northwest Yucatan does not prompt us to derive it in any direct fashion from earlier or contemporary manifestations in the Southern or Central Lowlands.

One of the most intriguing questions in northern Maya archaeology concerns the collapse of Formative social and political organization in the Dzibilchaltun area by about A.D. 250. The near-abandonment of Komchen by the end of the Xculul phase was followed by a hiatus that lasted until about A.D. 700. The reasons for this decline are unknown. Ball (1978b:216) argues that overpopulation, overtaxing of local subsistence systems, and disease were responsible. I hesitate to accept this explanation, for in later times this area supported far larger populations. Freidel (1978:260) suggests that the collapse of Dzibilchaltun coincided with the disintegration of a coastal trading pattern that prevailed in the Late Formative and its replacement by interior trade routes leading directly to the Central and Southern Lowlands. Like Ball's explanation, this reconstruction of events in the north is internally consistent, in that it traces the downfall of complex Formative communities to the same processes that caused their rise. But it, too, suffers from a lack of hard supporting evidence. We are not yet sure, for example, who controlled the northwestern salt beds in the Early Classic period. The collapse of Komchen coincided roughly with the rise of Teotihuacan, but no hard evidence links these events. (See Ball 1977b:182–187 for a detailed and innovative reconstruction of northern Maya prehistory in this interval, speculating on the roles of early Putun traders and the sites of Becan and Teotihuacan.)

## The Early and Middle Classic Hiatus (Piim and Early Copo 1 Phases, ca. a.d. 250–700)

Architecture of Early period I (ca. A.D. 250–600) and the first part of Early period II (ca. A.D. 600–700) at Dzibilchaltun consists of a few plaster floors and only one structure, oddly located in the Mirador Group, far to the west of the Late Classic center. Piim complex pottery, however, was encountered in 4 percent of the 392 unvaulted structures that were test-pitted (Kurjack 1974: Table 2).

Structure 612, period 1, was a small, Early period I platform supporting a one-room, unvaulted masonry superstructure on a low building platform (Fig. 11-8). The 55 cm thick walls of this building, oriented to the cardinal points, were of roughly shaped stones. Only the corner and jamb stones were pecked to a smooth surface. Fill contained late Piim polychrome sherds and a charcoal sample dating to A.D. 430 ± 200 (LJ-531). Burials and caches containing jade and obsidian were placed in small crypts, one vaulted, built against the back of the platform.

Several other mounds in the Mirador Group contained late Piim pottery, so that a small settlement must have been centered here, but we know nothing else of Early period I architecture. Polychrome pottery of early Piim is absent at Dzibilchaltun, a situation that Ball (1978a: 128–129) also reports along the Yucatan and Campeche coasts. Rovner notes that although the amount of obsidian from Piim contexts is small, there is relatively more than in the far larger Formative samples.

The subsequent construction phase at Structure 612 (Period 2), which dates to the beginning of Early period II, documents the intrusion into the Northwestern Lowlands of a pure Teotihuacan *talud-tablero* style that had previously been found in the Maya area only at Kaminaljuyu. This new 9 × 10 m platform had rear and side walls of a single *talud*; the front and part of the side bore a *tablero*

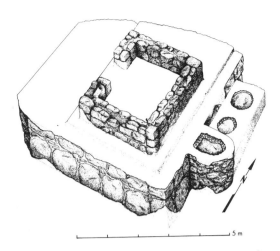

FIGURE 11-8. An Early period I structure in the Mirador Group, Dzibilchaltun. This one-room unvaulted superstructure on a low platform (Structure 612, period 1) is thought to date to A.D. 450–600. The small crypts attached to the back of the platform contained two burials and a cache. Only the corner and jamb stones of the superstructure show attempts at squaring.

atop a sharply battered *talud* (Fig. 11-9b). The platform apparently never carried a superstructure, and the stairway had been dismantled. Stones in the retaining wall were beautifully squared and pecked to a smooth surface, a technique that did not reappear in the Northern Lowlands until the Pure Florescent period.

Michael P. Simmons dates the ceramics associated with the Teotihuacan-style platform to the beginning of Copo 1, or about A.D. 600. The pottery is entirely of local origin.

The significance of this short-lived Teotihuacan architectural intrusion is not clear. The center of Dzibilchaltun seems to have been almost unoccupied at this time, and the new platform was constructed near the middle of a tiny hamlet. It is not known whether other structures in the Mirador Group were refurbished with similar foreign features; probably very few if any were. Its presence may have been largely symbolic—an indication of the arrival of a small, elite group of outsiders and their control over a scattered local population and perhaps local resources.

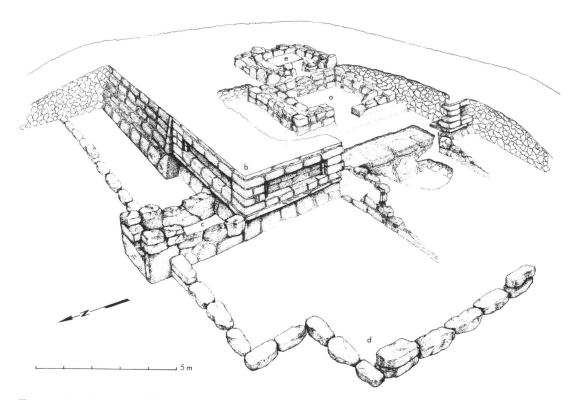

FIGURE 11-9. Structure 612, Dzibilchaltun: five periods of construction: *a*, the Early period I superstructure and platform illustrated in Fig. 11-8; *b*, the Early period II *talud-tablero* platform, probably dating to A.D. 600 or somewhat later (the stairway was missing); *c*, a rectangular projection added in Early period II, perhaps for a looted tomb; *d*, a badly ruined enlargement dating to late Early period II or the Pure Florescent; *e*, a Decadent period shrine.

The location of the structure a few kilometers south of the salt beds raises the possibility that it was this substance that engendered interest from such a distant region. Teotihuacan would probably not have needed to import salt from northern Yucatan, but representatives of this state may well have been vitally concerned with the distribution of this commodity throughout southern Mesoamerica, as they seem to have been with the production of cacao and other resources near Kaminaljuyu.

### EARLY PERIOD II: THE RISE OF A MAJOR POPULATION CENTER (LATE COPO 1 PHASE, CA. A.D. 700–830)

About A.D. 700 the area around Cenote Xlacah witnessed a massive and relatively sudden burst of activity. In less than a century Dzibilchaltun became one of the most populous and extensive communities in the Northern Lowlands. The Dzibilchaltun map, excluding the Formative Mirador and Komchen groups, covers 19 sq km. A total of 8,390 separate structures were plotted, ranging from huge temple-pyramids and multiroom vaulted structures to small, low platforms. About 90 percent of these (7,560) were occupied in Early period II and the Pure Florescent, ca. A.D. 700–1000. Most of the rest are Formative, and the others are Postclassic.

Edward B. Kurjack (1974:Tables 3, 6), who provides a detailed study of the architectural types and the form of the community, lists 240 vaulted buildings; 194 multiroom unvaulted structures; 1,706 single-room unvaulted buildings, of which 1,208 are apsidal and 498 are rectangular; 5,964 platforms without remains of a masonry superstructure; and 286 miscellaneous constructions, of which 272 are very small platforms, presumably too small to have supported a house. Most of these, except for the miscellaneous structures, a few of the most important vaulted buildings, some small vaulted shrines, and the very large platforms that were probably religious, Kurjack and I believe were residences. Differences in size and quality of construction are thought to reflect the relative status and wealth of the occupants, rather than different uses to which the structures were put. Most Maya houses today are small, perishable, apsidal structures with only a low wall base of stones. This house type was almost certainly prevalent in the past, and as the remains of most of these would have been obliterated with time, we think the actual number of buildings was higher than the above figures indicate.

Architectural remains are not scattered randomly throughout the mapped areas, but tend to cluster into more or less distinct groups of various sizes. Kurjack defines an architectural unit above the individual structure called the platform or terrace complex. These complexes range from two simple superstructures on a low, small platform to much larger platform-terrace combinations that may support several vaulted buildings, smaller unvaulted structures, and sometimes a temple-pyramid or shrine. The complexes are rectangular or form a combination of rectangular elements, and structures situated on them are almost always aligned with their axes. Some of the largest complexes are connected to the center of the site by raised masonry causeways. Kurjack counted 261 complexes that support a total of 846 structures. This figure does not include the large complexes near the core of the site that are connected by causeways.

Platform or terrace complexes often form the core of what are termed clusters (Fig. 11-10). About 30 such groups are "isolated from other clusters by space containing very few substantial ruins, very few ruins at all, or no ruins" (Kurjack 1974:91). These range in size from about 10 structures in a relatively small area to more than 100 structures covering several hectares, and they may include many platform or terrace complexes. Some large clusters are found far from the center of the site, but the largest tend to be closer to Cenote Xlacah. Most of them contain architecture of both Early period II and the Pure Florescent, usually in the form of vaulted buildings. Structures in a cluster are generally not arranged in any regular pattern or with any particular orientation, although clusters do exhibit internal concentric zoning. The most elaborate architecture is usually at their center, often on platform or terrace complexes, surrounded by smaller structures. Densities within clusters sometimes are as great as 20–30 structures per hectare.

Although Kurjack and I believe the difference in quality of architecture within clusters and throughout the site provides evidence of a class structure, platform and terrace complexes were probably also residential units for kin groups (Kurjack 1974: 92–93). Despite the fact that architectural remains in most clusters indicate the same internal social and economic stratification that is found at the site as a whole, I believe kinship was an important mechanism producing residential clustering at Dzibilchaltun. Some clusters are very large, and in many cases only the elite may have been actually related.

Recent research suggests that political power and offices at Yucatecan sites may have rotated among several kinship groups. An analysis of eighteenth-century church and *cabildo* records from the town of Tekanto by Philip C. Thompson (1978) documents a pattern of rotational movement from one office to another up the local hierarchy. The system was quadripartite, linked to Maya calendrical cycles, and controlled by a series of social groups, probably lineages. Thompson's study of the genealogies of *batabob*, the highest position in the *cabildo*, strongly suggests that this office rotated at 20-year intervals among a number of lineages.

This rotational pattern may have been an

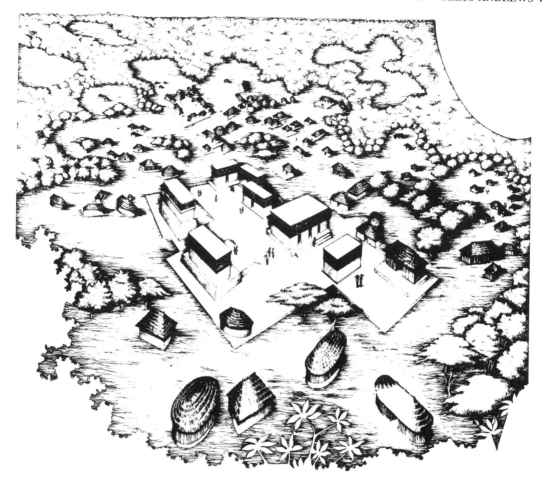

FIGURE 11-10. Reconstruction drawing of a typical cluster of buildings away from the center of Dzibilchaltun. This cluster, 2.6 km southeast of Cenote Xlacah, contained about 125 individual structures, not all of which are shown here. Drawing by John C. Scheffler.

ancient form of Maya social and political organization in northern Yucatan, and if it was, certain residential units, such as clusters, may have been lineage-affiliated (see Vogt 1961). The size of a cluster, the quality of its architecture, and its proximity to the center of the site may all reflect its importance and rank.

Other explanations for the clustering of architecture at Dzibilchaltun and other northern sites might include occupational specialization and perhaps ecological factors. The latter seems to me unlikely. The terrain is uniform, and I doubt that centrifugal tenden-

cies exerted by swidden farming could explain the internal arrangement of a major community such as Dzibilchaltun. Occupational or economic specialization, in addition to kinship, may have influenced residential clustering and dispersion, but archaeological data do not yet support this view. Clusters differ in size and in quality of architecture, and therefore presumably in wealth and importance, but neither artifact distribution nor burial offerings nor structure types suggest other kinds of specialization.

At Dzibilchaltun and elsewhere, distinct groups of ruins are connected to the community cores by raised causeways. The purposes of these roads undoubtedly varied, depending on their length, the nature of the constructions they joined, and other factors, but in the present context they could be interpreted as symbolic statements of alternating but continuing claims to local political power and therefore as indicators of internal sociopolitical organization.

Groups of ruins continue far beyond the mapped 19 sq km at Dzibilchaltun, and a crucial question concerns the definition and delimitation of the site. Kurjack (1974:84–89; 1978; 1979) defines four roughly concentric areas that differ in the amount of architecture they contain. A central group covering slightly more than ¼ sq km around Cenote Xlacah contains an extremely dense concentration of ruins, including many of the largest buildings at the site. Another 3 sq km around this core contain somewhat more dispersed but still massive aggregates of buildings, sometimes linked with the center by causeways, and an additional 13 sq km contain scattered clusters with vaulted buildings. Ruin groups continue at intervals beyond this area, but they lack vaulted superstructures. One must travel more than 10 km beyond these 16 sq km before reaching the closest site with traces of vaulting.

This definition of the extent of the site of course depends on the presence of vaulted architecture, which required vastly more time and resources than thinner-walled unvaulted buildings with thatch roofs. Vaulted structures in northwest Yucatan were clearly characteristic of population centers and not of intervening areas.

Kurjack (1974:94) originally estimated the population of Late Classic Dzibilchaltun at about 42,000, a figure reached by multiplying the number of structures mapped that are believed to have been occupied in the Late Classic (7,560) by 5.6. This estimate intentionally did not take into account a large number of variables, such as the number of perishable structures that left no trace; abandonment of smaller structures upon the death of an inhabitant; reuse of earlier, abandoned masonry in later structures; civic or ceremonial, rather than residential, use of some buildings; or the number of structures actually occupied at one time.

Modern demographic data (Kurjack 1979) indicate that an area of 325 sq km around Dzibilchaltun now has a population of about 13,500, averaging 40 persons per sq km. Kurjack believes this figure is not too different from what the land could have supported in the past, and he thinks a community of 40,000 is unlikely to have developed in such an area. His present suggestion is that Dzibilchaltun included no more than 10,000–20,000 persons.

It may be fruitless to strive for more precise estimates, but I believe that the revised figures may be too low and that even if only about 5,000 structures were used as residences at one time, we could posit a population of about 25,000. The present economy of this area is based on henequen production, not milpa farming, and we have little idea of the aboriginal carrying capacity of the land. The sustaining area of the site may have been on the order of 1,000 sq km, as Kurjack (1979) suggests, but Dzibilchaltun was a very big and complex community, almost certainly engaged in long distance commercial activities, and it may have imported maize and other crops from more productive zones far beyond its apparent sustaining area. If so, its population could easily have exceeded that allowed by the inferred modern carrying capacity, even without agricultural intensification, which would appear to have been difficult in this area.

Most of the largest buildings at Dzibilchaltun are grouped around several extensive open plazas and terraces near Cenote Xlacah, and the majority of these, of block-wall and slab-vault construction, date to Early period II, including large pyramidal platforms with superstructures and extensive vaulted buildings on platforms of varying shapes and sizes. Structure 44, on the south side of the Central Plaza, is probably the largest platform at the site, measuring 134 × 26 m × 8.5 m high. The ruined vaulted superstructure on its summit was 115 m long, or about 15 m longer than the Governor's Palace at Uxmal. Structure 55, on the South Plaza, contained at least 20 vaulted rooms.

Eleven masonry causeways (*sacbeob*) radiate from the center to large outlying complexes of buildings. Together their lengths total almost 4,000 m. Perhaps the most striking feature of the Dzibilchaltun map is the central east-west axis formed by Sacbe 1, which runs 431 m east to the Seven Dolls Group, and Sacbe 2, running 1,283 m west to a very similar ruin group. Together with the intervening surface of the Central Plaza and the terraces at their ends, these causeways form a road 2,263 m long.

The Seven Dolls Group (Fig. 11-11) consists of a huge terrace that supports 11 vaulted buildings and a stela platform. The core of the group, defined by a stone wall, includes a pyramidal platform (Structure 1-sub) with four stairways leading to a square temple with four wide doorways and a continuous corridor surrounding a central chamber that supported a low, hollow tower. In front of the temple are three sets of range structures in a line, each of which consists of 2 vaulted buildings, back to back. Structure 1-sub was built shortly after A.D. 700 and was greatly enlarged toward the end of Early period II.

Structures 64–66, at the west end of Sacbe 2, form almost a mirror image of the Seven Dolls Group, although only two, instead of three, ranges faced the temple-pyramid (Stuart et al. 1979). This group includes a stela platform but lacks other structures, and it was not enlarged in late Early period II.

Both groups are very similar to Southern Maya Lowland E-Groups, first defined at Uaxactun (Ricketson and Ricketson 1937:42–45, 105–109), and the central part of the Seven Dolls Group also distinctly recalls the late Early Classic arrangement of structures in the Structure A–V complex at that site (A. L. Smith 1950:Figs. 3a, 64). The Dzibilchaltun groups are much later than their prototypes, and it appears that their builders were consciously reviving an ancient southern architectural form.

Architectural parallels with the Western Maya Lowlands, especially with Palenque, are equally striking, but they are roughly contemporary, rather than revivals. Resemblances are both technical and stylistic (Andrews V 1974). Masonry at Palenque is generally similar to that in the Seven Dolls Group; vault spans and wall thickness show a similar standardization; rectangular inset corners show clear resemblances, as does the treatment of inset façade panels; and perhaps most striking, the ground plan of Structure 1-sub recalls that of the Palace Tower at Palenque. Several features, such as vaults that turn right angles, suggest ties also with Usumacinta sites, and the windows of Structure 1-sub may resemble large wall openings in the Western area, especially those at Comalcalco. In general, the Early period II architecture at Dzibilchaltun is more like that of Palenque and other Western sites than it is like contemporaneous sites in the Central and Southern Lowlands. It is of interest in this context that Fine Orange and Fine Gray wares, which appear during Early period II at Dzibilchaltun, are thought to derive ultimately from Western prototypes. I doubt that a significant portion, if any, of the Early period II population at Dzibilchaltun derived from the Western Lowlands, but important ties at the elite ceremonial and probably commercial level are evident.

A different kind of external influence becomes apparent later in Early period II (Andrews V 1979a). The orientation of the early plazas, causeways, and large buildings averages about 2–4° clockwise from the true cardinal directions, as is the case at many Classic sites to the south. Sometime after construction of the Seven Dolls Group and the early structures at the site center, this pattern changed. The orientation of Copo phase platform or terrace complexes provides the clearest guide to the overall pattern, since most buildings stood on substructures and followed their orientations. Alignments of these vary considerably, but a sample of the orientations of 150 of the 261 complexes on the map averaged 17.2° east of

330

FIGURE 11-11. The Seven Dolls Group, Dzibilchaltun (Strs. 1–12). The reconstruction differs from that presented in Andrews IV 1965a: Fig. 6 in showing slightly battered, rather than vertical upper façades. This group was started about A.D. 700; additions continued for about 100 years. Drawing by George E. Stuart and Lisa Biganzoli.

true north, with a standard deviation of 9.7°. This shift is unlikely to have been fortuitous, as an alignment of about 17° is characteristic of Central Mexican sites from Teotihuacan on. The central axis of Teotihuacan is 15.5° east of true north and that of Tula is 17°. Toltec period structures at Chichen Itza are aligned between about 16° and 21° east, averaging 17°. A number of Puuc (Pure Florescent) sites in Yucatan also show a strong shift in this direction.

A somewhat similar pattern has been reported at Mayapan (Carlson 1978), where the central group of large buildings has an average orientation of less than 5° east of true north and the residential structures average 11° to 18°. Here the two patterns are contemporary, but at Dzibilchaltun they were almost certainly sequential.

Dzibilchaltun was a coastal community, as was Komchen, its Formative predecessor. Like several other important Classic sites, such as Chunchucmil, Tzeme, and Dzilam Gonzalez, it was situated as close to the north coast as the rapidly diminishing soils would allow (Andrews V 1974:145). All these sites, and undoubtedly many others, must have been directly involved with the exploitation and exportation of salt from the seasonally inundated marshes that lie behind the barrier beaches in northern Yucatan (A. Andrews 1980a). In Early period II, Dzibilchaltun may have been the most powerful of these, and it

probably controlled a correspondingly large portion of the coast. Manipulation of this resource would have made it a formidable commercial power in northern Yucatan, linking it through coastal and overland trade, directly or indirectly, to many areas in southern Mesoamerica.

Salt was probably not the only major export from this area. Northern Yucatan in late Prehispanic times produced quantities of other perishable goods, the most important being cotton textiles (Roys 1943:46, 53, 56; J. E. S. Thompson 1970:127–128, 153), and cotton may have approached salt in commercial importance.

If Dzibilchaltun exported huge quantities of such items, it must have imported goods in turn. Some of these appear in the archaeological record; others surely do not. Jade was common in Copo phase deposits, and obsidian imports surpassed those of the Formative period. Rovner believes the latter derived from more than one source. Chert was of a higher quality than in the Formative. Much of this material Rovner believes came from nearby sources, but some artifacts were fashioned of Belizean honey-brown chert. Polychrome pottery was imported in significant amounts from areas to the south and the southeast.

In Early period II and the Pure Florescent, Dzibilchaltun may have been a major importer in northern Yucatan of highland ash temper for local pottery manufacture, if Simmons and Gerald F. Brem (1979) are correct. If ash was indeed imported, it would have been a high-volume trade, very likely conducted by canoe, rather than overland. A layer of windborne volcanic ash recently encountered deep in Loltun Cave, however, raises the possibility that ash temper may have been obtainable in northern Yucatan (N. González, personal communication, 1980).

On balance, however, export of salt and perhaps cotton could have created a favorable balance of trade, and the producers of these commodities may have been able to import foodstuffs from inland areas with higher soil productivity, as David T. Vlcek, Silvia Garza de González, and Kurjack (1978) have postulated was the case at Chunchucmil. This suggestion may help to explain how an area with seemingly marginal soils could have supported the extensive population indicated by the archaeological remains.

The nature of the political relationships of Dzibilchaltun with other centers in northwest Yucatan is problematical (Kurjack 1979; Kurjack and Garza T. 1981). The two largest were probably Izamal and Tiho, at the center of Merida. Izamal was an important site in Early period II and must have dominated a large regional polity, but although nearby Tiho was a much larger community than Dzibilchaltun in the Pure Florescent, it is not at all certain that this was true in Early period II. I believe that in Early period II Dzibilchaltun was paramount and that only later did Tiho establish its primacy in this part of northwest Yucatan.

That extensive, independent polities did exist in northern Yucatan is reasonably clear (Kurjack and Andrews V 1976; Kurjack and Garza T. 1981). Not only do causeways linking distant sites argue for powerful supralocal integration, but also the internal structure of different sites probably signifies autonomous regional groups. Chunchucmil (Vlcek, Garza de González, and Kurjack 1978), for example, is an extremely large Early period II site whose position in relation to soils and salt sources is comparable to that of Dzibilchal-

tun, although the Celestun salt beds near it were probably more productive than those north of Dzibilchaltun. But the settlement patterning at this site, about 100 km southwest of Dzibilchaltun, is quite different. The central group of about 1 sq km, part of which is enclosed by a stone wall, is surrounded by 6 sq km of dense domestic architecture, "all of it carefully subdivided by property walls" (ibid.: 217). Such walls were rare or absent at Dzibilchaltun, and the definitions of a dwelling unit and its associated land, and perhaps even concepts of land ownership, seem to have been distinct at the two sites. Such a basic cultural difference argues that important geographical divisions existed in northwest Yucatan and that these may have been related to the establishment of regional polities. An obvious consequence of this would be that at no time during Early period II did any one political unit control all coastal salt exploitation and export.

## THE PURE FLORESCENT PERIOD (COPO 2 PHASE, CA. A.D. 830–1000)

The Pure Florescent period at Dzibilchaltun is defined primarily by the Puuc architectural tradition, which replaced the block-wall and slab-vault techniques of Early period II at about the end of Tepeu 2 (A.D. 830). Vaulted buildings constructed after this time had walls of concrete, faced with carefully squared and pecked veneer stones, and vault soffits were faced with boot-shaped stones anchored into a concrete hearting. Geometric mosaics of pre-carved stones and three-dimensional masks replaced the modeled stucco façades of Early period II.

This style seems to have appeared relatively late at Dzibilchaltun. Various lines of reasoning suggest its earlier presence in the Puuc Hills, and its earliest manifestations in the western Puuc areas of eastern Campeche and western Yucatan probably go back as early as A.D. 750 (Andrews V 1979b). Although excavations in the Puuc Hills will surely refine this chronology, it is now reasonably clear that the tradition did not originate in northwest Yucatan, despite the presence of late Early period II buildings at Dzibilchaltun that show features transitional to the Puuc style.

Of the 240 vaulted buildings at Dzibilchaltun, 150 date to Early period II and 73 to the Pure Florescent (most of the rest combine features of both periods). Kurjack (1974:85–86, 91; 1978) demonstrates that the Pure Florescent vaulted buildings are concentrated closer to the center of the site. The greatest clusters are around the south side of the South Plaza, on the huge terrace that supports the Early period II Structure 89, and in the cluster around the end of Sacbe 5, 700 m south of the South Plaza. Kurjack argues that this pattern of increasing concentration or nucleation of wealth and power reflects the process of urbanization. He also suggests that Pure Florescent vaulted buildings, which tend to be somewhat larger and more elaborate than Early period II structures, were more costly and that fewer social groups could afford them. The wealthier groups that could tended to live nearer the center.

No reason exists to believe that population at Dzibilchaltun diminished during the early Pure Florescent, and in fact it may have increased, as Early period II buildings would have remained in use. Only about 35 percent of the vaulted architecture and a small proportion of the large pyramidal platforms date to the Pure Florescent, however, and since this period is estimated to have been as long as or longer than Early period II, the smaller number of new elite structures probably indicates a decline, at least by the late Pure Florescent, in the phenomenal Early period II construction rate.

A limited amount of evidence suggests that much, although certainly not all, Pure Florescent architecture dates from early in this span. Two late Pure Florescent excavated buildings at the center of the site show a degeneration of substructure and superstructure masonry, and before the end of the period deep middens had started to accumulate inside vaulted buildings near Cenote Xlacah. Toward the end of the Pure Florescent it is almost certain we have to deal not with increased nucleation, but rather with a population contraction.

Copo 1 and Copo 2 ceramic lots at Dzibilchaltun were distinguished by differing frequencies of types and wares that persisted from one subcomplex into the next and by rarer Copo 2 types that were probably imports. Ceramic samples from the test-pitting program beyond the site center tended to be small, and most lots identified as Copo could not be assigned to a facet within this complex. As a result, we cannot be confident about relative population levels at the site as a whole during Early period II and the Pure Florescent—most of the available information derives from identification of vaulted buildings and from intensive excavations near the center of the site.

The probable decrease in construction in the late Pure Florescent preceded the drastic depopulation and absence of significant construction in the early Modified Florescent, and it may have foreshadowed this collapse. The increasing use of vaulted buildings by groups that no longer kept them clean also provides evidence of a deterioration of the social and political fabric at Dzibilchaltun before the end of the Pure Florescent.

I think it also likely that the rise of Tiho 14 km to the south cast a shadow over Dzibilchaltun (cf. Kurjack 1979). Early descriptions of Tiho indicate that it was huge. The largest pyramidal substructure, now removed, may have been almost as large as the massive platform at Izamal. Diego de Landa (Tozzer 1941: 174) illustrated a Pure Florescent complex at Tiho similar in size and arrangement to the Monjas Quadrangle at Uxmal. Dzibilchaltun had no Pure Florescent buildings as large as the latter and no platforms in any period as large as those at Izamal.

No causeway ran south from Dzibilchaltun to Tiho, and unlike a number of sites in Yucatan that were fortified in the Pure Florescent (Kurjack and Andrews V 1976; Webster 1979), Dzibilchaltun was not walled. The absence of fortifications raises the possibility that Dzibilchaltun was dominated by its southern neighbor in the Pure Florescent, although almost certainly not in Early period II. A Pure Florescent wall around Dzibilchaltun would in contrast suggest that the site attempted for at least a time to remain independent of Tiho. The size of architecture at the center of Tiho and its inferred ability to control the thriving community at Dzibilchaltun hint that it was the center of a larger and more powerful political system than had existed previously in this area. Control of the salt beds north of Dzibilchaltun probably passed to Tiho in this period.

Joseph W. Ball argues that the Pure Florescent Cehpech (Copo 2) ceramic complex was an "elite class or fine wares subcomplex" that "seems actually to integrate and dominate those complexes with which it comes into persistent and/or intensive contact," and that it "represents . . . the actual movements of a small, mobile group of elite level warrior-merchants, ultimately of southern Campeche-Tabasco coastal plain origin" (1979: 27–30). Although the characteristic wares of the Copo 2 subcomplex, such as Fine Gray (not part of the Cehpech complex), Fine Orange, and Thin Slate, do appear to be intrusive at Dzibilchaltun, Michael Simmons' analysis shows that they appear at different times. Dzibilchaltun Orange pottery is present in small quantities by about A.D. 700; Balancan Orange may be present before the end of Early period II; Fine Gray appears in fill of later Early period II structures, sometime before A.D. 800; and Thin Slate, perhaps the most diagnostic Copo 2 ware, was not imported in quantity until late in the Pure Florescent, possibly as late as A.D. 900. Puuc architecture, associated with these wares in the Puuc Hills, begins about 10.0.0.0.0, or A.D. 830. At least at this site, the Copo 2 subcomplex was not introduced as a unit, and its diagnostic wares and types did not appear at the same time as concrete-veneer masonry.

The 17° east of north pattern of platform orientation adopted in Early period II continued during the Pure Florescent, and one Pure Florescent pyramidal platform, Structure 38, about 100 m north of Cenote Xlacah, was strongly influenced by Central Mexican construction styles (Fig. 11-12). Like that of the much earlier Structure 612, the lowest terrace of Structure 38 is a *talud-tablero*. The back and rear portions of the side walls consist of a high, almost vertical *talud*, and the front and part of the side walls present a recessed panel framed above and below by a double border. The panel probably lacked vertical borders, and the arrangement is more like the late *talud-tableros* at Cholula than like earlier examples at Teotihuacan. As before, ceramic and artifactual evidence of Central Mexican contacts is absent.

Several Early period II or early Pure Florescent carved stelae found on the north side of the Central Plaza seem to have been intentionally broken before the end of the Pure Florescent. Two were reset in the retaining wall of Structure 36, a large pyramidal platform that Simmons dates to the end of the Pure Florescent, and one of these (Stela 19, Fig. 11-13) shows a large hole chopped or drilled through the chest of a standing figure. Structure 36, at the northeast corner of the Central Plaza, is the latest major structure known at the site, and it indicates that at least in this area important construction continued until the end of the Pure Florescent.

## THE MODIFIED FLORESCENT COLLAPSE (ZIPCHE PHASE, CA. A.D. 1000–1200)

The early Modified Florescent (Zipche 1) is defined partly by ceramics characteristic of the Mexican period at Chichen Itza, such as Chichen Slate, Chichen Red, and Silho Orange, the last two of which were not common at Dzibilchaltun, and also by the greatly increased popularity of a coarse Puuc Slate type that Simmons has named Hunucma Slate. No large structures are known for Zipche 1. Only 3 percent of the platforms tested contained sherds of this span, but as Hunucma Slate was not recognized as distinct from Copo complex Muna Slate at the time of the survey, and as the sherds were not available for Simmons to study later, this figure may be slightly low. Only one Zipche 1 burial was found. Most of the inhabitants were probably squatters living in crumbling Copo buildings at the center of the site, as deep middens in several excavated structures attest.

The coincidence of this collapse with the introduction of Chichen Slate and related ceramic types makes it probable that this event was linked to the ascendancy of Chichen Itza. Our chronology for this period is weak, and the A.D. 1000 to 1100 or 1150 range assigned to Zipche 1 is based largely on traditional estimates.

The late Modified Florescent (Zipche 2, originally associated with what was termed the Haaz ceramic complex, also called the "Black-on-Cream transition") (see Andrews IV 1965b: Table 4) witnessed a modest revival of construction near the center of the site. Three vaulted buildings and a shrine enclosing a plain, perhaps reused, stela (Figs. 11-14, 11-15) probably date to this period, but the test-pitting program showed again that only about 3 percent of the structures at the site were inhabited at this time. Structure 39, on a platform faced with a *talud*, and Structure 36A were small vaulted buildings of reused Pure Florescent stones and cruder blocks built beside Structure 36, at the northeast corner of the Central Plaza (Andrews IV and Andrews V 1980; Figs. 183–186, 193). Structure 8000 was a larger, presumably residential structure south of Cenote Xlacah. At least one short section of Sacbe 2 near Structure 60, the stela shrine, was resurfaced in Zipche 2, but it is extremely doubtful that any major portion of the causeway system was refurbished.

The Zipche complex is believed to date within the Early Postclassic, corresponding in time to Robert E. Smith's (1971) Sotuta ceramic complex. Peto Cream is the important diagnostic ware in the Zipche 2 complex at Dzibilchaltun. This ware continues into the Decadent Chechem ceramic complex, but in Zipche 2 contexts it is mixed with Chichen Slate and never with Mayapan Red ware. The appearance of Mayapan Red at Dzibil-

FIGURE 11-12. Structures 38-sub and 38, Dzibilchaltun. Structure 38-sub, a shrine built during Early period II at the east edge of a residential complex near Cenote Xlacah, was covered by a large pyramidal platform in the Pure Florescent. The basal platform of the later structure shows a *talud-tablero* reminiscent of Cholula.

chaltun defines the beginning of the Chechem complex. Structure 39, a two-room vaulted building with a wide outer doorway supported by two columns, is very similar to a number of buildings at Chichen Itza but not to later structures at Mayapan. This link supports the placement of Zipche 2 before A.D. 1200.

The existence of a Modified Florescent period at Dzibilchaltun, corresponding approximately to George W. Brainerd's (1958) Early Mexican stage at Chichen Itza, is beyond any reasonable doubt. But it is far from certain that the stratigraphic sequence at Dzibilchaltun adequately depicts the true archaeological sequence at other sites in northern Yucatan. Recent interpretations by a number of workers in Yucatan, including Ball (1978a, 1979), Simmons (1973), Kurjack, Fernando Robles C., Norberto González C., Anthony P. Andrews (1978) and myself (Andrews V 1979b; Andrews IV and Andrews V 1980) have cast doubt on the traditional Classic-to-Postclassic sequence in northern Yucatan (see also Pollock 1952:238–239). In the old view, the arrival of a Mexican or Mexican-

FIGURE 11-13. Stela 19, Dzibilchaltun. This monument, dating to Early period II or the early Pure Florescent, was intentionally broken and reused in the retaining wall of the late Pure Florescent Structure 36. This composite photograph shows the hole cut in the figure's chest, but a small amount of carving is missing at the break line, where the two photographs meet.

related group at Chichen Itza and the subsequent spread of its influence throughout Yucatan brought an end to the Puuc tradition. The demise of the Puuc sites was followed by a period preceding the rise of Mayapan that saw Chichen Itza as the only important political and commercial center in the Northern Lowlands. The Modified Florescent, in other words, has been viewed as a discrete period that did not overlap with the Pure Florescent and Decadent periods.

This scheme, which resulted from extrapolation from sequences at relatively few sites and from inadequate chronological control over this limited information, is wrong. Recent evidence of several kinds, some of which is noted below, demonstrates that Mexican influence was present at Chichen Itza earlier than had been thought and that the Toltec domination at that site did overlap considerably with the florescence of Puuc sites elsewhere.

C14 dates from Balankanche Cave, near Chichen Itza (Andrews IV 1970), range from A.D. 860 to about 920, suggesting a Mexican presence much earlier than has usually been accepted. Sealed offerings in this cave document the coexistence of Pure Florescent Thin Slate, Modified Florescent Chichen Slate, late Modified Florescent Peto Cream, and Tlaloc censers.

Grave lots from Isla Cerritos, on the coast north of Chichen Itza, (Ball 1978a : 138; A. Andrews 1978 : 82–83) prove the contemporaneity of Pure Florescent Fine Gray ware with Sotuta complex types. Thin Slate and Tohil Plumbate wares are found together in Xcocom middens at Becan (Ball 1977a : 135–136; 1979 : 33), and Balancan or Altar Orange appears to have been contemporary with Silho Orange at Altar de Sacrificios (R. E. W. Adams 1971 : 196; Ball 1979 : 33).

It is clear that components of the Modified Florescent Sotuta ceramic complex were present much earlier than has been thought and that this complex coexisted and mingled in some areas with the Copo 2/Cehpech complex for perhaps more than 100 years. The big sites in the Puuc Hills were not aban-

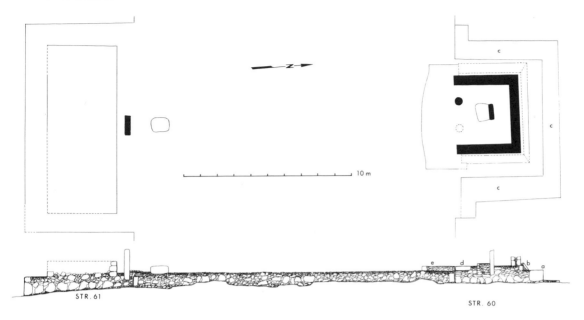

FIGURE 11-14. Structures 60 and 61 at Dzibilchaltun, a stela shrine and a stela platform built against Sacbe 2 in the late Modified Florescent and Decadent periods: *a*, original wall of basal platform; *b*, battered basal molding added subsequently; *c*, walkway and ramps; *d*, stela used as part of shrine floor; *e*, extension of shrine floor over causeway. Structure 60 dates to the late Modified Florescent, except for the Decadent floor extension (*e*), and Structure 61 dates to this time or to the Decadent period. The stelae, perhaps reused, are plain.

doned at the time Toltec features appeared at Chichen Itza, but considerably later.

A further possibility is that the Modified Florescent was not a pan-Yucatan period and that it was limited to Chichen Itza and the areas that fell under the sway of this polity (some as distant as Dzibilchaltun). If this was so, we would expect to find in some parts of the Northern Lowlands a ceramic sequence running from Puuc Slate (Copo 2) directly into Peto Cream (Zipche 2 and Hocaba) and eventually Mayapan Red. Preliminary results from excavations at Coba (Fernando Robles C., personal communication 1978, 1979) and Tancah (J. W. Ball, personal communication 1978) provide some support for this interpretation. The solution of this problem will require investigations in a number of new areas in northern Yucatan and intensive excavations at a large site in the Puuc.

## THE DECADENT PERIOD
## (CHECHEM PHASE, CA. A.D. 1200–1540)

Only 4 percent of the structures tested during the site survey contained sherds of the Chechem complex, but this total does not include excavated buildings at the center of the site, where debris from this period was more common. No Chechem burials are known, and Simmons suggests that the absence of Decadent wares such as Mayapan Red and San Joaquin Buff from Cenote Xlacah and the surrounding residential areas argues for a very small population.

The revival of ceremonial activity that began in Zipche 2 nevertheless continued into Chechem. No major structures date to this time, but at least two Early period II vaulted buildings (Structures 1-sub and 38-sub) that had been buried by larger pyramidal platforms were partially uncovered, cleared out, and used as shrines. The central chamber of

337

FIGURE 11-15. Structure 60, Dzibilchaltun. This late Modified Florescent stela shrine probably bore a thatch roof. Walls remained standing only to two courses. The plain stela is visible in the center of the shrine, and a second stela used as part of the shrine floor lies in front of it. On the latter is part of a column drum that formed part of the doorway. In the foreground is the Decadent period curving extension of the shrine floor built over the Early period II causeway. The low *talud* around the base of Structure 60 was removed before this photograph was taken.

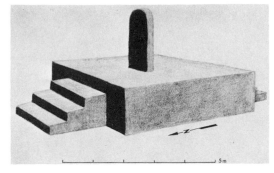

FIGURE 11-16. Structure 48, Dzibilchaltun, a Decadent period stela platform. Three such platforms were constructed in a north-south line east of the Central Plaza.

Structure 1-sub was emptied, an altar was constructed in its east doorway, and a series of polychrome hieroglyphic medallions was painted on its vertical face. The stairways to Structures 1, 36, and 39 were rebuilt several times during Chechem.

The stela cult, dormant until the late Zipche phase, is represented by three small stela platforms in a line east of the Central Plaza (Fig. 11-16). Like other Decadent constructions, these were of exceedingly crude masonry, unlike that used in earlier structures at Dzibilchaltun.

Mayapan-style shrines are lacking at Dzibilchaltun proper, but several were built on old, abandoned mounds far to the west in the Mirador Group. It is not certain whether they are earlier, contemporary, or later than the Decadent ceremonial constructions at the center of the site.

For the first time in its history, Dzibilchal-

tun seems to have been a true ceremonial center, with a very modest resident population. Its ritual importance in these late centuries is underscored by the construction of a large Spanish open chapel that may date to 1593 (Folan 1970:187). The site can probably be identified with the Preconquest town of Holtun Chable (Barrera Vásquez 1959), which is mentioned in the Chilam Balam of Chumayel.

## CONCLUDING REMARKS

Many aspects of the prehistory of Dzibilchaltun and its Formative neighbors remain veiled, and we are far from comprehending the events and processes that produced the fluctuations outlined above. But it is clear that the fortunes of this site must be understood partly in the context of forces that were shaping events elsewhere in southern Mesoamerica and also in relation to changing patterns of local resource exploitation.

Population in the Early Formative Northern Lowlands seems to have been minimal, but by about 800 B.C., small farming villages appeared throughout the area. Ball suggests early ceramic ties with the Gulf Coastal Lowlands and possibly with northern Belize.

Complex social and political systems began to develop in the last century or two of the Middle Formative in the zone around Dzibilchaltun. Komchen, north of Dzibilchaltun, had become an important population center by about 400 B.C., with large, formal architectural complexes at its center. Its growth accelerated in the Late Formative, and by about A.D. 100–200 it contained a 5 ha core of massive public buildings surrounded by 2 sq km of continuous settlement.

Komchen was by far the largest Formative community in the portion of the northern plains later controlled by Dzibilchaltun; the few sites that could be considered rivals cover less than half as much land and lack public architecture on a grand scale. Its obvious eminence presages the role Dzibilchaltun was destined to play and indicates that the Classic pattern in northern Yucatan of one community in an area overshadowing or dominating lesser centers around it is traceable far into the Maya past. Komchen indeed possessed several internal characteristics of large Classic sites, such as a concentrated core of civic-religious and elite buildings focused on a large plaza, rough orientation to the cardinal points, a masonry causeway, and concentric zoning.

Imported jade, ceramic and architectural ties with Belize, and architectural similarities to Chiapas, all concentrated in the early Late Formative, argue that Komchen participated in an extensive circumpeninsular trading network (Freidel 1978). The site undoubtedly controlled long stretches of the salt flat behind the coast, and exploitation and export of this resource must have provided one of the strongest commercial stimuli that catapulted this site to prominence in an environmentally marginal area.

Although ceramics and several rather general architectural features place Komchen squarely within the Preclassic Maya cultural tradition, we need not search elsewhere in the Maya area for the forces that caused its rise—the community was too big and too early to have been the result of colonization from the Southern Lowlands. Komchen interacted with sites in other areas, arguably forming part of an early Gulf and Caribbean coastal interaction sphere (Freidel 1979), but

it remained independent and apart, rejecting important elite iconographic traits, most obviously the Late Preclassic carved stucco façades and masks that were widespread in Belize and the Southern Lowlands, as well as many of the stylistic elements on monumental architecture that usually accompanied them.

The collapse of Komchen in the Terminal Formative appears to have left a partial vacuum in this area for several hundred years. Freidel (1978) suggests a concurrent collapse of a coastal interaction sphere that operated during the Late Formative, and he and Ball (1977b) argue that control of the northern coast passed to sites far to the interior, such as Becan. We may eventually find that power during the Early Classic shifted only slightly inland, perhaps to sites such as Izamal, Ake, and Acanceh, or to sites even closer than these to the coast, but in any case the tiny settlements around Dzibilchaltun probably depended on some larger polity in the interior.

Teotihuacan influence in this area is apparent by the end of the Early Classic, if not earlier, in the form of a *talud-tablero* platform in the Mirador Group. The absence of a large Maya site nearby may have encouraged this intrusion, the purpose of which may have been to secure a foothold behind the salt-producing areas along the coast.

The Central Highland presence was temporary, for by about A.D. 700, native Maya society reasserted itself at Dzibilchaltun and within a century had formed one of the largest communities in the Northern Lowlands. Population at this 15 sq km site probably exceeded 25,000, and the architectural remains indicate definite social stratification. An important part of the economic base must, as in the Late Formative, have been the salt trade, probably along with trade in other commodities, such as cotton.

Strong architectural and ceramic ties linked Dzibilchaltun with Campeche, Tabasco, and Chiapas, beginning about A.D. 700, and before the beginning of the Pure Florescent period (ca. A.D. 830) architectural features again point to influence from Central Mexico. The trading sphere in which Dzibilchaltun participated at this time seems to have been oriented to the Gulf Coast.

A community the size of Dzibilchaltun, situated near the coast on relatively unproductive land, probably needed to import food that its immediate sustaining area could not provide. It would as a result have developed an interdependence with a large area. Kurjack suggests that these economic relationships may have been instrumental in creating regional exchange systems and political structures.

Dzibilchaltun remained an important site during the early Pure Florescent, but between A.D. 900 and 1000 the community of Tiho just to the south probably surpassed it in size and influence. Before the end of this period, Dzibilchaltun was likely dominated by its neighbor, whose close architectural affiliation with sites in the Puuc Hills indicates increasing importance of a north-south commercial axis.

By A.D. 1000 the seat of power in northern Yucatan had passed to Chichen Itza, and the economic and political influence of this site is apparent over much of the northern peninsula. Anthony P. Andrews (1978) notes that a number of coastal sites north of Chichen Itza may have been affiliated with it, serving as ports and salt exploitation centers. Probably more than at any other time, control over this resource was centralized.

Dzibilchaltun was not a population center in the Postclassic, and nothing indicates that it possessed any economic significance. Coastal commerce and the salt trade were firmly in the hands of the sea-faring Putun and centers such as Mayapan and Cozumel (Scholes and Roys 1948; Sabloff and Rathje 1975). Even during the Decadent period, when regional political units appear to have regained a measure of autonomy, the site seems to have had primarily ritual importance.

## ACKNOWLEDGMENTS

I am indebted to many scholars, cited in note 2 below, whose work I have continuously relied on in this chapter. Most of them have commented on a preliminary version of this chapter. Our present understanding of Dzibilchaltun and of the Northern Lowlands as a whole is in large part the result of their efforts. The work of Anthony Andrews, Joseph Ball, Clemency Coggins, Edward Kurjack, and Michael Simmons has been especially influential, although I cannot attribute to them any errors that have crept into the preceding pages. For these and for any interpretations with which they may disagree, I take the blame.

The Dzibilchaltun project owes much to many persons, perhaps most of all to the National Geographic Society, the National Science Foundation, officials of the Instituto Nacional de Antropología e Historia in Mexico, and Robert Wauchope and Joann M. Andrews.

## NOTES

1. C14 dates cited are in radiocarbon years.

2. The final volumes on settlement patterns (Kurjack 1974) and on the excavations, architecture, chronology, burials, caches, and faunal remains (Andrews IV and Andrews V 1980) have been published, as has the map of the site (Stuart et al. 1979). A number of shorter final reports on various subjects are also available (Andrews IV 1969; Folan 1969, 1970; Andrews IV and Rovner 1973; Stewart 1974; Ball and Andrews V 1975). Monographs on other subjects are nearing completion, including the Formative pottery (Joseph W. Ball and E. W. Andrews V), Classic and Postclassic ceramics (Michael P. Simmons), artifacts (Jennifer Taschek), lithic artifacts (Irwin Rovner), sculpture and carved stucco (Clemency Coggins), and a botanical study of the site (Arthur Welden and Leonard Thien).

3. The 1980 Komchen Project has led to two revisions of the previously published Formative ceramic sequence for the Dzibilchaltun area. These changes, indicated in Fig. 11-1, result from a preliminary analysis, in consultation with Joseph W. Ball, of ceramic materials from Structure 500

and from survey test excavations. The first is the addition of a late facet to the Nabanche phase, called Nabanche 3, tentatively defined by sherds from the second major period of construction at Structure 500, which may date to 400–300 B.C. The previously published division between Nabanche 1 and 2 (450 B.C.) is now considered to be too late, but no alternative date is suggested here. Ball and I are currently unable to distinguish the two early facets of this complex, using either the new Komchen collections or the previous descriptions and type collections. Although further analysis may justify the retention of Nabanche 1 and 2, this chapter combines them as Nabanche 1–2, except when referring to chronological placements of architectural or stratigraphic units assigned to Nabanche 1 or Nabanche 2 before the 1980 project.

The second change is the deletion of the Komchen phase and its ceramic complex. Lots and architectural units previously thought to define this phase are now placed in the Xculul 1 phase. The pottery until now assigned to a separate Komchen complex cannot, in our opinion, be distinguished from that of the Xculul 1 complex. The transition between Nabanche 3 and Xculul 1 is believed to have occurred about 300 B.C. This date is in accord with currently available C14 dates from Komchen and the Xculul Group at Dzibilchaltun and is also close to previous estimates for the end of Nabanche. C14 analysis of several charcoal samples collected in 1980 may refine this estimate.

# Part III. Topical Syntheses

# 12. The Rise of Sedentary Life

*BARBARA L. STARK*

## INTRODUCTION

SETTLED AGRICULTURAL VILLAGES appeared in many areas of Mesoamerica between about 2500 and 1400 B.C. They represented a profound change in settlement-subsistence systems from the preceding millennia when mobile hunting and gathering had predominated. Sedentarization, plant cultivation, and plant domestication apparently were interrelated processes in many parts of Mesoamerica, despite the fact that sedentarization may have occurred independently of food production at some localities. This chapter examines new data on subsistence and settlement patterns during the millennia prior to and during the development of settled food production, relevant processes of change, theories which account for the changes, and some of the consequences of sedentary agricultural life.

The presentation is organized according to broad periods: (1) Paleoindian I, prior to about 14,000 B.C., (2) Paleoindian II, from about 14,000 to 7000 B.C., and (3) Archaic, from 7000 B.C. to the first appearance of pottery, ca. 2500 B.C. (initial dates for pottery differ in local regions). The subsequent Initial period, ca. 2500–1400 B.C., I will deal with very selectively. Time spans for these periods are based on radiocarbon years.[1]

I begin with a consideration of early hunting and gathering patterns because our ideas about antecedent conditions affect our viewpoints on the timing and reasons for the appearance of sedentary agriculture. For the Paleoindian I period, I review briefly the evidence and arguments about extremely early Mesoamerican sites, which have produced some evidence for small mobile groups of hunters who killed relatively large game. In Paleoindian II, evidence of big-game hunting in several areas of Mesoamerica is subject to fewer disputes, although the overall subsistence pattern is still unclear. Regardless of the importance of big-game hunting in the diet, there is a possibility that disappearance of the more varied array of Pleistocene prey required some readaptation in the Archaic period. During this period, the areas where we have an archaeological record of plant cultivation and domestication are the ones in which the use of wild plant resources had assumed an extensive role in subsistence.

345

Therefore, a shift away from the degree of hunting that had been characteristic in earlier periods may have engendered some of the preconditions for subsequent changes leading to village agriculture.

It is the preconditions and selective factors which fostered development of sedentary food production that are of particular interest in this review. I attempt to reconcile certain interpretations of the rise of sedentary Meso-american farming in a systemic, multicausal model. Population growth, sedentarization, food storage, distance costs, ecological conditions, and cultivation-domestication are the processes and factors I incorporate in the model. Finally, I explore briefly some of the probable consequences of settled farming in Mesoamerica. Throughout, I separate summaries of new archaeological evidence from discussion of processes of change. Earlier reviews of some of these topics appear in Aveleyra Arroyo de Anda 1964, MacNeish 1964b, and Mangelsdorf, MacNeish, and Willey 1964; Warwick Bray (1976, 1977) provides more recent surveys.

## PALEOINDIAN I

Two of the most sharply debated Paleoindian issues are the timing of the first Pleistocene occupations and, if very early occupations existed, whether they differed in settlement and subsistence patterns from later ones (Haynes 1969, 1974; Bryan 1973; Martin 1973; Lynch 1974; MacNeish 1976; Rouse 1976; Gruhn and Bryan 1977). Some sites in the New World, including some in Meso-america, have produced dates as early as about 20,000 B.C., antedating by several thousand years well-documented mammoth kill sites dated to ca. 10,000–9000 B.C., such as those where Clovis points have been found in North America. Some interpretations of lithic technology and subsistence associated with these early sites posit a simpler technology and less specialization in hunting than is found later. If a more generalized hunting and gathering subsistence prevailed, there is a possibility of greater resemblance to Ar-

346

chaic period patterns, and we would have to become more concerned with the reasons why plant domestication did not occur until much later in the prehistoric record. Otherwise, a relatively late peopling of the New World by specialized big-game hunters would suggest that the Post-Pleistocene timing of sedentarization and cultivation is less problematic.

The nature of the settlement patterns and subsistence practices of the earliest inhabitants of Mesoamerica remains unclear despite discovery in Mexico of two remarkable sites suggesting occupation as early as 20,000 B.C. Publication is incomplete in both cases, rendering my review provisional. Before describing these sites, I stress that we must shy from firm conclusions based on such a small sample of sites. Until the sites are completely published, it is useful to suspend final judgment about dating and cultural and faunal associations (Haynes 1969). My purpose is simply to indicate the nature of the evidence as it has been described and some of its possible implications if accepted.

### Archaeological Evidence

Investigations in the Valsequillo Reservoir area in Puebla by Cynthia Irwin-Williams and Juan Armenta Camacho (Irwin and Armenta Camacho 1963; Irwin-Williams 1967a, 1978; Szabo, Malde, and Irwin-Williams 1969; Armenta Camacho 1978) located Pleistocene kill and butchering sites and other cultural remains. At Tlapacoya in the Valley of Mexico, tools, chipping debris, and hearths were found in early levels (Goodliffe and Goodliffe 1966; Haynes 1967; Mirambell 1967, 1973, 1974, 1978). The current significance of Valsequillo and Tlapacoya lies in dating based on chronometric techniques, the great age of the dates, and the character of the artifacts. Faunal remains reveal some aspects of hunting but are not necessarily a balanced representation of subsistence pursuits.

In 1962 in the Valsequillo Gravels, known for their richness in Pleistocene fossils (Aveleyra Arroyo de Anda 1964:406–407), Irwin-

Williams and Armenta Camacho began a project which located five sites: Hueyatlaco, Caulapan, El Horno, El Mirador, and Tecacaxco. Hueyatlaco is the most completely published (Irwin-Williams 1967a), but Caulapan is the most adequately dated. Hueyatlaco proved to be an important site because it produced a stratified series of small assemblages associated with extinct fauna. José Luis Lorenzo (1969) subsequently challenged the associations for a number of reasons, but several scientists observed the artifacts and excavations and found no cause to doubt their validity, which also has been defended in detail by Irwin-Williams (1967b, 1969).

Of particular interest at Hueyatlaco is the technologically simple material from Deposit I, the oldest cultural stratum. Six artifacts were recovered—three flakes and three edge-retouched pointed pieces, probably projectile points, which were found near ungulate and proboscidean bones. This assemblage was stratigraphically below others with bifacially retouched projectile points.

Three other Valsequillo sites, which are stratigraphically earlier in the geology of the area, produced unifacially edge-retouched lithics also. The oldest is the mastodon kill and butchering site of El Horno; among the unifacially edge-retouched tools were implements described as scrapers, burins, and pointed pieces which may have been projectile points. El Mirador yielded a single edge-retouched point made on a blade, found in a stratum with horse, mammoth, camel, mastodon, and other fauna. Tecacaxco produced a number of chert flakes, some blades, and a few edge-retouched artifacts described as scrapers and knives. At Caulapan, located in a nearby barranca, a single edge-retouched flake appeared in a stratum with fossil mollusks which were radiocarbon dated to 21,850 ± 850 radiocarbon years (W-1895). A proboscidean vertebra from the same deposit was dated by uranium series to 20,000 ± 1,500 years and 22,000 ± 2,000 years. Another uranium series date and three other radiocarbon dates from the geological section at Caulapan are in appropriate relative order,

which lends credibility to the mollusk date associated with the flake. However, uranium series dates for the sites of Hueyatlaco and El Horno gave unreasonably old dates.

Early deposits at Tlapacoya in the Valley of Mexico lend support to the case for human occupation by 20,000 B.C. Beginning in 1965 a series of excavations probed the flanks of the Cerro de Tlapacoya beside Lake Chalco. At Tlapacoya I, a series of three radiocarbon dates agree in placing an early lakeshore between about 25,000 and 20,000 B.C. A large, rock-edged hearth intruded into this shore deposit from just above; it is the earliest such feature known from Mesoamerica, with a charcoal date of 24,000 ± 4,000 radiocarbon years (A-794B). Two additional hearths were discovered in subsequent excavations, one of which yielded a date of 21,700 ± 500 radiocarbon years (I-4449). Two piles of non-articulated bones occurred near the hearths (Mirambell 1978:224); black bear, a heavy species of deer, and white-tailed deer are among the fauna.

The slightly deeper lakeshore below the hearths contained a discoidal scraper made on a flake; most of the other artifacts from this stratum, which are reported to number over 2,500, have not been completely illustrated, but are described as flakes, blades, and cores made from both local and nonlocal materials (Mirambell 1973:8; 1974:61–62; 1978). Retouch is infrequent, and debitage is plentiful. Pleistocene fauna was abundant in the lakeshore deposit, but no direct associations have been announced between most of the fauna and artifacts.

At Tlapacoya II a lacustrine deposit contained a tree trunk dated to 23,150 ± 950 radiocarbon years (GX 0959); nearby was a well-made obsidian blade, which would further support the case for early human occupation, except that the fine quality of the blade seems anomalous.[2]

### Processes of Change

The two charcoal hearth dates from Tlapacoya have led many scholars to view at least

347

this Mesoamerican site as an indication of human occupation by about 20,000 B.C. even though a pattern of strong evidence indicating early occupation in the New World has not been achieved (Haynes 1969). Some archaeologists who accept the Paleoindian I data from Mesoamerica have developed generalizations about early culture and subsistence. One suggestion is that there was a distinctive and relatively simple lithic technology. This suggestion has been linked by Richard S. MacNeish (1976) with the idea of less specialized hunting, an interpretation ventured by others with different archaeological data (Bryan 1973; cf. Haynes 1974).

On the basis of Valsequillo evidence, Irwin-Williams (1967a) suggested there was an early unifacial flake or blade-point industry antecedent to much of the bifacial projectile point development in the New World. Expressing essential agreement, MacNeish (1976) groups the unifacial Valsequillo assemblages with others that are entirely or predominantly unifacial, including the Ayacucho phase from deep deposits at Pikimachay Cave near Ayacucho, Peru.[3] The brief descriptions of early Tlapacoya lithics hint that they may conform to a predominantly unifacial flake-blade technology, although the illustrated Tlapacoya scraper has some bifacial edge retouch (Mirambell 1967:39).[4]

Not all scholars accept the idea of an early, simpler lithic technology (e.g., Lynch 1974). Its acceptance implies a process of development toward later bifacial technology and more specialized tool forms even though we cannot document transitional steps. However, we should be cautious in accepting this technological generalization because these early industries, still incompletely described, share only what seem to be relatively unspecialized characteristics. Despite the fact that later lithic industries, e.g., Clovis in North and Middle America, clearly manifest stylistic and technological similarities over wide areas, the physical separation of the Mexican and Ayacucho sites and their unspecialized similarities make cultural comparisons tenuous. Moreover, some assemblages, such as

El Mirador, Caulapan, and Hueyatlaco Deposit I, have so few tools that sampling error may bias the lithic collections. There is also a problem of functional specialization in sites and tool kits, which makes it difficult to compare them. Kill and butchering stations, temporary campsites, and knapping locations are among the functional interpretations of the earliest sites.[5]

MacNeish (1976:316, 318) has suggested that these early cultures were not only technologically simpler, but also represented relatively unspecialized and unskilled hunting. If this were true, we could posit a process of improvement by the next period, when there is considerable evidence for successful big-game hunting. However, there are problems with the subsistence interpretation. Although later lithic tool kits became more specialized morphologically, this evidence of technological advance is not yet matched by faunal data indicating greater success in killing large animals. Preliminary reports on food remains suggest that the early hunters may have obtained much the same prey as in the next Paleoindian period, e.g., mastodon, horse, and sloth. True, the presence of bear and deer in bone piles at Tlapacoya perhaps gives some support to MacNeish's interpretation, but nonetheless it does not establish a general pattern. Some of the variation in game among sites may reflect local environmental and climatic conditions in the areas of the kill sites. Aside from the issue of whether hunting practices were less specialized in the earliest Paleoindian sites, the role of plant foods in subsistence is uncertain, as it is for Paleoindian II. Vegetal foods have not been found in the Mesoamerican sites, but lack of preservation or the limited activities performed at the sites may be the reasons.[6]

If Paleoindian I occupation is further substantiated and more subsistence information acquired, one question in relation to the rise of sedentary agriculture will be whether occupation in environments with wild potential domesticates involved any hunting and plant collecting practices analogous to Archaic period subsistence. The question is whether

348

the timing of sedentarization, cultivation, and domestication makes sense only for the Archaic period. Currently, we cannot say that Paleoindian I hunting closely resembled Archaic patterns, which in many cases involved carefully organized rotation among seasonal plant and animal resources.

The best summary for this period is a caution. Researchers have only begun to accumulate data and postulate processes of change. The bearing of these controversial discoveries on the rise of sedentary farming remains uncertain, but conceivably could raise a question like that often posed in the Old World—why did domestication occur when it did?

## PALEOINDIAN II

Mesoamerican data from the Paleoindian II period are widely scattered, although more plentiful than those from Paleoindian I (see Aveleyra Arroyo de Anda 1964 for review of earlier discoveries). Campsites and kill sites are among the archaeological contexts, and mobile hunting is the best-documented subsistence pursuit. Mammoth kill sites have been discovered on the margins of lakes in the Valley of Mexico, and there have been scattered surface finds of fluted projectile points, which in the U.S. Southwest and Great Plains are found in association with kill sites of mammoth (Clovis points) and extinct bison (Folsom points). Nonetheless, scholars disagree about the role of big-game hunting.

One school of thought tends to view the Paleoindian II period as a time when highly successful, specialized big-game hunting developed or was introduced—a pursuit which relied partly on the use of marshy areas and other natural aids to facilitate entrapping and dispatching animals (Martin 1973). However, many researchers have been skeptical of the prominent role of megafauna in subsistence, preferring to view the kill sites as one aspect of a seasonal or mixed subsistence strategy. Lorenzo (1975:32) argues against the idea that big-game hunting was feasible on a general basis because of the size and dangerous-

ness of prey like mammoth. He views killing big game as an occasional activity that took advantage of animals who became mired. Ruth Gruhn and Alan Lyle Bryan (1977) suggest that the functional distinctness of kill sites and campsites obscures the fact that more generalized hunting and collecting were part of subsistence in many areas.

In terms of Mesoamerican data themselves, perhaps the most telling argument against the prevalence of specialized big-game hunting has come from MacNeish's (1964b) and Kent V. Flannery's (1967:144) evaluation of paleoenvironmental and subsistence information from the Early Ajuereado phase in the Tehuacan Valley, Puebla. Prior to about 7600 B.C., cool, dry climatic conditions are indicated by Flannery's faunal analysis (see Schoenwetter 1974:297). In the semiarid Tehuacan Valley, this may imply a lack of extensive forage for the larger herbivores. Nor is there any indication from the cave deposits that people in Early Ajuereado times hunted mammoth or most other large Pleistocene forms. Rather, subsistence was closer to the mixed Archaic period pattern of hunting and gathering, with much of the prey consisting of small animals. However, some game was taken which later became locally or completely extinct, such as antelope, horse, and a large rabbit. Mesquite, grass seeds, and tree fruits were gathered plant foods in Ajuereado times. MacNeish (1964a: 532) aptly summarizes this subsistence pattern with the comment: "They probably found one mammoth in a lifetime and never got over talking about it." At issue in the debates about Paleoindian subsistence is the degree of contrast between the Paleoindian II and early Archaic periods and whether the timing of cultivation and domestication understandably awaited Post-Pleistocene extinctions. However, new Paleoindian II evidence does not yet resolve the debates.

### Archaeological Evidence

In the Basin of Mexico, recently discovered sites reveal a stratigraphic association of

349

Pleistocene megafauna and cultural remains, although actual kill sites have not been located. Angel García Cook (1975) reports the discovery of two pieces of worked or utilized bone at Los Reyes La Paz in a lakeside setting. Dates between 10,000 and 6000 B.C. are proposed. Associated fauna in the stratum included mammoth, among a variety of other animals. At Cerro Chimalhuaque in Chimalhuacan-Atenco, García Cook (1968) discovered an obsidian flake associated with Pleistocene fauna, mainly mammoth. However, there was no indication of butchering. The deposit is correlated with the Becerra Formation, which has produced other Terminal Pleistocene associations of mammoth and man. To date little has been published about cultural remains at Tlapacoya XVII, where a stratum dated to 7970 ± 220 B.C. (I-6897) yielded a variety of lithic artifacts and a human skull (Mirambell 1973:7–8; 1978: 224).

Outside the basin, the Valsequillo site of Hueyatlaco contained in its upper deposits artifacts with bifacial retouch, bipointed projectile points, and, in one case, a stemmed projectile point. One of the strata included a horse kill and butchering station (Irwin-Williams 1967a).

Between 1966 and 1969 four preceramic sites in Oaxaca were tested (Flannery 1970), but only one produced remains from the Paleoindian II period. At Cueva Blanca, zone F contained no artifacts, but it did produce Pleistocene animal bones including fox, rabbit, small rodents, and a gopher-tortoise. Some bones may have been artificially fractured and burned. The pollen record indicated a late Pleistocene date; because of overlying radiocarbon dates from zone E, Flannery suggested a date prior to 9050 B.C. and perhaps as early as 11,000 B.C.

Zone E produced an ash layer and at least one hearth, implying a brief occupation. The few stone tools recovered were not temporally diagnostic, but three radiocarbon dates from the hearth ranged between about 9000 and 8800 B.C. Deer and cottontail were among the bones of Post-Pleistocene fauna.

Thus, the scant Cueva Blanca remains resemble the kinds of evidence from Tehuacan—late Pleistocene and early Post-Pleistocene camps possibly used by groups of a few hunters who obtained relatively small animals. Lack of plant remains at Cueva Blanca probably is due to poor preservation rather than any marked difference from Tehuacan in subsistence.

New surface finds of fluted points have been reported elsewhere in Mexico. From the Laguna San Marcos and Laguna Zocoalco shores in Jalisco, Lorenzo (1964) examined obsidian fluted points that appeared Clovis-like. Phil C. Weigand (1970) found a fluted point fragment in the talus below a rockshelter near Mezquitic, Jalisco. Clovis points have been reported from sites in Sonora (Robles Ortiz 1974; Braniff 1976:26), and García Cook (1973b) found a fragment of one near San Juan Chaucingo, Tetla, Puebla (cited in Lorenzo 1975:37).

A campsite was discovered in highland Guatemala at Los Tapiales, but no bone or other indications about subsistence were preserved (Gruhn and Bryan 1977). Among the lithics were part of one fluted point and a channel flake. Unifacial points and leaf-shaped bifaces, possibly projectile points, were also part of the assemblage. Cutting, scraping, and woodworking tools are described by Gruhn and Bryan as well. The site contained four hearths, which produced some problematic radiocarbon dates on charcoal. The hearth dates seem too young to be associated with fluted points, but stratigraphic charcoal dates suggest a more reasonable figure of 9000–8000 B.C. for the occupation. The small size of the site and its artifactual remains bear out the notion of small mobile groups during this period. Two km away Gruhn and Bryan (1977:253–254) discovered La Piedra del Coyote, a site which yielded a few stone artifacts in its lower levels. Most of the associated radiocarbon dates were near 8000 B.C. Gruhn and Bryan suspect this is a site similar to Los Tapiales.

During a survey of the highland Quiche

Basin, Kenneth L. Brown (1980) identified additional Guatemalan Paleoindian sites, but has not specified the number because of the difficulty of segregating Paleoindian from early Archaic period occupations. Two sites had a Clovis-like projectile point, and two others had a leaf-shaped or Lerma point, suggesting a Paleoindian II date. Other kinds of artifacts were judged to be possibly of Paleoindian origin if they were heavily patinated like the diagnostic early projectile points. Unlike Brown's Archaic period sites, Paleoindian sites included few or no large "base camps," but were small sites which could have resulted from limited-activity occupations or temporary campsites. Brown suggests they could be remains of "small, scattered, and fairly nomadic bands."

A quarry and workshop site of Turrialba in eastern Costa Rica is a specialized site cross-dated to Paleoindian II (Snarskis 1979). Turrialba produced Clovis-like and fishtail points which helped define the antiquity of the component. However, the site does not clarify settlement or subsistence patterns.

At El Bosque, Nicaragua, geologic deposits yielded Pleistocene fossils and two enigmatic features which might be the result of human activity (Gruhn 1978). Until further information is obtained from the site, it cannot be evaluated.

In summary, none of these sites resolves dilemmas about Paleoindian II subsistence, although in several there is a juxtaposition of cultural remains and Pleistocene animals, including large game species. In general, for this period subsistence seems to have included a variety of prey, not all of which were as large as mammoth and several of which were small. The role of plant foods is uncertain. The size and content of sites suggest impermanent camps or activity stations left by small bands.

## Processes of Change

I have described the schism of opinion about Paleoindian II subsistence, which in turn determines whether the transition from Paleo-

indian to Archaic times involved marked readaptation from considerable hunting of a variety of large herb herbivores to hunting of smaller game, such as deer or rabbits, combined with plant collecting. This is a debate in which the middle ground appears more tenable than either extreme. Since early populations in Mesoamerica were small, groups could gravitate to environments with a combination of varied resources for easy hunting and collecting. Areas with herds of herbivores would presumably be attractive. Therefore, I am inclined to view Paleoindian subsistence as likely to have incorporated more hunting than many Archaic period occupations, although one need not conceive of this as implying predominantly big-game hunting.

For several reasons the Early Ajuereado phase data do not necessarily contradict this idea. The Tehuacan Valley may not have been particularly attractive to early hunters or hunter-gatherers during the Paleoindian II period if the climate was cooler and drier. In fact, occupation of the area may have been delayed until fewer and fewer groups could pursue large herbivore hunting in more desirable locations. The Early Ajuereado Phase is thought to date sometime between 10,000 and 7600 B.C. (Johnson and MacNeish 1972:18), but its placement is not well fixed within that span, and it is possible that the deposits are from the latter part of that period. Regardless of the timing of the Early Ajuereado phase, the presence of antelope and horse probably made the Tehuacan Valley more attractive for hunting than during the Archaic period. Even though these animals did not predominate as prey, their meat contribution to the diet in comparison to small animals like jackrabbits would have been greater than the minimum number of individuals would imply. This point generally has not received sufficient emphasis in the literature (e.g., Bray 1976:80–81). Loss of antelope and horse and their replacement with deer entailed no major dislocation of technology and subsistence, since a mixed hunting and gathering strategy was still prac-

351

ticable during Archaic times. But Archaic period subsistence is thought to have been difficult in the late winter season, a condition which may not have characterized the Early Ajuereado phase to the same degree because of the greater amount of winter fauna. MacNeish (1967b:300; 1978:140) infers a higher percentage of meat in the Ajuereado diet than in that of succeeding periods.

In summary, data from Paleoindian II are so scattered and variable that it is difficult to determine what regional shifts of population and subsistence may have occurred. Admittedly a generally greater reliance on hunting is hard to demonstrate during that time, but regardless of how much stress we place on big-game hunting per se, a decline in the role of hunting or of its feasibility in given seasons may help explain the establishment of more broadly based Archaic period subsistence, which included a considerable amount of seasonally organized plant collection. Early Archaic period subsistence patterns in turn form part of the ecological preconditions for the processes of cultivation and domestication.

## ARCHAIC PERIOD

Two key Archaic period changes, the development of sedentarism and agriculture, appear to have been interrelated in much of Mesoamerica, although there is reason to think that the link was not universal. By sedentarism I mean habitation in one location year-round, although special-purpose trips or seasonal, short-term activities may take some or most inhabitants away for brief periods. Ordinarily sedentarism also implies continuity of residence for at least a few years. Semisedentarism is a somewhat ambiguous term which can be applied two ways: to year-long habitation in a single place without necessary continuity from year to year, and to year-to-year habitation in a single place with departure of most of the inhabitants for no more than one season of the year. The latter pattern is rare in ethnographic records from Mesoamerica, but it is described elsewhere

in the literature. In general, nomadic versus sedentary settlement patterns are endpoints on the two separate continua of greater and lesser annual mobility and of degree of permanence of sites. There are ethnographic cases of biannual movement between villages; in these cases sites are relatively permanent and the settlement pattern is semisedentary. But if hunting and gathering groups follow a sufficiently regular annual subsistence-settlement cycle, their campsites can be reoccupied year after year—a mobile pattern with relatively permanent sites.

We are most familiar with sedentarism in the context of hamlets, villages, or even larger settlements, although it need not occur in aggregated communities (Flannery 1972b:24). But since sedentarism in aggregated settlements[7] eventually became typical in Mesoamerica, I will focus on the development of villages and agriculture.

I will use the term "agriculture" to refer to a subsistence pattern in which the majority of food is produced by plant cultivation—which ordinarily involves some clearing of land, sowing, perhaps weeding, and harvesting. However, early cultivation probably was quite minimal in effort, perhaps merely the weeding or extra watering of natural stands of economic plants. "Cultivation" means aiding plant growth through deliberate human action. "Domestication" involves genetic alteration of plant populations by human selection, whether conscious or not. A fairly substantial amount of cultivation over a sufficiently long time tends to result in some selection because seeds are saved to sow the following season. This activity can readily lead to selection of genetically different plants, even if inadvertently. However, limited cultivation need not result in domestication. A common example can be found with economic trees, which may be spared when land is cleared or may be favored as seedlings. The result may be an artificial increase in the density of the plants, not a change in their genotype.

Cultivation is a key to the development of agriculture, but domestication plays an important contributing role because it generally results in selection for greater productivity of edible plant parts. Greater productivity per unit labor is important in making food production more worthwhile energetically and more attractive as a subsistence strategy.

During the Archaic period we might reasonably expect nomadism or semisedentarism to have been characteristic in environments and time spans in which food production or localized wild resources did not suffice for a year-round diet, or did so infrequently. Certainly during the centuries when plant cultivation and domestication were beginning in the semiarid highland valleys of Mesoamerica, we might expect a sequence of changes leading to sedentarism like that described by MacNeish (1972; MacNeish, Peterson, and Neely 1975): an initial occupation by nomadic bands of hunter-gatherers who seasonally harvested wild plants, then a gradual lengthening and growth in size of summer harvest encampments, a process tied to plant cultivation and domestication, and, finally, establishment of semisedentarism and then sedentarism in small villages. This path to sedentarism is dependent on improvements in food production and is currently the accepted scenario for the rise of settled farming life in Mesoamerica.

There is a logic behind sedentarism which pertains both to its proposed interdependence with food production and to another pathway to sedentarism, one based on exploitation of certain naturally advantageous localities. If nearby resources suffice, sedentarism is an attractive least-cost solution to the energy expenditures associated with travel for getting food (Jochim 1976:17–19; G. Johnson 1977:489; Pyke, Pulliam, and Charnov 1977:144–145). Therefore, some favored natural localities may be suitable for sedentary life regardless of whether the inhabitants domesticated plants (or animals) and farmed, and sedentarism may precede plant cultivation or may occur independently of it. This is now a widely recognized ethnographic and archaeological fact (M. Coe and Flannery 1967:104; MacNeish 1967c:

311; Patterson 1971; Flannery 1972b; Moseley 1975; Niederberger 1979).

To recognize that the food supply determines whether groups can be sedentary is not to rule out the contribution of other factors to sedentarism or its lack. Obviously the adequacy of wild foods depends on the number of mouths to feed. Despite an adequate food supply, situations such as warfare or necessary exchanges with other groups may require a more mobile settlement pattern. There are other positive factors which make sedentarism attractive. It does not penalize people for heavy or bulky possessions, and it makes construction of more durable structures less costly in long-term effort. However, without an adequate localized food supply, groups cannot remain sedentary, a fact which makes this settlement option an energetic (and nutritional) issue. Since most highland localities in Mesoamerica from which we have adequate data either were not highly favorable for stationary hunting, fishing, and collecting or had marked seasonality in spatially distinct natural foods, sedentarism and food production tend to be linked. Archaeological data from the Archaic period do point to a causal interdependence of sedentarization and cultivation-domestication in some regions, but other information suggests the possibility of early sedentarism based on natural resources.

## Archaeological Evidence

Our archaeological evidence and ideas about the Archaic period derive principally from a series of concerted efforts to trace the origins of agriculture. Several major research projects investigated semiarid highland valleys with dry caves offering good preservation of organic substances, particularly plant remains. Consequently, our knowledge of the history of plant cultivation and domestication is biased toward upland crops. Some of the resulting information about the Archaic period from Tamaulipas and Chiapas has been reviewed previously (MacNeish 1958; MacNeish and Peterson 1962; MacNeish 1964b;

353

Mangelsdorf, MacNeish, and Willey 1964). In addition, we now have nearly completely published results from the major research program in the Tehuacan Valley (Byers 1967; MacNeish, Nelken-Terner, and Johnson 1967; MacNeish, Peterson, and Flannery 1970; F. Johnson 1972; MacNeish et al. 1975) and some information from investigations in the Valley of Oaxaca (Flannery 1970).

Excavated caves and a few open sites in the Tehuacan Valley provide the most extensive and detailed set of data on the Archaic period. There, nomadic hunting and gathering slowly gave way to settled farming through a long Archaic period sequence. Starting in the terminal Pleistocene and early Holocene Ajuereado phase (prior to 6800 B.C.), the Tehuacan sequence proceeds through the El Riego (6800–5000 B.C.), Coxcatlan (5000–3400 B.C.), Abejas (3400–2300 B.C.), Purron (2300–1500 B.C.), and Early Ajalpan phases (1500–1150 B.C.), by which time sedentary communities predominate in the settlement record. Pottery appears in Purron times, a convenient terminus for the Archaic period.

Throughout this sequence, the representation of ancestral wild and then domesticated plants in the diet increased, with cultivation apparently established in the El Riego phase. Tehuacan inhabitants probably themselves participated in the domestication process and also gradually adopted domesticates from other areas in Mesoamerica where selection of slightly different plants was underway. MacNeish (1978:163; MacNeish 1975:498) has proposed that increasing use of storable wild plants and cultivars allowed two changes in small band encampments: (1) bands were able to stay in one place for longer periods, as witnessed by increased numbers of multiseason occupations through time, and (2) larger bands were able to locate in the same place, witnessed by an increase in the number and size of larger occupation floors. MacNeish has suggested that there were a few sedentary pit house hamlets by the Abejas phase. In general, this Tehuacan pattern is fairly consistent with the less complete information from the Valley of Oaxaca (Flannery

354

1968a; 1970). In Oaxaca fewer components were investigated, but a cave and rockshelter suggest autumn collecting and hunting camps of small bands (Guila Naquitz) and winter deer hunting (Cueva Blanca). The open-air site of Gheo-Shih is thought to have been a summer camp perhaps occupied jointly by several of the smaller fall-winter bands. At the Texcal cave site in the Valsequillo area, Puebla, Roberto García Moll (1977) excavated levels pertaining to two Archaic phases, Texcal I (7000–5000 B.C.) and Texcal II (5000–2500 B.C.). No flora was preserved, but fauna indicated hunting of a variety of relatively small animals such as turtle and rabbits, along with some deer. The evidence suggests temporary camps.

Despite the greater comprehensiveness of the Tehuacan data, they contain ambiguities which affect interpretations of settlement and subsistence patterns. Relatively small occupation floors and activity areas constitute the early archaeological contexts. Determinations of seasonality and even of distinctions between some of the activity areas rely partly on a variety of perishable seasonal indicators. Because certain seasonal remains were found infrequently or in small numbers, there is a possibility for sampling error (see Bray 1976:77). Estimates of band size at particular encampments also pose problems, since the estimates depend on whether occupation floors are subdivided into separate, seasonally distinct components—a decision which also affects our view of the longevity of the occupation. Spatial segregation of clustered remains is potentially a good clue to separate occupation episodes. However, spatial segregation and composition of clusters vary, and some divergence of opinion is possible both about activity area definitions and about which areas within a stratum should be grouped into a single occupation (Brumfiel 1977:211).

For example, an El Riego stratum in Coxcatlan Cave (site Tc 50, stratum XVI) has several loci defined as activity areas by Melvin L. Fowler and MacNeish (1975:257–262; MacNeish, Peterson, and Neely 1975:

368). According to seasonal indicators, all seasons of the year are represented in the stratum.[8] Fowler and MacNeish divide the stratum into two seasonally distinct components, each of which contains more than one activity area; there is a fall-winter macroband camp and a summer-fall microband camp. Could this level represent a nearly year-long occupation by at least a few of the people? They note that the possibility cannot be ruled out. The possibility of year-long encampments by at least one or two families could signal an earlier appearance of occasional semisedentarism than has been generally acknowledged. The subsequent Coxcatlan phase has three components which include all seasons of the year (site Tc 50, stratum XIII, activity areas A–E; Tc 50, XII, A–D; and Tc 50, XI, A–F; see Flannery 1967:162; C. E. Smith 1967:233; but cf. Fowler and MacNeish 1975:273–285). This greater number is especially interesting in view of the fact that only twelve excavated components occur in the Coxcatlan phase, compared to thirty for El Riego.

I point out these possible year-long or nearly year-long components because they may move the onset of some semisedentarism back before the construction of pit houses in the Abejas phase. This interpretation does no great violence to MacNeish's developmental scenario, since clearly semisedentarism was not the dominant settlement mode earlier, and a gradual decrease in mobility is exactly what he has argued for. An all-season component in a thin cave stratum does not suggest great residential continuity in caves from year to year. However, neither is the one excavated pit house a completely convincing case for either sedentarism or a hamlet in Abejas times (Flannery 1972b:37). The pit house contained no evidence about seasonality, it was not a very substantial construction, and 17 test pits in the vicinity uncovered no other evidence of structures and only a few artifacts. Despite the fact that archaeologists clearly can disagree about what constitutes adequate evidence of sedentarism, in the Tehuacan Valley seasonal dietary

remains, the pattern of component sizes and lengths of occupation, and architecture all point to declining mobility during the Archaic period.

Up to this point, little has been said specifically about the subsistence patterns which underlay changing settlement patterns. In the Tehuacan and Oaxaca valleys, reconstructions of subsistence emphasize an annual round of activities tied to the summer rainy and winter dry season regime (MacNeish 1967b; Flannery 1967, 1968a, 1976b:114–115; C. E. Smith 1967). Deer hunting and rabbit trapping, cactus fruit and leaf collection, tree legume and fruit collection, and wild grass and amaranth harvesting were Archaic period subsistence pursuits. Fall acorn and piñon nut collecting also were part of the Oaxaca pattern (Flannery 1970). Flannery (1968a) outlines this seasonal cycle as an equilibrium system of Archaic period hunting and gathering, which eventually broke down as plant cultivation grew in importance. Originally, maize (*Zea mays*) and other grain constituted a minor part of the diet.

The nature and timing of Mesoamerican plant domestication has been reviewed elsewhere (Mangelsdorf, MacNeish, and Willey 1964; MacNeish 1967b; Flannery 1973; Pickersgill and Heiser 1977). I wish to concentrate on some general issues important for understanding plant domestication. Despite the wealth of relevant Archaic period discoveries in Tehuacan, Oaxaca, and elsewhere, there remain certain problems in chronicling domestication (Flannery 1973). Foremost among them are (1) the frequent lack of adequate samples of appropriate plant parts and (2) controversies about the characteristics of putative wild forms. Excellent preservation in dry caves has tended to obscure the fact that organic remains there do not necessarily have a one-to-one relationship with diet (Brumfiel 1977:209), and the preserved parts may not constitute an ideal sample for botanical analysis.

Botanical controversies particularly revolve around the antiquity of domesticated maize. The earliest cobs recovered from Coxcatlan Cave, ca. 5000 B.C., are wild maize according to Paul C. Mangelsdorf's reconstruction of the ancestral form, but are partially domesticated teosinte according to George W. Beadle's opposing view, which has a considerable amount of current evidence to support it (Flannery 1973; Beadle 1977). This debate has not been settled (MacNeish 1978:148–149). Since teosinte per se does not occur in the Tehuacan record, Beadle's view implies that partly domesticated teosinte was adopted from elsewhere, as was true of several of the domesticates used in early Tehuacan cultivation. In contrast, Mangelsdorf's and MacNeish's position implies that Tehuacanos were among those who domesticated the plant.

A palynological study is instructive about the problem of domestication from an archaeological standpoint. James Schoenwetter's (1974) identification of *Zea* pollen at Guila Naquitz Cave in Oaxaca, dated to ca. 7000 B.C., is accompanied by the argument that the ancient inhabitants selectively harvested and probably cultivated the plant, regardless of whether we choose to view it as wild teosinte or domesticated maize (which currently are classified as two species of the same genus). Cultivation and selection behaviors, along with subsequent changes in the processing characteristics or productivity of domesticates, are the archaeological topics of greatest interest in the early Archaic period. Any morphological changes in certain plant parts, taken as evidence of domestication, are a means to this end.

Because of the difficulty of inferring these behaviors, scholars have adopted slightly different positions about the timing of cultivation and domestication of particular plants. However, the presence of maize, avocado, chile, beans, amaranth, and cucurbits as probable cultivars or domesticates in the Coxcatlan phase in the Tehuacan Valley suggests that cultivation and selection occurred during the preceding El Riego phase and some of its temporal equivalents (MacNeish 1967b:293). Data from other localities in Mexico do not contradict this timing of culti-

vation and selection, although particular plants do not always appear at identical times in other sequences. Not surprisingly, in subsequent phases in the Tehuacan Valley, rough estimates of the relative contributions of wild and cultivated foods chronicle a slowly growing role of cultivated (and domesticated) foods in Archaic period subsistence (MacNeish 1967b:296–300).

The foregoing settlement and subsistence data indicate a close chronological relationship between cultivation-domestication and sedentarization, both of which proceeded very slowly. Similar processes may have been underway in other semiarid highland valleys in Mesoamerica. The introductions of nonlocal domesticates in Archaic period sequences and the natural distributions of the wild relatives of domesticates make it appear likely that people in multiple localities participated in early cultivation-domestication. However, there is considerable environmental variation among highland regions, and I presume that they also varied in their involvement in cultivation, domestication, and sedentarization. Perhaps in some regions cultivation was only sporadic or even nonexistent through most of the Archaic period; a transition to settled farming may have depended on inmigration of farming people or on conditions which favored adoption of a package of relatively productive domesticates from neighbors.

For example, it is possible that the relatively late evidence for maize in the pollen record from the cave of Santa Marta, Chiapas, is due to a relatively late adoption of domesticates there (macrofossil plant remains from the site have not yet been analyzed; MacNeish and Peterson 1962; García Barcena et al. 1976). If the Upper Grijalva Basin did follow a different pattern from the Tehuacan and Oaxaca valleys, it may have been due in part to greater rainfall there and different resource availability. In a similar vein, Brown's (1980) examination of surface survey data from the Quiche Basin leads him to speculate that Archaic period adaptation to that lusher environment differed from that in the Tehuacan and Oaxaca valleys because cultivation and domestication apparently were absent or scant until agricultural populations entered the area.

Before examining key processes of change during the Archaic period in the areas that did witness the development of settled farming, it is appropriate to consider a different set of evidence which derives from sites interpreted as sedentary or semisedentary occupations dependent on wild resources, not cultivars. These sites do not unequivocally demonstrate early sedentarism in Mesoamerica independent of plant cultivation, but they suggest its possibility.

In Latin America the idea of early forager sedentarism and semisedentarism historically has been associated with coastal archaeology (Sauer 1952:23–24; M. Coe and Flannery 1964, 1967:104; MacNeish 1967c:311; Binford 1968; Moseley 1975; but cf. Voorhies 1978:17–18; see Flannery 1972b and Niederberger 1979 for reviews of early noncoastal sedentarism elsewhere). River mouths with estuaries closely juxtapose plentiful brackish-water fauna with terrestrial plants and animals and have provoked the greatest amount of discussion of non-agricultural sedentarism, although other coastal aquatic environments may offer a similar subsistence richness (cf. Patterson 1971:319; Moseley 1975).

The Tlacuachero site during the Chantuto phase (3100–2000 B.C.) on the coast of Chiapas offers the best evidence to date. Barbara Voorhies' (1976:38–39, 99) excavations uncovered a clay stratum or floor with two possible post holes. A burial was placed through the floor, which later was a typical village practice. She interprets this Tlacuachero feature as a probable house floor, partly because special floors are not constructed for seasonal or temporary habitations ethnographically. The house interpretation forms the basis for her judgment that the Chantuto phase included sedentary habitation. However, lack of perishable organic materials or sufficient artifacts in association with the floor blocked conclusive demonstration of year-round occupation. It is possible that semisedentarism

or seasonal movements would lead to building of dual or multiple residences. A further complication is the complexity of the Chantuto settlement pattern; Voorhies found some evidence in fauna, soil analysis, and the bedding of strata for seasonal influxes of additional people with, by implication, either a semisedentary or mobile settlement pattern. Plant remains were not preserved in Chantuto deposits, but manos, metates, and obsidian chips did occur. The latter artifacts might have been used in plant food processing, but we do not know whether plant cultivation was involved. Subsistence foods included estuarine marsh clams, fish, reptiles, and a few land animals.

S. Jeffrey K. Wilkerson's (1975) Palo Hueco phase at Santa Luisa on the coast of northern Veracruz is also a late Archaic period occupation, dated to about 3000 B.C. Wilkerson interprets evidence of terrestrial hunting, mollusk gathering, and fishing as indicative of year-round village life, but no architectural features were found (but see Wilkerson 1972: 844–852 for discussion of alternatives). Palo Hueco lacked manos and metates, which makes use of plant foods doubtful (no plant fossils were preserved). The extent of the deposits, distributed along 1 km of a river bank, may have suggested a village occupation to Wilkerson, but there is no demonstration as yet that permanent residence occurred. With present evidence we cannot classify Palo Hueco as sedentary because it may have been a revisited camp location. Three or four other coastal sites in Veracruz may have Archaic period deposits (MacNeish 1967c:311; Wilkerson 1975; Medellín Zenil 1975:87–90), but we know too little about them to warrant their discussion here. Farther north, MacNeish (1958:173–193) identified coastal Archaic sites in Tamaulipas during survey but, again, we do not have much information about them. Only a few were subjected to limited testing. He regards the Archaic period components as brief camps.

The aceramic Matanchen shell midden deposits at Ceboruco (SB-4) in Nayarit are probably late Archaic period (ca. 1760 B.C.), but

357

appear to represent seasonal occupation, primarily for shellfishing (Mountjoy, Taylor, and Feldman 1972; Mountjoy 1974:114–115). Only four flakes and three worked cobbles definitely pertain to the Matanchen complex. Similarly, at Puerto Marquez in Guerrero the deepest levels lacked pottery and contained only a few obsidian and chert artifacts. A radiocarbon date of 2940 ± 130 B.C. came from the bottom of the preceramic deposit, termed the Ostiones phase (Brush 1965, 1969:90). Charles F. Brush (1969:97) interpreted the deposits as a village but, as Voorhies (1976: 6; 1978:8, 16) notes, his conclusion was supported only by the volume of unbedded deposits, which is insufficient evidence of sedentarism. However, MacNeish (1978:184; personal communication) reports there was a clay floor (from a house?) in the Ostiones deposits, which might strengthen the case.

Further southeast on the Pacific coast of Panama at the Archaic period coastal site of Cerro Mangote, both aquatic and terrestrial resources were used. The balance between the two is uncertain (Ranere and Hansell 1978:50–51). Probably some plant foods were prepared as well, but we do not know if they were cultivated since the only evidence is the presence of edge-ground cobbles and milling stones (McGimsey 1956). Recently inland rockshelters have been discovered which contain remains of both terrestrial and coastal aquatic animals, but the former predominate (Ranere and Hansell 1978). Anthony J. Ranere and Pat Hansell (1978:57) point out that a transhumant settlement pattern is a possibility, although permanent habitation of some sites such as Cerro Mangote cannot be ruled out.

Clearly coastal Archaic period remains have not provided conclusive evidence of early sedentarism independent of agriculture, although it is a subject of continued archaeological discussion (see Bray 1976 for an alternate view). Archaic period components are late enough that domesticates could have been adopted from highland groups. However, it is crucial that we keep in mind the limits of our information. Coastal and es-

tuarine biotopes, although they do manifest seasonal changes, do not show the discreteness and variety of seasonal markers that typify the semiarid highlands. Plant remains typically are not preserved. Archaeologists working with coastal components on all time horizons struggle to resolve whether occupations were seasonal or permanent (cf. Stark 1977:214). In preceramic times the suite of artifactual and architectural evidence that could bolster ambiguous food remains is extremely limited. We may never conclusively solve this problem—and certainly, for the early Archaic period, we may have great difficulty locating appropriate sites because of subsidence and/or rising sea level.

In view of this bleak outlook, it would be well to keep in mind ethnographic cases of semisedentary and sedentary non-agricultural occupation in favorable coastal locations, such as the historic Calusa on the west coast of southern Florida (Goggin and Sturtevant 1964). This instance establishes, I think, the ecological soundness of the concept of non-agricultural coastal sedentarism even though the example is tied to the availability of aquatic and terrestrial fauna and of wild roots in that part of Florida. Obviously we cannot indiscriminately generalize to all coastal situations, but since much of the southern Florida aquatic fauna is found in the Gulf of Mexico, the Calusa example is certainly pertinent.

In a noncoastal setting, recent work at the lakeside site of Zohapilco in the Basin of Mexico led Christine Niederberger (1976, 1979) to argue for sedentarism based on wild resources. At Zohapilco in the Playa phase (6000–4500 B.C.) food remains and artifacts were recovered in and around hearths (no architecture was encountered). Foods and pollen indicate that a supply of diverse resources was available locally year-round. Playa phase inhabitants hunted land animals such as deer and rabbits, they fished, and they captured summer amphibians and reptiles as well as winter migratory birds. They also gathered amaranth, teosinte, cucurbits, and other summer plants. Lorenzo and Lauro González

Quintero (1970) and Niederberger (1979) speculate that Zohapilcans may even have cultivated some of these plants.

The settlement pattern at Zohapilco is a subject of contention (MacNeish 1978:187), partly because full details on flora and fauna level by level have not been published yet. I suspect that even with a complete account there will be disagreement, since only three Playa levels appear to have adequate food preservation to allow seasonality assignments. Neiderberger's argument for sedentarism hinges on two things: (1) a hearth area in Layer 23 included both summer foods and winter migratory water fowl (Niederberger 1979:136); and (2) there were ample resources available year-round to support sedentarism. Other levels at Zohapilco are more ambiguous. Layer 25, for example, contained several winter migratory birds, but only teosinte grains represented summer or rainy season occupation (Niederberger 1976:43). Could the teosinte be from stored seeds? Layer 24 produced summer foods and bird remains, but whether from migratory or year-round fowl is not yet clear (Niederberger 1976:42–43). Despite these problems the notion of occasional nearly year-long occupation at a Zohapilco encampment is plausible to me. The safest interpretation would be that some of the levels derive from semisedentary base camps, since even a level with summer and winter indicators could have been produced by intermittent use occasioned by departures on hunting or gathering trips. Like the possible nearly year-long components in the Tehuacan Valley, Zohapilco does not suggest long year-to-year occupation in a single location. The reasons are a lack of architecture and relatively fine bedding of the strata. Apparently intermittent reoccupation of the site occurred.

## Processes of Change

I have briefly characterized settlement and subsistence evidence in the Mesoamerican Archaic period. At present I would argue that the following were key processes underway during that time: population growth; reduction in the diversity of exploited food resources and concomitantly the cultivation and domestication of some plants; sedentarization; increasing food storage; and, possibly, increasing exchange. I will discuss each of these, along with some of the explanations that have been offered to account for them. Most of these processes appear to be interrelated in the gradual economic transformation to sedentary agriculture that characterizes the Archaic period. The interrelationships will be summarized as a systemic model for the development of sedentary agriculture in the Mesoamerican highlands.

POPULATION GROWTH AND SEDENTARIZATION. Population growth cannot be demonstrated for all of Mesoamerica. Evidence for it comes from the steady increase in total site area in the Tehuacan Valley. Why, at least in some areas, might population have been growing? The question of demographic growth among hunter-gatherers has attracted considerable recent attention (see reviews by P. Smith 1976:19–25, Harris 1978). David R. Harris (1978:408–409) notes that a number of factors could disrupt the typically low population equilibria maintained by hunter-gatherers. An idea propounded by Lewis R. Binford (1968), Robert W. Sussman (1972), and Richard B. Lee (1972b) seems relevant to the Mesoamerican Archaic period. Among mobile groups relatively long birth spacing seems characteristic, maintained possibly by a variety of mechanisms such as long nursing periods, infanticide, or sexual abstinence. Its advantages derive from the fact that infants typically must be carried, and more than one small child poses a considerable logistic problem. If groups become less mobile, shorter birth spacing and consequently population growth might ensue.

Declining mobility (perhaps with occasional semisedentarism) characterized the Tehuacan Valley, and sedentarism may have existed exceptionally early in other favored locations. Declining mobility and especially semisedentarism may have reduced the advantages of maintaining longer birth spacing.

Without selective pressure in its favor, longer birth spacing and a low demographic equilibrium may have given way to slow growth. Admittedly the evidence for early semisedentarism is equivocal, but evidence for population growth does exist, and I suspect that the cause may have been sedentarization. As I will explain in the next section, population growth in areas like the Tehuacan Valley may have made seasonal food procurement more difficult, establishing a situation in which plant cultivation increasingly became a more attractive subsistence strategy (MacNeish 1978:227). Although there has been a tendency by some scholars to place undue emphasis on the single factor of population growth in the transformation to village farming, this does not mean that it played no role in all cases as Bronson notes (1977:30).

CULTIVATION-DOMESTICATION AND FOOD STORAGE. Reduction in the diversity of resources exploited for food went hand in hand with development of plant cultivation and domestication. As domesticated maize, squash, chile, avocados, beans, and other plants increased in the diet, wild foods declined. This change seems indisputable despite the crudeness of the measures used to gauge the relative contributions of different foods (MacNeish 1967b:296–300). The reasons for such a transformation have attracted world-wide archaeological attention. I note only a selected set of explanations for the origin of agriculture, concentrating on those that seem pertinent to Mesoamerica.

At the outset it is important to recognize the role of biological and ecological conditions. It is a truism that wild ancestral forms must be available and exploited by humans as a necessary antecedent condition. Moreover, as various biologists have emphasized, certain economically beneficial mutations must occur in wild populations if human selection of characteristics is to succeed (see summary in Flannery 1973). Many of the early mutations selected seem to have affected plant processing more than yield. For example, there was (1) softening of the seed coat in beans, which facilitates soaking to make

them edible and (2) softening of the glume around maize kernels and development of a nonshattering rachis which both allow easier threshing of maize kernels (provided we assume teosinte is ancestral to maize). MacNeish (1975:498) has suggested that the Tehuacan pattern of regular rotation among resource zones facilitated cultivation and selection because bands returned to previously occupied locations during the annual cycle. Thus, they could return to plots for harvesting.

Both seasonal procurement cycles and genetic mutations among plants are important ecological preconditions, the former for cultivation and the latter for selection. But these ecological conditions alone do not explain why plant selection and cultivation continued for millennia in a slow process of change away from the successful seasonal pattern of foraging and hunting (Meyers 1971:118). This is an especially puzzling change because increasing cultivation of plants generally requires more labor per unit yield than harvesting them in the wild, and, for a considerable time, plant productivity was not dramatically altered by the selection process. The issue we need to address is the nature and strength of incentives or selective pressures that would encourage increased cultivation-domestication as a subsistence strategy. I am not persuaded that plant cultivation on a minimal basis requires any radical inventions by hunter-gatherers, since it seems well within their botanical knowledge and skills. Therefore, it is crucial that we identify strong selective pressures that would encourage continuation of cultivation experiments.

Gregory A. Johnson (1977) observed that cultivation may have developed to increase the patch size or density of a collected resource or to move resources closer to settlements in order to reduce travel time to other patches. This suggestion is useful, but the energetic gain in travel saved has to be weighed against the costs of clearing, planting, and any other activities connected with cultivation. It has not been demonstrated that this alone is a powerful enough incentive, particularly in the Tehuacan Valley, where seasonal movements may have involved only a 10–15 km distance at most.

Another suggestion is population pressure (Meyers 1971; MacNeish 1975:498). Binford (1968) first raised the question of Post-Pleistocene population disequilibria and their possible effects on subsistence. This argument, as restated by Flannery (1973), is that optimal zones with sedentary populations will produce excess population. Resource stress will then appear in more marginal environments which absorb this population growth. It is in marginal areas that groups will experience subsistence difficulties and have reason to experiment with plant cultivation. But in Mesoamerica, as Flannery (1973:296) notes, we do not have evidence of rapidly expanding population in the areas where we have our earliest evidence of plant cultivation-domestication. However, the applicability of this model in a modified form is still open to question. There is evidence of population growth in the Tehuacan Valley, and it is best evaluated not on an absolute scale but on a relative one. Because the winter season is especially poor in wild food resources, even slight increases in population may have caused subsistence problems not strictly in relation to carrying capacity, but in relation to the returns to labor through hunting and gathering, perhaps by requiring longer or more frequent foraging trips. The winter season is a pressure point for population growth.

Aside from its effects in combination with population growth, the annual low period in the seasonal food cycle may have operated as an independent selective factor favoring cultivation. The late winter season in the Tehuacan Valley was the skimpiest in foods. While deer hunting continued in the winter it may have been less successful; stored foods were exhausted; and harvestable fruits and seeds were unavailable until near the start of the spring rains (Flannery 1968a, 1973:296). Year-round cactus foods, such as maguey, would have been the major "fail-safe" resource, but, in general, plant food diversity and quality would have been at their lowest during late winter foraging. One solution to a poor resource period is to increase collection of storable foods in an antecedent season (see Flannery 1973:296). Many plants which ultimately were domesticated were storable. MacNeish (1973:85) also notes that concentration of cultivated trees near camp would have abetted seed storage by facilitating use of fall tree fruits and delaying the use of cached seeds. Another reason that food storage might have been important is tied to risk. Rainfall variations create good and bad years in the semiarid highland valleys (MacNeish 1975:499; 1978:143; see also Chapter 3, this volume). Although cultivated plots even in favorable areas might suffer during a bad year, just as would wild resources, any yields they produced would be exceptionally valuable, especially if they mitigated the winter season.

Although the Archaic period record definitely shows food storage, evidence for increasing food storage is equivocal. For example, in the Tehuacan Valley, the ratio of cache pits and storage/refuse pits to excavated components jumps from 17 percent to 30 percent between the Ajuereado and El Riego phases, but it remains at about 30–36 percent through Abejas times.[9] Although we cannot clearly document an increase in food storage, I consider it reasonable. The presence of cultivars in some of the caves itself suggests storage (Flannery 1976b:116). Cultivation-selection consequently would be a solution to the need for storable resources, especially as population grew. Cultivation would have had the additional advantage of increasing the size and perhaps the density of stands of economic plants without extra increases in travel and transport costs, as Johnson has suggested. Population growth, the lean winter season, and annual rainfall fluctuations are three factors which would select for storage and cultivation.

The storability of different resources warrants further discussion because it also helps explain why agriculture developed so slowly

361

in Mesoamerica. Several resources which ripened in the late summer and early fall had excellent storage potential. Mesquite pods (mesocarp) and seeds can be dried and ground into flour (see recent review in Doelle 1976). Grass seeds such as *Setaria* and *Zea* dry and store well, as does amaranth. If my argument about the role of a poor winter season is correct, I would expect domestication and cultivation to emphasize storable wet-season products. This expectation is somewhat borne out because both amaranth and maize become important grain crops.[10] Several other cultivars were also storable; for example, cucurbit seeds, beans, and chile.

What about mesquite? Flannery (1973: 297–299) perceived this storable tree crop to be a major economic "block" to the expansion of maize cultivation. To move *Zea* from its natural barranca locations to adequately watered additional land would require clearing mesquite groves along waterways in the valley bottom. Flannery suggests that mesquite productivity would inhibit *Zea* expansion on the floodplains until grain production reached 200–250 kg/ha, thereby making the labor of clearing mesquite groves worthwhile. Based on Anne V. T. Kirkby's (1973: 126) estimates of maize yield from cob length, Flannery notes that this threshold of maize production was not reached until about 1500 B.C., close to the time when floodplain villages became characteristic in the archaeological record. I would agree that mesquite, a plentiful storable wild food, would slow down the development of food production based on grain staples.

Alternate or competing storable resources alone may account for the extreme slowness with which grain agriculture developed in Mesoamerica, but I question whether we should view the mesquite effect as a threshold tied to the end of the Initial period. First, sedentarization as a process antedates floodplain villages. Second, a more gradual expansion of maize may have occurred because of differences in harvesting patterns between the two foods. Teosinte-maize ripens relatively late in the season (Flannery

1973: 296), and the maize plants in a plot will tend to ripen together. James Schoenwetter (personal communication) pointed out that mesquite pods on different trees and even on the same tree ripen at slightly different times, which reduces the "peak load" of human harvesting, but which also exposes the pods to more animal predation in competition with humans.

A third reason to be cautious about the 1500 B.C. threshold is that comparison of the weight of shelled corn to the weight of (presumably dried) mesquite pods may be misleading, since, first, more than just maize may have been planted in fields and, second, we are not sure which parts of the mesquite pod generally were used. Ethnographic data in Northwestern Mexico and the U.S. Southwest suggest that so much labor is required to process the extremely hard seeds that often only the pod is used to make flour (Doelle 1976: 53–60). William H. Doelle (1976: 65) estimates that (conservatively) perhaps only 30 percent of the pod weight is edible and used among Pima Indians. Thus, maize farming may have been expanding onto river floodplains earlier than Flannery suggests, and Abejas phase waterway pit houses may reflect an early facet of such a slow shift.

Semiarid highland valleys with mobile hunter-gatherers are not the only settings which have been proposed for agricultural experimentation. Voorhies (1976: 30) and Niederberger (1979: 141) both suggest that early sedentary groups who made some marginal use of weedy grasses or of other potential domesticates, such as root crops, may have been predisposed to cultivate the plants because they were sedentary. This is a notion of preadaptation expressed by Coe and Flannery (1967: 104) in a different context (cf. Fowler 1971). A rather similar idea is embodied in Carl O. Sauer's (1952) concept of root crop domestication by South American, riverine-dwelling, tropical hunter-gatherers (see also Harris 1972). The argument is that an appropriate settlement pattern, sedentarism, allows ready selection and manipulation of locally available and exploited plants. Sedentary groups can more readily care for plots and be on hand at the right time for harvesting.

This explanation makes sense for some plant manipulation, but it does not account for a steady economic transformation into an agricultural economy. Agriculture generally requires greater labor investment than collection of wild resources because, minimally, clearing and planting are added steps. Thus, explanation of domestication clearly demands consideration of more than settlement pattern if we are to understand the origin of agriculture. Because we lack evidence about where or how sedentary groups may have begun to cultivate plants, I simply state some of the possible reasons for the step.

Bennet Bronson (1977) points out that in some cases locational constraints may have been important in addition to local population size, since the latter is important not so much in relation to carrying capacity as in relation to the relative costs of subsistence strategies. One of his examples of how locational constraints might operate is a situation in which a fixed attraction to settlement tends to keep people in one locality at the same time that they also use some plant resources which are distributed fairly evenly but infrequently over the landscape; an example of an attraction to settlement would be a rich protein source like fishing grounds. In such a situation, plant supplies near camp become quickly exhausted, requiring longer and longer foraging trips. As the labor investment in gathering food increases, the labor investment in cultivation may be offset, especially since the labor investment in early cultivation presumably was small.

This explanation seems apt for tropical root crop domestication. Individuals of a given species tend to be widely scattered in tropical forests, while concentrated protein supplies may exist only along rivers or coasts (Meggers 1971:6–38; Gross 1975). Although Mesoamerica is not generally identified as an area where root crop domestication occurred, coastal or riverine foragers in the lowlands may have been predisposed to adopt cultivars from other areas in part because of the same considerations. The key to this explanation is that if foraging travel costs are sufficiently high, some cultivation near favorable localities may not be more labor intensive than gathering.

There are other possible paths toward plant cultivation for sedentary groups. Although we might expect that sedentary groups would experience population growth, Binford (1968) noted that in optimal zones which allow sedentarization, groups can readily accommodate to population growth by shedding excess population to more marginal habitats. But there are other possibilities as well. It appears likely that early sedentarization, if it promoted plant cultivation, domestication, and agriculture, did so probably for a combination of sociological and economic reasons.

Population growth in optimal locations also could lead to competition for control of them; competition would make larger-sized groups advantageous (see Chagnon 1968:39–44). Once present, such groups might then find augmentation of natural resources attractive. This possibility does not seem particularly likely to me for Mesoamerica because none of the putative sedentary sites is necessarily very large nor are such sites plentiful around resource areas.

Barbara Bender (1978) argued for more attention to the role of social organization in stimulating greater food production and even sedentarization. Alliance systems and leaders who desire to increase their authority or status are singled out by her as independent factors which potentially could encourage increased food production through plant cultivation. Strong leadership incentives seem unlikely in Mesoamerican instances where small mobile bands have been reconstructed for the early Archaic; whether any sedentary groups may have had more complex social organization is unknown. However, it seems more likely that alliances or leadership positions would play a role later as farming spread or as larger and more settled groups increased their reliance on it. Rather, a dif-

363

ferent social organizational factor might have encouraged early cultivation among *small* sedentary groups: maintenance of necessary social relations.

Ethnographic studies of hunter-gatherers and, for that matter, many agriculturalists, show that mating networks, exchange, and mutual assistance, among other things, often require wider social contacts than does sheer economic self-sufficiency (see Wobst 1974, 1976 on mating networks). Seasonally mobile hunter-gatherers such as the Bushmen (R. Lee 1972a) typically maintain a flexible social group and broad-based social ties. Their social contacts are established and maintained in the course of seasonal movements and of frequent visiting. In contrast, small groups of sedentary hunter-gatherers would have an enduring economic tie to localized resources, but at the same time they would need to maintain social contacts with an adequate number of other people. These contacts would not be maintained automatically in the course of subsistence movements.

To reduce the travel costs of visiting and its possible disruption of local subsistence, people might opt for some increase in population density, presumably expressed both in growth of "contagious" distribution around favorable resource locations and of larger local groups. If declining natural food returns were reached (because of locational constraints) before group size exceeded the effectiveness of mechanisms of social control to settle disputes, individuals might find the labor costs of cultivation acceptable.

At present, Mesoamerican data are insufficient to shed light on the possible roles of locational constraints, competition, or social interaction in encouraging cultivation among sedentary hunter-gatherers. To substantiate these ideas would require careful study of relative energetic costs of a number of activities. At this point, we are still searching for unequivocal evidence of precocious sedentarism independent of plant cultivation (even though instances are known elsewhere). However, the fact that historic groups in the U.S. Northwest Coast and southern

Florida maintained stable villages without agriculture leads me to suggest that many environments naturally rich in food resources are unlikely to favor development of cultivation and domestication, although sedentary settlement may facilitate later adoption of agriculture.

EXCHANGE. I have deliberately left discussion of one other process, increasing product exchange, until last. Increased product exchange is poorly documented for the Archaic period, but plays a more definite role once sedentary farming is established. I focus on product exchange rather than shared styles, which can be interpreted as evidence of communication and exchange of ideas. Product exchange is subject to fewer disputes about the existence of the exchange process; it is easier to trace because degrees of stylistic resemblance and the historical origins of resemblances do not have to be assessed. However, among mobile or seasonally mobile groups, the distinction between product exchange and direct procurement may be particularly troublesome. It seems likely that during the Archaic period any exchange was reciprocal, perhaps in "down-the-line" patterns (Renfrew 1975:41–45), since we have evidence only of egalitarian social organization and small groups.

That Archaic period exchange did occur is indicated by two facts: (1) obsidian and shell occur in sites quite far from sources (MacNeish 1958:144; Voorhies 1976:93; Wilkerson 1975), and (2) some domesticates appear in local areas after they apparently were developed elsewhere earlier. Comparisons of the Tehuacan and Tamaulipas sequences are especially instructive about the spread of cultivars, for they show diversification of agriculture continuing up to the Spanish Conquest. The transition to agriculture during the Archaic period was probably as much dependent on exchange of early cultivars as it was on their domestication because each increased the flexibility and productivity of agricultural strategies.

Obsidian, a key commodity in Mesoamerican sourcing studies, clearly was exchanged by late Archaic times. Use of obsidian extends back into the Paleoindian period in Mesoamerica (e.g., Stross et al. 1977). In the Archaic period, for example, it occurs in the Chantuto phase in Chiapas and predominates among chipped stone in the Palo Hueco phase at Santa Luisa.[11] But no coastal sites provide a long sequence during which we can monitor exchange. Obsidian is scarce or absent until near the end of the Archaic period in the Tehuacan Valley, where local materials appear to predominate; their ready accessibility, in contrast to obsidian, may have reduced the demand for lithic exchange. The sequence at Zohapilco, which is nearer to obsidian sources, is intriguing because it exhibits a slight tendency for the percentage of obsidian among lithic artifacts to rise from Preceramic through Preclassic times (Niederberger 1976:56). Thus, obsidian exchange is indisputable during the Archaic period, but we need additional evidence to establish a general pattern of increase. However, I feel it is a possibility to which we should be alert. The reason is that increasing exchange may well prove to be closely connected to and dependent on the other processes I described, especially sedentarization. I will explore this relationship in greater detail as I examine the consequences of sedentary life.

SUMMARY. Explanations concerning processes of change in the Archaic period are interrelated. We can most appropriately conceptualize the relations among these changes in a multicausal systemic framework (Flannery 1968a), one which accommodates a slow shift in subsistence strategies (see Bray 1976, 1977:238). At the outset, least-cost travel considerations would lead to human occupation of localities with concentrated natural food resources sufficient for year-long or nearly year-long occupation. This seems to be a reasonable premise in general ecological terms (Pyke, Pulliam, and Charnov 1977: 144–145). This settlement-subsistence option, although not possible in most Mesoamerican environments, appears likely to lead to some population growth. Even in non-optimal areas, spatially limited seasonal

movement may have made slight population increase possible. Any such increase, if it were felt in areas like the Tehuacan Valley, could exacerbate seasonal food procurement problems by forcing more frequent or longer procurement trips. In such areas the low period in the annual diet cycle is itself an independent factor which likely selected for food storage by hunter-gatherers; the irregularity of annual precipitation presumably also encouraged storage. Any increase in the use of stored foods would, in turn, make some seasonal movements less frequent and would allow population growth in a "deviation amplifying" process (Flannery 1968a). To increase storable plant resources, some people may have begun a small amount of cultivation with a minimal investment of effort. If I am correct about the advantages of food storage, cultivation would have been adopted as a minor but expanding element of subsistence. As cultivation began to involve the storing and planting of seeds, selection and domestication became more probable outcomes and presumably began in a more consistent manner, gradually increasing the attractiveness of cultivation as a strategy. One result of these processes was slightly larger and less mobile local groups, which could not be maintained without continued cultivation. This is the only model of settlement-subsistence changes for which we have much evidence: slowly declining mobility, slow population growth, and slow plant cultivation-domestication in the Tehuacan Valley.

In other ecological situations, where greater sedentarism was possible initially, a different set of factors and processes of change might have occurred. At unusually favorable areas, such as lacustrine or riverine-estuarine settings, competition for resource access might have made larger local groups advantageous—a situation which under some conditions might lead to plant cultivation. Or perhaps the requisite social networks of sedentary hunter-gatherers would most easily be maintained by increasing group size and density—which, again, under some conditions, might lead to plant cultivation. Perhaps the spatial distributions of plant and animal resources acted to encourage cultivation. Each of these sequences of change would embody deviation amplification, since growing populations would become ever more dependent on food production in place of foraging. Improvements in the productivity of cultivars would have gradually offset some of the energetic costs of cultivation, making it an increasingly attractive strategy.

Thus, more than one developmental course toward sedentary farming life *may* be valid in Mesoamerica, although we have reason to be extremely cautious about models which are based on initial sedentarism. Even the Tehuacan-based explanatory model should not be viewed as proven. The pertinent archaeological and botanical evidence is subject to debate and continued study, and new data could pose dilemmas for this model of change. James Schoenwetter (personal communication) considers the Oaxaca Project palynological record from the Archaic period, soon to be more completely published, to reveal shifts in temperature, rainfall, 'and vegetation there. Since the Tehuacan-based model rests heavily on an assumption that the Archaic period paleoenvironment was similar to the modern one, it would have to be reevaluated if resources and their seasonality were altered by paleoecological change. We do not have evidence from the Tehuacan Valley that such a re-evaluation is warranted, but neither are our interpretations of the Archaic period so firmly grounded that we can risk complacency.

Ideas about domestication in other parts of the world incorporate some of the factors that may have been important in highland Mesoamerica, for example, population growth, subsistence preconditions, plant mutations, and marginal environments. Flannery (1973) has recently reviewed them (see also articles in Reed 1977; Bray 1976, 1977). However, it is unlikely that identical models will be appropriate for all instances of cultivation-domestication because details of ecological conditions vary widely in the areas where

cultivation-domestication apparently occurred (see Harris 1977).

## Consequences of Sedentary Life

During the Initial period (ca. 2500–1400 B.C.), we find evidence of settled communities in many parts of Mesoamerica: the Swasey phase in Belize in the Maya Lowlands (Hammond et al. 1979), and other ceramic phases which are slightly later in Chiapas, Guatemala, Veracruz, Oaxaca, the Valley of Mexico, Michoacan, Colima, and elsewhere. At least semisedentarism may have characterized early Initial period ceramic complexes such as Purron in the Tehuacan Valley and Pox on the coast of Guerrero (Brush 1965). For most ceramic phases in the Initial period, the evidence of stone tools, pottery, site architecture, and, in some cases, botanical remains conspire to indicate settled agricultural communities. There is not complete agreement about the basis for the earliest agriculture. In a few parts of the lowlands, investigators have suggested early root crop cultivation preceding maize-based farming (Lowe 1967b; Davis 1975).

However, I do not propose to review the settlement and subsistence data for this period in detail, but simply to point out what some of the consequences of sedentary farming life may have been. This question is not one which has yet received a great deal of attention, especially in Mesoamerica. The lapse is understandable because a very spotty record exists of terminal Archaic period and early ceramic sites. For example, only three complexes, Swasey, Purron, and Pox, are dated to the first part of the Initial period. Our information about Purron and Pox is quite scant, and Swasey has been defined only recently. In fact, the terminal Archaic and early Initial period is one of the most poorly documented time spans in Mesoamerican prehistory.

I consider it important to attempt to disentangle the specific effects of sedentary farming from the wealth of developments that follow it in time. Our understanding of the nature and causes of change will not be served by simply assuming that all changes in religion, social organization, technology, subsistence, and settlement pattern in the few centuries immediately following establishment of sedentary farming are somehow direct effects of it. Sedentary life may "permit" a number of developments to occur, but my purpose is to isolate what seem to be its more immediate effects without following their further consequences.

As a preface to my consideration of the effects of sedentary life, I note two descriptive observations by Flannery (1972b) about the nature of early Mesoamerican villages (combining hamlets and small villages). Flannery observed that the layout of early Mesoamerican villages indicates nuclear family units of food production and storage. Not all sedentary communities take this form; for example, circular hut compounds generally suggest more communal production and storage. Because production is not immediately pooled into a common store in nuclear familial villages, they can more readily allow surplus production for prestige-related social activities. This organizational feature Flannery traces back to the Archaic period, when small bands of seasonally mobile foragers had to divide into nuclear family groups in the dry season because of the nature of food resources and procurement.

Flannery also notes that once small farming villages are formed, they have a defensive and competitive advantage over isolated farming families (or less stable small foraging bands). Early villages would be unlikely to be deposed from their land and crops by smaller, less coherent social groups. Thus, we can view early small villages as a settlement-subsistence development which, once established, was not likely to disappear in favor of isolated farming families or mobile foragers unless there was a basic change in ecological conditions.

Given these preliminary observations about the nature of early sedentary commu-

nities in Mesoamerica, we can consider the consequences of this way of life. According to Flannery (1972b:47) and Robert D. Drennan (1976b:349), one consequence is changes in social institutions. They both comment that when disputes arising from regular face-to-face interactions cannot be resolved through the residential mobility of seasonal foraging, new ritual and social mechanisms to increase solidarity and perhaps to mediate disputes are advantageous, and such mechanisms appear early in the ceramic record in Oaxaca—e.g., possible dance or ritual sodalities. Flannery and Drennan reason that since agriculturalists are closely tied to fixed land and crop resources, greater territorial control is characteristic, and people are not as free economically to move away when disputes arise. Therefore, new methods of social integration are selected for, particularly the types of crosscutting social institutions characteristically found in egalitarian "tribal" societies (Service 1962; Fried 1967).

Many other processes of change during early sedentary farming times represent a continuation of those that began in the Archaic period. For example, MacNeish (1967b) and Paul Tolstoy et al. (1977:99–100) note that plant selection and the degree of reliance on food production, as opposed to hunting and gathering, continued to grow. These processes appear to be related to another, continued population growth, which can be argued to be an effect of sedentary farming (although initially it may also have been a cause).

Population growth may have occurred not only because of the relaxation of incentives for long birth spacing. Many agricultural systems have a peak load of labor during field preparation, planting, and harvesting, which makes the help of older children and close kin desirable; this constitutes a positive incentive for offspring. There is some evidence from surveys in the Basin of Mexico and Oaxaca that some slow population growth did characterize early ceramic periods (J. Parsons 1976; Tolstoy 1975; Feinman and Kowalewski 1979). Although I would agree that we cannot simply assume that population growth always occurs (Cowgill 1975b), there seem to be some reasonable economic bases for it in this area, and the archaeological record tends to verify it.

Undoubtedly population growth led to fissioning of social units as group size and consequently the incidence of disputes increased. Perhaps also there were some situations in which immediately accessible local food resources were sufficiently limited in returns to labor to prompt fissioning, although this notion has been called into question by studies in the Valley of Oaxaca (Flannery 1976b:111; Feinman and Kowalewski 1979). We do not have to conceive of the economic effects of population growth solely in terms of "carrying capacity" problems. Relative returns to energetic costs are a more realistic framework for human decision-making. In a more definite example of economic controls on settlement pattern, "filling in" of the landscape appears to have followed a progression from more desirable to less desirable farming habitats (Flannery et al. 1967; Tolstoy 1975; J. Parsons 1976).

It is in such a growth-dispersal situation that a further effect of sedentary farming life becomes apparent. Differentials in resource access and control arise among communities spreading through a nonhomogeneous environment. This may take the form of more and less advantageous access to the same sort of resource, e.g., poorer or better farmland (M. Coe 1974), or to different resources, such as localized minerological outcrops (Tolstoy et al. 1977:102). Out of these differentials may grow others. For example, some less desirable land may, with investment in irrigation facilities, prove to be highly productive. Michael H. Logan and Sanders (1976) provide a model for highland Mexico which incorporates the effects of irrigation in this fashion. A third kind of differential might apply to both relatively homogeneous and nonhomogeneous environments: if necessary social networks (e.g., for connubial or material exchange) extend beyond individual communities, then some settlements may be in a better relative spatial position than others (see Renfrew 1975; Wobst 1976). Central positions have received considerable attention for development of social and economic differences, although other possibilities have been raised (Brunton 1975). Additionally, the historical sequence of village founding and fissioning may make older communities and lineages social foci for intercommunity ritual, social, and economic relations (see Goldman 1963:292).

Obviously, economic or communication differentials can have social consequences among communities only if people in different settlements interact. Mating networks are one type of interaction. Others can be readily envisioned. Occasional, localized poor farming years would make intercommunity social ties and mutual aid advantageous. Erratic rainfall patterns in many of the semiarid highland valleys certainly allow for this eventuality. Differences in local foods or other resources could lead to exchange (Service 1962:133–143; 1975:75–76; Fried 1967:183 but cf. 115, 129; Sanders 1956).[12] Demand for nonlocal resources such as obsidian would also prompt contact and exchange among sedentary communities. For example, Voorhies (1978:18) has argued for the early importance of long distance exchange between upland and coastal groups. With increasing populations, exchange volume could be expected to grow proportionately. Three aspects of sedentary life facilitate elaboration of exchange. The increasing numbers of villages would reduce, per capita, the cost of transport of goods because of economies of scale; permanent dwellings would facilitate storage of goods; and fixed local groups would make communication and the organization of exchange easier. During the subsequent Early Horizon, studies of exchange in the Valley of Oaxaca and at San Lorenzo Tenochtitlan, Veracruz, tend to confirm growth of exchange as well as changes in its organization (Cobean et al. 1971; Flannery 1976a:283–328; Zeitlin 1978). Exchange in durable exotic products is the best-documented form of interaction during the Initial period and Early Horizon, aside from the spread of the Olmec style in the latter period.

It appears that the effects of economic or social differentials are visible, in at least some areas, quite early in the centuries following the Initial period. In the Tierras Largas phase (1400–1150 B.C.), in the Valley of Oaxaca, San Jose Mogote was much larger than surrounding villages, and it appears to have been the only one with public architecture (Flannery and Marcus 1976a; Feinman and Kowalewski 1979). The growth of the Olmec center of San Lorenzo between 1500 and 1150 B.C., by which time the Olmec style is clearly evident (M. Coe 1970), alerts us to the fact that complex society already had developed in some parts of Mesoamerica just after the Initial period. Presumably these developments reflect a series of social and/or economic changes in preceding centuries for which we currently lack archaeological documentation. It seems likely that social and economic differentials could have begun to have effects relatively early, as sedentarization and farming became more prominent in the settlement-subsistence system.

What remains to be determined is the manner in which these differentials affected communities and individuals in particular ecological situations. Local regions may differ in the factors which tended to differentiate communities and in the ways communities interacted (Renfrew 1975:24–35; Wright 1978). Processes of change may also vary, with population growth, agricultural intensification, and others playing different roles in different regions. Future research on social differentiation will have to identify the selective factors that favored social hierarchies in diverse settings. There already are many opinions about this set of subsequent changes, which I will not attempt to explore because they represent further consequences of sedentary agriculture in Mesoamerica.

## Conclusion

The widespread appearance of sedentary farming in Mesoamerica appears to be an outcome of a long series of changes in ecological and demographic variables. Although secure evidence is lacking, the timing of these changes in Mesoamerica may have been tied to particular environmental, demographic, and subsistence patterns in the early Archaic period. Only from semiarid upland valleys do we have an archaeological record of the steps involved. To account for this record, I used several general premises to construct a multicausal, systemic model of change which incorporates ecological preconditions, selective pressures, and changing settlement-subsistence strategies. The model is by no means the only one which could be argued to account for the Tehuacan data (cf. MacNeish 1975, 1978), and several aspects of it remain uncertain. However, the model incorporates many of the factors that scholars have argued to be relevant to the rise of sedentary farming, both in Mesoamerica and elsewhere. In its details, the model is tied to Mesoamerican ecology in upland valleys. There, the importance of plant food storage for winter was a factor that may have partly differentiated the highland Mesoamerican case from many others. Also, the role of *initial* sedentarism and population growth may have been less in Mesoamerica than, for example, in the Near East (cf. Flannery 1969; P. Smith and Young 1972).

Apparently it was in semiarid highland valleys in Mesoamerica that cultivation and domestication processes resulted in an agricultural complex which relied heavily on grasses and legumes. Unfortunately, the upland model does not cover the cultivation-domestication of lowland root crops, which also may have been important in early Mesoamerican agriculture, and we lack an archaeological record of the development of that agricultural complex.

In addition to changes leading to settled farming in semiarid upland valleys, there are other possible courses toward sedentary life.

369

Early sedentarism based on naturally available foods may have existed in Mesoamerica in some localities. Conceivably under certain conditions, such a settlement pattern predisposed people toward cultivation-domestication, an idea which is still largely conjectural. In any case, it seems clear that many groups in such favored locations eventually either adopted agriculture or engaged in exchange for agricultural products. The question of why sedentary agriculture spread to so many parts of Mesoamerica is one which I have not addressed in this article, and to which Mesoamericanists have given little attention. However, to understand the growth of sedentary farming as a predominant subsistence pattern in Mesoamerica, the reasons for its spread will have to be examined in future research. I identify this topic as a distinct research question on the grounds that initiation of cultivation-domestication was tied to particular ecological circumstances. Such situations need not be identical with the conditions under which agriculture spread or was adopted as a subsistence strategy by other hunter-gatherers.

In summary, within Mesoamerica there is no reason to assume that a single combination of conditions selected for cultivation-domestication or for sedentarization. By the same token, conditions appropriate to understanding the Mesoamerican case do not necessarily apply to other areas of the world where these processes occurred. However, I do not argue for the uniqueness of every instance of such change. Rather, I expect many of the same variables to prove to have been important, even though they may have interacted in slightly different ways.

After farming villages became widespread in Mesoamerica, certain processes underway in the Archaic period continued (at least in some areas). Population growth and continued plant selection and improvement are examples. Thus, there is reason to see considerable continuity in processes of change rather than a radical break signaling a completely new era in Mesoamerican prehistory. But despite continuities, the nature of in-tra- and intercommunity relations was profoundly altered both by new relations to more fixed resources and by changed conditions of resource exchange. The alteration undoubtedly became more pronounced as settled farming spread to more regions.

Social differentiation apparently developed relatively quickly in Mesoamerica under these conditions, but the development was confined initially to certain key regions. Presumably the Olmec "heartland" in the Gulf Coast lowlands was one of the most important. We do not have a record of the timing and nature of sedentarization, cultivation, and domestication there, and it may have been an area to which agriculture spread or to which agriculturalists moved. An important topic in future research should be acquisition of a better Archaic and Initial period archaeological record from the Gulf lowlands and identification of the conditions which promoted sedentary farming and social differentiation in that area. Currently we understand better the consequences of sedentary farming in the highlands than in the lowlands, and it is possible that different models will be required to account for each.

## ACKNOWLEDGMENTS

My colleagues whose good advice helped me improve this paper have my warmest thanks. James Eder, Gary Feinman, Sylvia Gaines, Richard MacNeish, Fred Plog, Reynold Ruppé, James Schoenwetter, Barbara Voorhies, Phil Weigand, and David Wilcox deserve credit for many improvements in it, although they have no responsibility for its shortcomings. I thank Joaquín García-Barcena, Ruth Gruhn, Cynthia Irwin-Williams, José Luis Lorenzo, Richard MacNeish, Carol Ruppé, Jeremy Sabloff, and Paul Tolstoy for their kind assistance with reference materials, and I appreciate Terri McCarty's having typed the manuscript on short notice.

NOTES

1. A slightly different periodization appears in Lorenzo 1975, which gives a useful review of preceramic Mesoamerican data. Another general review appears in MacNeish 1976, which offers a four-stage interpretation of early New World hunting and gathering, one subdivided according to technology and fauna. However, the data are still problematic, and periodization offers a more neutral framework than stages for assessing Mesoamerican information, in part because of variation in processes of change and in their timing in different regions (Rowe 1962). Tolstoy (1978) presents a period scheme and discussion of chronologies for western Mesoamerica which partly overlaps the time periods considered here.

The periods I use are expedient, justified by the fact that some sites have supplied early chronometric dates, on the order of 20,000 B.C., while other sites appear to be of Pleistocene antiquity but have been dated only by geologic strata in the Valley of Mexico between about 14,000 and 7000 B.C. The process of extinction of large Pleistocene fauna seems to have lasted into early Holocene times in at least some parts of Mesoamerica, such as the Valley of Mexico. This makes 7000 B.C. a useful temporal endpoint for Paleoindian II, one which also agrees approximately with the 7600 B.C. figure used for the end of Early Ajuereado times in the Tehuacan Valley sequence, when Pleistocene fauna disappeared (Flannery 1967; Johnson and MacNeish 1972:18). Although in many Mesoamerican regions the subsequent millennia produced evidence of plant cultivation and selection, the development of agriculture was a long process, which makes it difficult to isolate the beginning of farming as an endpoint for the Archaic period. In contrast, pottery is a convenient period marker.

2. Only brief notes are appropriate about other Mesoamerican finds, which, while possibly quite early, lack a sufficiently accurate chronology. There are some sites which Lorenzo (1975) and Mirambell (1974) have placed in Paleoindian I, but for which we lack direct dating. With one exception, they have been summarized previously: Laguna de Chapala in Baja California, Diablo Complex in Tamaulipas, and Chimalacatlan in Morelos (Aveleyra Arroyo de Anda 1964:390, 393, 305). The exception is the incompletely published surface site of Teopisca, Chiapas, which produced heavily patinated artifacts, including one burin

and some debitage (Lorenzo 1961; 1975:31). None of these four sites is dated chronometrically to Paleoindian I.

In addition, Richmond Hill, a large site with numerous heavily patinated stone artifacts, was discovered recently in Belize by the late Dennis E. Puleston (1975; A. V. Miller 1976). Although no chronometric dates are available, the site has a relatively crude lithic technology and apparently lacks projectile points, a situation which has provoked some comparisons to Paleoindian I assemblages (D. Puleston 1975:531; MacNeish 1978:181). Certainly this site is intriguing, not only because it extended over 5 km, but also because sandy knolls may have been habitation locations. However, there is insufficient evidence to determine to which of the preceramic periods Richmond Hill pertains, or whether it is a later aceramic occupation (Hammond et al. 1979:99).

3. A bipointed projectile point from a rodent burrow at Tlapacoya I contradicts this technological interpretation, but its provenience renders it suspect.

4. Since, like Valsequillo sites, the Ayacucho phase contained possible projectile points, Alex D. Krieger's (1964) proposal of an early pre-projectile point horizon is questionable not so much in respect to the suggested greater antiquity of early occupation but with regard to the associated tool kit (Irwin-Williams 1968:39–40).

5. MacNeish (1976:317) and MacNeish, Patterson, and Browman (1975:12–15) note that the earlier Paccaicasa phase and subsequent Ayacucho phase occupations of Pikimachay Cave may have been the result of hunters and their families killing giant sloths in their dens and remaining to butcher and eat the kill, as well as the result of more general hunting encampments, indicated by less frequent bones of other species including horse, carnivore, rodent, deer, and camelid. In cases where a context is clear, Valsequillo sites are kill and butchering stations, and this is the probable context of all the assemblages there. Lorena Mirambell (1973:8) reports that at least some of the Tlapacoya I lakeshore assemblage is the result of knapping, a third functional context, while the hearths there would suggest a campsite.

6. One other process suggested for this early period is continued migrations of people from Asia, possibly the source of some technological advances in lithics (MacNeish 1976). This is not the place to assess that topic, since most of the relevant data derive from sites outside Mesoamerica;

however, divergent opinions about migrations exist, depending on scholars' assessment of both Paleoindian periods (Gruhn and Bryan 1977). It is appropriate to note that the early sites from Mesoamerica, especially when considered in conjunction with the Ayacucho evidence, pose problems for Paul S. Martin's (1973) recent explanation of Pleistocene extinctions, which he attributes to a relatively late migration into the New World of highly skilled hunters who swept through both continents, decimating unwary game. Rather, these sites suggest there were earlier occupants who hunted some of these animals, although this fact does not eliminate human agency from some role in Pleistocene extinctions. Processes of population growth (and possibly decline) are tied to the Martin hypothesis (MacNeish 1976), but there are too few Mesoamerican and other Paleoindian I sites to allow cogent discussion of demographic change.

7. Archaeologists have not devoted much attention to possible exceptions or to the manner in which sedentarism was integrated with seasonal hunting, harvesting, or collecting trips. Later cave components in the Tehuacan and Oaxaca valleys show that such trips and encampments continued on a reduced scale in periods which were predominantly sedentary (MacNeish, Peterson, and Neely 1975; Flannery 1976b:111).

8. There are some differences of opinion about seasonal placement of a few of the diagnostics; MacNeish, Peterson, and Neely (1975:348–351) treat some tree pods, such as mesquite, and grasses and amaranth as spring indicators, but late summer–fall is a more common interpretation; see C. E. Smith 1967:232; Flannery 1967:159; but cf. Flannery 1976b:114–115.

9. I attempted also to calculate the frequency through time of dry season components which had milling stones because milling stones are associated predominantly with wet season plant food processing. Therefore, their occurrence in a dry season component might indicate their use on stored plants even if the plants were not preserved (of course, artifact curation cannot be ruled out). There are some dry season components with milling stones, but the marked growth of multi-season components results in too few components from only the dry season to give a meaningful sample.

10. Tropical root crops partly fit this argument because they can remain in the ground until needed, but a resource-poor season—and hence several aspects of a highland model—seems questionable for the tropical lowlands.

11. Voorhies (personal communication) reports that some Chantuto obsidian has been analyzed and assigned to sources. Tajulmulco may have been a source from which obsidian was obtained directly, but El Chayal was more distant and consequently a potential source of exchanged obsidian.

12. Timothy K. Earle (1977) questioned the general role of exchange in foods and other staples in the development of early chiefdoms, but his case example from Hawaii is in an area with relatively close spacing of different resource zones (within ca. 12 km), which makes them accessible from a single settlement. This need not be the case for all regions. For example, in the Lower Papaloapan Basin in Veracruz, zonation is on a larger scale (Stark 1978).

# 13. The Formative Period and the Evolution of Complex Culture

THE TRANSITION from small egalitarian communities to sociopolitically complex societies took place during the period from 2000 to 500 B.C. At the time of publication of the original volumes of the *Handbook of Middle American Indians* much of this transitional period was lumped under the poorly defined term "Middle Preclassic." Its culture history was viewed in terms of an "Olmec horizon" with Gulf Coast influences and/or colonists responsible for developments in many areas of Mesoamerica.

In actuality, the data base for that interpretation was very small. La Venta was the only Gulf Coast site to have undergone any extensive excavations, and the site's antecedents were still unclear. Mexico's Central Highlands were discussed primarily in terms of only three sites, Zacatenco, El Arbolillo, and Tlatilco. Investigations had just begun in the Tehuacan Valley, and the New World Archaeological Foundation was in the initial stages of its Chiapas program. In Oaxaca the earliest known complex culture levels were identified as Monte Alban I and thought to show "Olmec" influences.

Projects during the intervening two decades have altered the earlier interpretations regarding the development and diffusion of complex culture in Mesoamerica. This chapter will briefly summarize these recent developments for four areas of Mesoamerica: the Gulf Coast, the Valley of Oaxaca, the highlands of Central Mexico, and the Pacific Coast of Chiapas-Guatemala (see Fig. 13-1). The question of developments in the Maya area has been discussed at length in a recent book (R. E. W. Adams 1977) and will not be addressed in this chapter except to mention some new data from Belize. Furthermore, this synthesis cannot be exhaustive and will not concentrate on the finer points of chronological subdivisions or comparisons of pottery types. Both of these latter topics have received excellent treatments in articles by Gareth W. Lowe (1978) and Paul Tolstoy (1978).

Refinements in radiocarbon dating techniques, an increased reliance by archaeologists on radiocarbon for dating, and a reanalysis of dates from some sites (e.g., Berger, Graham, and Heizer 1967) have provided a greatly improved time frame and increased time depth for this period of Mesoamerican culture history. There is still the problem of the inconsistency with which archaeologists in Mesoamerica and elsewhere handle the numerical results. Some publish their data on the basis of the original 5,586-year half-life, others use the corrected 5,730-year half-life, while still others use additional correction factors without necessarily specifying those corrections taken. Thus, comparing dates between two sites is often impeded because the radiocarbon dates may not be comparable in terms of half-lives and adjustments.

For many years the time period under consideration has been labeled "Middle Preclassic." As the discussion below will demonstrate, the "Middle Preclassic" data were incorrectly interpreted, and a change in terminology has become appropriate to avoid the incorrect implications inherent in the older term. Michael D. Coe and Kent V. Flannery adopted the term "Formative" in their work at sites along the Guatemalan coast (M. Coe 1961a; M. Coe and Flannery 1967), and that usage has been continued in their individual projects on the Gulf Coast (M. Coe 1968) and in Oaxaca (Flannery 1968b). In their treatment of the Formative period, the Early and Middle Formative cover the time span previously termed "Middle Preclassic." Separation of the time period into Early (2000–900 B.C.) and Middle Formative (900–500 B.C.) segments fits well with the pattern of culture change in the archaeological record.

Because sociopolitical complexity is manifested so differently in societies throughout the world, it is difficult to ascertain which data in the archaeological record are pertinent to documenting the rise of complex culture. This chapter will focus on several basic archaeological traits which were part of the pattern exhibited by the complex societies of Mesoamerica. Such traits include civic or public structures arranged around plaza areas and/or within separate precincts; monumental and portable art which served ritual, dynastic, or other functions; ceramics bearing iconographic motifs; figurines; and the use

of jade and greenstone as precious, status items.

The relative noncomparability of the data among the four areas to be discussed is a problem which hampers any synthesis of this type. Excavations on the Gulf Coast have concentrated on ceremonial centers, while those in Central Mexico have stressed ceramic chronology, stratigraphy, and burial data. Published Formative period data from coastal Chiapas-Guatemala likewise have emphasized ceramic stratigraphy. Only Oaxaca has data covering both household and civic-public structures.

## THE GULF COAST

For decades Gulf Coast Olmec culture has been considered Mesoamerica's first complex culture, and perhaps its first civilization (M. Coe 1968:60; 1974:2). The antecedents to the development of complex culture on the Gulf Coast and elsewhere, the question of the uniqueness of the Gulf Coast developments, and the cultural impact of one region upon another are therefore topics of importance and will be addressed in this and other sections.

Until recently the antecedents to the elaborate stone monuments, ceramics, jades, mound architecture, and other traits which combine to form the archaeological culture termed Olmec have been an enigma. Some scholars felt that this archaeological culture "appeared suddenly" on the Gulf Coast. This is understandable since the only major excavations on the Gulf Coast, those at La Venta (P. Drucker, Heizer, and Squier 1959), uncovered no pre–La Venta I levels. Since Olmec-like ceramics, jades, and monumental carvings were known from Central Mexican sites, this was considered to be a possible source area for Olmec culture (see Grove 1974a).

An important breakthrough came with Michael Coe's excavations at San Lorenzo during the late 1960s (M. Coe 1968, 1970; M. Coe, Diehl, and Stuiver 1967), which uncovered a pre–La Venta stratigraphic record.

374

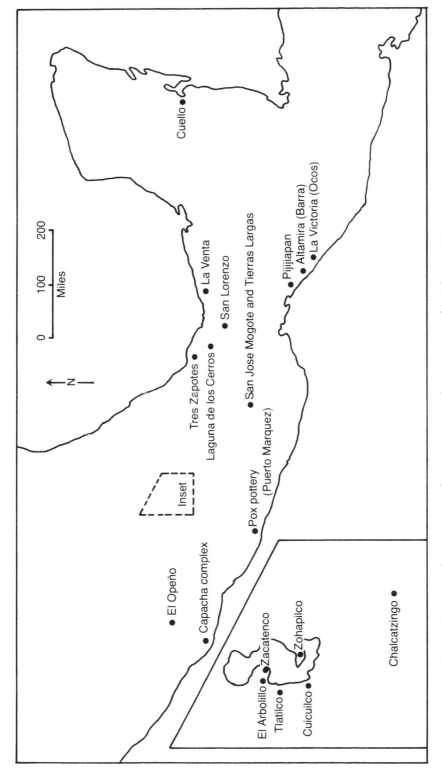

FIGURE 13-1. Map showing location of major sites and/or ceramic complexes mentioned in Chapter 13.

Olmec culture is now thought by Coe to begin with the Early Formative San Lorenzo phase (1150–900 B.C.). During this phase the site's archaeological inventory included colossal stone heads, monolithic table-top altars, and ceramic vessels decorated with iconographic motifs such as the "paw-wing" and "fire serpent." There are indications now that Early Formative levels do exist at La Venta (Hallinan, Ambro, and O'Connell 1968: 161–165), but these were not located during the 1955 research. In light of the newer San Lorenzo and La Venta data, it is not surprising that Olmec culture at La Venta seemed to appear suddenly with no antecedents. The sudden appearance was the result of archaeological sampling and not cultural reality.

A small farming community existed at San Lorenzo 300 to 400 years prior to the San Lorenzo phase. Archaeological material from this early occupation, Coe's Ojochi phase (1500–1350 B.C.), includes ceramic tecomates, narrow-necked bottles, and flat-bottom bowls with flaring walls. Ceramic decoration includes fluting, gadrooning, bands or stripes of red slip, and red rims on tecomates. Stone bowls, metates, obsidian chips, and a few figurine fragments have also been recovered.

Ojochi phase ceramics appear related to the Ocos phase ceramics of the Pacific Coast of Chiapas-Guatemala. Because the Pacific Coast's ceramics are far more elaborate, Coe has characterized Ojochi phase ceramics as "a kind of country cousin of that more spectacular culture" (1970:22). Actually, the entire Isthmian region and contiguous areas contain sites with Ocos-like ceramics (Lowe 1971: 223; 1977:207–212). The Ojochi phase occupation at San Lorenzo therefore was simply part of a larger, widespread early farming culture influenced by the Pacific Coast.

In attempting to determine if the early farming communities on the Gulf Coast evolved over time into the culture we call Olmec, it is possible to interpret the limited archaeological data in at least two ways. The common practice has been to view the Gulf Coast archaeological sequence in terms of its

changes and to interpret any major discontinuities as externally influenced. The alternative, which I prefer, is to analyze the record in terms of continuity between phases, allowing for internal differentiation through time as the culture becomes more complex and innovative. The two viewpoints are not mutually exclusive, since increasing complexity is often associated with increased external interactions.

The next phase at San Lorenzo, Bajio (1350–1250 B.C.), had certain vessel forms such as tecomates and flat-bottom bowls, which, together with decorative techniques such as fluting and gadrooning, indicate a continuum out of the Ojochi phase. Nevertheless, Coe sees the overall assemblage as "strikingly different" (1970:24). New traits within the assemblage include fluted bottles and decorative techniques such as zoned punctation and rocker-stamping. Differentially fired ceramics, an important constituent of the Olmec assemblage, began at this time. While differentially fired ceramics do not overtly display iconographic symbols, the black-white opposition they express may have been highly symbolic. Figurines increased in quantity, and one Bajio phase hollow figurine has been described by Coe (1970:24) as "identical in form to those considered typical of Olmec culture." Metates and obsidian chips continued from the Ojochi phase.

The Bajio phase ceramic assemblage is similar to the Ocos phase materials on the Pacific Coast but at the same time has a character all its own. Several lines of evidence demonstrate that a cultural impetus was developing on the Gulf Coast and that the Bajio phase occupation at San Lorenzo was far more than a simple egalitarian farming hamlet. The most significant evidence is a massive construction project during this phase which modified the San Lorenzo hilltop into a large artificial plateau over 1,000 m long and 600 m wide (M. Coe 1968:45; 1970: 22–23). This immense public works effort was apparently devoted to civic-religious functions rather than agricultural use. It was later to become the location of the major Olmec center at San Lorenzo.

The importance of this development lies in the fact that nothing of this magnitude is known from other areas of Mesoamerica at this time; thus, it was a local undertaking. Furthermore, the increasing cultural complexity demonstrated by the organization and labor investment necessary to modify the hilltop was far more of a "quantum jump" than many of the innovations a century or more later which initiated the San Lorenzo (Olmec) phase. The public works project was certainly one of the initial steps culminating in Olmec culture.

The evidence for Bajio phase public architecture is limited to one sand and clay platform disclosed by Coe's excavations (M. Coe 1968:46; 1970:24). Other structures may exist but are deeply buried under later cultural deposits.

If the San Lorenzo phase is Olmec, then the Chicharras phase (1250–1150 B.C.) is certainly proto-Olmec. Within the Chicharras phase assemblage are artifacts such as kaolin ceramics, hollow white-slipped figurines, the first "exotic" greenstone ornaments, and fragments of monumental stone carvings. All of these are "typical" artifacts of the San Lorenzo phase Olmec assemblage.

Although there are some continuities with the Bajio phase, Coe (1970:25) sees in the Chicharras phase ceramics a "host of new types and modes (which) suggests a significant influx of new ideas and/or people." The apparent discontinuities may be due to both innovation and borrowing. Obsidian source analyses (Cobean et al. 1971:Table 1) indicate expanding long distance exchange contacts during this phase, but since the Bajio phase plateau construction demonstrates a rapidly developing complexity on the Gulf Coast, the Chicharras developments can also be interpreted as indigenous and need not be attributed to external sources.

The subsequent San Lorenzo phase (1150–900 B.C.) has been described as "the sudden appearance of Olmec civilization in full flower" (M. Coe 1968:64), although the Chicharras–San Lorenzo phase transition can also be interpreted as a gradual and indigenous evolution. The San Lorenzo phase ceramic assemblage continues out of the Chicharras phase with the major addition of two pottery types which bear iconographic motifs and represent "ceramic markers" for the phase (M. Coe 1970:26). During this phase the site was quite elaborate, having monumental stone carvings, public architecture, and a network of buried stone drains connected to artificial ponds.

The significant differences between the Chicharras and San Lorenzo phases are primarily quantitative rather than qualitative. For example, stone monuments, which first appeared in the Chicharras phase, were far more abundant during the San Lorenzo phase. The principal change in ceramics was the appearance of iconographic motifs. Such iconography may have functioned in rituals of sanctification (Drennan 1976b), as status markers (Flannery 1968b:98–107), or to identify descent groups (Pyne 1976; Flannery and Marcus 1976b:380–382). The presence of iconography on ceramics reflects a higher level of sociocultural complexity, although it is not a necessary "marker" for Olmec culture nor should its appearance imply external influences. An increase in quantity is also seen in the figurine cult, which has greater numbers and varieties, and includes "ballplayers." Exotic imports likewise increase and include iron ore mirrors (M. Coe 1970:26–28).

Hereditary rulership sanctified by divine descent is common to chiefdoms (Flannery 1972a:402–403). The colossal stone heads for which Early Formative Olmec culture is famous are probably portraits of the rulers of major Olmec centers (M. Coe 1977:186; Grove 1981). Many other of the stone monuments demonstrate in their iconography the divine descent and supernatural power of the rulers (Grove 1973, 1981). A kinship tie between rulers at San Lorenzo and La Venta seems to be symbolized on one San Lorenzo altar (Grove 1981), a relationship which would also imply hereditary rulership and

377

suggest that one lineage may have ruled several Gulf Coast sites.

While the evolution of complex culture on the Gulf Coast may seem to have occurred relatively rapidly, the various traits constituting Olmec culture did not "appear suddenly" but rather were the outcome of a gradual development. The beginnings of sociocultural complexity can be traced to the Bajio phase. Stone monuments predate ceramic iconography, although both are used as "markers" for Olmec culture. These artifacts primarily served to symbolically demonstrate or sanctify certain beliefs. Such beliefs were almost certainly far older, and their eventual appearance in stone and ceramics was more a technological than an ideological achievement. All of these traits manifest the evolving complexity of Gulf Coast culture rather than a significant intrusion of new ideas.

The data on the transition from Early to Middle Formative on the Gulf Coast are inconclusive. Although San Lorenzo was still inhabited (Nacaste phase, 900–700 B.C.) (Chapter 5, this volume), it declined in importance. La Venta became a major Olmec center (P. Drucker, Heizer, and Squier 1959). Again there are at least two ways in which to interpret this transition. The first interpretation is that the transition was caused by internal revolt or invaders (M. Coe 1970:28); it relies on the fact that Early Formative monuments were mutilated and buried, presumably during this period of violence. An alternative view (Grove 1981) sees the transition as gradual. The mutilation of monuments is explained as essentially ritual activities over a long period of time. Any "abruptness" in the archaeological record reflects the quality of the present data.

Many areas of Mesoamerica similarly show an "abrupt" Early to Middle Formative transition, but the more recent data, for example those from the Valley of Mexico, reveal that a gradual evolution is a more tenable interpretation. This is probably also the case on the Gulf Coast. Because San Lorenzo and La Venta are the two best-known Olmec sites ar-

chaeologically, the transition seems to be one of San Lorenzo losing power and La Venta taking over. This interpretation is tenuous, however, because knowledge of such other sites as Laguna de los Cerros and Tres Zapotes is virtually nil.

The transition is marked in the artifact assemblage by a change from ceramics bearing iconographic motifs (e.g., the paw-wing, crossed-bands, fire-serpent, etc.), hollow baby-face figurines, colossal stone heads, and table-top altars, to white ware vessels with rims decorated in variations of the double-line-break motif, non-baby-face figurines, iconography prevalent on greenstone portable art rather than ceramics, and bas-relief carved stelae. These latter still expressed the divine descent and supernatural power of the rulers.

Ceramics with the double-line-break motif were almost pan-Mesoamerican at this time. These together with the increased use of jade and greenstone show increasing involvement of Gulf Coast sites in long distance interregional exchange networks. The jade and greenstone demonstrate the increasing differentiation in access to goods at major centers.

Middle Formative architecture seems more complex than that of the previous period, but this may only be so because Early Formative architecture is poorly known. During the Middle Formative, San Lorenzo had a large rectangular plaza area flanked by long mounds (M. Coe 1968:Fig. 2). A major pyramid mound was situated at the end of one plaza. Complex A at La Venta, the best known of that site's architectural groups, is likewise characterized by a plaza flanked by long mounds, with a pyramid at the plaza's south end (P. Drucker, Heizer, and Squier 1959:Fig. 3-5). A similar pattern occurs at Laguna de los Cerros (Bove 1978:Map A).

Middle Formative Gulf Coast public architecture varies from earthen to adobe brick–filled mounds. There are some instances of minor stone facing. A magnetometer survey of the large La Venta pyramid (Morrison,

Clewlow, and Heizer 1970) indicated the probability of a stone platform or construction in the pyramid's upper portion.

Within the plaza area termed Complex A at La Venta were special precincts and platforms surrounded by large basalt columns. Excavations uncovered tombs, "offering" groups of serpentine and jade celts (occasionally accompanied by iron ore mirrors), and associations of ceramics and jade beads (P. Drucker, Heizer, and Squier 1959:133–191) along the plaza's center line. The presence of "cinnabar" stains associated with some of these latter groups and their layout (beads, earspools, etc.) suggest that some may have been burial offerings. Other groups (e.g., Offering 10) (P. Drucker, Heizer, and Squier 1959:Fig. 51) are clearly ritual offerings. Underlying the plaza floor and small platforms within the plaza area were mosaic pavements and massive offerings of serpentine (P. Drucker, Heizer, and Squier 1959: 128–133, Fig. 4).

Gulf Coast Olmec sites are presumed to have been vacant centers, and because excavations have concentrated on the public or ceremonial areas, little is known about how the people themselves lived. If the sites followed the pattern of others in Mesoamerica, it is probable that certain elite residences were built on platforms adjoining the plaza areas. The tombs and possible nontomb burials along the Complex A plaza's center line may represent special individuals from the elite residences.

This section has viewed the evolution of complex culture on the Gulf Coast as indigenous, but has not ruled out stimuli due to external contacts. In an area of limited geological resources such as the Gulf Coast, external exchange contacts were always important, and they became increasingly significant both as the population with its need for basic technological materials (obsidian, grinding stones, etc.) grew, and as social complexity and its concomitant demand for socio-ideological artifacts (jade, serpentine, iron ore mirrors, cacao, etc.) increased.

Some borrowing of nontangible traits such as ideas, beliefs, symbols, etc., through these exchange interactions should be expected. The question of how significantly they may have influenced an already evolving culture should be treated with caution because of the small amount of archaeological data available.

Using the Gulf Coast evolutionary sequence as a base, we can now consider just how unique this development really was vis-à-vis other areas of Mesoamerica.

## OAXACA

An important contrast to the Gulf Coast developments is documented by research in the Valley of Oaxaca carried out by Kent Flannery and his associates (Flannery 1968b, 1970, 1976a; Flannery and Marcus 1976a, 1976b; Chapter 3, this volume). Their excavations have provided information on settlements and public architecture/public space which is relatively unavailable in other areas of Mesoamerica. The data are particularly interesting because they reveal a certain cultural precocity in this region.

The earliest identified "public space" occurs at the site of Gheo-Shih and dates to ca. 4000 B.C. (Flannery 1970:22–24; Flannery and Marcus 1976a:207). The creation of architecturally restricted access to special site areas is a common feature at later Mesoamerican ceremonial centers. Such a restricted public area occurred at the site of San Jose Mogote at the end of the first recognized ceramic-bearing phase, Espiridion, about 1400 B.C. (Chapter 3, this volume). This was a cleared area separated from the site's habitation zone by a double line of staggered posts (Flannery and Marcus 1976a: 208, Fig. 10.2). Ceramics from this phase are simple monochromes and include very thin walled hemispherical bowls. They show no strong similarities to other regions. One "feline" figurine fragment was recovered.

The first public structures appear in the Tierras Largas phase (1400–1150 B.C.) (Chapter 3, this volume). With the Tierras

Largas phase, the data on Formative period settlements greatly increase. The largest of the sites of this phase was San Jose Mogote, a village which remained central to Oaxaca's cultural development during the Early and Middle Formative. Tierras Largas phase ceramic forms and decorations are largely uninfluenced by other areas. The tecomate, a form typical of the widespread Ocos phase to the south, is rare. When tecomate sherds occur, they are Ocos-like "trade sherds" with rocker-stamped decoration (Flannery 1970: 96–97). Well-modeled clay figurines with elaborate headdresses and hair treatment (Marcus, personal communication) attest to the increasing importance of the figurine cult.

With the San Jose phase (1150–850 B.C.) (Flannery 1970:97), the village of San Jose Mogote experienced significant growth. Surface and house floor artifacts indicate the presence of part-time artisans who manufactured iron ore mirrors, made ornaments of shell and mica, and utilized other exotic raw materials (Flannery 1968b:85). No other site in the valley had such a large workshop area or specific iron ore workshops. The iron ore mirrors manufactured at San Jose Mogote were exported via interregional exchange networks to other regions (Pires-Ferreira 1975:31–35; 1976b). The presence of jade and greenstone ornaments with a limited number of burials suggests differential access to goods, which is an indication of social ranking.

Ceramics from this phase reflect a common Early Formative phenomenon in that although they were locally manufactured, some vessels have Olmec-like iconography. Thanks to the Oaxaca research, data are now available on the meaning of such pottery in contexts outside of the Gulf Coast. Analyses (Flannery and Marcus 1976b:381–382; Pyne 1976) indicate that two of the iconographic motifs, the "fire-serpent" and the "were-jaguar," do not co-occur in residential or burial contexts, and there is a positive correlation among the motifs, ceramic types, and barrios at the San Jose Mogote village. The east and west barrios have fire-serpent motifs executed on black or grey vessels, while the north and south barrios have white ceramics with were-jaguar motifs.

A similar separation is found, not among the barrios at other villages, but among the villages themselves. The San Jose phase occupations at Tierras Largas and Huitzo have ceramics with were-jaguar motifs, while Tomaltepec and Abasolo have fire-serpent decorated vessels. These data, presented here in abbreviated form, indicate that the widespread occurrence of the Olmec-like iconography is not necessarily the result of a direct imposition by outsiders. Rather the iconography was an integral part of the local societies and probably related to descent groups. Finding such pottery at an Early Formative site does not imply that the site was Olmec influenced.

During the Middle Formative Guadalupe (850–700 B.C.) and Rosario (700–500 B.C.) phases, public architecture appeared at secondary centers in the valley, such as Huitzo. The most significant change in public architecture did not occur until the Rosario phase, when San Jose Mogote was dominated by a large pyramid-like mound, ca. 15 m tall (a modified natural hill). North of this mound was a large plaza area, flanked on two sides by long mounds. A platform with an elite residence marked the plaza's north end. The mound-plaza arrangement exhibited at this site displays the general pattern found at Middle Formative Gulf Coast sites. Excavations atop the pyramid-like mound uncovered some areas of cut-stone façades and a carved danzante figure (Monument 3) (Flannery and Marcus 1976b:382).

Guadalupe and Rosario phase ceramics differ from their San Jose phase predecessors in the same general patterns that separate Early and Middle Formative Gulf Coast ceramics. Vessels with Olmec-like iconography give way to white wares with double-line-break motifs. As in other areas of Mesoamerica, the figurine cult, with stylistic changes, continues in importance.

The end of the Rosario phase marks the

380

end of the Middle Formative period, and with the Late Formative, political power shifted from San Jose Mogote to Monte Alban. By this time, however, the basic prototype for Monte Alban I—i.e., as the center of a religious-administrative hierarchy, with such features as mound-plaza-elite residence architectural patterns, *danzantes*, and calendrical hieroglyphs—had already been established by the people of San Jose Mogote.

## HIGHLAND CENTRAL MEXICO

Until recently the highland Central Mexican archaeological sequence was based primarily on the pioneering research of George Vaillant at Zacatenco (1930) and El Arbolillo (1935), and the somewhat later work by various investigators at Tlatilco (Covarrubias 1943; Piña Chan 1958a, 1958b; Porter 1953). These three sites all occur in the western Valley of Mexico. In the traditional interpretation of these data, Zacatenco and El Arbolillo were considered to be farming hamlets exemplifying the local culture and contemporaneous to Tlatilco. This latter site, however, had elaborate burial offerings, including ceramics bearing Olmec-like iconography. Tlatilco was thought to be a unique, highly developed village, a central focus in the Valley of Mexico, and even an Olmec colony (e.g., Bernal 1969:130–138).

The breakthrough in understanding the Formative period in the Central Highlands came with the demonstration that this long-established "Middle Preclassic" sequence was incorrect (Tolstoy and Paradis 1970). Excavations by Paul Tolstoy at El Arbolillo and Atoto (near Tlatilco) showed that Tlatilco ceramics were not contemporaneous with Zacatenco and El Arbolillo but in fact preceded them chronologically. Excavations at the same time in Morelos (Grove 1970, 1974a, 1974b) and more recent work in both areas (Grove et al. 1976; Niederberger 1976; Tolstoy 1975, 1978) have confirmed the revised sequence. The new data have initiated revisions in the interpretation of highland cultural development.

Much of the Formative period research in this region has been oriented to ceramics and ceramic chronology. The earliest fired clay object known from the Valley of Mexico is actually from the Archaic period. The object is a crude figurine found at Zohapilco (Tlapacoya) in the southeastern Valley of Mexico and dated to ca. 2300 B.C. (Niederberger 1976:213, Photo 11). Aside from this solitary example, the Zohapilco phase culture (2300–2000 B.C.) (Niederberger 1976:253–255) is aceramic. Furthermore, there were no corn grinding tools in the excavated sample.

The only data for ceramic-using Early Formative communities in the Valley of Mexico prior to 1400 B.C. are tenuous and come from ceramics recovered from mound fill at Cuicuilco (Heizer and Bennyhoff 1972:96–97). These ceramics, designated by the excavators as part of a Tlalpan phase (2100–1800 B.C.), include deep thin-walled bowls, the use of red paint and "wide channeling" for decoration, and several types of figurines. Unfortunately, there are severe problems with the Tlalpan phase data and radiocarbon dates (Tolstoy 1978:252–253), and they remain unconfirmed by twenty years of additional research in the same region.

The first good evidence for agricultural communities and ceramics is the Nevada complex (1400–1250 B.C.) (Niederberger 1976:256–257; Tolstoy [1978:253] gives a 1400–1150 B.C. time range). The ceramic assemblage includes red-rimmed tecomates and white ware vessels incised with Olmec-like iconographic motifs and rocker-stamped decoration (Niederberger 1976:114–123), and it exhibits some similarities with Early Nexpa subphase ceramics (1350–1250 B.C.) from Morelos (Grove 1974b:30–31, 36).

A variety of figurine types occur in the Nevada complex, one of which (Niederberger's "Pilli" type [1976:209–210, Figs. 74–76]) has facial features which would cause some scholars to classify it as "Olmec." Since the Early Formative figurines from San Lorenzo have not yet been published, critical comparisons cannot be made. Designating these or other non–Gulf Coast figurines as Olmec

381

ignores their function within the local context. They may have functioned in the same manner as the Olmec-like iconography on Oaxacan vessels, as descent or social markers, an interpretation with few if any implications of external influences.

Between 1250 and 900 B.C. the Valley of Mexico and Morelos were characterized archaeologically by a shared pattern in household and burial ceramics and figurines. Tolstoy (1978:253–255) has slightly refined the earlier Tolstoy-Paradis (1970) chronology, and now separates this period in the Valley of Mexico, the Ixtapaluca phase, into three subphases, Coapexco, Ayotla, and Manantial. Within the indigenous highland culture at this time two distinctive ceramic groups co-occur in domestic and burial contexts.

One group is a complex of red-on-brown bottles, often incised or gadrooned, and decorated with a smudge-resist technique (Grove 1974a:Fig. 3). This red-on-brown vessel complex changes through time, and distinctive forms, such as the stirrup-spout bottle and "belted" bottles, occur late in the Early Formative sequence (Manantial phase and its regional equivalents) (Grove 1974b:Fig. 9; Tolstoy 1978:254).

The second ceramic group is less abundant (less than 7 percent of the total assemblage) and comprises vessels with Olmec-like iconography, and tecomates. These vessels are not restricted to a single site but occur at sites throughout the region, in both large and small communities. They appear to be locally manufactured rather than imported, a situation identical to that of the Olmec-like ceramics described earlier for Oaxaca. Although the presence of these vessels at highland sites has been attributed to Olmec colonization (see Grove 1974a), the Oaxacan explanation (Flannery and Marcus 1976b:381–382; Pyne 1976) also seems appropriate in this instance. Tolstoy (1978:254–255; Tolstoy et al. 1977: 105) has dealt with these data in greater detail and has attempted to analyze differences in ceramic iconography between some Valley of Mexico sites.

The figurine cult became quite elaborate during the Ixtapaluca phase and included both solid and hollow figurines. Figurines which have been identified as "Olmec" are present in minor quantities, but, as with other artifacts, they should be considered as part of the local cultural milieu. Similar caution should be exercised with regard to the figurine types which seem similar to those from West Mexico.

The most famous Early Formative highland site is Tlatilco (Piña Chan 1958a, 1958b; Porter 1953), although its importance may be overemphasized in the literature. The site was a brickyard, and its first burials were "excavated" by brickyard workers who sold the artifacts they uncovered to collectors. Official excavations were begun in the early 1940s (Covarrubias 1943) and have been carried out only sporadically since then. Looting apparently continued between official excavations, and as Tlatilco's fame increased, looted Early Formative ceramics from other sites were sold as having been found at Tlatilco. Thus, more artifacts are alleged to come from Tlatilco than actually were recovered there.

The site today is covered by urban, industrial Mexico City, and its true spatial extent cannot be determined. The quantity of burial ceramics of alleged Tlatilco provenience, when added to burials and ceramics recovered by official excavations at the site, would imply that Tlatilco was one of Formative period Central Mexico's largest villages. This is probably an erroneous assumption. In fact, it is possible that the area called Tlatilco may have been the location of two or three small villages rather than one large site.

The archaeological data obtained by all Tlatilco excavations (legal or illegal) are biased. The main objective of the Tlatilco excavations was to locate burials in order to recover the associated artifacts. While biased to a "way of death" rather than a "way of life," the data are useful in that the variations in the quantity and quality of the mortuary goods (at Tlatilco and elsewhere in Central Mexico) indicate a ranked society. Jade and greenstone are present but quite rare. Among the burials receiving large quantities of offerings were women and children. Such offerings with children imply that ranking was ascribed rather than achieved.

Muriel Noé Porter (1953:34) has noted that some Tlatilco excavation units may have cut through earthen, clay-surfaced mounds. Working from field notes of previous archaeologists' excavations, Tolstoy (personal communication) has discovered that Tlatilco's burials tend to cluster in groups. This fact, together with Porter's observation, suggests that burials may have occurred around and under house platforms.

Although the earlier interpretation of "Middle Preclassic" culture history considered Tlatilco a unique site, the uniqueness has not been confirmed by more recent research. Early Formative sites in Morelos and the Valley of Mexico share a basic ceramic assemblage with Tlatilco, with some minor regional variations. In fact, there are far more Tlatilco-like Early Formative sites along the humid river valleys of Morelos than in the cooler lakeshore areas of the Valley of Mexico. Because of its better agricultural conditions, Morelos was more probably the focus of this regional culture.

In the discussions of the Gulf Coast and Oaxacan data, public architecture was one convenient marker for increasing social complexity. However, because research in the Central Highlands has focused on ceramics and burials, Early Formative public architecture is virtually unknown. Since, in contrast to Oaxaca, no Early Formative villages have been intensively excavated in the Central Highlands, the paucity of public architecture may be due to sampling rather than an actual absence. A stone-faced burial mound was found at one Morelos site (Grove 1970), and earthen mounds are suspected at Tlatilco, but the major exception to the presumed rarity of public architecture is found at Chalcatzingo in eastern Morelos.

Chalcatzingo is best known for its Middle Formative Olmec-style bas-relief carvings. Excavations at the site in the mid-1970s (Grove et al. 1976) concentrated on the extensive Middle Formative deposits, but two

Early Formative structures were located, although neither was excavated. One structure is a raised stone-faced platform, nearly 1 m in height. This platform may have been a public structure, or it may have served as the substructure for the residence of a high-ranking individual.

The second Chalcatzingo structure can definitely be classified as public architecture. It is an earthen mound slightly over 2 m in height, with a thin clay outer surface. This mound underlies the site's massive 70 m long, 4 m tall earthen Middle Formative platform structure and was located in test trenches excavated into the larger structure. Its exact dimensions are unknown. The Middle Formative platform mound probably represents a rebuilding and enlargement of the Early Formative mound. On the whole, however, the Early Formative component at Chalcatzingo is not well known, and aside from the architecture, there is little in the archaeological record to set Chalcatzingo apart from contemporaneous sites in Morelos and the Valley of Mexico.

For the Early Formative period, the Valley of Mexico–Morelos area can be subdivided into seven local subareas delimited by geographical boundaries such as ranges of hills. Available evidence indicates that within each subarea there was a simple hierarchy consisting of hamlets, several small villages, and one larger village. The larger village apparently served as a "center" in terms of being a focus for redistribution and exchange within the subarea. Chalcatzingo was the center for the eastern Morelos subarea. During the Early Formative, this subarea was lightly populated because of the relative inaccessibility of surface water. Chalcatzingo was the largest site in eastern Morelos. Located on good agricultural land and adjacent to a small spring, its central position in the valley also made it a natural focus for redistribution, for it was in close proximity to iron ore, kaolin, and chert sources, as well as to strategic communication routes.

Since most of Morelos has not been extensively surveyed, nor have any Early Formative villages been adequately excavated, comparisons cannot be made with Oaxacan settlement data. There are no current data to suggest that any of the larger villages in Morelos or the Valley of Mexico, including Chalcatzingo, attained the importance, size, or central character of San Jose Mogote during the Early Formative.

Although all of the local subareas were politically autonomous and only loosely integrated within the highland region, the data show a certain cohesion, not only in the artifact assemblage but also in the raw material exploitation pattern. Obsidian characterization studies (Pires-Ferreira 1975: Tables 2–4; Charlton, Grove, and Hopke 1978) demonstrate that 90 to 100 percent of the obsidian utilized by Early Formative communities in Morelos and the Valley of Mexico came from a set of two local sources, while the pattern outside of this area shows much greater variation. These data suggest that these two communities (which share a common cultural assemblage) controlled the obsidian sources in some way, and that the area's exchange network excluded obsidian from other sources. Interestingly, Oaxacan communities acquired obsidian from the Central Mexican sources and also from a source in Zinapecuaro, Michoacan (Pires-Ferreira 1976a: Tables 2–3). The Central Mexican communities are situated between Oaxaca and the Michoacan source, but they did not utilize that source themselves, although they may have been involved in exchanging Zinapecuaro obsidian with Oaxaca.

The transition from Early to Middle Formative is documented in the Manantial subphase (Tolstoy 1978:255–256). Both red-on-brown bottles and white wares with the double-line-break motif (so common during the Middle Formative) co-occur in Manantial subphase levels, indicating that one style did not abruptly replace the other. Such a transitional stage will probably be found at Gulf Coast sites as work continues there.

It is difficult to comment on evolving cultural complexity in the highlands during the Middle Formative because again there is a paucity of data. Middle Formative sites lack the more exotic-looking ceramic burial goods such as are found at Tlatilco, and the impression is conveyed that Middle Formative societies are not as complex. This impression is incorrect, as demonstrated by surface surveys of the Valley of Mexico (Blanton 1972b; J. Parsons 1971) and eastern Morelos (Hirth 1974) which document an increase in the number of communities and greater variation in community size (an expanding hierarchy) at this time. Although public architecture (including large platforms and mounds) was present in Oaxaca, Chiapas, and the Gulf Coast during the Middle Formative, it was still uncommon in the Central Highlands, and currently is only known at Chalcatzingo and sites in its immediate local area, and Cuicuilco in the Valley of Mexico.

Chalcatzingo is anomalous in the highlands not only because of its public architecture but also because it is the only Central Highland site with Olmec-style monumental art (Gay 1972a; Grove 1968; Grove et al. 1976; Piña Chan 1955a). During the Middle Formative Cantera phase (700–500 B.C.) the site featured a plaza area about 120 m long and 70 m wide, flanked on its north side by the previously mentioned 70 m long platform mound. An elite residence and several nonresidential buildings were located on the plaza's south side. In addition, two large stone-faced platforms, each with an erected carved stela, and an Olmec-style table-top altar within a small walled patio area, were found during excavations near the plaza (Grove et al. 1976: Fig. 5). Chalcatzingo's public or ceremonial area encompassed about 20 percent of the main site area.

Chalcatzingo's bas-relief carvings and newly discovered stelae have no highland antecedents and demonstrate significant relationships to Middle Formative carved art styles from La Venta. The Chalcatzingo Middle Formative ceramics show some similarities to the Tres Zapotes assemblage, but on the whole they are within the highland ceramic tradition. The figurine cult continues to be important. One highland figurine type, C8 (Vaillant 1930:112), is most abundant at Chalcatzingo and its immediate local area. Although most highland Middle Formative figurines seem to be generalized in features, my analysis of C8 figurines suggests that these are portrait figurines representing specific individuals, probably rulers.

Although Chalcatzingo is distinct from most Middle Formative highland sites because of its carvings, public architecture, and some highly restricted ceramic types, it basically reflects the highland culture pattern and reveals some insights into the indigenous culture. Chalcatzingo's Cantera phase burials clearly demonstrate social differentiation. The highest-ranked individuals were interred within stone-lined and stone-capped graves and accompanied by jade or other greenstone ornaments. These high-ranked burials were restricted primarily to the elite residence and 70 m platform mound, and are clearly separated both spatially and through mortuary practices from others in the community.

Such ranking may have typified other Central Highland communities as well. For example, although the majority of El Arbolillo's burials are direct interments, a number of slab-covered graves and one stone-lined and slab-covered grave also occur (Vaillant 1935: 168–188). Jade was found only with these latter burials, which are all located within a relatively small area outlined by wall lines. As in the case of Chalcatzingo, the wall lines may be the foundation walls of an elite residence. The presence of a child burial in association with jade earspools again indicates that ranking was ascribed.

In light of Chalcatzingo's uniqueness and obvious importance, the question of indigenous highland evolution during the Middle Formative depends on ascertaining the degree to which Gulf Coast contacts stimulated Chalcatzingo's development and thereby directly or indirectly stimulated the development of complex culture in the highlands. Available data suggest to me that Gulf Coast "influences" were not significant in the highlands (specifically Chalcatzingo) until the Middle Formative, but that by the Cantera phase the administration of Chalcatzingo was controlled either by a few Gulf Coast elite or by persons linked by marriage alliances to one or more Gulf Coast centers. Gulf Coast "influences" were probably not responsible for stimulating cultural developments in the highlands because the nature of the Middle Formative "influence" seems to have been exploitive, noncontributory, and highly localized. Both Chalcatzingo's growth and its Gulf Coast ties appear to have been directly related to the site's early and continuing role in the exploitation and redistribution of raw material resources.

The other locus of significant public architecture is Cuicuilco in the Valley of Mexico. Excavations in 1957 located several clay platform structures which have been assigned by the excavators to the Middle Formative (Heizer and Bennyhoff 1972:97–98). The earliest of these structures was unfaced, but stone-faced platforms appeared slightly later. Heizer and Bennyhoff suggest that these platforms had "ceremonial" functions and that Cuicuilco was "already very large" during the Middle Formative (1972:98). However, the data on Middle Formative Cuicuilco have "various problems" (1972:97) and also remain largely unpublished. Excavations carried out in 1967 during the construction of housing for Olympic athletes exposed a large area and uncovered several mounds which were subsequently reconstructed. These data are also unpublished.

The scarcity of data on Cuicuilco makes it difficult to comment on that site's possible relationships to Chalcatzingo and to compare their respective developments. If the Cuicuilco mounds found in 1957 are in fact Middle Formative, then they constitute evidence of an early foundation for what was to become a major Late Formative center. This development is highly relevant to the evolution of urban society in Central Mexico, particularly because of Cuicuilco's location in what was then the valley's prime agricultural area.

## SOUTHERN PACIFIC COAST

The Pacific Coast of Chiapas-Guatemala has been frequently mentioned in this chapter and compared to other areas, particularly for the Early Formative Ocos phase (1500–1150 B.C.) first defined by Michael D. Coe (1960, 1961a) at La Victoria, Guatemala. Ocos phase ceramics seem to be typical for early farming villages across the Isthmian region, and Ocos developments appear to have influenced early events on the Gulf Coast (M. Coe 1970:22; Lowe 1978:351). Probable Ocos phase trade sherds were found in Tierras Largas phase contexts in Oaxaca (Flannery 1970:96–97).

Recent stratigraphic evidence indicates that the Ocos phase was preceded by an earlier phase, Barra (Green and Lowe 1967; Lowe 1975), even though uncorrected radiocarbon dates (Lowe 1975:29–33) place the Barra phase at ca. 1400–1300 B.C. Barra phase ceramics are quite sophisticated and are unlike any others known in Mesoamerica from this time period. The vessels are primarily incurved-rim bowls. Decorative techniques include incising and grooving, attributes which also occur on the newly discovered Swasey phase ceramics from Belize (Hammond et al. 1976; Hammond et al. 1979). These are the earliest examples of such decorative attributes in Mesoamerica.

Lowe (1975:9–10, 21–23; Green and Lowe 1967:56–57) and others see strong affinities between Barra phase ceramics and those of coastal Ecuador. The similarities are primarily in the decorative attributes rather than in vessel forms.

Several figurine fragments also occur in the Barra sample (Green and Lowe 1967: Fig. 94m; Lowe, personal communication). This is the earliest occurrence of figurines in southern Mesoamerica. The Barra figurines are significant in that they are the initial segment of a continuing figurine tradition. By the Ocos phase this figurine tradition was being shared by Ojochi phase San Lorenzo. The Barra-Ocos figurine tradition may have been antecedent to Oaxaca's figurine cult as

well. The presence of figurines in the problematical Tlalpan phase in the Valley of Mexico may indicate a separate figurine tradition there, with different antecedents.

The Ocos phase (1500–1150 B.C.) is an elaboration out of Barra but with an increased variety of decorative attributes, most of which are shared with northern Ecuador (M. Coe 1960). The variety and sophistication of Ocos ceramics is unparalleled in other regions of Mesoamerica (e.g., Lowe 1977: 208). The figurine cult increased in importance in this phase.

There is no published evidence for public buildings during the Barra phase, and Ocos phase public architecture is poorly known. One Ocos phase site, Paso de Amada, has a "three meter high central mound surrounded by a quadrangular arrangement of very low platforms or house mounds covering several acres" (Lowe 1977:211). It is probable that at least the central mound constitutes public architecture.

A relatively rapid change in ceramic styles from the elaborate Ocos ceramics to vessels showing affinities to San Lorenzo phase ceramics on the Gulf Coast appears in the archaeological record late in the Early Formative. This marks the beginning of the Cuadros phase (1150–800 B.C.). Little mention is made in the literature concerning public architecture for this time period, and it is not until the following Middle Formative Conchas phase (800–600 B.C.) that architecture in quantity is known along the Pacific Coast. This consists primarily of clay platforms and pyramid mounds (M. Coe and Flannery 1967:89; S. Ekholm 1969).

As the Middle Formative progressed, architecture became increasingly abundant and complex, both on the coast and in portions of central Chiapas. Pyramid structures, long platform mounds, and occasionally ballcourts have been found in this latter area (Lowe 1977:224–226, Fig. 9.4). The layout of these sites, which exhibit the pyramid-plaza-platform arrangement, is reminiscent of Middle Formative Gulf Coast sites and Rosario phase Oaxaca.

Olmec-style carvings are also present along the Chiapas-Guatemalan coastal strip. The Pijijiapan and Padre Piedra reliefs have been assigned by Carlos Navarrete (1974:9–11) to the Early Formative Cuadros phase, while Andrew J. McDonald (1977) dates the Tzutzuculi carvings to the Middle Formative. It is my impression, based on stylistic grounds, that the scattered examples of Olmec-style bas-reliefs in Mesoamerica (San Miguel Amuco, Xoc, Chalchuapa, etc.), including those at Chalcatzingo and the coastal Chiapas examples, are Middle Formative. Their presence at the Pacific Coast sites, as at Chalcatzingo, may be related to resource exploitation, in these instances items such as cacao, salt, and Pacific Coast shell.

In summarizing cultural development in southern Mesoamerica, three points stand out. The first is that the earliest ceramics and figurines in the Isthmian region are found in Barra phase contexts. Second, no Mesoamerican antecedents are known today for these artifacts, whereas both Barra and Ocos ceramics show similarities to Ecuadorian materials. Finally, monumental architecture also appears early in the archaeological record on the Pacific Coast and could predate Gulf Coast architecture, although the current data are inconclusive.

## Other Areas

It is probable that, with sufficient data, an indigenous rise of complex culture could be traced in many other areas of Mesoamerica, such as the Huaxteca, central Veracruz, etc. At least two such areas deserve mention, however brief, in this chapter.

New data from the Cuello site in Belize (Hammond 1977; Hammond et al. 1976; Hammond et al. 1979) indicate a very early appearance there of sophisticated ceramics, jade beads, manos and metates, and platform structures with plaster floors. These platforms may have been the substructures for public buildings. Uncorrected radiocarbon dates for this archaeological manifestation, the Swasey phase, range from 2000 to 1000

B.C. There is some comparability between Swasey phase ceramics and certain ceramics from sites in Yucatan (Hammond 1977:96–97; Hammond et al. 1979:108; Lowe 1978:350), suggesting that sedentary communities in the Maya area may extend further back in time than was previously thought. At present there seems to be no relationship between Swasey phase developments and the rise of complex culture on the Gulf Coast or other areas discussed in this chapter.

The second area worthy of mention is Western Mexico. It has received little archaeological attention, although the data available suggest its Formative period developments may be potentially as interesting as those already discussed. José Arturo Oliveros' (1974) excavations of two chamber tombs at El Opeño, Michoacan, yielded highly sophisticated figurines, including a grouping of what may be ballgame players and spectators, together with red-on-brown ceramics decorated with a smudge-resist technique. A radiocarbon date places the El Opeño artifacts at ca. 1280 B.C. (Oliveros 1974:197). Many of the red-on-brown sherds are virtually identical (as sherd fragments) to Central Mexican Early Formative red-on-brown ceramics. These and other similarities have led Tolstoy (1971:26) and me (Grove 1974a:120; 1974b:59–60) to hypothesize ties between Western and Central Mexico during the Early Formative.

Investigations in Colima by Isabel Kelly (1970, 1974) have defined a Capacha complex which includes unusual stirrup-spout bottles and a *"bule"* form similar to the "belted" bottles which occur in Early Formative assemblages in the Central Highlands (Grove 1974a:Fig. 3d; Kelly 1974:Fig. 1; Greengo and Meighan 1976:Figs. 1–4). Capacha complex ceramics have recently been identified from a looted site in Jalisco as well (Greengo and Meighan 1976), indicating a wide distribution of the early sedentary villages which shared this style. A single radiocarbon date of 1450 B.C. (Kelly 1974:208) is all that is available for this material. Some doubt exists as to the validity of this date, but the ca.

500 B.C. obsidian hydration dates suggested by Robert E. Greengo and Clement W. Meighan (1976:15) appear to be too late. Stylistically the figurines and bottle forms of the Capacha complex suggest that it is Early Formative.

What is possibly Mesoamerica's earliest pottery, Pox pottery from coastal Guerrero (Brush 1965), has been dated by one radiocarbon assay to 2440 B.C. The Pox ceramics are similar to Barra and Ocos ceramics in two respects. The first is that although Pox derived its name from a pitted ("pock-marked") interior surface, its exterior surfaces are "well smoothed [and] occasionally red slipped" (Brush 1965:194). Red slip is a significant Early Formative decorative attribute present on both Barra and Ocos phase ceramics, and is also an attribute of the early ceramic traditions of coastal Ecuador, beginning at least a millennium earlier. Second, like Barra and Ocos, Pox pottery occurs on the Pacific Coast. The significance of these two points is explained below.

In the interior valleys of Guerrero there are also unusual and highly sophisticated Early Formative ceramics. The type site for this ceramic complex is Xochipala. Unfortunately, the material has been recovered primarily by looters, and the sole publication (Gay 1972b) concentrates on figurines. Although they have been identified as "Olmec" (Gay 1972b), only a few of the figurines and some of the ceramic vessels exhibit any Olmec-like attributes. I have discussed alternative explanations to such phenomena in previous sections of this chapter.

These limited data indicate that sedentary communities with highly sophisticated ceramic traditions existed in Western Mexico during the Early Formative period. Furthermore, the assemblages include a variety of exotic bottle forms and figurines nearly identical to Early Formative Central Mexican materials, as well as form and decorative attributes (e.g., red slip and smudge-resist) similar to Ecuadorian ceramics.

## MAIZE, AGRICULTURAL PRODUCTIVITY, AND THE RISE OF COMPLEX CULTURE

Although great strides have been made in the last two decades, there are still substantial gaps in the archaeological records of the areas of Mesoamerica that have been discussed here, and these gaps impede the construction of large-scale explanatory models. This is especially true because, as has been noted repeatedly, the data from the different areas are not always comparable.

Any discussion of the development of complex culture has to consider the agricultural subsistence base which permitted that development. This should be obvious, but questions regarding subsistence have not always been a priority among archaeologists working in Mesoamerica. The Gulf Coast is an example of an area in which until recently little attention was paid to the ecological potential and agricultural practices used to exploit that potential. One reason for this neglect is the long-standing bias against tropical areas as capable of sustaining large agricultural populations. Fortunately, recent research has been correcting this oversight (M. Coe 1968:57–60; 1974).

It is clear that tropical agriculture can be highly productive. Carl O. Sauer (1952) long ago suggested that the earliest New World agriculture developed in tropical South America and was based on root crops. The Gulf Coast is tropical, and much of the area requires slash-and-burn agriculture today. However, Gulf Coast sites are located adjacent to major rivers, and the river levee soils are replenished by annual flooding. Barbara J. Price (1977:212) has pointed out that with intensive slash-and-burn agriculture and river levee soils, the Gulf Coast peoples during the Early Formative would have enjoyed the "best of both worlds." Michael Coe (1974:10–11, 13), using the analogy of river levee land use today, has suggested that early in the Formative period these highly productive river levee soils could have come under the control of one small group of people, perhaps a family or lineage. The advantage they gained through this control would have provided them with political power, a power which could have served as the foundation for a ranked society.

The riverine setting alone may have provided San Lorenzo with an eventual low risk–high productivity advantage which lifted it from "country cousin" status to one of Mesoamerica's most spectacular early cultures. However, the archaeological record documents a second factor perhaps equally important: the production of improved hard-kernel maize.

Few archaeologists would question that manos and metates in Formative period archaeological assemblages, even in the absence of identifiable plant remains, suggest that maize constituted a subsistence item in the diet. On the other hand, the absence of corn grinding tools in the assemblage does not indicate the absence of maize because grinding is not the sole means of processing this food plant. Early maize varieties could have been eaten green, boiled, roasted on the cob, or even popped (Mangelsdorf 1974: 154).

Manos and metates are apparently absent in both the Barra and Ocos phases on the Pacific Coast (Green and Lowe 1967:59), and do not appear in quantity until the Cuadros phase (1150 B.C.), when corn remains also occur in the record (M. Coe and Flannery 1967:71–72). Lowe has suggested, on the basis of great quantities of obsidian chips in both the Barra and the Ocos phases, that manioc may have been a major subsistence item (1975:10–14; Green and Lowe 1967: 58–60). A simple, soft-kernel corn may also have been present (or perhaps was the major staple in the absence of manioc).

The appearance of manos and metates in the Cuadros phase and various other southern Mesoamerican assemblages implies the appearance of an economy based on an improved variety of maize, with larger and harder kernels, which is better processed by grinding. An important advantage of this improved maize, besides a probable increase in yield, is that it would store better and would allow for the accumulation of surpluses which could be utilized for a variety of purposes.

It is significant that on the Gulf Coast, manos and metates occur in the earliest known phase, Ojochi (M. Coe 1970:22), nearly 400 years prior to their appearance at Pacific Coast sites. When corn grinding tools appeared on the Pacific Coast, they were part of an assemblage which included Gulf Coast style ceramics, suggesting that tropically adapted hard-kernel corn passed from the Gulf Coast to the Pacific Coast. In sum, earlier access to a higher-quality storable maize, intensive slash-and-burn agriculture, the riverine setting, and rich river levee soils may have provided the Gulf Coast communities with an early advantage which eventually allowed them to surpass the Pacific Coast in complexity.

This advantage over the Pacific Coast may have been due in part to the differing natures of the long distance exchange networks for the two areas. These networks have been partially reconstructed using source analysis techniques on obsidian, a ubiquitous material at Early Formative sites. The data indicate that from the Ojochi phase onward, the Gulf Coast was interacting in an obsidian exchange network with areas on the eastern edge of the Central Highlands, close to the Tehuacan Valley (Cobean et al. 1971). By the Chicharras phase the interaction network had expanded to include the two obsidian sources controlled by the Valley of Mexico and Morelos Early Formative communities (Grove 1974a:125; Charlton, Grove, and Hopke 1978; Cobean et al. 1971). This highland-lowland exchange network most likely involved commodities other than obsidian and could have served to introduce improved plant varieties to Gulf Coast communities.

On the other hand, Pacific Coast obsidian exchange data for the Barra and Ocos phases indicate interaction with the Guatemala Highlands (Pires-Ferreira 1975:26). The archaeological record of this latter area apparently lacks maize grinding tools (manos and metates) in Early Formative contexts, suggesting that it had a subsistence economy (simple maize?) not substantially different from that of the Pacific Coast.

A similar argument can be made for improved maize and productive agricultural techniques as highly relevant factors for Oaxaca's cultural development. Manos and metates were present at Gheo-Shih, a site dating to ca. 5000–4000 B.C. (Flannery 1970: 23–24), although whether they were used to process corn can only be surmised. Hard-kernel corn is confirmed in the Tierras Largas phase by the occurrence of manos, metates, and maize (Winter 1972:150–157). There is also evidence that Tierras Largas and San Jose phase farmers were using highly efficient and productive agricultural techniques. Sites of these phases are located in areas with shallow water tables, where "pot irrigation" from in-field wells is still practiced today (Flannery 1968b:81; Kirkby 1973:42), and is inferred for the Early Formative. This irrigation technique provides two crops yearly.

In addition to a productive subsistence base, sites such as San Jose Mogote also benefited from productive exchange interactions. The Early Formative exchange systems in Oaxaca included both the Gulf Coast and Central Highlands (Pires-Ferreira 1975, 1976a, 1976b). San Jose Mogote's power grew at least partially through its virtual monopoly on local raw material exploitation and manufacturing. Its development appears similar to that of Chalcatzingo in the Central Highlands. Chalcatzingo also played a central role in raw material exploitation, originally for local and regional distribution. Later the site's exchange system enlarged to include long distance networks which probably involved not only local raw materials but a variety of nonlocal items as well.

Even with the Chalcatzingo data, the development of complex culture in the Central Highlands is more difficult to document in terms of advantages gained via agricultural productivity and interaction in exchange networks. The presence of manos and metates in the earliest Formative assemblages in the highlands implies the utilization of improved maize varieties. Settlement surveys show that sites were located adjacent to good water supplies and agricultural land, but such a pattern is typical of early Mesoamerican farming villages in general. Agricultural practices can only be inferred, but simple small-scale canal irrigation may have been practiced in some villages. Long distance exchange may have been important to the highland development, but the data available deal with this region as exporter, and items or ideas received in exchange transactions are unknown. The absence of public architecture at most Early and Middle Formative sites suggests that the subsistence technology vis-à-vis the ecology of the highlands may have been less productive than that of other regions discussed, and could not have supported the same size or number of centers as those regions.

During the Middle and Late Formative periods (900–0 B.C.), Price (1977:214) sees an "organizational revolution" as having taken place, which resulted in the development of social stratification and the state. She has hypothesized that an improving agricultural technology in the highlands ultimately allowed that region to surpass the Gulf Coast in productivity and in cultural complexity as well.

Cuicuilco is an important site in this regard, since it is located in what was probably the greatest expanse of good agricultural land in the southern Valley of Mexico. The southern area is the most suitable part of the valley for agriculture in terms of temperatures, humidity, water sources, etc. Cuicuilco also exhibits the improved agricultural technology which is part of Price's hypothesis, in this case irrigation canals which have been found covered by the 100 B.C. lava flow which also covered Cuicuilco (Palerm 1972:102–104). By the Late Formative, Cuicuilco had become the Valley of Mexico's largest site and may also have been its first city-state (e.g., Bennyhoff 1966:21). Cuicuilco may have set the pattern for the urbanization which soon followed at Teotihuacan.

## THE SOUTH AMERICAN CONNECTION

In this chapter the evolution of complex culture has been discussed in terms of essentially independent regional developments. While the available evidence seems to support this viewpoint, it is possible that some of the ideas which developed in Mesoamerica originally came from elsewhere, specifically South America. To date the earliest known ceramics in southern Mesoamerica (Swasey and Barra phases) have no Mesoamerican antecedents, although in time antecedents may be found. However, Michael Coe (1960) and Gareth Lowe (1975; Green and Lowe 1967) have detailed a number of co-occurrences of ceramic attributes on ceramics from Ecuador and from Barra and Ocos phase contexts at coastal Chiapas-Guatemala sites. The presence of red-slipped Pox ceramics on the coast of Guerrero and red-slipped bottles and other Ecuadorian-like ceramic traits in early assemblages in Michoacan, Colima, and Jalisco suggests widespread interaction via seaborne contacts along the Pacific Coast during the Early Formative.

If contacts of this type introduced sophisticated ceramics and a wide variety of decorative attributes to southern and western Mesoamerica during the Early Formative, then less tangible traits were probably introduced as well. Possible introductions into Mesoamerica include such diverse elements as manioc agriculture, cacao, improved corn varieties, pyramid mounds, mound-plaza site arrangements, the rubber ball game, cosmologies and ideologies, etc. If any or all of these traits were introduced, it must still be reiterated that, once in Mesoamerica, they were accepted (or rejected) and evolved on their own. While the antecedents to some Mesoamerican traits may ultimately lie elsewhere, these "borrowed ideas" were not responsible for the evolution of complex culture in Formative period Mesoamerica.

### ACKNOWLEDGMENT

While I am responsible for any shortcomings in this chapter, the comments and editorial assistance of Susan D. Gillespie left the manuscript greatly improved.

# 14. The Rise of Cities

ᔰᔰᔰᔰᔰᔰᔰᔰᔰᔰᔰᔰᔰᔰᔰᔰᔰᔰᔰᔰᔰᔰᔰᔰᔰᔰᔰᔰᔰᔰᔰᔰᔰᔰᔰᔰᔰᔰᔰᔰ

*RICHARD E. BLANTON*

THE GROWTH of cities is a manifestation of the growth of institutions capable of organizing large regions into integrated systems. These institutions can be either powerful, centralized governments or marketing institutions (or various combinations of the two). Cities are the focal points of the operation of such institutions. Thus a consideration of the rise of cities requires a consideration of the forces generating the growth of these institutions, a topic too vast for detailed treatment here. Because of space limitations, I have been forced to be highly selective and have, as a result, omitted much that is of value. I begin by discussing progress made in Mesoamerican archaeology in studies of the early development of cities, then briefly make a comparison of two of the earliest and most important cities, Teotihuacan and Monte Alban, in order to show that city growth cannot be explained in simple cultural ecological terms and that it was by no means a uniform phenomenon in different regions within Mesoamerica. Finally, I evaluate certain key features of a theory of the evolution of complex institutions—that of the cultural ecologists. Evaluation of this

theory is important, since it currently dominates the anthropological literature.

## BACKGROUND

Since the publication of the first series of *Handbook* articles in the 1960s, considerable progress has been made pertinent to the problem of the rise of cities in ancient Mesoamerica. A number of studies could be mentioned in this regard (see Haviland 1970; Kurjack 1974), but two projects in particular have special importance in contributing to an understanding of the growth of cities in two of Mesoamerica's most important nuclear zones—the Valley of Mexico Project (see R. Millon 1973; Wolf 1976a; Sanders, Parsons, and Santley 1979) and the Valley of Oaxaca Settlement Pattern Project (Blanton 1978; Blanton et al. n.d.). In both cases these projects have produced detailed maps of the dominant early cities, Teotihuacan and Monte Alban, respectively, and analyses of their patterns of growth (Blanton 1978; Cowgill 1974; R. Millon 1973).

Most of the information flowing from these projects has been collected by intensive, systematic surface survey, an extremely productive methodology in these high, semiarid valleys where most sites are visible on the surface and can be dated from surface-collected ceramic samples. Data of this sort can probably never be collected from the tropical lowland areas, although to a limited extent work done as part of the Tikal project is comparable (Fry 1969; Haviland 1970).

Recent progress in the study of early Mesoamerican cities has consisted of more than just the collection of new data. In addition, a new analytical perspective, the regional perspective, is being adopted and developed (Blanton 1976a, 1978; Blanton et al. n.d.; Flannery 1976a; Flannery 1972a; Hammond 1972; Marcus 1973, 1976a; M. Smith 1979). While this regional perspective has a number of facets (Hodder and Orton 1976; G. Johnson 1977), its most important contributions to the study of city development have to do with that part of it concerned with hierarchies of central places (Blanton 1976a; G. Johnson 1977; C. A. Smith 1976a; Skinner 1977). This approach focuses the researcher's attention on the disposition in space of those kinds of institutions that serve to bind together regional systems in complex societies—especially, as mentioned previously, administrative and marketing institutions. A region's system of central places (i.e., its cities and towns) are the focal points where most of the transactions pertaining to these institutions take place. These are communities with what are referred to as "central-place functions." Walter Christaller (1966), August Lösch (1954), and others (see the reviews by Peter Haggett [1966], Gregory A. Johnson [1977], and Carol A. Smith [1974]; see also Haggett, Cliff, and Frey 1977) have provided us with theories describing how central places and different kinds of central-place functions should be distributed over the landscape given the presence of certain "ideal" conditions—including such things as movement minimization decisions, flat terrain, and so forth. By comparing the actual distribution of central places in a region with the predictions of the theoretical constructs,

the researcher is able to make inferences concerning the major factors influencing the operation of the marketing and administrative institutions.

A critical component of central-place theories is the concept of hierarchy. A region's system of central places is a hierarchical system, reflecting the fact that administrative and exchange institutions in complex societies are themselves hierarchical. Local market centers, for example, cannot offer the "high-order" (i.e., costly, rarely consumed) goods that can be found in centers that service large regions. Similarly, local administrative places have a narrower and more local focus than does the regional capital, which, again, services a large region as a center of decision-making. "Lower-order" central places have few functions and serve only a local population. "Higher-order" central places are fewer in number, have more such functions, and serve a wider region (including the populations of the lower-order centers). Since the higher-order places have more functions, they will have larger population sizes, and are referred to as the region's cities; lower-order places have fewer functions, smaller populations, and are referred to as towns (or local market centers, etc.) (Blanton 1976a; Wheatley 1963). The settlements of an area with such regional institutions will consist primarily of agricultural settlements lacking central-place functions plus the centers. Of course not every resident of every center will necessarily be an administrator or merchant. Other kinds of communities may be found in a region which are not agricultural settlements, but which are not central places either. Resort towns, pilgrimage centers, and mining towns, for example, are places that service large regions but which are not necessarily central places. The existence of places of this sort could, potentially, lead to misinterpretations of archaeological settlement pattern data, but, in my opinion, the problems presented are minimal. My impression is that in the early civilizations such communities occurred relatively rarely, and it is probably the case that when encountered their functions would be relatively easy to identify.

Christaller (1966) first pointed to the fact that the ideal spatial arrangements of marketing centers will not be the same as the ideal spatial arrangements of administrative places. This means that administrative and commercial hierarchies should not show a great deal of overlap. In reality, however, there can exist various degrees of "embeddedness" of commercial and administrative central-place hierarchies (Blanton 1976a; Skinner 1977). This can happen, for example, when a regional economy is highly administered so that many commercial transactions take place in administrative centers. The settlement patterns that result can be identified in that they are "distortions" of the theoretically predicted patterns. This can give the archaeological researcher a clue concerning the extent to which a region's economy was administered, and how it may have been administered. I will illustrate how this can be done below in my discussion of Teotihuacan and the Valley of Mexico.

Cross-culturally, of course, the forms of central-place hierarchies will vary. Thus the cities of one society will not necessarily contain the same mix or number of central-place functions as those of another society. These differences will be reflected in cross-cultural differences in population sizes, internal organization, layout, and architecture (although of course other kinds of cultural differences will also be reflected in cities, relating to such things as ideology and style). In spite of these outward differences, however, it is nonetheless the case that we should refer to the higher-ranking places in any system of central places as cities. This functional definition of cities avoids the kinds of ethnocentric errors made by researchers who have tried to establish other kinds of definitional criteria for cities, such as the presence of a literate elite (Childe 1942; Sjoberg 1960), or the presence of autonomous municipal government (Weber 1958). It also avoids the kind of ethnocentric error involved in denying the existence of cities in Lowland Maya civiliza-

tion—denials that have been made because these Maya central places don't look like what the archaeologist thinks a city should look like (Blanton 1976a; Fox 1977:23; cf. M. Coe 1961b). The work of Joyce Marcus (1976a) is an important first step to understanding the nature of the hierarchy of centers among the Classic period Lowland Maya.

It is not exactly clear how the term "urbanism" fits into all of this, although it obviously has something to do with cities and their institutions (Wheatley 1971, 1972). Perhaps it would be best to use the term "urban center" interchangeably with the term "city," since it seems to me that the arbitrary definitions of urbanism that have been suggested which specify such things as minimum population size and density (e.g., Sanders and Price 1968:46–47) are potentially as ethnocentric as the definitions of cities supplied by Childe, Sjoberg, and Weber.

## EARLY CITIES IN MESOAMERICA: A COMPARISON OF TEOTIHUACAN AND MONTE ALBAN

An advantage of a regional perspective in analyzing settlement pattern data is that it enables the researcher to go far beyond the overly simple explanations of site size and site location based on a consideration of local environment and agricultural productivity alone, in the manner of the cultural ecologists (cf. Sanders and Santley 1978; J. Parsons 1971; Santley 1980). The regionally oriented researcher is interested primarily in the spatial organization of marketing and administrative institutions. As an example of how this approach will result in conclusions different from those of the cultural ecologists, I will briefly discuss Teotihuacan's role in the Valley of Mexico during its period of hegemony, then compare this with Monte Alban during the period of its regional dominance in the Valley of Oaxaca.

The cultural ecologists have emphasized the importance of the irrigability of the Teotihuacan Valley and the local obsidian sources in explanations of the growth and dominance of Teotihuacan (Sanders, Parsons, and Logan 1976:167). As René Millon (1973, 1976) has pointed out, however, these factors cannot fully explain why Teotihuacan became Mesoamerica's most important political, commercial, and religious capital (a "repository of symbols"). More powerful explanations, he argues, will be necessary. The following discussion of Teotihuacan, and comparison with Monte Alban, will show, I hope, how a regional perspective can be a contribution to the development of these more powerful explanations.

From a regional perspective, the key feature of the Valley of Mexico during the hegemony of Teotihuacan is the region's extreme primacy—that is, the fact that the regional capital was far larger than lower-ranking centers (by an order of magnitude of ten or more) (Blanton 1976c; Sanders, Parsons, and Santley 1979). This kind of size-rank distribution of centers is not at all predicted from central-place theory when all of its assumptions are met. Nor can this distribution be explained in environmental terms. Other localities in the valley were fully capable agriculturally of supporting large centers (as they had prior to Teotihuacan's expansion, and would again after its decline). In part the extreme primacy of the Teotihuacan system was no doubt due to the fact that in topographically bounded regions such as the Valley of Mexico, competing central places at the edge of the region fail to develop fully, since their sustaining areas are truncated by sparsely inhabited mountainous terrain, which means that they service only a limited population (see Blanton 1976a; Skinner 1977; C. A. Smith 1974). While this factor may be important in explaining some of Teotihuacan's size dominance, we can infer that it by no means constitutes a complete explanation. Certainly primacy as extreme as that of the Teotihuacan system is not the only possible pattern of regional integration in the Valley of Mexico. Michael E. Smith (1979), for example, points out that the hierarchy of marketing centers in the valley in the Late Postclassic was close to the predictions of Christaller.

This is consistent with the fact that by the Late Postclassic the rank-size distribution for the region was much less primate than it had been under Teotihuacan's hegemony (Blanton 1976c). This means that by the end of the Prehispanic sequence there was a better developed commercial central-place hierarchy, not so "distorted" by the presence of an excessively large capital center.

Not only was Teotihuacan much larger than other places in the Valley of Mexico, but its population was also much wealthier than the populations of other communities. The foremost manifestation of this is in residential architecture. The elaborate walled compounds in which most Teotihuacanos resided (R. Millon 1973) are found outside the city only within a limited radius (of about 30 km at most), involving those few communities that were obviously directly keyed into the city's economic system (Sanders, Parsons, and Santley 1979). Further away from the capital, sites are generally small, lack any evidence for walled compounds, and have sparse and incomplete ceramic assemblages (Blanton 1972b; J. Parsons 1971; Sanders, Parsons, and Santley 1979).

The parallels between this mode of regional organization and what Carol A. Smith (1974:176) refers to as "solar" marketing systems are striking. Solar systems are a deviation from the kind of ideal marketing systems posited by Christaller and others in that there is poor development of a hierarchy of marketing places. In such a system there are basically only rural villages, on the one hand, and a single urban center, on the other. These systems are described as having poorly developed hierarchies because only one major marketing place exists—unlike the ideal situation in which multiple marketing centers exist, serving the population efficiently and providing marketing choices. Since only one center services the region, some participants in the system are disadvantaged because they reside far away from the center; and all of the rural population is disadvantaged because marketing choices are absent. Given this situation, the urban center dominating the region has a monopoly, so that prices for the products of rural producers (mostly food) remain low, while the cost of city-supplied goods remains relatively high.

One would imagine that in a solar system, competing market centers better situated to service distant populations would develop. This does not happen, however, because the solar systems are highly administered. As Carol Smith relates it, in a solar system,

. . . if they are to survive, the urban merchants *must* have monopoly control of some goods necessary for peasants and *must* price them high enough to call forth sufficient surplus foodstuffs, for both themselves and the administrative elite (who will take their cut in market and other urban taxes). As a result, merchants expend considerable effort attempting to "convert" the peasantry to the use of some urban monopolies—often religious—ceremonial goods . . . They are supported in this by the administrative elite who have the same interests and who force the peasants to use urban markets by suppressing horizontal peasant marketing arrangements, among other means. (1976c: 341)

The peculiarities of the Teotihuacan-dominated Valley of Mexico, I suggest, are the result of a regional economy managed in this way. This could account for the extreme primacy as well as other features. As Carol Smith (1976c:364) points out, one of the consequences of the solar pattern is a highly dichotomous system of social stratification—consisting basically of urban dwellers and rural peasants. This rings true with my impression of the Valley of Mexico during the domination by Teotihuacan. As I mentioned before, rural sites are vastly poorer-looking as a whole (architecturally and artifactually) than Teotihuacan.

If this regional model is appropriate, then within Teotihuacan one would not expect to find evidence of direct state control of marketplaces and production (at least not totally), but instead a kind of mutually symbiotic relationship between the state and urban producers and merchants, the latter producing goods (or services, such as ritual, a point I return to below) for which rural peasants

would produce an agricultural surplus, while the state, in turn, protected the monopoly of the merchants by suppressing the growth of competing centers in the region. Working independently from me, Michael W. Spence has arrived at essentially this same conclusion based on his analyses of obsidian workshops in Teotihuacan. As he sees it: "The role of the state seems to have been aimed at facilitating the successful operation of a set of independent and somewhat entrepreneurial craftsmen, rather than at organizing and running a state industry. . . . The contributions of the state [to the obsidian industry] were . . . guarantees of safe travel, exclusion of potential rivals from access to sources, etc." (Spence 1979b:13).

In order to explain the emergence of a solar system in the Valley of Mexico, we will probably have to go beyond considering local environmental features of the Teotihuacan Valley, and, instead, discover the kinds of conditions favoring the growth of regional systems organized in that particular way.

The growth of cities and towns in the Valley of Oaxaca presents a set of problems distinct from those we encounter in the Valley of Mexico. Although our settlement pattern survey in Oaxaca is only half completed at this writing, we are already sure of the existence of major differences in modes of regional organization between these two nuclear zones. Our data indicate very clearly that it would be misleading to apply the adjective "solar" to marketing and production systems in the Valley of Oaxaca during the period of Monte Alban's hegemony. Although Monte Alban was, during some periods, much larger than lower-order centers, the gap in population size between it and the smaller places was never as great as was the gap in size between Teotihuacan and other central places in the Valley of Mexico. For example, we have traced the histories of two major centers in the Valley of Oaxaca (Zaachila and Santa Inez Yatzeche—both in the valley's southern district) which have occupational sequences going well back into the Formative, and which, after the formation of

Monte Alban, not only continued to be occupied but continued as important central places and increased in population size and architectural complexity (Santa Inez was finally abandoned just before Monte Alban's collapse). Contrast this with the Valley of Mexico, where virtually all of the Formative period central places were abandoned at the time Teotihuacan began its rapid growth (Blanton 1972b; J. Parsons 1971).

The nature of the evolving regional system under Monte Alban's hegemony is treated in detail in Blanton et al. n.d. This sequence is too complex to be related in a meaningful way here (see Chapter 4, this volume, for additional details), but it will be possible to illustrate some of the major differences between the Valley of Oaxaca and the Valley of Mexico in a general sense by listing some of the major contrasts in the respective regional capitals during the latter part of the Formative and during the Classic:

(1) Monte Alban was more marginally located vis-à-vis agricultural or other resources (the implications of this are discussed in Chapter 4) than Teotihuacan was, and, in all periods when both cities were regional capitals, had a substantially smaller population than Teotihuacan. While the latter had already reached a population of 50,000–60,000 during the Terminal Formative Tzacualli phase (Cowgill 1974), and a maximum of probably 200,000 later in its history (R. Millon 1973), Monte Alban had a Terminal Formative (period II) population of only about 15,000 and a maximum population of less than 30,000 during the Late Classic period IIIb. In part this reflects the fact that Monte Alban was the capital center of a region somewhat smaller than Teotihuacan's region, but it is largely a reflection of the fact that Monte Alban was never the region's only large central place. Central-place transactions in the Valley of Oaxaca were more decentralized than those in the Teotihuacan system. In other words, in Oaxaca there was a better-developed hierarchy of cities and towns with administrative as well as commercial functions.

(2) No feature at Monte Alban is comparable in size or architectural complexity to Teotihuacan's major marketplace, the Great Compound (R. Millon 1973). Monte Alban's Main Plaza is an extremely large feature, but my analysis indicates it functioned as a center of government, not market activities (Blanton 1978). Related to this is the nature of Monte Alban's road system. Roads in the city are narrow and winding, obviously not built to handle more than a minimal amount of traffic, and certainly not sufficient for an important marketing center. Teotihuacan is different. The Great Compound sits at the intersection of two substantial avenues that would have been capable of handling a heavy flow of commercial traffic. And, finally, the evidence from the Valley of Mexico indicates that Teotihuacan had been the region's only important center of craft production. Monte Alban had some production activities within its bounds, but we have found evidence for such production activities in a number of other valley localities, as well.

(3) Other than Monte Alban's Main Plaza complex, which is not duplicated in any other site in the Valley of Oaxaca, residential and other architecture in the city is not notably different from that in other valley sites. This is no doubt a reflection of the fact that in the Valley of Oaxaca, the strong rural-urban dichotomy never developed in the way it developed in the Valley of Mexico under Teotihuacan's control.

Thus the Valley of Oaxaca under Monte Alban's hegemony came closer to some of the theoretical predictions of central-place theory, at least when compared with the highly distorted solar pattern of the Valley of Mexico at that time. This is not to say that there was no administrative management of the Oaxacan economic system (see Feinman n.d.), but this management took a form unlike that of the Valley of Mexico.

One last point can be mentioned in this comparative exercise. It is interesting to note that in the ethnographic cases used by Carol Smith in the development of her solar marketing concept, an important component of the products supplied to peasant agricultural producers by urban dwellers consists of ritual items. Evon Z. Vogt (1969:59), for example, noted this in connection with the exchanges of the rural Zinacantecos in the Ladino urban center of San Cristobal: "The Zinacantecos bring in corn, beans, and salt for the Ladinos, and the Ladinos provide the Zinacantecos with liquor, ribbons, candles, sky rockets, beef, pork, and Catholic priests—all for ritual." This phenomenon may help explain why Teotihuacan was, in addition to being an important center commercially and politically, an important center religiously—a "repository of symbols" to use Millon's phrase again. Perhaps it is the case that solar systems in general cannot operate unless the state and the urban merchants are able to monopolize ties to the supernatural and monopolize the production and distribution of ritual items that filter down to rural producers. Such monopolization would help assure that the otherwise economically disadvantaged rural groups will continue producing a surplus and will continue directing it to the city. Monte Alban, in contrast, cannot be described as a repository of symbols. In fact, especially during the first 500 or 600 years of Monte Alban's dominance, themes on carved stone monuments in the capital were almost exclusively militaristic, while themes on such monuments from other centers in the valley were often ritualistic as well (Marcus 1976b).

## THE RISE OF CITIES

Although brief, the discussion to this point has demonstrated the distinctness in patterns of early city development in two of Mesoamerica's pre-eminent core zones. If I were to add here a discussion of early Lowland Maya cities, a third pattern would be apparent. The parallels between this latter area— with its graded hierarchies of central places (Marcus 1976a)—and the Valley of Oaxaca are more obvious than those with the Valley of Mexico with its dichotomous primate system. One might suggest that the presence of

these distinct patterns in the development of the first cities reflects differing causes at work area to area in cultural evolution. To date no one has explored this possibility. In fact, at this time there is only one theory for the growth of complex societies in Mesoamerica that is prominent in the literature, that of the cultural ecologists (Sanders and Price 1968; Logan and Sanders 1976; Sanders, Parsons, and Logan 1976; Sanders and Webster 1978; Sanders, Parsons, and Santley 1979). This is a theory which ignores or denies the variability that is so obvious in the various evolutionary sequences (cf. Sanders and Santley 1978; Santley 1980).

It is difficult to accept the validity of a theory of cultural evolution which cannot account for interregional variation, but this is only one of the oversimplifications inherent in the cultural ecologist's ideas. Although the cultural ecologists have made the claim that their theorizing has an eclectic base and that it pays attention to a number of variables simultaneously (Logan and Sanders 1976:31), they themselves then state that "the primary cause of increasingly complex social and political patterns" is population pressure (ibid.:32). Virtually every feature of evolving complex societies, they argue, is the result of this one causal factor: agricultural intensification, warfare, social differentiation, the evolution of control institutions, and specialized production. It would be nice, I suppose, if such complex topics in cultural evolution could be explained in such simple, linear terms (a comrade-in-arms, Robert Carneiro [1970] is able to relate his entire theory of the evolution of the state in five pages!), but, as Eric R. Wolf (1976b:7) has noted, "when interest turns to an analysis of the critical turning points in the spiral which connects population–technology–societal differentiation–controls, more complex models will be required."

Even a passing familiarity with the literature in demography is enough to convince one that population growth is as much a reflection of changes in societal structure as a cause of those changes (see Blanton 1976d; Cowgill 1975a; White 1973). Not only are the cultural ecologists' claims unsupportable from demographic theory, but they also cannot claim any support from researchers who have gone out to the field and collected data making possible an evaluation of the role of population pressure in cultural evolution (Chapter 4, this volume; Earle 1978; Kowalewski n.d., 1980; Wright and Johnson 1975). Sanders' own calculations of carrying capacity and population density for the Valley of Mexico do not support his contentions (Sanders 1976b: Table 11, pp. 146, 148). In this table, Sanders lists the results of calculations of carrying capacity of the regions that had been surveyed at that time in the Valley of Mexico during the critical First Intermediate (phases 2 and 3) (the Ticoman and Tezoyuca-Patlachique ceramic phases), when, so far as we can tell, the region's first central places developed (cf. Blanton 1972b; J. Parsons 1971, 1976).

In this table, Sanders expresses the carrying capacity as a range of population values. Since there is no a priori reason to favor either the high or the low values of this range, it seems most reasonable to calculate a mean value. Doing this, the mean value for carrying capacity of the combined Ixtapalapa, Chalco, Xochimilco (when only 50 percent of this zone is assumed to be irrigated), and Teotihuacan Valley survey areas is 99,597 people. The mean value of the total population estimates for the First Intermediate phase 2 for these same regions is only 46,200. The actual value is probably lower than this, since in his calculations Sanders elevated the population totals (in my opinion, needlessly) by his so-called "preservation factor" of 20 percent. Even so, this is a population estimate which amounts to only 46 percent of the region's potential capacity during a period of rapid sociocultural change manifested in the growth of a number of central places. It is likely that this same period of rapid change was also a period of intense rivalry between autonomous, competing sociopolitical units (Blanton 1972b; J. Parsons 1971), in which one could reasonably expect that the local elite in each case might have urged their re-

spective populations to increase in number in order to increase the number of both producers and warriors. Even so, the population growth from the First Intermediate phase 2 to the First Intermediate phase 3 was very slow. It could be accounted for with an instantaneous growth rate (r) of only .002. The mean total for phase 3 is 70,480. This is a value which, even after some 300 years of evolution in complexity in central-place systems, amounts to only 71 percent of the region's estimated carrying capacity.

We may conclude that population pressure was not an important prime mover in cultural evolution in the Valley of Mexico, either during those periods when the first central places evolved or later, when Teotihuacan's dominance began to be felt in the region. In fact, this latter period of development was accompanied by population declines everywhere in the valley except in and directly adjacent to the Teotihuacan Valley itself. This conclusion is what one would expect given the large body of ethnographic evidence for systematic underuse of agricultural resources (see Sahlins 1972: Chapter 2), even in simple hierarchical systems analogous to those that developed in Mesoamerica toward the end of the Formative period (cf. Fallers 1964: 126).

What, then, led to the development of these complex societies? To date no adequate explanations exist, in my opinion, but it will be possible to construct theories without making oversimplified assumptions about the inevitability of population growth or the causal primacy of population pressure. Warfare, for example, may have had an important role to play in cultural evolution under certain circumstances (R. McC. Adams 1966: 140), but it is not always necessary to see warfare as a product of land shortages as the cultural ecologists do. Warfare can occur in a variety of circumstances even in the absence of land shortages—for example, in response to unpredictable agricultural deficits (Ford 1972), or as a means of counteracting labor shortages through abduction (Goody 1978; Ruyle 1973). Population decline and labor shortages, in other words, may be as important a reason for warfare as population growth and land shortages.

## CONCLUSION

It is suggested that in dealing with evolving complex societies the adoption of a regional perspective will permit analyses that are more sophisticated and more productive than those that have been offered by the cultural ecologists. To illustrate this point, I have briefly discussed the Teotihuacan regional system, concluding that its form is not explicable in terms of agricultural-environmental variables. The particular form of this system, I have suggested, was the result of a kind of administrative management of the region in which the development of competing marketing/production centers was suppressed, leading to a situation in which the capital was the region's only commercial focus—a solar system. This is contrasted with the Monte Alban system, one that evolved in a highly distinct manner, with a better-developed central-place hierarchy.

Finally, I suggest that in addition to better methods and theory for analyzing settlement pattern data, a major need now is new and better theories of cultural evolution, given that the theoretical position most frequently expressed in our literature today, the cultural ecological, is oversimplified and misleading. It is my hope that when the next update of the *Handbook of Middle American Indians* is done, the author of the article with this subject matter will be discussing and evaluating theories of cultural evolution which are more powerful, logical, and satisfactory from the point of view of data collected from the field than those that now dominate our literature.

## ACKNOWLEDGMENTS

I thank Eva Fisch, Steve Kowalewski, Gary Feinman, and Jill Appel for suggestions and stimulation, although all errors and misinterpretations are my responsibility. The Valley of Oaxaca Settlement Pattern Project has been supported primarily through NSF grants GS-28547, GS-38030, and BNS76-19640.

# Bibliography and Index

# VOLUME BIBLIOGRAPHY

ABASCAL, RAFAEL, AND ANGEL GARCÍA COOK
1975   Sistemas de cultivo, riego y control de agua en el área de Tlaxcala. In *XIII Mesa Redonda* 1:199–212. Mexico City: Sociedad Mexicana de Antropología.

ACOSTA, JORGE R.
1940   Exploraciones en Tula, Hidalgo, 1940. *Revista Mexicana de Estudios Antropológicos* 4:172–194.

1941   Los ultimos descubrimientos arqueológicos en Tula, Hidalgo, 1941. *Revista Mexicana de Estudios Antropológicos* 5:239–248.

1945   Las cuarta y quinta temporadas de exploraciones arqueológicas en Tula, Hidalgo, 1943–1944. *Revista Mexicana de Estudios Antropológicos* 7:23–64.

1956a   El enigma de los Chac Mooles de Tula. In *Estudios Antropológicos Publicados en Homenaje al Doctor Manuel Gamio*, pp. 159–170. Mexico City: Universidad Nacional Autónoma de México and Sociedad Mexicana de Antropología.

1956b   Resumen de los informes de las exploraciones arqueológicas en Tula, Hidalgo, durante las VI, VII, y VIII temporadas, 1946–1950. *Anales del Instituto Nacional de Antropología e Historia* 8:37–115. Mexico City.

1956–1957   Interpretación de algunos de los datos obtenidos en Tula relativos a la época tolteca. *Revista Mexicana de Estudios Antropológicos* 14:75–110.

1957   Resumen de los informes de las exploraciones arqueológicas en Tula, Hidalgo, durante las IX y X temporadas, 1953–54. *Anales del Instituto Nacional de Antropología e Historia* 9:119–169. Mexico City.

1959   Exploraciones arqueológicas en Monte Albán, XVIII temporada, 1958. *Revista Mexicana de Estudios Antropológicos* 15:7–50.

1960   Las exploraciones en Tula, Hidalgo, durante la XI temporada, 1955. *Anales del Instituto Nacional de Antropología e Historia* 11:39–72. Mexico City.

1961a   La doceava temporada de exploraciones en Tula, Hidalgo. *Anales del Instituto Nacional de Antropología e Historia* 13:29–58. Mexico City.

1961b   La indumentaria de las cariátides de Tula. In *Homenaje a Pablo Martínez del Río*, pp. 221–228. Mexico City: Instituto Nacional de Antropología e Historia.

1964a   La decimotercera temporada de exploraciones en Tula, Hgo. *Anales del Instituto Nacional de Antropología e Historia* 16:45–76. Mexico City.

1964b   *El Palacio del Quetzalpapalotl.* Memorias del Instituto Nacional de Antropología e Historia 10. Mexico City.

1965 Preclassic and Classic Architecture of Oaxaca. In *Handbook of Middle American Indians*, vol. 3, edited by Robert Wauchope and Gordon R. Willey, pp. 814–836. Austin: University of Texas Press.

1966 Una clasificación tentativa de los monumentos arqueológicos de Teotihuacán. In *Teotihuacán: Onceava Mesa Redonda* 1: 45–55. Mexico City: Sociedad Mexicana de Antropología.

ADAMS, RICHARD E. W.

1971 *The Ceramics of Altar de Sacrificios*. Papers of the Peabody Museum, Harvard University 63(1).

1977 (ed.) *The Origins of Maya Civilization*. Albuquerque: University of New Mexico Press.

1978 Routes of Communication in Mesoamerica: The Northern Guatemalan Highlands and the Peten. In *Mesoamerican Communication Routes and Cultural Contacts*, edited by Thomas A. Lee, Jr., and Carlos Navarrete. Papers of the New World Archaeological Foundation No. 40:27–35. Provo, Utah.

ADAMS, RICHARD E. W., AND AUBREY S. TRIK

1961 *Tikal Report No. 7: Temple I (Str. 5D-1): Post-constructional Activities*. Museum Monographs, The University Museum. Philadelphia: University of Pennsylvania.

ADAMS, ROBERT McC.

1965 *Land behind Baghdad: A History of Settlement on the Diyala Plains*. Chicago: University of Chicago Press.

1966 *The Evolution of Urban Society: Early Mesopotamia and Prehispanic Mexico*. Chicago: Aldine.

1972 Patterns of Urbanization in Southern Mesopotamia. In *Man, Settlement and Urbanism*, edited by Peter J. Ucko, Ruth Tringham, and G. W. Dimbleby, pp. 735–749. London: Duckworth.

1974 Anthropological Perspectives on Ancient Trade. *Current Anthropology* 15:239–258.

1975 The Emerging Place of Trade in Civilizational Studies. In *Ancient Civilization and Trade*, edited by Jeremy A. Sabloff and C. C. Lamberg-Karlovsky, pp. 451–465. Albuquerque: University of New Mexico Press.

ADAMS, ROBERT McC., AND HANS J. NISSEN

1972 *The Uruk Countryside: The Natural Setting of Urban Societies*. Chicago: University of Chicago Press.

AGRINIER, PIERRE

1964 *The Archaeological Burials at Chiapa de Corzo and Their Furniture*. Papers of the New World Archaeological Foundation No. 16. Provo, Utah.

AGUILERA, CARMEN

1974 La Estela (Elemento 7) de Tlalancaleca. *Comunicaciones* 10:1–4. Puebla: Fundación Alemana para la Investigación Científica.

ALTSCHUL, JEFFREY H.

1978 TE28: Test Excavations in the Cave underneath the Pyramid of the Sun at Teotihuacán. MS, University of Rochester.

ANDREWS, ANTHONY P.

1978 Puertos costeros del Postclásico Temprano en el Norte de Yucatán. *Estudios de Cultura Maya* 11:75–93.

1980a Salt-making, Merchants and Markets: The Role of a Critical Resource in the Development of Maya Civilization. Ph.D. dissertation, Department of Anthropology, University of Arizona. Ann Arbor: University Microfilms.

1980b The Salt Trade of the Ancient Maya. *Archaeology* 33:24–33.

ANDREWS, E. WYLLYS, IV

1942 Yucatan: Architecture. *Carnegie Institution of Washington, Year Book*, 41:257–263.

1959 Dzibilchaltun: Lost City of the Maya. *National Geographic Magazine* 115:90–109.

1960 Excavations at Dzibilchaltun, Northwestern Yucatan, Mexico. *Proceedings of the American Philosophical Society* 104:254–265. Philadelphia.

1961 *Preliminary Report on the 1959–60 Field Season, National Geographic Society–Tulane University Dzibilchaltun Program*. Middle American Research Institute, Tulane University, Miscellaneous Series 11. New Orleans.

1962 Excavaciones en Dzibilchaltun, Yucatán, 1956–1962. *Estudios de Cultura Maya* 2:149–183.

1965a Archaeology and Prehistory in the Northern Maya Lowlands: An Introduction. In *Handbook of Middle American Indians*, vol. 2, edited by Robert Wauchope and Gordon R. Willey, pp. 288–330. Austin: University of Texas Press.

1965b  Progress Report on the 1960–1964 Field Seasons, National Geographic Society–Tulane University Dzibilchaltun Program. In *Archaeological Investigations on the Yucatan Peninsula*. Middle American Research Institute, Tulane University, Pub. 31:23–67. New Orleans.

1968  Dzibilchaltun: A Northern Maya Metropolis. *Archaeology* 21:36–47.

1969  *The Archaeological Use and Distribution of Mollusca in the Maya Lowlands*. Middle American Research Institute, Tulane University, Pub. 34. New Orleans.

1970  *Balankanche: Throne of the Tiger Priest*. Middle American Research Institute, Tulane University, Pub. 32. New Orleans.

1972  National Geographic Society–Tulane University Program of Archeological Research at Dzibilchaltun, Yucatán, Mexico. In *National Geographic Society Research Reports: 1955–1960 Projects*, pp. 7–18.

ANDREWS, E. WYLLYS, IV, AND E. WYLLYS ANDREWS V

1980  *Excavations at Dzibilchaltun, Yucatan, Mexico*. Middle American Research Institute, Tulane University, Pub. 48. New Orleans.

ANDREWS, E. WYLLYS, IV, AND IRWIN ROVNER

1973  Archaeological Evidence on Social Stratification and Commerce in the Northern Maya Lowlands: Two Masons' Tool Kits from Muna and Dzibilchaltun, Yucatan. In *Archaeological Investigations on the Yucatan Peninsula*. Middle American Research Institute, Tulane University, Pub. 31:81–102. New Orleans.

ANDREWS, E. WYLLYS, V

1974  Some Architectural Similarities between Dzibilchaltun and Palenque. In *Primera Mesa Redonda de Palenque, Part I: A Conference on the Art, Iconography, and Dynastic History of Palenque*, edited by Merle Greene Robertson, pp. 137–147. Pebble Beach, Calif.: Robert Louis Stevenson School.

1978  The Northern Maya Lowlands Sequence. Endnote to Eastern Mesoamerica, by Gareth W. Lowe. In *Chronologies in New World Archaeology*, edited by R. E. Taylor and Clement W. Meighan, pp. 377–381. New York: Academic Press.

1979a  Early Central Mexican Architectural Traits at Dzibilchaltun, Yucatan. In *Actes du XLII^e Congrès International des Americanistes* (Paris, 1976) 8:237–249.

1979b  Some Comments on Puuc Architecture of the Northern Yucatan Peninsula. In *The Puuc: New Perspectives*, edited by Lawrence Mills, pp. 1–17. Pella, Iowa: Central College.

ANGULO V., JORGE

1972  Reconstrucción etnográfica a través de la pintura. In *Teotihuacán: XI Mesa Redonda* 2:43–68. Mexico City: Sociedad Mexicana de Antropología.

APENES, OLA

1936  Possible Derivation of the 260-Day Period of the Maya Calendar. *Ethnos* 1:5–8.

APPEL, JILL

n.d.a  Obsidian Production and Distribution in Periods IIIA through V. *In* Monte Albán's Hinterland, Part 1: The Prehispanic Settlement Patterns of the Central and Southern Parts of the Valley of Oaxaca, Mexico, edited by Richard E. Blanton, Stephen A. Kowalewski, Gary Feinman, and Jill Appel. In preparation.

n.d.b  A Summary of the Ethnohistoric Information Relevant to the Interpretation of the Late Postclassic Settlement Pattern Data, the Central and Valle Grande Survey Zones. *In* Monte Alban's Hinterland, Part 1: The Prehispanic Settlement Patterns of the Central and Southern Parts of the Valley of Oaxaca, Mexico, edited by Richard E. Blanton, Stephen A. Kowalewski, Gary Feinman, and Jill Appel. In preparation.

ARMENTA CAMACHO, JUAN

1978  *Vestigios de labor humana en huesos de animales extintos de Valsequillo, Puebla, Mexico*. Puebla: Consejo Editorial de Gobierno del Estado.

ARMILLAS, PEDRO

1944  Exploraciones recientes en Teotihuacán, México. *Cuadernos Americanos* 16(4): 121–136.

1948  A Sequence of Cultural Development in Meso-America. In *A Reappraisal of Peruvian Archaeology*, edited by Wendell C. Bennett, pp. 105–112. Memoirs of the Society for American Archaeology 4. Menasha, Wisc.

1950  Teotihuacán, Tula, y los toltecas: Las culturas post-arcáicas y pre-aztecas del centro de México: Excavaciones y estudios, 1922–1950. *RUNA* 3:37–70. Buenos Aires.

1964   *Northern Mexican Prehistoric Man in the New World* Chicago: University of Chicago Press.

1971   Gardens in Swamps. *Science* 174:653–661.

*Artes de México*

1965   Anahuacalli: Museo Diego Rivera. *Artes de México* 1964–1965.

AVELEYRA ARROYO DE ANDA, LUIS

1963   *La estela teotihuacana de La Ventilla*. Cuadernos, Museo Nacional de Antropología, 1. Mexico City: Instituto Nacional de Antropología.

1964   The Primitive Hunters. In *Handbook of Middle American Indians*, vol. 1, edited by Robert Wauchope, and Robert C. West, pp. 384–412. Austin: University of Texas Press.

AVENI, ANTHONY, AND SHARON L. GIBBS

1976   On the Orientation of Precolumbian Buildings in Central Mexico. *American Antiquity* 41:510–517.

BAILEY, J. W.

1972   A Preliminary Investigation of the Formal and Interpretive Histories of Monumental Relief Sculpture from Tikal, Guatemala: Pre-, Early and Middle Classic Periods. Ph.D. dissertation, Department of Anthropology, Yale University. Ann Arbor: University Microfilms.

BAKER, GEORGE T., III, HUGH HARLESTON, JR., ALFONSO RANGEL, MATTHEW WALLRATH, MANUEL GAITÁN, AND ALFONSO MORALES

1974   *The Subterranean System of the Sun Pyramid at Teotihuacán: A Physical Description and Hypothetical Reconstruction*. Mexico City: Grupo UAC-KAN, Apartado 6-857.

BALL, JOSEPH W.

1974   A Teotihuacán-Style Cache from the Maya Lowlands. *Archaeology* 27(1):2–9.

1977a   *The Archaeological Ceramics of Becan, Campeche, Mexico*. Middle American Research Institute, Tulane University, Pub. 43. New Orleans.

1977b   An Hypothetical Outline of Coastal Maya Prehistory: 300 B.C.–A.D. 1200. In *Social Process in Maya Prehistory: Studies in Honour of Sir Eric Thompson*, edited by Norman Hammond, pp. 167–196. London: Academic Press.

1977c   The Rise of the Northern Maya Chiefdoms: A Socioprocessual Analysis. In *The Origins of Maya Civilization*, edited by Richard E. W. Adams, pp. 101–132. Albuquerque: University of New Mexico Press.

1978a   Archaeological Pottery of the Yucatan-Campeche Coast. In *Studies in the Archaeology of Coastal Yucatan and Campeche, Mexico*, pp. 69–146. Middle American Research Institute, Tulane University, Pub. 46. New Orleans.

1978b   The Rise of the Northern Maya Chiefdoms: A Socioprocessual Analysis, Part II. *Estudios de Cultura Maya* 10:209–222.

1979   Ceramics, Culture History, and the Puuc Tradition: Some Alternative Possibilities. In *The Puuc: New Perspectives*, edited by Lawrence Mills, pp. 18–35. Pella, Iowa: Central College.

BALL, JOSEPH W., AND E. WYLLYS ANDREWS V

1975   The Polychrome Pottery of Dzibilchaltun, Yucatan, Mexico: Typology and Archaeological Context. In *Archaeological Investigations on the Yucatan Peninsula*. Middle American Research Institute, Tulane University, Pub. 31:227–247. New Orleans.

BARBOUR, WARREN T. D.

1976   The Figurines and Figurine Chronology of Ancient Teotihuacán, Mexico. Ph.D. dissertation, Department of Anthropology, University of Rochester. Ann Arbor: University Microfilms (BWH76-23976).

BARRERA VÁSQUEZ, ALFREDO

1959   *El misterio de Dzibilchaltun: El ángulo histórico-filológico del problema*. Merida: Universidad de Yucatán, Instituto Nacional de Antropología e Historia, Centro de Estudios Mayas.

BATRES, LEOPOLDO

1906   *Teotihuacan*. Mexico City: Fidencio S. Soria.

BEADLE, GEORGE W.

1977   The Origin of *Zea mays*. In *Origins of Agriculture*, edited by Charles A. Reed, pp. 615–635. The Hague: Mouton.

BECKER, MARSHALL JOSEPH

1971   The Identification of a Second Plaza Plan at Tikal, Guatemala, and Its Implications for Ancient Maya Social Complexity. Ph.D. dissertation, Department of Anthropology, University of Pennsylvania. Ann Arbor: University Microfilms (BWH71-25982).

1973a   The Evidence for Complex Exchange Systems among the Ancient Maya. *American Antiquity* 38:222–223.

1973b   Archaeological Evidence for Occupational

Specialization among the Classic Period Maya at Tikal, Guatemala. *American Antiquity* 38:396–406.

BENDER, BARBARA
1978 Gatherer-hunter to Farmer: A Social Perspective. *World Archaeology* 10:204–222.

BENFER, ROBERT A.
1974 The Human Skeletal Remains from Tula. In *Studies of Ancient Tollan: A Report of the University of Missouri Tula Archaeological Project*, edited by Richard A. Diehl. University of Missouri Monographs in Anthropology No. 1:105–121. Columbia.

BENNYHOFF, JAMES A.
1966 Chronology and Periodization: Continuity and Change in the Teotihuacan Ceramic Tradition. In *Teotihuacan: Onceava Mesa Redonda* 1:19–29. Mexico City: Sociedad Mexicana de Antropología.

BENSON, ELIZABETH
1968 (ed.) *Dumbarton Oaks Conference on the Olmec*. Washington, D.C.: Dumbarton Oaks.

BERDAN, FRANCES FREI
1978 Ports of Trade in Mesoamerica: A Reappraisal. In *Mesoamerican Communication Routes and Cultural Contacts*, edited by Thomas A. Lee, Jr., and Carlos Navarrete. Papers of the New World Archaeological Foundation No. 40:187–198. Provo, Utah.

BERGER, RAINER, JOHN A. GRAHAM, AND ROBERT F. HEIZER
1967 A Reconsideration of the Age of the La Venta Site. *Contributions of the University of California Archaeological Research Facility* 3:1–24. Berkeley.

BERLIN, HEINRICH
1958 El glifo "emblema" en las inscripciones mayas. *Journal de la Société des Américanistes* 47:111–120. Paris.

BERNAL, IGNACIO
1949 La cerámica grabada de Monte Albán. *Anales del Instituto Nacional de Antropología e Historia* 3:59–77. Mexico City.
1959 *Tenochtitlán en una isla*. Serie Historia, Instituto Nacional de Antropología e Historia, 2. Mexico City.
1963 (ed.) *Teotihuacán: Descubrimientos, reconstrucciones*. Mexico City: Instituto Nacional de Antropología e Historia.
1965 Archaeological Synthesis of Oaxaca. In *Handbook of Middle American Indians*, vol. 3, edited by Robert Wauchope and Gordon R. Willey, pp. 788–813. Austin: University of Texas Press.
1966a The Mixtecs in the Archaeology of the Valley of Oaxaca. In *Ancient Oaxaca*, edited by John Paddock, pp. 345–366. Stanford: Stanford University Press.
1966b Teotihuacán ¿Capital de imperio? *Revista Mexicana de Estudios Antropológicos* 20:95–110.
1967 La presencia olmeca en Oaxaca. In *Culturas de Oaxaca I*. Mexico City: Instituto Nacional de Antropología e Historia.
1968a The Ball Players of Dainzú. *Archaeology* 21:246–251.
1968b The Olmec Presence in Oaxaca. *Mexico Quarterly Review* 3(1):5–22.
1969 *The Olmec World*. Translated by Doris Heyden and Fernando Horcasitas. Berkeley: University of California Press.

BERNAL, IGNACIO, AND LORENZO GAMIO
1974 *Yagul: El palacio de los seis patios*. Mexico City: Instituto de Investigaciones Antropológicas, Universidad Nacional Autónoma de México.

BINFORD, LEWIS R.
1968 Post-Pleistocene Adaptations. In *New Perspectives in Archaeology*, edited by Sally R. Binford and Lewis R. Binford, pp. 313–341. Chicago: Aldine.

BITTMAN, BENTE, AND THELMA D. SULLIVAN
1978 The Pochteca. In *Mesoamerican Communication Routes and Cultural Contacts*, edited by Thomas A. Lee, Jr., and Carlos Navarrete. Papers of the New World Archaeological Foundation No. 40:211–218. Provo, Utah.

BLANTON, RICHARD E.
1972a Prehispanic Adaptation in the Ixtapalapa Region, Mexico. *Science* 175:1317–1326.
1972b *Prehispanic Settlement Patterns of the Ixtapalapa Peninsula Region, Mexico*. Occasional Papers in Anthropology, Pennsylvania State University, No. 6.
1976a Anthropological Studies of Cities. *Annual Review of Anthropology* 5:249–264. Palo Alto.
1976b Appendix: Comment on Sanders, Parsons, and Logan. In *The Valley of Mexico: Studies in Pre-Hispanic Ecology and Society*, edited by Eric R. Wolf, pp. 179–180. Albuquerque: University of New Mexico Press.
1976c The Role of Symbiosis in Adaptation and

Sociocultural Change in the Valley of Mexico. In *The Valley of Mexico: Studies in Pre-Hispanic Ecology and Society*, edited by Eric R. Wolf, pp. 181–201. Albuquerque: University of New Mexico Press.

1976d The Cybernetic Analysis of Human Population Growth. In *Population Studies in Archaeology and Biological Anthropology: A Symposium*, edited by Alan C. Swedlund. Memoirs of the Society for American Archaeology 30:116–126. Washington, D.C.

1976e The Origins of Monte Alban. In *Cultural Change and Continuity*, edited by Charles Cleland, pp. 223–232. New York: Academic Press.

1978 *Monte Albán: Settlement Patterns at the Ancient Zapotec Capital*. New York: Academic Press.

1980 Cultural Ecology Reconsidered. *American Antiquity* 45:145–151.

BLANTON, RICHARD E., JILL APPEL, LAURA FINSTEN, STEVE KOWALEWSKI, GARY FEINMAN, AND EVA FISCH

1979 Regional Evolution in the Valley of Oaxaca, Mexico. *Journal of Field Archaeology* 6:369–390.

BLANTON, RICHARD E., STEPHEN A. KOWALEWSKI, GARY FEINMAN, AND JILL APPEL

n.d. Monte Albán's Hinterland, Part 1: The Prehispanic Settlement Patterns of the Central and Southern Parts of the Valley of Oaxaca, Mexico. In preparation.

BLUCHER, DARLENA K.

1971 Late Preclassic Cultures in the Valley of Mexico: Pre-Urban Teotihuacan. Ph.D. dissertation, Department of Anthropology, Brandeis University. Ann Arbor: University Microfilms (BWH71-30116).

1972 The Critical Patlachique Phase in the Growth of Teotihuacán, Mexico. Paper presented at the 71st annual meeting of the American Anthropological Association, Toronto.

BOCK, KENNETH

1956 The Acceptance of Histories. *University of California Publications in Sociology and Social Institutions* 3(1):1–132. Berkeley: University of California Press.

1963 Evolution, Function and Change. *American Sociological Review* 28:229–237.

1978 Theories of Progress, Development, Evolution. In *A History of Sociological Analysis*, edited by Tom Bottomore and Robert Nisbet, pp. 39–79. New York: Basic Books.

BOSERUP, ESTHER

1965 *The Conditions of Agricultural Growth: The Economics of Agrarian Change under Population Pressure*. Chicago: Aldine.

BOVE, FREDERICK J.

1978 Laguna de los Cerros: An Olmec Central Place. *Journal of New World Archaeology* 2(3).

BRAINERD, GEORGE W.

1942 Yucatan: Pottery. *Carnegie Institution of Washington, Year Book*, 41:253–257.

1958 *The Archaeological Ceramics of Yucatan*. University of California, Anthropological Records, No. 19. Berkeley.

BRANIFF, C. BEATRIZ

1976 Notas para la arqueología de Sonora. *Cuadernos de los Centros* 25. Mexico City: Dirección de Centros Regionales, Instituto Nacional de Antropología e Historia.

BRAY, WARWICK

1976 From Predation to Production: The Nature of Agricultural Evolution in Mexico and Peru. In *Problems in Economic and Social Archaeology*, edited by G. de G. Sieveking, I. H. Longworth, and K. E. Wilson, pp. 74–95. London: Duckworth.

1977 From Foraging to Farming in Early Mexico. In *Hunters, Gatherers and Forest Farmers beyond Europe*, edited by J. V. S. Megaw, pp. 225–250. Leicester: Leicester University Press.

1978 Review of *The Valley of Mexico: Studies in Pre-Hispanic Ecology and Society*, edited by Eric R. Wolf. *American Antiquity* 43:127–128.

BREINER, SHELDON, AND MICHAEL D. COE

1972 Magnetic Exploration of the Olmec Civilization. *American Scientist* 60:566–575.

BROCKINGTON, DONALD L.

1973 *Archaeological Investigations at Miahuatlan, Oaxaca*. Vanderbilt University Publications in Anthropology 7. Nashville.

BROCKINGTON, DONALD L., MARÍA JORRÍN, AND J. ROBERT LONG

1974 *The Oaxaca Coast Project Reports: Part I*. Vanderbilt University Publications in Anthropology 8. Nashville.

BROCKINGTON, DONALD L., AND J. ROBERT LONG

1974 *The Oaxaca Coast Project Reports: Part II*. Vanderbilt University Publications in Anthropology 9. Nashville.

BRONSON, BENNET

1977   The Earliest Farming: Demography as Cause and Consequence. In *Origins of Agriculture*, edited by Charles A. Reed, pp. 23–48. The Hague: Mouton.

1978   Angkor, Anuradhapura, Prambanan, Tikal: Maya Subsistence in an Asian Perspective. In *Pre-Hispanic Maya Agriculture*, edited by Peter D. Harrison and B. L. Turner II, pp. 255–300. Albuquerque: University of New Mexico Press.

BROWN, KENNETH L.

1975   The Valley of Guatemala: A Highland Port of Trade. Paper presented at the 40th annual meeting of the Society for American Archaeology, Dallas.

1980   A Brief Report on Paleoindian-Archaic Occupation in the Quiche Basin, Guatemala. *American Antiquity* 45:313–324.

BRUMFIEL, ELIZABETH M.

1977   Archaeological Research 2: Tehuacan. *Latin American Research Review* 12(1): 203–212.

BRUNTON, RON

1975   Why Do the Trobriands Have Chiefs? *Man* 10:544–558.

BRUSH, CHARLES F.

1965   Pox Pottery: Earliest Identified Mexican Ceramic. *Science* 149:194–195.

1969   A Contribution to the Archeology of Coastal Guerrero, Mexico. Ph.D. dissertation, Department of Anthropology, Columbia University. Ann Arbor: University Microfilms (BWH69-17575).

BRYAN, ALAN L.

1973   Paleoenvironments and Cultural Diversity in Late Pleistocene South America. *Quaternary Research* 3:237–256.

BURLAND, COTTIE A.

1948   *Art and Life in Ancient Mexico*. Oxford: Cassirer.

BYERS, DOUGLAS S.

1967   (ed.) *The Prehistory of the Tehuacan Valley*, vol. 1, *Environment and Subsistence*. Austin: University of Texas Press.

CALNEK, EDWARD

1970   The Population of Tenochtitlán in 1519. Paper presented at the 69th annual meeting of the American Anthropological Association, San Diego.

1972   Settlement Pattern and Chinampa Agriculture at Tenochtitlan. *American Antiquity* 37:104–115.

1974a  Conjunto urbano y modelo residencial en Tenochtitlan. In *Ensayos sobre el desarrollo urbano de México*, pp. 11–65. Mexico City: Secretaría de Educación Pública.

1974b  The Sahagún Texts as a Source of Sociological Information. In *Sixteenth-Century Mexico: The Work of Sahagún*, edited by Munro S. Edmonson, pp. 189–204. Albuquerque: University of New Mexico Press.

1976   The Internal Structure of Tenochtitlan. In *The Valley of Mexico: Studies in Pre-Hispanic Ecology and Society*, edited by Eric R. Wolf, pp. 287–302. Albuquerque: University of New Mexico Press.

1979   Kinship, Settlement Pattern and Domestic Groups in Tenochtitlan. MS, University of Rochester.

CANCIAN, FRANK

1976   Social Stratification. *Annual Review of Anthropology* 5:227–248. Palo Alto.

CARLSON, JOHN B.

1975   Lodestone Compass: Chinese or Olmec Primacy? *Science* 189:753–760.

1978   Maya City Planning and Archaeoastronomy. *Archaeoastronomy Bulletin* 1(3): 4–5. Center for Archaeoastronomy, University of Maryland.

CARNEIRO, ROBERT

1970   A Theory of the Origin of the State. *Science* 169:733–738.

CARR, ROBERT F., AND JAMES E. HAZARD

1961   *Tikal Report No. 11: Map of the Ruins of Tikal, El Peten, Guatemala*. Museum Monographs, The University Museum. Philadelphia: University of Pennsylvania.

CARRASCO, PEDRO

1971   Social Organization of Ancient Mexico. In *Handbook of Middle American Indians*, vol. 10, edited by Robert Wauchope, Gordon F. Ekholm, and Ignacio Bernal, pp. 349–375. Austin: University of Texas Press.

1978   La economía del México prehispánico. In *Economía política e ideología en el México prehispánico*, pp. 15–76. Mexico City: Centro de Investigaciones Superiores del Instituto Nacional de Antropología e Historia.

CARRASCO, PEDRO, AND JOHANNA BROADA

1976   (eds.) *Estratificación social en la Mesoamérica prehispánica*. Mexico City: Instituto Nacional de Antropología e Historia.

CASO, ALFONSO
1938 *Exploraciones en Oaxaca, quinta y sexta temporadas, 1936–37*. Instituto Panamericano de Geografía e Historia, Pub. 34. Mexico City.
1947 Calendario y escritura de las antiguas culturas de Monte Albán. In *Obras completas de Miguel Othón de Mendizábal* 1:5–102. Mexico City.
1965 Sculpture and Mural Painting of Oaxaca. In *Handbook of Middle American Indians*, vol. 3, edited by Robert Wauchope and Gordon R. Willey, pp. 849–870. Austin: University of Texas Press.
1966 Dioses y signos teotihuacanos. In *Teotihuacán: Onceava Mesa Redonda* 1:249–275. Mexico City: Sociedad Mexicana de Antropología.
1967 *Los calendarios prehispánicos*. Instituto de Investigaciones Históricas, Serie Cultura Náhuatl, Monograph 6. Mexico City: Universidad Nacional Autónoma de México.
1969 *El tesoro de Monte Albán*. Memorias del Instituto Nacional de Antropología e Historia 3. Mexico City.

CASO, ALFONSO, AND IGNACIO BERNAL
1952 *Urnas de Oaxaca*. Memorias del Instituto Nacional de Antropología e Historia 2. Mexico City.

CASO, ALFONSO, IGNACIO BERNAL, AND JORGE ACOSTA
1967 *La cerámica de Monte Albán*. Memorias del Instituto Nacional de Antropología e Historia 13. Mexico City.

CASTANEDA SALDAÑA, HILDA
1976 Los utensiles de molienda de Teotihuacán. Tesis profesional, Escuela Nacional de Antropología e Historia. Mexico City.

CHADWICK, ROBERT
1971a Native Pre-Aztec History of Central Mexico. In *Handbook of Middle American Indians*, vol. 11, edited by Robert Wauchope, Gordon F. Ekholm, and Ignacio Bernal, pp. 474–504. Austin: University of Texas Press.
1971b Postclassic Pottery of the Central Valleys. In *Handbook of Middle American Indians*, vol. 10, edited by Robert Wauchope, Gordon F. Ekholm, and Ignacio Bernal, pp. 228–257. Austin: University of Texas Press.

CHADWICK, ROBERT, AND RICHARD S. MACNEISH
1967 Codex Borgia and the Venta Salada Phase. In *The Prehistory of the Tehuacan Valley*, vol. 1, *Environment and Subsistence*, edited by Douglas S. Byers, pp. 114–131. Austin: University of Texas Press.

CHAGNON, NAPOLEON A.
1968 *Yanomamö: The Fierce People*. New York: Holt, Rinehart and Winston.

CHANDLER, TERTIUS, AND GERALD FOX
1974 *3000 Years of Urban Growth*. New York: Academic Press.

CHAPMAN, ANNE M.
1971 Commentary on: Mesoamerican Trade and Its Role in the Emergence of Civilization. In *Observations on the Emergence of Civilization in Mesoamerica*, edited by Robert F. Heizer and John A. Graham. Contributions of the University of California Archaeological Research Facility 11:196–211. Berkeley.

CHARLTON, THOMAS H.
1970a Contemporary Settlement Patterns: The Cerro Gordo-North Slope and Upper Valley Areas. In *The Teotihuacan Valley Project Final Report*, vol. 1. Occasional Papers in Anthropology, Pennsylvania State University, 3:181–252.
1970b Contemporary Agriculture of the Valley. In *The Teotihuacan Valley Project Final Report*, vol. 1. Occasional Papers in Anthropology, Pennsylvania State University, 3:253–383.
1978a Formative Trade and Cultural Transformations in the Basin of Mexico. *Human Mosaic* 12:121–129. New Orleans: Tulane University.
1978b Teotihuacán, Tepeapulco, and Obsidian Exploitation. *Science* 200:1227–1236.
1979a Production and Exchange: Variables in the Evolution of a Civilization. Revised version of a paper presented at the 76th annual meeting of the American Anthropological Association, Houston, 1977.
1979b Teotihuacán: Trade Routes of a Multi-Tiered Economy. In *Los procesos de cambio: XV Mesa Redonda* 2:285–292. Mexico City: Sociedad Mexicana de Antropología and Universidad de Guanajuato.

CHARLTON, THOMAS H., DAVID C. GROVE, AND PHILIP K. HOPKE
1978 The Paredon, Mexico, Obsidian Source

and Early Formative Exchange. *Science* 201:807–809.

CHEEK, CHARLES D.

1976 Teotihuacan Influence at Kaminaljuyu. In *Las fronteras de Mesoamérica: XIV Mesa Redonda* 2:55–71. Mexico City: Sociedad Mexicana de Antropología.

CHI CH'AO TING

1936 *Key Economic Areas in Chinese History.* American Council Institute of Pacific Relations. London: George Allen and Unwin.

CHILDE, V. GORDON

1942 *What Happened in History.* Baltimore: Penguin Books.

CHRISTALLER, WALTER

1966 *Central Places in Southern Germany.* Translated by C. W. Baskin. Englewood Cliffs, N.J.: Prentice-Hall.

CLEWLOW, C. WILLIAM, JR.

1974 *A Stylistic and Chronological Study of Olmec Monumental Sculpture.* Contributions of the University of California Archaeological Research Facility 19. Berkeley.

COBEAN, ROBERT H.

1974a Archaeological Survey of the Tula Region. In *Studies of Ancient Tollan: A Report of the University of Missouri Tula Archaeological Project*, edited by Richard A. Diehl. University of Missouri Monographs in Anthropology 1:6–10. Columbia.

1974b The Ceramics of Tula. In *Studies of Ancient Tollan: A Report of the University of Missouri Tula Archaeological Project*, edited by Richard A. Diehl. University of Missouri Monographs in Anthropology 1:32–41. Columbia.

1978 The Pre-Aztec Ceramics of Tula, Hidalgo, Mexico. Ph.D. dissertation, Department of Anthropology, Harvard University. Ann Arbor: University Microfilms.

1979 Tula's Ancient City and Its Obsidian Industry. MS on file, Department of Anthropology, University of Missouri.

COBEAN, ROBERT H., MICHAEL D. COE, EDWARD A. PERRY, JR., KARL K. TUREKIAN, AND DINKAR P. KHARKAR.

1971 Obsidian Trade at San Lorenzo Tenochtitlan, Mexico. *Science* 174:666–671.

COE, MICHAEL D.

1960 Archaeological Linkages with North and South America at La Victoria, Guatemala. *American Anthropologist* 62:363–393.

1961a *La Victoria, an Early Site on the Pacific Coast of Guatemala.* Papers of the Peabody Museum, Harvard University, 53. Cambridge, Mass.

1961b Social Typology and the Tropical Forest Civilizations. *Comparative Studies in Society and History* 4:65–85.

1962 *Mexico.* London: Thames and Hudson; New York: Frederick A. Praeger.

1965a Archaeological Synthesis of Southern Veracruz and Tabasco. In *Handbook of Middle American Indians*, vol. 3, edited by Robert Wauchope and Gordon R. Willey, pp. 679–715. Austin: University of Texas Press.

1965b The Olmec Style and Its Distributions. In *Handbook of Middle American Indians*, vol. 3, edited by Robert Wauchope and Gordon R. Willey, pp. 739–775. Austin: University of Texas Press.

1965c *The Jaguar's Children: Pre-Classic Central Mexico.* New York: Museum of Primitive Art.

1966 *The Maya.* London: Thames and Hudson.

1967 Solving a Monumental Mystery. *Discovery* 3(1):21–26. New Haven.

1968 San Lorenzo and the Olmec Civilization. In *Dumbarton Oaks Conference on the Olmec*, edited by Elizabeth P. Benson, pp. 41–77. Washington, D.C.: Dumbarton Oaks.

1970 The Archaeological Sequence at San Lorenzo Tenochtitlan, Veracruz, Mexico. *Contributions of the University of California Archaeological Research Facility* 8:21–34. Berkeley.

1974 Photogrammetry and the Ecology of Olmec Civilization. In *Aerial Photography in Anthropological Field Research*, edited by Evon Z. Vogt, pp. 1–13. Cambridge: Harvard University Press.

1977 Olmec and Maya: A Study in Relationships. In *The Origins of Maya Civilization*, edited by Richard E. W. Adams, pp. 183–195. Albuquerque: University of New Mexico Press.

COE, MICHAEL D., AND RICHARD A. DIEHL

1980 *In the Land of the Olmec.* 2 vols. Austin: University of Texas Press.

COE, MICHAEL D., RICHARD A. DIEHL, AND MINZE STUIVER

1967 Olmec Civilization, Veracruz, Mexico: Dating of the San Lorenzo Phase. *Science* 155:1399–1401.

411

COE, MICHAEL D., AND KENT V. FLANNERY

1964 Microenvironments and Mesoamerican Prehistory. *Science* 143:650–654.

1967 *Early Cultures and Human Ecology in South Coastal Guatemala*. Smithsonian Contributions to Anthropology 3. Washington, D.C.

COE, WILLIAM R.

1958 Two Carved Lintels from Tikal. *Archaeology* 11:75–80.

1959 Tikal 1959. *Expedition* 1(4):7–11.

1962a Maya Mystery in Tikal. *Natural History* 71:10–12, 44–53.

1962b Priestly Power and Peasant Corn: Excavations and Reconstructions at Tikal. *Illustrated London News* 240:103–106, 135–137.

1962c A Summary of Excavation and Research at Tikal, Guatemala: 1956–1961. *American Antiquity* 27:479–507.

1963a Current Research (Tikal). *American Antiquity* 28:417–419.

1963b A Summary of ·Excavation and Research at Tikal, Guatemala: 1962. *Estudios de Cultura Maya* 3:41–64.

1964 Current Research (Tikal). *American Antiquity* 29:411–413.

1965a Current Research (Tikal). *American Antiquity* 30:379–383.

1965b Tikal, Guatemala, and Emergent Maya Civilization. *Science* 147:1401–1419.

1965c Tikal: Ten Years of Study of a Maya Ruin in the Lowlands of Guatemala. *Expedition* 8(1):5–56.

1967 *Tikal: A Handbook of the Ancient Maya Ruins*. Philadelphia: The University Museum, University of Pennsylvania. (Spanish version, 1971, Asociación Tikal, Guatemala.)

1968 Tikal: In Search of the Maya Past. *The World Book Year Book*, pp. 160–176. Chicago.

1971 El Proyecto Tikal: 1956–1970. *Anales de La Sociedad de Geografía e Historia de Guatemala* 42:185–202. (Bears 1969 dateline.)

1972 Cultural Contact between the Lowland Maya and Teotihuacan as Seen from Tikal, Peten, Guatemala. In *Teotihuacán: XI Mesa Redonda* 2:257–271. Mexico City: Sociedad Mexicana de Antropología.

1975 Resurrecting the Grandeur of Tikal. *National Geographic* 148:792–795.

COE, WILLIAM R., AND VIVIAN L. BROMAN

1958 *Tikal Report No. 2: Excavations in the Stela 23 Group*. Museum Monographs, The University Museum. Philadelphia: University of Pennsylvania.

COE, WILLIAM R., AND J. J. McGINN

1963 Tikal: The North Acropolis and an Early Tomb. *Expedition* 5(2):24–32.

COE, WILLIAM R., EDWIN M. SHOOK, AND LINTON SATTERTHWAITE

1961 *Tikal Report No. 6: The Carved Wooden Lintels of Tikal*. Museum Monographs, The University Museum. Philadelphia: University of Pennsylvania.

COGGINS, CLEMENCY C.

1975 Painting and Drawing Styles at Tikal: An Historical and Iconographic Reconstruction. Ph.D. dissertation, Department of Fine Arts, Harvard University. Ann Arbor: University Microfilms (BWH76-03783).

1979a The Manikin Scepter: Emblem of a Foreign Elite. Paper presented at the annual College Art Association meeting, Washington, D.C.

1979b A New Order and the Role of the Calendar: Some Characteristics of the Middle Classic Period at Tikal. In *Maya Archaeology and Ethnohistory*, edited by Norman Hammond and Gordon R. Willey, pp. 38–50. Austin: University of Texas Press.

1979c Teotihuacan at Tikal in the Early Classic Period. In *Actes du XLII<sup>e</sup> Congrès International des Américanistes* (Paris, 1976) 8:251–269.

1980 The Shape of Time: Some Political Implications of a Four-Part Figure. *American Antiquity* 45:727–739.

CONTRERAS S., EDUARDO

1965 La zona arqueológica de Manzanilla, Pue. *Boletín del Instituto Nacional de Antropología e Historia* 21:18–24. Mexico City.

COOK DE LEONARD, CARMEN

1956 Dos atlatl de la época teotihuacana. In *Estudios antropológicos publicados en homenaje al Doctor Manuel Gamio*, pp. 183–200. Mexico City: Universidad Nacional Autónoma de México and Sociedad Mexicana de Antropología.

CÓRDOVA, JUAN DE

1578 *Arte en lengua zapoteca*. Mexico City: Pedro Balli.

COVARRUBIAS, MIGUEL

1943 Tlatilco: Archaic Mexican Art and Culture. *Dyn* 4–5:40–46.

COWGILL, GEORGE L.

1968 Computer Analysis of Archaeological Data from Teotihuacan, Mexico. In *New Perspectives in Archaeology*, edited by Sally R. Binford and Lewis R. Binford, pp. 143–150. Chicago: Aldine.

1974 Quantitative Studies of Urbanization at Teotihuacan. In *Mesoamerican Archaeology: New Approaches*, edited by Norman Hammond, pp. 363–396. Austin: University of Texas Press.

1975a On Causes and Consequences of Ancient and Modern Population Changes. *American Anthropologist* 77:505–525.

1975b Population Pressure as a Non-explanation. In *Population Studies in Archaeology and Biological Anthropology: A Symposium*, edited by Alan C. Swedlund. Memoirs of the Society for American Archaeology 30:127–131. Washington, D.C.

1979a Processes of Growth and Decline at Teotihuacan: The City and the State. In *Los Procesos de Cambio: XV Mesa Redonda*, 1: 183–193. Mexico City: Sociedad Mexicana de Antropología y Universidad de Guanajuato.

1979b Teotihuacan, Internal Militaristic Competition, and the Fall of the Classic Maya. In *Maya Archaeology and Ethnohistory*, edited by Norman Hammond and Gordon R. Willey, pp. 51–62. Austin: University of Texas Press.

CRESPO, ANA MARÍA

1976 Uso del suelo y patrón de poblamiento en el área de Tula, Hgo. In *Proyecto Tula, segunda parte*, coordinated by Eduardo Matos Moctezuma. Colección Científica, Arqueología, 33:35–48. Mexico City: Instituto Nacional de Antropología e Historia.

CRESPO, ANA MARÍA, AND ALBA GUADALUPE MASTACHE DE ESCOBAR

1976 La presencia en el área de Tula, Hidalgo, de grupos relacionados con el Barrio de Oaxaca en Teotihuacán. Paper presented at the 41st annual meeting of the Society for American Archaeology, St. Louis.

CULBERT, T. PATRICK

1963 Ceramic Research at Tikal, Guatemala. *Cerámica de Cultura Maya* 1(2–3):34–42.

1967 Preliminary Report of the Conference on the Prehistoric Ceramics of the Maya Lowlands (1965). *Estudios de Cultura Maya* 6:81–109.

1973a (ed.) *The Classic Maya Collapse*. Albuquerque: University of New Mexico Press.

1973b The Maya Downfall at Tikal. In *The Classic Maya Collapse*, edited by T. Patrick Culbert, pp. 63–92. Albuquerque: University of New Mexico Press.

1974 *The Lost Civilization: The Story of the Classic Maya*. New York: Harper and Row.

1977 Early Maya Development at Tikal, Guatemala. In *The Origins of Maya Civilization*, edited by Richard E. W. Adams, pp. 27–43. Albuquerque: University of New Mexico Press.

CURRAN, MARGARET E.

1978 An Examination of the Relationship between Population Density and Agricultural Productivity in the Prehispanic Valley of Oaxaca, Mexico. Paper presented at the 43rd annual meeting of the Society for American Archaeology, Tucson.

CUTLER, HUGH C., AND THOMAS W. WHITAKER

1967 Cucurbits from the Tehuacan Caves. In *The Prehistory of the Tehuacan Valley*, vol. 1, *Environment and Subsistence*, edited by Douglas S. Byers, pp. 212–219. Austin: University of Texas Press.

DAHLIN, BRUCE H.

1976 An Anthropologist Looks at the Pyramids: A Late Classic Revitalization Movement at Tikal, Guatemala. Ph.D. dissertation, Department of Anthropology, Temple University. Ann Arbor: University Microfilms (BWH76-22086).

DAVIES, NIGEL

1968 *Los señoríos independientes del imperio azteca*. Mexico City: Instituto Nacional de Antropología e Historia.

1977 *The Toltecs until the Fall of Tula*. Norman: University of Oklahoma Press.

1978 The Military Organization of the Aztec Empire. In *Mesoamerican Communication Routes and Cultural Contacts*, edited by Thomas A. Lee, Jr., and Carlos Navarrete. Papers of the New World Archaeological Foundation No. 40:223–230. Provo, Utah.

DÁVILA, PATRICIO

1974 Cuauhtinchan: Estudio arqueológico de un área. Tesis profesional, Escuela Nacional de Antropología e Historia, Mexico City.

DÁVILA, PATRICIO, AND DIANA Z. DE DÁVILA

1976 Periodificación de elementos culturales para el área del Proyecto Arqueológico Cuautinchán. *Comunicaciones* 13:85–98.

Puebla: Fundación Alemana para la Investigación Científica.

DAVIS, DAVE D.

1975 Patterns of Early Formative Subsistence in Southern Mesoamerica, 1500–1100 B.C. *Man* 10:41–59.

DIEHL, RICHARD A.

1970 Contemporary Settlement Patterns in the Teotihuacan Valley: An Overview. In *The Teotihuacan Valley Project Final Report*, vol. 1. Occasional Papers in Anthropology, Pennsylvania State University, 3:103–179. University Park.

1974 (ed.) *Studies of Ancient Tollan: A Report of the University of Missouri Tula Archaeological Project*. University of Missouri Monographs in Anthropology No. 1. Columbia.

1976 Pre-Hispanic Relationships between the Basin of Mexico and North and West Mexico. In *The Valley of Mexico: Studies in Pre-Hispanic Ecology and Society*, edited by Eric R. Wolf, pp. 249–286. Albuquerque: University of New Mexico Press.

DIEHL, RICHARD A., AND ROBERT A. BENFER

1975 Tollan, the Toltec Capital. *Archaeology* 28:112–124.

DIEHL, RICHARD A., ROBERT A. BENFER, AND DAN M. HEALAN

1974 Methodology and Field Techniques. In *Studies of Ancient Tollan: A Report of the University of Missouri Tula Archaeological Project*, edited by Richard A. Diehl. University of Missouri Monographs in Anthropology No. 1:3–5. Columbia.

DIEHL, RICHARD A., AND LAWRENCE H. FELDMAN

1974 Relaciones entre la Huasteca y Tollan. In *Proyecto Tula, 1ª parte*, coordinated by Eduardo Matos Moctezuma. Colección Científica, Arqueología, 15:105–108. Mexico City: Instituto Nacional de Antropología e Historia.

DIEHL, RICHARD A., ROGER LOMAS, AND JACK T. WYNN

1974 Toltec Trade with Central America: New Light and Evidence. *Archaeology* 27:182–187.

DIEHL, RICHARD A., AND EDWARD G. STROH, JR.

1978 Tecali Vessel Manufacturing Debris at Tollan, Mexico. *American Antiquity* 43:73–79.

DIXON, KEITH A.

1959 *Ceramics from Two Preclassic Periods at Chiapa de Corzo, Chiapas, Mexico*. Papers of the New World Archaeological Foundation No. 5. Provo, Utah.

1966 Progress Report on Excavation of Terminal Late Preclassic Ceremonial Architecture, Temesco, Valley of Mexico. MS.

DOELLE, WILLIAM H.

1976 *Desert Resources and Hohokam Subsistence: The Conoco Florence Project*. Arizona State Museum Archaeological Series 103. Tucson.

DORAN, JAMES

1970 Systems Theory, Computer Simulations and Archaeology. *World Archaeology* 1:289–298.

DOW, JAMES W.

1967 Astronomical Orientations at Teotihuacán. *American Antiquity* 32:326–334.

DRENNAN, ROBERT D.

1976a *Fábrica San José and Middle Formative Society in the Valley of Oaxaca*. Vol. 4 of *Prehistory and Human Ecology of the Valley of Oaxaca*, edited by Kent V. Flannery. Memoirs of the Museum of Anthropology, University of Michigan 8. Ann Arbor.

1976b Religion and Social Evolution in Formative Mesoamerica. In *The Early Mesoamerican Village*, edited by Kent V. Flannery, pp. 345–368. New York: Academic Press.

n.d. Oaxaca Radiocarbon Dates Associated with Ceramic Phases. In *The Cloud People: Evolution of the Zapotec and Mixtec Civilizations of Oaxaca, Mexico*, edited by Kent V. Flannery and Joyce Marcus.

DREWITT, BRUCE

1966 Planeación en la antigua ciudad de Teotihuacán. In *Teotihuacán: Onceava Mesa Redonda* 1:79–94. Mexico City: Sociedad Mexicana de Antropología.

1969 Data Bearing on Urban Planning at Teotihuacán. Paper presented at the 68th annual meeting of the American Anthropological Association, New Orleans.

DRUCKER, PHILIP

1943 *Ceramic Sequences at Tres Zapotes, Veracruz, Mexico*. Smithsonian Institution, Bureau of American Ethnology, Bulletin 140. Washington, D.C.

1952 *La Venta, Tabasco: A Study of Olmec Ceramics and Art*. Smithsonian Institution,

Bureau of American Ethnology, Bulletin 153. Washington, D.C.

DRUCKER, PHILIP, ROBERT F. HEIZER, AND ROBERT J. SQUIER

1959 *Excavations at La Venta, Tabasco, 1955*. Smithsonian Institution, Bureau of American Ethnology, Bulletin 170. Washington, D.C.

DRUCKER, R. DAVID

1973 The Shortest Day of the Year at Teotihuacan and the Solution to the Problem of the Orientation of the Ancient City and the Location of Its Major Structures. Paper presented at the joint meeting of the Consejo Nacional de Ciencia y Tecnología and the American Association for the Advancement of Science, June 20–July 4, 1973, Mexico City.

1974 Renovating a Reconstruction: The Ciudadela at Teotihuacan, Mexico: Construction Sequence, Layout, and Possible Uses of the Structure. Ph.D. dissertation, Department of Anthropology, University of Rochester. Ann Arbor: University Microfilms (BWH74-22572).

1977 A Solar Orientation Framework for Teotihuacan. Paper presented at XV Mesa Redonda of the Sociedad Mexicana de Antropología, Guanajuato.

DUMOND, DON E.

1972 Demographic Aspects of the Classic Period in Puebla-Tlaxcala. *Southwestern Journal of Anthropology* 28:101–130.

1976 An Outline of the Demographic History of Tlaxcala. In *The Tlaxcaltecans: Prehistory, Demography, Morphology and Genetics*, edited by Michael H. Crawford. University of Kansas Publications in Anthropology 7:13–23.

DUMOND, DON E., AND FLORENCIA MULLER

1972 Classic to Postclassic in Highland Central Mexico. *Science* 175:1208–1215.

DUTTON, BERTHA P.

1955 Tula of the Toltecs. *El Palacio* 62:195–251.

DYSON, ROBERT H., JR.

1962 The Tikal Project—1962. *Archaeology* 15:131–132.

EARLE, TIMOTHY K.

1977 A Reappraisal of Redistribution: Complex Hawaiian Chiefdoms. In *Exchange Systems in Prehistory*, edited by Timothy K. Earle and Jonathan E. Ericson, pp. 213–229. New York: Academic Press.

1978 *Economic and Social Organization of a Complex Chiefdom: The Halelea District, Kaua'i, Hawaii*. Anthropological Papers, Museum of Anthropology, University of Michigan, 63. Ann Arbor.

EATON, JACK D.

1978 Archaeological Survey of the Yucatan-Campeche Coast. In *Studies in the Archaeology of Coastal Yucatan and Campeche, Mexico*, pp. iii–67. Middle American Research Institute, Tulane University, Pub. 46. New Orleans.

EDWARDS, EMILY

1966 *Painted Walls of Mexico*. Austin: University of Texas Press.

EKHOLM, GORDON F.

1944 *Excavations at Tampico and Panuco in the Huasteca, Mexico*. Anthropological Papers, American Museum of Natural History, 38(5). New York.

EKHOLM, SUSANNA M.

1969 *Mound 30a and the Early Preclassic Ceramic Sequence of Izapa, Chiapas, Mexico*. Papers of the New World Archaeological Foundation No. 25. Provo, Utah.

ESTER, MICHAEL R.

1976 The Spatial Allocation of Activities at Teotihuacán, Mexico. Ph.D. dissertation, Department of Anthropology, Brandeis University. Ann Arbor: University Microfilms (BWH76-25301).

FALLERS, LLOYD A.

1961 Are African Cultivators to Be Called "Peasants"? *Current Anthropology* 2:108–110.

1964 Social Stratification and Economic Processes. In *Economic Transition in Africa*, edited by Melville J. Herskovits and Mitchell Harwitz, pp. 113–130. Evanston: Northwestern University Press.

FEINMAN, GARY

n.d.a Ceramic Production Sites. *In* Monte Albán's Hinterland, Part 1: The Prehispanic Settlement Patterns of the Central and Southern Parts of the Valley of Oaxaca, Mexico, edited by Richard E. Blanton, Stephen A. Kowalewski, Gary Feinman, and Jill Appel. In preparation.

n.d.b Patterns in Ceramic Production and Distribution, Periods Early I through V. *In* Monte Albán's Hinterland, Part 1: The Prehispanic Settlement Patterns of the Central and Southern Parts of the Valley of Oaxaca, Mexico, edited by Richard E. Blanton,

Stephen A. Kowalewski, Gary Feinman, and Jill Appel. In preparation.

FEINMAN, GARY, AND STEPHEN A. KOWALEWSKI

1979  Valley of Oaxaca Settlement Pattern Project Progress Report 1979. Submitted to the National Science Foundation.

FELDMAN, LAWRENCE H.

1974a  Tollan in Hidalgo: Native Accounts of the Central Mexican Tolteca. In *Studies of Ancient Tollan: A Report of the University of Missouri Tula Archaeological Project*, edited by Richard A. Diehl. University of Missouri Monographs in Anthropology 1:130–149. Columbia.

1974b  Tollan in Central Mexico: The Geography of Economic Specialization. In *Studies of Ancient Tollan: A Report of the University of Missouri Tula Archaeological Project*, edited by Richard A. Diehl. University of Missouri Monographs in Anthropology 1:150–189. Columbia.

FERREE, LISA

1970  The Pottery Censers of Tikal, Guatemala. Ph.D. dissertation, Department of Anthropology, Southern Illinois University. Ann Arbor: University Microfilms (BWH73-06203).

FEUCHTWANG, STEPHEN

1974  Domestic and Communal Worship in Taiwan. In *Religion and Ritual in Chinese Society*, edited by Arthur P. Wolf, pp. 105–129. Stanford: Stanford University Press.

1975  Investigating Religion. In *Marxist Analyses and Social Anthropology*, edited by Maurice Bloch, pp. 61–82. New York: Wiley.

1977  School-Temple and City God. In *The City in Late Imperial China*, edited by G. William Skinner, pp. 581–608. Stanford: Stanford University Press.

FISCH, EVA

1978  The Early Formative in the Valley of Oaxaca, Mexico: A Regional Analysis. Paper presented at the 43rd annual meeting of the Society for American Archaeology, Tucson.

n.d.  The Early and Middle Formative Periods. *In* Monte Albán's Hinterland, Part 1: The Prehispanic Settlement Patterns of the Central and Southern Parts of the Valley of Oaxaca, Mexico, edited by Richard E. Blanton, Stephen A. Kowalewski, Gary Feinman, and Jill Appel. In preparation.

FLANNERY, KENT V.

1967  The Vertebrate Fauna and Hunting Patterns. In *The Prehistory of the Tehuacan Valley*, vol. 1, *Environment and Subsistence*, edited by Douglas S. Byers, pp. 132–177. Austin: University of Texas Press.

1968a  Archaeological Systems Theory and Early Mesoamerica. In *Anthropological Archaeology in the Americas*, edited by Betty J. Meggers, pp. 67–87. Washington, D.C.: Anthropological Society of Washington.

1968b  The Olmec and the Valley of Oaxaca: A Model for Interregional Interaction in Formative Times. In *Dumbarton Oaks Conference on the Olmec*, edited by Elizabeth P. Benson, pp. 79–110. Washington, D.C. Dumbarton Oaks.

1969  Origins and Ecological Effects of Early Domestication in Iran and the Near East. In *The Domestication and Exploitation of Plants and Animals*, edited by Peter J. Ucko and G. W. Dimbleby, pp. 73–100. Chicago: Aldine.

1970  (ed.) Preliminary Archaeological Investigations in the Valley of Oaxaca, Mexico, 1966–1969. Mimeographed report to the National Science Foundation.

1972a  The Cultural Evolution of Civilizations. *Annual Review of Ecology and Systematics* 3:399–426. Palo Alto.

1972b  The Origins of the Village as a Settlement Type in Mesoamerica and the Near East: A Comparative Study. In *Man, Settlement and Urbanism*, edited by Peter J. Ucko, Ruth Tringham, and G. W. Dimbleby, pp. 23–31. London: Duckworth.

1973  The Origins of Agriculture. *Annual Review of Anthropology* 2:271–310. Palo Alto.

1976a  (ed.) *The Early Mesoamerican Village*. New York: Academic Press.

1976b  Empirical Determination of Site Catchments in Oaxaca and Tehuacán. In *The Early Mesoamerican Village*, edited by Kent V. Flannery, pp. 103–117. New York: Academic Press.

1976c  Interregional Religious Networks: Introduction. In *The Early Mesoamerican Village*, edited by Kent V. Flannery, pp. 329–333. New York: Academic Press.

1976d  Contextual Analysis of Ritual Paraphernalia from Formative Oaxaca. In *The Early Mesoamerican Village*, edited by Kent V.

416

Flannery, pp. 333–345. New York: Academic Press.

1977 A Setting for Cultural Evolution: Review of *The Valley of Mexico: Studies in Pre-Hispanic Ecology and Society*, edited by Eric R. Wolf. *Science* 196:759–761.

n.d. (ed.) Guilá Naquitz Cave: A Study of Hunting, Gathering, and Incipient Agriculture in Preceramic Oaxaca, Mexico. In preparation.

FLANNERY, KENT V., ANNE V. T. KIRKBY, MICHAEL J. KIRKBY, AND AUBREY W. WILLIAMS, JR.

1967 Farming Systems and Political Growth in Ancient Oaxaca. *Science* 158:445–454.

FLANNERY, KENT V., AND JOYCE MARCUS

1976a Evolution of the Public Building in Formative Oaxaca. In *Cultural Change and Continuity*, edited by Charles Cleland, pp. 205–222. New York: Academic Press.

1976b Formative Oaxaca and the Zapotec Cosmos. *American Scientist* 64:374–383.

n.d. (eds.) *The Cloud People: Evolution of the Zapotec and Mixtec Civilizations of Oaxaca, Mexico.*

FLANNERY, KENT V., AND MARCUS C. WINTER

1976 Analyzing Household Activities. In *The Early Mesoamerican Village*, edited by Kent V. Flannery, pp. 34–47. New York: Academic Press.

FLANNERY, KENT V., MARCUS C. WINTER, SUSAN LEES, JAMES A. NEELY, JAMES SCHOENWETTER, SUZANNE KITCHEN, AND JANE C. WHEELER

1970 Preliminary Archaeological Investigations in the Valley of Oaxaca, Mexico, 1966–1969. Report to the National Science Foundation and the Instituto Nacional de Antropología e Historia.

FOLAN, WILLIAM J.

1969 Dzibilchaltun, Yucatan, Mexico: Structures 384, 385, and 386: A Preliminary Interpretation. *American Antiquity* 34:434–461.

1970 The Open Chapel of Dzibilchaltun, Yucatan. In *Archaeological Studies in Middle America*. Middle American Research Institute, Tulane University, Pub. 26:181–199. New Orleans.

FORD, RICHARD I.

1972 Barter, Gift, or Violence: An Analysis of Tewa Intertribal Exchange. In *Social Exchange and Interaction*, edited by Edwin Wilmsen. Anthropological Papers, Museum of Anthropology, University of Michigan, 46:21–45. Ann Arbor.

FORD, RICHARD I., AND JOEL N. ELIAS

1972 Teotihuacán Paleoethnobotany. Paper presented at the 37th annual meeting of the Society for American Archaeology, Miami.

FOWLER, MELVIN L.

1968 *Un sistema preclásico de distribución de agua en la Zona Arqueológica de Amulacan, Puebla*. Instituto Poblano de Antropología e Historia Pub. 2. Puebla.

1971 The Origin of Plant Cultivation in the Central Mississippi Valley: A Hypothesis. In *Prehistoric Agriculture*, edited by Stuart Struever, pp. 122–128. Garden City, N.Y.: Natural History Press.

FOWLER, MELVIN L., AND RICHARD S. MACNEISH

1975 Excavations in the Coxcatlan Locality in the Alluvial Slopes. In *The Prehistory of the Tehuacan Valley*, vol. 5, *Excavations and Reconnaissance*, by Richard S. MacNeish et al., pp. 219–340. General Editor: Richard S. MacNeish. Austin: University of Texas Press.

FOX, RICHARD G.

1977 *Urban Anthropology*. Englewood Cliffs, N.J.: Prentice-Hall.

FRANCO, JOSÉ LUIS

1970a Trabajos y excavaciones arqueológicos. In *Minería prehispánica en la Sierra de Querétaro*, pp. 23–26. Mexico City: Secretaría del Patrimonio Nacional.

1970b Material recuperado. In *Minería prehispánica en la Sierra de Querétaro*, pp. 27–36. Mexico City: Secretaría del Patrimonio Nacional.

FREEDMAN, MATTHEW S.

1976 Barrio Definition at Teotihuacán: A Preliminary Examination. Paper presented at the 41st annual meeting of the Society for American Archaeology, St. Louis.

FREIDEL, DAVID A.

1978 Maritime Adaptation and the Rise of Maya Civilization: The View from Cerros, Belize. In *Prehistoric Coastal Adaptations: The Economy and Ecology of Maritime Middle America*, edited by Barbara L. Stark and Barbara Voorhies, pp. 239–265. New York: Academic Press.

1979 Culture Areas and Interaction Spheres: Contrasting Approaches to the Emergence of Civilization in the Maya Lowlands. *American Antiquity* 44:36–54.

FRIED, MORTON H.

1967   *The Evolution of Political Society: An Essay in Political Anthropology.* New York: Random House.

FRIEDMAN, JONATHAN

1974   Marxism, Structuralism and Vulgar Materialism. *Man*, n.s. 9:444–469.

FRIEDMAN, JONATHAN, AND M. J. ROWLANDS

1978   Notes towards an Epigenetic Model of the Evolution of "Civilization." In *The Evolution of Social Systems*, edited by Jonathan Friedman and M. J. Rowlands, pp. 201–276. Pittsburgh: University of Pittsburgh Press.

FRIEDMANN, JOHN

1961   Cities in Social Transformation. *Comparative Studies in Society and History* 4:86–103.

FRY, ROBERT E.

1969   Ceramics and Settlement in the Periphery of Tikal, Guatemala. Ph.D. dissertation, Department of Anthropology, University of Arizona. Ann Arbor: University Microfilms (BWH70-05245).

1972   Manually Operated Post-Hole Diggers as Sampling Instruments. *American Antiquity* 37:259–261.

1979   The Economics of Pottery at Tikal, Guatemala: Models of Exchange for Serving Vessels. *American Antiquity* 44:494–512.

FRY, ROBERT E., AND S. C. COX

1973   *Late Classic Pottery Manufacture and Distribution at Tikal, Guatemala.* Working Paper No. 70. Institute for the Study of Social Change, Purdue University.

1974   The Structure of Ceramic Exchange at Tikal, Guatemala. *World Archaeology* 6:209–225.

FUENTE, BEATRIZ DE LA

1973   *Escultura monumental olmeca: Catálogo.* Mexico City: Instituto de Investigaciones Estéticas, Universidad Nacional Autónoma de México.

FUNDACIÓN ALEMANA PARA LA INVESTIGACIÓN CIENTÍFICA

1973   Primer simposio, proyecto Puebla-Tlaxcala. *Comunicaciones* 7, 8. Puebla.

GALINAT, WALTON C.

1970   The Cupule and Its Role in the Origin and Evolution of Maize. *Massachusetts Agro-nomic Experimental Station Bulletin* 585:1–18.

1971   The Origin of Maize. *Annual Review of Genetics* 5:447–478.

GALLEGOS, ROBERTO

1962   Exploraciones en Zaachila, Oax. *Boletín del Instituto Nacional de Antropología e Historia* 8:6–8. Mexico City.

1963   Zaachila: The First Season's Work. Translated by Dudley T. Easby, Jr. *Archaeology* 16:226–233.

GAMIO, MANUEL

1922   *La población del valle de Teotihuacán.* 3 vols. Mexico City: Secretaría de Agricultura y Fomento.

GARCÍA BARCENA, JOAQUÍN, DIANA SANTAMARÍA, TICUL ALVAREZ, MANUEL REYES, AND FERNANDO SÁNCHEZ

1976   *Excavaciones en el Abrigo de Santa Marta, Chis. (1974).* Informes, Departamento de Prehistoria, No. 1. Mexico City: Instituto Nacional de Antropología e Historia.

GARCÍA COOK, ANGEL

1968   *Chimalhuacán: Un artefacto asociado a megafauna.* Instituto Nacional de Antropología e Historia, Departamento de Prehistoria, Pub. 21. Mexico City.

1973a   Algunos descubrimientos en Tlalancaleca, Edo. de Puebla. *Comunicaciones* 9:25–34. Puebla: Fundación Alemana para la Investigación Científica.

1973b   Una punta acanalada en el Estado de Tlaxcala, Mexico. *Comunicaciones* 9:39–42. Puebla: Fundación Alemana para la Investigación Científica.

1974a   Una secuencia cultural para Tlaxcala. *Comunicaciones* 10:5–22. Puebla: Fundación Alemana para la Investigación Científica.

1974b   Transición del "Clásico" al "Postclásico" en Tlaxcala: Fase Tenanyecac. In *Cultura y Sociedad* 1(2):83–98. Mexico City.

1975   Dos artefactos de hueso en asociación con restos pleistocénicos en Los Reyes La Paz, México. *Anales del Instituto Nacional de Antropología e Historia*, epoca 7, 4:237–250. Mexico City.

1976a   Cronología de la tumba y comentarios generales. In *El proyecto arqueológico Puebla-Tlaxcala*, coordinated by Angel García Cook, vol. 1. Suplemento, *Comunicaciones* 3:53–62. Puebla: Fundación Alemana para la Investigación Científica.

1976b   *El desarrollo cultural prehispánico en el*

norte del Valle Poblano-Tlaxcalteca: In-
ferencias de una secuencia cultural, espa-
cial y temporalmente establecida. Serie Arqueología, Departamento de Monumentos
Prehispánicos, 1. Mexico City: Instituto
Nacional de Antropología e Historia.

1976c   Fronteras culturales en el Area Tlaxcala-
Puebla. In Las fronteras de Mesoamérica:
XIV Mesa Redonda 1:49–50. Mexico City:
Sociedad Mexicana de Antropología.

1976d   Notas sobre orejeras de cerámica. Comunicaciones 13:41–48. Puebla: Fundación
Alemana para la Investigación Científica.

1976e   El proyecto arqueológico Puebla-Tlaxcala:
Orígen, finalidad y logros. In El proyecto
arqueológico Puebla-Tlaxcala, coordinated
by Angel García Cook, vol. 1. Suplemento,
Comunicaciones 3:5–12. Puebla: Fundación Alemana para la Investigación
Científica.

1978   Tlaxcala: Poblamiento prehispánico. Comunicaciones 15:173–187. Puebla: Fundación Alemana para la Investigación
Científica.

GARCÍA COOK, ANGEL, MARTHA ARIAS M. G.,
AND RAFAEL ABASCAL M.
1976   Una tumba de la fase Tenanyecac en Tlaxcala, Mexico. In El proyecto arqueológico
Puebla-Tlaxcala, coordinated by Angel
García Cook, vol. 1. Suplemento, Comunicaciones 3:13–27. Puebla: Fundación Alemana para la Investigación Científica.

GARCÍA COOK, ANGEL, AND B. LEONOR MERINO
C.
1974   Malacates de Tlaxcala: Intento de una secuencia evolutiva. Comunicaciones 11:
27–36. Puebla: Fundación Alemana para la
Investigación Científica.

1976   Los tipos de asentamientos prehispánicos
en Tlaxcala. Paper presented at 42nd International Congress of Americanists, Paris,
1976.

1977   Notas sobre caminos y rutas de intercambio
al este de la Cuenca de México. Comunicaciones 19:71–82. Puebla: Fundación Alemana para la Investigación Científica.

1979   Grupos huaxtecos en el norte de Tlaxcala.
Comunicaciones 17:57–64. Puebla: Fun-
dación Alemana para la Investigación
Científica.

GARCÍA COOK, ANGEL, AND RAZIEL MORA
LÓPEZ
1974   Tetepetla: Un sitio fortificado del "Clásico"

en Tlaxcala. Comunicaciones 10:23–30.
Puebla: Fundación Alemana para la Investigación Científica.

GARCÍA COOK, ANGEL, AND FELIPE RODRÍGUEZ
1975   Excavaciones arqueológicas en "Gualupita
las Dalias," Puebla. Comunicaciones 12:
1–8. Puebla: Fundación Alemana para la
Investigación Científica.

GARCÍA COOK, ANGEL, AND ELIA DEL CARMEN
TREJO
1977   Lo teotihuacano en Tlaxcala. Comunicaciones 14:57–70. Puebla: Fundación Alemana para la Investigación Científica.

GARCÍA MOLL, ROBERTO
1976   El Monumento 13 de Tlalancaleca, Puebla.
Boletín del Instituto Nacional de Antropología e Historia, Epoca II, 17:47–50. Mexico City.

1977   Análisis de materiales arqueológicos,
Cueva de Texcal, Puebla. Colección Científica, Departamento de Prehistoria, 56.
Mexico City: Instituto Nacional de Antropología e Historia.

GARCÍA PAYÓN, JOSÉ
1965   (ed.) Descripción del pueblo de Gueytlal-
pan (Zacatlan, Juxupango, Matlatlan, y
Chila, Papantla) por el Alcalde Mayor Juan
de Carrión, 30 de Mayo de 1581. Jalapa:
Universidad Veracruzana.

1966   Prehistoria de Mesoamérica: Excavaciones
en Trapiche y Chalahuite, Veracruz, Mexico, 1942, 1951, y 1959. Jalapa: Universidad Veracruzana.

1971   Archaeology of Central Veracruz. In Handbook of Middle American Indians, vol. 11,
edited by Robert Wauchope, Gordon F.
Ekholm, and Ignacio Bernal, pp. 505–542.
Austin: University of Texas Press.

GAXIOLA GONZÁLEZ, MARGARITA
1976   Excavaciones en San Martín Huamelulpan:
Un sitio de la Mixteca Alta, Oaxaca, Mexico, 1974. Tesis profesional, Escuela Nacional de Antropología e Historia, Mexico
City.

GAY, CARLO T. E.
1972a   Chalcacingo. Portland: International
Scholarly Book Services. (Originally, Graz:
Akademische Druck, 1971.)

1972b   Xochipala: The Beginnings of Olmec Art.
Princeton: Princeton University Press.

GEERTZ, CLIFFORD
1957   Ethos, World-View and the Analysis of Sacred Symbols. Antioch Review 17:421–
437.

419

1963 *Agricultural Involution: The Process of Ecological Change in Indonesia.* Berkeley: University of California Press.

1964 Ideology as a Cultural System. In *Ideology and Discontent*, edited by David E. Apter, pp. 47–76. Glencoe, Ill.: Free Press.

1966 Religion as a Cultural System. In *Anthropological Approaches to the Study of Religion*, edited by Michael Banton. Association of Social Anthropologists, Monograph 3:1–46. New York: Praeger.

GIBSON, CHARLES

1952 *Tlaxcala in the Sixteenth Century.* New Haven: Yale University Press.

1964 *The Aztecs under Spanish Rule.* Stanford: Stanford University Press.

GILBERT, B. MILES

n.d. Faunal Remains in the UMC Tula Archaeological Project Collections. In preparation.

GINSBURG, NORTON

1979 Review of *The City in Late Imperial China*, edited by G. William Skinner. *American Ethnologist* 6:143–148.

GOGGIN, JOHN M., AND WILLIAM C. STURTEVANT

1964 The Calusa: A Stratified, Nonagricultural Society (with Notes on Sibling Marriage). In *Explorations in Cultural Anthropology*, edited by Ward H. Goodenough, pp. 179–219. New York: McGraw-Hill.

GOLDMAN, IRVING

1963 *The Cubeo: Indians of the Northwest Amazon.* Illinois Studies in Anthropology 2. Urbana.

GONZÁLEZ APARICIO, LUIS

1973 *Plano reconstructivo de la Región de Tenochtitlán.* Mexico City: Instituto Nacional de Antropología e Historia.

GOODLIFFE, ELIZABETH AND MICHAEL

1966 Un sitio pleistocénico en Tlapacoya, Estado de Mexico. *Boletín del Instituto Nacional de Antropología e Historia* 23:30–32. Mexico City.

GOODY, JACK

1978 Population and Polity in the Voltaic Region. In *The Evolution of Social Systems*, edited by Jonathan Friedman and M. J. Rowlands, pp. 535–546. Pittsburgh: University of Pittsburgh Press.

GOTTSCHO [SLOAD], REBECCA

1977 Toward More Precise Status Categories at Teotihuacán, Mexico. *Newsletter of Computer Archaeology* 13(1):1–16.

GRAHAM, IAN

1975 *Corpus of Maya Hieroglyphic Inscriptions*, vol. 1, *Introduction to the Corpus.* Cambridge: Peabody Museum, Harvard University.

GREEN, DEE F., AND GARETH W. LOWE

1967 *Altamira and Padre Piedra, Early Preclassic Sites in Chiapas, Mexico.* Papers of the New World Archaeological Foundation No. 20. Provo, Utah.

GREEN, ERNESTENE L.

1970 The Archaeology of Navajuelal, Tikal, Guatemala, and a Test of Interpretive Method. Ph.D. dissertation, Department of Anthropology, University of Pennsylvania. Ann Arbor: University Microfilms (BWH71-19229).

GREENE, VIRGINIA, AND HATTULA MOHOLY-NAGY

1966 A Teotihuacán-Style Vessel from Tikal: A Correction. *American Antiquity* 31:432–434.

GREENGO, ROBERT E., AND CLEMENT W. MEIGHAN

1976 Additional Perspective on the Capacha Complex of Western Mexico. *Journal of New World Archaeology* 1(5):15–23.

GRENNES-RAVITZ, RONALD A., AND G. H. COLEMAN

1976 The Quintessential Role of Olmec in the Central Highlands of Mexico: A Refutation. *American Antiquity* 41:196–206.

GROSS, DANIEL R.

1975 Protein Capture and Cultural Development in the Amazon Basin. *American Anthropologist* 77:526–549.

GROVE, DAVID C.

1968 Chalcatzingo, Morelos, Mexico: A Reappraisal of the Olmec Rock Carvings. *American Antiquity* 33:486–491.

1970 The San Pablo Pantheon Mound: A Middle Preclassic Site in Morelos, Mexico. *American Antiquity* 35:62–73.

1973 Olmec Altars and Myths. *Archaeology* 26:128–135.

1974a The Highland Olmec Manifestation: A Consideration of What It Is and Isn't. In *Mesoamerican Archaeology: New Approaches*, edited by Norman Hammond, pp. 109–128. Austin: University of Texas Press.

1974b *San Pablo, Nexpa, and the Early Formative Archaeology of Morelos, Mexico.*

Vanderbilt University Publications in Anthropology 12. Nashville.

1981 Olmec Monuments: Mutilation as a Clue to Meaning. In *The Olmec and Their Neighbors: Essays in Memory of Matthew W. Stirling*, edited by Elizabeth P. Benson, pp. 49–68. Washington, D.C.: Dumbarton Oaks.

GROVE, DAVID, KENNETH HIRTH, DAVID BUGE, AND ANN CYPHERS

1976 Settlement and Cultural Development at Chalcatzingo. *Science* 192:1203–1210.

GRUHN, RUTH

1978 A Note on Excavations at El Bosque, Nicaragua, in 1975. In *Early Man in America from a Circum-Pacific Perspective*, edited by Alan Lyle Bryan. Occasional Papers of the Department of Anthropology, University of Alberta, 1:261–262. Edmonton: Archaeological Researches International.

GRUHN, RUTH, AND ALAN LYLE BRYAN

1977 Los Tapiales: A Paleo-Indian Campsite in the Guatemalan Highlands. *Proceedings of the American Philosophical Society* 121: 235–273.

GUEVARA, JONATHAN

1975 Presencia de las culturas del occidente de México en la región de Tlaxcala. In *XII Mesa Redonda* 1:137–146. Mexico City: Sociedad Mexicana de Antropología.

GUILLEMIN, GEORGE F.

1967 Tikal: Formación y evolución del centro ceremonial. *Anales de la Sociedad de Geografía e Historia de Guatemala* 40(3,4): 203–224.

1968a Development and Function of the Tikal Ceremonial Center. *Ethnos* 33:1–39.

1968b Un "yugo" de madera para el juego de pelota. *Antropología e Historia de Guatemala* 20:25–33.

1970a Some Aspects of Function and Symbolism at the Ceremonial Centers of Tikal and Copan. In *Verhandlungen des XXXVIII. Internationalen Amerikanistenkongress* (Stuttgart-Munich, 1968) 1:173–174. Munich.

1970b Artefactos de madera en un entierro clásico tardío de Tikal. In *Verhandlungen des XXXVIII. Internationalen Amerikanistenkongress* (Stuttgart-Munich, 1968) 1: 175–178. Munich.

1970c Notas sobre restauración y reconstrucción en los sitios de Tikal e Iximche, Guatemala. In *Verhandlungen des XXXVIII. Internationalen Amerikanistenkongress* (Stuttgart-Munich, 1968) 2:119–123. Munich.

HAGGETT, PETER

1966 *Locational Analysis in Human Geography.* New York: St. Martin's Press.

HAGGETT, PETER, ANDREW CLIFF, AND ALLAN FREY

1977 *Locational Analysis in Human Geography.* 2d ed. London: Edward Arnold.

HALL [MILLON], CLARA

1962 A Chronological Study of the Mural Art of Teotihuacán. Ph.D. dissertation, Department of Anthropology, University of California, Berkeley. Ann Arbor: University Microfilms.

HALLINAN, P. S., R. D. AMBRO, AND J. F. O'CONNELL

1968 La Venta Ceramics, 1968. *Contributions of the University of California Archaeological Research Facility* 5:155–170. Berkeley.

HAMMOND, NORMAN

1972 Locational Models and the Site of Lubaantún: A Classic Maya Centre. In *Models in Archaeology*, edited by David L. Clarke, pp. 757–800. London: Methuen.

1974 The Distribution of Late Classic Maya Major Ceremonial Centres in the Central Area. In *Mesoamerican Archaeology: New Approaches*, edited by Norman Hammond, pp. 313–334. Austin: University of Texas Press.

1977 The Early Formative in the Maya Lowlands. In *Social Process in Maya Prehistory: Studies in Honour of Sir Eric Thompson*, edited by Norman Hammond, pp. 77–101. London: Academic Press.

1978 Cacao and Cobaneros: An Overland Trade Route between the Maya Highlands and Lowlands. In *Mesoamerican Communication Routes and Cultural Contacts*, edited by Thomas A. Lee, Jr., and Carlos Navarrete. Papers of the New World Archaeological Foundation No. 40:19–25. Provo, Utah.

HAMMOND, NORMAN, DUNCAN PRING, RAINER BERGER, V. R. SWITSUR, AND A. P. WARD

1976 Radiocarbon Chronology for Early Maya Occupation at Cuello, Belize. *Nature* 260:579–581.

HAMMOND, NORMAN, DUNCAN PRING, RICHARD WILK, SARA DONAGHEY, FRANK P. SAUL, ELIZ-

ABETH S. WING, ARLENE V. MILLER, AND LAWRENCE H. FELDMAN
1979 The Earliest Lowland Maya: Definition of the Swasey Phase. *American Antiquity* 44:92–110.

HARDOY, JORGE E.
1973 *Pre-Columbian Cities*. Translated by Judith Thorne. New York: Walker.

HARLESTON, HUGH, JR.
1974 *A Mathematical Analysis of Teotihuacán*. Paper presented at the 41st International Congress of Americanists, Mexico. Mexico City: privately published.

HARRIS, DAVID R.
1972 The Origins of Agriculture in the Tropics. *American Scientist* 60:180–193.

1977 Alternative Pathways toward Agriculture. In *Origins of Agriculture*, edited by Charles A. Reed, pp. 179–243. The Hague: Mouton.

1978 Settling Down: An Evolutional Model for the Transformation of Mobile Bands into Sedentary Communities. In *The Evolution of Social Systems*, edited by Jonathan Friedman and M. J. Rowlands, pp. 401–417. Pittsburgh: University of Pittsburgh Press.

HARRISON, PETER D.
1963 A Jade Pendant from Tikal. *Expedition* 5(2):12–13.

1970a The Central Acropolis, Tikal, Guatemala: A Preliminary Study of the Functions of Its Structural Components during the Late Classic Period. Ph.D. dissertation, Department of Anthropology, University of Pennsylvania. Ann Arbor: University Microfilms (BWH71-19235).

1970b Form and Function in a Maya "Palace" Group. In *Verhandlungen des XXXVIII. Internationalen Amerikanistenkongress* (Stuttgart-Munich, 1968) 1:165–172. Munich.

HARRISON, PETER D., AND B. L. TURNER II
1978 (eds.) *Pre-Hispanic Maya Agriculture*. Albuquerque: University of New Mexico Press.

HARTUNG, HORST
1970 *Notes on the Oaxaca Tablero*. Boletín de Estudios Oaxaqueños 27. Mitla, Oaxaca.

HAVILAND, WILLIAM A.
1962 A "Miniature Stela" from Tikal. *Expedition* 4(3):2–3.

1963 Excavation of Small Structures in the Northeast Quadrant of Tikal, Guatemala. Ph.D. dissertation, Department of Anthropology, University of Pennsylvania. Ann Arbor: University Microfilms (BWH63-07050).

1965 Prehistoric Settlement at Tikal, Guatemala. *Expedition* 7(3):14–23.

1966a Maya Settlement Patterns: A Critical Review. In *Archaeological Studies in Middle America*. Middle American Research Institute, Tulane University, Pub. 26:21–47. New Orleans.

1966b Social Integration and the Classic Maya. *American Antiquity* 31:625–631.

1967 Stature at Tikal, Guatemala: Implications for Ancient Maya Demography and Social Organization. *American Antiquity* 32:316–325.

1969 A New Population Estimate for Tikal, Guatemala. *American Antiquity* 34:429–433.

1970 Tikal, Guatemala, and Mesoamerican Urbanism. *World Archaeology* 2:186–198.

1972a Family Size, Prehistoric Population Estimates, and the Ancient Maya. *American Antiquity* 37:135–139.

1972b Estimates of Maya Population: Comments on Thompson's Comments. *American Antiquity* 37:261–262.

1972c A New Look at Classic Maya Social Organization at Tikal. *Cerámica de Cultura Maya* 8:1–16.

1974 Occupational Specialization at Tikal, Guatemala: Stoneworking–Monument Carving. *American Antiquity* 39:494–496.

1975 Tikal Report No. 22: Excavations in Residential Areas of Tikal: Group 7E-1, an Elite Residential Group. MS, University Museum, University of Pennsylvania, Philadelphia.

1977 Dynastic Genealogies from Tikal, Guatemala: Implications for Descent and Political Organization. *American Antiquity* 42:61–67.

1978 On Price's Presentation of Data from Tikal. *Current Anthropology* 19:180–181.

1981 Dower Houses and Minor Centers at Tikal, Guatemala: An Investigation into the Identification of Valid Units in Settlement Hierarchies. In *Lowland Maya Settlement Patterns*, edited by Wendy Ashmore. Albuquerque: University of New Mexico Press.

HAVILAND, WILLIAM A., D. E. PULESTON, R. E. FRY, AND E. GREEN
1967   The Tikal Sustaining Area: Preliminary Report on the 1967 Season. MS, University Museum, University of Pennsylvania, Philadelphia.

HAYNES, C. VANCE, JR.
1967   Muestras de C14, de Tlapacoya, Estado de México. *Boletín del Instituto Nacional de Antropología e Historia* 29:49–52. Mexico City.
1969   The Earliest Americans. *Science* 166:709–715.
1974   Paleoenvironments and Cultural Diversity in Late Pleistocene South America: A Reply to A. L. Bryan. *Quaternary Research* 4:378–382.

HEALAN, DAN M.
1974a   Residential Architecture and Household Patterning in Ancient Tula. Ph.D. dissertation, Department of Anthropology, University of Missouri, Columbia. Ann Arbor: University Microfilms (BWH75-05750).
1974b   Residential Architecture at Tula. In *Studies of Ancient Tollan: A Report of the University of Missouri Tula Archaeological Project*, edited by Richard A. Diehl. University of Missouri Monographs in Anthropology 1:16–24. Columbia.
1977   Architectural Implications of Daily Life in Ancient Tollán, Hidalgo, Mexico. *World Archaeology* 9:140–156.
1979   Functional, Technological, and Developmental Aspects of Obsidian Workshop Production at Tula, Mexico. Research proposal submitted to the National Science Foundation.

HEIZER, ROBERT F., AND JAMES A. BENNYHOFF
1972   Archaeological Investigations at Cuicuilco, Mexico, 1957. In *National Geographic Society Research Reports: 1955–1960 Projects*, pp. 93–104.

HELLMUTH, NICHOLAS
1975   *The Escuintla Hoards: Teotihuacán Art in Guatemala*. Progress Reports, Foundation for Latin American Anthropological Research 1(2). Guatemala.
1978   Teotihuacan Art in the Escuintla, Guatemala Region. In *Middle Classic Mesoamerica: A.D. 400–700*, edited by Esther Pasztory, pp. 71–85. New York: Columbia University Press.

HERRERA Y TORDESILLAS, ANTONIO DE
1944   *Historia general de los hechos de los castellanos en las islas y tierra-firme de el Mar Océano*, vol. 1. Asunción, Paraguay: Editorial Guaranía. (First published by Imprenta Real, Madrid, 1601.)

HESTER, THOMAS R., ROBERT N. JACK, AND ALICE BENFER
1973   Trace Element Analyses of Obsidian from Michoacan, Mexico: Preliminary Results. *Contributions of the University of California Archaeological Research Facility* 18:167–176. Berkeley.

HEYDEN, DORIS
1973   ¿Un Chicomostoc en Teotihuacán? La cueva bajo la Pirámide del Sol. *Boletín del Instituto Nacional de Antropología e Historia*, Epoca II, 6:3–18. Mexico City.
1975   An Interpretation of the Cave underneath the Pyramid of the Sun in Teotihuacán, Mexico. *American Antiquity* 40:131–147.

HIRTH, KENNETH G.
1974   Precolumbian Population Development along the Rio Amatzinac: The Formative through Classic Periods in Eastern Morelos, Mexico. Ph.D. dissertation, Department of Anthropology, University of Wisconsin, Milwaukee. Ann Arbor: University Microfilms (BWH75-17808).
1977   Toltec-Mazapan Influence in Eastern Morelos, Mexico. *Journal of New World Archaeology* 2(1):40–46.
1978a   Interregional Trade and the Formation of Prehistoric Gateway Communities. *American Antiquity* 43:35–45.
1978b   Teotihuacán Regional Population Administration in Eastern Morelos. *World Archaeology* 9:320–333.

HIRTH, KENNETH G., AND WILLIAM SWEZEY
1976   The Changing Nature of the Teotihuacán Classic: A Regional Perspective from Manzanilla, Puebla. In *Las fronteras de Mesoamérica: XIV Mesa Redonda* 2:11–23. Mexico City: Sociedad Mexicana de Antropología.

HODDER, IAN, AND CLIVE ORTON
1976   *Spatial Analysis in Archaeology*. Cambridge: Cambridge University Press.

HOLE, FRANK
n.d.   The Chipped Stone Artifacts. *In* Guilá Naquitz Cave: A Study of Hunting, Gathering, and Incipient Agriculture in Pre-

ceramic Oaxaca, Mexico, edited by Kent V. Flannery. In preparation.

HOLIEN, THOMAS, AND ROBERT B. PICKERING
1978    Analogues in Classic Period Chalchihuites Culture to Late Mesoamerican Ceremonialism. In *Middle Classic Mesoamerica: A.D. 400–700*, edited by Esther Pasztory, pp. 145–157. New York: Columbia University Press.

HOLLAND, JOHN H.
1975    *Adaptation in Natural and Artificial Systems: An Introductory Analysis with Applications to Biology, Control, and Artificial Intelligence.* Ann Arbor: University of Michigan Press.

HOUSTON, MARGARET, AND JUDITH CARSON WAINER
1971    *Pottery-Making Tools from the Valley and Coast of Oaxaca.* Boletín de Estudios Oaxaqueños 36. Mitla, Oaxaca.

HUNT, EVA
1972    Irrigation and the Socio-Political Organization of Cuicatec Cacicazgos. In *The Prehistory of the Tehuacan Valley*, vol. 4, *Chronology and Irrigation*, edited by Frederick Johnson, pp. 162–259. General Editor: Richard S. MacNeish. Austin: University of Texas Press.

IRWIN, CYNTHIA, AND JUAN ARMENTA CAMACHO
1963    Explorations and Excavations near Valsequillo, Mexico. *American Philosophical Society Yearbook 1963*, pp. 550–553.

IRWIN-WILLIAMS, CYNTHIA
1967a   Associations of Early Man with Horse, Camel, and Mastodon at Hueyatlaco, Valsequillo (Puebla, Mexico). In *Pleistocene Extinctions: The Search for a Cause*, edited by Paul S. Martin and Henry E. Wright, pp. 337–347. New Haven: Yale University Press.

1967b   *Comments on Allegations by J. L. Lorenzo Concerning Archaeological Research at Valsequillo, Puebla.* Miscellaneous Publications, PaleoIndian Institute, Eastern New Mexico University. Portales, N.M.

1968    Archaeological Evidence on Early Man in Mexico. *Eastern New Mexico University, Contributions in Anthropology* 1(4):39–41. Portales, N.M.

1969    Comments on the Associations of Archaeological Materials and Extinct Fauna in the Valsequillo Region, Puebla, Mexico. *American Antiquity* 34:82–83.

1978    Summary of Archaeological Evidence from the Valsequillo Region, Puebla, Mexico. In *Cultural Continuity in Mesoamerica*, edited by David Browman, pp. 7–22. The Hague: Mouton.

JEFFERSON, MARK
1939    The Law of the Primate City. *Geographical Review* 29(2):226–232.

JIMÉNEZ MORENO, WIGBERTO
1941    Tula y los toltecas según las fuentes históricas. *Revista Mexicana de Estudios Antropológicos* 5:79–83.

1966    Los imperios prehispánicos de Mesoamérica. *Revista Mexicana de Estudios Antropológicos* 20:179–195.

1974    Los portadores de la cultura teotihuacana. *Historia Mexicana* 24(1):1–12. Mexico City: El Colegio de México.

JOCHIM, MICHAEL A.
1976    *Hunter-gatherer Subsistence and Settlement: A Predictive Model.* New York: Academic Press.

JOESINK-MANDEVILLE, LeROY V.
1970    The Comparative Cultural Stratigraphy of Formative Complexes in the Maya Area: A Reappraisal in Light of New Evidence from Dzibilchaltun, Yucatan. Ph.D. dissertation, Department of Anthropology, Tulane University. Ann Arbor: University Microfilms (BWH71-8058).

JOESINK-MANDEVILLE, LeROY V., AND SYLVIA MELUZIN
1976    Olmec-Maya Relationships: Olmec Influence in Yucatan. In *Origins of Religious Art and Iconography in Preclassic Mesoamerica*, edited by H. B. Nicholson. UCLA Latin American Studies Series 31:87–105. UCLA Latin American Center and the Ethnic Arts Council of Los Angeles.

JOHNSON, FREDERICK
1972    (ed.) *The Prehistory of the Tehuacan Valley*, vol. 4, *Chronology and Irrigation*. General Editor, Richard S. MacNeish. Austin: University of Texas Press.

JOHNSON, FREDERICK, AND RICHARD S. MACNEISH
1972    Chronometric Dating. In *The Prehistory of the Tehuacan Valley*, vol. 4, *Chronology and Irrigation*, edited by Frederick Johnson, pp. 3–55. General Editor: Richard S. MacNeish. Austin: University of Texas Press.

424

JOHNSON, GREGORY A.

1973 *Local Exchange and Early State Development in Southwestern Iran*. Anthropological Papers, Museum of Anthropology, University of Michigan 51. Ann Arbor.

1977 Aspects of Regional Analysis in Archaeology. *Annual Review of Anthropology* 6: 479–508.

JONES, CHRISTOPHER

1969 The Twin-Pyramid Group Pattern: A Classic Maya Architectural Assemblage at Tikal, Guatemala. Ph.D. dissertation, Department of Anthropology, University of Pennsylvania. Ann Arbor: University Microfilms (BWH69-21375).

1977 Inauguration Dates of Three Late Classic Rulers of Tikal, Guatemala. *American Antiquity* 42:28–60.

in press Tikal as a Trading Center: Why It Rose and Fell. In *Acts of the 43rd International Congress of Americanists* (Vancouver, 1979).

JONES, CHRISTOPHER, WENDY ASHMORE, AND ROBERT J. SHARER

in press The Quirigua Project: 1977 Report. In *Quirigua Reports*, vol. 2. Museum Monographs, The University Museum. Philadelphia: University of Pennsylvania.

JORALEMON, P. DAVID

1971 *A Study of Olmec Iconography*. Studies in Pre-Columbian Art and Archaeology 7. Washington, D.C.: Dumbarton Oaks.

1976 The Olmec Dragon: A Study in Pre-Columbian Iconography. In *Origins of Religious Art and Iconography in Preclassic Mesoamerica*, edited by H. B. Nicholson. UCLA Latin American Studies Series 31:27–71. UCLA Latin American Center and the Ethnic Arts Council of Los Angeles.

KAMPEN, MICHAEL E.

1972 *The Sculptures of El Tajín, Veracruz, Mexico*. Gainesville: University of Florida Press.

KAPLAN, LAWRENCE

1967 Archaeological Phaseolus from Tehuacan. In *The Prehistory of the Tehuacan Valley*, vol. 1, *Environment and Subsistence*, edited by Douglas S. Byers, pp. 201–211. Austin: University of Texas Press.

KELLEY, J. CHARLES

1971 Archaeology of the Northern Frontier: Zacatecas and Durango. In *Handbook of Middle American Indians*, vol. 11, edited by Robert Wauchope, Gordon F. Ekholm, and Ignacio Bernal, pp. 768–801. Austin: University of Texas Press.

KELLOGG, SUSAN M.

1979 Social Organization in Early Colonial Tenochtitlán-Tlatelolco: An Ethnohistorical Study. Ph.D. dissertation, Department of Anthropology, University of Rochester. Ann Arbor: University Microfilms.

KELLY, ISABEL

1970 Vasijas de Colima con boca de estribo. *Boletín del Instituto Nacional de Antropología e Historia* 42:26–31. Mexico City.

1974 Stirrup Pots from Colima: Some Implications. In *The Archaeology of West Mexico*, edited by Betty Bell, pp. 206–211. Ajijic, Jalisco: West Mexican Society for Advanced Study.

KIDDER, ALFRED V., JESSE JENNINGS, AND EDWIN M. SHOOK

1946 *Excavations at Kaminaljuyu, Guatemala*. Carnegie Institute of Washington Pub. 561. Washington, D.C.

KIRCHHOFF, PAUL

1943 Mesoamerica. *Acta Americana* 1:92–107.

KIRKBY, ANNE V. T.

1973 *The Use of Land and Water Resources in the Past and Present Valley of Oaxaca, Mexico*. Vol. 1 of *Prehistory and Human Ecology of the Valley of Oaxaca*, edited by Kent V. Flannery. Memoirs of the Museum of Anthropology, University of Michigan, 5. Ann Arbor.

KOVAR, ANTON J.

1966 Problems in Radiocarbon Dating at Teotihuacan. *American Antiquity* 31:427–430.

1970 The Physical and Biological Environment of the Basin of Mexico. In *The Teotihuacán Valley Project Final Report*, vol. 1. Occasional Papers in Anthropology, Pennsylvania State University, 3:13–67.

KOWALEWSKI, STEPHEN A.

1976 Prehispanic Settlement Patterns of the Central Part of the Valley of Oaxaca, Mexico. Ph.D. dissertation, Department of Anthropology, University of Arizona. Ann Arbor: University Microfilms (BWH77-07333).

1980 Population-Resource Balances in Period I of the Valley of Oaxaca, Mexico. *American Antiquity* 45:151–165.

n.d. Population and Agricultural Potential: Early

I through V. *In* Monte Albán's Hinterland, Part 1: The Prehispanic Settlement Patterns of the Central and Southern Parts of the Valley of Oaxaca, Mexico, edited by Richard E. Blanton, Stephen A. Kowalewski, Gary Feinman, and Jill Appel. In preparation.

KOWALEWSKI, STEPHEN A., AND MARCIA TRUELL

1970 *"Tlaloc" in the Valley of Oaxaca.* Boletín de Estudios Oaxaqueños 31. Mitla, Oaxaca.

KRIEGER, ALEX D.

1964 Early Man in the New World. In *Prehistoric Man in the New World*, edited by Jesse D. Jennings and Edward Norbeck, pp. 23–81. Chicago: University of Chicago Press.

KROTSER, PAULA H.

1976a The Ceramic Industry at Teotihuacan. Paper presented at the 41st annual meeting of the Society for American Archaeology, St. Louis.

1976b The Potters of Teotihuacán. Paper presented at the 41st annual meeting of the Society for American Archaeology, St. Louis.

1979 Production and Distribution of San Martín Orange Ware: An Example of Prehistoric Specialization. Paper presented at the 44th annual meeting of the Society for American Archaeology, Vancouver.

KUBLER, GEORGE

1962 *The Art and Architecture of Ancient America: The Mexican, Maya, and Andean Peoples.* Baltimore: Penguin.

1967 *The Iconography of the Art of Teotihuacán.* Studies in Pre-Columbian Art and Archaeology No. 4. Washington, D.C.: Dumbarton Oaks.

1973 Iconographic Aspects of Architectural Profiles at Teotihuacan and in Mesoamerica. In *The Iconography of Middle American Sculpture*, pp. 24–39. New York: Metropolitan Museum of Art.

1978 Review of *Urbanization at Teotihuacán, Mexico*, vol. 1, by René Millon, R. Bruce Drewitt, and George L. Cowgill. *Journal of the Society of Architectural Historians* 37:58–59.

KURJACK, EDWARD B.

1974 *Prehistoric Lowland Maya Community and Social Organization: A Case Study at Dzibilchaltun, Yucatan, Mexico.* Middle American Research Institute, Tulane University, Pub. 38. New Orleans.

1978 The Distribution of Vaulted Architecture at Dzibilchaltun, Yucatan, Mexico. *Estudios de Cultura Maya* 10:91–101.

1979 *Introduction to the Map of the Ruins of Dzibilchaltun, Yucatan, Mexico.* Middle American Research Institute, Tulane University, Pub. 47. New Orleans.

KURJACK, EDWARD B., AND E. WYLLYS ANDREWS V

1976 Early Boundary Maintenance in Northwest Yucatan, Mexico. *American Antiquity* 41:318–325.

KURJACK, EDWARD B., AND SILVIA GARZA T.

1981 Pre-Columbian Community Form and Distribution in the Northern Maya Area. In *Lowland Maya Settlement Patterns*, edited by Wendy Ashmore. Albuquerque: University of New Mexico Press.

LATHRAP, DONALD W.

1977 Our Father the Cayman, Our Mother the Gourd: Spinden Revisited, or a Unitary Model for the Emergence of Agriculture in the New World. In *Origins of Agriculture*, edited by Charles A. Reed, pp. 713–751. The Hague: Mouton.

LEE, RICHARD B.

1972a Population Growth and the Beginnings of Sedentary Life among the !Kung Bushmen. In *Population Growth: Anthropological Implications*, edited by Brian Spooner, pp. 329–343. Cambridge: MIT Press.

1972b The Intensification of Social Life among the !Kung Bushmen. In *Population Growth: Anthropological Implications*, edited by Brian Spooner, pp. 343–350. Cambridge: MIT Press.

LEE, THOMAS A., JR.

1978 Introduction. In *Mesoamerican Communication Routes and Cultural Contacts*, edited by Thomas A. Lee, Jr., and Carlos Navarrete. Papers of the New World Archaeological Foundation No. 40:1–4. Provo, Utah.

LEE, THOMAS A., JR., AND CARLOS NAVARRETE

1978 (eds.) *Mesoamerican Communication Routes and Cultural Contacts.* Papers of the New World Archaeological Foundation No. 40. Provo, Utah.

LEES, SUSAN H.

1973 *Sociopolitical Aspects of Canal Irrigation*

*in the Valley of Oaxaca, Mexico*. Vol. 2 of *Prehistory and Human Ecology of the Valley of Oaxaca*, edited by Kent V. Flannery. Memoirs of the Museum of Anthropology, University of Michigan 6. Ann Arbor.

LEONE, M. P.

1971 Late Classic Burial Ceramics from Tikal, Guatemala. Master's thesis, University of Arizona.

LINNÉ, SIGVALD

1934 *Archaeological Researches at Teotihuacán, Mexico*. Ethnographic Museum of Sweden, n.s., Pub. 1. Stockholm.

1942 *Mexican Highland Cultures: Archaeological Researches at Teotihuacán, Calpulalpan, and Chalchicomula in 1934–35*. Ethnographic Museum of Sweden, n.s., Pub. 7. Stockholm.

LITTMANN, EDWIN R.

1973 The Physical Aspects of Some Teotihuacán Murals. In *The Mural Painting of Teotihuacán*, by Arthur G. Miller, Appendix 2, pp. 175–189. Washington, D.C.: Dumbarton Oaks.

LITVAK KING, JAIME

1970 Xochicalco en la caída del clásico: Una hipótesis. *Anales de Antropología, Instituto de Investigaciones Históricas*, 7: 131–144. Mexico City: Universidad Nacional Autónoma de México.

1972 Las relaciones externas de Xochicalco: Una evaluación de su posible significado. *Anales de Antropología, Instituto de Investigaciones Históricas*, 9:53–76. Mexico City: Universidad Nacional Autónoma de México.

1973 Los patrones de cambio de estadío en el Valle de Xochicalco. *Anales de Antropología, Instituto de Investigaciones Históricas*, 10:93–110. Mexico City: Universidad Nacional Autónoma de México.

1974 Algunas observaciones acerca del clásico de Xochicalco, México. *Anales de Antropología, Instituto de Investigaciones Históricas*, 11:9–17. Mexico City: Universidad Nacional Autónoma de México.

1975 En torno al problema de la definición de Mesoamérica. *Anales de Antropología* 12: 171–195.

1978 Central Mexico as a Part of the General Mesoamerican Communications System. In *Mesoamerican Communication Routes and Cultural Contacts*, edited by Thomas

A. Lee, Jr., and Carlos Navarrete. Papers of the New World Archaeological Foundation No. 40:115–122. Provo, Utah.

LOGAN, MICHAEL H., AND WILLIAM T. SANDERS

1976 The Model. In *The Valley of Mexico: Studies in Pre-Hispanic Ecology and Society*, edited by Eric R. Wolf, pp. 31–58. Albuquerque: University of New Mexico Press.

LOMBARDO DE RUIZ, SONIA

1973 *Desarrollo urbano de México-Tenochtitlán según las fuentes históricas*. Mexico City: Instituto Nacional de Antropología e Historia.

LORENZO, JOSÉ LUIS

1958 *Un sitio precerámico en Yanhuitlán, Oaxaca*. Dirección de Prehistoria, Pub. 6. Mexico City: Instituto Nacional de Antropología e Historia.

1960 Aspectos físicos del Valle de Oaxaca. *Revista Mexicana de Estudios Antropológicos* 16:49–63.

1961 Un buril de la cultura precerámica de Teopisca, Chiapas. In *Homenaje a Pablo Martínez del Río*, edited by Ignacio Bernal et al., pp. 75–90. Mexico City: Instituto Nacional de Antropología e Historia.

1964 Dos puntos acanaladas en la región de Chapala, México. *Boletín del Instituto Nacional de Antropología e Historia* 18:1–6. Mexico City.

1967 *La etapa lítica en Mexico*. Departamento de Prehistoria, Pub. 20. Mexico City: Instituto Nacional de Antropología e Historia.

1968a (ed.) *Materiales para la arqueología de Teotihuacán*. Serie Investigaciones, Instituto Nacional de Antropología e Historia, 17. Mexico City.

1968b Clima y agricultura en Teotihuacán. In *Materiales para la arqueología de Teotihuacán*, edited by José Luis Lorenzo. Serie Investigaciones, Instituto Nacional de Antropología e Historia, 17:51–72. Mexico City.

1969 Sobre métodos arqueológicos. *Boletín del Instituto Nacional de Antropología e Historia* 28:48–51. Mexico City.

1975 Los primeros pobladores. In *Del nomadismo a los centros ceremoniales*, coordinated by Román Piña Chan, pp. 15–59. Mexico City: Departamento de Investigaciones Históricas, Instituto Nacional de Antropología e Historia.

LORENZO, JOSÉ LUIS, AND LAURO GONZALES QUINTERO

1970 El más antiguo teosinte. *Boletín del Instituto Nacional de Antropología e Historia* 42:41–43. Mexico City.

LORENZO, JOSÉ LUIS, AND MIGUEL MESSMACHER

1963 Hallazgo de horizontes culturales precerámicos en el Valle de Oaxaca. In *Homenaje a Pedro Bosch-Gimpera*, edited by Santiago Genovés, pp. 289–301. Mexico City: Instituto Nacional de Antropología e Historia and Universidad Nacional Autónoma de México.

LÖSCH, AUGUST

1954 *The Economics of Location*. Translated by William H. Woglom. New Haven: Yale University Press.

LOTEN, H. STANLEY

1970 The Maya Architecture of Tikal, Guatemala: A Preliminary Seriation of Vaulted Building Plans. Ph.D. dissertation, Department of Anthropology, University of Pennsylvania. Ann Arbor: University Microfilms (BWH70-25686).

LOUNSBURY, FLOYD G.

1978 Maya Numeration, Computation, and Calendrical Astronomy. In *Dictionary of Scientific Biography*, vol. 15, Supplement I, Topical Essays, pp. 759–818. New York: Charles Scribner's Sons.

LOWE, GARETH W.

1962 *Mound 5 and Minor Excavations, Chiapa de Corzo, Chiapas, Mexico*. Papers of the New World Archaeological Foundation No. 12. Provo, Utah.

1966 (ed.) Current Research (Tikal). *American Antiquity* 31:460–463.

1967a (ed.) Current Research (Tikal). *American Antiquity* 32:137.

1967b Discussion. In *Altamira and Padre Piedra: Early Preclassic Sites in Chiapas, Mexico*, by Dee F. Green and Gareth W. Lowe. Papers of the New World Archaeological Foundation No. 20:53–79. Provo, Utah.

1968 (ed.) Current Research (Tikal). *American Antiquity* 33:418–420.

1969 (ed.) Current Research (Tikal). *American Antiquity* 34:354.

1971 The Civilizational Consequences of Varying Degrees of Agricultural and Ceramic Dependency within the Basic Ecosystems

of Mesoamerica. In *Observations on the Emergence of Civilization in Mesoamerica*, edited by Robert F. Heizer and John A. Graham. Contributions of the University of California Archaeological Research Facility 11:212–248. Berkeley.

1975 *The Early Preclassic Barra Phase of Altamira, Chiapas*. Papers of the New World Archaeological Foundation No. 38. Provo, Utah.

1977 The Mixe-Zoque as Competing Neighbors of the Early Lowland Maya. In *The Origins of Maya Civilization*, edited by Richard E. W. Adams, pp. 197–248. Albuquerque: University of New Mexico Press.

1978 Eastern Mesoamerica. In *Chronologies in New World Archaeology*, edited by R. E. Taylor and Clement W. Meighan, pp. 331–393. New York: Academic Press.

LOWE, GARETH W., AND PIERRE AGRINIER

1960 *Mound 1, Chiapa de Corzo, Chiapas, Mexico*. Papers of the New World Archaeological Foundation No. 8. Provo, Utah.

LYNCH, THOMAS F.

1974 The Antiquity of Man in South America. *Quaternary Research* 4:356–377.

McBRIDE, HAROLD W.

1969 The Extent of the Chupícuaro Tradition. In *The Natalie Wood Collection of Pre-Columbian Ceramics*, edited by Jay D. Frierman, pp. 33–47. Los Angeles: University of California and the Los Angeles Museum and Laboratories of Ethnic Arts and Technology.

1975 Middle Formative Ceramics from the Cuauhtitlan Region, Valley of Mexico. In *XIII Mesa Redonda* 2:231–238. Mexico City: Sociedad Mexicana de Antropología.

McCLUNG DE TAPIA, EMILY

1974 Pre-Columbian Ethnobotany of Teotihuacán, Mexico: A Summary of Preliminary Findings. MS, Department of Anthropology, Brandeis University.

1977 Recientes estudios paleoetnobotánicos en Teotihuacan, México. *Anales de Antropología, Instituto de Investigaciones Históricas*, 14:49–61. Mexico City: Universidad Nacional Autónoma de México.

1978 Aspectos ecológicos del desarrollo y la decadencia de Teotihuacan. *Anales de Antropología, Instituto de Investigaciones Históricas*, 15:53–65. Mexico City: Universidad Nacional Autónoma de México.

1979 Plants and Subsistence in the Teotihuacán

Valley: A.D. 100–750. Ph.D. dissertation, Department of Anthropology, Brandeis University. Ann Arbor: University Microfilms.

MCDONALD, ANDREW J.

1977 Two Middle Preclassic Engraved Monuments at Tzutzuculi on the Chiapas Coast of Mexico. *American Antiquity* 42:560–566.

MCGIMSEY, CHARLES R., III

1956 Cerro Mangote: A Preceramic Site in Panama. *American Antiquity* 22:151–161.

MACNEISH, RICHARD S.

1954 An Early Archaeological Site near Pánuco, Veracruz. *Transactions of the American Philosophical Society* 44:539–641.

1958 Preliminary Archaeological Investigations in the Sierra de Tamaulipas, Mexico. *Transactions of the American Philosophical Society* 48(6). Philadelphia.

1962 *Second Annual Report of the Tehuacán Archaeological-Botanical Project.* Andover, Mass.: R. S. Peabody Foundation for Archaeology.

1964a Ancient Mesoamerican Civilization. *Science* 143:531–537.

1964b The Food-gathering and Incipient Agriculture Stage of Prehistoric Middle America. In *Handbook of Middle American Indians*, vol. 1, edited by Robert Wauchope and Robert C. West, pp. 413–426. Austin: University of Texas Press.

1967a An Interdisciplinary Approach to an Archaeological Problem. In *The Prehistory of the Tehuacan Valley*, vol. 1, *Environment and Subsistence*, edited by Douglas S. Byers, pp. 14–24. Austin: University of Texas Press.

1967b A Summary of the Subsistence. In *The Prehistory of the Tehuacan Valley*, vol. 1, *Environment and Subsistence*, edited by Douglas S. Byers, pp. 290–309. Austin: University of Texas Press.

1967c Mesoamerican Archaeology. In *Biennial Review of Anthropology, 1967*, edited by Bernard Siegel and Alan Beals, pp. 306–331. Stanford: Stanford University Press.

1971 Speculations about How and Why Food Production and Village Life Developed in the Tehuacan Valley, Mexico. *Archaeology* 24:307–315.

1972 The Evolution of Community Patterns in the Tehuacan Valley of Mexico and Speculations about the Cultural Processes. In *Man, Settlement and Urbanism*, edited by Peter J. Ucko, Ruth Tringham, and G. W. Dimbleby, pp. 23–31. London: Duckworth.

1973 The Scheduling Factor in the Development of Effective Food Production in the Tehuacan Valley. In *Variation in Anthropology: Essays in Honor of John C. McGregor*, edited by Donald W. Lathrap and Jody Douglas, pp. 75–89. Urbana: Illinois Archaeological Survey.

1975 Summary of the Cultural Sequence and Its Implications in the Tehuacan Valley. In *The Prehistory of the Tehuacan Valley*, vol. 5, *Excavations and Reconnaissance*, by Richard S. MacNeish et al., pp. 496–504. General editor: Richard S. MacNeish. Austin: University of Texas Press.

1976 Early Man in the New World. *American Scientist* 64:316–327.

1978 *The Science of Archaeology?* North Scituate, Mass.: Duxbury Press.

MACNEISH, RICHARD S., MELVIN L. FOWLER, ANGEL GARCÍA COOK, FREDERICK A. PETERSON, ANTOINETTE NELKEN-TERNER, AND JAMES A. NEELY

1975 *The Prehistory of the Tehuacan Valley*, vol. 5, *Excavations and Reconnaissance*. General Editor: Richard S. MacNeish. Austin: University of Texas Press.

MACNEISH, RICHARD S., ANTOINETTE NELKEN-TERNER, AND IRMGARD W. JOHNSON

1967 *The Prehistory of the Tehuacan Valley*, vol. 2, *Nonceramic Artifacts*. General Editor, Douglas S. Byers. Austin: University of Texas Press.

MACNEISH, RICHARD S., THOMAS C. PATTERSON, AND DAVID L. BROWMAN

1975 *The Central Peruvian Prehistoric Interaction Sphere*. Papers of the Robert S. Peabody Foundation for Archaeology 7. Andover, Mass.

MACNEISH, RICHARD S., AND FREDERICK A. PETERSON

1962 *The Santa Marta Rock Shelter, Ocozocoautla, Chiapas, Mexico*. Papers of the New World Archaeological Foundation No. 14. Provo, Utah.

MACNEISH, RICHARD S., FREDERICK A. PETERSON, AND KENT V. FLANNERY

1970 *The Prehistory of the Tehuacan Valley*, vol.

3, *Ceramics*. General Editor, Richard S. MacNeish. Austin: University of Texas Press.

MacNeish, Richard S., Frederick A. Peterson, and James A. Neely
1975    The Archaeological Reconnaissance. In *The Prehistory of the Tehuacan Valley*, vol. 5, *Excavations and Reconnaissance*, by Richard S. MacNeish et al., pp. 341–495. General Editor, Richard S. MacNeish. Austin: University of Texas Press.

Malmstrom, Vincent H.
1973    Origin of the Mesoamerican 260-Day Calendar. *Science* 181:939–941.
1978    A Reconstruction of the Chronology of Mesoamerican Calendrical Systems. *Journal of the History of Astronomy* 9(2)(25): 105–116.

Mandeville, Margaret
n.d.    Excavations in the Corral Locality Residential Complex at Tollan. In preparation.

Mangelsdorf, Paul C.
1974    *Corn: Its Origin, Evolution and Improvement*. Cambridge: Harvard University Press.

Mangelsdorf, Paul C., Richard S. MacNeish, and Walton C. Galinat
1967    Prehistoric Wild and Cultivated Maize. In *The Prehistory of the Tehuacan Valley*, vol. 1, *Environment and Subsistence*, edited by Douglas S. Byers, pp. 178–200. Austin: University of Texas Press.

Mangelsdorf, Paul C., Richard S. MacNeish, and Gordon R. Willey
1964    Origins of Agriculture in Middle America. In *Handbook of Middle American Indians*, vol. 1, edited by Robert Wauchope and Robert C. West, pp. 427–445. Austin: University of Texas Press.

Marcus, Joyce
1973    Territorial Organization of the Lowland Classic Maya. *Science* 180:911–916.
1974    The Iconography of Power among the Classic Maya. *World Archaeology* 6(1):83–94.
1976a   *Emblem and State in the Classic Maya Lowlands: An Epigraphic Approach to Territorial Organization*. Washington, D.C.: Dumbarton Oaks.
1976b   The Iconography of Militarism at Monte Albán and Neighboring Sites in the Valley of Oaxaca. In *Origins of Religious Art and Iconography in Preclassic Mesoamerica*, edited by H. B. Nicholson. UCLA Latin American Studies Series 31:123–139. UCLA Latin American Center and the Ethnic Arts Council of Los Angeles.
1976c   The Origins of Mesoamerican Writing. *Annual Review of Anthropology* 5:35–67. Palo Alto.
1976d   The Size of the Early Mesoamerican Village. In *The Early Mesoamerican Village*, edited by Kent V. Flannery, pp. 79–90. New York: Academic Press.
1978    Archaeology and Religion: A Comparison of the Zapotec and Maya. *World Archaeology* 10(2):172–191.
1980    Zapotec Writing. *Scientific American* 242: 50–64.
n.d.    Rethinking the Zapotec Urn. In *The Cloud People: Evolution of the Zapotec and Mixtec Civilizations of Oaxaca, Mexico*, edited by Kent V. Flannery and Joyce Marcus.

Marcus, Joyce, and Ronald Spores
1978    The *Handbook of Middle American Indians*: A Retrospective Look. *American Anthropologist* 80:85–100.

Marquina, Ignacio
1951    *Arquitectura prehispánica*. Memorias del Instituto Nacional de Antropología e Historia 1. Mexico City.
1970a   (coord.) *Proyecto Cholula*. Serie Investigaciones, Instituto Nacional de Antropología e Historia, 19. Mexico City.
1970b   Pirámide de Cholula. In *Proyecto Cholula*, coordinated by Ignacio Marquina. Serie Investigaciones, Instituto Nacional de Antropología e Historia, 19:31–45. Mexico City.

Martin, Paul S.
1973    The Discovery of America. *Science* 179: 969–974.

Mason, Roger D., Dennis E. Lewarch, Michael J. O'Brien, and James A. Neely
1977    An Archaeological Survey on the Xoxocatlan Piedmont, Oaxaca, Mexico. *American Antiquity* 42:567–575.

Mastache de Escobar, Alba Guadalupe
1976    Sistemas de riego en el área de Tula, Hgo. In *Proyecto Tula, segunda parte*, coordinated by Eduardo Matos Moctezuma. Colección Científica, Arqueología, 33:49–70. Mexico City: Instituto Nacional de Antropología e Historia.

Mastache de Escobar, Alba Guadalupe, and Ana María Crespo
1974    La ocupación prehispánica en el área de

Tula, Hgo. In *Proyecto Tula, 1ª parte*, coordinated by Eduardo Matos Moctezuma. Colección Científica, Arqueología, 15: 71–103. Mexico City: Instituto Nacional de Antropología e Historia.

1976 Mazapan Period Occupation of the Tula Region. Paper presented at the 42nd International Congress of Americanists, Paris.

1979 Análisis sobre el trazo general de Tula, Hidalgo. Paper presented at the Simposia sobre Tula, Pachuca, Hidalgo.

MATOS MOCTEZUMA, EDUARDO

1974a (coord.) *Proyecto Tula, 1ª parte*. Colección Científica, Arqueología, 15. Mexico City: Instituto Nacional de Antropología e Historia.

1974b Excavaciones en la microárea: Tula Chico y la Plaza Charnay. In *Proyecto Tula, 1ª parte*, coordinated by Eduardo Matos Moctezuma. Colección Científica, Arqueología, 15:61–69. Mexico City: Instituto Nacional de Antropología e Historia.

1976 (coord.) *Proyecto Tula, segunda parte*. Colección Científica, Arqueología, 33. Mexico City: Instituto Nacional de Antropología e Historia.

MAYER-OAKES, WILLIAM J.

1959 A Stratigraphic Excavation at El Risco, Mexico. *Proceedings of the American Philosophical Society* 103:332–373.

MEDELLÍN ZENIL, ALFONSO

1975 Tribus y aldeas en el centro de Veracruz. In *Del nomadismo a los centros ceremoniales*, coordinated by Román Piña Chan, pp. 87–102. Mexico City: Departamento de Investigaciones Históricas, Instituto Nacional de Antropología e Historia.

MEGGERS, BETTY J.

1971 *Amazonia: Man and Culture in a Counterfeit Paradise*. Chicago: Aldine-Atherton.

MENDIETA, GERÓNIMO DE

1945 *Historia eclesiástica indiana*, vol. 1. Mexico City: Editorial Salvador Chávez Hayhoe. (Reprint of first ed., 1870. MS completed, 1596.)

MERINO C., B. LEONOR

1980 La Cultura Tlaxco: Un aporte sobre los grupos humanos que vivieron en el norte-noreste de Tlaxcala del siglo X a.n.e. al siglo XVI d.n.e. Tesis profesional, Escuela Nacional de Antropología, Mexico City.

MESSER, ELLEN

1978 *Zapotec Plant Knowledge: Classification, Uses, and Communication about Plants in Mitla, Oaxaca, Mexico*. Vol. 5(2) of *Prehistory and Human Ecology of the Valley of Oaxaca*, edited by Kent V. Flannery. Memoirs of the Museum of Anthropology, University of Michigan, 10. Ann Arbor.

MEYERS, J. THOMAS

1971 The Origins of Agriculture: An Evaluation of Three Hypotheses. In *Prehistoric Agriculture*, edited by Stuart Struever, pp. 101–121. Garden City, N.Y.: Natural History Press.

MILLER, ARLENE V.

1976 Arti-fact or Fiction? The Lithic Objects from Richmond Hill, Belize. In *Maya Lithic Studies: Papers from the 1976 Belize Field Symposium*, edited by Thomas R. Hester and Norman Hammond. Special Report, Center for Archaeological Research, University of Texas at San Antonio 4:119–135. San Antonio.

MILLER, ARTHUR G.

1973a Architectural Sculpture at Tikal, Guatemala: The Roof-Comb Sculpture on Temple I and Temple IV. In *Actas del 22nd Congreso Internacional de Historia del Arte* (Granada), pp. 177–183.

1973b *The Mural Painting of Teotihuacán*. Washington, D.C.: Dumbarton Oaks.

1978 A Brief Outline of the Artistic Evidence for Classic Period Cultural Contact between Maya Lowlands and Central Mexican Highlands. In *Middle Classic Mesoamerica: A.D. 400–700*, edited by Esther Pasztory, pp. 63–70. New York: Columbia University Press.

MILLON, CLARA

1972a Commentary about *A Lost Teotihuacán Mural* by Arthur G. Miller. *Boletín Bibliográfico de Antropología Americana* 35(1): 85–89.

1972b The History of Mural Art at Teotihuacan. In *Teotihuacán: XI Mesa Redonda* 2:1–16. Mexico City: Sociedad Mexicana de Antropología.

1973 Painting, Writing, and Polity in Teotihuacán, Mexico. *American Antiquity* 38: 294–314.

1978 Religion and State in Teotihuacán. MS, University of Rochester.

MILLON, RENÉ F.

1955 *When Money Grew on Trees: A Study of Cacao in Ancient Mesoamerica*. Ph.D. dissertation, Department of Anthropology, Columbia University. Ann Arbor: University Microfilms (BWH00-12454).

1957  New Data on Teotihuacán I in Teotihuacán. *Boletín del Centro de Investigaciones Antropológicas de México* 4:12–17.

1960  The Beginnings of Teotihuacán. *American Antiquity* 26:1–10.

1961  The Northwestern Boundary of Teotihuacan: A Major Urban Zone. In *Homenaje a Pablo Martínez del Río*, edited by Ignacio Bernal et al., pp. 311–318. Mexico City: Instituto Nacional de Antropología e Historia.

1964  The Teotihuacán Mapping Project. *American Antiquity* 29:345–352.

1966a  Cronología y periodificación: Datos estratigráficos sobre períodos cerámicos y sus relaciones con la pintura mural. In *Teotihuacán: Onceava Mesa Redonda*, pp. 1–18. Mexico City: Sociedad Mexicana de Antropología.

1966b  Extensión y población de la ciudad de Teotihuacán en sus diferentes períodos: Un cálculo provisional. In *Teotihuacán: Onceava Mesa Redonda* 1:57–78. Mexico City: Sociedad Mexicana de Antropología.

1966c  El problema de integración en la sociedad teotihuacana. In *Teotihuacán: Onceava Mesa Redonda* 1:149–155. Mexico City: Sociedad Mexicana de Antropología.

1967a  Teotihuacán. *Scientific American* 216(6): 38–48.

1967b  Urna de Monte Albán IIIA encontrada en Teotihuacan. *Boletín del Instituto Nacional de Antropología e Historia* 29:42–44. Mexico City.

1968a  Urbanization at Teotihuacán: The Teotihuacán Mapping Project. In *XXXVII Congreso Internacional de Americanistas: Actas y Memorias* (Buenos Aires, 1966) 1:105–120. Buenos Aires.

1968b  Urban Revolution II: Early Civilizations of the New World. *International Encyclopedia of the Social Sciences* 16:207–217.

1970a  Progress Report 10 on Teotihuacán Mapping Project for Departamento de Monumentos Prehispánicos, Instituto Nacional de Antropología e Historia. Department of Anthropology, University of Rochester.

1970b  Teotihuacán: Completion of Map of Giant Ancient City in the Valley of Mexico. *Science* 170:1077–1082.

1973  *Urbanization at Teotihuacán, Mexico*, vol. 1, *The Teotihuacán Map*, part 1, Text. Austin: University of Texas Press.

1974  The Study of Urbanism at Teotihuacan, Mexico. In *Mesoamerican Archaeology: New Approaches*, edited by Norman Hammond, pp. 335–362. Austin: University of Texas Press.

1976  Social Relations in Ancient Teotihuacán. In *The Valley of Mexico: Studies in Pre-Hispanic Ecology and Society*, edited by Eric R. Wolf, pp. 205–248. Albuquerque: University of New Mexico Press.

MILLON, RENÉ F., BRUCE DREWITT, AND JAMES A. BENNYHOFF

1965  The Pyramid of the Sun at Teotihuacán: 1959 Investigations. *Transactions of the American Philosophical Society*, n.s. 55(6). Philadelphia.

MILLON, RENÉ, R. BRUCE DREWITT, AND GEORGE L. COWGILL

1973  *Urbanization at Teotihuacán, Mexico*, vol. 1, *The Teotihuacán Map*, part 2, Maps. Austin: University of Texas Press.

MIRAMBELL, LORENA

1967  Excavaciones en un sitio pleistocénico de Tlapacoya, México. *Boletín del Instituto Nacional de Antropología e Historia* 29:37–41. Mexico City.

1973  El hombre en Tlapacoya desde hace unos 20 mil años. *Boletín del Instituto Nacional de Antropología e Historia*, Epoca II, 4:3–8. Mexico City.

1974  La etapa lítica. In *Historia de México*, vol. 3, coordinated by Miguel León-Portilla, José Luis Lorenzo, and Ignacio Bernal, pp. 55–76. Mexico City: Salvat.

1978  Tlapacoya: A Late Pleistocene Site in Central Mexico. In *Early Man in America from a Circum-Pacific Perspective*, edited by Alan Lyle Bryan. Occasional Papers of the Department of Anthropology, University of Alberta 1:221–230. Edmonton: Archaeological Researches International.

MOHOLY-NAGY, HATTULA

1962  A Tlaloc Stela from Tikal. *Expedition* 4(2):27.

1963a  The Field Laboratory at Tikal. *Expedition* 5(3):12–17.

1963b  Shells and Other Marine Material from Tikal. *Estudios de Cultura Maya* 3:65–83.

1966  Mosaic Figures from Tikal. *Archaeology* 19(2):84–89.

1976 Spatial Distribution of Flint and Obsidian Artifacts at Tikal, Guatemala. In *Maya Lithic Studies: Papers from the 1976 Belize Field Symposium*, edited by Thomas R. Hester and Norman Hammond. Special Report, Center for Archaeological Research, University of Texas at San Antonio 4:91–108. San Antonio.

1978 The Utilization of *Pomacea* Snails at Tikal, Guatemala. *American Antiquity* 43: 65–73.

MORA, RAZIEL, AND A. GARCÍA COOK

1975 Restos precerámicos y acerámicos en el área. In *XIII Mesa Redonda* 1:83–96. Mexico City: Sociedad Mexicana de Antropología.

MORRISON, FRANK, C. W. CLEWLOW, JR., AND ROBERT F. HEIZER

1970 Magnetometer Survey of the La Venta Pyramid. *Contributions of the University of California Archaeological Research Facility* 8:1–20. Berkeley.

MOSELEY, MICHAEL E.

1975 *The Maritime Foundations of Andean Civilization*. Menlo Park, Cal.: Cummings Publishing Co.

MOSER, CHRIS L.

1969 La Tumba 1 del barrio del Rosario, Huitzo, Oaxaca. *Boletín del Instituto Nacional de Antropología e Historia* 36:41–47.

MOUNTJOY, JOSEPH B.

1974 San Blas Complex Ecology. In *The Archaeology of West Mexico*, edited by Betty Bell, pp. 106–119. Ajijic, Jalisco: West Mexican Society for Advanced Study.

MOUNTJOY, JOSEPH B., R. E. TAYLOR, AND LAWRENCE H. FELDMAN

1972 Matanchén Complex: New Radiocarbon Dates on Early Coastal Adaptation in West Mexico. *Science* 175:1242–1243.

MULLER, FLORENCIA

1970 La cerámica de Cholula. In *Proyecto Cholula*, coordinated by Ignacio Marquina. Serie Investigaciones, Instituto Nacional de Antropología e Historia, 19:129–142. Mexico City.

1978 *La cerámica del centro ceremonial de Teotihuacán*. Mexico City: Instituto Nacional de Antropología e Historia.

MUÑOZ CAMARGO, DIEGO

1947 *Historia de Tlaxcala*. 2d ed. Mexico City.

NADER, LAURA

1969 The Zapotec of Oaxaca. In *Handbook of Middle American Indians*, vol. 7, edited by Robert Wauchope and Evon Z. Vogt, pp. 329–359. Austin: University of Texas Press.

NALDA, ENRIQUE, AND ALEJANDRO PASTRANA

1976 Una proposición para la investigación de los "talleres de lítica" en Tula, Hgo. In *Proyecto Tula, segunda parte*, coordinated by Eduardo Matos Moctezuma. Colección Científica, Arqueología, 33:75–83. Mexico City: Instituto Nacional de Antropología e Historia.

NAVARRETE, CARLOS

1974 *The Olmec Rock Carvings at Pijijiapan, Chiapas, Mexico, and Other Olmec Pieces from Chiapas and Guatemala*. Papers of the New World Archaeological Foundation No. 35. Provo, Utah.

NEELY, JAMES A.

1967 Organización hidráulica y sistemas de irrigación prehistóricos en el Valle de Oaxaca. *Boletín del Instituto Nacional de Antropología e Historia* 27:15–17. Mexico City.

NICHOLS, DEBORAH

1975 The Early Postclassic Ceramic Complex from the Xometla Mound Excavation. Master's thesis, Department of Anthropology, Pennsylvania State University.

NICHOLSON, H. B.

1976 Preclassic Mesoamerican Iconography from the Perspective of the Postclassic: Problems in Interpretational Analysis. In *Origins of Religious Art and Iconography in Preclassic Mesoamerica*, edited by H. B. Nicholson. UCLA Latin American Studies Series 31:157–175. UCLA Latin American Center and the Ethnic Arts Council of Los Angeles.

NIEDERBERGER, CHRISTINE

1975 Excavaciones en Zohapilco-Tlapacoya, México. In *Actas del XLI Congreso Internacional de Americanistas* (Mexico City, 1974) 1:403–411. Mexico City.

1976 *Zohapilco: Cinco milenios de ocupación humana en un sitio lacustre de la Cuenca de México*. Colección Científica, Arqueología, 30. Mexico City: Instituto Nacional de Antropología e Historia.

1979 Early Sedentary Economy in the Basin of Mexico. *Science* 203:131–142.

NOGUERA, EDUARDO

1925 La cerámica tlaxcalteca de Tizatlán. *Bole-*

tín, Secretaría de Educación Pública, vol. 4 (June). Mexico City.

1927 Altares de Tizatlán, Tlaxcala. *Boletín, Secretaría de Educación Pública*, 6(3):195–203. Mexico City.

1934 Las pinturas de Tizatlán. *Mapa* 1:7–9. Mexico City: Editorial Mercurio.

1964 El sarcófago de Tlalancaleca. *Cuadernos Americanos* 134:139–148.

NUTTALL, ZELIA

1928 Nouvelles lumières sur les civilisations américaines et le système du calendrier. In *Atti del XXII Congresso Internazionale degli Americanisti* (Rome, 1926) 1:119–148. Rome.

OLIVEROS, JOSÉ ARTURO

1974 Nuevas exploraciones en El Opeño, Michoacán. In *The Archaeology of West Mexico*, edited by Betty Bell, pp. 182–201. Ajijic, Jalisco: West Mexican Society for Advanced Study.

OLSON, G. W.

1969 Descriptions and Data on Soils of Tikal, El Peten, Guatemala, Central America. *Cornell Agronomy News* 69(2). Ithaca, N.Y.

PADDEN, R. C.

1967 *The Hummingbird and the Hawk*. Columbus: Ohio State University Press.

PADDOCK, JOHN

1966 (ed.) *Ancient Oaxaca: Discoveries in Mexican Archaeology and History*. Stanford: Stanford University Press.

1978 The Middle Classic Period in Oaxaca. In *Middle Classic Mesoamerica: A.D. 400–700*, edited by Esther Pasztory, pp. 45–62. New York: Columbia University Press.

n.d. Lambityeco. In *The Cloud People: Evolution of the Zapotec and Mixtec Civilizations of Oaxaca, Mexico*, edited by Kent V. Flannery and Joyce Marcus. Albuquerque: University of New Mexico Press.

PADDOCK, JOHN, JOSEPH R. MOGOR, AND MICHAEL D. LIND

1968 *Lambityeco Tomb 2: A Preliminary Report*. Boletín de Estudios Oaxaqueños 25. Mitla, Oaxaca.

PALACIOS, ENRIQUE

1941 Teotihuacan, los toltecas, y Tula. *Revista Mexicana de Estudios Antropológicos* 5:113–134.

PALERM, ANGEL

1972 Sistemas de regadío prehispánico en Teotihuacán y en el Pedregal de San Angel. In *Agricultura y civilización en Mesoamérica*, edited by Angel Palerm and Eric Wolf. SepSetentas 32:95–108. Mexico City: Secretaría de Educación Pública.

1973 *Obras hidráulicas prehispánicas en el sistema lacustre del Valle de México*. Mexico City: Instituto Nacional de Antropología e Historia.

PALERM, ANGEL, AND ERIC R. WOLF

1957 Ecological Potential and Cultural Development in Mesoamerica. In *Studies in Human Ecology*. Anthropological Society of Washington and Pan American Union Social Science Monograph 3:1–37. Washington, D.C.: Pan American Union.

1961 La agricultura y el desarrollo de la civilización en Mesoamérica. *Revista Internacional de Ciencias Sociales* 1. Washington, D.C.: Organization of American States.

PARSONS, JEFFREY R.

1968 Teotihuacan, Mexico, and Its Impact on Regional Demography. *Science* 162:872–877.

1969 Patrones de asentamiento prehispánico en la región texcocana. *Boletín del Instituto Nacional de Antropología e Historia* 35:31–37. Mexico City.

1971 *Pre-Hispanic Settlement Patterns in the Texcoco Region, Mexico*. Memoirs of the Museum of Anthropology, University of Michigan, 3. Ann Arbor.

1973 Reconocimiento superficial en el sur del Valle de México: Temporada 1972. Mimeographed report to the Instituto Nacional de Antropología e Historia, Mexico City.

1974a The Development of a Prehistoric Complex Society: A Regional Perspective from the Valley of Mexico. *Journal of Field Archaeology* 1:81–108.

1974b Patrones de asentamientos prehispánicos en el noroeste del Valle de México, región de Zumpango. Report to the Instituto Nacional de Antropología e Historia, Mexico City.

1976 Settlement and Population History of the Basin of Mexico. In *The Valley of Mexico: Studies in Pre-Hispanic Ecology and Society*, edited by Eric R. Wolf, pp. 69–100. Albuquerque: University of New Mexico Press.

1977 The Demographic Structure of the Teotihuacán Heartland. Paper presented at the

434

XV Mesa Redonda of the Sociedad Mexicana de Antropología, Guanajuato.

PARSONS, LEE A.
1969    *Bilbao, Guatemala: An Archaeological Study of the Pacific Coast Cotzumalhuapa Region*, vol. 2. Milwaukee Public Museum Publications in Anthropology 42. Milwaukee.
1978    The Peripheral Coastal Lowlands and the Middle Classic Period. In *Middle Classic Mesoamerica: A.D. 400–700*, edited by Esther Pasztory, pp. 25–34. New York: Columbia University Press.

PARSONS, LEE A., AND BARBARA J. PRICE
1971    Mesoamerican Trade and Its Role in the Emergence of Civilization. In *Observations on the Emergence of Civilization in Mesoamerica*, edited by Robert F. Heizer and John A. Graham. Contributions of the University of California Archaeological Research Facility 11:169–195. Berkeley.

PARSONS, MARY H.
1972    Spindle Whorls from the Teotihuacán Valley, Mexico. In *Miscellaneous Studies in Mexican Prehistory*. Anthropological Papers, Museum of Anthropology, University of Michigan, 45:45–80. Ann Arbor.

PASO Y TRONCOSO, FRANCISCO DEL
1905    (ed.) *Papeles de Nueva España, segunda serie: Geografía y estadística*, vol. 4. Madrid: Sucesores de Rivadeneyra.

PASTRANA CRUZ, ALEJANDRO
1977    Producción de instrumentos de obsidiana—División del trabajo (Proyecto Tula). Tesis profesional, Escuela Nacional de Antropología e Historia. Mexico City.

PASZTORY, ESTHER
1973    The Gods of Teotihuacán: A Synthetic Approach in Teotihuacan Iconography. In *Atti del XL Congresso Internazionale degli Americanisti* (Rome and Genoa, 1972) 1:147–159. Genoa.
1974    *The Iconography of the Teotihuacan Tlaloc*. Studies in Pre-Columbian Art and Archaeology 15. Washington, D.C.: Dumbarton Oaks.
1976    *The Murals of Tepantitla, Teotihuacan*. New York: Garland Publishing.
1978a   (ed.) *Middle Classic Mesoamerica: A.D. 400–700*. New York: Columbia University Press.
1978b   Historical Synthesis of the Middle Classic Period. In *Middle Classic Mesoamerica:*

*A.D. 400–700*, edited by Esther Pasztory, pp. 3–22. New York: Columbia University Press.
1978c   Artistic Traditions of the Middle Classic Period. In *Middle Classic Mesoamerica: A.D. 400–700*, edited by Esther Pasztory, pp. 108–142. New York: Columbia University Press.

PATTERSON, THOMAS C.
1971    Central Peru: Its Population and Economy. *Archaeology* 24:316–321.

PAYNE, WILLIAM O.
1970    *A Potter's Analysis of the Pottery from Lambityeco Tomb 2*. Boletín de Estudios Oaxaqueños 29. Mitla, Oaxaca.

PEÑA, AGUSTÍN, AND MARÍA CARMEN RODRÍGUEZ
1976    Excavaciones en Daini, Tula, Hgo. In *Proyecto Tula, segunda parte*, coordinated by Eduardo Matos Moctezuma. Colección Científica, Arqueología, 33:85–90. Mexico City: Instituto Nacional de Antropología e Historia.

PENDERGAST, DAVID M.
1971    Evidence of Early Teotihuacan–Lowland Maya Contact at Altun Ha. *American Antiquity* 36:455–460.

PETERSON, DAVID ANDREW
1976    Ancient Commerce. Ph.D. dissertation, Department of Economics, State University of New York, Binghamton.

PETERSON, FREDERICK A.
1959    *Ancient Mexico: An Introduction to the Pre-Hispanic Cultures*. New York: Putnam.

PICKERSGILL, BARBARA, AND CHARLES B. HEISER, JR.
1977    Origins and Distribution of Plants Domesticated in the New World Tropics. In *Origins of Agriculture*, edited by Charles A. Reed, pp. 803–835. The Hague: Mouton.

PIÑA CHAN, ROMÁN
1955a   *Chalcatzingo, Morelos*. Informes, Dirección de Monumentos Prehispánicos, 4. Mexico City: Instituto Nacional de Antropología e Historia.
1955b   *Las culturas preclásicas de la Cuenca de México*. Mexico City: Fondo de Cultura Económica.
1958a   *Tlatilco I*. Serie Investigaciones, Instituto Nacional de Antropología e Historia, 1. Mexico City.
1958b   *Tlatilco 2*. Serie Investigaciones, Instituto Nacional de Antropología e Historia, 2. Mexico City.

1960 *Mesoamérica: Ensayo histórico cultural*. Memorias del Instituto Nacional de Antropología e Historia 6. Mexico City.

1972 Teotenango prehispánico. *Boletín del Instituto Nacional de Antropología e Historia*, Epoca II, 2:17–20. Mexico City.

1974a Las culturas preclásicas del México antiguo. In *Historia de México* 1:135–184. Mexico City: Salvat.

1974b Teotenango y la región de Toluca. Paper presented at the 41st International Congress of Americanists, Mexico City.

PIRES-FERREIRA, JANE W.

1975 *Formative Mesoamerican Exchange Networks with Special Reference to the Valley of Oaxaca*. Vol. 3 of *Prehistory and Human Ecology of the Valley of Oaxaca*, edited by Kent V. Flannery. Memoirs of the Museum of Anthropology, University of Michigan, No. 7. Ann Arbor.

1976a Obsidian Exchange in Formative Mesoamerica. In *The Early Mesoamerican Village*, edited by Kent V. Flannery, pp. 292–306. New York: Academic Press.

1976b Shell and Iron-Ore Mirror Exchange in Formative Middle America, with Comments on Other Commodities. In *The Early Mesoamerican Village*, edited by Kent V. Flannery, pp. 311–328. New York: Academic Press.

PLOG, STEPHEN

1976 Measurement of Prehistoric Interaction between Communities. In *The Early Mesoamerican Village*, edited by Kent V. Flannery, pp. 255–272. New York: Academic Press.

POLLOCK, H. E. D.

1952 Department of Archaeology. *Carnegie Institution of Washington, Year Book*, 51: 235–243.

PORTER, MURIEL NOÉ

1953 *Tlatilco and the Pre-Classic Cultures of the New World*. Viking Fund Publications in Anthropology 19. New York: Wenner-Gren Foundation.

PRICE, BARBARA J.

1976 A Chronological Framework for Cultural Development in Mesoamerica. In *The Valley of Mexico: Studies in Pre-Hispanic Ecology and Society*, edited by Eric R. Wolf, pp. 13–21. Albuquerque: University of New Mexico Press.

1977 Shifts in Production and Organization: A Cluster-Interaction Model. *Current Anthropology* 18:209–233.

1978 Commerce and Cultural Process in Mesoamerica. In *Mesoamerican Communication Routes and Cultural Contacts*, edited by Thomas A. Lee, Jr., and Carlos Navarrete. Papers of the New World Archaeological Foundation No. 40:231–245. Provo, Utah.

PROSKOURIAKOFF, TATIANA

1960 Historical Implications of a Pattern of Dates at Piedras Negras, Guatemala. *American Antiquity* 25:454–475.

PULESTON, DENNIS E.

1965 The Chultuns of Tikal. *Expedition* 7(3): 24–29.

1968 *Brosimium Alicastrum* as a Subsistence Alternative for Classic Maya of the Central Southern Lowlands. Master's thesis, Department of Anthropology, University of Pennsylvania.

1971 An Experimental Approach to the Function of Classic Maya Chultuns. *American Antiquity* 36:322–335.

1973 Ancient Maya Settlement Patterns and Environment at Tikal, Guatemala: Implications for Subsistence Models. Ph.D. dissertation, Department of Anthropology, University of Pennsylvania. Ann Arbor: University Microfilms (BWH74-14128).

1974 Intersite Areas in the Vicinity of Tikal and Uaxactun. In *Mesoamerican Archaeology: New Approaches*, edited by Norman Hammond, pp. 303–311. Austin: University of Texas Press.

1975 Richmond Hill: A Probable Early Man Site in the Maya Lowlands. In *Actas del XLI Congreso Internacional de Americanistas* (Mexico City, 1974) 1:522–533. Mexico City.

1978 Terracing, Raised Fields, and Tree Cropping in the Maya Lowlands: A New Perspective on the Geography of Power. In *Pre-Hispanic Maya Agriculture*, edited by Peter D. Harrison and B. L. Turner II, pp. 225–245. Albuquerque: University of New Mexico Press.

PULESTON, DENNIS E., AND DONALD W. CALLENDER, JR.

1967 Defensive Earthworks at Tikal. *Expedition* 9(3):40–48.

PULESTON, DENNIS E., AND G. W. OLSON

1970 Examples of Ancient and Modern Use and

Abuse of Soils. In *New York's Food and Life Sciences*, pp. 27–29.

PULESTON, DENNIS E., AND OLGA S. PULESTON
1971 An Ecological Approach to the Origins of Maya Civilization. *Archaeology* 24:330–337.

PULESTON, OLGA S.
1969 Functional Analysis of a Workshop Tool Kit from Tikal. Master's thesis, Department of Anthropology, University of Pennsylvania.

PYKE, G. H., H. R. PULLIAM, AND E. L. CHARNOV
1977 Optimal Foraging: A Selective Review of Theory and Tests. *The Quaternary Review of Biology* 52(2):137–154.

PYNE, NANETTE M.
1976 The Fire-Serpent and Were-Jaguar in Formative Oaxaca: A Contingency Table Analysis. In *The Early Mesoamerican Village*, edited by Kent V. Flannery, pp. 272–282. New York: Academic Press.

QUIRARTE, JACINTO
1973 Izapan and Mayan Traits in Teotihuacán III Pottery. *Contributions of the University of California Archaeological Research Facility* 18:11–29. Berkeley.

RABIN, EMILY
1970 *The Lambityeco Friezes: Notes on Their Content with an Appendix on C14 Dates*. Boletín de Estudios Oaxaqueños 33. Mitla, Oaxaca.

RAINEY, FROELICH G.
1956 The Tikal Project. *University Museum Bulletin* 20(4):2–24. Philadelphia: University of Pennsylvania.
1970 Tikal: A Fourteen Year Program Now Completed. *Expedition* 12(2):2–9.

RALPH, ELIZABETH K.
1965 Review of Radiocarbon Dates from Tikal and the Maya Correlation Problem. *American Antiquity* 30:421–427.

RANERE, ANTHONY J., AND PAT HANSELL
1978 Early Subsistence Patterns along the Pacific Coast of Central Panama. In *Prehistoric Coastal Adaptations: The Economy and Ecology of Maritime Middle America*, edited by Barbara L. Stark and Barbara Voorhies, pp. 43–59. New York: Academic Press.

RAPPAPORT, ROY A.
1968 *Pigs for Ancestors: Ritual in the Ecology of a New Guinea People*. New Haven: Yale University Press.
1969 Sanctity and Adaptation. Paper read at Burg Wartenstein Symposium No. 44, "The Moral and Ethical Structure of Human Adaptation."
1971a Ritual, Sanctity, and Cybernetics. *American Anthropologist* 73:59–76.
1971b The Sacred in Human Evolution. *Annual Review of Ecology and Systematics* 2: 23–44.
1978 Maladaptation in Social Systems. In *The Evolution of Social Systems*, edited by Jonathan Friedman and M. J. Rowlands, pp. 49–71. Pittsburgh: University of Pittsburgh Press.

RATHJE, WILLIAM L.
1971 The Origin and Development of Lowland Classic Maya Civilization. *American Antiquity* 36:275–285.

RATHJE, WILLIAM L., DAVID A. GREGORY, AND FREDERICK M. WISEMAN
1978 Trade Models and Archaeological Problems: Classic Maya Examples. In *Mesoamerican Communication Routes and Cultural Contacts*, edited by Thomas A. Lee, Jr., and Carlos Navarrete. Papers of the New World Archaeological Foundation No. 40:147–175. Provo, Utah.

RATTRAY, EVELYN C.
1966 An Archaeological and Stylistic Study of Coyotlatelco Pottery. *Mesoamerican Notes* 7–8:87–211.
1973 The Teotihuacán Ceramic Chronology: Early Tzacualli to Early Tlamimilolpa Phases. Ph.D. dissertation, Department of Anthropology, University of Missouri. Ann Arbor: University Microfilms (BWH74-18619).
1978a Los contactos Teotihuacan-Maya vistos desde el centro de México. *Anales de Antropología, Instituto de Investigaciones Históricas*, 15:33–52. Mexico City: Universidad Nacional Autónoma de México.
1978b Los entierros de Teotihuacán: Informe para el Museo Nacional de Antropología, México. MS, Instituto de Investigaciones Antropológicas. Mexico City: Universidad Nacional Autónoma de México.
n.d. The Teotihuacán Ceramic Chronology. MS.

RATTRAY, EVELYN C., AND MARÍA ELENA RUIZ
1977 Interpretaciones de La Ventilla, Teotihuacán. Paper presented at the Congreso Interno of the Instituto de Investigaciones

Antropológicas, Universidad Nacional Autónoma de México, Mexico City.

REED, CHARLES A.
1977    (ed.) *Origins of Agriculture*. The Hague: Mouton.

RENFREW, COLIN
1975    Trade as Action at a Distance: Questions of Integration and Communication. In *Ancient Civilization and Trade*, edited by Jeremy A. Sabloff and C. C. Lamberg-Karlovsky, pp. 3–59. Albuquerque: University of New Mexico Press.

REYES, LUIS
1975    *Cuautinchán del siglo XII al XVI: Formación y desarrollo histórico de un señorío prehispánico*. El Proyecto México de la Fundación Alemana para la Investigación Científica. Wiesbaden: Frans Steiner Verlag.

REYNOLDS, ROBERT G.
1979    An Adaptive Computer Model of the Evolution of Agriculture for Hunter-Gatherers in the Valley of Oaxaca, Mexico. Ph.D. dissertation, Department of Computer Science, University of Michigan.
n.d.    Q-mode and R-mode Analyses of Living Floor Distributions. *In* Guilá Naquitz Cave: A Study of Hunting, Gathering, and Incipient Agriculture in Preceramic Oaxaca, Mexico, edited by Kent V. Flannery. In preparation.

RICKETSON, OLIVER G., JR., AND EDITH BAYLES RICKETSON
1937    *Uaxactun, Guatemala, Group E—1926–1931*. Carnegie Institution of Washington, Pub. 477. Washington, D.C.

ROBLES ORTIZ, MANUEL
1974    Distribución de artefactos clovis en Sonora. *Boletín del Instituto Nacional de Antropología e Historia*, Epoca II, 9:25–32. Mexico City.

RODRÍGUEZ, FELIPE
1975    Motivos incisos de la cerámica de Tlaxcala. In *XII Mesa Redonda* 1:179–188. Mexico City: Sociedad Mexicana de Antropología.

ROMERO FRIZZI, MA. DE LOS ANGELES
1974    Bibliografía antropológica del Estado de Oaxaca. *Cuadernos de los Centros* 5. Mexico City: Dirección de Centros Regionales, Instituto Nacional de Antropología e Historia.

ROSSMAN, DAVID L.
1976    A Site Catchment Analysis of San Lorenzo, Veracruz. In *The Early Mesoamerican Village*, edited by Kent V. Flannery, pp. 95–103. New York: Academic Press.

ROUSE, IRVING
1976    Peopling of the Americas. *Quaternary Research* 6:597–612.

ROVNER, IRWIN
1975    Lithic Sequences from the Maya Lowlands. Ph.D. dissertation, Department of Anthropology, University of Wisconsin, Madison. Ann Arbor: University Microfilms (BWH75-28813).

ROWE, JOHN H.
1960    Cultural Unity and Diversification in Peruvian Archaeology. In *Men and Cultures*, edited by A. F. C. Wallace, pp. 627–631. Philadelphia: University of Pennsylvania Press.
1962    Stages and Periods in Archaeological Interpretation. *Southwestern Journal of Anthropology* 18:40–54.

ROYS, RALPH L.
1943    *The Indian Background of Colonial Yucatan*. Carnegie Institution of Washington, Pub. 548. Washington, D.C.
1957    *The Political Geography of the Yucatan Maya*. Carnegie Institution of Washington, Pub. 613. Washington, D.C.

RUYLE, EUGENE E.
1973    Slavery, Surplus, and Stratification on the Northwest Coast: Ethnoenergetics of an Incipient Stratification System. *Current Anthropology* 14:603–617.

SABLOFF, JEREMY A., AND WILLIAM L. RATHJE
1975    The Rise of a Maya Merchant Class. *Scientific American* 233(4):72–82.

SAHAGÚN, BERNARDINO DE
1952    *Florentine Codex: General History of the Things of New Spain*, Book 3, *The Origin of the Gods*. Translated by Arthur J. O. Anderson and Charles F. Dibble. Monographs of the School of American Research and Museum of New Mexico 14(4). Santa Fe: School of American Research and the University of Utah.
1953    *Florentine Codex: General History of the Things of New Spain*, Book 7, *The Sun, the Moon, and Stars, and the Binding of the Years*. Translated by Arthur J. O. Anderson and Charles E. Dibble. Monographs of the School of American Research and Museum of New Mexico 14(8). Santa Fe: School of American Research and the University of Utah.

1961    *Florentine Codex: General History of the Things of New Spain*, Book 10, *The People.* Translated by Arthur J. O. Anderson and Charles F. Dibble. Monographs of the School of American Research and Museum of New Mexico 14(11). Santa Fe: School of American Research and the University of Utah.

SAHLINS, MARSHALL D.
1972    *Stone Age Economics.* Chicago: Aldine-Atherton.

SAHLINS, MARSHALL D., AND ELMAN R. SERVICE
1960    (eds.) *Evolution and Culture.* Ann Arbor: University of Michigan Press.

SALMON, MERRILEE H.
1978    What Can Systems Theory Do for Archaeology? *American Antiquity* 43:174–183.

SANDERS, WILLIAM T.
1956    The Central Mexican Symbiotic Region. In *Prehistoric Settlement in the New World*, edited by Gordon R. Willey. Viking Fund Publications in Anthropology 23:115–127. New York: Wenner Gren Foundation.

1965    *The Cultural Ecology of the Teotihuacán Valley: A Preliminary Report of the Results of the Teotihuacán Valley Project.* University Park: Department of Anthropology, Pennsylvania State University.

1966    Life in a Classic Village. In *Teotihuacán: Onceava Mesa Redonda* 1:123–147. Mexico City: Sociedad Mexicana de Antropología.

1970    The Population of the Teotihuacán Valley, the Basin of Mexico and the Central Mexican Symbiotic Region in the 16th Century. In *The Teotihuacán Valley Project Final Report*, vol. 1. Occasional Papers in Anthropology, Pennsylvania State University, 3:385–457. University Park.

1971    Settlement Patterns in Central Mexico. In *Handbook of Middle American Indians*, vol. 10, edited by Robert Wauchope, Gordon F. Ekholm, and Ignacio Bernal, pp. 3–44. Austin: University of Texas Press.

1974    Chiefdom to State: Political Evolution at Kaminaljuyú, Guatemala. In *Reconstructing Complex Societies: An Archaeological Colloquium*, edited by Charlotte B. Moore. Supplement, *Bulletin of the American Schools of Oriental Research* 20:97–121. Cambridge, Mass.

1976a   The Natural Environment of the Basin of Mexico. In *The Valley of Mexico: Studies in Pre-Hispanic Ecology and Society*, edited by Eric R. Wolf, pp. 59–67. Albuquerque: University of New Mexico Press.

1976b   The Agricultural History of the Basin of Mexico. In *The Valley of Mexico: Studies in Pre-Hispanic Ecology and Society*, edited by Eric R. Wolf, pp. 101–159. Albuquerque: University of New Mexico Press.

1977    Environmental Heterogeneity and the Evolution of Lowland Maya Civilization. In *The Origins of Maya Civilization*, edited by Richard E. W. Adams, pp. 287–297. Albuquerque: University of New Mexico Press.

1978    Ethnographic Analogy and the Teotihuacan Horizon Style. In *Middle Classic Mesoamerica: A.D. 400–700*, edited by Esther Pasztory, pp. 35–44. New York: Columbia University Press.

1979    Procesos ecológicos y la evolución cultural de la Meseta Central. In *Actes du XLII^e Congrès International des Americanistes* (Paris, 1976). Paris.

SANDERS, WILLIAM T., AND JOSEPH W. MICHELS
1977    (eds.) *Teotihuacan and Kaminaljuyu: A Study in Prehistoric Culture Contact.* Pennsylvania State University Press Monograph Series on Kaminaljuyu. University Park.

SANDERS, WILLIAM T., JEFFREY R. PARSONS, AND MICHAEL H. LOGAN
1976    The Valley as an Ecological System: Summary and Conclusions. In *The Valley of Mexico: Studies in Pre-Hispanic Ecology and Society*, edited by Eric R. Wolf, pp. 161–178. Albuquerque: University of New Mexico Press.

SANDERS, WILLIAM T., JEFFREY R. PARSONS, AND ROBERT S. SANTLEY
1979    *The Basin of Mexico: Ecological Processes in the Evolution of a Civilization.* New York: Academic Press.

SANDERS, WILLIAM T., AND BARBARA J. PRICE
1968    *Mesoamerica: The Evolution of a Civilization.* New York: Random House.

SANDERS, WILLIAM T., AND ROBERT S. SANTLEY
1978    A Mesoamerican Capital. Review of *Monte Albán*, by Richard E. Blanton. *Science* 202:303–304.

SANDERS, WILLIAM T., AND DAVID WEBSTER
1978    Unilinealism, Multilinealism, and the Evolution of Complex Societies. In *Social Ar-*

*chaeology*, edited by Charles Redman et al., pp. 249–302. New York: Academic Press.

SANDERS, WILLIAM T., MICHAEL WEST, CHARLES FLETCHER, AND JOSEPH MARINO

1975    *The Formative Period Occupation of the Valley.* Vol. 2 of *The Teotihuacan Valley Project Final Report* (2 parts). Occasional Papers in Anthropology, Pennsylvania State University, 10. University Park.

SANTAYANA, GEORGE

1905–1906    *The Life of Reason; or, The Phases of Human Progress*, vol. 2, *Reason in Religion.* London: Constable.

SANTLEY, ROBERT S.

1977    Intra-site Settlement Patterns at Loma Torremote and Their Relationship to Formative Prehistory in the Cuauhtitlan Region, State of Mexico. Ph.D. dissertation, Department of Anthropology, Pennsylvania State University.

1980    Disembedded Capitals Reconsidered. *American Antiquity* 45:132–145.

SATTERTHWAITE, LINTON

1956    Maya Dates on Stelae in Tikal "Enclosures." *University Museum Bulletin* 20(4): 25–40. Philadelphia: University of Pennsylvania.

1958a    *Tikal Report No. 3: The Problem of Abnormal Stela Placements at Tikal and Elsewhere.* Museum Monographs, The University Museum. Philadelphia: University of Pennsylvania.

1958b    *Tikal Report No. 4: Five Newly Discovered Carved Monuments at Tikal and New Data on Four Others.* Museum Monographs, The University Museum. Philadelphia: University of Pennsylvania.

1960    Maya "Long Count" Numbers. *Expedition* 2(2):36–37.

1963    Note on Hieroglyphs on Bone from the Tomb below Temple I, Tikal. *Expedition* 6(1):18–19.

1964    Dates in a New Tikal Hieroglyphic Text as Katun-Baktun Anniversaries. *Estudios de Cultura Maya* 4:203–222.

1967    Radiocarbon and Maya Long Count Dating of "Structure 10" (Str. 5D-52, First Story), Tikal. *Revista Mexicana de Estudios Antropológicos* 21:225–249.

SATTERTHWAITE, LINTON, VIVIAN L. BROMAN, AND WILLIAM A. HAVILAND

1961    *Tikal Report No. 8: Miscellaneous Investigations.* Museum Monographs, The Uni-

versity Museum. Philadelphia: University of Pennsylvania.

SATTERTHWAITE, LINTON, AND WILLIAM R. COE

1968    The Maya-Christian Calendrical Correlation and the Archaeology of the Peten. In *XXXVII Congreso Internacional de Americanistas: Actas y Memorias* (Buenos Aires, 1966) 3:3–21. Buenos Aires.

SATTERTHWAITE, LINTON, AND ELIZABETH K. RALPH

1960    New Radiocarbon Dates and the Maya Correlation Problems. *American Antiquity* 26:165–184.

SAUER, CARL O.

1952    *Agricultural Origins and Dispersals.* New York: American Geographical Society.

SAYRE, EDWARD V., AND GARMAN HARBOTTLE

1979    The Analysis by Neutron Activation of Archaeological Ceramics Related to Teotihuacán: Local Wares and Trade Sherds. MS.

SCHOENWETTER, JAMES

1974    Pollen Records of Guila Naquitz Cave. *American Antiquity* 39:292–303.

in press    The Pollen Records from Guila Naquitz Cave, Oaxaca, Mexico. In *Prehistory and Human Ecology of the Valley of Oaxaca*, edited by Kent V. Flannery. Memoirs of the Museum of Anthropology, University of Michigan. Ann Arbor.

SCHOENWETTER, JAMES, AND LANDON D. SMITH

n.d.    Pollen Analysis of the Oaxacan Preceramic. *In* Guilá Naquitz Cave: A Study of Hunting, Gathering, and Incipient Agriculture in Preceramic Oaxaca, Mexico, edited by Kent V. Flannery. In preparation.

SCHOLES, FRANCE V., AND RALPH L. ROYS

1948    *The Maya Chontal Indians of Acalan-Tixchel.* Carnegie Institution of Washington, Pub. 560. Washington, D.C.

[SCHWERIN, KARL]

1977    Review of *The Valley of Mexico: Studies in Pre-Hispanic Ecology and Society*, edited by Eric R. Wolf. *Journal of Anthropological Research* 33:350–352.

SECRETARÍA DEL PATRIMONIO NACIONAL

1970    *Minería prehispánica en la Sierra de Querétaro.* Mexico City.

SEELE, ENNO

1973    Restos de milpas y poblaciones prehispánicas cerca de San Buenaventura Nealtican, Pue. *Comunicaciones* 7:77–86. Puebla: Fundación Alemana para la Investigación Científica.

SÉJOURNÉ, LAURETTE
1954    Tula, la supuesta capital de los toltecas. *Cuadernos Americanos* 73:153–169.
1959    *Un palacio en la ciudad de los dioses: Exploraciones en Teotihuacán, 1955–58.* Mexico City: Instituto Nacional de Antropología e Historia.
1960    *Burning Water: Thought and Religion in Ancient Mexico.* Translated by Irene Nicholson. New York: Grove Press.
1962    *El universo de Quetzalcóatl.* Mexico City: Fondo de Cultura Económica.
1966a   *Arquitectura y Pintura en Teotihuacán.* Mexico City: Siglo XXI Editores.
1966b   *El lenguaje de las formas en Teotihuacán.* Mexico City: Gabriel Mancera 65.

SÉJOURNÉ, LAURETTE, AND GRACIELA SALICRUP
1965    Arquitectura y arqueología. *Revista de la Universidad de Mexico* 19(7):4–8.

SEMPOWSKI, MARTHA
1979    TE27: Test Excavation in the Puma Mural Group—Plaza and Main Temple–Pyramid (73A:N4E1), Teotihuacán. MS, Department of Anthropology, University of Rochester.

SERVICE, ELMAN R.
1962    *Primitive Social Organization: An Evolutionary Perspective.* 2d ed. New York: Random House.
1975    *Origins of the State and Civilization: The Process of Cultural Evolution.* New York: Norton.

SHARER, ROBERT J., AND WILLIAM R. COE
1979    The Quirigua Project: Origins, Objectives and Research in 1973 and 1974. In *Quirigua Reports*, vol. 1, edited by Wendy Ashmore; general editor, Robert J. Sharer. Museum Monograph 37, The University Museum. Philadelphia: University of Pennsylvania.

SHARP, ROSEMARY
1970    *Early Architectural Grecas in the Valley of Oaxaca.* Boletín de Estudios Oaxaqueños 32. Mitla, Oaxaca.
1978    Architecture as Interelite Communication in Preconquest Oaxaca, Veracruz, and Yucatan. In *Middle Classic Mesoamerica: A.D. 400–700*, edited by Esther Pasztory, pp. 158–171. New York: Columbia University Press.

SHOOK, EDWIN M.
1951    The Present Status of Research on the Pre-Classic Horizons in Guatemala. In *The Civilizations of Ancient America*, edited by Sol Tax, pp. 93–100. Chicago: University of Chicago Press.
1957    The Tikal Project. *University Museum Bulletin* 21(3):36–52. University of Pennsylvania, Philadelphia.
1958a   *Tikal Report No. 1: Field Director's Report: The 1956 and 1957 Seasons.* Museum Monographs, The University Museum. Philadelphia: University of Pennsylvania.
1958b   The Temple of the Red Stela. *Expedition* 1(1):26–33. (Spanish translation, 1958, *Antropología e Historia de Guatemala* 11:7–14.)
1960    Tikal Stela 29. *Expedition* 2(2):28–35.
1962    Tikal: Problems of a Field Director. *Expedition* 4(2):11–26.
1964    Archaeological Investigations in Tikal, Peten, Guatemala. In *XXXV Congreso Internacional de Americanistas: Actas y Memorias* (Mexico City, 1962) 1:379–386. Mexico City.

SHOOK, EDWIN M., AND WILLIAM R. COE
1961    *Tikal Report No. 5: Tikal: Numeration, Terminology, and Objectives.* Museum Monographs, The University Museum. Philadelphia: University of Pennsylvania.

SHOOK, EDWIN M., AND ALFRED KIDDER II
1961    The Painted Tomb at Tikal. *Expedition* 4(1):2–7. (Spanish translation, 1962, *Antropología e Historia de Guatemala* 14:5–10.)

SIMMONS, MICHAEL P.
1973    External Trade and Ash Temper in Northern Yucatan. Paper presented at the 38th annual meeting of the Society for American Archaeology, San Francisco.

SIMMONS, MICHAEL P., AND GERALD F. BREM
1979    The Analysis and Distribution of Volcanic Ash–tempered Pottery in the Lowland Maya Area. *American Antiquity* 44:79–91.

SISSON, EDWARD B.
1973–1974    First and Second Annual Reports of the Coxcatlan Project. Andover, Mass.: R. S. Peabody Foundation.
1976    Survey and Excavation in the Northwestern Chontalpa, Tabasco, Mexico. Ph.D. dissertation, Department of Anthropology, Harvard University.

SJOBERG, GIDEON
1960    *The Preindustrial City, Past and Present.* Glencoe, Ill.: The Free Press.

SKINNER, G. WILLIAM
1964    Marketing and Social Structure in Rural

China, Part I. *Journal of Asian Studies* 24: 3–43.

1965 Marketing and Social Structure in Rural China, Part II. *Journal of Asian Studies* 24:195–228.

1977 The City in History, Introduction: Urban Development in Imperial China, pp. 3–31; Regional Urbanization in Nineteenth-Century China, pp. 211–249; The City in Space, Introduction: Urban and Rural in Chinese Society, pp. 253–273; Cities and the Hierarchy of Local Systems, pp. 275–351; The City as a Social System, Introduction: Urban Social Structure in Ch'ing China, pp. 521–553. In *The City in Late Imperial China*, edited by G. William Skinner. Stanford: Stanford University Press.

SMITH, A. LEDYARD

1950 *Uaxactun, Guatemala: Excavations of 1931–1937.* Carnegie Institution of Washington, Pub. 588. Washington, D.C.

SMITH, CAROL A.

1974 Economics of Marketing Systems: Models from Economic Geography. In *Annual Review of Anthropology* 3:167–201. Palo Alto.

1976a (ed.) *Regional Analysis.* 2 vols. New York: Academic Press.

1976b Regional Economic Systems: Linking Geographical Models and Socioeconomic Problems. In *Regional Analysis*, edited by Carol A. Smith, 1:3–63. New York: Academic Press.

1976c Exchange Systems and the Spatial Distribution of Elites: The Organization of Stratification in Agrarian Societies. In *Regional Analysis*, edited by Carol A. Smith, 2:309–374. New York, Academic Press.

SMITH, C. EARLE, JR.

1967 Plant Remains. In *The Prehistory of the Tehuacan Valley*, vol. 1, *Environment and Subsistence*, edited by Douglas S. Byers, pp. 220–255. Austin: University of Texas Press.

1978 *The Vegetational History of the Oaxaca Valley.* Vol. 5(1) of *Prehistory and Human Ecology of the Valley of Oaxaca*, edited by Kent V. Flannery. Memoirs of the Museum of Anthropology, University of Michigan, 10. Ann Arbor.

SMITH, MICHAEL E.

1975 Temples, Residences and Artifacts at Clas-

sic Teotihuacán. Senior honors thesis, Department of Anthropology, Brandeis University.

1976 A Multivariate Analysis of Temples and Residences of Classic Teotihuacán, Mexico. Paper presented at the 41st annual meeting of the Society for American Archaeology, St. Louis.

1979 The Aztec Marketing System and Settlement Pattern in the Valley of Mexico: A Central Place Analysis. *American Antiquity* 44:110–125.

SMITH, PHILIP E. L.

1976 *Food Production and Its Consequences.* Menlo Park, Cal.: Cummings Publishing Co.

SMITH, PHILIP E. L., AND T. CUYLER YOUNG, JR.

1972 The Evolution of Early Agriculture and Culture in Greater Mesopotamia. In *Population Growth: Anthropological Implications*, edited by Brian Spooner, pp. 1–59. Cambridge: MIT Press.

SMITH, ROBERT E.

1971 *The Pottery of Mayapan Including Studies of Ceramic Material from Uxmal, Kabah, and Chichen Itza.* 2 parts. Papers of the Peabody Museum, vol. 66.

SNARSKIS, MICHAEL J.

1979 Turrialba: A Paleo-Indian Quarry and Workshop Site in Eastern Costa Rica. *American Antiquity* 44:125–138.

SNOW, DEAN R.

1969 Ceramic Sequence and Settlement Location in Pre-Hispanic Tlaxcala. *American Antiquity* 34:131–145.

SNOW, MICHAEL E., AND ELIZABETH F. SNOW

1969 Report on the First Season of Archaeological Investigations in the Tulancingo Valley, Hgo., Mexico. MS, Department of Anthropology, University of Toronto.

1970 Report of the Second (1969) Season of Archaeological Investigations in the Tulancingo Valley, Hgo., Mexico. MS, Department of Anthropology, University of Toronto.

SOCIEDAD MEXICANA DE ANTROPOLOGÍA

1966 *Teotihuacán: Onceava Mesa Redonda*, vol. 1. Mexico City.

1972 *Teotihuacan: XI Mesa Redonda*, vol. 2. Mexico City.

SOMOLINOS-D'ARDOIS, GERMÁN

1968 La medicina teotihuacana. *Gaceta Médica de México* 98(3):359–369. Mexico City: Academia Nacional de Medicina.

SOUSTELLE, JACQUES
1937 *La Famille Otomí-Pame du Mexique Central*. Université de Paris, Institut d'Ethnologie, Travaux et Memoires 26. Paris.

SPENCE, MICHAEL W.
1966 Los talleres de obsidiana de Teotihuacán. In *Teotihuacán: Onceava Mesa Redonda* 1:213–218. Mexico City: Sociedad Mexicana de Antropología.

1967 The Obsidian Industry of Teotihuacán. *American Antiquity* 32:507–514.

1971 Skeletal Morphology and Social Organization in Teotihuacán, Mexico. Ph.D. dissertation, Department of Anthropology, Southern Illinois University. Ann Arbor: University Microfilms (BWH72-10302).

1974a The Development of the Teotihuacán Obsidian Production System. MS, Department of Anthropology, University of Western Ontario, London.

1974b Residential Practices and the Distribution of Skeletal Traits in Teotihuacán, Mexico. *Man*, n.s. 9:262–273.

1976 Human Skeletal Material from the Oaxaca Barrio in Teotihuacán, Mexico. In *Archaeological Frontiers: Papers on New World High Cultures in Honor of J. Charles Kelley*, edited by Robert B. Pickering. Southern Illinois University Museum Studies 4:129–148. Carbondale.

1979a Human Skeletal Material from Teotihuacán: Analyses and Observations. MS.

1979b Obsidian Production and the State in Teotihuacan, Mexico. MS on file, Department of Anthropology, University of Western Ontario, London.

1979c Teotihuacán y el intercambio de obsidiana en Mesoamérica. In *Los procesos de cambio: XV Mesa Redonda*, 2:293–300. Mexico City: Sociedad Mexicana de Antropología and Universidad de Guanajuato.

SPENCE, MICHAEL W., AND JEROME KIMBERLIN
1979 Obsidian Procurement Systems of Teotihuacán, Mexico. Paper presented at the 44th annual meeting of the Society for American Archaeology, Vancouver.

SPENCE, MICHAEL W., AND JEFFREY R. PARSONS
1972 Prehispanic Obsidian Exploitation in Central Mexico: A Preliminary Synthesis. In *Miscellaneous Studies in Mexican Prehistory*. Anthropological Papers, Museum of Anthropology, University of Michigan, 45:1–44. Ann Arbor.

SPENCER, CHARLES S.
n.d. Descriptive Statistics of the Guilá Naquitz Living Floors. In Guilá Naquitz Cave: A Study of Hunting, Gathering, and Incipient Agriculture in Preceramic Oaxaca, Mexico, edited by Kent V. Flannery.

SPENCER, CHARLES S., AND ELSA M. REDMOND
n.d.a A Middle Formative Elite Residence and Associated Structures at La Coyotera. In *The Cloud People: Evolution of the Zapotec and Mixtec Civilizations of Oaxaca, Mexico*, edited by Kent V. Flannery and Joyce Marcus.

n.d.b The Cuicatlán Cañada and the Period II Frontier of the Zapotec State. In *The Cloud People: Evolution of the Zapotec and Mixtec Civilizations of Oaxaca, Mexico*, edited by Kent V. Flannery and Joyce Marcus.

SPORES, RONALD
1972 *An Archaeological Settlement Survey of the Nochixtlan Valley, Oaxaca*. Vanderbilt University Publications in Anthropology No. 1. Nashville.

1973 Research in Mexican Ethnohistory. In *Research in Mexican History*, edited by Richard E. Greenleaf and Michael C. Meyer, pp. 25–48. Lincoln: University of Nebraska Press.

1974 *Stratigraphic Excavations in the Nochixtlan Valley, Oaxaca*. Vanderbilt University Publications in Anthropology No. 11. Nashville.

SPRANZ, BODO
1966 *Las pirámides de Totimehuacán: Excavaciones 1964–65*. Instituto Poblano de Antropología e Historia Pub. 1. Puebla.

1967 Descubrimiento en Totimehuacán, Puebla. *Boletín del Instituto Nacional de Antropología e Historia* 28:19–22. Mexico City.

1970 *Las pirámides de Totimehuacan y el desarrollo de las pirámides preclásicas en Mesoamérica*. Wiesbaden: Franz Steiner Verlag.

SQUIER, ROBERT J.
1964 A Reappraisal of Olmec Chronology. Ph.D. dissertation, Department of Anthropology, University of California, Berkeley. Ann Arbor: University Microfilms (BWH64-09093).

STARBUCK, DAVID R.
1975 Man-Animal Relationships in Pre-Columbian Central Mexico. Ph.D. dissertation, Department of Anthropology, Yale Univer-

sity. Ann Arbor: University Microfilms (BWH75-24604).

1977 Animal Utilization and Urban Adaptations in the City of Teotihuacán, Mexico. *The Western Canadian Journal of Anthropology* 7:151–162.

STARK, BARBARA L.

1977 *Prehistoric Ecology at Patarata 52, Veracruz, Mexico: Adaptation to the Mangrove Swamp.* Vanderbilt University Publications in Anthropology No. 18. Nashville.

1978 An Ethnohistoric Model for Native Economy and Settlement Patterns in Southern Veracruz, Mexico. In *Prehistoric Coastal Adaptations: The Economy and Ecology of Maritime Middle America*, edited by Barbara L. Stark and Barbara Voorhies, pp. 211–238. New York: Academic Press.

STARK, BARBARA L., AND BARBARA VOORHIES

1978 (eds.) *Prehistoric Coastal Adaptations: The Economy and Ecology of Maritime Middle America.* New York: Academic Press.

STEWARD, JULIAN H.

1938 *Basin-Plateau Aboriginal Sociopolitical Groups.* Smithsonian Institution, Bureau of American Ethnology, Bulletin 120. Washington, D.C.

1955 *Theory of Culture Change.* Urbana: University of Illinois Press.

STEWART, T. DALE

1974 Human Skeletal Remains from Dzibilchaltun, Yucatan, Mexico, with a Review of Cranial Deformity Types in the Maya Region. In *Archaeological Investigations on the Yucatan Peninsula.* Middle American Research Institute, Tulane University, Pub. 31:199–225. New Orleans.

STIRLING, MATTHEW W.

1955 *Stone Monuments of the Rio Chiquito, Veracruz, Mexico.* Smithsonian Institution, Bureau of American Ethnology, Bulletin 157. Washington, D.C.

STOCKER, TERRANCE L.

1974 A Small Temple in the Tula Residential Zone. In *Studies of Ancient Tollan: A Report of the University of Missouri Tula Archaeological Project*, edited by Richard A. Diehl. University of Missouri Monographs in Anthropology 1:25–31. Columbia.

n.d. Excavation of a Temple in the Canal Locality Residential Complex at Tollan. In preparation.

STOUTAMIRE, JAMES

1974 Archaeological Survey of the Tula Urban Zone. In *Studies of Ancient Tollan: A Report of the University of Missouri Tula Archaeological Project*, edited by Richard A. Diehl. University of Missouri Monographs in Anthropology 1:11–15. Columbia.

1975 Trend Surface Analysis of Survey Data from Tula, Mexico. Ph.D. dissertation, Department of Anthropology, University of Missouri. Ann Arbor: University Microfilms (BWH76-01051).

STROSS, F. H., H. V. MICHEL, F. ASARO, AND R. GRUHN

1977 Sources of Some Obsidian Flakes from a Paleoindian Site in Guatemala. *American Antiquity* 42:114–118.

STRUEVER, STUART

1968 Flotation Techniques for the Recovery of Small-Scale Archaeological Remains. *American Antiquity* 33:353–362.

STUART, GEORGE E., JOHN C. SCHEFFLER, EDWARD B. KURJACK, AND JOHN W. COTTIER

1979 *Map of the Ruins of Dzibilchaltun, Yucatan, Mexico.* Middle American Research Institute, Tulane University, Pub. 47. New Orleans.

STUCKENRATH, ROBERT, JR., WILLIAM R. COE, AND ELIZABETH K. RALPH

1966 University of Pennsylvania Radiocarbon Dates IX: Tikal Series. *Radiocarbon* 8: 371–385.

SUSSMAN, ROBERT W.

1972 Child Transport, Family Size, and Increase in Human Population during the Neolithic. *Current Anthropology* 13:258–259.

SWASEY, WILLIAM

1975 Mound 91, Lambityeco, a Description of an Ancient Kiln. In *XIII Mesa Redonda.* Mexico City: Sociedad Mexicana de Antropología.

SZABO, BARNEY J., HAROLD E. MALDE, AND CYNTHIA IRWIN-WILLIAMS

1969 Dilemma Posed by Uranium-Series Dates on Archaeologically Significant Bones from Valsequillo, Puebla, Mexico. *Earth and Planetary Science Letters* 6:237–244. Amsterdam: North-Holland Publishing Co.

TAYLOR, R. E., AND CLEMENT W. MEIGHAN

1978 (eds.) *Chronologies in New World Archaeology.* New York: Academic Press.

TEJERA, NOEMI CASTILLO

1970 Tecnología de una vasija en travertino.

*Boletín del Instituto Nacional de Antropología e Historia* 41:48–52. Mexico City.

TESCH, MONIKA, AND RAFAEL ABASCAL M.
1974 Azadas. *Comunicaciones* 11:37–40. Puebla: Fundación Alemana para la Investigación Científica.

THOMAS, DAVID H., JR.
1971 Prehistoric Subsistence-Settlement Patterns of the Reese River Valley, Central Nevada. Ph.D. dissertation, Department of Anthropology, University of California at Davis. Ann Arbor: University Microfilms (BWH72-03608).
1972 A Computer Simulation Model of Great Basin Shoshonean Subsistence and Settlement Patterns. In *Models in Archaeology*, edited by David L. Clarke, pp. 671–704. London: Methuen.
1973 An Empirical Test for Steward's Model of Great Basin Settlement Patterns. *American Antiquity* 38:155–176.

THOMPSON, J. ERIC S.
1970 Trade Relations between Maya Highlands and Lowlands. In *Maya History and Religion*, pp. 124–158. Norman: University of Oklahoma Press.

THOMPSON, PHILIP C.
1978 Tekanto in the Eighteenth Century. Ph.D. dissertation, Department of Anthropology, Tulane University. Ann Arbor: University Microfilms.

TOLSTOY, PAUL
1971 Recent Research into the Early Preclassic of the Central Highlands. In *Observations on the Emergence of Civilization in Mesoamerica*, edited by Robert F. Heizer and John A. Graham. Contributions of the University of California Archaeological Research Facility 11:25–28. Berkeley.
1975 Settlement and Population Trends in the Basin of Mexico (Ixtapaluca and Zacatenco Phases). *Journal of Field Archaeology* 2:331–349.
1978 Western Mesoamerica before A.D. 900. In *Chronologies in New World Archaeology*, edited by R. E. Taylor and Clement W. Meighan, pp. 241–284. New York: Academic Press.

TOLSTOY, PAUL, SUZANNE K. FISH, MARTIN W. BOKSENBAUM, KATHRYN BLAIR VAUGHN, AND C. EARLE SMITH
1977 Early Sedentary Communities of the Basin of Mexico. *Journal of Field Archaeology* 4:91–106.

TOLSTOY, PAUL, AND LOUISE I. PARADIS
1970 Early and Middle Preclassic Culture in the Basin of Mexico. *Science* 167:344–351.

TOMPKINS, PETER
1976 *Mysteries of the Mexican Pyramids*. New York: Harper and Row.

TOZZER, ALFRED M.
1921 *Excavation of a Site at Santiago Ahuitzotla, Mexico, D.F.* Smithsonian Institution, Bureau of American Ethnology, Bulletin 74. Washington, D.C.
1941 (ed.) *Landa's Relación de las cosas de Yucatán*. Translated and edited with notes. Papers of the Peabody Museum, vol. 18. Cambridge, Mass.

TREJO ALVARADO, ELIA DEL CARMEN
1975 Figurillas características de la secuencia cultural de Tlaxcala. In *XIII Mesa Redonda* 1:147–158. Mexico City: Sociedad Mexicana de Antropología.

TREJO ALVARADO, ELIA DEL CARMEN, AND MARÍA ELENA RUIZ AGUILAR
1975 Los comales en el material cerámico del área Puebla-Tlaxcala. *Comunicaciones* 12:9–16. Puebla: Fundación Alemana para la Investigación Científica.

TRIK, AUBREY S.
1963 The Splendid Tomb of Temple I at Tikal, Guatemala. *Expedition* 6(1):2–18.

VAILLANT, GEORGE C.
1930 *Excavations at Zacatenco*. Anthropological Papers of the American Museum of Natural History 32(1). New York.
1935 *Excavations at El Arbolillo*. Anthropological Papers of the American Museum of Natural History 35(2). New York.
1941 *Aztecs of Mexico*. New York: Doubleday Doran.

VARNER, DUDLEY M.
1974 Prehispanic Settlement Patterns in the Valley of Oaxaca, Mexico: The Etla Arm. Ph.D. dissertation, Department of Anthropology, University of Arizona. Ann Arbor: University Microfilms (BWH75-04115).

VIDARTE DE LINARES, JUAN
1964 Exploraciones arqueológicas en el Rancho "La Ventilla." Informe al Departamento de Monumentos Prehispánicos, Instituto Nacional de Antropología e Historia. Mexico City.
1968 Teotihuacán, la ciudad del quinto sol. *Cuadernos Americanos* 158:133–145.

445

VILLAGRA CALETI, AGUSTÍN

1951 Las pinturas de Atetelco en Teotihuacán. *Cuadernos Americanos* 55:153–162.

1955 Trabajos realizados en Teotihuacán: 1952. *Anales del Instituto Nacional de Antropología e Historia* 6(1):67–78.

1971 Mural Painting in Central Mexico. In *Handbook of Middle American Indians*, vol. 10, edited by Robert Wauchope, Gordon F. Ekholm, and Ignacio Bernal, pp. 135–156. Austin: University of Texas Press.

VLCEK, DAVID T., SILVIA GARZA DE GONZÁLEZ, AND EDWARD B. KURJACK

1978 Contemporary Farming and Ancient Maya Settlements: Some Disconcerting Evidence. In *Pre-Hispanic Maya Agriculture*, edited by Peter D. Harrison and B. L. Turner II, pp. 211–223. Albuquerque: University of New Mexico Press.

VOGT, EVON Z.

1961 Some Aspects of Zinacantan Settlement Patterns and Ceremonial Organization. *Estudios de Cultura Maya* 1:131–145.

1969 *Zinacantan*. Cambridge: Harvard University Press.

VOORHIES, BARBARA

1976 *The Chantuto People: An Archaic Period Society of the Chiapas Littoral, Mexico*. Papers of the New World Archaeological Foundation No. 41. Provo, Utah.

1978 Previous Research on Nearshore Coastal Adaptations in Middle America. In *Prehistoric Coastal Adaptations: The Economy and Ecology of Maritime Middle America*, edited by Barbara L. Stark and Barbara Voorhies, pp. 5–21. New York: Academic Press.

WASHBURN, SHERWOOD L., AND JANE LANCASTER

1968 Evolution III: Human Evolution. *International Encyclopedia of the Social Sciences* 5:215–221. New York: Macmillan.

WAUCHOPE, ROBERT

1950 A Tentative Sequence of Pre-Classic Ceramics in Middle America. In *Middle American Research Records* 1:211–250. Middle American Research Institute, Tulane University, Pub. 15. New Orleans.

1954 Implications of Radiocarbon Dates from Middle and South America. In *Middle American Research Records* 2:17–39. Middle American Research Institute, Tulane University, Pub. 18. New Orleans.

WAUCHOPE, ROBERT, AND GORDON R. WILLEY

1965 (eds.) *Handbook of Middle American Indians*, vol. 3. Austin: University of Texas Press.

WEAVER, MURIEL PORTER

1972 *The Aztecs, Maya, and Their Predecessors*. New York: Seminar Press.

WEBER, MAX

1958 *The City*. Translated and edited by Don Martindale and Gertrud Neuwirth. Glencoe, Ill.: The Free Press.

WEBSTER, DAVID L.

1977 Warfare and the Evolution of Maya Civilization. In *The Origins of Maya Civilization*, edited by Richard E. W. Adams, pp. 335–371. Albuquerque: University of New Mexico Press.

1979 Three Walled Sites of the Northern Maya Lowlands. *Journal of Field Archaeology* 5:375–390.

WEBSTER, HELEN T.

1963 Tikal Graffiti. *Expedition* 6(1):36–47.

WEIGAND, PHIL C.

1968 The Mines and Mining Techniques of the Chalchihuites Culture. *American Antiquity* 33:45–61.

1970 Huichol Ceremonial Reuse of a Fluted Point. *American Antiquity* 35:365–367.

WEIGAND, PHIL C., GARMAN HARBOTTLE, AND EDWARD V. SAYRE

1977 Turquoise Sources and Source Analysis: Mesoamerica and the Southwestern U.S.A. In *Exchange Systems in Prehistory*, edited by Timothy K. Earle and Jonathan E. Ericson, pp. 15–34. New York: Academic Press.

WEST, MICHAEL

1965 Transition from Preclassic to Classic at Teotihuacán. *American Antiquity* 31:193–202.

WETHERINGTON, RONALD K.

1978 (ed.) *The Ceramics of Kaminaljuyu, Guatemala*. Pennsylvania State University Press Monograph Series on Kaminaljuyu. University Park.

WHALEN, MICHAEL E.

n.d. Excavations at Santo Domingo Tomaltepec: Evolution of a Formative Community in the Valley of Oaxaca, Mexico. Vol. 6 of *Prehistory and Human Ecology of the Valley of Oaxaca*, edited by Kent V. Flannery. Memoirs of the Museum of Anthropology, University of Michigan 11. Ann Arbor.

WHALLON, ROBERT, JR.

1973 Spatial Analysis of Occupation Floors I: Application of Dimensional Analysis of Variance. *American Antiquity* 38:266–278.

WHEATLEY, PAUL

1963 What the Greatness of a City Is Said to Be: Reflections on Sjoberg's "Preindustrial City." *Pacific Viewpoint* 4:163–188.

1971 *The Pivot of the Four Quarters: A Preliminary Enquiry into the Origins and Character of the Ancient Chinese City.* Chicago: Aldine.

1972 The Concept of Urbanism. In *Man, Settlement and Urbanism,* edited by Peter J. Ucko, Ruth Tringham, and G. W. Dimbleby, pp. 601–637. London: Duckworth.

WHITAKER, THOMAS

n.d. Cucurbits from Guilá Naquitz Cave. In *Guilá Naquitz Cave: A Study of Hunting, Gathering, and Incipient Agriculture in Preceramic Oaxaca, Mexico,* edited by Kent V. Flannery.

WHITE, BENJAMIN

1973 Demand for Labor and Population Growth in Colonial Java. *Human Ecology* 1(3): 217–236.

WHITECOTTON, JOSEPH W.

1977 *The Zapotecs: Princes, Priests, and Peasants.* Norman: University of Oklahoma Press.

WILKERSON, S. JEFFREY K.

1972 Ethnogenesis of the Huastecs and Totonacs: Early Cultures of North-central Veracruz at Santa Luisa, Mexico. Ph.D. dissertation, Department of Anthropology, Tulane University. Ann Arbor: University Microfilms (BWH73-12064).

1975 Pre-agricultural Village Life: The Late Preceramic Period in Veracruz. *Contributions of the University of California Archaeological Facility* 27:111–122. Berkeley.

WILKES, H. GARRISON

1967 *Teosinte: The Closest Relative of Maize.* Cambridge: Buessy Institute of Harvard University.

WILLEY, GORDON R.

1950 Growth Trends in New World Cultures. In *For the Dean: Essays in Anthropology in Honor of Byron Cummings on His Eighty-ninth Birthday, September 20, 1950,* edited by Erik K. Reed and Dale S. King, pp. 223–247. Tucson and Santa Fe: Hohokam Museums Association and the Southwestern Monuments Association.

1955 The Prehistoric Civilizations of Nuclear America. *American Anthropologist* 57: 571–593.

1962 The Early Great Styles and the Rise of the Pre-Columbian Civilizations. *American Anthropologist* 64:1–14.

1966 *An Introduction to American Archaeology,* vol. 1, *North and Middle America.* Englewood Cliffs, N.J.: Prentice-Hall.

1978a Developmental Stages in Ancient Mesoamerican Society: Reflections and Impressions. In *Codex Wauchope,* pp. 155–162. *Human Mosaic* 12. New Orleans: Tulane University.

1978b A Summary Scan. In *Chronologies in New World Archaeology,* edited by R. E. Taylor and Clement W. Meighan, pp. 513–564. New York: Academic Press.

WILLEY, GORDON R., GORDON F. EKHOLM, AND RENÉ F. MILLON

1964 The Patterns of Farming Life and Civilization. In *Handbook of Middle American Indians,* vol. 1, edited by Robert Wauchope and Robert C. West, pp. 446–501. Austin: University of Texas Press.

WILLEY, GORDON R., AND PHILIP PHILLIPS

1955 Method and Theory in American Archaeology II: Historical-Developmental Interpretation. *American Anthropologist* 57: 723–819.

1958 *Method and Theory in American Archaeology.* Chicago: University of Chicago Press.

WINNING, HASSO VON

1976 Late and Terminal Preclassic: The Emergence of Teotihuacan. In *Origins of Religious Art and Iconography in Preclassic Mesoamerica,* edited by H. B. Nicholson. UCLA Latin American Studies Series 31:141–156. UCLA Latin American Center and the Ethnic Arts Council of Los Angeles.

WINTER, MARCUS C.

1972 Tierras Largas: A Formative Community in the Valley of Oaxaca, Mexico. Ph.D. dissertation, Department of Anthropology, University of Arizona. Ann Arbor: University Microfilms (BWH73-13325).

1974 Residential Patterns at Monte Albán, Oaxaca, Mexico. *Science* 186:981–987.

1978 *Cerro de la Cueva: Una zona arqueológica del Clásico en Santa Cruz Mixtepec y San*

*Bernardo Mixtepec, Distrito de Zimatlan, Oaxaca.* Estudios de Antropología e Historia 12. Oaxaca: Centro Regional, Instituto Nacional de Antropología e Historia.

WINTER, MARCUS C., DARIA DERAGA, AND RODOLFO FERNÁNDEZ

1975 *Tumba 74-1 de San Sebastián Teitipac, Tlacolula, Oaxaca.* Oaxaca: Centro Regional, Instituto Nacional de Antropología e Historia.

1977 *Una tumba postclásica en San Pablo Etla, Oaxaca.* Estudios de Antropología e Historia 3. Oaxaca: Centro Regional, Instituto Nacional de Antropología e Historia.

WINTER, MARCUS C., AND WILLIAM O. PAYNE

1976 Hornos para cerámica hallados en Monte Albán. *Boletín del Instituto Nacional de Antropología e Historia* 16:37–40. Mexico City.

WINTER, MARCUS C., AND JANE W. PIRES-FERREIRA

1976 Distribution of Obsidian among Households in Two Oaxacan Villages. In *The Early Mesoamerican Village,* edited by Kent V. Flannery, pp. 306–311. New York: Academic Press.

WITTFOGEL, KARL A.

1957 *Oriental Despotism.* New Haven: Yale University Press.

WOBST, H. MARTIN

1974 Boundary Conditions for Paleolithic Social Systems: A Simulation Approach. *American Antiquity* 39:147–178.

1976 Locational Relationships in Paleolithic Society. *Journal of Human Evolution* 5: 49–58.

WOLF, ERIC R.

1959 *Sons of the Shaking Earth.* Chicago: University of Chicago Press.

1976a (ed.) *The Valley of Mexico: Studies in Pre-Hispanic Ecology and Society.* Albuquerque: University of New Mexico Press.

1976b Introduction. In *The Valley of Mexico: Studies in Pre-Hispanic Ecology and Society,* edited by Eric R. Wolf, pp. 1–10. Albuquerque: University of New Mexico Press.

WOLFMAN, DANIEL

1973 A Re-evaluation of Mesoamerican Chronology: A.D. 1–1200. Ph.D. dissertation, Department of Anthropology, University of Colorado at Boulder. Ann Arbor: University Microfilms (BWH73-32609).

WOODBURY, RICHARD B., AND JAMES A. NEELY

1972 Water Control Systems of the Tehuacan Valley. In *The Prehistory of the Tehuacan Valley,* vol. 4, *Chronology and Irrigation,* edited by Frederick Johnson, pp. 81–153. General Editor: Richard S. MacNeish. Austin: University of Texas Press.

WRIGHT, HENRY T.

1977 Recent Research on the Origin of the State. *Annual Review of Anthropology* 6:379–397. Palo Alto.

1978 Toward an Explanation of the Origin of the State. In *Origins of the State: The Anthropology of Political Evolution,* edited by Ronald Cohen and E. R. Service, pp. 49–68. Philadelphia: Institute for the Study of Human Issues.

WRIGHT, HENRY T., AND GREGORY A. JOHNSON

1975 Population, Exchange, and Early State Formation in Southwestern Iran. *American Anthropologist* 77:267–289.

YADEÚN ANGULO, JUAN

1975 *El estado y la ciudad: El caso de Tula, Hgo. (Proyecto Tula).* Colección Científica, Arqueología y Antropología Social, 25. Mexico City: Instituto Nacional de Antropología e Historia.

YOFFEE, NORMAN

1979 The Decline and Rise of Mesopotamian Civilization: An Ethnoarchaeological Perspective on the Evolution of Social Complexity. *American Antiquity* 44:5–35.

ZEITLIN, JUDITH F.

1978 Changing Patterns of Resource Exploitation, Settlement Distribution, and Demography on the Southern Isthmus of Tehuantepec, Mexico. In *Prehistoric Coastal Adaptations: The Economy and Ecology of Maritime Middle America,* edited by Barbara L. Stark and Barbara Voorhies, pp. 151–177. New York: Academic Press.

ZEITLIN, ROBERT N.

1978 Long-Distance Exchange and the Growth of a Regional Center: An Example from the Southern Isthmus of Tehuantepec, Mexico. In *Prehistoric Coastal Adaptations: The Economy and Ecology of Maritime Middle America,* edited by Barbara L. Stark and Barbara Voorhies. New York: Academic Press.

# INDEX

INDEX